Enlightenment, Passion, Modernity

CULTURAL SITINGS

Elazar Barkan, Editor

CULTURAL SITINGS will present focused discussions of major contemporary and historical cultural issues by prominent and promising scholars, with a special emphasis on multidisciplinary and transnational perspectives. By bridging historical and theoretical concerns, CULTURAL SITINGS will develop and examine narratives which probe the spectrum of experiences that continuously reconfigure contemporary cultures. By rethinking chronology, agency, and especially the siting of historical transformation, the books in this series will go beyond disciplinary boundaries and notions of what is marginal and what is central to knowledge. By juxtaposing the analytical, the historical, and the visual, this challenging new series will provide a venue for the development of cultural studies and for the rewriting of the canon.

PETER GAY.

Enlightenment, Passion, Modernity Historical Essays in European Thought and Culture

INTRODUCED AND EDITED BY

Mark S. Micale and Robert L. Dietle

STANFORD
UNIVERSITY
PRESS

Stanford,
California

2000

Stanford University Press
Stanford, California
© 2000 by the Board of Trustees of the
Leland Stanford Junior University
Chapter 16, "Opposite the Pantheon:
Fantasy about a Picture Postcard Sent by
Sigmund Freud," © Ilse Grubrich-Simitis

Photograph of Peter Gay by Janet Malcolm

Printed in the United States of America
CIP data appear at the end of the book

For Peter Gay

Contents

Contents

Contents

Notes on Contributors

W. F. BYNUM is professor of the history of medicine at University College, London, and the Wellcome Institute for the History of Medicine. His recent books include *Science and the Practice of Medicine in the Nineteenth Century* (Cambridge University Press, 1994) and, as co-editor, the *Companion Encyclopedia of the History of Medicine*, 2 vols. (Routledge, 1993). He is presently working on the history of malaria in British India.

DAVID CANNADINE is professor of history and director of the Institute of Historical Research at London University. Among his many books are *The Pleasures of the Past* (Collins, 1989), *The Decline and Fall of the British Aristocracy* (Yale University Press, 1990), *G. M. Trevelyan: A Life in History* (Harper Collins, 1992), *Class in Britain* (Yale University Press, 1998), and *History in Our Time* (Yale University Press, 1998).

STEFAN COLLINI is reader in intellectual history and English literature at the University of Cambridge. He is author most recently of *Public Moralists: Political Thought and Intellectual Life in Britain, 1850–1930* (Oxford University Press, 1991) and *Matthew Arnold: A Critical Portrait* (Oxford University Press, 1994). He is currently working on a book about intellectuals in twentieth-century Britain.

ROBERT DARNTON is professor of history at Princeton University. His most recent books are *The Forbidden Best-Sellers of Prerevolutionary France* and its companion volume *The Corpus of Clandestine Literature in France, 1769–1789*, both published by Norton in 1996. He is also author of *The Business of the Enlightenment: A Publishing History of the Encyclopédie, 1775–1800* (Harvard University Press, 1979), *The Literary Underground of the Old Regime* (Harvard University Press, 1982), and *The Great Cat Massacre and Other Episodes in French Cultural History* (Basic Books, 1984).

ROBERT L. DIETLE teaches eighteenth-century European intellectual and political history at Western Kentucky University.

Contributors

ILSE GRUBRICH-SIMITIS is a psychoanalyst in private practice in Frankfurt am Main. She is a member of the International Psychoanalytical Association and a training and supervising analyst at the Frankfurter Psychoanalytisches Institut. She is co-editor of *Sigmund Freud: His Life in Pictures and Words* (Harcourt Brace Jovanovich, 1978), editor of and contributor of an essay to Sigmund Freud, *A Phylogenetic Fantasy: Overview of the Transference Neuroses* (Harvard University Press, 1987), and author of *Back to Freud's Texts: Making Silent Documents Speak* (Yale University Press, 1997) and *Early Freud and Late Freud* (Routledge, 1997).

JUDITH M. HUGHES is professor of history at the University of California, San Diego, and is also clinical associate at the San Diego Psychoanalytic Institute. Among her recent works are *Reshaping the Psychoanalytic Domain: The Work of Melanie Klein, W. R. D. Fairbairn, and D. W. Winnicott* (University of California Press, 1989), *From Freud's Consulting Room: The Unconscious in a Scientific Age* (Harvard University Press, 1994), and *Freudian Analysts/Feminist Issues* (Yale University Press, 1999).

MARTIN JAY is Sidney Hellman Ehrman professor and chairman of the history department at the University of California at Berkeley. Among his most recent works are *Downcast Eyes: The Denigration of Vision in Twentieth-Century French Thought* (University of California Press, 1993); *Force Fields: Between Intellectual History and Cultural Critique* (Routledge, 1993); and *Cultural Semantics: Keywords of Our Age* (University of Massachusetts Press, 1998).

PETER JELAVICH teaches modern European intellectual and cultural history at the University of Texas at Austin. He is author of *Munich and Theatrical Modernism: Politics, Playwriting and Performance, 1890–1914* (1985) and *Berlin Cabaret* (1993), both published by Harvard University Press.

MARION A. KAPLAN is professor of modern European history at Queens College and the Graduate Center, City University of New York. She is author of *The Jewish Feminist Movement in Germany: The Campaigns of the Jüdischer Frauenbund, 1904–1938* (Greenwood Press, 1979), *The Making of the Jewish Middle Class: Women, Family, and Identity in Imperial Germany* (Oxford University Press, 1991), and *Between Dignity and Despair: Jewish Life in Nazi Germany* (Oxford University Press, 1998). She has also edited books in European women's history and is currently editing a history of Jewish daily life in Germany from the eighteenth century until 1945.

THOMAS A. KOHUT is the Sue and Edgar Wachenheim III professor of history at Williams College. He is author of *Wilhelm II and the Germans: A Study in Leadership* (Oxford University Press, 1991). He is currently working on a book about the history of twentieth-century Germany as experienced by Germans who were active in the youth movement during the 1920s.

PETER LOEWENBERG is professor of history and political psychology at the University of California, Los Angeles. He is author of *Fantasy and Reality in History* (Oxford University Press, 1995) and *Decoding the Past: The Psychohistorical Approach* (Transaction Books, 1996). He is currently working on a study of the Bauhaus as a creative group. He is a training and supervising analyst of the Southern California Psychoanalytic Institute and is chair of the Committee on Research and Special Training of the American Psychoanalytic Association.

MARK S. MICALE is associate professor of history at the University of Illinois in Champaign-Urbana. He is author of *Approaching Hysteria: Disease and Its Interpretations* (Princeton University Press, 1995), editor and translator of *Beyond the Unconscious* (Princeton University Press, 1993), and co-editor of *Discovering the History of Psychiatry* (Oxford University Press, 1994), *Traumatic Pasts: History, Psychiatry, and Trauma in the Modern Age, 1860–1930* (Cambridge University Press, 2000), and *The Mind of Modernism: Psychology and the Cultural Arts in Europe and America, 1870–1930* (Cambridge University Press, 2000).

HARRY C. PAYNE is president of Williams College and professor of history. He is author of *The Philosophes and the People* (Yale University Press, 1976) and editor of *Studies in Eighteenth-Century Culture*, vols. 10–12 (University of Wisconsin Press, 1980–82). He has published extensively on European intellectual history, 1750–1930.

QUENTIN SKINNER is the Regius professor of modern history at the University of Cambridge. His books include *The Foundations of Modern Political Thought*, 2 vols. (1978), *Reason and Rhetoric in the Philosophy of Hobbes* (1996), and *Liberty Before Liberalism* (1998), all published by Cambridge University Press.

JOHN E. TOEWS is professor of history and chair of the Program in the Comparative History of Ideas at the University of Washington. He is author of *Hegelianism: The Path toward Dialectical Humanism, 1805–1841* (Cambridge University Press, 1981) and has written numerous articles on the history of psychoanalysis, contemporary historiography, and historical theory. He is currently completing a book on the production of historical consciousness and public memory in Berlin during the 1840s.

R. K. WEBB is professor of history, emeritus, at the University of Maryland, Baltimore County. He is co-author with Peter Gay of *Modern Europe*, 2 vols. (Harper & Row, 1973) and has also written *The British Working-Class Reader, 1790–1850* (A. M. Kelley, 1955), *Harriet Martineau: A Radical Victorian* (Heinemann, 1960), *Modern England* (Harper & Row, 1968, 1980), and a series of essays on English religion in the eighteenth and nineteenth centuries. A larger work on English Unitarianism is in preparation.

DORA B. WEINER is professor of the medical humanities and professor of history at the University of California, Los Angeles. She recently published *The Citizen-Patient in Revolutionary and Imperial Paris* (Johns Hopkins University Press, 1993), edited *Jacques Tenon's Memoirs on Paris Hospitals* (Science History Publications, 1997), and co-edited *The World of Dr. Francisco Hernández* (Stanford University Press, in press). She is now preparing an English translation of her book *Comprendre et soigner: Pinel (1745–1826) et la médecine de l'esprit,* just published by Arthème Fayard, Paris.

JAY WINTER is reader in modern history at the University of Cambridge and a fellow of Pembroke College. He is author of *Sites of Memory, Sites of Mourning: The Great War in European Cultural History* (Cambridge University Press, 1995) and, with Jean-Louis Robert, of *Capital Cities at War: Paris, London, Berlin, 1914–1919* (Cambridge University Press, 1997).

Preface

This gathering of original essays has two independent but related purposes. It is intended, first, as a collection of new historical studies of modern European culture and thought. During the 1970s and 1980s, it was not uncommon for historians to denigrate the study of intellectual and cultural history for its alleged elitist and canonical character: the academic history of ideas, it was widely claimed, was little more than an uncritical celebration of the "great thoughts" of "great men." For a variety of reasons, this situation has changed dramatically today. Enriched by the methods and insights of neighboring areas of inquiry, including social history, the history of *mentalités*, anthropology, literary theory, linguistics, art history, gender studies, and the study of popular culture, intellectual and cultural history in the late 1990s is among the most dynamic and creative fields of Anglo-American historical studies. *Enlightenment, Passion, Modernity* offers a generous sampling of these new studies written by a distinguished group of international scholars at the end of the twentieth century.

In the second place, this book is a testimonial volume to Peter Gay. Since the early 1950s, Professor Gay has been among intellectual and cultural history's most able and ambitious practitioners. Spanning more than four decades, Professor Gay's career as a publishing scholar has reflected — indeed, has helped to determine — the paradigmatic development of the field during this period. The sections of the book, like the book's title, reflect themes running through Professor Gay's many writings. Because his scholarly output has been exceptionally diverse and far-ranging, the essays deal with the eighteenth, nineteenth, and twentieth centuries and with British, French, Central European, and North American history.

In our introductory essay, Chapter 1, we have avoided the customary practice of summarizing the contents of the book's constituent chapters. With essays as lucid and literate as these, we believed that to do so would be a tedious and unnecessary exercise. Rather, we introduce the volume with a brief intellectual biography of Professor Gay. Given his field of historical study, this approach seemed particularly appropriate. Furthermore, in Chapter 1 we highlight the meaning of and interconnections among the book's themes as they emerged in Professor Gay's career. Clearly, we have not provided a complete or comprehensive biography there. These pages are intended rather as the sketch of an intellectual biography with special attention to the formative experiences of Professor Gay's early maturity, the turning points of his professional career, and the development of his major scholarly projects.

Festschrift, we learned in the course of assembling these essays, is a dirty word in the world of contemporary academic publishing. No matter how distinguished the honoree, how eminent the contributors, and how engaging the essays, publishers today tend to regard such commemorative volumes in purely economic terms. Many publishing houses now enforce inflexible prohibitions against *Festschriften*. For this reason, we are immensely pleased and grateful to have worked with Stanford University Press in producing this book. Michael S. Roth alerted us to SUP's new Cultural Sitings series. Elazar Barkan, the series editor, was enthusiastically and indispensably supportive at every stage. And Muriel Bell, Kate Washington, Harrison Shaffer, and Mary Severance shepherded the book through production.

Many essays in the book were presented as lectures at a two-day conference in Professor Gay's honor at Williams College, Williamstown, Massachusetts, on 2–3 October 1998. This highly memorable event would not have been possible without the efforts of Tom Kohut. We are additionally grateful to Hank Payne, president of Williams College, whose extraordinary hospitality and generosity made the conference possible.

For close and critical readings of the Introduction, we thank David Cannadine, Martin Jay, Tom Kohut, John Merriman, Hank Payne, Bob Webb, Dora Weiner, and Ferrel Rose (who also provided crucial help in compiling the bibliography). Janet Malcolm graciously supplied the photograph for the frontispiece. From her special perspective, Ruth Gay donated ideas and information while keeping the project secret. Perhaps our greatest debt of gratitude is to the book's celebratory cast of contributors: on short notice, and often under difficult and trying circumstances, the seventeen authors of the book took time from their own crowded and prodigiously productive careers to salute one of their own. We offer our deep thanks to them all.

M S. M.

R. L. D.

Enlightenment, Passion, Modernity

ROBERT L. DIETLE

MARK S. MICALE

1. Peter Gay

A *Life in History*

Emotions and ideas are the sparks that fly when the
mind meets difficulties.
—Lionel Trilling, *The Liberal Imagination* (1950)

Scanning the shelf of Peter Gay's published works, we are reminded forcibly
of the scholars and authors of the Victorian age — those indefatigable writers
who seem never to have wasted a moment or an idea. Gay published his first
book in 1952. Since then, articles and books have poured forth with astonishing regularity. Mere volume, of course, is no virtue. What makes Gay's career especially remarkable is the consistently high and imaginative quality of
his work combined with a great diversity of subject matter. Far from cultivating a single field of study, Gay has staked out as his historical garden European ideas, culture, and politics of the past three centuries. The cumulative
result is one of the largest and most diverse oeuvres created by a historian in
the twentieth century.

Such a prolific and varied author presents a challenge to the intellectual
biographer in search of a way to present an intelligible unity without imposing a false coherence. At the very least, a personal case can be made for the
unity of Gay's work: no matter how different in subject matter, Gay's historical writings "as the product of a single mind, have a certain stamp upon them;
they must be, at least in their style of thought and their concerns, unified by
some underlying intellectual intent." [1] This essay examines some of the elements that have gone into Gay's style of history and explores the intellectual
intent underlying his career.

Peter Gay has suggested that all historical scholarship starts with polemic, and his writing lends support to this dictum; it is suffused with a revisionist impulse. Gay likes nothing better than to undermine historical dogmas. He has defended Voltaire and the eighteenth-century philosophes against charges of intellectual shallowness and political ineffectiveness, argued against the avant-garde's portrayal of the bourgeoisie as a class of repressed philistines, urged skeptical colleagues to exploit the insights of psychoanalysis, confronted what he sees as the excesses and oversights of a generation of social history, and countered the attacks of current anti-Freudian critics. In the face of historians' fascination with relativism, he unapologetically defends "perspectival realism," insisting that "the objects of historical study are really that — objects — to be studied and understood, and that objectivity, though difficult, is possible."[2]

Gay's drive to revise, however, goes well beyond his willingness to challenge the assumptions of fellow scholars. He prefers to study individuals or groups that revised their beliefs in the light of experience, historical figures who in their attempts to change the world rejected the comfortable answers provided by contemporary orthodoxies. His first book set the tone: published in 1952, when he was 29, *The Dilemma of Democratic Socialism: Eduard Bernstein's Challenge to Marx* was based on Gay's Columbia University dissertation in political science. A study of German revisionist socialism of the later nineteenth century, the book is a fairly traditional intellectual biography of Bernstein. What is revealing is the type of politician and intellectual that Gay in his formative years chose to study. As a young man, Bernstein had found security in Marxism — a theory of history and politics that both explained the world and held out the promise of transforming it. Yet Bernstein's study and experiences led him away from Marxist orthodoxy until, in the 1890s, he rebelled against theories that had hardened into dogma. Reminding his colleagues that "Marx and Engels were, in their time, Revisionists too," Bernstein insisted that the socialist movement awake from its dream of a world revolution and accept the less dramatic but more realistic goal of a representative democratic state based upon the ideas of social and economic equality. In *The Dilemma of Democratic Socialism*, Gay shows how Bernstein's encounter with reality forced him to reevaluate and revise his ideas.

In the mid 1950s, Gay's attraction to revisionism caused him to shift the focus of his inquiry to the eighteenth-century Enlightenment. As a part-time lecturer and then assistant professor in Columbia's government department, Gay was responsible for teaching a survey course on political theory. While reading and gathering material for lectures, he was frustrated by the lack of systematic and sympathetic studies of the political ideas of the philosophes, that loose, eighteenth-century coalition of cultural critics, religious skeptics, and political reformers. A colleague recommended to him Carl Becker's influential *The Heavenly City of the Eighteenth-Century Philosophers* (1932), which argued that Locke, Hume, Voltaire, and Diderot had demolished the medieval Christian worldview only to replace it with an uncritical, quasi-religious faith in reason and science. Then, in 1952, J. L. Talmon's voluminous *The Origins of Totalitarian Democracy* appeared. In the genre of Cold War studies of political tyranny, Talmon's book traced the paternity of twentieth-century dictatorships to the French philosophes, particularly to the "proto-totalitarian" Rousseau. To similar effect, Irving Babbitt's *Rousseau and Romanticism* (1919), which excoriated Rousseau in defense of classicism, was still influential in literary and historical criticism.[3] Gay found the interpretations of Becker, Talmon, and Babbitt, like the larger "literature of denunciation" about the Enlightenment, utterly perverse;[4] he began to conclude that views of the Enlightenment were in serious need of reworking.[5]

Gay wanted to salvage the Enlightenment from its detractors because he found much in the movement worthy of admiration. The philosophes "championed free inquiry, they upheld the right to free thought and expression, they believed in diversity, they were secular, they despised superstition and fanaticism, they believed in the possibilities of reform, and they were passionately humane."[6] He found the ideals of "the party of humanity" worthy of political vindication as well as of serious scholarship.[7] Furthermore, Gay first organized his ideas about the Enlightenment in the 1940s and 1950s; against the backdrop of twentieth-century challenges to freedom by fascism and communism, the Western liberal-rationalist tradition, he believed, very much deserved affirmation.

In Gay's interpretation, the Enlightenment engaged in a systematic revision of its own; determined to change the world, the philosophes challenged received ideas and entrenched institutions. Explicitly rejecting the view of Enlightenment politics as uselessly abstract and irresponsibly utopian, Gay saw the Enlightenment as both a philosophical and an empiricist movement. The philosophes lived "in the world of affairs and the world of ideas with equal ease."[8] Gay's *Voltaire's Politics: The Poet as Realist* (1959), *The Party of Humanity: Essays in the French Enlightenment* (1964), and two-volume study *The Enlightenment: An Interpretation* (1966–69) describe a climate of criticism that allowed the philosophes the freedom of mind necessary to challenge oppressive political traditions and repressive Christianity. Their self-liberation enabled them to imagine a world organized on the basis of reason in which humanity's natural passions would be cultivated instead of rejected. The use of reason to harness the passions for practical and sometimes noble ends marked the philosophes as pioneers of modernity and helps explain Gay's reading of Sigmund Freud as the direct heir of the secular Enlightenment.[9]

If criticism was the means, mastery was the goal. According to Gay, "the Enlightenment may be summed up in two words: criticism and power."[10] In the hands of the philosophes, criticism became a weapon in two related fields of struggle: their desire to gain intellectual and emotional mastery over themselves was inextricably bound up with their attempt to control the external world. The struggle for mastery surfaces as another recurrent theme in Gay's historical work. The importance Gay placed on mastery stems in part from his growing use of psychoanalysis to understand the past. Freud spoke more than once about a kind of instinct to mastery that was part of the human urge to control the natural environment by means of science, technology, and social inventions. A generation later, in the work of psychoanalytic ego psychologists, mastery took the form of the successful mediation between instinctual impulses and the social world by the ego. And, in the early 1940s, the struggle for mastery was conceptualized as a formal psychological category by the Boston psychoanalyst Ives Hendrick. Hendrick argued that analysts too often neglected the infant's "inborn drive to do and to learn how to do." Distinct from the sexual and aggressive drives, this instinct is manifested by manipulation, locomotion, comprehension, and reasoning—all "various ways to serve the ultimate purpose of adjusting the environment to oneself."[11] For both child and adult, the instinct to mastery plays a crucial role in learning how to deal with a recalcitrant world, a reality that seems adept at frustrating efforts to control it.

Less explicit than Gay's revisionist impulse, the drive for mastery emerges from his work like the figure in the carpet. To Gay, the European Enlightenment, the rise of modernity, and the discovery of psychoanalysis all represent recoveries of nerve, historically specific refusals to submit passively to forces that seemed uncontrollable. In these efforts, the defeated are as likely to capture Gay's historical interest as the victors. He frequently portrays persons who failed in their attempt to gain mastery. His 1966 study of American puritan historians' abandonment of Renaissance and early Enlightenment historical methods and drift back toward a "mythopoetic" and Christian worldview is titled *A Loss of Mastery*; *Weimar Culture*, his account of the culture of interwar Germany published in 1968, offers an object lesson in how an attempt to exert political mastery through the use of reason proved tragically unable to withstand the forces arrayed against it; and his collection of essays *Freud, Jews, and Other Germans* (1978) bears the subtitle *Masters and Victims in Modernist Culture*. Conversely, in *The Bourgeois Experience*, his multivolume study of the middle classes in the nineteenth century, Gay labels the struggles of Victorian bourgeois to gain control over nature, society, and themselves "the most sustained campaign for mastery of the world ever undertaken."[12] And in his biography of Freud, which appeared in 1988, he presents Freud's life as a lifelong and largely successful quest for self-mastery.

The mastery theme in Gay is also partly autobiographical. The progress of Gay's own work represents an assertion of mastery over a widening range of historical sources. In the 1950s and 1960s, as Gay read deeply in the eighteenth-century Enlightenment, he began to see problems with traditional approaches to intellectual history. While admiring the celebrated work of Arthur O. Lovejoy and his followers, Gay thought their "austere analysis of 'unit ideas'" too closely allied to the history of philosophy and too prone to treat ideas as independent, unchanging entities. For Gay the sociology of knowledge as practiced by Max Weber and Karl Mannheim offered a way in which intellectual historians could focus on the encounter of ideas with reality.[13] He labeled this combination of Lovejoy and Weber "the social history of ideas"—an attempt to grasp ideas in both their intellectual and social contexts.[14] Such a project, needless to say, enormously expanded the range and quantity of sources historians would have to consult, but Gay was equal to the challenge. Beginning with the first volume of *The Enlightenment: An Interpretation*, published in 1966, Gay's work has displayed an amazing ability to synthesize vast and diverse materials into a compelling interpretation of a historical era. And from *Voltaire's Politics* (1959) onward, his books have included what has become a trademark feature: extended bibliographical essays that coordinate masses of scholarship into an interpretative unity.

Gay's desire for mastery also helps explain his attraction to very large historical topics, his desire to bring order and meaning to an entire culture or epoch. By the early 1970s, his publications about the Enlightenment consisted of a monograph, a collection of essays, a set of dialogues, translations from French and German, book introductions, three anthologies, and a two-volume synthetic study.[15] The first volume of *The Enlightenment: An Interpretation*, which received a National Book Award in 1967, established Gay as the leading American student of the Anglo-French Enlightenment and a historical writer of formidable literary gifts. Such a record would have sustained the careers of many scholars. Gay, however, only in his mid-forties, began casting about for a new project.

Unexpectedly, in 1968, the editors of the Harvard-based *Perspectives in American History* invited Gay to contribute a prefatory essay to a volume of studies on the migration of European intellectuals to America during the 1920s, 1930s, and 1940s. The topic had personal as well as academic resonance for him: he was born in Berlin on 20 June 1923, and at Columbia University during the late 1940s and the 1950s, he had encountered many scholars who were refugees from fascism. Asked to write specifically on the culture of the Weimar Republic, Gay willingly interrupted his work on the second volume of *The Enlightenment: An Interpretation* and quickly began to explore the "spirit of Weimar." The project involved an entirely different historical setting and many new sources; but he immersed himself in the task. The result was an elegant and richly suggestive 80-page essay titled "Weimar Culture: The Outsider as Insider," which he later expanded into a book with the same title.[16]

The publication of the second volume of *The Enlightenment: An Interpretation* in 1969 marks a clear transition in Gay's career. Subtitled *The Science of Freedom*, the volume completed Gay's reassessment of the eighteenth-century philosophes. Although he would occasionally return to the topic in lectures and articles, the Enlightenment henceforth ceased to be a major object of study for Gay. Throughout the 1970s, in lectures, essays, and collections, he probed aspects of European cultural Modernism.[17] He regarded Modernism, of which Weimar culture was such a dazzling part, as an international movement of enormous cultural vitality that had transformed the arts, literature, and thought; he likened the movement alternatively to the Periclean age and the Renaissance.[18] Characteristically, Gay was interested in Modernism in all of its branches — painting, sculpture, architecture, music, the novel, drama, philosophy, psychology, and the social sciences. Unlike the scholarship on the topic by literary critics and literary historians, who by and large had dominated the inquiry into Modernism, Gay's writings situated the movement in its contemporary social and political contexts. Furthermore, whereas commentators such as Lionel Trilling and Irving Howe had dwelled on the themes of rebellion, alienation, and anti-rationalism, Gay sought a more balanced account that took stock of Modernism's constructive energies. In its spirit of criticism, its secularity, and its unmasking tendencies, Modernism, in his view, shared important features with the Enlightenment.[19]

Moreover, whereas Gay's presentation of eighteenth-century thought had centered on France and Britain, he now insisted on the key and distinctive role of Germany, particularly of Berlin, which in the years after 1890 had developed into a vibrant cultural center. The Modernist experiment involved special promises and problems in Germany. Gay pleaded for an understanding of German Modernism that was not distorted by retrospective knowledge of the later Nazi trauma.[20] His writings on Modernism offer preliminary studies in the cultural history of our own century; he intended them equally as "explorations in a region of our recent past of which we know much, and which is documented to an almost bewildering degree, but which we have mastered neither intellectually nor emotionally."[21]

In 1968, Gay presented *Weimar Culture* as "a first attempt to organize my ideas on the culture of Weimar; I hope to devote some years to an extensive study of what I propose to call the 'Weimar Renaissance.'"[22] A decade later, in the introduction to *Freud, Jews and Other Germans*, he mentioned a projected multivolume "cultural history of Imperial Germany on which I am now engaged."[23] Clearly, he was in search of a new unifying project. Despite these hints of a larger project, Gay's writings of the 1970s never coalesced into a large-scale undertaking the way his work of the preceding two decades merged to become *The Enlightenment: An Interpretation*. It is difficult to know exactly why a satisfying synoptic project eluded him at this point. The explanation may hinge in part on his need for an overarching revisionist theme; only a historical topic with an overt revisionist element seems fully to engage his energies. Or, perhaps, in the end, despite his brave defense of modern German culture, against the logic of his own personal experience, Gay could not face spending decades of his life studying the subject. Whatever the reasons, this was in retrospect a great pity. Gay was superbly, perhaps uniquely, well equipped to write on this subject, and a generation afterward, we still lack a major interpretative study of German culture during the Wilhelminian and Weimar eras.

By the late 1970s, Gay had begun to close in on quite a different scholarly project. Up to this point in his career, he had studied the eighteenth and the early twentieth centuries. He now turned his attention to the vast terrain between these two earlier enterprises. As before, Gay was as much provoked as inspired into the project. While reading about Modernism, he had explored the historical world of the cultural avant-garde, and had come away dissatisfied. In particular, he was struck by how many historians and critics accepted as historical fact the avant-garde's own vocal and unrelenting attacks on the bourgeoisie of its time. For Gay, the familiar picture of the nineteenth-century bourgeois as economically obsessed, artistically philistine, and sexually hypocritical appeared to be yet another dogma in need of critical scrutiny.[24]

Reinforcing his discontent were aspects of "the new social history" and women's studies. During the 1970s and 1980s, social history, buttressed by quantitative techniques and theoretical work from the social sciences, became the most dynamic branch of Anglo-American historical studies. Gay believed that, while it brought a welcome broadening of the field, the new wave of social-historical scholarship dwelled rather too narrowly on the working classes, especially when engaged in strikes or rebellions, and on the peasantry. Even though the 1800s were dubbed "the bourgeois century," remarkably little was actually known about the ideas, attitudes, and sensibilities that dominated the emergent middle classes of the nineteenth century. Many of the new social historians used the term "bourgeois" as little more than a derisive epithet. Drawing on Marx, its practitioners seemed content with a narrowly economic image of the middle classes as monolithically capitalist and forever rising. To similar effect, Gay found that early feminist-informed historiography tended to present the Victorian era as one-dimensionally patriarchal, oppressive, and even misogynistic.

By the late 1970s, Gay had come to believe that these new scholarly literatures were creating a skewed and superficial historical picture. Here was an opportunity for revision on a grand scale. Seizing the opportunity, Gay has devoted the second half of his career to an expansive, multivolume study of the middle classes in Europe and North America from the defeat of Napoleon in 1815 to the outbreak of World War I in 1914. The five substantial volumes of *The Bourgeois Experience: Victoria to Freud* published between 1984 and 1998 reconstruct less the social and economic history of middle-class Victorians than the inner workings of their minds.

This approach was possible because during the same years in which Gay was searching for a new project, his historical method continued to evolve. Although he had always been a reader of Freud, it was in the mid 1970s that he "decided to rise above my amateur status" by undergoing a program of formal psychoanalytic training.[25] This led Gay to broaden his subject matter from ideas to mentalities and enabled him to explore the instinct for mastery in a fuller, more multidimensional fashion. In the process, he transformed the social history of ideas into a cultural history of the passions.

The Bourgeois Experience: Victoria to Freud is a remarkably nuanced and wide-ranging attempt to show how men and women of the nineteenth-century middle classes struggled for control over their erotic and aggressive drives by "translating destructive wishes into productive occupations" and by using their rational faculties to heed the call of desire.[26] By the end of the nineteenth century, the goal of a stable, civilized culture seemed within reach to many Westerners. Yet, in Gay's exposition, the bourgeois attempt at mastery of self and society ultimately failed. The outbreak of World War I in August 1914 marked a massive regression, an orgiastic outbreak of misguided aggression amounting to a tragic abandonment of the bourgeoisie's hard-won, century-long gains.

In commerce, technology, science, medicine, education, the arts, imperialism, and war, the energy and accomplishments of the Victorians were clearly extraordinary. Gay sought to reconstruct the emotional, psychological, and sexual dimensions of these achievements. Gay's Enlightenment scholarship of the 1950s and 1960s had concentrated on the elite intellectual class, but he now took as his historical actors not only well-known figures but physicians, lawyers, men of business, teachers, journalists, housewives, artisans, novelists, painters, and politicians. He interrogated an immense range of sources, including family papers, diaries, letters, medical texts, biographies, autobiographies, self-portraits, paintings, novels, history writing, editorials, sermons, religious tracts, and courtship manuals. *Education of the Senses* (1984) and *The Tender Passion* (1986) chronicled an emotional life among the bourgeoisie far richer and more sexually charged than had been previously thought to exist.[27] Arguably the most original book in the series, *The Cultivation of Hatred* (1993) traces the complex, culturally legitimized forms of aggression that lurked beneath the civilized surface of Victorian bourgeois society.[28] And *The Naked Heart* (1995) studies the introspective, self-analytical impulse in middle-class life and thought. Uniting the series with Gay's earlier work on Modernism, *Pleasure Wars* (1998) examines social and cultural relations between the middle classes and the avant-garde.[29]

The first two volumes of *The Bourgeois Experience* appeared in the middle of the 1980s, just when gender studies, the history of sexuality, and the history of the body were emerging as new and politically charged fields of academic history. Heavily indebted to the writings of Michel Foucault, much of this new literature construed the impulse to mastery as an attempt at social repression between different individuals and groups. In contrast, Gay viewed mastery more subtly and complexly, as a partially internalized drama; he refused to reduce all of culture to a mechanism for social control. As a result, practitioners of the new studies frequently criticized these two books. Similarly, some critics among his readers of the series were troubled by what they perceived as the diffuse chronological and geographical scope of Gay's global class portrait. Nevertheless, there is little doubt that more than any other English-language historian Gay opened up the middle class as a domain of historical investigation. He successfully challenged many dominant historical stereotypes and brought to the subject far greater empirical resources than any previous scholar. Collectively, his five volumes have magisterially enriched our historical picture of bourgeois civilization.

Like his earlier work, Gay's psychocultural history of the Victorian bourgeoisie seeks to combine exacting scholarly standards with a personal commitment to certain values. The link between Gay's core values and his study of both the nineteenth-century middle classes and the Enlightenment is best represented by the ideal of the "liberal temper." Gay laid out this ideal during the early stages of his work on the bourgeoisie. His most concise description of the "liberal temper" is contained in a talk he delivered in May 1981 to the American Psychoanalytic Association.[30] Entitled "Liberalism and Regression," the lecture integrates classic Anglo-American political liberalism and psychoanalytic ego psychology. Implicitly rejecting recent trends that saw psychoanalysis as an insidious form of social control, Gay opened with the blunt statement that "psychoanalysis is the psychology of liberalism." He then went on to define liberalism:

I am principally referring to what I want to call the liberal temper: a capacity for tolerating the delays, disappointments, and ambiguities attendant upon any open society; an unimpaired capacity for reality testing, for curbing one's aggressiveness without turning it against oneself, for a reliance on defensive stratagems that remain moderate in scope and flexible in application. The liberal I am sketching here is the modern edition of Aristotle's political animal, magnanimous in victory and patient, though not passive, in defeat; a stranger alike to apathy and fanaticism; a judge of men and situations for whom complexity does not breed anxiety; an urbane observer endowed with a sense of the absurd who does not exploit his humorous distance from the world as a defense against assuming responsibility.[31]

In the face of a threatening and all too illiberal world, such a temper is difficult to achieve and easy to abandon.

In light of this passage, it becomes clear that, in a real sense, Gay has devoted his entire career to studying the historical vicissitudes of the modern liberal temper with the goal of bolstering that temper. His allegiance to this heritage flows above all from personal experience. As a Jew growing up in Berlin during the 1930s, Gay confronted the greatest assault ever mounted against modern liberalism. Under the Nazis, large portions of Germany's population regressed to tribal primitivism, investing imaginary enemies with mythical powers in order to wallow in the pleasures of destroying them. Between 9 and 15, Gay lived in the German capital of the Third Reich. These were years that witnessed the ever-tighter domestic consolidation of the Nazi state, including the expulsion of Jews from the civil service, the courts, trade unions, political parties, the legal and medical professions, schools and universities, and the arts. Random street assaults on Jews by bands of SA thugs were not uncommon. Gay remembers as an adolescent "being told, with ugly and emphatic reiteration, that he was Jewish—which meant, in the official vocabulary, subhuman."[32] By 1936, his family was actively planning to emigrate to America. Originally Gay's parents, Moritz and Helga Gay, envisioned emigrating sometime in the early 1940s. But as the Nazi regime became more actively hostile toward Germany's Jews, they realized that they would have to accelerate their timetable. In 1938, Nazi anti-Jewish economic legislation prevented Moritz Gay from earning a livelihood as a regional representative for various German porcelain and glassware manufacturers. In October of that same year, a cousin of Peter Gay's was the first member of the family's younger generation to emigrate to the United States.

Not until April 1939, almost the last possible moment, were Gay's parents able to obtain the life-saving visas admitting them to Cuba.[33] Gay's last full year in Berlin witnessed the Anschluss of Austria, the annexation of the Czech Sudetenland, the infamous Kristallnacht, in which thousands of Jewish businesses, synagogues, and organizations were destroyed, and the passage of edicts permitting the seizure of Jewish property and possessions. Four months after Gay's departure, Hitler invaded Poland, and World War II began.[34]

Even after their escape, the family's future remained uncertain. The United States, where they had relatives, was their ultimate destination, but by the late 1930s the U.S. government had severely curtailed the number of European refugees admitted into the country. Consequently, Gay and his parents spent almost two years in Cuba before they were granted permission to enter the United States. In the spring of 1941, the eve of his eighteenth birthday, Gay finally arrived in Roosevelt's America, eager to find in reality a home he had already created in his imagination.

The family's decision at this point legally to change its name from Fröhlich to Gay marked both their enthusiasm for their new home and their rejection of a German identity. The youthful years under Hitler's Reich left Gay with a deep fund of rage toward all things German. For years after his family's escape, he "refused to read anything in the German language." During World War II, he admits that he "welcomed air raids on my native country with satisfaction: the more destruction the better. And during all this time I guarded my memories of Nazi Germany, like secret, privileged wounds, to preserve, with them, my hatred." Gradually, however, Gay's "rage abated, and my ideas changed. The only good German was no longer a dead German." Gay's self-release from his burden of anger was aided by the realization that "it is liberating to recapture the complexity of the past instead of living by slogans and melodrama."[35]

Through the 1950s and 1960s, Gay was largely silent about his experiences in Nazi Germany. However, for those who had lived through it, the Nazi era remained "a brooding omnipresence, a decisive experience."[36] By the late 1970s, Gay had gained sufficient distance to allow him to reflect on it in print. Yet he carefully avoids overdramatization, pointing out that his family was among the fortunate minority that eventually escaped the Nazi nightmare. Throughout his published works evidence can be found of Gay's struggle to attain intellectual and emotional control over this part of his own past. His *A Loss of Mastery: Puritan Historians in Colonial America*, published in 1966, contains what may be his first published reference to his experience of the 1930s. The book's dedication consists of a single page-length sentence:

To the many thousands of pilgrims, Jewish and not Jewish, German and Austrian and Polish, whom Hitler compelled to discover America—to the memory of my father who never made a good living here but so passionately loved his adopted country that he could not bear to hear it criticized, to the spoiled, idle wives who supported their unemployable husbands by washing floors, making candy and selling underwear, to first-rate professors who preferred exile in second-rate American institutions to success in Nazi universities purchasable at the price of divorcing their Jewish wives, to the physicians forced to waste precious years as laboratory assistants and to pass humiliating examinations that they might practice their calling once again, to the prosperous lawyers and businessmen who took menial jobs and made new lives without losing, in the midst of their isolation and their suffering, their will to adapt to a new country, to the D.P.s [Displaced Persons] who came out of the camps without their families and who, with the indelible numbers on their arms and their indelible memories, delighted in the open society of America and started new families . . . to all of these, I, a fortunate man, dedicate this book, part of my own discovery of America, offering these few words, and this small volume, in honor of men and women who were in their own ways heroes, who are in danger of being forgotten and who deserve to be remembered.[37]

Profoundly felt and beautifully crafted, the passage reveals the future historian of the great migration from Nazi Germany in the making.

Gay's youth in Europe was essential for his ability to believe himself a "fortunate man," to make himself "at home in America."[38] The enormous challenge of exile forced him to develop to the fullest his own drive for mastery. Gay did not begin to study English until 1937, at age 14. Once his family decided to emigrate, he began private lessons — one hour a week supplemented by intensive reading. While in Cuba in 1939–41, he took classes in business English and in typing at the Havana Business Academy, and he read serialized novels in American magazines sent by an uncle who lived in northern Florida. Gay still recalls dreaming in English for the first time while in Cuba. In the fall of 1941, when his family settled in Denver — a city chosen in the hope that the mountain air would benefit his mother's tuberculosis — his English was advanced enough to allow him to enter East High School.

Gay vividly remembers 8 December 1941, when students gathered in the school auditorium to hear the radio broadcast of FDR's "Day of Infamy" speech. Soon afterward, the family's financial situation compelled him to leave school and seek work. From late 1941 to early 1943, he worked in the shipping room of a factory that made caps. He lost this job when his employer discovered Gay's involvement in an attempt at union organization. He then found employment with a magazine distributor. Despite these menial jobs, he never lost confidence in his own future. Forty years later, he reflected that this belief "represented a confluence of causes: from some unarticulated inner resources, from my parents' high opinion of my talents, and, powerfully, from the American world in which I was so rapidly learning to find my way." [39]

From 1943 until 1946, Gay attended the University of Denver, where he majored in philosophy. His first encounter with eighteenth-century authors occurred during his junior year there in a reading course on philosophical empiricism in which he discovered David Hume. Living at home, he continued to work in the evenings, on weekends, and during summer vacations. He admits to having been "ignorant of what to do" when he finished college, but his one clear goal was to be a writer with a commitment to public issues. Near the end of his undergraduate studies, he was able to attend a summer seminar for students interested in politics in Salisbury, Connecticut. While in the northeast, he took the opportunity to travel to Harvard University, where he met, quite by chance, Raphael Demos, a professor of philosophy who specialized in Plato. After an enjoyable chat, Gay decided to apply to study philosophy at Harvard. Warned by friends that he needed a "safety school," he also applied to Columbia University's School of Public Law and Government. Although he was accepted by both institutions, Columbia's financial offer was the more generous. With his family in Colorado still facing financial difficulties, he took Columbia's offer and moved to New York City in the fall of 1946.

Gay chose better than he might have realized at the time. For a young person with lively political and cultural interests, New York in the late 1940s and the 1950s was an intensely stimulating environment. The city was now home to a larger community of émigré artists, scholars, and intellectuals than any place in the world.[40] The "New York intellectuals," that brilliant and contentious circle of erstwhile radical critics, were at the high tide of influence and fame. Their favorite forum, *The Partisan Review*, had become "a kind of house organ of the American intellectual community."[41] Against the background of the Cold War abroad and anticommunism at home, Irving Howe, Mary McCarthy, Delmore Schwartz, Sidney Hook, and other members of the group debated the most urgent political and cultural issues of the day. In the visual arts, Clement Greenberg and Harold Rosenberg were providing intelligent criticism of Modernist art. Centered in New York, the Abstract Expressionist movement of Gorky, Pollock, de Kooning, Rothko, and Motherwell reached its height in the early 1950s. With the expansion of the Museum of Modern Art in 1939 and 1953, and the opening of the Guggenheim Museum in 1959, Modernist painting and sculpture was entering the American cultural mainstream. The city's skyline was a panoramic artifact of architectural Modernism. In the literary domain, Philip Rahv, William Phillips, and Edmund Wilson were championing the modern American, French, and Russian novel.[42] In addition, American psychoanalysis, which had been greatly enriched by the influx of refugee analysts, was experiencing its golden age. Every branch of the academic humanities and social sciences was touched by Freud. The neo-Freudianism of Erich Fromm, Karen Horney, and Wilhelm Reich was being widely discussed, and the New York Psychoanalytic Institute was the most powerful training center in the country.[43] In all these cultural domains, the central and eastern European Jewish émigré presence was palpable.

In parallel fashion, Columbia University during the years 1945–65 could plausibly claim to be the United States' greatest university for study of the humanities and social sciences. In the English and comparative literature department, Lionel Trilling was a literary historian and cultural critic of international stature. Published in 1950, Trilling's *The Liberal Imagination* sparked a wide-ranging debate about the definition, meaning, and value of liberalism.[44] The art historian Meyer Schapiro, a Lithuanian Jew who had taught at Columbia since the late 1920s, was mesmerizing audiences with lectures on Modernist painting. Paul Henry Lang taught music history. As professor of history and, later, dean of the graduate school and then provost of the university, Jacques Barzun reached a broad public readership with books on nineteenth-century European culture and contemporary cultural issues. Barzun and Walter Dorn powerfully carried on a tradition at Columbia of studying intellectual history that had been established earlier in the century by James Harvey Robinson. And Barzun and Trilling taught a much-sought-after undergraduate colloquium that dealt with central texts in Western civilization. Paul Oskar Kristeller, another refugee professor, was emerging as the world authority on Italian Renaissance thought. Garrett Mattingly was gaining international recognition as a historian of early modern Spain. And, against the backdrop of McCarthyite conservatism, Richard Hofstadter was writing on American Progressivism and anti-intellectualism.[45]

A similar environment pertained in the fields of social theory and the social sciences. Paul Lazarsfeld, Robert Merton, and C. Wright Mills dominated Columbia's department of sociology. Furthermore, Columbia was then affiliated with the Institute of Social Research, staffed mainly by Jewish Marxist intellectuals from the Frankfurt School who had earlier fled Nazi Germany. In the early 1950s, Herbert Marcuse, a prominent academic representative of the institute, was a notable figure in New York intellectual circles. Marcuse's *Reason and Revolution* (1941) had sought to rescue Hegel from association in American minds with Nazism, and his *Eros and Civilization* (1955) attempted to synthesize Freudianism and neo-Marxism.[46] In short, these were heady days on campus.

At Columbia, Gay encountered the spirit of Weimar most directly in the person of Franz Neumann, who taught in the political science department. As a Jew, a labor lawyer, and an adviser to the Social Democratic Party, Neumann had been an early target of the Nazis. In 1933, stripped of his citizenship and driven into exile, Neumann settled in England, where he hoped to remain in touch with developments in Germany. By 1936, however, he was forced to admit that the Nazi regime was unlikely to fall in the near future. In an attempt to make a clean break, he decided to move to the United States, considering it "the sole country where, perhaps, an attempt would be successful to carry out the threefold transition: as a human being, an intellectual, and a political scholar."[47]

During the war, Neumann had served as a specialist on Germany for the Office of Strategic Services in Washington. There he met and inspired a group of extraordinary younger scholars who would later become influential historians of modern Europe, among them Franklin Ford, H. Stuart Hughes, Leonard Krieger, and Carl Schorske. After the war, Neumann's influence on historical studies continued through his teaching at Columbia. Fritz Stern, like Gay a graduate student there in the late 1940s, recalls how Neumann "communicated to his students his interest in the social origin and relevance of ideas."[48] A collateral member of the Frankfurt School who later took up a post on the Columbia faculty, Neumann became a key participant in debates of the 1940s and 1950s about the politics and economics of totalitarianism.[49]

It seems almost inevitable that Gay soon numbered himself among Neumann's "devoted following." Here was an exile whose intellectual and emotional resilience had enabled him to make a home and career in America while maintaining an active interest in European affairs. Neumann's hold upon the imagination and loyalty of his students was underscored in 1950 when word circulated that he (along with his wife Inge and his close friend Marcuse) was reading Freud with a view to applying psychoanalytic concepts to political theory and political history.[50] After an initial astonishment that "this severe and consistent Marxist" would study Freud, Gay and a group of fellow graduate students quickly followed Neumann's lead.[51] As he began to read psychoanalytic texts, Gay was at first drawn to Erich Fromm's theories, partly because of Fromm's socialism and partly because of his emphasis on control over the environment as a way to alleviate neuroses. In 1953, however, Marcuse published an attack on Fromm's "total environment" approach and, convinced by Marcuse's arguments, Gay turned to Freud.[52]

Gay's encounter with the spirit of Weimar continued throughout the 1950s, albeit in a less personal fashion. The writings of émigré intellectuals such as Ernst Cassirer, Erich Auerbach, and Erwin Panofsky enriched his developing approach to intellectual and cultural history and left an enduring imprint on his work. The influence of the brilliant neo-Kantian Cassirer, who had been visiting professor at Columbia the year before Gay arrived as a student, was the most significant. Cassirer's philosophy of symbolic forms, which described "the birth of modern self-consciousness from the matrix of pre-historic myth and medieval metaphysics" as a gradual process of self-liberation, provided a framework for Gay's own conceptualization of the history of thought and culture.[53] Gay was attracted to the way in which Cassirer had applied these ideas to the eighteenth century in his highly regarded study *The Philosophy of the Enlightenment* (1932). Focusing on intellectual criticism as a necessary creative act, Cassirer had presented the Enlightenment as a movement that "joined, to a degree scarcely ever achieved before, the critical with the productive function and converted the one directly into the other."[54] Gay also drew assurance from Cassirer that a historian could achieve some degree of objectivity when viewing the past. For Gay, the philosopher's insistence on "the objectivity of imagination" offered a way out of

the persistent but often sterile debate over the possibility of reliable historical knowledge.[55] Cassirer's work suggested that an individual's subjectivity
was not necessarily fatal to the attempt to gain knowledge about the world or
the past. Rather than a barrier, individual imagination, properly disciplined,
could be a source of true insight into the past. Gay's *Style in History* (1974)
built upon Cassirer's views by using Gibbon, Ranke, Macaulay, and Burckhardt as examples of how "perception is part of the total person, and the
dominant direction of the person may be, not toward myth or self-protection,
but toward mastery and reality."[56]

While teachers, books, and ideas are rightly considered the central aspect
of a scholar's education, friendship also plays a role. In this regard, Gay's
encounter at Columbia with Richard Hofstadter was of decisive importance.
The two men first met in 1950 when Gay, then an instructor in the government department, served on a committee with Hofstadter. Their acquaintance quickly grew into a deep friendship. Slightly older than Gay and already
well established in Columbia's history department, Hofstadter combined the
roles of personal friend and professional mentor. Gay gladly acknowledges
that "Hofstadter was an authority for me, as he was for so many who were fortunate enough to enter his ambiance, with his unsurpassed sense of style, his
refreshing intellectual boldness, to say nothing of his contempt for boundaries."[57] In his writings, Hofstadter imaginatively explored the intersection
of political and intellectual history, an approach Gay found congenial to his
own developing views.[58]

Hofstadter was crucial in helping Gay make the professional transition
from political science to history. During the fall of 1955, Columbia's department of history decided not to promote an assistant professor who specialized
in eighteenth-century Europe. To fill the gap, Hofstadter suggested Gay be
invited to shift to the history department. The invitation came at an oppor-
tune moment, since Gay's own future in Columbia's government department
was in doubt. Although Gay had studied philosophy as an undergraduate and
received his Ph.D. in political science, he had studied the sweep of modern
history through his work during the late 1940s and early 1950s in Columbia's
Contemporary Civilization course, a collaboratively taught, interdisciplinary
program in which each instructor led his section of students through the history of Western ideas and institutions.[59] Moreover, while at the Institute for
Advanced Study in Princeton in 1955, Gay met R. R. Palmer, who was then
teaching in the Princeton history department and who guided him through
a program of readings on early modern France. From the start Gay had found
himself consistently drawn to a historical approach, reflecting a growing con-

viction that, for him, history provided the most meaningful way to understand the world. In 1955, Gay's abilities and Hofstadter's influence secured Gay an assistant professorship in Columbia's history department.[60] The publication of *Voltaire's Politics* in 1959, dedicated to Neumann, was the transitional text between his careers in political science and intellectual history.

Columbia's history department provided Gay with an institutional and intellectual home where his career would develop for the next fifteen years. It was there that he accomplished all his work on Europe during the eighteenth century. By the later 1950s, the key elements of Gay's intellectual outlook were in place, including a grounding in the ideas of the Enlightenment, an interest in the cultural and intellectual aspects of modernity, the belief that Freud was an unsurpassed source of insight, and a view of modern Western history as a titanic confrontation between the forces of reason and unreason.

During the late 1950s, while visiting the Hofstadters at their summer home in Wellfleet, Gay came to know another individual who would play a crucial role in his life and career—Ruth Glazer. After a courtship lasting several years, the two married on 30 May 1959. A dyed-in-the-wool New Yorker and a published author, Ruth Gay has focused her attention on the history of European and American Jews.[61] It would be difficult to articulate the precise ways in which Peter and Ruth Gay have influenced each other; there is little doubt, however, that their marriage has been a remarkable four-decade partnership. In ways that the many dedications and acknowledgments to her in his books only hint, Gay's wife became an intimate personal and intellectual presence in his life.

Despite his happy marriage and despite the arrival of a dynamic group of younger historians at Columbia, including John Garraty, Eugene Rice, and R. K. Webb, Gay by the mid 1960s was becoming restless. Successively as student, instructor, assistant professor, and professor, he had been at Columbia for over twenty years. Many older faculty members who distinguished the school at mid-century had retired, dispersed, or died. By the late 1960s, faculty were becoming more focused on their individual careers.[62] As a result, the sense of intellectual community that had been the hallmark of Columbia's faculty began to fade. Also, as Gay aged and his financial situation improved, he dreamt of owning a home designed to his own specifications, which was not possible in Manhattan. And New York, including the Morningside Heights neighborhood around Columbia, was becoming a less livable place than before. Therefore, in the late 1960s, Hofstadter contacted C. Vann Woodward at Yale University on Gay's behalf. The academic world of the 1960s was very different than it is today: in 1969, the year he published volume two of

The Enlightenment: An Interpretation, Gay left Columbia to take up a chair at Yale in "comparative European intellectual history."[63] Socially and culturally, New Haven was much less vibrant than New York, but nonetheless Peter and Ruth Gay characteristically made a life for themselves there. The year they moved to New Haven, the Gays employed the architect Don Metz to construct for them a house derived from the Bauhaus style, the leading Modernist Weimar school of design.[64] Ten years later, they moved into a second, larger home built by the same architect in the same style. The Gays worked closely with the architect in designing the house and hung it with their growing collection of artworks, including etchings by Picasso and Kandinsky and a Motherwell print. Cultural Modernism was no longer just an object of textual analysis for Gay; it became his daily living environment as well.

At work, Gay once again joined a department that was entering an exceptionally strong period. In the 1960s, the Yale department of history had managed to shed the social elitism traditionally associated with the more conservative Ivy League universities and to assemble a highly impressive contingent of historical scholars. Gay counted among his new colleagues John Blum, J. H. Hexter, Howard Lamar, Edmund S. Morgan, R. R. Palmer, Jaroslav Pelikan, Jonathan Spence, Robin Winks, and C. Vann Woodward. Furthermore, during the 1980s, the department acquired a number of gifted, younger scholars — Ivo Banac, John Boswell, Linda Colley, Nancy Cott, Bill Cronon, and John Merriman — who were exploring new historical methods and subjects. Gay's intellectual personality was largely in place when he came to New Haven; Yale nonetheless provided a congenial and stimulating atmosphere in which he could work.

Perhaps most important, there was one area in which Gay found New Haven nearly as rich as New York: its psychoanalytic community. The department of psychiatry at Yale–New Haven Hospital was then heavily analytical. Until his death in 1957, the renowned psychoanalytic art historian Ernst Kris was a faculty member at the Yale Child Study Center. In the late 1960s and early 1970s, Anna Freud herself maintained close working ties with both the Yale Law School and the Yale Child Study Center. The Western New England Institute for Psychoanalysis was located in New Haven. And distinguished personalities such as Theodore Lidz, Hans Loewald, Ernst Prelinger, and Albert Solnit were local psychoanalytic illuminati. Yale, furthermore, had a rich tradition of cross-fertilization between psychoanalysis and the humanities. Among others, Harold Bloom, Peter Brooks, Joseph Goldstein, Robert Jay Lifton, and Geoffrey Hartmann were major scholars who brought creative and highly individual readings of Freud to their work. In

1974, Gay joined Yale's newly established Mark and Viva Kanzer Program in Psychoanalysis and the Humanities, a loosely associated and highly interdisciplinary cadre of scholars and physicians who shared an interest in the reciprocal study of psychoanalysis and the traditional humanities. At the same time, he enrolled as a nonmedical research candidate in the Western New England Institute for Psychoanalysis. He was in his early fifties. Altogether, Gay spent seven years in training, taking classes on Freud's writings and on specialized clinical topics, listening in on case seminar presentations, and undergoing personal analysis.

Gay's psychoanalytic study during the Yale years has spawned two lines of scholarship, one "psychohistorical," the other biographical. Since his graduate student days, Gay had been interested in the idea of applying depth psychology to history and politics. He had been impressed by a number of earlier studies, including Erich Fromm's psychological critique of fascism in the 1940s, Neumann's late essay "Anxiety and Politics," and Hofstadter's well-known analysis "The Paranoid Style in American Politics."[65] In 1961, he experimented with this approach in an *American Historical Review* article about the political mentality of the Jacobins.[66] During the later 1960s and the 1970s, the subfield of psychohistory emerged, inspired chiefly by Erik Erikson's writings. Gay, however, judged most formally psychohistorical work, with its emphasis on the extreme psychopathologies and Oedipal backgrounds of world-historical figures, to be dreary and reductionist.[67] He was interested in studying the psychology of everyday life and past collective as well as individual experience.

In *The Bourgeois Experience: Victoria to Freud*, Gay chose selectively to combine Freudian theories and techniques with the conventional modes of inquiry of social and cultural history in order to explore the subterranean emotional and sexual life of a past society. His study and personal analysis at the Western New England Institute for Psychoanalysis sharpened his sensitivity to the themes of sexuality, love, aggression, and introspection, to each of which he devoted a substantial historical volume. The very subject matter of the series — the desires, passions, anxieties, and ambivalences of people in the past — as well as his view of history as the grand working out of instinctual drives in conflict are key aspects of the Freudian dispensation.[68] Gay knew that psychoanalysis was not popular among his fellow historians, and he was aware of the decline in scientific and professional standing of psychoanalysis within American psychiatry during this period. Nevertheless, continuing to find the Freudian perspective extremely valuable, he proceeded fearlessly. Between 1984 and 1998, in the five thick volumes of *The Bourgeois Experience*, he illustrated his vision of "history informed by psychoanalysis."[69]

In a separate statement, he polemicized energetically about a role for psycho-analysis in the historical interpretation of human experience.[70] By 1990, he was arguably the best-known "psychoanalytic historian" in North America.

A second line of Freud scholarship was biographical.[71] Gay had long found Freud's life as important and compelling as his ideas. In 1976, he wrote an extended introductory essay to a collection of photographs of Freud's Vienna home and offices.[72] Then, in the mid 1980s, he temporarily suspended his work on the bourgeoisie in order to accept an invitation from the W. W. Norton Company to write a biography of Freud. While writing his 800-page *Freud: A Life for Our Time*, he described it as "the book I've spent my entire life not writing."[73] Translated into ten languages and nominated for the National Book Award, the biography was the most significant account of Freud's life since Ernest Jones's *Life and Work of Sigmund Freud* (1953–57). The fit between subject and author was superb. Gay's portrait of Freud represents a synthesis of themes that had dominated Gay's thinking and research for forty years: Freud as secular German Jew, psychological Modernist, cultural critic, lifelong self-revisionist, twentieth-century *Aufklärer*, and, finally, émigré to the free English-speaking world. By the early 1990s, Gay had complemented the biography with a collection of essays about Freud and an anthology of Freud's writings.[74]

Gay's years at Yale, between 1969 and 1993, were immensely productive. He published nearly all of his work beyond the Enlightenment while there. In 1984, he was appointed to one of the university's prestigious Sterling professorships. By the time of his mandatory retirement in 1993, however, the Yale department of history was entering a period of intellectual and professional change owing to the departure, retirement, or death of many of its most eminent members. Gay had effectively managed to participate in the golden ages of two of the country's greatest institutions of higher learning. His retirement brought to an end forty years in academe, during which he lectured to thousands of undergraduates and mentored scores of graduate students; it has, however, had no perceptible effect on his energies. He continues to lecture widely, to hold visiting professorships, and to publish. *Pleasure Wars*, the fifth and final volume of *The Bourgeois Experience*, appeared in January 1998. In 1997, Gay, at 74, became founding director of the new Dorothy and Lewis B. Cullman Center for Scholars and Writers at the New York Public Library.[75]

From the perspective of the late 1990s, Peter Gay belongs to the remarkable coterie of Germanic scholar-teacher-intellectuals who established the professional study of postmedieval European ideas and culture in North America during the third quarter of the twentieth century. This group—which includes Felix Gilbert, Leonard Krieger, George Mosse, Carl Schorske, and Fritz Stern—contributed mightily to establishing this tradition of scholarship in the United States during the decades following World War II.[76] Many younger scholars in the field today, including the editors of this volume, were their students. To be sure, there are notable differences in the work of these men. Nevertheless, their biographies and their basic vision of history share a number of features: as a cohort, they or their families have central European origins; they are drawn to the study of modern European history, with special attention to the German experience; they study the interactions among politics, culture, and thought; they are enormously knowledgeable generalists with descriptive and synthetic turns of mind who do not shy from depicting entire past cultures and ages; their work is highly and creatively cross-disciplinary; they pursue what today would be called contextual (as opposed to theoretical) approaches to their subjects; in their personal politics, they are liberals who study past liberal cultures and polities in crisis; they view the writing of history as a moral and political as well as scholarly endeavor; their ideological outlook has been centrally formed by the two world wars and the Cold War; they are vitally interested in contemporary affairs and maintain a strong sense of civic duty; and they combine passionate scholarly interests with great personal cosmopolitanism. As a species of scholar, the cultured humanist historian in the best tradition of *Mitteleuropa* is vanishing in an age of academic specialization and cultural fragmentation. As these individuals approach the end of their careers or their lives, and as "the short twentieth century" comes to a close,[77] we are in an excellent position to appreciate and to appraise their work, to historicize *their* achievement as a cultural phenomenon in its own right.[78]

Of these founding figures of modern European intellectual and cultural history, Gay is perhaps the most provocative and venturesome. Revisionism, his preferred mode of intellectual engagement, necessarily entails confrontation with other scholars. In his writing and in his person, Gay is very much an active political being. He has formed many judgments and has expressed them firmly in print. He has not been inhibited by prevailing fashions of method or interpretation; nor has he made concessions to contemporary critical correctness. With notable intellectual courage, he has taken up some of the most warmly contested topics in modern historiography. He regards the clash of ideas as a fundamental feature of the life of the mind in a free, liberal, individualist, and pluralist society.

Of the group, Gay is assuredly the most wide-ranging and prolific. He has written in every scholarly genre — essays, monographs, biographies, general interpretative syntheses, translations, textbooks, and anthologies. He has commented authoritatively on German, Austrian, French, and British history, and he has ranged across 300 years of the past. Methodologically, his work has moved from the history of political theory, to "high" intellectual history, to sociocultural history, and finally to psychocultural history and psychoanalytic biography. He has distilled his immense and imaginative learning into writings spanning half a dozen fields of knowledge, any one of which might have sustained the career of most professional scholars. As the bibliography appended to this volume records, he has written unceasingly about these subjects for nearly four decades. Measuring the influence of a contemporary author is a notoriously difficult exercise. However, Gay remains a leading voice in all five areas of scholarship that comprise the sections of this volume.[79] A remarkably large amount of what he has written, from the late 1950s to the present, remains in print today. Clearly, he stands proudly in the best tradition of Jacob Burckhardt, Johan Huizinga, and Ernst Cassirer. We believe that the book readers hold in their hands — a collection of studies, written by some of the world's leading historians of ideas and culture, that rationally and critically engage the themes to which he has devoted his life's work — is the best possible tribute to Peter Gay.

PART I

The Enlightenment and Its Heritages

2. Thomas Hobbes's Changing Conception of Civil Science

I

Although Peter Gay has never written at length about Hobbes, a number of highly perceptive remarks about the author of *Leviathan* are to be found in the two volumes of *The Enlightenment: An Interpretation*, Gay's masterpiece of the 1960s. Hobbes is hailed in the chapter on "The Science of Man" as one of the leading thinkers whom "the philosophes chose as their intellectual ancestors, in the study of man as elsewhere."[1] Commenting on their admiration, Gay adds that Hobbes's importance for the philosophes stemmed from the fact that he "had distrusted reason without exalting unreason."[2] In what follows I should like to explore and comment on this characterization of Hobbes's understanding of the place of reason in the human sciences.[3] I shall argue that, while it is certainly true that Hobbes came to distrust our powers of reasoning, he arrived at this distrust by way of an earlier and strongly contrasting willingness to speak about the methods of reason and science in the most confident terms. His initial faith and his later skepticism form my underlying theme.

II

While Hobbes undoubtedly regarded his political theory as a contribution to the science of man, he generally described himself more specifically as engaged in the writing of *scientia civilis*, or civil science. In the Epistle Dedicatory to his first work on politics, *The Elements of Law* of 1640, he promises to explain "the true and only foundation of such Science."[4] In the 1647 Preface to *De Cive*, he begins by speaking of his treatise as a contribution to *scientia civilis*, adding that this is the most valuable of all the sciences.[5] In the *Leviathan* of 1651, he reiterates that his aim is to demonstrate the benefits of "Morall and Civill Science,"[6] and in the revised Latin edition of 1668, he speaks of the dangers incurred by those who lack the *scientiae* needed for appreciating the duties of citizenship.[7]

By the time Hobbes began his formal schooling in the 1590s, the humanist educational theorists of Elizabethan England had put into widespread currency a distinctive view about the nature of civil science.[8] The sources from which they principally drew their understanding were the major rhetorical treatises of ancient Rome, especially Cicero's *De inventione* and *De oratore*, together with Quintilian's great summarizing work of the next century, the *Institutio oratoria*. These treatises chiefly offered expositions of *inventio, dispositio*, and *elocutio*, the basic techniques necessary for speaking and writing in the most persuasive style.[9] But they also embodied an explanation of why the acquisition of these rhetorical arts should be regarded as a matter of social and cultural importance. The influence of this explanation upon those who, like Hobbes, began their education in the grammar schools of Elizabethan England can hardly be overestimated.

To be an Elizabethan grammar school pupil was to receive an intensive training in the two primary elements of the classical "humanistic" syllabus.[10] First came the study of grammar, the goal of which was to memorize the vocabulary and structure of Latin and (sometimes) Greek in sufficient detail to be able to read the language with fluency. Then came rhetoric, the principal subject taught in the senior classes. Pupils were expected to master the leading classical handbooks on the art of rhetoric in conjunction with learning to imitate the best classical authors, the goal in this case being that of learning not merely to read but to write Latin — in verse as well as prose — in the best and most eloquent style.[11]

To study the art of rhetoric meant studying the undisputed masters of the ancient *Ars rhetorica*, Cicero and Quintilian. While their works were often merely expounded by schoolmasters or read in the form of extracts and digests, a number of Elizabethan grammar school statutes make it clear that serious pupils were expected to read these texts in full for themselves.[12] As a consequence, any grammar school pupil of Hobbes's generation would have studied the views of Cicero and Quintilian on the nature of *scientia civilis* more closely than those of anyone else. As Hobbes himself later insists in his own works on civil science, the impact of this classical education on the moral and political sensibility of his generation was at once overwhelmingly strong and, he came to believe, largely detrimental to the public good.[13]

Cicero had initially articulated his views about *scientia civilis* at the start of *De inventione*, which opens with an account of the founding of cities that was destined to be endlessly repeated by the humanists of the Renaissance. He begins by assuming that individuals, the substance or *materia* out of which cities are constructed, must come together in a union of an honorable and mutually beneficial kind if they are to realize their highest potentialities.[14] He further assumes that, at some determinate moment, some mighty leader must have recognized this fact and resolved to force the available human material into just such a unified shape.[15] This leads him to ask about the nature of the talents required by those who aspire to advise their fellow citizens on how to live together in friendship and peace. To put the same question the other way round, he asks about the character of *scientia civilis*, or civil science.

It goes without saying that for Cicero a good citizen is always and necessarily male. His thesis is that such men are distinguished by the possession of three linked qualities necessary and jointly sufficient for the effective practice of civil science. We must be capable in the first place of instructing our fellow citizens in the truth, and must therefore be persons of *sapientia*, or wisdom, the primary talent required of those who aspire to advise or teach. When reflecting on the origins of cities, Cicero declares that wisdom is the key quality that every founding father and lawgiver must undoubtedly have possessed.[16] Next, we must equally acquire a proper knowledge of the subjects on which we propose to speak, and must therefore be possessed of *ratio*, the power to reason and comprehend aright. Cicero declares in his account of the origins of cities that reason must therefore be of even greater significance than wisdom, since it can only have been through the highest reasoning faculties that founding fathers were able to counsel their fellow citizens and legislate wisely on their behalf.[17]

Cicero's further and contrasting argument is that civil science can never be a matter of wisdom and reason alone. If we wish to discharge the highest duties of citizenship — pleading successfully for justice in the law courts and beneficial policies in the assemblies[18] — it will never be sufficient to reason wisely about the issues involved. It will always be necessary to move or impel our hearers to accept our arguments. This in turn means that, besides being a wise man capable of reasoning aright, the good citizen must be a man of the highest eloquence, someone capable of arousing his listeners and persuading them by the sheer force of "winning" speech to acknowledge the truths that his reasoning brings to light.

The ideal citizen is accordingly seen as the possessor of two preeminent qualities: reason to find out the truth and eloquence to make his hearers accept it.[19] This is the essence of both the civic ideal and the conception of civil science put forward at the start of the *De inventione*. Cicero concedes that "eloquence in the absence of wisdom is frequently very disadvantageous and never of the least advantage to civil communities."[20] But he insists that, since "wisdom in itself is silent and powerless to speak," wisdom in the absence of eloquence is even less use.[21] What is needed "if a commonwealth is to receive the greatest possible benefit" is *ratio atque oratio*, powerful reasoning allied with powerful speech.[22] We can thus be sure that "cities were originally established not merely by the reason of the mind but also, and more readily, by means of eloquence."[23]

As a result, Cicero goes on, "a large and crucial part" of *scientia civilis* must be occupied by the art of eloquence, and especially by "that form of artistic eloquence which is generally known as rhetoric, the function of which is that of speaking in a manner calculated to persuade, and the goal of which is that of persuading by speech."[24] Cicero's further contention, in short, is that rhetoric is the key to eloquence. If we are to plead or deliberate effectively, we must learn the techniques of the *Ars rhetorica*, above all the technique of "ornamenting" or "adorning" the truth in such a way as to arouse our listeners to accept it. As Crassus puts it in book 3 of the *De oratore*, "the greatest praise for eloquence is reserved for the amplification of argument by means of *ornatus*."[25] The addition of such "adornment" provides the best means "either of conciliating the minds of our hearers or else of exciting them."[26] And the capacity to arouse the emotions in this way is what enables us to win our hearers over to the cause of justice and truth.

Why are Cicero and Quintilian so insistent that, in the absence of these rhetorical arts, even the wisest reasoning can never hope to carry us to victory in the law courts and assemblies? They regard the answer as particularly obvious in the case of "deliberative" oratory. The aim of writing or speaking in the deliberative mode[27] is to counsel or advise the adoption of a certain policy, a policy at once honorable and advantageous to the commonwealth. The speaker's aim is to reason in such a way as to persuade his fellow citizens to follow one course of action rather than another. But Cicero and Quintilian both adopt what modern philosophers like to call the "Humean" view that, even if I succeed in presenting you with good reasons for acting in some particular way, I can never hope by force of reason alone to motivate you so to act. Cicero gives powerful expression to this difficulty at the start of *De inventione* when praising the founding fathers of cities. The wisdom of these visionary figures enabled them to perceive "that there was an opportunity for men to achieve the greatest things"[28] if only they would abandon their lawless reliance on natural ferocity in favor of learning "to keep faith, to recognize the need to uphold justice and be ready to submit their wills to others."[29] But as he adds, it is impossible to believe that such legislators could ever have induced uncivilized multitudes to change their settled habits simply by reason and argument. We can be sure that "at first they cried out against such unfamiliar plans," even though it was undoubtedly in their interests to accept them.[30]

This reminds us why counselors and lawgivers must be masters of the rhetorical arts. They need to call on something more powerful than "mute and voiceless wisdom" if they are to alter our behavior; they need to supply us in addition with a desire to act rationally. But the only means of empowering wisdom in this way is to lend it the force of eloquence. "Eloquence," as Cicero repeats, "is essential if men are to persuade others to accept the truths that reason finds out."[31] This is why "I find that many cities have been founded, and even more wars have been ended, while the firmest alliances and the most sacred friendships have been established not simply by rational argument but also, and more readily, by means of eloquence."[32]

The rhetoricians add that it is not merely when speaking in the deliberative mode that orators will find it necessary to deploy the rhetorical arts. They will encounter the same necessity even when their sole concern, as in forensic oratory,[33] is to persuade their hearers to accept the justice of some particular verdict. This is because the force of reason is not merely insufficient to motivate action; it is also insufficient in a large number of cases to induce belief.

The rhetoricians are mainly led to this further conclusion by reflecting on the subject matter of forensic and of deliberative speech. An orator performing in the law courts will be engaged in prosecuting or defending in circumstances in which it will often be possible for a skillful adversary to mount a no less plausible case on the other side. An orator advising an assembly will similarly be attempting to show that some particular course of action ought to be followed in circumstances in which it will often be no less reasonable to propose a contradictory policy. In such situations there will be no possibility of demonstrating beyond question that one side is in the right. As Quintilian puts it, these are the sort of cases "in which two wise men may with just cause take up one or another point of view, since it is generally agreed that it is possible for reason to lead even the wise to fight among themselves."[34] These are instances, in other words, in which "the weapons of powerful speech can always be used *in utramque partem*— on either side of the case."[35] By the time Cicero came to write his *De oratore*, he was ready to insist that the subject matter of oratory makes the capacity to speak *in utramque partem* the most important skill of all. The figure of Crassus summarizes in book 3 by proclaiming that "we ought to have enough intelligence, power and art to speak on either side of the case" on all the leading commonplaces: "on virtue, duty, equity, goodness, dignity, benefit, honor, ignominy, reward, punishment, and all the rest." [36]

Once again, the moral is said to be that it will never be sufficient to reason wisely in order to win over an audience. Given that we can always hope to speak with plausibility *in utramque partem*, it will always be necessary in addition to have mastered the art of rhetoric, and thus to have learned how to deploy its techniques of adornment to allure or impel our audience round to our side. It is true that these considerations are not thought to apply in the natural as opposed to the moral sciences. As the figure of Scaevola concedes at the start of the *De oratore*, "we can pass over the mathematicians, the grammarians, and the followers of the muses, with whose arts this capacity for powerful speaking has no connection at all." [37] But Scaevola's main contention is that, in cases where we cannot look for certainty — as in most of the arguments characteristic of civic life — the need for eloquence becomes paramount, and with it a need for a mastery of the rhetorical arts. You cannot do without these skills "if you want the case you are pleading in the courts to seem the better and more plausible one, or if you want the speeches you deliver in the assemblies to have the greatest persuasive force, or if you merely want your utterances to appear truthful to the uninstructed and skillful to the wise." [38] If, in short, your arguments fall in any way within the purview of civil science, you will always find it necessary to supplement your reasoning with the moving force of eloquence.

III

When Hobbes reissued his *De cive* of 1642 in an expanded version in 1647, he inserted a new preface outlining his philosophical method and summarizing what he believed himself to have achieved. [39] He begins by stressing that, like the sages of antiquity, he is primarily concerned with the concept of civil science, [40] and he names Cicero among "the philosophers of Greece and Rome" who took pride in the contributions they made to "what is unquestionably the most valuable of all the sciences." [41] He follows their account of its subject matter, arguing as Cicero had done that civil science is chiefly concerned with the doctrine of public duties, or *officia*, [42] and can therefore be described (in Cicero's own words) as a science of justice. [43] He also endorses the classical view that such a science must be purposive in character. [44] He marks a sharp distinction, that is, between civil and natural science, although he allows that both are capable of amounting to genuine sciences. The aim of natural science is to understand the behavior of physical bodies, and in this case we need to adopt a purely mechanistic approach. But the aim of civil science is to understand the behavior of one particular type of artificial body, the body of the commonwealth. The peculiarity of such bodies stems from the fact that men are at once their artificers and their material.[45] And this means, for Hobbes no less than for Cicero, that we cannot avoid asking about the purposes for which they are brought into existence.[46]

When Hobbes turns to ask about these purposes, he again voices his agreement with the classical point of view. Cities are founded primarily "in order to preserve life," and more specifically to enable us, by reasoning firmly about our common concerns, to follow "the royal road to peace."[47] This is why we are justified in singling out the exceptional utility of civil science. "For nothing could be more useful than to find out how this can be done." Finally, Hobbes reiterates the classical belief that what a student of civil science needs above all to comprehend is the nature and range of the qualities that enable men, the material of cities, to mold themselves successfully into those particular shapes.[48] We need "rightly to understand the character of human nature, what makes men either fit or unfit to bind themselves together into a commonwealth, and how far men need to agree among themselves if they wish to form such a unity."[49]

There is a sense in which Hobbes continues to uphold these classical allegiances when he turns to inquire into the nature of the qualities required. He fully agrees that, as Cicero had put it at the start of *De inventione*, among the attributes we must possess if we are to succeed in bringing people together in civic unity are wisdom and the powers of reasoning to which it gives rise.[50] Beyond this point, however, Hobbes suddenly parts company with, and turns violently against, the presuppositions of classical and humanist civil science. The rest of his analysis, not merely in *De cive* but in his earlier *Elements of Law*, takes the form of a frontal attack on the assumptions about the character of *scientia civilis* put forward by the most revered humanist authorities.

The attack is launched at the outset of *The Elements of Law*,[51] the manuscript of which Hobbes completed and circulated in May 1640.[52] As we have seen, one of the two governing assumptions of humanist civil science had been that reason possesses no inherent power to persuade. Hobbes's superbly confident Epistle Dedicatory responds with the lie direct. His own ambition, he retorts, is to construct a science of justice and policy on the basis of right reason alone; to "reduce this doctrine to the rules and infallibility of Reason." The possibility of creating such a science arises from the fact that there are "two principall parts of our Nature."[53] One is admittedly passion; but the other is reason, "which," as he later adds in discussing the laws of nature, "is noe less of the nature of man than passion, and is the same in all men," since "God Almighty hath given reason to a man to be a light unto him."[54] This being so, there need be no barrier in principle to our employing our reason to lay the foundations for a science of civil life which, "Passion not mistrusting, may not seek to displace." As a result, we can hope to produce a form of learning, even in matters of justice and policy, that will finally be "free from controversies and dispute."[55]

Hobbes presses home his attack in the body of *The Elements*. Against the view that reason is impotent in the absence of powerful speaking, he insists in chapter 17 that reason is capable of dictating conclusions, of obliging us to follow particular arguments.[56] To this he adds in the opening chapter of part 2 that "reason teacheth us" about such matters as the value of government.[57] But he has already explained in chapter 13 that to teach is to beget in the mind of others a conception they will have no inclination to dispute.[58] What he is again affirming is that reason is capable of producing conclusions beyond controversy or doubt. He insists, moreover, that these "dictates" of reason are such that even those of the meanest capacity can hope to follow them without difficulty.[59] He accordingly repudiates with considerable asperity the rhetorical assumption that we must always make a special effort, as Quintilian had claimed, to win the attention and benevolence of our audience.[60] Reversing the usual argument, Hobbes declares that "if reasoning aright I winne not Consent (which may very easily happen) from them that being confident of their owne Knowledge weigh not what is said, the fault is not mine but theirs." This is because "as it is my part to show my reasons, so it is theirs to bring attention."[61]

Hobbes is no less vehemently opposed to the other governing assumption of humanist civil science, the assumption that no moral or political conclusion can ever be established with demonstrative certainty, since there will always be room to mount a plausible argument on either side of the case. To these contentions he responds even more polemically. The polemics in this case begin with his title, *The Elements of Law*. This is surely intended to recall *The Elements of Geometry*, the title given to Euclid's great treatise by Sir Henry Billingsley when he published the first English translation in 1571.[62] Hobbes's initial move is thus to associate his own treatise in the minds of his readers with one of the most celebrated works of deductive and demonstrative reasoning ever written.

The Epistle Dedicatory to *The Elements* continues in no less polemical vein. Hobbes is explicit in claiming that he has discovered the principles of a fully demonstrative science "of Justice & Policy," and that he will be able to explain for the first time "the true and only foundation of such Science."[63] He concedes that anyone writing about these matters will be dealing with issues in which he "compareth Men, & medleth with their Right and Profitt." But there is no reason to leave the study of civil science in its present state, in which "they that have written of Justice & Policy in generall do all invade each other, & themselves, with contradiction."[64] We can hope to proceed in a genuinely scientific manner, thereby arriving at conclusions that are "not slightly proved." We can hope in consequence, simply by force of scientific reasoning, to build up a set of political principles that, as Hobbes revealingly puts it, will be "inexpugnable" — incapable of being challenged or dislodged by an opposing force in the manner usually assumed to be inevitable.[65]

This second line of attack is also kept up in the body of the text. Hobbes's opening chapter begins by reaffirming that, when we are told that "true knowledge" is impossible to acquire in matters of justice and policy, this merely reveals "that they which have heretofore written thereof have not well understood their owne subject."[66] The fact is that we can lay down "necessary and demonstrable rules" about how to produce good and peaceful government.[67] We can hope in consequence to construct a science "from which proceed the true and evident conclusions of what is right and wronge, and what is good and hurtfull to the being and welbeing of mankinde."[68] We are not condemned to follow those who have merely "insinuated their opinions by eloquent Sophistry"; we can hope to write "concerning morallity and policy demonstratively."[69] Unlike the rhetoricians, whose art depends on insinuations and emotional appeals, we can hope to ground our arguments on principles of truth.

If we turn from *The Elements* to *De cive*, first published two years later, we encounter a still more confident effort to challenge and supersede the presuppositions of humanist civil science. Hobbes is even more emphatic that the methods of right reason carry with them an inherent power to persuade and convince, and thus that the idea of an alliance between reason and rhetoric is an irrelevance. He first assures us in his Epistle Dedicatory — in a direct allusion to the rival rhetorical doctrine — that he aims to persuade his readers "not by any outward display of *oratio* but rather by the firmness of *rationes*."[70] He speaks at several subsequent points about the "dictates" of right reason, and thus about its power to order, command, and enforce particular conclusions upon us.[71] And, in examining the duties of sovereigns in chapter 13, he adds that "the opinions they need to insert into the minds of men" can and ought to be inserted "not by commanding but by teaching, not by fear of penalties but by perspicuity of reasons."[72] The implication is unmistakable: if reason is sufficient to insert opinions into the minds of men, there is no place for the techniques of persuasion associated with the art of eloquence.

Hobbes likewise reiterates his earlier attack on the connected belief that, in matters of civil science, we can only hope to discuss the issues in a "probable" way, since it will always be possible to mount a plausible case *in utramque partem*. The Epistle Dedicatory begins by identifying, as the position to be overcome, the view that in discussions about justice an effective argument "can always be sustained on either side of the case."[73] Hobbes mentions that orators habitually "fight with contrary opinions and speeches,"[74] and alludes to the view that in politics (as Quintilian had conceded), we can only reach conclusions "worthy of being debated."[75] But he retorts that, so long as we follow the methods of science, we can argue "in such a way that no space is left for contrary disputes."[76] We can hope to reach conclusions capable not merely of being defended as probable but of being systematically proved.[77] And this, he claims, is what he has achieved. By contrast with all previous writers on civil science, "I have followed a proper principle of teaching," as a result of which "it seems to me that I have succeeded in this brief work in demonstrating the character of moral virtue and the elements of civic duties by connecting them together in a completely self-evident way."[78]

Soon afterward, Hobbes underlined this categorical distinction between the methods of rhetoric and science in his *Critique* of Thomas White's *De mundo*, the manuscript of which he drafted between the winter of 1642 and the spring of 1643.[79] White, like Hobbes, wished to distinguish between two kinds of philosopher. On the one hand, White asserted, "there are those who truly philosophise, that is, proceed by a certain way and the fixed route of demonstration";[80] on the other hand, "there are those who merely make a show of philosophy, but in fact confine themselves to logic, that is, exercise the faculty of debating *in utrumque* when dealing with philosophical material."[81] Hobbes in reply pounces on what he takes to be White's confusion between logic and rhetoric. "The fact is," Hobbes retorts, "that 'the capacity to proceed by a certain way and the fixed route of demonstration' belongs entirely to logic; by contrast, the ability to debate *in utramque partem* arises out of the discipline of rhetoric."[82] Having reaffirmed this distinction, Hobbes takes the opportunity to insist once more that the methods of rhetoric must be avoided. "Certainly," he concludes, "everything I have said seems to me to have been demonstrated."[83]

Hobbes summarizes his anti-rhetorical stance in a passage of magnificent effrontery in chapter 12 of *De cive* when discussing the dissolution of commonwealths. He recurs to the idea that wisdom can be acquired simply "by contemplating things as they are in themselves," and "by gaining an understanding of words in their true and proper definitions," thereby ensuring that our statements of belief are founded on principles of truth.[84] If we follow this route, we shall be able to produce "an expression of any propositions or conceptions in our mind which is at once perspicuous and elegant." As a consequence, we shall be able to express ourselves not merely with wisdom but with true eloquence.[85] This ability to speak with eloquence, and thereby to offer an explication of our beliefs at once elegant and perspicuous, was of course exactly what the theorists of rhetoric had always promised those capable of mastering the techniques of *inventio, dispositio,* and *elocutio.* But Hobbes insists that the key to elegance and perspicuity lies not in studying the art of rhetoric but in following the methods of science. With this contention, he finally turns the tables on the rhetoricians and their assumptions about the need to adorn the truth. He willingly accepts their central contention that eloquence is indispensable to civil science. But he maintains that genuine eloquence arises from "the Art of logic, not the Art of rhetoric."[86] It follows that, when we acknowledge the indispensability of eloquence, we are merely saying that it is necessary to reason logically; we are not in the least saying that it is necessary to call on the artificial aids associated with "that form of powerful eloquence which is separated from a true knowledge of things."[87]

A number of recent commentators have interpreted Hobbes's drive toward demonstrative certainty in the moral sciences as a response to the growing popularity of Pyrrhonian skepticism and associated arguments of a supposedly relativist kind.[88] I have been arguing, in contrast, that his project is best understood as a reaction not to skepticism as an epistemological doctrine but to the modes of argument characteristic of the rhetorical culture of Renaissance humanism. Hobbes is seeking to replace the dialogical and anti-demonstrative approach to moral reasoning encouraged by the humanist assumption that there are two sides to any question, and thus that in civil science it will always be possible to argue on either side of the case. He is chiefly reacting, in short, against what the English version of *De cive* calls the "rhetorication" of moral philososphy.[89] One of his fundamental purposes is to transcend and supersede the entire rhetorical structure on the basis of which the humanist conception of civil science had been raised. To understand his own vision of civil science as he first articulated it, we need to see it as framed in large part as an alternative to prevailing humanist orthodoxies, and as an attempt to replace them with a theory of politics based on authentically scientific premises.

IV

After the publication of *De cive* in 1642, Hobbes returned to his interrupted researches in the natural sciences. As we have just seen, the first significant piece of writing to which this gave rise was his examination of White's *De mundo*, a massive manuscript treatise that he finished in the spring of 1643. Thereafter he settled down to complete his *De corpore*, the first of three projected volumes into which he had decided to divide his general system of philosophy. He continued to labor on this text throughout most of the 1640s,[90] returning to his work on civil science only after the constitutional crisis in England reached its resolution with the execution of Charles I and the abolition of the monarchy in 1649. Spurred into action by the new and intractable problems raised by the establishment of the Commonwealth, Hobbes stopped work on *De corpore* and, in the space of less than eighteen months, completed what he described in a letter to his friend Robert Payne in 1650 as a new "trifle," his theme being "Politique in English."[91] Within a year Payne was able to report that Hobbes's trifle had arrived in the bookshops of Oxford, and that "he calls it *Leviathan*."[92]

It is commonly said that the political theory of *Leviathan* is "substantially the same" or "almost exactly the same" as in *The Elements of Law* and *De cive*, the changes between the earlier and later texts being "relatively minor" and "of secondary importance."[93] This seems an orthodoxy well worth challenging.[94] If we focus on Hobbes's account in *Leviathan* of the concept of civil science itself, what we find is not a new version of his earlier theory; we find a new and contrasting theory, evidently motivated by a desire to reappropriate much of what he had earlier cast aside. *The Elements* and *De cive* had been based on the conviction that civil science must transcend and repudiate the purely persuasive techniques associated with the art of rhetoric and the "adornment" of truth. By contrast, *Leviathan* reverts to the humanist assumption that, if the truths of reason are to be widely believed, the methods of science will need to be supplemented and empowered by the moving force of eloquence.

This is not to say that *Leviathan* should be accounted a work of rhetoric as opposed to a work of science. While it reflects a remarkable change of mind on Hobbes's part about the proper relations between reason and rhetoric, it also embodies a continuing conviction that civil philosophy can and ought to aspire to demonstrative certainty. In chapter 5, Hobbes reaffirms that what it means to master "the Science of any thing" is to possess the capacity to "demonstrate the truth thereof perspicuously to another."[95] In chapter 15, he applies his general argument to the case of civil science, repeating that moral and civil philosophy must take the form of "the Science of what is *Good*, and *Evill*, in the conversation, and society of man-kind."[96] He brings book 2 to a resounding close by declaring that he has in fact "put into order, and sufficiently or probably proved all the Theoremes of Morall doctrine," thereby articulating the principles of "the Science of Naturall justice."[97]

What Hobbes undoubtedly abandons in his later works, however, is his earlier confidence in the unaided powers of demonstrative reasoning to alter people's beliefs and behavior.[98] His first published hint of this new skepticism occurs in one of the annotations to the 1647 edition of *De cive*.[99] Describing what we can hope to discover by the light of natural reason alone, he now lays a somber emphasis on the fact that most people "are either not accustomed to, or else not capable of, or else not interested in arguing properly."[100] He subsequently enlarges on this insight in analyzing the concept of reason in chapter 5 of *Leviathan*. First he observes that even those who understand how to argue properly are highly fallible and prone to self-deceit:

And as in Arithmetique unpractised men must and Professors themselves may often erre and cast up false; so also in any other subject of Reasoning the ablest, most attentive and most practised men may deceive themselves and inferre false conclusions; Not but that Reason it selfe is always Right Reason, as well as Arithmetique is a certain and infallible Art: But no one mans Reason, nor the Reason of any one number of men makes the certaintie; no more than an account is therefore well cast up because a great many men have unanimously approved it.[101]

To this he adds, even more despondently, that most people have no understanding of right reasoning at all. At this juncture he revives a complaint not uncommon among scientific writers of the previous generation to the effect that ordinary people are actually afraid of the sciences. John Dee had lamented in his preface to Billingsley's translation of Euclid that anyone who devoted himself to mathematics was liable to be denounced as a "conjurer."[102] Hobbes makes exactly the same point, declaring that most people are so far from understanding science "that they know not what it is," the most obvious instance being the fact that "Geometry they have thought Conjuring"—"a magic art," as the Latin *Leviathan* adds.[103]

Hobbes also speaks with new frustration of what follows from such neglect of reason and science. The most obvious outcome is that people fall "vehemently in love with their own new opinions (though never so absurd)," and become "obstinately bent to maintain them."[104] A further consequence, as he later observes in discussing miracles, is that "such is the ignorance and aptitude to error generally of all men, but especially of them that have not much knowledge of naturall causes" that they are susceptible of being deceived "by innumerable and easie tricks."[105] Worst of all, as he adds in his critique of demonology, "wee see daily by experience in all sorts of People, that such men as study nothing but their food and ease, are content to beleeve any absurdity, rather than to trouble themselves to examine it."[106]

Given this ever-deepening skepticism about the capacity of reason to win assent, Hobbes found himself obliged in *Leviathan* to confront a new set of questions about the nature of *scientia civilis*, a set of questions he had earlier seen no reason to ask. If the findings of civil science possess no inherent power to convince, how can we hope to empower them? How can we hope to win attention and consent, especially from those whose passions and ignorance lead them to repudiate even the clearest scientific proofs?

These were exactly the questions that the classical and Renaissance theorists of eloquence had always addressed. As we have seen, Cicero in particular had argued that, in the quest for wise and peaceable government, the faculty of unaided reason *parum prodesse*, can scarcely hope to be of much benefit.[107] He had inferred that, if reason is to have any effect, it will need to be empowered by the *vis*, or moving force of eloquence, and thus by the rhetorical techniques of "adorning" and "amplifying" the truth.[108] Developing the same line of thought, Quintilian had underpinned Cicero's mechanistic imagery by arguing that, if the claims of justice and truth are to be vindicated, it will always be necessary to use the force of eloquence to pull or draw—*trahere*—our fellow citizens toward accepting them.[109] He had thus been led to identify the ideal citizen with the perfect orator, the figure whose rhetorical prowess enables him to arouse and attract us to the truth by way of adorning it.[110]

Returning in *Leviathan* to the humanist roots from which he had cut himself off in *The Elements* and *De cive*, Hobbes not only arrives at the same conclusions but expresses them in terms that echo with fascinating closeness these classical formulations of the case. He first hints at this new commitment in analyzing the concept of power in chapter 10. "The Sciences are small Power," he now concedes, but "Eloquence is Power," and is indeed to be numbered among the most eminent faculties of the human mind.[111] He develops the argument in chapter 25, in the course of which he introduces the play on words lying at the heart of the classical and Renaissance art of rhetoric. The reason why eloquence is so powerful, he now explains, is that those who listen to eloquent speakers find themselves "moved" to endorse their side of the argument. The effect of eloquence can thus be described by saying—and here he actually invokes Quintilian's terminology—that it "drawes" our hearers into accepting our point of view.[112]

A remarkable passage in the conclusion to *Leviathan* points the moral for the proper conduct of civil science. Hobbes begins by associating the argument he now wishes to put forward with the two leading *genera* of rhetorical utterance: the *genus iudiciale*, here described as "Pleadings," and the *genus deliberativum*, here described as "Deliberations." He closely follows the language used by the rhetoricians in the accounts they had given of the skills required for speaking with success in either of these genres. As we have seen, they had begun by acknowledging that the possession of *ratio* is indispensable. As Hobbes puts their claim, "the faculty of solid Reasoning is necessary: for without it, the resolutions of men are rash, and their sentences unjust." But they had added that, while *ratio* is necessary, it will never be sufficient to win round an audience. This is because, as Hobbes expresses their further claim, "if there be not powerfull Eloquence, which procureth attention and Consent, the effect of Reason will be little."[113] Here Hobbes echoes their language with particular closeness. When he remarks that, in the absence of eloquence "the effect of reason will be little," he offers a virtual translation of Cicero's *ratio parum prodesse*. And when he infers that reason will need to be supplemented with "powerfull eloquence," he similarly alludes to Cicero's image of the *vis*, or power, of eloquent speech.

Turning to reconsider this humanist understanding of civil science, Hobbes first observes that a number of writers have rejected it on the grounds of its apparent incoherence. The specific objection he mentions is exactly the one he had earlier voiced himself in *The Elements* and *De cive*. As he now states it, the alleged difficulty is that, if we call on solid reasoning as well as powerful eloquence, we shall be founding our civil science on "contrary Faculties." This is because the faculty of reasoning is "grounded upon principles of Truth," whereas the faculty of persuasion, and hence the art of eloquence, depend "upon Opinions already received, true, or false; and upon the Passions and Interests of men, which are different and mutable."[114]

As we have seen, Hobbes had initially drawn the conclusion that this does indeed render the humanist account incoherent, and that any civil science worthy of the name must therefore hold itself aloof from the art of rhetoric and the distorting influence of eloquence. Now, however, his ruminations on the *genus iudiciale* and the *genus deliberativum* lead him in the opposite direction, and thus to a startling rapprochement with the rhetorical tradition he had earlier sought to discredit and supersede. The right response, he now declares, is to recognize that "these are indeed great difficulties, but not Impossibilities: For by Education, and Discipline, they may bee, and are sometimes reconciled." The basis for this reconciliation, he goes on, lies in accepting the fundamental principle on which the classical rhetoricians had always insisted:

Reason, and Eloquence, (though not perhaps in the Naturall Sciences, yet in the Morall) may stand very well together. For wheresoever there is place for adorning and preferring of Errour, there is much more place for adorning and preferring of Truth, if they have it to adorn.[115]

He now endorses, in short, the very conclusion he had earlier denied: that the technique of adding rhetorical "adornment" to the truth can after all be made compatible with the methods of right reasoning, and can thus be employed to lend persuasive force to the findings of science.

Announcing this change of mind, Hobbes mirrors the language he had previously used to mount the opposite case. He had declared in *The Elements* that, so long as his readers "bring attention," it ought to be sufficient for him "to show my reasons" to win their assent.[116] He now acknowledges that the only way to win "attention and consent" may be to write with powerful eloquence.[117] In *The Elements*, he had concluded that, because rhetoricians "derive what they would have to be believed from somewhat believed already" and in doing so "must have Aide from the passions of the Hearer," the art of rhetoric must be outlawed from civil science.[118] In *Leviathan*, he concludes that, although it is true that rhetoricians rely "upon Opinions already received, true or false; and upon the Passions and Interests of men," the science of politics may nevertheless be founded on an alliance between reason and these apparently contradictory faculties.[119]

Hobbes continues to allow that eloquence is "not perhaps" suited to the natural sciences,[120] although even here his tone is so tentative as to imply that some rapprochement with the art of rhetoric may be necessary even in this case. But his principal contention is that, in the moral if not in the natural sciences, the ornamentation of truth should be attempted wherever possible. Drawing this last and crucial inference in the conclusion to *Leviathan*, he reverts once more to the language he had earlier used to mount the opposite case. He had argued in *The Elements* that the art of rhetoric is almost inherently treasonous, and had emphasized "how want of wisedome, and store of Eloquence, may stand together." [121] Now he not only affirms that reason and eloquence "may stand very well together," but adds the purely Ciceronian advice that, in the moral sciences, we should aim to adorn the truth "wheresoever there is place" for such adornment. [122]

None of this implies that Hobbes ever came to feel any positive admiration for the art of eloquence. On the contrary, it is clear from many observations in *Leviathan* that he largely retained his earlier anxieties about its irrational and potentially subversive character. [123] What he eventually felt obliged to acknowledge, however, was that the methods of science will need to be supplemented by the techniques of rhetoric if they are to have any beneficial effects. We cannot hope after all to outlaw the art of eloquence from the domain of civil science.

HARRY C. PAYNE

3. Wisdom at the Expense of the Dead

Thinking about History in the French Enlightenment

Introduction

What follows is a set of reflections on what might simply be called the "strangeness" of statements about the intellectual nature of writing and studying history in the French Enlightenment.[1] This way of looking at Enlightenment historiography — perhaps not necessarily a characteristic of the thing studied so much as of my own expectations — came to me a few summers ago while I was reading Rousseau's *Emile* (1762). I was struck by the powerful way in which history as an intellectual enterprise is progressively narrowed as Rousseau ponders its uses and limits, and by his striking juxtaposition and association of history and fables, and even of history and lies. But if the passages in *Emile* that systematically reduce history to anecdotes about great men undoubtedly mirror Rousseau's idiosyncratic approach to culture, the only other major statements by leaders of the philosophes that I have found —Voltaire's article "Histoire" in the *Encyclopédie* (1758) and d'Alembert's *Réflexions sur l'histoire, et sur les différentes manières de l'écrire* (1761) — present equally intriguing difficulties. These statements certainly move toward a broader range for history, but they also present a historical enterprise in some ways marginalized and undercut by epistemological convictions, rhetorical assumptions, and pedagogical imperatives.

The puzzles are deeper because we know well that the French Enlightenment was hardly as "unhistorical" as was once asserted. As we shall see, within Enlightenment culture at large, enormous energy was expended in unearthing and debating the past. Moreover, although the somewhat Cartesian philosophes rejected any controlling power of past practice or thought for the future, they certainly constructed numerous visions of the past in sup-

44

port of their inquiries, from the wide-ranging philosophical inquiries of Voltaire to the sociological-humanist explorations of Montesquieu, from the hypothetical histories of society and language of Rousseau to the broad vision of progress of Turgot and Condorcet. They theorize very little about the intellectual enterprise they and we call "history," however, and when they do, the results can only be described as thinly reasoned and oddly conservative compared to their otherwise bold explorations of the past in service of *les lumières*.

What follows cannot in any way claim to be final. First, I shall present the basic logic and rhetoric of the documents. From these readings we can discern the puzzles as we measure the Enlightenment's discourse on the writing and study of *histoire* compared to our more modern assumptions about the nature and tasks of academic history. These questions will then force us to consider the cultural situation in which the philosophes wrote history—a strikingly unstructured and miscellaneous collage of inherited approaches to the historical enterprise. Ultimately, this excursion should help us better describe and understand what divides the French Enlightenment, for all its potential modernity, from the modern era of historicist and professional history writing that followed, and what links its difficulties to the postmodern period in which we reside.

Texts

Rousseau's 'Emile'

Rousseau's educational "novel" portrays the hypothetical upbringing of a young Emile in isolation from society. The technique is "negative education," designed to preserve and nurture Emile's inherent goodness—the birthright of us all—from the corruption of human vanity. The method requires learning by working through highly controlled situations or "facts" in a progressive unfolding of the student's potential. Hence the study of history presents a structural dilemma. It offers ostensible facts, but at secondhand, and Rousseau, hostile to such learning in general, sees little immediate use for such artificially acquired learning.

The first encounter with history in *Emile* is predictably quite negative. While Emile is still a child, Rousseau asks whether this is the time to start teaching him history, as often proposed by educators in the eighteenth century.[2] Such an approach, Rousseau insists, is mistaken. He rejects the idea that the young can confront historical facts intelligently, because such facts depend on understanding their relations: "Can anyone believe that the relations which determine historical facts are so easy to grasp that ideas are effortlessly formed from the facts in children's minds? Can anyone believe that the true knowledge of events is separable from that of their causes or of their effects and that the historical is so little connected to the moral that one can be known without the other?"[3]

The study of history requires, for Rousseau, penetration beneath outward movement to the inner springs and meaning of action. The young student, incapable of such effort, will, as Rousseau goes on to illustrate by a story, childishly misinterpret any story.[4] Ignorance for Rousseau is always far preferable to error, and the teaching of history at this age is bound to inscribe in children's minds "a catalogue of signs which represent nothing for them."[5] Memorization of names, dates, places, and the like is simply a misuse of the capacities of the child's brain. Memorization just to show erudition corrupts the child, sowing the seeds of Rousseau's original sin, amour propre, or vanity: "It is with the first word the child uses in order to show off, it is with the first thing he takes on another's word without seeing its utility himself, that his judgment is lost."[6]

Rousseau next moves by an important association to the related question of fables, demonstrating in a manner parallel to his discussion of history how children who memorize fables, such as those by La Fontaine, are incapable of deriving proper lessons and, indeed, might just as easily learn the wrong lessons. Learning from stories at secondhand, whether ostensibly true (history) or knowingly false (fables), is not for the Rousseauian child. History and fable have the same lowly pedagogical standing.

The argument changes dramatically, however, when Emile enters adolescence. The greatest danger of childhood is the acquisition of empty words and signs and the vanity of hollow erudition. The greatest danger of adolescence is corruption of innocence, and Emile does not yet have the strength of mind to learn directly from involvement in human affairs. Hence Rousseau chooses this moment to alter his method from one of learning by controlled experience to learning at secondhand through the study of history, followed, as before, by consideration of the study of fables.

In these passages the controlling metaphor is that of the theater.[7] In order "to put the human heart in reach without risk of spoiling his own," the tutor endeavors "to show him men from afar, to show them in other times or other places and in such a way that he can see the stage without ever being able to act on it."[8] Through the study of history, one is able to move beyond words to deeds and their consequences and can thus strip away their masks. Immediately, however, Rousseau sees obstacles.[9]

First, it is hard to find, as it were, the right seat in the right theater for the right play. Most history recounts tales of evils, disasters, and decline: "History, like philosophy, ceaselessly calumniates humankind."[10]

Second, the facts are far from truthfully presented, as human interests and prejudices shape their presentation by the historian. Even if the pure fact is recounted, it can be radically altered by the context and perspective in which it is placed. "Critical history," which seeks to analyze the facts, is likely to distort. The will to find causes and meanings is genuine, but doing so is fraught with difficulty: "Of what importance to me are the facts in themselves when the reason for them remains unknown to me, and what lessons can I draw from an event of whose true cause I am ignorant? The historian gives me one, but he counterfeits it; and critical history itself, which is making such a sensation, is only an art of conjecture, the art of choosing among several lies the one best resembling the truth."[11]

Hence, one can argue that there is little difference between historical novels and what purport to be true histories, except that the novelist consciously sets a moral goal, for better or worse, while the historian is often morally indifferent. One could also argue (indeed Rousseau himself appears to do so in an earlier footnote)[12] that veracity is not all that important as long as "the portraits are well rendered according to nature." Rousseau agrees, but sees a renewed difficulty: now the student is slave to the imagination of the writer rather than learning directly from facts.[13]

Having posed the epistemological difficulties, Rousseau turns to the problem of content—which stories can provide the proper reservoir of factual experience for Emile. Rousseau proceeds to weed out most existing texts.[14] All modern historians appear afflicted with the desire to be brilliant, hence display the vice of vanity. Philosophical historians are too afflicted with "systems" to present facts simply and accurately. The ancients offer more hope, but Polybius and Sallust are inappropriate for the young, and Tacitus is far too philosophical. Thucydides comes closest to the right approach of bare factual recounting: "Far from putting himself between the events and his readers, he hides himself. The reader no longer believes he reads; he believes he sees."[15] Unfortunately, however, Thucydides talks only of wars. As for Herodotus, his laudable naïveté degenerates too often into "puerile simplicities," and the "political" and "rhetorical" Livy is more appropriate for a later age.

That leaves only Plutarch, and specifically that writer's ability to describe the great in private, intimate settings and anecdotes. Giving an example from the life of Turenne, Rousseau appears to envisage a curriculum composed of a sequence of dissociated moral tales from the lives of the great for the young adult. Emile will confront the world of action at secondhand, from backstage as it were, and see the masks, levers, pulleys, and costumes.[16] More complex rumination, in the manner of Livy and Tacitus, is in the distant future, once Emile is mature and secure in his own moral judgment.

Prepared by history, Emile will now take his first preliminary steps onto ʰ stage of social experience itself. At this juncture, the learning of fables is also introduced, as Emile is now capable of drawing proper moral conclusions. Fables, like history, will attach vivid images to moral principles, appropriate as long as the pupil develops the lessons for himself.[17] Viewed from the perspective of Rousseau's pedagogical moralism, therefore, both history and fable provide equivalent perils for the child and equivalent virtues for the young adult.

Voltaire's "Histoire"

Voltaire received the commission to work on the article "Histoire" for the *Encyclopédie* and, after several revisions, submitted a final version in 1758.[18] Like much of Voltaire's writing about history and the past, it sorts out alternatives with strong and firm judgments. He begins with a striking and ambiguous definition: "History is the recital of facts presented as true; as opposed to fable, which is the recital of facts presented as false."[19]

Rather than continue with epistemology, however, Voltaire distinguishes three kinds of content: the history of opinions, which is the gathering together of human errors; the history of the arts, which might be the most useful, because it combines knowledge of their invention and mechanisms; and finally natural history, which is actually part of physical sciences, not history properly understood. He then makes a bow to the traditional distinction between sacred and profane history (as a gesture to the censor), vowing not to touch the former.

Once again we have a path not followed, however, as Voltaire turns to the question of the origins of history, finding its roots in the stories told by fathers to children, transmitted over the generations, and losing probability with each retelling. It is in fact here that Voltaire finds his principal theme, being deeply interested neither in the question of truth and fiction in narratives nor in the taxonomies of history. The largest part of the article dwells on the unreliability of most supposed "history," especially from the times before printing. Most history, therefore, is presented as true but is really "fable" and ought to be presented as false. That is his principal mission here, as in many of his historical writings.[20]

Speaking against those antiquarians who put great stock in the testimony of monuments, coins, and other remains of antiquity, Voltaire insists that there are only three incontrovertible monuments of historical interest: the Babylonian astronomical tables, the Chinese calculations of the solar eclipse, and the Arundel marbles. Of written accounts, only two strike him as having any high degree of probability: the chronicles of the Chinese and the *History* of Herodotus. And indeed the latter must be carefully discounted: "Almost everything he recounts based on the testimony of strangers is fabulous; but everything he saw is true."[21]

And so it goes for several pages, the greater part of the article, a series of cautionary judgments on most of what had passed for history in his times. Most history becomes fable.

Only then does Voltaire return to some of the questions that were familiar to his readers an   nmon to most discussions of history in this period: What is the use of history? It consists largely in the citizen and the public authorities learning from the *mœurs* and laws of other lands. Most of all, one can learn from the horrors of the past: "One can never place before their eyes too often the crimes and miseries caused by absurd quarrels. Certainly by refreshing the memory of these quarrels one hinders them from returning."[22] Modern history offers a special lesson for princes, that is, that there will always be a balance of power, a tendency for states to join together to prevent one from dominating.[23]

From these basic lessons, Voltaire returns to epistemology, the question of "certitude" in history, which had been the stuff of discussion in learned circles for more than a century. He avers that there can never be the certitude of "mathematical demonstration," but only, at best, "extreme probability." That can best be achieved, he implies, by eyewitnesses. We must not believe what is against the "ordinary course of nature."[24] Sometimes even true but incredible tales must await eyewitness accounts to confirm them, such as Marco Polo's account of the Chinese empire and the story of the man with the iron mask.[25] On the other hand, if all of Paris indicates that a man has been resurrected from the dead, one still cannot give that credit.[26]

Voltaire then returns to his more comfortable theme—the profound lack of certainty in history, and, through a series of queries, casts doubts on many of the received stories from antiquity: "One could create immense volumes out of all of the famous and accepted facts that must be doubted."[27] This includes those monuments, ceremonies, medals, and the like that were so much the focus of erudite thought about antiquity and the Middle Ages. Only direct contemporary testimony deserves credence; the rest is too vulnerable to fabrication. So, too, one must distrust the tendency of ancient historians to embellish, through orations and portraits, standard topoi of humanist historiography. These are poetic remnants of Homeric style. Literal orations might well be the most useful part of history. "But what is fiction in a poem becomes, strictly speaking, a lie in a historian." And even if the ancients did this, one need not imitate them. All it shows is that "several ancients wanted to display their eloquence at the expense of truth."[28]

He then considers the injurious role so-called *histoires* can play in public life. Commenting on Cicero's assertion that the historian should neither speak falsely nor hide any truth, Voltaire argues that truths likely to help the state should be revealed, but that truths with no bearing on public affairs may simply become material for satire and should be avoided, whatever their factual basis. So much of what bears the title *histoires*, he indicates, is actually scurrilous libel unworthy of the name.[29]

As to the style of history, Voltaire has surprisingly little to say. Each of the ancients has virtues to be emulated. But the modern historian has a greater burden because of the accumulation of data and the desire for accuracy in details of laws, manners, commerce, finance, agriculture, and population. Indeed, Voltaire seems deeply ambivalent about the advent of printing and the concomitant growth of access to facts; such factual surfeit threatens to clutter historical accounts. But he offers no guidance on how to resolve this dilemma. Histories of foreign lands must pay more attention to geography, and all histories need pay more attention to the wider world of what we would call culture and society: "If you have nothing more to tell us but that one barbarian succeeded another barbarian on the banks of the Oxus and the Iaxarte, what use is that to the public?" With that limited, characteristically negative guidance, Voltaire commends a style that is "serious, pure, varied, and agreeable," ending with the expectation that few can achieve that mastery.[30]

D'Alembert's 'Réflexions'

The context of Jean Le Rond d'Alembert's major statement on the nature of history is quite different—a discourse to the Académie française dating from 1761. His ostensible posture is that of one defending the study and teaching of history against those who are hostile or indifferent to it. He also ridicules those for whom history is a low-level pastime—"this multitude, too vacuous to ponder deeply, too vain simply to vegetate."[31]

More seriously, perhaps, d'Alembert ridicules those who reject the study of history outright, presenting for argument a composite straw man possessed by Cartesian and Rousseauian disdain for and distrust of the past. This hypothetical detractor rejects history on many grounds: the burdens of the present are heavy enough; the story of the past gives examples almost exclusively of foolishness, from which there is little to learn, since they simply replicate the lessons of everyday life; the truth is almost always obscured by the passions and interests of those who report or retell a story; knowledge of God, nature, and self are the true objects of philosophy; the edifying feats of the past go largely unchronicled, and we have no need of the stories of violence, passion, and stupidity handed down to us. Those who pass on such tales resemble "the naturalists who describe without feeling the battles of spiders who devour each other, and who would forget to make us aware of the industry with which they constructed their web."[32] To all this d'Alembert counters:

Let us attempt, in [history's] defense, to set over against our cynic the wise and moderate philosopher who reads history *to assure himself that past generations have nothing with which to reproach the current one; to find consolation in this life, by viewing the spectacle of so many illustrious and respectable unfortunates who have lived before him; to search in the annals of the world for those precious traces, albeit weak and sparse, of the efforts of the human spirit, and the much more visible marks of the care taken in all times to stifle it; to observe, without being overcome, in the fate of his predecessors, what will come to him, if he unites the same courage with the same success, and if he has the fortune or misfortune to add a few stepping-stones to the edifice of reason.* History seems to reiterate at each instant what the Mexicans used to say to their children at the moment of their birth: *Remember that you have come into this world to suffer; therefore suffer and be silent.* In this way history instructs, consoles and encourages him. He forgives it for being unsure about what it teaches him, because that is the destiny of human knowledge, and because the obscurities of the physical universe console him for not seeing more clearly within the moral universe.[33]

At the very least, the accumulation of fact is a "conventional necessity" to fill vacant points in conversation—"one of those very necessary useless things that serve to fill the immense and frequent voids in society."[34] History is most useful, therefore, to philosophers as a consolation, and to princes as a fount of cautionary wisdom and lessons.

Having thus established his basic justification, d'Alembert proceeds to wrestle in rather random form with a number of issues on his mind and presumably on the minds of his learned listeners:

If history above all is to serve princes, and if it is a given that one must never write untruths, is one obliged to tell all, or is silence sometimes justifiable? His resolution is avoidance — a recommendation that one never be put in that position by scrupulously avoiding contemporary history, where the motives to hide things are greatest. Indeed, he speculates that by forbidding the writing of current history, princes would do their times a courageous favor.[35]

How, then, should history be written? "The simplest," he writes, "and at the same time the most appropriate [way] for the person who wishes to write on history, that is *the truth*, is the writing of *chronological summaries*." That approach alone would leave history on incontestable grounds.[36] D'Alembert recognizes a human thirst for more, however, "and finds only too many pens ready to serve and deceive them." He proceeds to ridicule those who are too eager to fill gaps in our knowledge of facts and causes with their own specu- lations, undaunted by the clear difficulties of doing so. He also finds deep fault with models of ancient rhetoric and its suspicious desire to invent ora- tions for major actors.[37]

D'Alembert recognizes that his own century has moved away from rhe- torical history in the strict humanist mode, although he finds difficulty here as well, for narrative history is thus delivered into the hands of mediocrities who "write history the same way most people read it, in order not to have to think."[38]

Trying to find a middle ground, but obviously not comfortable with either, d'Alembert suggests two models, all the while cautioning how easily they can slip into error. One is the "abridged universal history" that gives general sum- maries of facts together with the writer's reflections: "a reduced but colored picture of events, foreshortened but animated." The other is "philosophical and reasoned" history, in the manner of Montesquieu's *Consideration of the Grandeur and Decadence of the Romans* (1734), which tries to find "in their first principles the causes of the growth and decay of empires."[39] D'Alembert cautions at some length, however, on the precariousness of these enterprises. In a startling move, he then suggests that "of all the ways of writing history, that which merits perhaps the most confidence, by the simplicity that must be at its core, is that of individual memoirs and letters." The virtue of these mediums is that, although possibly careless, verbose, and disorderly, they carry the "air of truth," especially if they were not written with publication in mind.[40]

D'Alembert then turns to the pedagogical question of how to teach history, offering two major suggestions. The first, which he had ventured earlier in his *Encyclopédie* article "Collège," is that history be taught backward, from the current and most detailed to the more distant, less interesting, and less certain. In this way students "would not learn the names of Dagobert and Chilperic before those of Henry IV and Louis XIV."[41] The second suggestion is that one compile a collection of edifying words and deeds from history, in the manner of Plutarch, to instill the values of "humanity, justice, and kindness" into students. This would provide a necessary corrective to the tendency of the republic of letters to dwell on the negative and scandalous.[42]

Contexts

Although the philosophes were without doubt capable of striking commentaries on the past, one cannot help but be struck by the curiously limited, defensive, unambitious, and occasionally self-contradictory nature of their statements on the historical enterprise, which bespeak both confused thinking and an apparent lack of interest in trying to create coherence. To understand the individual statements of these authors — their *parole*, in the parlance of elementary linguistics, one must understand the larger context, the *langue* as it were, offered to them by their surrounding culture. These texts are repositories and symptoms of larger cultural discussions and confusions. Several interrelated contexts appear most germane: the received assumptions of Renaissance humanism; the conditions of the production of history; the situation of the teaching of history; changing ideas about the possibilities of knowing the past; and the challenge of a different kind of storytelling, the novel.

Humanism

One must first remember that the major intellectuals of the Enlightenment received a strictly classical education and that assumptions from antiquity and from humanist Renaissance letters were deeply inbred.[43] The assumptions of the humanist's rhetorical model of history as a branch of rhetoric were tested in the Enlightenment but never substantially rejected. What were these assumptions?

First, it was assumed that history is a branch of rhetoric, part of the art of description and persuasion using a specific content, the near and distant past. Antiquity provided a few different models — from the biographical-anecdotal approach of Plutarch, to the purportedly straightforward narrative of Thucydides, to the more reflective and philosophical Tacitus. This inheritance received a powerful recasting in the civic humanist world of the fifteenth-century Renaissance in Italy, where writers such as Machiavelli,

Guicciardini, and later Paolo Sarpi provided examples of a rhetoric attempting to capture the dynamic flux of power, fortune, and virtue.[44]

Second, historians must tell the truth. Cicero's injunctions that historians must tell the truth and hide nothing were treated as sacred and often quoted, although, as we shall see, in an era of censorship and official historiography, the hold of the second injunction was somewhat tenuous.

Third, telling the truth did not mean that there was no room for invention, which was a rhetorical virtue. Truthfulness meant, to some extent, empirical accuracy, but it also meant verisimilitude and truthfulness to the character and the situation. Hence the famous invented orations, often the literary high points of humanist narrative, that came to vex a more properly empirical age.

Fourth, history existed to teach virtue, to promote wisdom among those in authority by providing exemplars of action, success, failure, propriety, and corruption from the past. As opposed to philosophers who wanted to teach virtue by precept, the humanists of antiquity and the Renaissance held out the need to learn from experience through stories of the past.[45] Statements of this standard were routine in all discussions of the nature and practice of history in the rhetorical mode.[46] One should not take these simply as mandatory tropes. That the study of history should yield moral fruit in a traditional vein shaped all discussions of its theory and practice. The notion of a historical practice motivated by disinterested aesthetic or scientific principles simply was not conceived of, even though the Enlightenment saw the amplification of such notions in the approach to material nature and the fine arts.[47]

Last, the ideal historian is someone who has participated in affairs of state and had direct contact with the events described or those who participated in them. Many of the historians of antiquity and the Italian Renaissance fit the pattern of an aristocratic retired man of action providing analysis of affairs of state close to his experience for those destined for such action in the future.[48]

Very little about these cultural assumptions was added to or modified in the education of the philosophes. As we shall see, antiquarian, erudite approaches to the past provided a dramatic new model, one that they received with ambivalence. Speculative thinkers such as Jean Bodin (1530–1596), in a secular vein, and Bishop Jacques-Bénigne Bossuet (1627–1704), in a religious one, exemplify attempts to transcend the history of individual events and states, looking to derive grand patterns from the flow of so-called "universal history." Such attempts ran counter to the Enlightenment horror of systems, however, and were rarely emulated, except perhaps in Condorcet's late-

Enlightenment model for a universal history of the progress of humankind. Much of thinking portrayed in the documents here must, therefore, be seen as modifications and adjustments to Renaissance humanist assumptions in the context of the evolving political and intellectual conditions of eighteenth-century France.

Production

One must also look at the specific context of the production of historical works in eighteenth-century France. The writing of history took place under clear institutional constraints of patronage, ideology, and censorship. Insofar as philosophes speculated about history writing, they did so largely within these inherited limitations.

There was no way to earn significant income as a professional writer of history. One writer, Nicolas Lenglet-Dufresnoy (1674–1755), did make a manual for the study of history a significant part of his publication repertoire, frequently re-editing it and earning reasonable sums. He was the exception. The principal "professional" historians were official "historiographers." The office of royal historiographer was established in the seventeenth century as part of the crown's attempt to control its own reputation in history. In the eighteenth century, it was used in the battle for public opinion, both through official accounts of events and wars and in the legal-historical documentary war over the origins of the monarchy and the history of its legal powers.[49] Needless to say, the range of play for the official historiographers was narrow. Indeed, Voltaire, who served briefly in that office and who wrote the article "Historiographe" for the *Encyclopédie*, distinguishes between the work of the historiographer and that of a historian as two different enterprises.[50]

The Académie des inscriptions, reconstituted in 1701 by Louis XIV, provided a base of support for some scholars of the past, who could combine their payments from it with various offices in the production of royal and other princely historiography, as well as positions as tutors and librarians. Most members who were not simply honorific devoted their efforts to antiquarian and documentary research or to the composition of manuals for the study of history, rather than narrative accounts. As pensioners drawn largely from the third estate, they needed to be cautious and royalist in their judgments.[51]

Official and self-censorship shaped much of what could be done, even within the confines of documentary and annalistic presentations. History was, in the official words of the censoring officials, to devote itself to *vérités utiles* from the perspective of the state. Censorship in the eighteenth century had a peculiarly intermittent character, and so authors could, through clever framing, anonymity, or foreign publication still dance in these chains. But the chains were real enough and the consequences, as many French intellectuals learned, could be imprisonment or exile.[52]

Hence a large part of the production of writing about the past circled around the kind of mixture of scientific exploration, narrative shaping, and implicit judgment we imagine as the heart of the historical enterprise. Documentary collections burgeoned, sponsored both by the state and by corporate entities — nobility, *parlements*, monasteries, religious orders, towns — for establishing moral and legal bases. Erudition flourished in local and national academies, focused on local documents, monuments, customs, and geography.

There was also a large and continuing market for chronologies, *abrégés*, manuals (called *ars historicae*), historical tables, and the like. These were designed for the tutor, the autodidact, and the schools, although, as we shall see, there was no comfortable place for history in the curriculum per se.[53]

This structure left room on the margins for numerous official and unofficial memoirs, as well as encouraging a lively market for various shades of scandalous accounts on the periphery of the censorship system. So, too, letter-writing with a view to historical posterity was a cottage industry among intellectuals, and the unofficial circulation of letters was quite common.

As we can see, therefore, the recounting of the past, under the very broad umbrella of *histoire*, went on in many separate venues. The expanding world of publishing and small, but evident, increases in literacy of the eighteenth century only enhanced this plurality. This has remained true ever since, but there was then no historiographical paradigm, similar to those in the modern academy, to provide a controlling focus for theorizing the endeavor.

Teaching

The teaching of history posed peculiar problems to the French eighteenth century. While philosophes and other educators recognized that there was some importance to historical study, especially the history of more recent times, it fitted nowhere comfortably into the curriculum of the *collèges* where the young adult men of the eighteenth-century French elite were to be educated. Indeed, François Furet has gone so far as to speak of the "impossibility of teaching history in the eighteenth century."[54]

Of course, the term "impossibility" is a bit exaggerated, but it makes the essential point that we cannot take our categories for granted. Furet describes history as a "stowaway aboard official curricula,"[55] in the sense that it was rarely a formally designated part of the sequence of subject matter in the *collèges.* Rather, the content of history appeared largely within the study of Latin and Greek letters. History as a mode of inquiry or as a locus of epistemological problems could not and did not arise in that context, nor the notion of training students to go on to be "historians" in any professional sense, there being, as we have seen, no profession of history per se. History was overwhelmingly taught as a branch of letters in the classic rhetorical exemplary mode of learning by example. In the one case where a major philosophe approached the design of a history course for his pupil, the abbé Condillac adheres very closely to the exemplar tradition in his explanation of his aims and goals.[56]

The leverage for a history outside of classical letters was provided by the growing sentiment among educational reformers that students needed a sense of *national* history in more recent centuries — to inculcate relevant lessons, build national identification, and teach loyalty to the monarchy. Hence a large portion of history writing in the eighteenth century was devoted to the design of manuals, chronologies, annals, and the like to aid the young student and the willing teacher to build this knowledge into study.[57] Most were to be used in the context of private tutoring as the curricula of the schools proved generally impenetrable in any formal way until the revolutionary period. "Rarely," one historian has written, "has a historiography had such a preponderantly pedagogical character." These manuals varied greatly in depth of information, but tended to present the information very much in an annalistic fashion, rigidly organized around chronology and dynasty.[58] The demands of censorship kept judgments bland and politics largely loyal.[59]

Epistemology

As rigid as were the conditions for writing and teaching history, the philosophes inherited a rich and evolving structure of discussion with regard to theories of knowing the past. Before the mid seventeenth century, the question of knowing the past as object does not appear to have been a significant cultural issue. One might say that the past was a subject to be represented, and the humanist project of the Italian Renaissance gave that rhetorical problem new shape and dynamism with its concern for the role of human strength and uncontrollable circumstance in the shaping of human affairs.[60] The seventeenth century saw a burgeoning of interest in the problem of *knowing* as prior to the problem of *representing.* The discussion took place under four major headings: philological criticism, antiquarian erudition, a revived Pyrrhonism, and a nascent interest in the concept of probability. All but the last had strong relationships to humanist interest in the past, but paradoxically raised significant problems vis-à-vis the essence of the original humanist model of doing history in the ancient rhetorical mode.

Philology

The role of philological criticism, growing out of the humanist desire to recover the ancient past, cannot be underestimated in terms of the long-term trajectory of the development of academic history as a discipline of knowing a distant object. The impulse came from the Renaissance humanists, such as Lorenzo Valla (1406–1457), who were concerned with the need to establish critical versions of ancient texts. This awareness that the leavings of the past were at once vulnerable to erroneous copying and interpretation provided the basis for more disciplined approaches to the past in several directions. Flavio Biondo (1392–1463) strenuously urged the need to look beyond texts to objects — monuments, medals, coins, and the like — as crucial evidence, indeed evidence less susceptible to the whims of copyists and interpretive distortion.[61] French legal humanists, such as Etienne Pasquier (1529–1615), applied the same methods to the ancient and medieval past of France and gave the first full arguments for the need to interpret documents carefully in the context of the language, customs, and meanings of their times.[62]

Old-regime French legal scholars were often impelled by political concerns to justify various versions of the French monarchy through deep research into political and legal documents — a tradition that continued down through the French Revolution — as the status of the monarchy and its relationships to other orders were periodically debated as a central motif of French political history. Other scholars, such as the Oratorian Dom Jean Mabillon (1632–1707), whose *De re diplomatica* (1681) is the classic guide to the establishment of texts, sought justification for a variety of religious doctrines, rights, and properties.

Such philological erudition could easily develop a momentum of its own, independent of political or religious conflicts. The French Académie des inscriptions was largely devoted to such documentary and antiquarian enterprises, although often commissioned in service to the history or glory of the monarchy. Local societies and individual scholars, often known as *érudits* or *antiquaires*, pursued local subjects with great passion.[63]

The *érudits* developed a critical stance toward traditional rhetorical history in the antique mode. Many were lawyers who took a critical, interrogatory approach to the credulity and inventiveness of literary history. Several asserted that nonliterary evidence was far superior to literary, and that inquiry into the past can only be pursued with surety through the testimony of things not actively trying to persuade or tell a story. Most were distrustful of narrative history generally. The mode of the antiquaries fed most comfortably into the style of the philologist and chronologist. Partisans of rhetorical antiquity often took umbrage, and the battle could verbally become quite fierce, especially in England.[64] While most philosophes shared a distrust of the excesses of the rhetorical style, they found the labors and passions of the antiquaries, however seemingly scientific, foreign to their passion for a history of moral usefulness. Hence, one can find many unkind comments about antiquaries, albeit occasional grudging admiration for their empirical work.[65]

Pyrrhonism

The antiquarians found ideological support in the broader questions of historical knowledge raised by the revival of historical Pyrrhonism, so-named for the work of the skeptic philosopher Pyrrho of Alexandria, resurrected by humanist scholars and given wide publicity in the seventeenth century. Pyrrhonic skeptics expressed deep suspicion of the human capacity for reaching sure knowledge, and the historical field provides perhaps the most fruitful fodder — as it was relatively simple to show how passion and interest shaped humans' accounts of their own actions, and how those accounts, suspicious from the beginning, could be warped and distorted in the retelling. In the Cartesian vein, one could wonder about the usefulness of any attempt to know the past, but more typical Phyrrhonism focused on the critical task of casting doubt on all that was fabulous and improbable from received accounts of the past. In an age of deep political and religious conflicts, during which validation by historical precedent was still considered the principal means of establishing rights, the aggressive potential of Pyrrhonism had a particular appeal, which could and did lead to radical and heterodox positions. The *Philosophical and Critical Dictionary* of Pierre Bayle from the late 1690s was the *locus classicus*, gathering many decades of skeptical wisdom to all manner of reports, reducing the circle of reasonably certain statements about the past to a startlingly narrow domain.[66]

Probability

Pyrrhonism found its counterpart, and to some extent its corrective, in the form of a growing discussion of the role of probability in human knowledge, both generally and of the past. As important recent studies have shown,[67] the period from 1650 on saw a remarkable flowering of interest in the idea of probability — driven by an intriguing combination of interests. Those in business and finance wanted better ways to conceive of the problems of aleatory contracts such as insurance and annuities. Those in law wanted better ways to assess the probability that accounts of past actions were true. Those in mathematics sought better ways to measure both what we think of as the proper domain of probability, the predictability of events based on combinatorics, and, in ways we might consider less convincing, the mathematics of the probability of the veracity of human testimony and decisions. These discussions were at one level theoretical, to be found in all of the classic works about human knowing in such thinkers as Antoine Arnauld, Leibniz, and Locke.

Mathematicians even attempted to provide a practical method of calculation for this enterprise. John Craig's *Rules of Historical Evidence* (1699), with its elaborate mathematics of the credibility of oral testimony, is one oft-cited example,[68] and in his *Ars conjectandi* (1713), Jacob Bernoulli developed a calculus of probabilities that sought to place all knowledge on a continuum of probabilities, rather than dividing it between the certain and uncertain.[69] Mathematicians also took on questions of deep religious urgency, above all in religious debates about the testimony from Scripture as to miracles and prophecies.[70]

The world of probability was a comfortable one for the philosophes, hostile as they were to metaphysical systems and claims of religious certitude. To the Pyrrhonist, the concept of probability provided a pathway to reason, in the sense that even though all knowledge of things human is uncertain, life, common sense, and history appear to require some awareness that certainty is not a matter of all or nothing.

Novels

Nor was the distinction between history and fiction. By the mid eighteenth century, the discussion of history was surrounded by a parallel, and in many ways more complex and richer, discussion of the nature of what we call the "novel." By the time these philosophes' statements on history were composed, the boundaries of literary fact and fiction had been blurred. As we have seen, the uncomfortable nearness of history to fable had been raised by the resurgence of historical Pyrrhonism. By the mid eighteenth century, it was now common currency that the *roman*—or other invented prose works labeled *histoires, nouvelles,* or *mémoires*—could be highly truthful (albeit wholly invented) and, in some ways have even more integrity than *histoire*.[71]

Since the second half of the seventeenth century, writers who invented prose stories had increasingly sought to escape the image and reality of creators of what in classical rhetoric would be called "fable"—romances with no pretense to verisimilitude. Rather they sought to create stories with *vraisem-blance* (verisimilitude). In the terms of classical rhetoric, this would mean a shift from *fabula* to *argumentum*, from invented stories of no realism to ficti-tious but plausible stories.[72] (It is intriguing that *argumentum* was also a form of weak judicial proof based on circumstantial evidence; as we have seen, in many ways history writing was moving, through its reliance on probability and on a judicial-style approach to witnesses, toward the same category.)

Rather than express this shift in the terms of classical rhetoric, however, the new prose writers and their supporters staked their claims on the status of history with regard to both verisimilitude and moral worthiness. Associa-tion with the genre of history gave the new *roman/nouvelle/histoire* a higher status. Few doubted that history served a moral function. Few doubted that invented tales also could serve a moral function, in the manner of Aesop or La Fontaine. Few doubted either, however, that the old *roman* lacked moral seriousness. But what of fables that increasingly took on all of the appearances of history, having the paradoxical added advantage of none of its epistemo-logical uncertainties, because they made no claims to being representations of actual thoughts and events? By the mid eighteenth century, these argu-ments were well established, so much so they were already the subject of self-reflexive parody in works such as Diderot's *Jacques le fataliste* and Sterne's *Tristram Shandy*.[73] Some samples from the discussion might help give the texture of the conversation.

In 1683, Du Plaisir pondered the relationships of history and other forms of writing, puzzling through the question of verisimilitude, a rhetorical vir-tue made problematic in traditional history writing in two ways: the classical tradition of invented speeches (also considered a virtue) and the unbeliev-able things that actually do occur.

[V]erisimilitude consists of only saying what is morally believable. . . . Truth is not al-ways probable [*vraisemblable*], and yet the author of a true story [*une histoire vraie*] is not always obliged to modify his material to make it believable. He is not responsible for its verisimilitude, because he has only to report things as they have happened . . . but the author of a fiction [*histoire fabuleuse*] himself creates his heroes' actions and he does not want to leave himself open to contradiction.[74]

In 1734, Nicolas Lenglet-Dufresnoy, a prolific historian and author of prob-ably the most reprinted book on standard historical method, wrote a work en-titled *De l'usage des romans*, in which at one point he compares novels to his-tory, making plausible arguments for the superiority of the former. He found the evolving novel superior in four respects. First, novels do not deceive, or if one is deceived, it is willingly and for one's moral profit, whereas history is beset by problems of accuracy and veracity. Second, in the novel, "nothing is equivocal, nothing is doubtful," because it is wholly invented according to the will of the writer. Third, history, in order to be truthful, must generally portray vice rewarded and virtue punished; history is the "portrait of human misery," whereas the novel "is the tableau of human wisdom." Last, whereas history does not portray half the human race, women, the novel can give them equal place as admirable and strong moral actors.[75] Or consider Diderot's praise of Samuel Richardson from 1761:

O Richardson! I shall dare to say that the truest history is full of lies, and that your novel is full of truths. History paints a picture of a few individuals; you paint the human race; history ascribes to a few individuals things they neither said nor did; everything you ascribe to man he has said or done; history only depicts a small period of time, a small part of the world; you have embraced all places and times. . . . From this perspective, I dare to say that often history is a bad novel, and that the novel, as you have written it, is a good history. O painter of human nature, it is you who never lies.[76]

Needless to say, this statement begs many questions, but the categories it plays with were commonplace by the mid 1700s. The juxtaposition of history and fable in the texts of the philosophes we have examined recognizes both their natural relationship as modes of storytelling and the growing association of history and novels by their readers.

Conclusion

Such then is the interconnected but fragmented assembly of approaches to the past that the philosophes inherited and imbibed in their own studies. What emerges is hardly a coherent picture, indeed, the opposite. Still, if our goal has been to understand the awkwardness and intellectual thinness of French Enlightenment statements about the enterprise of recounting the past, then this background creates a much clearer frame for the statements we first encountered. In short, we have:

• an intellectual milieu that inherited the Cartesian sense that the past can and should have no binding authority, yet a milieu that also saw the usefulness of the past for making arguments about the prospects for the future;

• an awareness of an epistemological situation in which the past has become an object like other objects, except that, unlike the objects of the natural world or the contemporary social world, the object of study is irretrievably gone and is known only through often fragile and unreliable traces;

- an evolving discussion surrounding the novel and history that raised difficult questions about the kinds of truth sought in each genre, the adequacies of each, and the relationship of the inventions of the novel to the inventions, deceptions, and misapprehensions endemic to the historical enterprise;

- a pedagogical world that retained the desire to provide exemplary and politically useful stories, but in which an evolving scientific approach to antiquarian-empirical history fitted awkwardly at best into a traditionally humanist curriculum;

- a paradoxical legacy of humanism that created both the mechanisms for critical attention to the leavings of the past, and a traditional commitment to a traditional rhetoric at cross-purposes to such efforts; and

- an ideological world that nurtured an interest in arguing for certain versions of the past rather than others, but kept the foci of interest generally on rather narrow political and religious lines.

Rousseau, Voltaire, and d'Alembert grappled with these crosscurrents in their idiosyncratic ways, according to their intellectual habits, the requirements of the occasion of writing, and their own individual stakes in the past.

Rousseau's commentary is in many ways the simplest to understand. Unconvinced that the past has much to teach, and fully convinced that the moral value of history was equivalent to the moral value of fable, he was simply indifferent to most of what the contemporary historical enterprise had to offer. So he leads us through an exercise of progressive limitation of relevance, as narrow and self-enclosed as the world of Emile himself. For the moral purist, looking to protect the innocence of his charge, history offered the safety of theatrical spectacle, but all of the problems of theatrical illusion.

Voltaire offers the most paradoxical solution. In one sense, he had a deep interest in the past, and he wrote voluminously about it. But his writings largely have a kind of exorcistic quality, in which tales are told in order to wonder at their horror and reject their models, exemplary history in the negative sense. Epistemology mirrors its object. The weakness and foolishness of much historical "knowledge" is appropriate to the weakness and foolishness of most human behavior recounted in the problematic retellings. Descartes had rejected interest in the past on rationalist principles. The past was neither accessible to true knowledge nor relevant to the seeker after truth in the present or future. In a way, Voltaire was the empirical agent of Descartes's project, disinclined to argue from a geometric rationalism but ultimately taking the long road to the same conclusion by showing over and over again the folly and brutishness of most human history. While he outlined a project for a positive history of culture, he was drawn obsessively to the negative themes.[77]

D'Alembert is surely the most symptomatic of the three. Mathematical by inclination and determined in principle to find the simplest patterns and laws in all that was studied,[78] he clearly was uncomfortable in the fragmented and counterintuitive world of the study of the past. Rather than trying to resolve the difficulties, he simply restates them without resolution and without recognition of his failure to resolve them. Hence we have a highly rhetorical performance, one of whose principal themes is distrust of rhetoric. We find both reiteration of old statements about the need to discover the causes of human events and equally bold ridicule of such attempts. (Indeed, at one juncture, d'Alembert equates the attempt to ascribe causes to past events with the attempt to predict future ones.) We find a sense that human history offers enormous richness of data, but no sense that it would allow any scientific organization in lawlike patterns or rhetorical organization through humanist rhetoric; hence a reliance on chronology, whether running forward or backward. We find a disgust with mediocre minds who simply list and arrange, but deep fear that anything that transcends such patterns results in mere pandering to a public demanding amusement. We find both a demand for objectivity and the paradoxical conclusion that the most personal statements — memoirs and letters contemporary with events and innocent of public rhetoric — may be the best form of historical expression.

It is not surprising, therefore, that the milieu of the French Enlightenment created no particularly stable paradigm for theories of historical inquiry. We find no new theory for the activity named *histoire*, for the philosophes found their preferred niche largely outside received wisdom in their idiosyncratic, often radical foraging through the past for purposes of philosophy and social visions. Montesquieu's humanistic yet sociological inquiry into the causes of the grandeur and decadence of Rome, Rousseau's hypothetical histories of inequality and language, Voltaire's free-ranging philosophical histories and commentaries, and Turgot's and later Condorcet's multi-staged visions of human progress — these have little or no relation to the formal definitions and analyses of history we have discussed. The situation created neither motive nor direction for a cogent theory of a critical, scientific, emotionally distanced reconstruction of the past in all its fullness, in the manner of the historicist-academic paradigm of the nineteenth and twentieth centuries.

Indeed, the opposite. The French philosophes approached the past as curious, critical, and imaginative intellectual opportunists. The results for the literature of Enlightenment were striking. The results for stated theory are those odd mixtures of Enlightenment critical thought, contemporary discussions, and personal idiosyncrasy we see in the texts with which we began. Intriguing in their own right, their situation might also be instructive for our own, as the academic-historicist paradigm that stands between them and us has crumbled in recent decades under the weight of epistemological doubts and a reopening of the relationship of history to fable.

DORA B. WEINER

4. A Provincial Doctor
Faces the Paris Establishment

Philippe Pinel, 1778–1793

In his early days at Columbia University, when Peter Gay was still essentially a *dix-huitièmiste* with his heart in France, he published a book of essays entitled *The Party of Humanity* whose heroes are Voltaire, the rationalist, Rousseau, the Romantic, and Diderot, the encyclopedist.[1] The only doctors mentioned in that volume are Servetus, La Mettrie, and Sigmund Freud, and Freud has of course remained the major medical figure in Peter Gay's world.

Yet Philippe Pinel, the humane physician of the Enlightenment, might have joined that "Party of Humanity," for he embodied cultural values that Gay treasures, and that he accentuates in his subsequent, magisterial study, *The Enlightenment: An Interpretation.*[2] Pinel was an accomplished classicist, intimately familiar with the Latin medical literature. Fluent in English, he especially admired Scottish psychology and Edinburgh medicine. He translated William Cullen and chose him as a mentor. As a medical philosophe, Pinel constructed an encyclopedic overview of diseases, his *Nosographie philosophique*, which became the textbook of internal medicine for a generation of French medical students. His belief in the citizen-patient's right to equal access to health care motivated his remarkable thirty-year career in public service as physician-in-chief of the Salpêtrière Hospice: in revolutionary, imperial, and Bourbon Paris, he applied the philosophy of the Enlightenment. Furthermore, religious toleration was Pinel's response to the fanaticism that for centuries had torn his native region between Albi and Toulouse. The persecution of the Cathari, the Albigensian crusade, the Wars of Religion, and the Revocation of the Edict of Nantes had left scars and many thousands of dead. Pinel's maternal ancestors were Protestants from Castres; his father's family were Catholics in St. Paul Cap-de-Joux, where he grew up. Toleration was his preferred option.

Like Voltaire and numerous others, Pinel received a fine education from a Catholic teaching order, in his case the Fathers of the Christian Doctrine at Lavaur. Pinel earned a bachelor's degree at Lavaur and then a master of arts degree in the humanities at the Doctrinaires' college in Toulouse. He then spent two and a half years in the pursuit of a doctorate of theology at the University of Toulouse. But on his 25th birthday, in April 1770, he changed direction abruptly, opting instead for medicine. Pinel thus joined the family profession, but at a learned level, far above their traditional practice of surgery. And he eventually pursued medicine as a calling, living behind the forbidding walls of the Salpêtrière in Paris. The early experience of the tonsured cleric thus shaped the life of the mature physician. But we cannot account for the uniquely empathic and sensitive understanding of patients that characterized the writings and practice of the mature Pinel: that was his personal gift.

As a newly certified doctor in December 1773, he left narrow-minded provincial Toulouse — scene of the "affaire Calas" that Voltaire pilloried — for Occitan Montpellier. Here learning and academic controversy, a rich library, access to hospital patients, and the chance to present papers to the Royal Society of Sciences prodded and spurred the young doctor. In Montpellier, he learned the intricacies of nosology according to Boissier de Sauvages and absorbed the new philosophy of vitalism that Bordeu and Barthez infused into medical thinking. Here he acquired a lasting admiration for British achievements in philosophy, medicine, and politics — an attitude that the Party of Humanity deemed essential.

We do not know whether Pinel ever thought of settling in Montpellier: he must have known that for an impecunious outsider, Paris offered far better chances. Coming to the capital in 1778 at the age of 33, Pinel evolved into a cosmopolitan medical writer with an interdisciplinary outlook. This essay studies the eventful fifteen-year initiation of this newcomer and outsider into the Parisian world of the Enlightenment in the 1770s and 1780s.

Turmoil in the Paris Medical World

On New Year's Eve 1773, a murderous fire had destroyed a wing of the Hôtel-Dieu hospital near the Petit Pont, on the City Isle in Paris. Since that disaster, two conflicting points of view had vied for general endorsement. One opinion held that the Hôtel-Dieu should be rebuilt in the center of town so as to be accessible to the ailing poor and to injured workers, despite lack of space and the well-known unhealthiness of the site, polluted air and water. On the other side of the controversy stood the Académie des sciences. The deliberations of a blue-ribbon committee — Lavoisier, Laplace, Condorcet, and Coulomb were among its members — led to the well-documented conclusion that the Hôtel-Dieu should be subdivided into four hospitals to be established on the periphery of the capital. That environment was healthy, and there was room for expansion. Projects soon multiplied, with instructive architectural drawings, but Louis XVI, always hesitant, failed to reach a decision. Like all physicians interested in hospital reform, Pinel profited from reading the report of the Académie des sciences, *Mémoires sur les hôpitaux de Paris*, published by the surgeon Jacques Tenon, the most active member of the Académie's hospital committee.[3] As physician-in-chief of the Salpêtrière for thirty years, Pinel would eventually help implement many of Tenon's recommendations.

One year after the fire at the Hôtel-Dieu, Paris inaugurated the sumptuous neoclassical building of the new Académie de chirurgie. The newly won importance of surgeons intensified the ongoing debate about the training of all doctors. It was high time, reformers argued, to merge the two groups of students, to add practical experience to the education of physicians and theoretical teaching to the training of surgeons. Social distinctions between the two groups should be abolished. For a young medical man like Pinel, descended from a long line of master surgeons, these discussions carried very personal meaning. In an essay of 1793, he was to make detailed recommendations on the clinical training of doctors.[4]

Also among the Parisian controversies that touched provincial medical newcomers most closely were attacks on the Société royale de médecine, created by the king in 1776. Here the permanent secretary, the distinguished comparative anatomist Félix Vicq d'Azyr, attempted to forge a national medical profession. To stimulate the activity of provincial physicians, the society proposed numerous questions, offering prizes for the best essays submitted. Pinel competed three times for such a prize, and it seems clear that his first official position, as "physician of the infirmaries" at Bicêtre Hospice, resulted from the distinction of his prize essay in the spring of 1793.

The society's success excited the envy of the medical faculty. To publicize their power and preclude contamination with newfangled attitudes, the professors prevented young members of the Société royale such as the chemist Antoine François Fourcroy, the protégé of Vicq d'Azyr, from obtaining a medical diploma. Lacking 6,000 livres, the cost of the parchment, Fourcroy decided to compete for the Diest prize, which provided the winner with tuition-free study of medicine in Paris. When the jury rejected him in 1780, Vicq d'Azyr undertook a collection among the society's members, thus enabling Fourcroy to pay for his diploma. But the young man would never accede to the *régence*, the right to teach. What memories for the future director-general of public instruction! And what a source of worry for other young doctors who were equally anxious to obtain a Paris diploma, required for the legal practice of medicine in the capital! Pinel tried his luck, competing twice for the Diest prize. Was it his friendship with Fourcroy that caused his repeated failure?

It is obvious that the three medical controversies we have mentioned, around the Hôtel-Dieu, the Académie de chirurgie, and the Société royale de médecine, aroused lively discussion in Parisian learned societies, in the salons, and in periodical publications interested in medicine. It was equally obvious to a medical newcomer, anxious to involve himself in these issues, that he must gain access to these academies and societies or to journals such as the *Recueil périodique d'observations en médecine* or the *Gazette de santé*.[5] Pinel decided to begin by obtaining the right to practice his profession.

First Steps of a Newcomer

In 1778, three men welcomed Pinel to Enlightenment Paris: his brother Louis, who would soon return home to St. Paul Cap-de-Joux to practice surgery; Jean Antoine Chaptal, a recently minted physician, at that moment a student of chemistry in Paris, but soon to leave for Montpellier; and the mathematician Jacques Antoine Joseph Cousin, a member of the Académie des sciences, to whom Pinel had a letter of recommendation. Cousin found two mathematics students for Pinel, thus enabling him to earn his living.[6] Familiar with the ways of the capital and impressed with Pinel's grasp of mathematics, Cousin advised that he give up medicine and pursue a career in mathematics instead. Such was not Pinel's plan. Rather, he tried four different strategies to penetrate the official world of Paris medicine. In all four he failed, but in doing so he acquired highly useful experience. Eventually he ended up practicing his profession illegally in a private clinic (*maison de santé*) that cared for the mentally ill.[7]

The story of Pinel's attempts, in February 1782 and 1784, to win the Diest prize has repeatedly been told. The first time, the prize was awarded to a certain Desmarescaux, a former student at Montpellier, who had bought a thesis written for him by Pinel, "Tentamen medicum de equitatione."[8] (This was a well-practiced way for a scholar to earn money.) Michel Caire has recently published the details of Pinel's second attempt to win this prize,[9] and Pierre Chabbert provides a partial translation of the disastrous evaluation of the candidate by the judges, speaking Latin. Reading this judgment, it is difficult to believe that it portrays a future professor and member of the Académie des sciences. It reads:

We conclude that Monsieur Pinel has little knowledge and cannot easily be declared a winner. In anatomy his baggage is light; in physiology he is better, but not remarkable. In surgery he does not stand out, either in theory or in manual dexterity. He knows little chemistry, a bit more medicine and pharmacy, but he has many shortcomings. . . . Adequate in general pathology, he seems to rely on it to answer every question . . . he seemed to turn in endless circles. . . .

. . . in the midst of all these difficulties, one hope remained: to explore and develop the written questions and demonstrate a wealth of information about medicine, indicating a method and insight that the oral examination failed to show. That hope, alas, was not fulfilled.[10]

Chabbert argues that Pinel's friendship with Michel Augustin Thouret and François Fourcroy, both members of the Société royale de médecine, may have caused this fiasco. Possibly the judges knew that Pinel had "magnetized" with Deslon in 1784 and held this interest in Mesmer against him.[11] Among the members of the hostile jury, it is surprising to find not only Louis Desbois de Rochefort, physician at Charité hospital, but also Jean Nicolas Corvisart, who may have been embarrassed when he met Pinel as professor and colleague at the Paris Health School ten years later.

Seeing these disappointing encounters, the naturalist René Louich Desfontaines, a close friend of Pinel's, asked his friend Lemonnier, first physician to the king, to present Pinel to Louis XVI's aunts Adélaïde and Victoire, who were looking for a new doctor. Alas, Pinel did not utter a word during the interview.

We might imagine Pinel returning from Versailles more relieved than disappointed, for the role of courtier would not have suited him. In addition he was devastated at this time by the suicide of a young friend, whose death he thought he might have prevented. Pinel returned several times to the history and the diagnosis of the friend's fatal illness, even seventeen years later, in the first edition of his celebrated *Traité médico-philosophique sur l'aliénation mentale ou la manie*, in which a footnote specifies "this happened in 1783." He also expressed his sense of responsibility for the tragedy in the chapter subtitle "A Case of Mania Where Moral Treatment Would Have Been Necessary."[12] Seeing his discouragement and trying to distract him, friends drew Pinel's attention to a prize proposed by the Société royale de médecine for the best essay on the topic "Determine the characteristics of nervous diseases properly so called, such as hysteria and hypochondriasis; how do they differ from analogous illnesses such as melancholia; what are their principal causes and the general remedies one should propose for their treatment."[13] Pinel did not compose an essay in 1783, but the subject became the focal theme of his intimate and continuing reflections. Indeed, five years later he submitted to the Société royale a manuscript entitled "Distinctions Among Various Species of Madness and Among the Therapeutic Means to Be Used in Their Treatment." But he withdrew the memoir because, Professor Pinel told the Société médicale d'émulation ten years later, it "does not seem to me worthy of publication in its initial version."[14] The "worthy" version would become chapter 4 of the *Traité médico-philosophique sur l'aliénation mentale.*

We do not know whether Pinel overcame the discouragement of 1783 by his own efforts or with the help of friends. Whatever the means, he next published several brief articles in a modest periodical titled the *Gazette de santé.* These articles won him the esteem of the editor, Jacques Paulet, and in 1784 Pinel was asked to take over the journal's editorship. He filled this position successfully for almost six years.

The Editorial Policy of the *Gazette de Santé*, 1784–1789

With the arrival of the new editor, the horizon of the *Gazette de santé* broadened greatly. The journal was soon discussing hygiene and medical psychology and developed interests in surgery, chemistry, pharmacy, natural history, and botany. It published reviews of foreign books and verbatim reports of the public meetings of learned societies; it announced the prize competitions of academies and societies; and it denounced the work of charlatans. The *Gazette de santé* thus grew into a publication with encyclopedic interests, modest, but reflective of Enlightenment ideals. "The quality of the *Gazette* and the change of tone during this period are remarkable," comments Roselyne Rey.[15] The contrast with the Paulet years enhanced Pinel's merit, for indeed the *Gazette* had declined in 1783, when it filled its pages for six months with the text of Albrecht von Haller's *Bibliotheca medicinae practicae.* In contrast, from May 1784 to December 1789, the *Gazette* appeared weekly and presented a varied program of high quality.

Discussing health, the *Gazette de santé* welcomed letters from its readers and emphasized issues of prevention and hygiene. Discussing medicine, the journal asked professionals to send in their clinical observations, their questions, and their opinions about suspect "secret" remedies. It is impossible accurately to identify all the articles written by Pinel, especially in the mid 1780s, when few are signed. But gradually we pass from a contributor identified as "one of our subscribers, . . . as knowledgeable as he is modest"[16] to "M.P., doctor of medicine." It is often possible, moreover, to identify Pinel's convictions and his style. Sometimes he repeats an argument voiced elsewhere. In 1785, he defends his translation of Cullen against a rival. And once "the editor" comments on an "Observation sent by M. Pinel, master of surgery at St. Paul in Languedoc" (his brother Louis). One can thus observe the editor at work.

Hygiene is a central theme about which Pinel intended to write a book. It was a subject that authors like Tissot were popularizing at that time. "I am working hard on my Hygiene," Pinel wrote to his friend Desfontaines, "and, to try it out on the public, I include occasional articles in the *Gazette de santé*. . . . I have announced . . . my work on medical gymnastics and I am absolutely determined to complete it and to publish it by the spring or summer."[17] The concept of "hygiene" elaborated by Pinel in the 1780s deserves our attention. On the one hand, it reflects Montpellier Hippocratism, a physician's attitude that prizes moderation in all things, relies on the *vis medicatrix naturae*, looks skeptically on potent medications, and discourages venesection. On the other hand, we should consider Pinel's early concept of "hygiene" the basis for a therapy valid for all of "internal pathology" (the chair Pinel was to occupy for thirty years), applicable to illnesses of both mind and body. Pinel's attitude toward hygiene and toward his readers' involvement with this subject thus reveals a physician who addressed the human being as a whole rather than a specialist concerned with only a part of the patient's body or afflictions.[18]

As we would expect of an eighteenth-century student of the classical humanities, Pinel frequently conveys the advice of the ancients, such as Celsus, Seneca, Galen, Suetonius, Plutarch, and especially Pliny. Regarding diet, Pinel reports that the Romans thought oysters excellent to start a meal and served them on snow. He advocates cool food as more digestible than hot, denounces hard liquor, and warns that tea causes tooth decay.

Food led Pinel to discuss fresh air, man's natural environment. Citing Plato, he specifies that "[c]old air is a powerful stimulant and tonic if not used excessively or for too long. Nothing is more important than to get accustomed to it young." Then he adds:

How many nervous diseases, nurtured during the winter in a sedentary life near the fire, could easily be cured if one had the courage to go out jogging regularly in the fresh air. The play of the muscles could thus be reactivated; respiration and appetite would be newly energized, and one would thus find new enjoyment returning to a warm and comfortable apartment.

Pinel was in fact advocating winter sports as excellent for health:

A few years ago a medical thesis praised the advantages of exercising on ice, called *skating*. The speed of this kind of motion, disregarding any accidents, is well suited to active and restless young people; it requires alternate contractions of all the muscles, provides fun and good spirits, and transmits strength stimulated by the cold. Skill in skating builds a healthy and robust constitution.[19]

While Pinel praises fresh air, he disliked cold baths, even for therapeutic purposes.[20] This opinion is interesting, in light of how much nineteenth-century psychiatry would use and abuse baths, cold or lukewarm, often for many hours, descending and ascending showers, and surprise "ducking" as shock treatment. Pinel never changed his opinion on this matter, remaining the advocate of mild, moderate therapies.

Soon afterward a subscriber wrote: "You will not expect, Sir, to be asked about a topic as frivolous as dreams. . . . I should like to know whether medicine can prescribe a regimen that will free nervous and overly imaginative persons from the torment of exhausting and stressful dreaming." Pinel's reply, alas! does not teach us anything new. Against bad dreams "Hippocrates counseled reducing food intake by one-third"; Pinel also recommends "walking, exercise, singing, and declamation."[21] He evidently did not recognize the potential diagnostic value of dreams.

Hygiene was thus fundamental to Pinel's medical thought. But there is another theme in the *Gazette de santé* of equal importance, because it can be seen as the starting point of what would later be called psychiatry. A Spanish scholar, Pedro Marset, has devoted a medical thesis and two articles to this topic.[22] Pierre Chabbert provides a general overview, and Jacques Postel's commentaries are enriched by clinical experience.[23]

Marset believes, as I do, that one can identify many of Pinel's unsigned contributions to the *Gazette de santé* owing to his ideas, his style, and certain allusions. Marset analyzes numerous articles on Mesmerism, underlining the fact that Mesmer's French critics saw only the charlatan without appreciating the experimental or therapeutic possibilities of hypnosis. Pinel was at first intrigued, but then joined the near-totality of French doctors against Mesmer.[24] Marset then singles out Pinel's interest in the power of habit over human behavior. He extracts this theme from two articles on sexual impotence as a possible consequence of masturbation.[25] Then, appearing from 1785 onward, Marset identifies Pinel's first five articles on mental maladies.

The first of Pinel's articles concerning mental illness is a book review of *Disputatio medica de mania* by the Virginian David Stuart.[26] Pinel reports that the author thought he had found the cause of mania in organic alterations of the brain. Expressing for the first time a skepticism that would only grow, Pinel demanded much more substantial proof before accepting such an explanation.[27]

His second article refers to a case of temporary dementia evidently cured by an attack of malignant fever. The doctor who reported this case explained the cure on the basis of humoral theories. Pinel sounds indignant: "We must observe that this manner of reasoning based entirely on humoral pathology and on gratuitous assumptions such as acrid or viscous humors is no longer appreciated by persons who argue with some precision."[28] Here is an early example of the severity and demand for high scientific standards that Pinel expresses in his numerous reports to the Académie des sciences after 1803.

In a third case, published in 1786, Pinel explores the effects of habit combined with feelings of fear or sadness. He believed that such repeated experiences may "raise nervous sensitivity to the extreme" until "one believes oneself the victim of imaginary maladies and constantly fears to be facing one's last moments."[29]

It was in 1785 that Pinel began to think seriously about melancholia; his close friend who had committed suicide appears repeatedly in his writings. Pinel's regrets on this score even led him to write that "one should have used force to subject him to a regular treatment, but no one had enough authority over him to exert such violence."[30] This question of the physician's authority over the mental patient haunted psychiatry in the nineteenth and twentieth centuries. Pinel insisted on firmness, because certain patients require it, but he vigorously condemned any brutality toward the mentally ill.

Like many others before him, Pinel noted the influence of climate and weather on mental health and the prevalence of suicides, mainly, it seemed, in England. Thus a piece he inserted into the rubric "Hygiene" explains why "[t]he numerous class of melancholics fear the approach of winter." But then Pinel grows pensive and underlines "the apathy and a kind of concentration of interest in oneself that renders [one] incapable of affectionate feelings." This concentration on a single idea remained for Pinel the characteristic trait of melancholics. He applied this idea to the difficulties that very active persons may experience when they suddenly face retirement. "It seems as if persons used to a certain sphere of activity acquire the need to continue living in this manner. They cannot give it up lest their moral faculties develop a lethargy that tortures them."[31] We find here an example, as early as 1785, of that empathic understanding typical of Pinel as he approached the mentally ill.

Spurred by his increasing expertise, Pinel harbored the growing conviction that mental illness, or, as he would name it, "mental alienation," is an integral part of medicine, and that doctors are the only appropriate guardians of the mentally ill. With the unfolding of revolutionary events in the late 1780s, his humanitarian propensities developed an activist, even political, edge. We can foresee this attitude when he took charge of a particular group of patients, namely, the mentally ill at Bicêtre, and then at the Salpêtrière. He would define their place among many other groups of patients accommodated in the same hospital, in contrast to other specialists who aimed at their isolation and confinement in asylums, far from "normal" society. At the Salpêtrière, Pinel for thirty years presided over a "hospital within the Hospice."[32] In the course of 1789, his last year as editor of the *Gazette de santé*, the influence of the political climate on health also intrigued Pinel — but he recorded his reflections on this timely topic in other periodicals, as we shall see shortly.

In addition to publishing original articles, the *Gazette de santé* kept its readers abreast of the contemporary medical literature. Book reviews frequently dealt with foreign works — German, Italian, Spanish, even American, but mainly British. Pinel the editor never hesitated to be critical, as in the case of the *Observations on Insanity* of Thomas Arnold, which he rightly described as "an imposing apparatus of general divisions, a multitude of superfluous species and of laboriously fashioned definitions,"[33] or of *A History of the Origins of Medicine* by John Coakley Lettsom, which "seems more interested in heaping up a profusion of quotations than making a judicious choice and respecting the limits of his subject."[34] Pinel also mentions a curious book titled *An Account of the Effects of Swinging* by James Carmichael Smyth.[35] The *Gazette de santé* often listed translations into French — for example, John Hunter's *Treatise on the Venereal Disease*, John Gregory's *Observations on the Duties and Offices of a Physician*,[36] William Cumberland Cruikshank's *Anatomy of the Absorbing Vessels of the Human Body*, and John Aikin's *Thoughts on Hospitals*.[37] Pinel also regularly printed notices of important articles published in foreign, mainly British, journals such as the *London Medical Journal* and the *Critical Review*. He had an interest in the reform of medical teaching and in the free courses available in Paris. An example is an account of the "Public course in botany offered at the Jardin du Roi" by René Louich Desfontaines, obviously written by the teacher's intimate friend Pinel, who was also an observant auditor.[38]

Finally, in the pages the *Gazette de santé*, Pinel also paid close attention to the programs of learned societies. The proceedings of public meetings of the Société royale de médecine are regularly printed, as well as those of assemblies at the Académie des sciences relevant to medicine. "All in all," concludes Roselyne Rey, "the promises made in the Advertisement and Prospectus of 1785 have been kept, as concerns the variety of subject matter and the quality of the articles, not only in medicine and surgery, but in natural history, chemistry and botany as well."[39] Perusing the pages of this weekly over six years, we can see the *Gazette de santé* transformed from a boring and pedantic paper into a small but vital journal, avid for news and filled with accounts of the medical events of the day. We observe the editor take pride in stimulating and satisfying popular curiosity and calming the anxieties of intelligent readers who lacked medical knowledge. The *Gazette de santé* clearly communicates its editor's characteristically late-eighteenth-century convictions that medicine is an encyclopedic science; that health and illness concern the entire human person, and not just the mind *or* the body; that many sciences contribute to the physician's expertise, and that the practice of medicine requires an open mind; that maintaining one's health presupposes knowledge; and that each citizen must care for his or her own health and the health of the community.

If Pinel improved the *Gazette de santé*, the *Gazette* also transformed its editor. By 1789, Pinel had become extensively acquainted with the Paris medical world; he was well informed about recent developments, since he read books and journals fresh from the presses. His perspective on medicine had become cosmopolitan and encyclopedic, and dialogue with his readers had emboldened him to state his opinions.

At the end of 1789, Pinel announced that the *Gazette de santé* would merge with the much larger *Journal de médecine, chirurgie et pharmacie* of Philippe Joseph Roux.[40] He cites a number of reasons for this move: the public's attention was now being absorbed by political, rather than scientific, events; in order to hold the readers' attention and keep them informed of the impressive recent strides made by the medical sciences, a journal with more powerful resources than the *Gazette de santé* was needed; and the editor's "other occupations have been increasing." Pinel's professional fortunes were finally improving.[41]

The Road to Medical Power

While serving as editor of the *Gazette de santé*, Pinel sought to find his way toward the important institutions and personalities of the Paris medical world. He presented his work to the Académie des sciences and to the Société royale de médecine; he edited several books and published numerous articles in important medical and general periodicals; he acquired some clinical experience; and he nurtured friendships that widened his social circle. A key event, typical of Enlightenment Parisian society, was his introduction to Madame Helvétius at her famous salon in Auteuil. Here Pinel met not only Benjamin Franklin (who wanted to lure him to America) but the marquis de Condorcet (whom Pinel would later try to save from the guillotine) and future academic colleagues such as François Fourcroy, Pierre Jean Georges Cabanis, and Michel Augustin Thouret, who eventually were to open a career to his talents. We will return to this salon below.

At the Académie des sciences, Pinel read four memoirs in 1785 and 1786. On 1 June 1785, colleagues proposed his candidacy for the class of anatomy and zoology; only eighteen years later, however, was he finally elected.[42]

Memoirs Read by Philippe Pinel at the Académie des sciences, 1785–1786

2 April 1785: "On the Dislocations of the Clavicle" (*commissaires* MM. Tenon and Portal), *Procès-verbaux de l'Académie des sciences* 104: 69.

1 June 1785: "On the Dislocations of the Humerus" (*commissaires* MM. Tenon and Portal), ibid. 104: 106.

27 August 1785: "On the Dislocations of the Humerus and Cubitus" (*commissaires* MM. Poissonnier, Vicq d'Azyr and Broussonet), ibid. 104: 191.

5 August 1786: "On a Human Monster" (*commissaires* MM. Portal and Sabatier), ibid. 105: 300.

Comparing Pinel's first Paris publications with manuscripts from his Montpellier days, we find that a professional medical investigator has replaced the student who reveled in pedantic demonstrations. Mathematics and mechanics are no longer his subject matter, but only working tools for scientific inquiry. The scholar reveals himself as a physician interested, not so much in normal articulations, as in their pathology. To prepare the papers he was presenting, Pinel had studied patients, not only at the Hôtel-Dieu St. Eloi of Montpellier, but at the hospital of the Paris School of Surgery, the Charité Hospital in the service of Alexis Boyer, and the Hôtel-Dieu of Paris with Pierre Desault. At his first visit to the Académie, he brought a copy of his recent translation of William Cullen's *First Lines of the Practice of Physic*.[43] In 1786, he used six anatomical pieces not only to demonstrate how nature attempts to repair a damaged joint but also to comment on the position, the reaction, the pain of the patient. "Did the blow speed this person's death?" he asked.[44] Surely an unusual question for an anatomical demonstration.

Pinel went on to publish these four memoirs in the *Journal de physique*, which was more prestigious than his own *Gazette de santé*. He also contributed to the *Journal de physique* the results of his volunteer work at the Jardin du roi, where he collected zoologic specimens, experimented in the laboratory, guided Sunday excursions, and presented conferences on "zootomy." One of these memoirs dealt with the articulation of the jaw as a possible criterion for a new classification of quadrupeds.[45] In that context he also studied the skull of a young elephant and the ossified brain of an ox.[46] In addition, he helped campaign for the establishment of a menagerie at the Muséum d'histoire naturelle (the new name for the Jardin du roi),[47] and helped write the instructions for the naturalists who were to accompany an expedition to search for the explorer La Pérouse in 1791: his memoir concerns the preservation of rare animals or their parts on board ship and is entitled "How to Prepare Quadrupeds and Birds for Natural History Collections."[48]

Questions of classification were on the mind of every naturalist in eighteenth-century Paris, but they also preoccupied physicians. During Pinel's four years at Montpellier, the detailed nosology of François Boissier de Sauvages reigned supreme. Surely Pinel had also encountered William Cullen's *Synopsis nosologiae methodicae* at that time, since the book was published in 1772. But Cullen's *First Lines of the Practice of Physick* did not appear until 1777, and it aroused immediate and sustained interest for its careful clinical methodology, solid structure, and clear prose. Knowing Pinel's proficiency in English and his fine writing style, the publisher Duplain commissioned a translation from him.[49]

Cullen's book rested on vast clinical experience, precisely the type of experience that Pinel lacked. The translator, turned student, now walked the wards with the great Edinburgh physician and watched closely as he observed, examined, diagnosed, and treated his patients. Cullen thus became Pinel's teacher of clinical medicine. Cullen contributed an idea of great importance to the nosologic thought of the eighteenth century, for he insisted on the fundamental role of the nervous system in transmitting sensation and irritation. "His whole pathology derives from spasm and atony," comments François Gabriel Boisseau; "he usually considered one or the other of these states as uniformly present in the whole organism."[50] Cullen's neurocentric conception of mental disease was congenial to Montpellier vitalism: it explained how the nervous system and its illnesses, which Cullen called "neuroses," play a central role in human physiology, thought, and behavior. Pinel adopted these views and underscored them by defining the "neuroses" as the

fourth of five classes of diseases in his *Nosographie philosophique, ou Méthode de l'analyse appliquée à la médecine* of 1798. As is well known, Pinel's
Nosographie philosophique became the textbook of internal medicine for a
whole generation of French medical students and was printed in six successive editions between 1798 and 1818.[51]

This kind of publishing success, however, still lay in the future. Sales of
Pinel's translation of Cullen in 1785 fared poorly and Pinel was once again
the victim of bad luck. Chabbert reports that "a few weeks after the publication of his book, another translation appeared, done by [Edouard François
Marie] Bosquillon, who was not only a physician at the Hôtel-Dieu of Paris
and professor of Greek at the Collège de France, but a royal reader and,
moreover, a censor of the library." And there was worse: "Bosquillon commissioned poisonous articles depreciating Pinel's translation and, in the ensuing
polemic, Pinel experienced the unpleasant surprise of seeing his publisher
abandon him and back Bosquillon, doubtless because he feared the powers
of censorship."[52]

This left Pinel with his honorarium of 1,000 livres and the modest revenge
of a critical book review of Bosquillon's translation, published in the *Gazette
de santé* at the end of 1785.[53] It was perhaps in compensation for this fiasco
that the publisher Duplain asked Pinel for a new edition of the *Opera omnia*
of Giorgio Baglivi. These two projects freed him from having to give mathematics lessons.

Pinel had become acquainted with the work of the Italian physician Giorgio Baglivi at Montpellier where Baglivi's *Opera omnia* formed part of the
library that professor Henri Haguenot had bequeathed to the medical students.[54] Pinel admired Baglivi, who had been professor of clinical medicine
at Rome, especially his book *De praxi medica* of 1696, because it demonstrated Baglivi's great qualities as a clinical observer. Pinel and his Ideologue
friends often repeated maxims of Baglivi's : "Patients are the best professors of
medicine"; "Hypotheses and systems should be discarded"; "To study medicine, one must examine and compare precise cases, one patient to another."[55]
A new edition of Baglivi, corrected, annotated, and provided with a new preface, appeared in 1788.[56]

It is possible that his close reading of Cullen made Pinel keenly aware
of his lack of clinical experience. At any rate, we read in a letter to his
friend Desfontaines, dated 1784, of "several commercial houses whose physician I am."[57] Furthermore, in the second edition of his *Traité médico-
philosophique sur l'aliénation mentale* (1809), Pinel mentions a "pension in
the faubourg St. Antoine that often calls on me (that was in 1786)."[58] Pinel

here refers to the establishment of the ex–cabinet maker Jacques Belhomme at Charonne, which is known to history precisely because it was there that Pinel began his psychiatric practice in earnest. Belhomme seems to have been quite uninterested in seeing his paying patients recover, and there is questionable evidence that he sheltered some political suspects, under cover of presumed mental illness and at astronomic prices. Such allegations are of course difficult to document, given the discretion that is de rigueur under such circumstances. Nor does the Register of the pension Belhomme (now deposited in the Biomedical Library at UCLA) mention money.[59] Pinel complained bitterly about interference by Belhomme, who prevented or countermanded his therapeutic prescriptions. Pinel remained on the staff until 6 August 1793 — the day (strange coincidence?) — when the establishment became a prison and when Pinel was appointed as physician of the infirmaries at Bicêtre.[60] During this first decade of his life in Paris, and while subject to all kinds of setbacks, Pinel thus nevertheless experienced a number of qualified successes as medical journalist, editor, researcher, and practitioner. These modest successes finally placed him on the road to medical power.

With the help of the *Gazette de santé* and in the environment of the Jardin du roi, the Académie des sciences, and the hospitals and libraries that he regularly visited, Pinel finally found himself in the company of his professional peers. We do not know who introduced him to the famous salon of Madame Helvétius at Auteuil, but scholars agree on the crucial importance of this salon in the intellectual life of Paris around 1800. Pinel's most helpful contacts were Thouret, a member of the Société royale de médecine and the son-in-law of the medical reformer Jean Colombier, and the philosopher and future senator Cabanis. A procession of well-known philosophers, scientists, physicians, and reform-minded thinkers appeared at the Auteuil salon between 1780 and 1800. We can only imagine the sparkling conversations that filled these elegant drawing rooms. Although Pinel was probably ill at ease in the worldly ambience of a Parisian salon, the serious talk of reform in politics, society, and medicine may have helped him overcome his awkward shyness.[61]

For Pinel, participation in the life of the Helvétius salon was important for both intellectual and political reasons: it introduced him to a large number of men who harbored avant-garde views about what needed to be changed in contemporary French society and how to change it. Interesting ideas abounded. Everyone talked, listened, argued. Outstanding among the regular visitors — apart from Cabanis, Franklin, Condorcet, and Thouret — were friends of Pinel's such as the medical writer Pierre Roussel, author of *Système physique et moral de la femme*, and the orientalist Ch. E. Savary, and men as different as Nicolas François de Neufchâteau, a future minister of internal affairs, the chemist Antoine Laurent de Lavoisier, the lawyer-legislator C. E. J. P. Pastoret. Among these intellectuals, whom Napoleon later famously dubbed "ideologues," there was much talk about a "science of man," about new methods and projects for altering the social environment in order to improve human life.[62] Although Pinel knew A. L. C. Destutt de Tracy, the author of *Eléments d'idéologie* (1804), it was Cabanis's interests that paralleled his views most closely. The two men did not always agree, but they shared a detailed knowledge about the clinical training of doctors, hospital reform, and health care for the ailing poor.[63]

Apart from the great intellectual stimulation that Pinel's new acquaintances offered, they might be of help in case the political situation changed. Their various reform projects would require appropriate staffing if these individuals achieved power. By 1793, Cabanis and Thouret were members of the Paris hospital committee: they called Pinel to his first important and regular position, at Bicêtre. To the friendships formed at the Helvétius salon, he owed the beginning of his career.

New Beginnings: The Medical Press

At the very beginning of the Revolution, Pinel published several short articles in periodicals that had only a peripheral interest in medicine and health, such as the *Journal de Paris* and the *Journal gratuit*,[64] but he also proved himself as a serious investigator. To study those activities, we must turn to François Fourcroy's *La Médecine éclairée par les sciences physiques ou Journal des découvertes relatives aux différentes parties de l'art de guérir*, published in four volumes in 1791–92. Like the *Gazette de santé*, this periodical had encyclopedic scope, but in contrast to the *Gazette*, it was meant exclusively for scientists. The work of well-known contributors filled its pages.

The editor directed readers' attention to two different activities engaged in by Pinel: to illustrate work in zoology at the Muséum d'histoire naturelle, Fourcroy reprinted "Extrait d'un Mémoire lu à la Société d'histoire naturelle sur une nouvelle méthode de classification des quadrupèdes."[65] He also pointed to volume 6 of *Abrégé des transactions de la Société philosophique de Londres*, to be examined at some length in a moment.[66] To Fourcroy's journal, Pinel contributed two book reviews, three articles critical of medical or pharmacological therapies — on the abuse of venesection, the disastrous effects of a "topical disorganizing agent" used against a cancerous growth, and the preparation of a "divine plaster"[67] — and three original articles.

The diverse contents of these writings indicate that as late as 1793, Pinel was still searching for his way to a career: his literary production seems to lack a center of gravity. Here we find a new article on dislocations, this time of the jaw.[68] Then Pinel surprises us with lengthy "Reflections on Laundry."[69] The third article, however, reveals the deep and lasting preoccupations that weighed on Pinel's mind. In "Observations on a Special Kind of Melancholia Leading to Suicide," Pinel presents the cases of three men whose doctor he had been or whose illnesses he had followed since 1783.[70] Respectively 36 and 22 years of age, the first two had yielded to an insuperable disgust of life and, despite care and good counsel, had sought death by drowning. The third man, about 36 years old, was about to do the same when he was attacked by robbers. He "managed to tear loose from their hold. . . . This kind of struggle totally changed his trend of thought," Pinel writes, and the man recovered. These case histories troubled Pinel, who recalled them in the *Traité médico-philosophique sur l'aliénation mentale*,[71] seemingly puzzled, as Jacques Postel reminds us, by the fact that melancholics may act in a logical manner.[72]

Pinel's publications in Fourcroy's journal thus show us a man with wide-ranging interests, including mental medicine, classification, public health, materia medica, the practice of medicine, surgery, and pharmacy. During this period, Pinel received constant stimulation from his co-authors, among them his future academic colleagues Andry, Daubenton, Doublet, Portal, Sabatier, and Vauquelin. Indeed, we learn from the introduction to *La médecine éclairée par les sciences physiques*, that "the most distinguished scientists," contributors to the journal, met regularly. "This is perhaps the first time that members of a free society of Physicians, Surgeons and Pharmacists, meeting every other week for this useful purpose, have collaborated toward the advancement of Science whose parts are so intimately interconnected that they can no longer be separated," Fourcroy comments.[73] There is no doubt that Pinel shared Fourcroy's sentiments, but he no longer had much free time to write articles, for he had taken on a huge new editorial project.

The naturalist Jacques Gibelin had been entrusted by the editor Buisson with the preparation of an abridgment of the *Philosophical Transactions* of the Royal Society of London. The work turned out to be exhausting, and Gibelin only managed to complete the twelve volumes in his series with the help of five collaborators, one of them Pinel. What complicated the undertaking, Gibelin explains in his preface, was that the *Transactions* follow a chronological order, whereas he wished to present his abridgment thematically. "Imagine the work and the complications," Gibelin pleaded, "involved in the choice, editing, and ordering of innumerable pieces dealing with all the sciences, piled up helter-skelter in 75 large quarto volumes and, what is more, written in a foreign language!"[74] For this work, Pinel took charge of volume 5, on chemistry, volume 6, on anatomy and animal physics, volume 7, on medicine and surgery, and volume 9, that is, the second half of materia medica and pharmacy. What was more, he had to undertake this last volume in collaboration with . . . Bosquillon!

For the volume on chemistry, Pinel confronted a strange situation, because "the defenders of the ancient phlogiston theory had written almost all the articles," whereas the language of that science had been completely renewed.[75] Volume 6, on anatomy, presented another problem: an abundance of articles about unnatural occurrences, human monsters, or unbelievable events. A French scientist of the 1790s used to the seriousness of the Académie des sciences had to remind himself that the Royal Society of London, at least at the beginning, was composed in large part of amateurs and wealthy "virtuosi." Volume 7, on medicine and surgery, offered Pinel a more satisfying experience "because the authors were content simply to relate facts, indicating their practical consequences."[76] In volume 9, the second part of materia medica and pharmacy, Pinel should have followed the plan established for volume 8 by Bosquillon. However, he took considerable liberties, commenting at length on air, oxygen, the atmosphere, the "epidemic constitution," and the discoveries of Alessandro Volta and Jan Ingenhousz. In other words, the editor turned cultural ambassador, introducing foreign knowledge to France. But the years 1790–91 were badly chosen for the publication of this abridgment, since more pressing matters than British scientific activities preoccupied Pinel's countrymen. Upon publication, the work aroused little interest.

In the meantime, Pinel had the great satisfaction of being asked by the famous Vicq d'Azyr to contribute to the *Encyclopédie méthodique*, where the anatomist, since 1787, was editing the part on *Médecine*. Pinel began in 1792 with an article on medical dosage, "Dose et doser," in which he proclaimed his Hippocratic faith.[77] He insisted on the need to observe patients closely and to prescribe medications in appropriate amounts and at the right moment, because "one can easily obtain good results with a small dose where a stronger dose would have been useless or would have acted imperfectly at any other moment in the course of the illness."[78] This admonition to time and titrate the administration of medicines carefully reveals Pinel's clinical acumen. He repeatedly insists on the importance of understanding the history of the individual illness, as well as the natural history of the disease, and expresses his lifelong interests in applying botany and chemistry to therapy and in the therapeutic significance of hygiene and diet. Pinel considered "Dose et doser" important and republished the article with small changes twenty years later in the *Dictionnaire des sciences médicales*.[79]

On 30 August 1791, the Société royale de médecine again announced an essay competition, this time on the subject: "Indicate the most effective means of treating patients whose minds have become deranged before old age." The judges thought no entry deserved the prize of 600 livres, but Pinel received a medal worth 100 livres, with honorable mention, for "skillful observations and very sound views."[80] Having been recognized as noteworthy, his essay was read aloud to the society's members on 28 September 1792. In this manner, all those present learned of Pinel's ideas, and a decade later, he incorporated this essay into the *Traité médico-philosophique sur l'aliénation mentale*.

In September 1792, Pinel was already at work on a third memoir to compete for a prize offered by Vicq d'Azyr's society. This time the subject was: "Determine the best method to teach practical medicine in a hospital." Pinel's memoir led to his professorial appointment. Thus three times, in the course of six years, the Société royale motivated Pinel to order, refine, and express his thoughts on the varieties of mental illness, their treatment, and on medical education. These thoughts provided the foundation for his three books.

In an article entitled "A Doctor Surveys the Effects of the French Revolution," published in the *Journal de Paris* on 18 January 1790 and republished a month later in *L'Esprit des journaux*,[81] Pinel now addressed the public at large for the first time. In this piece, he superimposed his personal experience of the fifteen years he had spent "in *my* capital" before the Revolution on the contemporary political situation, observing that "the nefarious increase of selfishness [had] made people hard-hearted and the arbitrariness of the government caused sadness and discouragement." He goes on to draw a parallel between the human body and the body politic, both susceptible to illness, asserting that "it was easy to observe in the capital all the infirmities of a moribund social order . . . man's body wasting away in idleness, indolence, and luxury."

Differing from Jean Jacques Rousseau, whom he cites in this article, Pinel voices his reliance on a doctor's opinion. "The observant physician could easily recognize the salutary effects of the progress of liberty," he asserts. Freedom had "rendered character more resilient and imbued the whole animal economy with increased vigor and energy . . . Emotional upsets [*affections vaporeuses*] and a thousand ever-recurring anxieties . . . have seemed to vanish." He also takes note of "a sizable drop in morbidity and the death rate," but reports "a great many more madmen than usual." Pinel goes on to analyze the effects of the Revolution on the "true patriot" in contrast to "the faint-hearted," especially on women, who, he says, are subject to "realistic or imagined fears" and suffer from "a painful tightening at the base of the chest with intense anxiety . . . a gloomy despondency . . . suffocations, spasmodic headaches, tremors of the extremities and all the complex sequelae of consternation and fear."

Writing at the beginning of 1790, Pinel appears to have been overjoyed at the newfound freedom of expression. Political analysis was obviously not his métier: he took personal impressions for facts and repeated rumors as if they were evidence. Nevertheless, he spoke as a physician. His observations on the psychologic impact of violent political events, particularly on women, would resurface ten years later when he conducted a historic four-year experiment applying humane management, dubbed "moral treatment," to the mentally ill women hospitalized at the Salpêtrière.

Pinel also made two other notable comments on politics that foreshadow his attitudes toward the successive republican, Napoleonic, and Bourbon regimes under which he lived until his death in 1826. In politics he assumed a stance of indifference and silent compliance; but as a physician with a public appointment, he never shied away from admonishing the government to improve patient care.

On 21 January 1793, Pinel attended the execution of Louis XVI. "To my great regret," he wrote to his brother Louis that same evening, "I had to be present, armed, with the other citizens of my section, and I am writing with pain in my heart and in the stupor of a profound consternation." He was far from being a royalist, Pinel states, but he believed that the Convention had committed "the most serious infraction of the eternal laws of justice." The majority of the nation, he adds, would have voted for incarceration of the king. Then he turned to recent personal experiences:

You know that at the beginning of the Revolution I also had the ambition [of being active in politics]. But my life and those of my colleagues were in such danger, when all I was asking for was justice and the good of the people, that I developed a profound horror toward clubs and popular assemblies. I have since then kept my distance from all public positions that are not connected with my profession as doctor.[82]

Once Pinel had attained an official medical position, as physician of the infirmaries at Bicêtre Hospice, he composed a dramatic document that analyzed the condition of the mentally ill, proposed measures for improving their management, and appealed directly to the government to implement such measures. This document contained all the major ideas of his subsequent publications. It was his "Memoir on Madness: A Contribution to the Natural History of Man," read to the Society for Natural History on 11 December 1794. The society voted to transmit the text to the Committee of Public Safety but it has yet to be found in the committee's files.[83] Pinel's appearance before the Society for Natural History late in 1794 marked his long-delayed access to public visibility and to a prominent professional career. Twelve days after the reading, he was named to a professorship at the Paris Health School.

This essay sketches the portrait of a French provincial physician on the fringes of medical power at the end of the ancien régime, who was preoccupied with the fate of a group of patients whom official medicine then ignored. Following a record of initial failures — refusal of the Diest prize, of a position at court, of admission to the Académie des sciences or the Société royale de médecine — Pinel achieved modest successes as medical journalist, editor and translator, and practicing scientist and physician. Along the way, his circle of friends and colleagues expanded. During this formative period, it was above all his mastery of the English language and of British, particularly Scottish, writings, as well as his proficiency in the life sciences that opened the way to his subsequent career. Nonetheless, he still had to wait for the Revolution to obtain two other conditions: freedom to practice and teach medicine, and a reform of the Paris hospitals.[84]

Critics have argued that Pinel is but an eponym, that any humane physician in the right place at the right time — that is, revolutionary Paris — could have become the "liberator of the insane." However, in perusing the relevant works by contemporary physicians, such as Joseph Daquin, Andrés Piquér, Vincenzo Chiarugi, Johann Christian Reil, Benjamin Rush, and more than a half-dozen Englishmen who kept "mad-houses" and reported on their patients, one does not find a single physician with the combination of aptitudes and experience that qualified Pinel for the career he embarked on in 1793. Pinel forged that career by the choices he made, the work he accomplished, the quality of his writing, and the demonstration of an extraordinary empathy with human pain and anguish.

Although Pinel made an impact primarily in the nineteenth century, his principles stemmed directly from the Enlightenment and qualify him as a member of the "Party of Humanity." In his company, that Party might even have shed its distrust of doctors and agreed that, if equality is indeed a natural human right, then a human being born sick or handicapped is not equal to a healthy one and requires the assistance of society and of a physician.[85] Pinel's enduring message is that medicine must encompass the mental as well as the physical aspects of human illness and not only deal with a diseased body part or with symptoms traceable to an anatomical lesion. The humane management of patients, including the mentally ill, is a goal that was defined for medicine by Pinel and by the Enlightenment.

5. "Philosophical Sex"

Pornography in Old Regime France

In 1984, Peter Gay trained his sharp eye for promising subjects on the history of pornography. "Scholarship on the subject, though growing, remains limited and its result, so far, frustrating," he lamented.[1] Since then, his frustration has probably increased, because pornography has turned into a political football, kicked around by presidential candidates who want to demonstrate their devotion to family values and by radical feminists who want to eradicate what they take to be the root of all evil. Evil there may be in obscene texts and images that degrade women, children, and even men. But pornography, or erotic literature that has been treated as taboo, also contains a great deal of value. Like most forbidden fruit, it has served as food for thought. Yet this aspect of its history has never been taken seriously; and it deserves to be considered, if one is ever to make sense of pornography as an element in Western civilization.

In reconsidering the history of pornography, one might begin with a proposition derived from Claude Lévi-Strauss: sex is good to think—or, to phrase it in more acceptable English, sex provides excellent material for working over in the mind. In *La Pensée sauvage* and other works, Lévi-Strauss argues that many peoples do not think in the manner of philosophers, by manipulating abstractions. Instead, they think with things—concrete things from everyday life, like housing arrangements and tattoos, or imaginary things from myth and folklore, like Brer Rabbit and his briar patch. Just as some materials are particularly good to work, some things are especially "good to think" (*bonnes à penser*). They can be arranged in patterns, which bring out unsuspected relationships and define unclear boundaries.

Sex, I submit, is one of them. As carnal knowledge worked into cultural patterns, it supplies endless material for thought, especially when it appears in narratives—dirty jokes, male braggadocio, female gossip, bawdy songs, and erotic novels. In all these forms, sex is not simply a subject but also a tool, used to pry the top off things and explore their inner works. It does for ordinary people what logic does for philosophers: it helps make sense of things. And it did so with greatest effect during the golden age of pornography, from 1650 to 1800, primarily in France.

I

Fortunately, this proposition can be tested, because for the past ten years, French publishers have been reprinting whole shelfloads of the most illegal and most erotic works from the Old Regime. They have capitalized on the freer attitudes toward sex among the public and police, and they have drawn on an endless supply of copy from the famous "Enfer" section of the Bibliothèque Nationale.

The librarians created "l'Enfer" ("Hell") sometime between 1836 and 1844 in order to cope with a contradiction. On the one hand, they needed to preserve the fullest possible record of the printed word; on the other, they wanted to prevent readers from being corrupted by bad books. The answer was to cull all the most offensive erotic works from the library's various collections and shut them up in one spot, which was declared off limits to ordinary readers.[2]

This policy belonged to the bowdlerization of the world that took place in the nineteenth century. As part of the general buttoning-up and locking-away, librarians everywhere put certain kinds of books beyond the reach of readers and invented codes to classify them: the "Private Case" of the British Museum, the Delta callmark of the Library of Congress, the ***** of the New York Public Library, and the Bodleian's Greek letter φ, which when pronounced in Oxford English sounded like "Fie!"[3]

The greatest collection of them all was generally believed to be in the Bibliothèque Nationale, because Paris—the naughty Paris of the Regency and the rococo—passed as the capital of pornography. Downstairs in the Nationale's cavernous Salle des Imprimés, readers sometimes allowed their thoughts to wander upstairs, where, curiously, "Hell" was located. Instead of trudging through the sermons of Bourdaloue or the histories of Rollin, they imagined themselves climbing up two flights into a Baudelairean realm of *luxe, calme, et volupté*. "Hell" therefore became something more than a storage space defined by call numbers—the D2 series devised in 1702 and the extraordinary Y2, which goes back to 1750. "Hell" was heaven, an escape fantasy charged with poetic energy.

One of France's greatest poets, Guillaume Apollinaire, visited l'Enfer and cataloged its holdings in 1919: 930 works, one apparently more delicious than the other. A more scholarly catalog produced by Pascal Pia in 1978 lists 1,730 titles, although many are modern reprints, the originals having disappeared from the stacks at various times since the seventeenth century. Evidently Hell contained a huge supply of forbidden fruit, but most of it remained beyond the reach of ordinary readers until 1980, when l'Enfer was abolished and the publishers began to reprint its contents.[4]

Now all this literature has fallen into the public domain. You can pick some up in any Paris bookstore and sample vast amounts in the seven-volume selection from the *Enfer* published by Fayard: 29 novels complete with scholarly introductions and illustrations. The Fayard series does not include many of the most important works, such as *Margot la ravaudeuse*, *Les Lauriers ecclésiastiques*, and *La Chandelle d'Arras*, which were best-sellers in the clandestine book trade of the Old Regime. But some of them can be found in an excellent anthology published last year by Raymond Trousson, *Romans libertines du XVIIIe siècle*: a dozen novels and stories crammed into one volume of 1,300 pages. So now at last one can take a fairly complete tour of France's literary Hell. What does it reveal about the history of pornography and pornography's place in the history of thought?

The word, like the thing, is a matter of dispute. For some, "pornography" should be restricted to its etymological root, meaning writing about prostitutes, as distinct from eroticism in general. For others, it involves descriptions of sexual activity that are meant to arouse the reader or beholder and that violate conventional morality. A postmodernist might argue that the thing did not come into existence until the word was coined — that is, not until the first half of the nineteenth century (the earliest use of a related term seems to be in Restif de la Bretonne's tract about public prostitution, *Le Pornographe*, of 1769). Only then, through measures like the creation of the Enfer, did the public discourse on sex define a category of erotica as peculiarly worthy of repression.[5]

The difficulty with such definitions is that sexual practices and cultural taboos keep shifting. Indeed, it is their very shiftiness that made sex so good to think, because it served as a way to explore ambiguities and establish boundaries. No one in the sixteenth and early seventeenth centuries thought of banning books because of bawdiness that might be considered pornographic today. Religion, not sex, determined the main limits of the licit. But it is impossible to separate sex from religion in the earliest works of modern pornography: Aretino's *Ragionamenti* (1536), where the most lascivious scenes are set in a convent; *L'Ecole des filles* (1655) and *L'Académie des dames* (1680), which adapts Aretino's themes to French anticlericalism; and *Vénus*

dans le cloître (1682?), where free love promotes freethinking. At the high tide
of pornography in the eighteenth century, best-selling works like *Thérèse
philosophe* (1748) employed eroticism in the cause of the Enlightenment.
And on the eve of the Revolution, sex books such as *La Correspondance
d'Eulalie* (1784) served above all as vehicles of social criticism.

After 1789, pornography provided a whole arsenal of weapons for bash-
ing aristocrats, clergymen, and the monarchy. But after turning political
(e.g., *Dom Bougre aux Etats-Généraux*, an indictment of deputies in the Es-
tates General), it became trivial (*Les Quarante manières de foutre*, a pseudo-
sex manual that reads like a recipe book, most of it for fast food: "Take a thigh,
add butter, cover, heat to simmering . . . "). True, the century ended with the
marquis de Sade, whom some have hailed as a prophet of the modern avant-
garde. But the endless permutation of copulating bodies in the work of a
more typical author, André-Robert Andréa de Nerciat, suggests a genre that
had exhausted itself. In the nineteenth and twentieth centuries, Baudelaire
and Bataille made sex good to think in new ways; and the new era of mass literacy and mass production turned pornography into a phenomenon of mass
consumption.[6]

In short, pornography has a history. It grew within a body of literature
whose contours kept changing but that maintained a certain coherence. The
works in the Enfer constantly refer back to the same sources, especially Aretino and the ancient phallic cult of Priapus. They cite one another, sometimes describing "gallant libraries" used as sexual props. They exploit the
same devices, above all voyeurism (the reader is made to look over the shoulder of someone looking through a keyhole at a couple copulating in front of
a mirror or pictures of copulating couples on the wall). They use the same
narrative strategies: first-person autobiographies by courtesans, dialogues between sexual veterans and innocent beginners, pseudo sex manuals, and tours
of convents and brothels (which are always presented as two versions of the
same thing, a usage preserved in the slang term *abbaye* for whorehouse). In
many cases, they even give their characters the same names—Nana, Agnes,
Suzon were favorites—and advertise their wares by means of the same false
addresses on their title pages: "à Rome, de l'imprimerie du Saint Père"; "à
Gratte-mon-con, chez Henri Branle-Motte"; "à Tribaldis, de l'imprimerie de
Priape"; "à Cythère, au Temple de la Volupté"; "à Lèche-con, et se trouve
dans les coulisses de tous les théâtres."

Yet despite these conventions, which cast the reader in the role of voyeur
and oriented his expectations toward an erotic experience, early modern
pornography did not stand out in the eyes of its contemporaries as a clear

and distinct genre of literature. Instead, it belonged to the general category known at the time as "philosophical." Eighteenth-century publishers and booksellers used the term "philosophical books" to designate illegal merchandise, whether it was irreligious, seditious, or obscene. They did not bother about finer distinctions, because most forbidden books gave offense in several ways. *Libre* in the jargon of their trade sometimes meant lascivious, but it invoked the libertinism of the seventeenth century — that is, freethinking. By 1750, libertinism had become a matter of the body and the mind, of pornography and philosophy. Readers could recognize a sex book when they saw one, but they expected sex to serve as a vehicle for attacks on the Church, the crown, and all sorts of social abuses.[7]

Consider *Thérèse philosophe*, one of the two or three most important pornographic works of the eighteenth century. It begins with a fictitious version of a notorious scandal in which a Jesuit priest seduced a young woman who had come to him for spiritual guidance. In the novel, the Jesuit preaches a radical variety of Cartesianism. He expounds Descartes's dichotomy between spirit and matter by instructing his pupil, Mlle Eradice, to detach her soul from her body through spiritual exercises, such as lifting her skirts while he flagellates her buttocks and she concentrates on the Holy Ghost. If she concentrates hard enough, he assures her, she won't feel any pain. Instead, her soul will abandon her body and soar to heaven on a wave of spiritual ecstasy.

After an adequate flogging, Eradice is ready for the ultimate spiritual exercise: sexual intercourse. The Jesuit explains that, thanks to the use of a relic — a stiff remnant of the rope that Saint Francis wore around his habit — she will undergo a pure form of spiritual penetration. Then, as she prays from a nearly prostrate position, he mounts her from behind. The scene is described by Thérèse, the heroine and narrator of the novel, as she witnesses it from a hiding place:

Oh, father! cried Eradice. Such pleasure is penetrating me! Oh, yes, I'm feeling celestial happiness; I sense that my mind is completely detached from matter. Further, father, further! Root out all that is impure in me. I see . . . the . . . an . . . gels. Push forward . . . push now . . . Ah! . . . Ah! . . . Good . . . Saint Francis! Don't abandon me! I feel the cord . . . the cord . . . the cord . . . I can't stand it any more . . . I'm dying![8]

This episode provides Thérèse with more than a lesson in the dangers of priestcraft. It is the first step in her education. Having learned to throw off the authority of the Church, she pursues the pleasure principle, which leads through physics, metaphysics, and ethics to a happy ending in the bed of a philosophic count. Strange as it may seem to a modern reader, the sex and the philosophy go hand in hand throughout the novel. The characters masturbate and copulate, then discuss ontology and morality, while restoring their forces for the next round of pleasure. This narrative strategy made perfect sense in 1748, because it showed how carnal knowledge could open the way to enlightenment—the radical enlightenment of La Mettrie, Helvétius, Diderot, and d'Holbach.

In the end, Thérèse becomes a philosophe of their stripe. She learns that everything can be reduced to matter in motion, that all knowledge derives from the senses, and that all behavior should be governed by a hedonistic calculus: maximize pleasure and minimize pain. But she is a female philosophe. The greatest pain she can imagine is childbirth, all the more so as her mother and her female mentor almost died in labor. Therefore, much as she enjoys sex and wants to make love with the count when he courts her, she decides that intercourse is not worth the risk. Given the character of eighteenth-century demography and obstetrics, her calculation makes perfect sense, and so does her answer: masturbation at first and contraception by means of coitus interruptus in the end.

Because Thérèse is a poor commoner and her lover a count, she cannot expect to marry him. But she strikes a good bargain: a generous annuity of 2,000 livres a year and the run of his château. She even calls the tune in their lovemaking—and in an earlier episode repulses a rapist by seizing him by the throat. Instead of accepting her lot in life, Thérèse refuses the role of wife and mother and pursues her own happiness on her own terms—as a materialist, atheist, liberated woman.

She was also a figment of a male imagination, because, like most pornography, Thérèse philosophe was written by a man—probably Jean-Baptiste de Boyer, marquis d'Argens, possibly a certain D'Arles de Montigny, or perhaps even Diderot. Thérèse herself belongs to a long line of female narrators that stretches back to Aretino's Nanna. They express men's fantasies, not the long-lost voice of early modern feminism. As prostitutes, kept women, and nuns, they perpetuate the myth of the female voluptuary who accepts her subjection in order to give full rein to her lasciviousness. Nothing could be further from the horrors of prostitution than the fiction of the happy whore.

But the fictitious females represented a challenge to the subordination of women under the Old Regime. Above all, they challenged the authority of the Church, which did more than any other institution to keep women in their place. The pornography is so shot through with anticlericalism that it often seems more irreligious than obscene. Priests are always abusing the confessional to seduce their parishioners. Monks are always turning convents into harems. Country curates always abuse the peasantry, deflowering, cuckolding, and shipping their victims off to cities, where they become the prey of prelates. Bishops and abbots have their own pimps and houses of pleasure. Even so, they fail to protect themselves from venereal disease, which is consuming the upper clergy along with the upper nobility.

These themes can be put abstractly as a matter of corruption and exploitation, but the pornography makes them effective by embodying them in sex stories. The heroine of *Vénus en rut, ou vie d'une célèbre libertine* (1771?) cites Mme de Pompadour's famous remark about the bishop of Condom (no less), who had contracted syphilis: "Why didn't he stay in his diocese?" And then she reveals what she did with a bishop of her own when she got him between the sheets. In order to make him believe that he was a great lover, she called out as he humped away, "Ah! Monseigneur, what voluptuousness!" "Shut up!" he replied, "or I won't be able to come." After limping to an orgasm, he explained that any reference to his title, Monseigneur, was enough to spoil his erection for the rest of the evening. "A Monsieur would be too much."[9]

In *La Correspondance d'Eulalie*, a bishop buys a few nights with the kept woman of a marquis. Tipped off by a spy, the marquis surprises them in bed. But instead of flying into a rage, he presents the bishop with a bill for 15,000 livres, the sum he has spent on the woman for the last three months (and the equivalent of 300 years' wages for a skilled artisan), threatening to expose his conduct if he refuses to pay. The bishop coughs up the blackmail, but is made a laughingstock in the Paris rumor mill and therefore is obliged to retreat to his see. Margot in *Margot la ravaudeuse* soaks a prelate for even more: 24,000 livres in two weeks, and sends him back to his parishioners with a case of venereal disease — his just reward, she claims, for having extorted the money from the common people in the first place.

True, one could find similar anecdotes in earlier anticlericalism, especially the bawdy variety of Boccaccio, Rabelais, and Aretino. But those authors remained fundamentally Christian — Aretino nearly became a cardinal and wrote saints' lives as well as pornography — while the pornographers of the eighteenth century used sex to express all the key ideas of the Enlightenment: nature, happiness, liberty, equality. Like Margot, the courtesan narrator of *Vénus en rut* exposes the artificiality of social distinctions by sleeping her way from the bottom of society to the top. She learns that all men are equal, once you get them in bed — or, rather, that they vary according to the gifts they have received from nature: "temperament" (but the lower classes always outdo the upper; three orgasms of a servant are worth more than eight of a count) and physique (but penises should not be rated according to their length; "seven or eight inches should amuse any woman of taste"). The conclusion is clear: "In the state of nature, all men are equal; that assuredly is the state of the courtesan." As a proposition, the idea was common enough; but it came across with uncommon force, because it was embodied in narratives with a strong story line: that is how sex helped readers think equality in a deeply inegalitarian society.[10]

The same line of thought applied to the relations between men and women. By stripping everyone of their social distinctions, pornography exposed similarities and differences in the sexuality of the sexes, at least as they were understood by male authors writing as female narrators. At their most basic, in *Thérèse philosophe*, for example, the differences came down to little or nothing, because all humans were "machines" composed of the same tiny particles of matter. Pleasure simply set the matter in motion, first as a stimulus of the sense organs, then as a sensation transmitted through the nervous system, and finally as an idea to be stored and combined in the brain.

The differences between men and women are also minimal in seventeenth-century pornography, which draws on Galen and Descartes to advance a physiological view of sex. In *L'Ecole des filles*, the vagina is an inverted penis, complete with "testicles" and "spermatic canals," and women ejaculate the same "thick, white liquor" in the same way as men. Fecundation occurs by means of mutual orgasm, when the two liquors meet; so the woman's pleasure is crucial to reproduction. She can also prevent conception by controlling "the combat of semen against semen" through movements of her thighs and buttocks. She should direct the action and mount the man when she pleases, both to maximize pleasure and to develop his "humility."[11] By bestriding her lover, the heroine of *Histoire de Marguerite* (1784) "ejaculated so amply that she drowned me with her delicious semen from my belly button to the middle of my thighs."[12]

Behind the mechanics and hydraulics of this sexology was a utopian notion of men and women copulating and ejaculating endlessly, in perfect synchrony. *L'Ecole des filles* even revives the ancient myth that men and women are divided halves of the same androgynous whole, which seek forever to reunite. It dismisses the sexual doctrines of the Catholic Church as so much nonsense, invented by men in order to dominate women, despite the self-evident truths of the order of nature. A century and a half later, *Eléonore, ou l'heureuse personne* (1798) pursues the same theme in a fable about a hermaphrodite who switches sexes once a year, moving back and forth between monasteries and nunneries while experimenting with every conceivable sexual combination. In its wildest fantasies as well as its most scientific fictions, early modern pornography therefore made it possible to think about sexual equality in ways that challenged the basic values of the Old Regime.

In some cases, the thought experiments came close to themes in modern feminism. In 1680, *L'Académie des dames* protests against the skewed social code that subjects women to the "inhumanity of men." [13] Although women have greater capacity for sexual pleasure, men are given greater freedom to indulge in it. Therefore, it argues, women should avenge themselves by pretending to honor society's absurd conventions in public while giving full vent to their natural instincts in secret — in a word, by cuckolding their husbands.

In 1740, *Histoire de Dom B . . .* condemns "the captivity in which [the female] sex is kept." [14] The hero's mother delivers a remarkable sermon on courtship and marriage, denouncing conventional morality as a way of subjecting women to men. And in 1784, *Correspondance d'Eulalie* plays with a fanciful solution to the problem of male dominance: women could withdraw to self-sufficient lesbian communities in the country. It repeats the well-worn theme of women's superior capacity for multiple orgasms and celebrates their general superiority in verse:

> Par des raisons, prouvons aux hommes
> Combien au-dessus d'eux nous sommes
> Et quel est leur triste destin.
> Nargue du genre masculin.
> Démontrons quel est leur caprice,
> Leur trahison, leur injustice.
> Chantons et répétons sans fin:
> Honneur au sexe feminin.[15]

> By reasons, let us prove to men
> How superior we are to them
> And what is their sad fate.
> Phooey to the male gender.
> Let us demonstrate their capriciousness,
> Their treason, their injustice.
> Sing and repeat endlessly:
> Honor to the female sex.

II

After reading through 150 years of early modern pornography, it is difficult to resist the conclusion that some feminists have got it wrong. Instead of condemning all pornography outright, they could use some of it to advance their cause. Catharine MacKinnon may be correct in associating modern pornographers with the proposition that "having sex is antithetical to thinking." [16] But that claim contradicts arguments developed three centuries ago in "philosophical books" that sex is "an inexhaustible source of thought." [17] And Andrea Dworkin's indictment of pornography rests on a breathlessly ahistorical view of culture:

In the intimate world of men and women, there is no mid-twentieth century distinct from any other century. There are only the old values, women there for the taking, the means of taking determined by the male. It is ancient and it is modern; it is feudal, capitalist, socialist; it is caveman and astronaut, agricultural and industrial, urban and rural. For men, the right to abuse women is elemental, the first principle. . . . In pornography, men express the tenets of their unchanging faith, what they must believe is true of women and of themselves to sustain themselves as they are.[18]

Instead of refusing historical reflection and restricting their arguments to culture-bound notions of gender, feminists could draw on the history of pornography to show how male dominance has been exerted and resisted over time. While asserting the right of women to defend themselves against men, early modern pornography frequently castigates the male animal as a predator who paws every female within reach and feels no compunctions about rape. Dom B . . . masturbates while taking confession, then rapes his most succulent parishioner. His violence and her resistance are described in excruciating detail. But as soon as he penetrates her, she responds passionately and outdoes him in lasciviousness. By fighting him off, she had really been trying to turn him on — that is, she had meant yes by saying no, another stock theme in the literature, but one that is not invoked in a way that mitigates male rapaciousness. When the heroine's first lover in *La Cauchoise* catches her with another man, he avenges himself by arranging for her to be gang-raped by eight of his friends while he urges them on. The women in the prostitute narratives are frequently raped; and one of them, Mlle Rosalie in *Correspondance d'Eulalie*, is found dangling from a noose in the Bois de Boulogne with her breasts cut off.

Some of these episodes seem to have been inspired by the sensationalist fiction of penny dreadfuls (*canards, feuilles volantes*, and chapbooks). One should not take them literally, just as one should not read *Fanny Hill* (*La Fille de joie* in the inadequate French translation) as a clinical account of female sexuality. But taken as literature, such pornography expresses the assumption that women are in constant danger of rape, especially when exposed to men of superior power and status. It favors violent metaphors. A bride's virginity is a fortress to be stormed, the bed a battlefield, the deflowering a slaughter. *L'Académie des dames* describes the hymen as "a victim . . . that must be sacrificed or massacred and torn to pieces with plenty of bloodshed." A groom instructs his bride to surrender "that part of your body that is no longer yours but mine"; and by entering her vagina, he "takes possession of a thing that belongs to me."[19]

Male dominance could hardly be put more bluntly. True, the sex books often seem to condone as well as to condemn the brutal treatment of women. It would be silly to read a modern argument for women's liberation into ancient texts designed primarily to arouse men. Yet the texts also advance ideas that undercut simplistic notions of phallocracy. After losing their virginity, the heroines of early modern pornography often gain a kind of independence, not legal or professional or social autonomy, which was virtually impossible under the conditions of the Old Regime, but self-reliance of an intellectual sort, because once they discover that sex is good to think, they learn to think for themselves. In *L'Ecole des filles*, Fanchon remains silly and servile until she makes love. Then she awakens to a new power in herself:

Formerly I was only good for sewing and holding my tongue, but now I can do all sorts of things. When I speak with my mother, I now find reasons to support what I say; I hold forth as if I were another person, instead of fearing to open my mouth as I used to do. I am beginning to use my mind and to stick my nose into things that were almost unknown to me before.[20]

In *L'Académie des dames*, the *ingénue*, Octavie, gains intellectual maturity as soon as she loses her virginity; for as she observes, to open the vulva is to open the mind.[21] In *Vénus dans le cloître*, Sister Dosithée, a religious fanatic, flagellates herself so violently that she ejaculates, bursting her hymen with a discharge released from deep within her womb. Then suddenly her mind clears, she recognizes the superstition at the core of Catholicism, and she converts to deism. In *Histoire de Dom B . . .* , Sister Monique frees herself of ignorance and opens her mind to the light of reason by means of masturbation. Dom B . . . himself first becomes aware of the rational order of nature by watching a couple copulate. And in *Thérèse philosophe*, voyeurism and masturbation clear a way through the claptrap of religion, making it possible for Thérèse to become a philosopher.[22]

The theme appears everywhere in early modern pornography. In fact, the literature of the Enfer uses a special verb to convey it: *déniaiser*, to lose one's silliness by gaining carnal knowledge. At the other end of the process, the heroines in the sexual success stories become *savantes*—not the kind of *femmes savantes* satirized by Molière and not necessarily learned, but critical and intellectually independent. "I became *savante*," declares the narrator of *La Cauchoise* after an account of her initiation in the mysteries of sex. She therefore rejects religion and refuses to accept "any authority other than nature itself."[23]

The narrator of *Vénus en rut* pursues the knowledge of nature even further by seducing a doctor and compelling him to give her lessons in physiology, complete with wax models of the inner workings of the sexual organs. The heroines of *Margot la ravaudeuse* and *Correspondance d'Eulalie* set up salons and rule over the literary world. They do not all embrace the cause of the Enlightenment, but all of them pursue enlightened self-interest and fight their way to the top of the Old Regime by refusing to accept its prejudices and by exploiting its corruption.

In the end, therefore, sex turns out to be good for thinking, not merely in order to resist the exploitation of women by men, but to oppose exploitation in general. The pornography provides a general indictment of the Old Regime, its courtiers, manor lords, financiers, tax collectors, and judges, as well as its priests. Everyone who lives off the labor of the common people receives a drubbing at one point or another. Not that the sex books call for a revolution. Some of them—*Lucette ou les progrès du libertinage*, for example— even satirize freethinkers and philosophers. But by pursuing standard themes like a harlot's progress and the corruption of country youth, they expose the web of wealth and influence that constituted *le monde*, France's all-powerful elite. *La Correspondance d'Eulalie* can be read as a map of *le monde* and also as a *chronique scandaleuse*, or underground journal. It provides a running commentary on plays and operas, exhibitions of paintings, ministerial intrigues, foreign affairs, and all sorts of current events, along with the sex lives of the rich and powerful. The sex merely serves as a vehicle for social criticism, and the criticism runs in many directions, not merely along the Great Divide separating men and women.

By concentrating exclusively on the victimization of women, feminist critics of pornography fail to recognize the part it played in exposing other kinds of social abuses. But its history also confirms some of their central arguments, notably their claim that "pornography is masturbation material."[24] Not only do works like *Thérèse philosophe* take masturbation as a major theme, they also encourage the reader to masturbate along with the characters in the stories. The comte de Mirabeau puts it at its crudest in the introduction to *Ma conversion ou le libertin de qualité* (1783): "May the reading [of this book] make the whole universe beat off."[25]

Such remarks seem to assume a male audience, although they do not necessarily exclude women. In claiming to be written for the edification of girls, *L'Ecole des filles* and *Lucette ou les progrès du libertinage* are probably trying to tickle the imagination of men. But *La Cauchoise* includes women servants in a more straightforward description of the reading public;[26] and the narrator of *Eléonore, ou l'heureuse personne* refers casually to "my women readers" as if she expected to have some.[27] Iconographic evidence such as Emmanuel de Ghendt's notorious *Le Midi* shows women using books for stimulation while masturbating. And the texts themselves stress female masturbation, often in connection with reading. The nuns in *Vénus dans le cloître* excite themselves by reading *L'Académie des dames*; the prostitutes in *La Correspondance d'Eulalie* by reading Aretino; the female philosophers in *Thérèse philosophe* by reading *Histoire de Dom B . . .* ; and the lesbians in *Les Progrès du libertinage* by reading *Thérèse philosophe*. "Gallant libraries" are often described in the novels.[28] The intertextuality is so thick and so shot through with autoeroticism that it can be sensed on every page, but it cannot be identified exclusively with men.

III

The issue is not whether pornography was meant to arouse sexual desire or meant to arouse only males, but rather whether it can be reduced to its function as masturbation material. In order to argue their case more effectively, the feminists could find some unexpected allies in the camp of literary theory. Above all, they could draw on the work of Jean-Marie Goulemot, which represents the best in the current scholarship on pornography.

Goulemot argues that eighteenth-century pornography came closer than any other genre to realizing the aim of all literature before Mallarmé— namely, to create a "reality effect" so powerful that it seemed to obliterate the distinction between literature and life.[29] In pornographic novels, unlike other kinds of narrative, the words printed on paper produce an unmediated, involuntary response in the body of the reader. The fiction works physically, as if it could insinuate itself into flesh and blood, abolishing time and language and everything else that separates reading from reality. Goulemot's argument fits perfectly with Catharine MacKinnon's contention that "pornography is often more sexually compelling than the realities it presents, more sexually real than reality."[30] But the thesis has drawbacks.

It combines theories of reader-response and of genre to advance the notion of an ideal type, something that might be called "pure" pornography, because it operates exclusively on the reader's libido. Any disruption (*brouillage*)—in the form of plot development, psychological complexity, philosophy, humor, sentiment, or social comment—will mitigate the effect and detract from the pornography's pureness. Unfortunately for the theory, however, early modern pornography consists mainly of *brouillage*—that is, of the very ingredients that create impurities. Its greatest successes, *Histoire de Dom B . . .* and *Thérèse philosophe*, go to the furthest extremes in steering the reader through narrative and philosophical complexities. And its founding father, Aretino, shifts from sex to social criticism in the course of his *Ragionamenti*.

True, Aretino is famous for the explicit descriptions of copulating techniques in his *Sonetti lussuriosi*. But it seems unlikely that the sonnets were widely read in France; and it is inaccurate to claim, as Goulemot does, that Aretino was "tirelessly translated and retranslated" into French under the Old Regime.[31] Aside from some of his religious writings and one fragment of the *Ragionamenti*, the French did not publish a single translation of his work between 1660 and 1800.[32] Instead, they printed and reprinted *L'Arrétin moderne* by Henri-Joseph Du Laurens (first edition, 1763, and at least thirteen others before 1789), a scandal sheet that was three parts gossip to one part sex.[33] The "modern Aretino" of eighteenth-century France actually had a lot in common with his Italian ancestor from the sixteenth century. But he was above all a *libelliste*—that is, a specialist in slandering eminent figures of the Church and state. Libel, like irreligion, can hardly be distinguished from pornography in the "philosophical" works of the Old Regime. If pornography was a genre, it was such a mixed genre that it defies any attempt to isolate a pure variety. Its impurities are the very elements that made sex so good for thought.

In the end, then, literary theory fails to account for the defining characteristics of early modern pornography. Jean-Marie Goulemot comes close to acknowledging this failure in the conclusion to his book, where he toys with the fantasy of a "golden age of reading."[34] He locates it in eighteenth-century France, a time when readers could plunge into texts like adolescents, free of the inhibitions produced by training in literary criticism. Thanks to their passionate primitivism, he fancies, they may have used pornography as a way of abandoning themselves to the call of the wild. (Indeed, some librarians are said to have found spermatic traces, possibly from the eighteenth century, on the leaves of eighteenth-century sex books.) Could a modern researcher follow in the steps of those long forgotten readers and, by divesting himself of enough sophistication, respond in the same way? The proof of his success would be, to put it bluntly (but Goulemot steers his argument around all such coarseness), an orgasm. In that case, the books from Hell could function as time machines, propelling their readers into sensations that burned out two centuries ago, and pornography could provide historians with an experience that has hitherto eluded them: direct access to passions in the past.

IV

This fantasy should not be taken too seriously, but it illustrates a serious impediment to understanding the history of pornography: the illusion of immunity from anachronism. No matter how erotic a text may be, it can hardly affect readers today in the same way that it affected them centuries earlier; for reading now takes place in a mental world that differs fundamentally in its assumptions, values, and cultural codes from the world of the Old Regime. Therefore, instead of searching through early modern pornography for parallels to modern varieties of male dominance, one could take the opposite tack and read it for what it says about mentalities that no longer exist. Take one step into an obscene novel from seventeenth- or eighteenth-century France, and you enter an unfamiliar landscape. Read through several shelves, and you find yourself on an ethnographic journey through a vast museum of foreign folkways. In this way, too, sex is good for thinking—not just for primitives from the Old Regime but for anyone who wants to understand them.

Consider the question of beauty. Like natives in many developing countries, the characters in early modern pornography fancied fat: fat in general and fat in particular places—on arms, for example, and in the small of the back. Back fat produced dimples at the *chute de reins*, a sensuous spot just above the buttocks immortalized by François Boucher in paintings of his famous model, Mademoiselle O'Murphy. It is Eradice's "admirable *chute de reins*" that makes her so irresistible to her Jesuit confessor in *Thérèse philosophe*[35] and Lucette's arms that make her fortune as a courtesan in *Les Progrès du libertinage*: "Her chubby arms make cupid smile; one longs to fix one's mouth to them and to be squeezed in their soft bondage."[36] Women used their arms more than their legs as means of seduction. "No doubt Monsieur likes to see the movement of a naked arm," Mme C . . . says to arouse her lover in *Thérèse philosophe*.[37] But legs mattered, too, especially on men, because men's breeches left their calves exposed, and spindly calves disgusted women. Thus Margot's populist scorn for the leg of one of her clients in *Margot la ravaudeuse*: "He had the leg of a man of breeding—that is to say, skinny and meatless."[38] Men were also repelled by "hideous thinness."[39] They found breasts and buttocks alluring, but only if abundantly upholstered: the more meat, the better, although they preferred Boucher-like fleshiness (*embonpoint*) to Rubenesque obesity. The heroine of *Vénus en rut* puts the ideal succinctly when she describes herself as "a little ball of fat." [40]

Of course, one must allow for literary conventions in the descriptions of beautiful women. So it is not surprising that the narrator of *Vénus en rut* presents herself to the reader as having the "freshness of a new rose." [41] But she immediately goes on to praise her teeth. Teeth stand out everywhere in the descriptions, probably because of the prevalence of rotting jaws and stinking breath in early modern society. In *Le Rut ou la pudeur éteinte* (1676), Dorimène has skin like a lily and a mouth like a rose. "Her teeth were white, so equal and perfectly aligned that this part of her alone would have sufficed to inspire love in a soul less sensitive than [Céladon's]." [42]

What do they do, these two sensitive souls, when they get past the self-presentation and the foreplay? They organize an orgy with two other couples in a prison, where the hero, Céladon, holds court after being locked up by a nasty attorney. In order to hump more effectively, one of the gallants props his feet against a cupboard. But he thrusts so hard that he knocks it over onto one of the ladies, Hiante, who is copulating on the floor — and having some difficulty, because her lover, Le Rocher, cannot sustain an erection, and she is enormously pregnant. The blow causes her to have a stillbirth on the spot. The ladies then withdraw, and the cavaliers give themselves over to a poetry contest.

Le Rocher wins the contest by improvising all sorts of verse, including a sonnet on the poor performance of his penis. It went limp, he explains in perfect Petrarchan style, because after penetrating Hiante it found Death waiting for it in the person of the fetus at the far end of her womb. While the poets woo their muse, the prison guard dog eats the baby's body, all except its head, and promptly dies of indigestion. The poets realize what has happened, when they spot the prison cat playing with the head as if it were a ball. "This spectacle gave them great pleasure," the narrator observes. [43] It stimulates their appetites and also their creativity; so they sit down to a hearty meal and produce epitaphs for the dog, improvising rhymes around the theme of birth and death. Then they send a lackey to nail the baby's head on the front door of the attorney's house.

When the attorney looks out his window the next morning, he sees a crowd gathered in front of his door. Assuming they are a lynch mob, he confesses all the crimes he has committed at the expense of the local peasants. But then he notices the head and realizes that the crowd is a collection of bumpkins venting its "joy" at the sight of something strange.[44] So he retracts his confession and explains that the head came from a monkey that his brother killed in the forest—a creature that had been unaccountably swinging through the trees outside of Alençon. The bumpkins then disperse, delighted at having seen, for free, the kind of curiosity that would have cost them a penny at a village fair.

What makes this episode so strange for the modern reader is not its violence—we have more than enough of that in pornography today—but its humor. It is clearly meant to be funny. While stringing together one horror after another, the text describes the incidents as "comic," "funny," and "buffoonish."[45] If we have absorbed an adequate supply of picaresque novels, we might recognize some themes. If we have mastered enough Shakespeare and Cervantes, we might begin to get our bearings. But none of us today can laugh at those jokes. Our inability to get them should tip us off to the difficulty of "getting" a culture fundamentally different from ours, although it might have some specious familiarity if it appeared under the heading "Renaissance" or "Baroque" in a textbook on Western civilization.

Early modern pornography grew out of a culture that seems unthinkable today, just as the car crashes and shoot-outs of our television will look baffling to researchers three centuries from now. In the seventeenth century, works like *Le Rut ou la pudeur éteinte* belonged to a Rabelaisian world that combined the rough-and-tumble of the street with the sophistication of the court. In the eighteenth century, the street culture continued to leave its mark on bawdy books, but it changed in character. It became concentrated on the boulevards that had replaced the medieval walls of Paris, providing a setting for a new kind of popular theater and a new kind of prostitute: the *grisette* who graduated from clothes shops along the rue Saint Honoré to fancy apartments behind the boulevards in the rue de Cléry and the rue Tiquetonne.

All of the prostitute narratives after 1750 take their readers on tours of this territory, describing the food in the bistros, the furniture in the *bordels*, the music in the dance halls, the gestures in the pantomimes, and the farces in the theaters. *Correspondance d'Eulalie* reads in places like a guidebook, complete with footnotes for the edification of ignorant provincials. At one point, Mlle Julie, a high-class courtesan, amuses herself by picking up a man from the low life in Nicolet's vaudeville theater. She lets him think "that I was one of those girls who is willing to accept a supper in a good boulevard bistro as the price of their favors." So she sends him off to order a meal chez Bancelin and then disappears. A footnote explains that Bancelin's is the most famous tavern on the boulevard and that to spice up a meal, one can order bawdy songs from *joueuses de veille* (girl street-singers who accompanied themselves on a hurdy-gurdy), who also provide sexual services.[46] At another point, Julie goes dining on the boulevard and orders an evening's worth of off-color ballads, which she then transcribes into the text; so the prostitute's memoirs briefly turn into an anthology of street music.

This is the milieu that would later evolve into the Balzacian world of *Splendeurs et misères des courtisanes*, the bohemian world of *La Bohème*, and the poetic world of *Les Enfants du Paradis*. But in the eighteenth century, it remained far removed from the sentiments that still resonate today. Suzon in the *Mémoires de Suzon* becomes a dancer in a boulevard cabaret. One night on her way home, she comes across two soldiers, who carry her off to a field on the road to Montmartre and rape her. It is quite an ordinary occurrence, except for the fact that one soldier has such a monstrous penis that he cannot get inside her. On their way back, they spot a grindstone in a wheelbarrow left outside a tavern by an itinerant knife sharpener, and Suzon suggests a solution to the soldier's problem. She climbs on the wheelbarrow and urinates on the grindstone to reduce the heat from the friction while he grinds his penis down to a usable size. This "funny scene," as Suzon calls it, amuses a crowd of 200 onlookers, but it doesn't seem funny to a modern reader.[47] Nor do Suzon's other experiences on the boulevards: gymnastic group sex with some Spanish acrobats and "comic" copulating backstage with the Harlequin and Pierrot of a pantomime.[48]

Equally unfunny are the deflowerings that bring comic relief to the sexual tension throughout the literature. The whores often joke about how they use astringents to fake virginity and thereby dupe their clients into paying supplements. One of them, Mlle Felmé in *Correspondance d'Eulalie*, retires to the provinces under a false name, marries a magistrate, and describes her burlesque wedding night with professional expertise: the tiny packet of blood slipped up her vagina, the vinegar treatment, the hiding under the covers, the insistence on blowing out the candles, the faked resistance, the faked frigidity, and the groom's triumphal cry the morning after, when he finds the fake blood on the bedclothes: "Ah! my wife was a virgin! How happy I am!"[49]

One can see the joke, but one cannot really get it—any more than one can laugh at cuckolding and the transmission of venereal disease, two other inexhaustible subjects of hilarity in the sex books. To see deeper into the humor, it is crucial to know more about the serious scenarios for wedding nights, and they, too, are available in the pornography. The best of many examples comes in *L'Académie des dames*. It takes place in the house of the bride's parents. Her mother undresses her in front of the groom, puts her to bed naked, and joins the rest of the family in the next room, locking the door behind her. After stripping, the groom turns back the covers and checks the bride's virginity by sticking his finger up her vagina. She freezes, then resists as he fondles and kisses; so he forces open her thighs and mounts her. While he batters his way into her, she screams in pain and terror, much to the satisfaction of her family listening next door.

A preliminary orgasm slows the groom down before he can penetrate far. But his second "attack" strikes deeper, and the third breaks through the hymen, so that the "fortress" is taken. The groom demands that the vagina, "all broken and torn," acknowledge his penis "as its sovereign." Then he attacks again, making the bed groan and the bride scream so loudly that when at last the room falls silent her mother reenters it. She presents the groom with some perfumed wine and acknowledges him formally as her son: "My son," she says, "how valiantly you fought! You are a hero! The screams of my daughter bear irrevocable witness to her defeat. I congratulate you on your victory." [50]

Another wedding night later in the book follows the same scenario, which is described with the same profusion of military metaphors. When the mother arrives with the drink, she says, "Brave soldier . . . I now recognize you as my son and my son-in-law." [51] And still later, a third groom deflowers his bride according to the identical ritual, but this time it is parodied. She is a simple peasant girl, he the servant of an aristocratic lady, who uses him as a stud. In order to exert her power and enjoy a practical joke, the lady indoctrinates the girl with the wrong information about how to behave. So instead of freezing, the bride grabs the groom's penis, moves her buttocks wildly, and lifts her legs in the air. She gives off all the wrong signals, as if she were a prostitute rather than a virgin: that is the joke, but it is funny only to those who share the cultural code.

To be sure, *L'Académie des dames* is a sex book, not the field notes of an ethnographer. It provides a literary version of an ideal wedding night as imagined in the seventeenth century, not a reliable account of how people actually behaved in bed. But that ideal still served as a foil for jokes a hundred years later. Even if it did not correspond closely to actual behavior, it defined a certain mentality—that is, a world we have (fortunately) lost, lost so completely that we must consult pornography in order to catch a glimpse of it.

As a final example of the foreignness of this literature, consider *Histoire de Dom B . . .* , the greatest and most outrageous of all the books in the Enfer.

This time, exceptionally, the narrator is a man, the monk Dom B . . . (the B . . . stands for bugger; his name is actually Saturnin). As an oversexed adolescent peering through a hole in his bedroom wall, Saturnin spots his mother copulating with a monk. He wants to do the same with his sister, Suzon. (It turns out later that none of them are blood relatives, but the text plays with every variety of the incest taboo.) In order to excite Suzon, he leads her to his peephole; and while she observes the next round of copulation, he slides to the floor and looks up her skirt. Then he slips his hand up her leg, higher and higher, following the rhythm of her thighs, which tighten and loosen in response to the humping in the next room. At last he pushes into her vagina: "I've got you, Suzon; I've got you!"[52]

While Suzon remains glued to the peephole, Saturnin masturbates her and pulls off her clothes. She spreads her legs, and he tries to take her from behind. But the position is impossible, so he spins her around and pulls her to the bed. He penetrates, she pushes, and just as they begin to heave with abandon the bed collapses under them. Their mother rushes in, furious; but when she spots Saturnin's erection, she changes her tune and drags him to the bed in the other room, while the monk takes Saturnin's place with Suzon. Thus, after violating his sister's virginity, Saturnin cuckolds his father and concludes with a defiant address to the reader:

Here is plenty of food for thought for readers whose glacial temperament has never felt the furies of love! Go ahead, Messieurs, think away, give full vent to your moralizing! I abandon the field to you, and want to say just one thing: if you had a hard-on as unbearable as mine, who would you fuck? The devil himself.[53]

Today's reader might reply: very well, here we have some eighteenth-century hard-core; what makes it so surprising? The rest of the novel continues in the same manner, at a breathless pace, piling social criticism on anticlericalism as one orgy leads to another. Each episode tops the previous one, until all inhibition seems to be destroyed. The sexual escalation sweeps everything before it, and in the end it deposits the hero in a particularly crapulous whorehouse. There, after years of separation, he meets Suzon again. Having been seduced and dumped in the road by a priest, she has survived a near-fatal miscarriage, a term in a pestilential poorhouse, and a horrific career as a hooker. Now she is in the terminal stage of a vicious case of syphilis.

Yet Saturnin loves her. He has always loved her, with a visceral passion that has never loosened its grip on his soul. So he wants to make love with her once more. She refuses, knowing that she will kill him with her disease. But he insists, and they unite their bodies for the last time, all through the night, deep in the dark and decrepit brothel. Not a foul word in the text. Not a hint of lasciviousness.

Suddenly, the police burst in. They seize Suzon. Saturnin fells one of them with a blow from an andiron, but the others drag him down the stairs, knocking him unconscious. Suzon disappears into one prison, where she immediately dies of her disease. Saturnin wakes up in another, feverish from the onset of the syphilis. He passes out again. Again he regains consciousness, this time awakened by a pain between his legs. He reaches down with his hand, and discovers he has been castrated. From deep within his bowels, a sound forms, rises through his throat, and breaks out as a scream, beating at the ceiling: Saturnin has ceased to be a man; he has nothing more to live for.

The surgery saves him, although he wants to die, having learned of Suzon's death. He does not know where to turn or what to do with his new freedom. So he takes to the road, abandoning himself to Providence. He comes upon a Carthusian monastery and suddenly has a vision of a life to be lived outside the agony of passion. After hearing his story, the superior takes him in; and Saturnin becomes Dom B . . . , gatekeeper to the Carthusians:

I am waiting here for death, without fearing or desiring it. After it releases me from the world of the living, they will carve in golden letters on my tomb: *Hic situs est Dom Bougre, fututus, futuit.* [Here lies Dom Bugger, fucked, he fucked.] [54]

It is an astounding story, one that deserves a place beside *Manon Lescaut* and *La Nouvelle Héloïse.* In it, eroticism is swallowed up in asceticism, pornography in religiosity. Of course, the burlesque epitaph leaves everything unsettled. The note of passion at the end could be one more trick of priestcraft; the moralizing could be specious. But the unsettling character of the story is part of its point. Sex may lead to love, love to salvation, and salvation to closure in a narrative of escalating surprises. Or everything could be a joke. The novel is so rich that it permits many readings. But if it is a joke, it cannot be grasped by anyone who has never had a brush with Augustinian piety, especially the kind known as Jansenism in the seventeenth and eighteenth centuries.

Seen in this light, the entire story leads to a spectacular non sequitur: the monastery, instead of being a brothel, turns out to be a genuine refuge from the torments of the flesh; and Saturnin, after working through every conceivable kind of sexual sin, finds his true vocation as a monk. Is he saved, or is he, as his epitaph says, merely fucked? Whether a send-up of religion or a confirmation of it, his story illustrates the precariousness of the struggle to find some solid meaning in life — in the mid eighteenth century, when Jansenism and the Enlightenment threatened to cancel one another out, and also today; for one cannot close a pornographic masterpiece like *Histoire de Dom B . . .* without thinking that sex is good for thought.

BIBLIOGRAPHY

This essay is an expanded version of an essay published in *The New York Review of Books*, 22 December 1994, 65–74. It is based on the following French texts from the seventeenth and eighteenth centuries, reprinted with full bibliographical information in *L'Enfer de la Bibliothèque Nationale*, 7 vols. (Paris: Fayard, 1984–88).

VOLUME I: *Oeuvres érotiques de Mirabeau*

Ma Conversion ou le libertin de qualité
L'Abbé IL-ET-ELLE (HIC-ET-HAEC) ou l'Elève des Révérends Pères Jésuites d'Avignon
Le Rideau levé ou l'éducation de Laure
Erotika Biblion

VOLUME II: *Oeuvres érotiques de Restif de la Bretonne*

Le Pornographe ou idées d'un honnête homme sur un projet de règlement pour les prostituées
L'Anti-Justine ou les délices de l'amour
Dom Bougre aux Etats-Généraux ou doléances du Portier des Chartreux
Les Revies, histoires refaites sous une autre hypothèse du coeur humain dévoilé

VOLUME III: *Oeuvres anonymes du XVIIIᵉ siècle (I)*

Histoire de Dom B . . . , portier des Chartreux, écrite par lui-même
Mémoires de Suzon, soeur de D . . B . . . , portier des Chartreux, écrits par elle-même
Histoire de Marguerite, fille de Suzon, nièce de D . . B . . . .
La Cauchoise ou mémoires d'une courtisane célèbre

VOLUME IV: *Oeuvres anonymes du XVIIIᵉ siècle (II)*

La courtisane anaphrodite ou la pucelle libertine
Correspondance d'Eulalie, ou tableau du libertinage de Paris
Lucette ou les progrès du libertinage

VOLUME V: *Oeuvres anonymes du XVIIIᵉ siècle (III)*

Thérèse philosophe ou mémoires pour servir à l'histoire du Père Dirrag et de Mademoiselle Eradice
Le Triomphe des religieuses ou les nones babillardes
Lettres galantes et philosophiques de deux nones
La Messaline française ou les nuits de la duchesse de Pol . . . et aventures mystérieuses de la princesse d'H . . . et de la . . .

La Liberté ou Mlle Raucour
Les Quarante Manières de foutre, dédiées au clergé de France

VOLUME VI: *Oeuvres anonymes du XVIIIe siècle (IV)*

Eléonore, ou l'heureuse personne
Vénus en rut ou vie d'une célèbre libertine
Décrets des sens sanctionnés par la volupté
Requêt et décret en faveur des putains, des fouteuses, des maquerelles et des branleuses contre les bougres, les bardaches et les brûleurs de paillasses
Ordonnance de police de Messieurs les officiers et gouverneurs du Palais Royal
Le Degré des âges du plaisir ou jouissances voluptueuses de deux personnes de sexes différents, aux différentes époques de la vie

VOLUME VII: *Oeuvres érotiques du XVIIe siècle*

Le Rut ou la pudeur éteinte
L'Ecole des filles ou la philosophie des dames
Vénus dans le cloître ou la religieuse en chemise
L'Académie des dames

PART II

Mind and Culture in the Victorian
Middle Classes

6. Miracles in English Unitarian Thought

To most people to whom the word "Unitarian" is in some degree familiar, the subject of this chapter may seem astonishing: what could a denomination so liberal as sometimes to seem no religion at all have to do with miracles? Here, in barest outline, is the answer: in the latter part of the eighteenth century, Unitarians accepted and confidently defended miracles; by the end of the nineteenth century, miracles had been largely explained away; but in the roughly one hundred years between, they were a problem.

Some setting of the scene is required. Originally a theological doctrine or tendency, organized Unitarianism took its place in the early nineteenth century among the so-called Dissenting or Nonconformist denominations that emerged in the century or so after the Act of Uniformity of 1662 shattered the formal unity of English Protestantism. There are not many Unitarians in Britain today, and while there were more a century ago — perhaps 20,000, a decline from a possible 30,000 in the early 1830s — they were a tiny minority compared with the Evangelical legions of Congregationalists, Baptists, and Methodists.[1] But for most of the nineteenth century, in the happy phrase of a Unitarian journalist,[2] they weighed more than they measured — in Parliament, local government, educational and cultural institutions, journalism, and the economy.

Descended primarily from the English Presbyterians, but incorporating some splinter groups within Dissent and a very important accession from Anglican Latitudinarians, English Unitarians carried the eighteenth-century tradition of Rational Dissent into the nineteenth century.[3] Rejecting human formularies or creeds, they stood for individual interpretation of the Bible, accepted the symbiosis of religion and nature, and sought to eliminate corruption and mystery from the Christian faith — in this, most characteristically, by rejecting the Trinity, the sacrificial view of atonement, and eternal punishment. To most Anglicans and all Evangelical Dissenters, denying these doctrines meant denying the essence of Christianity, but Unitarians insisted that, as believers in Christ's teachings and Resurrection and in the divinity of His mission, if not His person, they *were* Christians, and the most enlightened of them.

Incomparably the most important figure in the emergence of denominational Unitarianism over some fifty years after about 1770 was the celebrated scientist, theologian, and radical Joseph Priestley, who, from a background of Independency (or Congregationalism), had become an Arian while a student at Daventry Academy in the early 1750s and then in 1769 abandoned that limited view of the divinity of Christ for belief in His full humanity. The extraordinary polemics that Priestley published in the 1770s and the 1780s carried conviction to many Rational Dissenters and Latitudinarians, and the force of his message was made yet more powerful by martyrdom, following the destruction of his house, library, and laboratory in the church-and-king riots in Birmingham in 1791 and his emigration to the United States three years later. Unitarians were particularly suspect during the French Revolution, and their congregations, already reduced by the mid-century flight from heterodoxy, dwindled yet again. But the small band of survivors, their faith strengthened and sharpened by real or threatened persecution, regained their optimism early in the new century, and their numbers began to grow.

What I shall refer to, in convenient shorthand, as Priestleyanism involved more than a distinctive Christology. Priestley's philosophy and much of his theology were shaped by the writings of the physician David Hartley, who, in his *Observations on Man* of 1749, had developed a suggestion of Sir Isaac Newton's into a highly original theory in what would now be called neurophysiology and used that in turn to expand the rudimentary associationism of John Locke into the system that dominated English psychology for more than a hundred years. While not acceptable to all Unitarians, the philosophical determinism known as Necessarianism, identified with Hartley and Priestley, also proved persuasive to many, both ministers and laymen. Chief among the ministers was Thomas Belsham, a convert from Congregationalism who in the early nineteenth century occupied the premier Unitarian pulpit in Essex Street, London. He wrote the authoritative Hartleian textbook and turned a stunning polemical style to the defense and advancement of Unitarianism.

Shortly after Belsham's death in 1829, James Martineau, destined to become the most important figure in nineteenth-century Unitarianism, turned on the Necessarianism that he, like so many ministers in his generation, had absorbed at Manchester College, York. A brilliantly destructive (but also appreciative) article on Priestley in 1833 pointed the way, and his *Rationale of Religious Enquiry* in 1836 launched half a century of intellectual exploration.[4] He was joined in the leadership of what came to be known as the New School of Unitarianism, as against the Old School of the Priestleyans, by John Hamilton Thom, in Liverpool, and John James Tayler, in Manchester. From 1857 on, Martineau and Tayler — against strenuous initial opposition — were firmly in control of Manchester College, by then settled in London. In making it a forcing house for their views, they won a victory of attrition of the kind that happens between generations, but in the last quarter of the century, their views were in turn supplanted by new and disparate enthusiasms of an essentially untheological age.

Martineau's doctrinal evolution was less precipitous than Tayler's — George Eliot's friend Sara Sophia Hennell describes him as "wriggling his way forward"[5] — but his formidable controversial style made him seem more radical than in fact he was; he thus alienated many old friends and introduced a bitterness into the conflict that was seriously counterproductive. Particular offense was given by his attack on the Unitarian name, arguing that, in defining themselves by a perhaps transient doctrine, Unitarians became a sect rather than a church — a distinction in which Martineau anticipated Ernst Troeltsch by fifty years.[6] To his older coreligionists, however, the Unitarian name carried great historical and theological significance, while newer recruits tended to see it as proudly proclaiming their liberation from orthodoxy.

The central concern of the New School, however, was to ground religion in an inner perception of the divine, and not in the natural religion and evidences so dear to the Priestleyans. In this view, closer to recent developments in theology and biblical criticism, especially in Germany, the historicity of miracles became a focal point. Yet, however fervently Martineau's opponents clung to a belief in miracles, their Priestleyan predecessors had already begun to undermine that faith.

Today, the question of miracles cannot be thought of apart from David Hume's famous chapter in the *Philosophical Essays* of 1748.[7] But Unitarians were less preoccupied with Hume, even with his broader subversion of religion, than might be expected. Certainly, Hume on miracles had brought up some very big guns from all points of the religious compass: William Adams, rector of St. Chad's, Shrewsbury, and later master of Pembroke College, Cambridge, in 1752; George Campbell, principal of Marischal College, Aberdeen, ten years later; and the anti-Trinitarian Arian minister and philosopher Richard Price in 1768.[8] Their arguments, substantially similar, suggest that whatever problem there was lay with Hume, not with miracles.

In his somewhat later replies, Priestley noted that Hume had himself said that his greatest ambition was fame and that his writings seemed intended chiefly to amuse. Neither Hume's philosophy nor his efforts to undermine religion could be taken seriously, Priestley insisted: "Compared with Dr. Hartley, I consider Mr. Hume as not even a child."[9] As to miracles, Priestley argued that, if we take Hume at his word that all we know comes from experience, then our having experienced no interruption of the laws of nature must still allow for such interruptions in an earlier age, if testified to by sufficient witnesses. Hume had insisted that testimony to a miracle could be accepted only if the likelihood of delusion were more incredible than the reported event. Priestley countered with the unanimity of the apostles who, as eyewitnesses, could not be gainsaid; moreover, their testimony was accepted by friends and, even more strikingly, by enemies, both in their own time and in succeeding generations (e.g., by St. Paul). There was yet further proof in the miraculous spread of Christianity in so short a time: thus, the testimonial arithmetic that Hume had balanced in fifties and hundreds, Priestley trumped with thousands and millions. Christ's Resurrection and the miracles of the apostles were "received as true by such numbers of persons in the age in which they were published, and the account was never confuted, but Christianity kept gaining ground from that time to the present," confirming that "the great *facts* on which its credit stands" are unquestionably true. Similar arguments were mustered in defense of the Old Testament miracles and the prophecies. If the miraculous delivery of the Jews from Egyptian bondage were not true, how could the Jewish nation have been so uniformly persuaded that it was? Would not a thousand writers who maintained that in 1755 France had conquered all of North America and Ireland and had reduced England to a colony have been utterly discredited by the tens of thousands who, having lived at that time, knew differently?[10]

Priestley and his contemporaries held certain axioms that they believed could be contested only by men who were ipso facto irrational or evil: the infinite power and benevolence of God, His desire to reveal divine truth to men, the Bible as that revelation, and the accuracy of both the Old and New Testaments as records of historical events—whatever small fallibilities or inconsistencies might appear in accounts written by men, who, as men, were prone to err. From that security, Priestley took on Holbach, Gibbon, and other fashionable successors to the Deists. Hume on miracles continued to

offer an occasional target of opportunity for Unitarians in the next generation, but they did not move the arguments further.[11]

I shall deal with three stages in the evolution of the Unitarian controversy
over miracles, the first being the gradual emergence of the problem. In the
Theological Repository, a vehicle for Priestley and his friends that appeared
irregularly between 1769 and 1788, Hume is scarcely in the picture: on the
few occasions when miracles are written about, it is not as a general or ultimate question, but rather to propose textual or commonsense solutions that
would make individual miracles more comprehensible and less subject to
carping.

An instance is the discussion (1: 381–86) of the blasting of the fig tree, in
which "Eusebius" (the Rev. William Turner of Wakefield) seeks to contribute to a continuing debate by proposing a reconciliation of the accounts in
Matthew 21: 18–21 and Mark 11: 12–14, and by drawing attention to points on
which understanding might be helped by further clarification of facts—the
meaning of "the season of figs," the number of crops a fig tree bears in a season, and whether fruit precedes or follows the leaves. A far more substantial
article by "Ebionita" (Priestley himself) casts doubt on the miraculous conception (4: 245–305), concluding that while a virgin birth was doubtless
in the power of God, "we ought not lightly to give credit to accounts of miracles for which we cannot imagine any good reason, and the very report of
which is calculated to expose christianity to ridicule"; the Rev. John Wiche
of Maidstone objected and was in turn rebutted by Gilbert Wakefield (5: 83–
107, 129–58).[12]

This approach to miracles, like much in the *Repository*, reflects a characteristic activity of the time: the construction of chronologies and harmonies:
chronologies to solve vexed questions like the great ages of the patriarchs
or conflicting genealogies of David and Jesus, harmonies to reconcile apparent contradictions or impossibilities in the texts and to preclude their being turned to subversive uses. While these were not novel forms of commentary, they held particular appeal in the eighteenth century. Locke and Newton compiled them, as did Hartley and Priestley, and there are two much
grander, now-forgotten instances. One of the most respected scholars of the
age, among Anglicans and Dissenters alike, was the Dissenting minister
Nathaniel Lardner, who between 1727 and 1757 published fifteen large volumes on *The Credibility of the Gospel History*, while William Warburton,
now remembered chiefly for *The Alliance Between Church and State* (1736),

was in his own time far more celebrated for *The Divine Legation of Moses* (1737–41), a display of prodigious learning that, as Joseph Estlin Carpenter wryly observes, rests upon a single sentence, asserting without proof the Mosaic authorship of the Pentateuch.[13]

This preoccupation, understandable given the Deist attack on absurdities and contradictions in the Bible, was important, not only in published apologetics,[14] but in teaching and as a means to devotion. John Jebb—whose increasingly heterodox views led university authorities to forbid undergraduates to attend his theology lectures at Cambridge—devoted much space in his justificatory letter to the archbishop of Canterbury to explaining the importance he attached to reconciling the gospel narratives and the extensive part the practice played in his lectures and in student exercises.[15] And harmonizing was sufficiently ingrained as a learning device, if not an instinctive response, that toward the end of the second decade of the nineteenth century, Harriet Martineau, at sixteen or seventeen, well before she had had any exposure to Priestley or Hartley, was "making 'Harmonies,' poring over the geography [of the Holy Land], and greedily gathering up every thing I could find in the way of commentary and elucidation, and gladly working myself into an enthusiasm with the moral beauty and spiritual promises I found in the sacred writings."[16] The impulse flowed naturally into efforts at the end of the eighteenth century and into the nineteenth to seek psychological explanations of miracles.

It may already have become evident that the truth of miracles was embedded in a larger question: the status and authority of the Bible. When Priestley insisted that the truth of Christianity is founded "only upon the *leading facts* in the gospel history"—facts that included properly supported miracles—he was making Christian truth hostage to something that was about to dissolve. To Priestley and his contemporaries, the Bible was emphatically not, in the famous later phrase, "like any other book." But once the balance of criticism shifted from texts to text, fundamental assumptions were under threat.

Of course, the first, instinctual impulse was to explain and reconcile by bettering the text—an activity in which Unitarians were pioneers. In the first number of the distinguished Unitarian periodical, the *Monthly Repository*, in 1806, a reviewer offered a powerful justification:

Unbelievers have been eminent as philosophers and fine writers, but we do not remember that even one of them is known to have been a great Biblical scholar! We have always rejoiced, therefore, when able and learned men have applied themselves to the improvement of our vernacular version of the Scriptures, for by no other means could they so effectually lower the pride and narrow the conquests of scepticism.[17]

That was surely a justification, if not an advertisement, for the publication in 1808, by a Unitarian committee with Thomas Belsham in the lead, of an "Improved Version" of the New Testament. Having determined against a new translation and unable to secure the rights to a recent version by Gilbert Wakefield, a classicist who had left Cambridge after finding it impossible to subscribe the Thirty-nine Articles, they turned to a translation by William Newcome, archbishop of Armagh. Newcome (whose first published work had been a harmony that provoked some debate with Priestley)[18] had based his translation on the first edition of the authoritative Greek text by Johann Jakob Griesbach; printed in Dublin in 1796, it was published after Newcome's death in 1800.

The committee, over Belsham's objections, made several hundred changes in Newcome's text, some to give preference to his marginalia, some to accommodate Griesbach's second edition, and others to provide a Unitarian rendering or, as Belsham put it in a subsequent defense, "to explain the scriptures in a rational sense, and to shew that the New Testament, properly understood[,] gives no countenance to those strange and heathenish systems of theology, which have been grafted upon it." Nearly half a century later, Harriet Martineau, recalling her youthful enthusiasm, was scornful of such "shallow scholarship," and marveled that in Belsham's later interpretation of the Epistles, which explained away so much "about heaven and hell, the end of the world, salvation and perdition, &c. . . . it never seems to have occurred to him that that could hardly be a revelation designed for the rescue of the human race from perdition, the explanation of which required all this ingenuity at the hand of a Belsham, after eighteen centuries."[19] Harriet Martineau wrote that from the splendid simplicity of her newfound atheism and positivism; Belsham and his contemporaries could hardly have advanced so far so soon.

The critical but not unfriendly reviewer of the Improved Version in the *Monthly Repository*—whom James Martineau later identified as his teacher, the Bristol minister Lant Carpenter[20]—suggested, echoing Bishop Butler, that cultivating moral excellence *required* difficulties in knowing God's dispensations.

And why should we expect the more peculiar occurrences in the grand order of Providence to be free from them? or that the records of revelation should have been miraculously preserved from all those causes of obscurity and perplexity which must ever accompany all human methods of communication? or that every intellect when employed upon those records should be miraculously preserved from the darkness and error to which every one is more or less subject?

Over the next few years, the pages of the magazine were full of quibbles about translation and interpretation, arguments that were surely thought to underlie further progress.[21]

Inexorably, textual criticism expanded to more and more serious questions. We have seen Priestley's doubts about the Virgin Birth, which Belsham was to dismiss as "no more entitled to credit, than the fables of the Koran, or the reveries of Swedenborg." But by 1807, Belsham had already concluded that the Pentateuch was of composite authorship; by 1819, he had doubts about the present form of the gospels, and by 1821, he had concluded that the account of Creation in Genesis was inconsistent with modern scientific knowledge.[22]

Some German scholarship was being mediated to England early in the nineteenth century — notably by Herbert Marsh in Cambridge and by William Taylor of Norwich in the pages of the *Monthly Review*, for an audience largely made up of liberal-minded Dissenters[23] — but Unitarians remained largely insulated from it. In 1819, Belsham professed himself delighted with the German historical critics and wished that he might hear lectures by J. G. Eichhorn, the celebrated Göttingen theologian, who sought naturalistic explanations of miracles; but Belsham dismissed German theology and philosophy — he said he had tried Kant but could make nothing of him[24] — and deplored efforts to account for the miracles that went beyond his own ventures and fell over into anti-supernaturalism. What man of understanding, he wrote, could be satisfied with explaining the stilling of the tempest as settling a quarrel between the disciples and the boatmen or the Ascension as an imposture? "Must they not certainly know, that to deny the miracles of Christ is to deny his divine mission, which is itself a miracle; and that, in fact, it is downright infidelity?"[25]

For the second of the three stages, I shall deal only with the difficulties and opportunities presented to Unitarians by the publication in 1835–36 of David Friedrich Strauss's *Das Leben Jesu*.[26] George Eliot's definitive translation in 1846 was anticipated in 1841–44 by four cheaply printed volumes, issued in penny parts, from the radical publisher Henry Hetherington. This English version was based on a French translation of Strauss, interestingly by Comte's principal successor in the Positivist movement, Emile Littré.

Much of this phase in the story is dealt with helpfully in an article by Valerie A. Dodd on "Strauss's English Propagandists and the Politics of Unitarianism, 1841–45."[27] She is concerned with, and relieves me from recounting, the intersection of the episode with the history of English literature, the complex web of radical publishing tied to the advanced Unitarianism of the capital, and the varieties of political and social radicalism refracted through the story. Dodd rightly concentrates, as shall I, on six lectures on Strauss given in 1841 by Philip Harwood. For the purposes of this chapter, I shall isolate certain themes in the substance of the lectures, their religious and intellectual context, and the apologetic aftermath.

For a decade, between 1833 and 1843, we know quite a lot about Harwood, but his early life is obscure, and his move into journalism in 1843 was followed by his almost complete disappearance into anonymity, despite the distinguished place he held in Victorian intellectual life as subeditor and then editor of the *Saturday Review* from its founding in 1855 until his retirement for reasons of ill health in 1883. That known decade is dramatic. Having entered the University of Edinburgh in 1833, Harwood, who had recently joined Lant Carpenter's Bristol congregation, was reportedly so appalled by lectures on the Atonement given by Thomas Chalmers, then professor of divinity, that he withdrew from the university and became a Unitarian minister. From 1834 to 1840, he served the small, wealthy, and radical congregation at Bridport in Dorset. In his published sermons from those years, he showed himself a bitter opponent of establishment as it existed in England, the advocate of a semi-Coleridgean view setting national cultivation at the center of things, and a preacher with increasingly advanced theological views.[28] In sermons delivered while visiting Edinburgh in 1839, he dismissed miracles and splintered the congregation.

In 1840, Harwood moved from Bridport to London to become assistant to W. J. Fox in his chapel in South Place, Finsbury. Fox's irregular domestic arrangements had separated him from the main body of Unitarians, but his influence in the greater world of early- and mid-Victorian politics and journalism was as wide as it has been under-studied in the past fifty years.[29] In 1841–42, Harwood was one of two lecturers — the other was Thomas Wood, minister of the new Unitarian chapel at Brixton — at the Beaumont Institution, newly established in Mile End by a wealthy insurance merchant for promoting self-culture and, in particular, the views of a now-forgotten advocate of natural religion named Robert Fellowes, whose liturgy was used in weekly services in the chapel connected with the Institution. The diarist Henry Crabb Robinson thought Harwood "an inferior Carlyle," but was nonetheless impressed by his oratory.[30] Beaumont's death within a year of the opening of the Institution and the unacceptability of the lecturers' heterodoxy to Beaumont's son and heir forced Harwood's resignation and his change of · career.[31]

Harwood's six lectures at South Place — common Unitarian practice was to confine doctrinal exposition to lectures apart from sermons — are distinguished by remarkable clarity and a stunning eloquence. Every one of them deals in some way with miracles. Like Strauss, Harwood is impatient with the rationalistic critics, such as Eichhorn and H. E. G. Paulus, who had attempted to explain the miracles on naturalistic or psychological grounds. The further critical step was to query both the dating of the gospels and their informing purpose. As Harwood puts it, where Eichhorn saw Abraham gazing into the heavens and seeing an augury that his family would become as numerous as the stars, De Wette (professor at Basel) had wondered if there was any reality to it at all; where Eichhorn accepted the antiquity of the record of Genesis and sought to confirm it in fact, De Wette had dated the record some centuries later and abandoned Genesis to poetry.

Strauss's central contribution was the idea of *mythus*, tied to expectation of the Messiah. Abandoning all the ingenuities of the rationalists, Strauss's general principle, in Harwood's words, was that "*given the Messiahship of Jesus, the miracles would follow of course* . . . all pre-arranged and prefigured." "Given some thirty, forty, or fifty years (to ask no more) before the floating, traditionary recollections of the Christ came to be fixed in writing, and it would have needed a miracle to keep down the growth of miracles."

Harwood is even harder, if anything, on the uses of biblical narrative as a source for history; myths and fables he sees as "expressing a religious faith rather than an historical reminiscence" (3). The traditional rationalist "speculates upon the minutiae of the history; the other asks, Are we sure that it is history at all?" (10). "Is it a history at all? is it even a fiction founded on facts? And, having negatived that, [Strauss] proceeds to examine, not what facts are at the root of the recorded facts, but what ideas are at the root of the record itself" (23). The gospels "are the most difficult books in the world to make anything of in the way of a history — a clearly developed succession of events that can be supposed to have actually occurred. . . . It must have been a work of time to produce versions so different as we again and again have of one event; so that repeatedly it is a question with harmonists, whether we have two facts, or only two various readings of one fact" (34); "inconsistency, contradiction, psychological impossibility everywhere. Reconcilement of such incongruities is obviously out of the question" (41). "There is little or nothing, in the gospels, of that *marking of the epochs* of Christ's outer or inner life, which one looks for in a history" (75). Most terribly, Harwood says of the accounts of the Resurrection: "Call this 'Evidence!' evidence of 'eye-witnesses!'

It is evidence of nothing but that of which we ourselves are eye-witnesses — that a whole world of tradition and legend is between us and the reality" (81).

It is difficult to overstate the stark conclusions that these assertions entailed for the traditional Unitarian view, not only of the history so deeply queried in the quoted passages, not only of the miracles of Moses and Christ and the apostles, but of the central miracle of them all, the Resurrection, which Unitarians clung to, with perhaps greater urgency than more orthodox believers, who had other assurances, as the guarantee of man's own resurrection and eternal life.

Some indirect sense of Harwood's impact can be gathered from a response to a lecture given in the chapel in Brixton by Harwood's associate in the Beaumont Institution, Thomas Wood. It is a sermon preached in Stamford Street Chapel in London by William Hincks, on 17 January 1841.[32] Hincks had only recently taken up that pulpit after a distinguished career as a minister in Exeter and Liverpool and something over a decade as tutor in mathematics and philosophy in Manchester College, York. His important role as editor of a new Unitarian newspaper, *The Inquirer*, lay a year in the future. In his five years in that post, Hincks (who later became professor of natural history at Queen's College, Cork, and then in the University of Toronto) was a steady, forthright defender of the older, Priestleyan understanding of Unitarianism and Necessarianism.

In the 1841 sermon, Hincks reiterated the uniqueness of Christ, who was more than a great moral teacher like Socrates or Milton. What set Jesus apart was his own affirmation that *"as a proof of his Divine commission,* God enabled him to command certain results contrary to the ordinary course of nature, and not to be obtained by mere human powers. . . . Such is miracle! the proper proof of Divine communication,"* that is, of Revelation. "Give up the miracles," Hincks said, "and you lose most of your illustrations of the personal character of Christ; affirm them to be deceptions, and you destroy that character; maintain that the narratives were produced or altered with corrupt views, and you leave us no reason for believing in Christ's character at all; since amidst so much falsehood, on what can we rest?" Hincks readily granted Wood's right to speak as he saw fit, although he questioned the seemliness of his advocating his peculiar views under the Unitarian or even the Christian name. For all Hincks's certainty, there is desperation in that cry.

Four years passed, and there was another, more wide-ranging rebuttal of Strauss and Harwood by the Rev. John Relly Beard. Beard was a phenomenon in Victorian Unitarianism. From a humble General Baptist background in Sussex, he was educated at Manchester College, York, and spent the rest of his life as a minister in the vicinity of Manchester. He founded the Unitarian Home Missionary Board, later Unitarian College, Manchester, initially to train men as domestic missionaries but in time to become a northern and more conservative counterpart of Manchester College in London and, later, Oxford. Beard was a denominational politician and a prolific writer and publisher; he was, moreover, well versed in German biblical and critical scholarship.

From the preface to *Voices of the Church, in Reply to Dr. D. F. Strauss*, it is clear that Beard was concerned about Hetherington's enterprise, but he concentrates on the first "set effort" to introduce Strauss to an English audience—Harwood's lectures, which not only failed to confute Strauss's views but made them worse by obscuring Strauss's good points in dangerous rhetoric. There had been, Beard said, a growing awareness of German scholarship, which, without direct knowledge, had been taken as wild and destructive; in particular, the opinion was abroad that one great work of German scholarship, which Christian ministers feared to allow people to read or even to study themselves, had undermined the foundations of Christianity. He hoped, by drawing on the wider corpus of German scholarship and on authoritative replies to *Leben Jesu*, to enable readers to judge for themselves the extent of the damage from Strauss's attack "on the historical foundations of our common faith."

The first of the book's eight chapters is Beard's summary of the opinions of Strauss and Hegel, to which he added a later chapter on the moral argument for the credibility of the gospels. George Vance Smith, a distinguished conservative biblical scholar and Unitarian minister, also contributed two chapters. One summarizes the argument for gospel credibility advanced in 1837 in a refutation of Strauss by F. A. G. Tholuck, a professor at Halle; the other refutes the mythical theory. In addition, there are translations of two answers to Strauss by celebrated French writers (the liberal historian Edgar Quinet and the Protestant minister Athanase Coquerel), and extracts from the life of Jesus by the great church historian in Berlin, J. A. W. Neander, chosen specifically to rebut Strauss. By the time George Eliot's translation appeared in 1846, the biblical and historical faith of the Priestleyans had been thrown on the defensive.

An even better indicator of this sea-change is *An Essay on Primaeval History*, published in the same year by John Kenrick. After taking a degree at the University of Glasgow, Kenrick had become tutor in classics, history, and literature at Manchester College, York; on the college's return to Manchester in 1840, he became professor of history, holding the post until 1850. He was held in the deepest respect throughout the denomination and was genuinely beloved by his students, who included partisans of both factions in the widening rift in Unitarianism.[33] The *Essay* is a calm, elegant, and utterly authoritative distillation, not only of German scholarship — Kenrick had studied in Germany almost three decades earlier — but of the immense recent advances in geology, philology, ethnography, and history to force a reevaluation of the Old Testament as a basis for understanding the origins of the world and of man and the history of the ancient peoples of the Near East. Belsham's tentative and simplistically argued hunches about the relevance of Genesis to science are confirmed and generalized; Priestley's assumptions about the Old Testament as an authentic historical source are exploded.

For the third phase of my account, I return to the growing estrangement between Old and New Schools. In *Unitarianism Defended*, the massive answer to Liverpool orthodoxy undertaken by three Unitarian ministers in 1839, Martineau had lectured on "The Bible: What It is and What It Is Not." He denied infallibility and inspiration, suggested a relative ranking of the books of the New Testament in terms of authority, and, while he continued to accept miracles, did so with a difference: miracles were "simply awakening facts: demanding and securing reverential and watchful regard to something, or to everything, in the parties performing them; but not specifically singling out any portion of their doctrinal ideas, and affording them infallible proof."[34]

In notes for congregational lectures given in Liverpool in the early 1840s, he rejects some miracles and accepts others and concedes that it may not be necessary for a Christian to believe in miracles at all. Yet there remains the miracle of creation, and even if the "successive birth" of animals and plants is shown to be mere natural events, yet we must acknowledge "one powerful God, possessing a prior claim to our homage, as having powers and exercising them before the order of nature was established." Perhaps some miracles were invented by Christ's followers, but, even so, His mind must have inspired their capacity to imagine such wonders. "So I do not think that whether or not they are really true is a matter of much moment; for they showed the belief that Christ was capable of working such miracles, and this is the impression that ought to be left on our minds. By whatever means this impression is effected is . . . of but little consequence."[35]

In the preface to the third edition (1845) of his *Rationale*, which with some reluctance he reprinted unchanged, he notes that one opinion maintained in the preface to the second edition (also 1836) had now to be revised. He had then known only one class of persons who could be described as anti-supernaturalists—those who pretended to explain Christ and religion as results of second causes, as mere products, and to whom he would still deny the name of Christian. He had also thought that rejection of the gospel miracles was a disqualification, but he had since encountered anti-supernaturalists who recognized "what is beyond nature in Christ" and so could be seen as true disciples, even though they might doubt or even disbelieve in the miracles recorded in the Scriptures. Behind this change of view stood the compelling figure of Joseph Blanco White, a former Spanish priest and a member of the Oriel common room in the 1830s. In the years before his death in Liverpool in 1841, White deeply influenced the leaders of the New School and, as Tony Cross has neatly put it, moved Martineau off the miracles.[36]

Traditionalist contemporaries watched the course of Martineau's gradualism with increasing alarm. But even toward the end of his long life, he was still circling the question with both bluntness and delicacy. In a letter in 1885, he referred to "the old Unitarian or, as I should call it, *Deistical* conception of God," who worked only through necessary laws in nature while reserving to Himself all that is supernatural, unless He saw fit to intervene with exceptional acts called miracles: "This resolution of Christianity into Deism *plus* Miraculous history . . . I cannot accept. The Divine Life . . . presents itself to me as twofold, like our humanity," both natural and supernatural, physical and spiritual. All religion is supernatural, "and there is a Revealing Presence of God in every Soul that is not sunk in slavery to the mere 'Natural Man'." But the supernatural elements have become inward instead of outward, and extended to all humanity, rendering them "homogeneous with [Christ], and through this harmony at one with God."[37]

In 1844, Hincks had written an editorial in the *Inquirer* praising Priestley's clear reasoning and his union "of philosophic calmness of investigation, with ardour in the pursuit and diffusion of truth" and deploring the tendency "to substitute the fanciful speculations and bold assumptions of German metaphysics, for his lucid statements and solid deductions. . . . [The] imputation of coldness . . . seems but a passing wave of public opinion which will sink as it rose and leave scarcely a trace behind."[38] Vain hope!

With Hincks's departure for Ireland and Canada, the most outspoken representative of the Old School was Samuel Bache, Martineau's brother-in-law and minister to Priestley's old congregation in Birmingham.[39] After reading one of Martineau's sermons, Bache exploded: "But oh! what a strange compound of crude & erroneous notions . . . what a substitution of *abstractions* for real persons & relations, such as, if logically carried out, wd lead to athe-

ism just as it here seems to lead to a renouncement of historical Christianity."
By 1861, he was insisting "that the time is *fully* arrived when the essentially
miraculous character of the Mission & Gospel of Christ must be distinctly
and unequivocally maintained." He himself did so as to the Messiahship,
which Martineau and his friends had given up, but which Bache maintained
in the pure Lockean sense, by defiantly naming his new Gothic church the
Church of the Messiah; and in 1863, he published five lectures he had given
at the new church on *Miracles, the Credentials of Christ*.[40]

Finally, in 1865, he gave notice of intention to move at the next meeting
of the British and Foreign Unitarian Association that the rules of the Association require that members recognize, along with the unity of God, the "special divine mission and authority, as a Religious Teacher, of Jesus Christ"—
the term "divine mission" entailing for Bache both the Messiahship and the
miracles. In seconding the motion, Thomas Madge, Martineau's minister
in Norwich, who had succeeded Belsham at Essex Street, argued that any
church that denied the greatest of miracles, the Resurrection, was built on
sand. Bache and Madge did not deny the right of Unitarians to disagree, but
they insisted that dissidents could claim no right to associate with those who
held to the principles of Unitarianism as understood at the time of the association's founding in 1825. The motion was resoundingly defeated in May 1866.
It was thought that a majority of those present at the meeting agreed with
Bache and Madge on the theology, but they could not accept the implicit interference with the right of private judgment through the imposition of any
fixed principles in what amounted, however circumscribed, to a creed.[41]

There was much in the Unitarian scene in the early 1860s to confirm
Bache in his determination to bring matters to a head. The general theological ferment of the time, most evident in the controversy over *Essays and
Reviews*, clearly affected a sermon preached in 1864 by William Binns, a
Methodist local preacher turned Unitarian minister, before the Provincial
Assembly of Lancashire and Cheshire. Binns maintained that "all speculative
questions are open, and all theological questions are speculative. In them
there is no orthodoxy and no heterodoxy, for to no man have the secrets of
the Infinite been revealed so as to make him an unerring judge of truth." He
went on to proclaim the triumph of science and to discern a possible church
of the future that would abandon what nine-tenths of the Christian world now
deemed essential, which would rest on the bedrock of man's "native consciousness of God." Then the only miracle would be a believer in miracles.[42]

John Wright was minister at Bury in Lancashire and in the early 1860s
was one the editors of the *Unitarian Herald*, a newspaper founded in Man-

chester in 1861 to provide a counterweight, in both price and doctrine, to the London-based *Inquirer*, which by then was strongly inclined to the New School. In 1864, Wright, using only the initial W., published in the *Herald* a series of articles — not editorials — on a number of theological issues; in one of them he said he had come to regard the gospel miracles as a hindrance, not a help, to reverence for Christ and Christianity. In an editorial reply to the many correspondents, including Bache who had challenged W. to give up his claim to Christianity, the *Herald* noted that differences among the four editors had widened and that W.'s independent series grew out of his need to articulate his views. And while the author of the editorial thought that a majority of ministers still believed in the miracles, he concluded that "the question of the miraculous is an open one among us."[43]

In the same year Charles Beard — the son of John Relly Beard — founded a new periodical, the *Theological Review*, with the specific intention of lessening the hostility between the two opposed camps by being open to both. Having noted the controversy in the *Herald*, he began "meditating a manifesto on the subject that would appeal to moderates by exploring the center that lay between "Bain and Bache" — the atheism of the psychologist Alexander Bain and dogmatic historicism. His choice as author fell on J. H. Thom, whose article appeared in January 1865. It is a difficult, even refractory essay, which seeks, in notably Romantic language, to establish a spiritual validity for miracles that would supersede historical claims that could no longer be sustained. Thom had given up on harmonies as the eighteenth century had understood their function. Surely, he said, if the portraiture of the New Testament had been done by the hand of God, we would have had "one perfect, and not four imperfect delineations. . . . We have to combine and unite the features, silently dropping, rather than rejecting, what we cannot combine, to know him more and more as really he was." Miracles in themselves cannot be established by testimony, can serve as evidences for nothing external to themselves, and are "objects of faith, not grounds of faith," witnessing to larger spiritual truth. Even less can they be a test for Christian fellowship:

If from what we discern of the life of God in Christ we believe *every thing* of the living God willing and working in our own spirits which we could believe if we believed that Christ wrought Miracles, it is vain to tell us that we remain outside the temple because we cannot feel certain about the scaffolding by which it is raised.

Beard thought Thom had succeeded in giving the conservative party a resting place, but Bache was having none of it. He demanded the right of reply, which Beard was willing to grant but only if the reply took the form of an independent article and not an ad hominem attack. Not being allowed (in Beard's words) "to pitch into Mr. Thom, [Bache] has shaken off the dust from his feet against me" and elected the political route of his motion about the BFUA.[44]

By the end of the century, we have entered a different world of discourse. James Drummond—the most admired and beloved of Unitarian theologians at the turn of the century, and far from a theological radical—was telling his students at Manchester College (by then in Oxford) that miracles were indeed to be tried by testimony. Assuming that, some (such as the miracles of healing) might be accepted as explicable in nature, if exaggerated in the telling; but the testimony to raising the dead was too weak to bear the burden of truth, while the evidence for interfering with inanimate nature, even when all three synoptic authors agreed, would simply not stand up against rigorous historical criticism. Even the Resurrection itself could not survive that test. To Drummond (in Dawes Hicks's words), Christianity in its whole conception was utterly alien to the evidential theory, and the spontaneous response of Christ's followers to His "holiness and love and self-sacrifice . . . is a surer witness to spiritual things than ten thousand miracles could be."[45] Although Drummond did not publish directly on the miracles, there seems to me something remarkably revealing in this closely observed and affectionate account: here, as in everything that Drummond wrote, there is not a sign of the wrestling in prose that characterizes the efforts of Martineau and Thom to come to terms with historical Christianity.

A final test. Robert Spears had emerged from the humblest of backgrounds in Northumberland to become one of the most remarkable preachers and organizers that Victorian Unitarianism produced. He was a constant defender and advocate of the Unitarian name that Martineau disavowed and a champion of biblically based Christianity. In 1876, he resigned the secretaryship of the British and Foreign Unitarian Association because his committee had decided over his objections to republish the works of the radical American theologian Theodore Parker. With the handsome purse he was given by his admirers, he at once founded *The Christian Life*, a newspaper that, until its absorption in 1929 into its rival, *The Inquirer*, was the wonderfully lively voice of conservative Unitarianism.

In the paper's early years,[46] there was considerable discussion of the question of miracles, concerned principally with refuting as a logical insufficiency the simplistic "scientific" rejection of miracles as contrary to known law. But coupled with this reiterated theme was a defense of the gospel miracles on grounds of the strength of testimony and of the larger miracle of the

Christian faith that they subserved. But gradually and unevenly, even before Spears's death in 1899, the subject was canvassed in fewer and fewer leaders. By the 1890s, it appears, with rare exceptions, only in occasional editorials at Eastertide on the centrality of the Resurrection. In the first decade of the twentieth century, they too have disappeared. Even for their stoutest advocates, the miracles had moved to the margins of Unitarian awareness.

7. The Cardinal's Brother

Francis Newman,
Victorian Bourgeois

The principle of the nineteenth century, that the
children are wiser than their fathers, was working in
all classes.   —J. A. Froude[1]

Religious belief was a powerful force shaping the lives, loves, and labors of the
nineteenth-century bourgeoisie. Amid the dramatic changes in material culture, class relationships, and economic expectations, religion still mattered.
Despite the intellectual challenges to biblical cosmology offered by geology,
paleontology, evolutionary biology, and the higher criticism, church-going
held up in Britain until the century's end.[2] In spite of secularism, socialism,
materialism, and anticlericalism, giving up one's faith rarely happened without a struggle, and movement was often between established creeds rather
than the abandonment of belief in some purpose or plan in the universe. The
editor and publisher Charles Kegan Paul's (1828–1902) journey from high
Anglicanism, through Comte and positivism to Unitarianism, before ending
his life as a convert to Rome, is but one example of the plethora of Victorian
religious trajectories.[3]

Belief mattered, partly because the Victorians could never entirely shake
the notion that high moral conduct and formal belief were intimately and
causally connected. But the nuances of doctrine were also of import, shaping family life and sometimes turning brother against brother, father against
daughter, friend against friend. George Eliot came to regret defying her father by refusing to go to chapel when her own faith became frail.[4] In his *Autobiography*, Charles Darwin treated his own religious evolution with discretion, not wishing to cause pain to his devout wife. Even so, he was sufficiently
frank that his family censored the document when it was published shortly

after his death.[5] Henry Manning, the future cardinal, effectively walked out of the life of William Gladstone when he fled rather than take communion with him at the Anglican chapel off Buckingham Palace Road.[6] John Henry Newman did not go over to Rome until both of his parents were dead.

The varieties of faith and, especially, doubt are prominent in Peter Gay's pioneering study of the Enlightenment, with its birth of modern paganism.[7] Religion is less central to his equally monumental analysis of the bourgeois experience in Victoria's century, although Annie Besant, W. R. Greg, Charles Kingsley, Philip Henry Gosse, and other tormented souls make their moving appearances.[8] There can be little doubt of the persistent hold of religion throughout the century, even on those for whom doctrine seemed irrelevant.[9] This is particularly striking in early Victorian Britain, when the fervor of the Evangelical movement helped mold many bourgeois psyches, and the Oxford Movement convulsed the nation. Evangelicals such as William Wilberforce (1759–1833) and Hannah More (1745–1833) left their indelible marks on the generation that followed.[10] The daily totting up of works good and bad, temptations resisted or succumbed to, was a ritual too fraught for many. In their turn, the Tractarians provoked a crisis within the Established Church, generating more heat than Darwin's *Origin of Species* some thirty years later.

Among those who passed through evangelicalism to other resting places were the Newman brothers. This footnote to Peter Gay looks principally at the younger Newman, who has not yet appeared among Gay's formidable group of Victorian bourgeois.

> Francis Newman, a pathetic figure of shambling
> ineffectiveness who had the uncanny knack of
> saying the wrong thing at the wrong time in the
> wrong way. . . .
> —David Newsome, *Two Classes of Men*[11]

Francis Newman (1805–1897) always stood in his elder brother's shadow. He followed John Henry Newman (1801–1890) to school and to Oxford, where he relied on his brother's financial support, since the family's fortunes had suffered in the aftermath of the Napoleonic Wars. Their father's bank had failed, and although he managed to find work as the manager of a brewery, he was not very successful at his second career. The family was conventionally pious, but at school both brothers came under the influence of the evangelical clergyman Walter Mayers. Even at Oxford, where Francis Newman's legendary Double First contrasted with John Henry Newman's failure to achieve high honors, the younger brother always lived in the elder's shadow. While John Henry Newman was achieving fame (and notoriety) as a molder of young men, a Tractarian and, eventually, the most sensational Victorian convert to Roman Catholicism, Francis was undergoing his own religious pilgrimage, first as a participant in a chaotic evangelical mission to the Middle East, then as a peripatetic teacher and tutor, before accepting the chair in Latin at University College, London, the "godless institution in Gower Street," in 1846. Francis did precede his brother in producing an autobiographical account of his own spiritual development: *Phases of Faith* (1850) was more than simply a nine-days' wonder, going through six editions in ten years and producing a good deal of spirited discussion before Victorian reviewers turned their attention to other matters. It is one of only two of his books that has been deemed worthy of reprinting in our own century.[12]

By contrast, John Henry Newman's *Apologia pro Vita Sua* (1864) has never gone out of print and is widely regarded as a classic of high Victorian literature. Peter Gay cites it as an exemplary exercise in Victorian self-definition, Linda Peterson as a major instance of Victorian self-interpretation.[13] A. O. J. Cockshut treats John Henry Newman's biography by W. G. Ward as a peak of the nineteenth-century genre, and major and minor biographies of him have appeared with great regularity since.[14] John Henry Newman's *Collected Works* were published in thirty-six volumes toward the end of his life, and his *Letters and Diaries* are still being lovingly edited.

Francis Newman was unfortunate in his contemporary biographer: I. G. Sieveking's *Memoir and Letters of Francis W. Newman* (1907) might best be described as a trough of the genre, useful principally for its quotations from Newman's correspondence and the reminiscences of those who had known him.[15] Sieveking had limited sympathy for her subject, her main reason for writing the book apparently being the fact that Newman had once been in love with her aunt, Maria Rosina Giberne (who subsequently became a nun).[16] William Robbins's fine comparative intellectual biography of the two brothers treats them both fully and fairly,[17] but many J. H. Newman admirers have never forgiven Francis for outliving his brother and having the last word in public. Francis published *Contributions Chiefly to the Early History of the Late Cardinal Newman* within a year of his brother's death and in his own eighty-sixth year. Maisie Ward (W. G. Ward's daughter) described it as an "odd book," manifesting a "strong bias" against its subject;[18] Father Tristram, J. H. Newman's editor and biographer, insisted that Francis had "dipped his pen in slime" before beginning to write.[19] Certainly, the volume did nothing to foster Francis's reputation, since John Henry had become a national institution long before his death. Lytton Strachey once wrote that "[i]f [J. H.]Newman had died at the age of sixty, to-day he would have been already forgotten, save by a few ecclesiastical historians; but he lived to write his *Apologia*, and to reach immortality."[20] Above all, Victorians, even those who continued to be suspicious of Rome, admired the style of Newman's writing. As Samuel Butler remarked, "Men like Newman and R. L. Stevenson seem to have taken pains to acquire what they called a style as a preliminary measure — as something that they had to form before their writings could be of any value."[21]

The younger brother may have lived too long for his historical reputation. Espousing theological rationalism in his middle age was an awkward way to penetrate the English establishment; taking up the many causes he did in old age further marginalized him. He published widely but wrote, for the most part, too quickly and inelegantly. He was against vaccination, animal experimentation, alcohol, meat-eating, and the Contagious Diseases Acts, a sharp critic of British imperial aspirations and Irish policy, and contemptuous of most politicians. He was notoriously without humor, although he at least did have the lightness to describe himself as "anti-slavery, anti-alcohol, anti-tobacco, anti-*everything*."[22] That he included slavery alongside the demon rum and the sot weed reminds us that many of his causes were admirable, if not always popular; they also included higher education for women and land reform. These social causes, principally the activities of his long retirement (he retired from his chair at University College in 1869), were often dominated by dissenters.[23] They frequently brought him into contact with ordinary individuals, and despite Newman's undoubted populist sympathies, he was never able to adapt the common touch with any ease. He was once pained when the audience at a vegetarian meeting he was addressing was uninterested in his proposal that vegetarians call themselves "anti-creophagists," since only two or three of those present understood the term's Greek derivation (from kreva, "flesh").[24]

If the causes Newman took up were not always those near to the hearts of the Victorian bourgeoisie, his eccentricities would have further marked him out as an oddball. Ever sensitive to the cold, he was commonly to be seen in three outer layers indoors and out, the top layer consisting of a rug with a hole cut in the middle to admit his head. He kept the same dirty greatcoat for years, and sometimes walked to University College in his academic cap and gown. He was a natural prey for student pranks, and his mannerisms and absentmindedness detracted from his effectiveness as a teacher. When a former Hungarian minister of justice was a guest in one of his classes, he spent his hour inquiring of the bewildered foreigner why the Bactrian camel had never been introduced to Hungary, well suited as it was to the climate and conditions of that country.[25]

Much of his academic output was also singular. Convinced that the ancient languages needed to be made more relevant, he translated *Robinson Crusoe* and Henry Wadsworth Longfellow's poems into Latin as student texts. His translation of Homer brought down Matthew Arnold's wrath upon him.[26] Newman's dictionary and grammar of modern Arabic, and his Libyan and Kabyle vocabularies might have consolidated his reputation as a linguist, but would hardly have placed him in the mainstream of intellectual life. He was mathematically adept even at school, and his volumes on plane geometry and elliptic integrals were published almost sixty years apart. Few of his contemporaries had such wide interests or more formidable talents, yet when he died, most remembered him simply as Cardinal Newman's eccentric and acid-tongued younger brother.

Francis Newman has not found his way into Peter Gay's monumental study of the bourgeois experience in the nineteenth century. Nevertheless, this curiously God-intoxicated rationalist embodied a number of quintessential bourgeois characteristics: the high sense of purpose, the moral earnestness, the consciousness of historical change, the appreciation of decorum, the awareness of class. I shall focus on Newman's three autobiographical writings: his *Phases of Faith*, a little volume of letters written while he was in the Middle East, and his reflections on his own brother's early development. In its own way, each was about phases of faith. Religious belief was so often central to our Victorian forebears' sense of self that it deserves an entire volume in *The Bourgeois Experience: Victoria to Freud*, Gay's analysis of their passions and aspirations.

> We fancy that we are free agents. We are conscious
> of what we do; we are not conscious of the causes
> which make us do it; and therefore we imagine that
> the cause is in ourselves. The Oxford [Movement]
> leaders believed that they were fighting against the
> spirit of the age. They were themselves most com-
> pletely the creatures of their age.
>
> —J. A. Froude[27]

> [A] quadruple biography, comprising the Newmans
> and Froudes, might be even more revealing.
> — Gertrude Himmelfarb, *Victorian Minds* [28]

There is not much evidence that James Froude and Francis Newman were ever particularly close. Froude was thirteen years younger, and so missed meeting Francis at Oxford. Froude gets no mention in Sieveking's biography, and there are only occasional references to Newman in W. H. Dunn's two-volume modern study of the historian. Nevertheless, the Newman and Froude families powerfully interacted with each other, largely through the elder sons. John Henry Newman described Richard Hurrell Froude's (1803–1836) influence on him as "powerful beyond all others"; they were fellows of Oriel College together, shared a passion for celibacy,[29] jointly wrote a volume of religious poems, *Lyra Apostolica*, and, with William Wilberforce's second son, Robert Isaac Wilberforce (1802–1857), made headlines when they resigned their fellowships at Oriel in 1832.

When Hurrell's health broke down in the same year, John Henry went with Hurrell and his father, a West Country archdeacon with a taste for riding and outdoor pursuits, on a tour of the Mediterranean. It was a turning point in the future cardinal's life: in Rome, the Froudes and Newman met the English Cardinal Nicholas Wiseman, and when he returned alone to Sicily in April 1833, Newman himself suffered from an almost-fatal illness, which left him with a heightened sense of religious destiny. His autobiographical account, not published until after his death, is a moving and graphic depiction of the episode.[30] He was convinced that he was too sensitive to the cold ever to be suited to the life of a missionary, but his bout with death reinforced his sense of calling. On his way back to England, he penned "Lead, Kindly Light."

Many date the formal beginning of the Oxford Movement to a sermon that John Keble preached shortly after Newman returned to Oxford. Hurrell Froude's involvement in it was to be short-lived, for the warm climates had failed to ameliorate his consumption. "I shall truly be widowed," Newman wrote in February 1836, when hearing that his friend was dying.[31] Almost as hard for Newman to bear was the virtually simultaneous news that Keble had suddenly married ("marriage is a very second rate business," was Newman's acid comment).[32] Newman and Keble did dubious homage to their late friend by publishing his literary and theological *Remains*, together with a biographical memoir. The public was scandalized by the revelations of fastings, flagellations, and Mariolatry.[33]

If Hurrell's death left Newman "widowed," it was the making of James Anthony Froude. Owen Chadwick has provided a powerful psychological reading of the younger Froude's religious and social development:

The Oxford Movement meant Hurrell Froude [to J. A. Froude] and Hurrell meant father and home. He admired the memory of Hurrell and knew that he ought to have loved him. But what he remembered was Hurrell watching with approval while his father flogged him, Hurrell examining his lessons and finding them lamentable, Hurrell holding his heels over a stream and his head under water. The memory of his dead brother was a cell in the family prison. To the Oxford Movement he knew he owed the highest in his soul. And the Oxford was a thrall whence he must flee for his very life.[34]

Although the future historian came briefly under John Henry's spell, producing a famous life of St. Neot for Newman's series on the Lives of the Saints, during the early 1840s, he underwent his own crisis of faith. His two autobiographical novels, the pseudonymous *The Spirits Trials* in 1847, followed by *The Nemesis of Faith*, with his name on the title page, record, in vaguely fictional form, his doubts about the Anglican Church, in which he had taken orders in 1844. *Nemesis* was a brave novel, but not a very good one, and it pleased neither wing of the established Church, nor people like Thomas Carlyle and Francis Newman, who were not then part of it. Carlyle snorted that Froude ought to consume his own smoke, and not let it get up other people's nostrils.[35] For his own part, Francis Newman always thought Froude a little too soft on John Henry: "My first book won me the regard of Frank Newman. My second has forfeited it, or nearly so. Strange he most resents my admiration of his brother," he wrote to another apostate, Arthur Clough, just after the publication of *Nemesis*.[36]

> If one man is cast out of God's favour for eliciting
> error while earnestly searching after truth, and an-
> other remains in favour by passively receiving the
> word of a Church, or a Priest, or of an Apostle, then
> to search for truth is dangerous; apathy is safer; then
> the soul does not come directly into contact with
> God and learn of him, but has to learn from, and
> unconvincedly submit to, some external authority.
> This is the germ of Romanism: its legitimate devel-
> opment makes us Pagans outright.
> —Francis Newman, *Phases of Faith*[37]

Francis Newman never turned his hand to the genre of autobiographical fiction. However, he did duplicate the epistolary structure of Froude's *Nemesis* in the second of his own autobiographical writings. With a short title, *Personal Narrative*, recalling Alexander von Humboldt's monumental account of his travels in South and Central America, Newman's slim volume consists of sixty-six letters written to several unidentified individuals at home between 1830 and 1833 from his ill-fated missionary endeavor in the Near East. The book bears the imprint of the radical publisher George Jacob Holyoake, although it hardly seems to have been aimed at a working-class readership, and its radicalism has to be teased out. In virtually all of his other writings, Newman paraded his academic positions on the title pages, but in *Personal Narrative*, his name appears unadorned, with no reference to his earlier fellowship at Balliol or his chair in Latin at University College, which he held at the time of publication, 1856.[38] The work seems to have sunk virtually without trace. It is not mentioned in a long and largely favorable retrospective of Newman's work in the *Westminster Review*, and neither does the *Christian Examiner* list it in what was admitted to be an "imperfect" bibliography of his writings between 1836 and 1864.[39]

Newman traveled to the Near East with a strange troop of evangelical souls whom he had met in England and Ireland. The years after he resigned his Balliol fellowship and declined to take his M.A. because of his doubts about infant baptism and his growing concern about whether the doctrine of the Trinity was actually scriptural had been restless ones. He had spent over a year in Ireland as a tutor in the household of Sir Henry Brooke Parnell (1776–1842), later the first Baron Congleton. There, both he and Parnell's eldest son had come under the influence of John Nelson Darby (1800–1882), a founder of the sect of Plymouth Brethren, the unnamed "Irish clergyman" of *Phases of Faith*. It is clear that during this evangelical phase of Newman's life, he was desperately seeking someone who combined simple spiritual piety and absolute moral behavior. According to the testimony of *Phases*, the closest model was not Darby but one of Darby's converts, Anthony N. Groves.

The most dramatic demonstration of one's conversion was to become a missionary, and this Newman and his companions sought to do. The party was headed and largely financed by John Parnell (1805–1883), later the second Baron Congleton, and included Parnell's fiancée, Nancy Cronin, her brother (a medical man), and his infant daughter, as well as the Cronins' mother and a Mr. Hamilton. Dr. Cronin's wife had died while preparations for the journey were in train. Parnell's father had purchased an army commission for his son, but the younger Parnell refused to give up his religious ways for the army. "Fearing his Christianity would bring discredit on his military profession," the elder Parnell gave up the commission and let his son get on with his missionary work.[40]

The group set out from Dublin on 18 September 1830, intending to go directly to Baghdad, where Anthony Groves (a "distinguished dentist") and his wife were busy converting souls. Parnell wanted to marry his sweetheart en route in France, but he discovered he could not do so without residing there for a month. Anxious to begin the good work, the party pressed on, although hampered at every turn by their bulky and heavy luggage, the weather, and their inability to find an Arabic-speaking interpreter. They traveled in the cheapest cabins, Parnell being reluctant to spend "the Lord's money in self-indulgence." It took them four weeks to sail from Cyprus to the Syrian coast ("the captain of the vessel had only one old French map, the names of which he could not read"). The overland journey to Aleppo in late December and early January was wet, cold, and generally miserable. Old Mrs. Cronin kept falling off her mule and had to ride astride. "It was to her, morally and physically, a great trial. 'Ach, Edward,' said she to her son, 'I expected they would persecute and murdher [sic.] us, but I never thought to ride across a mule.'"[41]

Civil unrest prevented them from continuing on to Baghdad, which was just as well, since plague broke out there shortly afterward, carrying off Mrs. Groves. In Aleppo, Parnell finally married his fiancée, who herself died a few months after the wedding. She was already pregnant. Newman wrote home:

We have received the afflicting intelligence of the death of Mrs P. at Ladakîa. She had been somewhat shaken by a fall from her ass (a very nice animal), and a slight illness, aggravated by very improper medicines which she fancied were good for her, ended in violent inflammation of the bowels. Alas, to possess English drugs without English physicians at hand, is a dreadful power. The brother and mother here are so deeply affected, that I ask: what does the noble hearted husband suffer, but so lately a bridegroom? I am astounded at the reverse. Two months back she was hanging over my pillow, weeping and kissing me as a dying man: now here am I in youthful vigour, and she is in her grave.[42]

His own grave illness is but briefly described in his published letters, but Groves's journal offers another perspective:

When Mr Newman was at the worst, and they had given up all hopes of him, they anointed him with oil according to the 14th of the 5th of James, and prayed over him, and the Lord had mercy on them, yea, and on me also, and restored him. It seems to me truly scriptural, and if the Church of Rome has perverted it to superstitious ends, ought we therefore to cast aside so plain a precept. By many it would be called plain

popery, but this we must bear. With regard to miracles my mind is not at present prepared to embrace them fully: but this I do feel that the Apostle Paul, in Corinthians
12 and 14, when speaking for supernatural gifts for the edifying the Church and doing the work of God, points them out as things to be desired and prayed for then, and
if they were desired to be prayed for then, why not now?[43]

According to Newman's published testimony, his illness was but a serious
fever, from which he recovered, subsequently gaining his strength by taking
up horse riding.

In Aleppo, Mr. Hamilton decided that his linguistic abilities were not
up to missionary work, and he returned to England. Worse still, the party
seemed to have made virtually no converts, although Mr. Cronin found
plenty of work as a doctor, taking Newman with him to act as interpreter. The
party's vague plan seems to have been to translate and distribute religious
tracts. To that end, Newman applied himself to learning Arabic, and he became fascinated with the whole range of Near Eastern languages. Parnell also
busied himself studying Arabic and Persian, but the Cronins were content to
conduct their missionary efforts in English, which undoubtedly contributed
to their ineffectiveness. The party attracted a bit of favorable attention when
they sang their hymns — two of them had particularly fine voices — but attention did not lead to conversion. This showy demonstration of religious
zeal had embarrassed Newman on the boat in the Mediterranean — "where
there were other Englishmen" — but it seemed acceptable when surrounded
by the public trappings of Islamic worship.

After almost fifteen months in Aleppo, the political and epidemiological
situation was stable enough for the party to set off to Baghdad, to meet up
with Groves, by then a widower. The journey was fraught with incident.
Their cook pulled out at the last minute, after a dispute over his wages. Tribal
princes demanded tribute in exchange for safe passage, made more difficult
by their shortage of cash, since bills of credit were almost impossible to negotiate. Unsurprisingly, since they were carrying more than 3,000 pounds
of luggage (mostly Syrian and Armenian Bibles), travel was slow. Because of
the heat, they often had to travel at night, and Mrs. Cronin found she could
not sleep during the day. In Aintab, they were accosted by the governor for
selling four Turkish New Testaments. "This is not a town of Christians, but
a town of Moslems," he told them,[44] ordering them to leave immediately. On
the way out, they were stoned, and Cronin was left for dead. Miraculously,
he was only bruised and able to continue after a rest. At Mardin, a promise
of an escort by Turkish soldiers was frustrated because they were unable to
obtain their cash in time to leave with them.

After almost three months on the road, they finally reached Baghdad in late June 1832. Mrs. Cronin announced to Groves that "she had come hither to die," and, true to her word, she did so three days later. As Newman notes grimly, "Her work was done already, and neither the loss nor the grief are like those previously suffered." Newman spent most of his brief time in Baghdad acting as tutor to Groves's two motherless sons, although both Groves and Parnell soon acquired new wives before deciding that India offered a riper field for their evangelical endeavours.[45] After three months in Baghdad, Newman returned to England via Teheran, Tabriz, Erzurum, and Istanbul, his missionary days over.

The contrast between Newman's letters home and the accounts of those years in the religious biographies of Groves and Parnell could not be starker. The latter are recorded in the tones of providential fundamentalism. God was always looking after his disciples. Henry Groves (the missionary's son and biographer of Parnell) interpreted the promise of the Turkish escort from Mardin to Baghdad as the work of God, although he had to admit that the delay in obtaining money left the offer unfulfilled. He sums up the whole endeavor as a wonderful fulfillment of God's grand plan, although the lack of converts was disappointing. Typical of the descriptions is the following episode:

During the journey [from Aleppo to Baghdad] they were exposed to frequent dangers from the wandering Arabs bent on plunder. On one occasion Mr. Parnell and his friends saw a large body of Arabs in the distance, and felt as if they would certainly fall a prey into their hands. God was their only help in the matter; and so, dismounting, they knelt in prayer, seeking His protection, and on arising from their knees they saw the Arabs going off in an opposite direction, and they were permitted to pursue their journey without molestation.[46]

Newman did not regard the incident as worth recounting, at least in the published volume of letters.

Although it is clear that Newman edited the letters before he put them before the world, what remains is almost entirely secular. He was interested in people, history, culture, and, above all, language. He practiced his Arabic by translating Gibbon, and midway through the journey from Aleppo to Baghdad, he concluded, "Mussulmans are not to be converted by translations of the New Testament."[47] Newman came away with no great fondness for Islam — he found the Koran "tedious and shallow" — but he met local people whom he liked and respected. Above all, he became conscious of the power of culture to transform an individual. The party adopted Eastern styles of dress, partly to avoid attracting undue attention, partly because of the climate. He thought this practical, but found the garments so effeminate that he grew a mustache to avoid being mistaken for a woman. In England, he had detested smoking; in Aleppo, it seemed the natural thing to do. He was exposed to new taste sensations: "I then first tasted potatoes fried in oil, and in spite of my prejudices found them excellent."[48] The fruit and vegetables were very good, and he drank, even if he did not particularly enjoy, the local wines.

Newman's linguistic talents made it easier for him to assimilate, although he was never able to get rid of his own Englishness. Indeed, that cultural identity made him conclude that they would never be able to make converts. "I should tell you: neither Moslems nor Franks think of us as Christians, but as English." Although "[a]n Ottoman at bottom is very like a John Bull," Turkish culture and religion were so firmly intertwined and deeply rooted that neither cultural nor religious imperialism was possible. As he had recounted in *Phases of Faith*,

When we were at Aleppo, I one day got into religious discourse with a Mohammedan carpenter, which left on me a lasting impression. Among other matters, I was peculiarly desirous of disabusing him of the current notion of his people, that our gospels are spurious narratives of late date. I found great difficulty of expression; but the man listened to me with much attention, and I was encouraged to exert myself. He waited patiently till I had done, and then spoke to the following effect: "I will tell you, sir, how the case stands. God has given to you English a great many good gifts. You make fine ships, and sharp penknives, and good cloth and cottons; and you have rich nobles and brave soldiers; and you write and print many learned books: (dictionaries and grammars:) all this is of God. But there is one thing that God has withheld from you, and has revealed to us; and that is, knowledge of the true religion, by which one may be saved." When he thus ignored my argument, (which was probably quite unintelligible to him,) and delivered his simple protest, I was silenced, and at the same time amused. But the more I thought it over, the more instruction I saw in the case.[49]

Newman's anti-imperialism was consolidated by his experiences in the Middle East.

The thing Newman found most oppressive about Islam was the way it stifled the individual conscience: in this it was as successful "as any mummery of Rome."[50] Indeed, Newman's *Personal Narrative* records almost as many encounters with Catholic clergymen as with followers of Islam. It was perhaps natural that he and his Protestant colleagues would look upon Catholic missionaries as rivals, but Newman's loathing of Rome and all that it stood for are ongoing themes in his letters home. Romanists had never been able to get out of the Middle Ages, that period of semi-barbarism when men had tried to perfect their art without perfecting their tools. He was disgusted at a "monk in sackcloth with a rope around his loins, a picture of gaunt ugliness." While he found horse riding with a Catholic bishop pleasant enough, he noted: "I really think he breathes more freely in my company, than when monks or high professors of his church are near. What a misery is a constrained religion!"[51]

For Newman, then, his Eastern encounters with Catholicism were just as formative as his realization that dialogue between religionists of incompatible persuasions was likely to prove sterile. If one system was true, the other was by definition false, and if each believer was equally sincere, compromise was impossible. Groves and Parnell responded to the impasse by transferring their energies to India:

No one can imagine the disheartening feelings that often try the missionary's heart in the countries where Mohammedanism is professed and dominant, and where your mouth is sealed. Among heathens, and especially in India, you can publish your testimony, and this is a great comfort to the heart that knows what a testimony it is, and what promises are connected with its publication.[52]

Although Newman later remarked that he had sometimes "yearned to proceed to India, whither my friend Groves had transferred his labours and his hopes," his own spiritual journey was henceforth to be more personal.[53] Although he returned to England with the vague idea of securing more recruits for the cause, he also returned a changed man. Unlike Richard Burton and a few other Victorian travelers in the Middle East, he had hardly gone native; unlike Flaubert, he had not indulged in the sensual opportunities presented by the area.[54] But as with Darwin, whose own voyage of discovery overlapped with Newman's, the experience of other lands and peoples was crucial.

> There lives more faith in honest doubt,
> Believe me, than in half the creeds.
> —Alfred, Lord Tennyson,
> *In Memoriam A. H. H.*[55]

It is not hard to see that the correspondent of the *Personal Narrative* had also been the author of *Phases of Faith*. Coinciding in its publication with volumes such as Froude's *Nemesis* and W. R. Greg's *Creed of Christendom* (1851), it belongs to a group of works reflecting what has been called a mid-century "Victorian crisis of faith."[56] It remains the most visible of Newman's books,[57] and it is certainly the most reflective. Although uncompromising in its minute dissection of scriptural passages that puzzled Newman, it also makes effective use of the personal pronoun. Newman was not afraid of exposing his emotions, even while emphasizing the rational doubt that had led from his early evangelicalism to his mature religious position. Along the way, he had cast doubt, inter alia, on infant baptism, the Trinity, the perfection of Jesus, and the biblical miracles.

In Newman's lifelong search for what he always called "primitive Christianity," one theme stands out: the primacy of the individual, in his relationship both to Scripture and to God. In that, of course, he stood within a well-marked Protestant tradition, even if he went much further along the path of critical inquiry than many of his predecessors. Within that individualistic tradition, the real enemy was Rome, the real Antichrist, the pope. The perniciousness of blind acceptance of authority in matters religious was the dominant motif in Newman's spiritual quest. From his evangelical youth, when a "kinsman" (his father) had attempted to quell his Sabbatarian leanings "by mere authority, not by instruction"; to his discovery, at Oxford, that few undergraduates actually cared about the Thirty-nine Articles they had just signed in order to be admitted; to his abandonment of the Nicene and Athanasian Creeds; to his doubts about the received meanings of many passages within the Bible: in these and a hundred other instances, Newman asserted his right and his duty as a rational, moral creature to think for himself. "Faith at Second Hand Found to Be Vain," as one of his chapter titles puts it.

By 1850, Newman had passed through six "Phases of Faith." He had abandoned the evangelical Calvinism of his youth, even while attempting to put into practice an essential Christianity in the Middle East. He had come to believe that modern science had rendered biblical fundamentalism untenable (Darwinism subsequently seems to have left him unmoved), and that the morality of the Bible was not absolute, for example, in its approach to the detestable institution of slavery. Having come to doubt that the doctrine of the Trinity was actually scriptural, he argued that even Jesus had been liable to error. Nevertheless, he was never comfortable with a secular humanism. Rather, he wanted to strip away all later additions to Christian doctrine and return to the "the tenderness, humility, and disinterestedness, that are the glory of the purest Christianity, [combined] with that activity of intellect, untiring pursuit of truth, and strict adherence to impartial principle, which the schools of modern science embody." In short, he sought to marry practical devotion and free thought.[58] It is not surprising that neither secularists nor churchmen could cope with him.

Although Newman could not have known it, he still had more than half his life before him when he wrote *Phases of Faith*. The later decades of his life tended to be devoted to the various social causes mentioned earlier, but this was consistent with his notion that Christianity had been too other-worldly, to the cost of active involvement in the here and now. He wanted men and women to be judged by their actions, not their beliefs, asking only that individuals show the "moral peculiarities of a Christian."[59] Neither heaven nor hell seems to have interested him much, and the Calvinistic doctrine of eternal punishment was one of the doctrines from which he first fled. And given the intensity of his individualism, it is not surprising that his relationship with all organized religions, even Unitarianism, was problematic. Many of his closest friends were to be found within the Unitarian community, however. These included James Martineau, the doyen of Victorian Unitarianism, whom he met during his brief stint at Manchester New College in the early 1840s; and Anna Swanwick, the pioneer of higher education for women, whom he had taught. According to Sieveking, Newman let these two old friends know late in his life that he wished it to be known that he had died a Christian.[60] Whether many Christians would have recognized Newman's interpretation of what their religion meant is another matter.

In one thing he never wavered: his "pure hatred of Popery."[61] Together with Islam, Roman Catholicism represented to him all that was wrong with organized religion, taking away from the individual the spirit of free inquiry. Given his brother's different trajectory, it was inevitable that their relationship, which had already begun to cool at Oxford, did not survive unscathed. In Francis Newman's account of his own spiritual development, he describes his elder brother as "warm-hearted and generous," but also unsympathetic to Francis's evangelical questioning of episcopal authority: why should bishops, Newman had asked, "*as such*, . . . be more reverenced than common clergymen; or Clergymen, *as such*, more than common men"? And, in a foretaste of what was to be a major theme of his late-life reminiscences of his brother, he insists that John Henry had worked out full-blown popish views as early as 1823–26. His brother's Tractarianism showed how plainly he was prepared to "sacrifice private love to ecclesiastical dogma," a sin to which Francis Newman also confessed, although not in turning family members against one of their own, as his own brother had done to him.[62] The final step, John Henry Newman's conversion to Catholicism, could have not come as a surprise to his family, and although it strained his relationship with his sisters, that with Francis had already reached an impasse. Their letters in the years after both travelers had returned to England document a growing theological and emotional distancing. There was "no halfway house between Rome and rationalism" (or pantheism or atheism),[63] John Henry came to believe, and the brothers put flesh on the pronouncement.

There was never a formal breach, however, and blood proved thicker than even holy water, in that they continued to share the collective family distress at the behavior of the middle Newman son, Charles Robert, who renounced his family as religion-crazed, but was himself so erratic that he could never hold down any of the various posts that his brothers procured for him. This black sheep would figure prominently in any study of the Newman family dynamics: he at least had the salutary effect of providing a common focus of agreement amid so much religious turmoil.[64] His two brothers generously supported him during much of his life, despite the fact that he reportedly wrote a whole book denouncing Francis. Like most of the things he touched in his life, he never followed it through, and it remained unpublished.[65] His "wasted life," Francis remarked, "were better buried in silence."[66]

Both John Henry and Francis refrained from denouncing their brother in public, but Francis's late sketch of John Henry was received in some quarters as a public betrayal. His ostensible reason for writing it was reasonable enough: John Henry had become part of "*English history*,"[67] and no one then alive knew the cardinal's early history as intimately as his surviving brother. Curiously, J. H. Newman had believed that only a Protestant could properly assess his life up until his flight to Rome in 1845. One assumes that he did not have his brother in mind.

Contributions is a strange work, especially from one of such meticulous scholarship. Newman relied almost entirely on memory, not bothering to reread the printed record of his brother's Anglican period. Consequently, it is not a particularly reliable guide to the events it describes. Nevertheless, its gossipy tone is effective in reinforcing the themes that had long been part of Newman's agenda. John Henry is presented as a fastidious, manipulative schoolboy who declined to participate in games and was already fascinated by secret societies. In defending (in contrast to his father) George IV and his government against the hapless Queen Caroline, John Henry had justified his father's retort: "Well, John! I suppose I ought to praise you for knowing how to rise in this world. Go on! Persevere! Always stand up for men in power, and in time you will get promotion."[68] In his brother's judgment, John Henry was the ultimate corporation man.

If authority is the bugbear of *Phases*, dissembling is the key to *Contributions*. Newman spends almost half the volume arguing that his brother had developed Romish views as early as 1825, and thus for two decades had lived a lie. It was a character flaw that could be only partially redeemed by his conversion: "I should have vastly preferred entire oblivion of him and his writings of the first forty years, but that is impossible."[69] His brother lacked that open manliness so prized by the Victorians, and it was this, as much as the Mariolatry or the power of the priesthood, that alienated him from all that Francis held dear. After all, it was Catholicism, not Catholics, that Francis despised. He had shared the platform with Cardinal Manning at temperance meetings.

Edmund Gosse described *Father and Son* as "A Study of Two Temperaments." The same could be said of the Newman brothers: the one conservative, the other liberal; the one otherworldly, the other this-worldly; the one drawn toward authority, the other always his own man. That they drifted apart is not surprising. More surprising, perhaps, is the extent to which Francis has been written out of history, even if he was sometimes careless of his own place within it.

In conclusion, it might be asked if Francis Newman was "born to rebel"?[70] At first glance, Frank J. Sulloway's work on birth order seems to provide an attractive framework for both the Newman and Froude brothers. After all, both Francis Newman and J. A. Froude left their testimonies of honest doubt, and in espousing the causes he did, Francis became something of a professional protester in his later life. Paradoxically, however, it could be argued that Hurrell Froude and John Henry Newman were the real rebels. Within the context of early Victorian society, with the Catholic Emancipation Bill being hotly debated, and anti-Catholic sentiment running high, theirs was the more rebellious course. Hurrell Froude died before the logic of his position could work itself out, and John Henry Newman hesitated for years before going over to Rome. Nevertheless, despite the zeal for authority that the elder Newman brother always possessed, there was a core of self-assurance that gave his life a remarkable consistency.

8. The Bourgeois Experience as Political Culture

The Chamberlains of Birmingham

Between the accession of Queen Victoria and the demise of Sigmund Freud, the Chamberlains of Birmingham were a quintessentially middle-class family — in their ancestry, their clannishness, their education, their sources of income, their religious beliefs, their styles of life, their choices of marriage partners, their cultural aspirations, and their attitude to honors. Thus described, theirs was a conventional part of the nineteenth- and twentieth-century "bourgeois experience" that Peter Gay has recreated with such verve and erudition.[1] But the Chamberlains were less than typically bourgeois in their political importance and their worldly success. Joseph, who was born a year before Victoria became queen, was the greatest mayor of Birmingham, an inveterate opponent of Irish Home Rule, and a famously forceful colonial secretary, who raised British imperial consciousness to unprecedented heights. His eldest son, Austen, an M.P. for more than forty years, was twice chancellor of the exchequer, served as foreign secretary from 1924 to 1929, and won the Nobel Peace Prize for negotiating the Locarno Treaty in 1925. And Joseph's younger son Neville, who died one year after Freud, was the most successful of all: lord mayor of Birmingham from 1915 to 1917 (following his father), twice chancellor of the exchequer (following his half brother), and prime minister from 1937 to 1940 (outdoing them both).[2]

This meant that in their time, the Chamberlains were the most prominent middle-class dynasty in British politics. During the past two hundred years, they have been rivaled in this only by the Cannings before them and the Hoggs since. Not surprisingly, their sense of family pride and collective identity was exceptionally well developed, and in private and public, Austen and Neville remained abidingly loyal to "the clique" and especially to their father's memory.[3] But the Chamberlains were also unusual in that they were so closely identified, across the generations, with one particular British city.

For it was Birmingham that provided the source of their considerable wealth, an unrivaled arena for municipal endeavor, and the base from which they sustained themselves in parliamentary politics. Much has been written about these three men as local worthies and as national figures. The purpose of this essay is to take a fresh look at the Chamberlains in their civic setting: to reevaluate their political position in Birmingham across the decades, to outline the cultural and ceremonial resources they mobilized in stamping their mark on the city, and to explore the interconnections between their local standing and their national endeavors. It seeks, in short, to describe the rise, zenith, and decline of something that disappeared from Birmingham's collective civic consciousness in 1945, but that in its heyday was an integral and defining element in the city's political and cultural life: "the Chamberlain tradition."

I

When Joseph Chamberlain became mayor of Birmingham in 1873, having been elected to the council only four years before, he inaugurated a municipal revolution that was of lasting significance in his adopted town, and that set so successful an example to the nation and empire that Birmingham became recognized as a "municipal Mecca" and the "best-governed city in the world."[4] The outlines of this story are well known. Along with his nonconformist relatives and friends, many of whom were important local businessmen, Chamberlain elevated the status and standing of the office of mayor, and transformed the city council from a byword for myopic incompetence into "the pivot on which the whole life of the community has turned." During his three-year mayoralty, the gas and water supply were taken into municipal ownership and the Corporation Street improvement scheme was inaugurated. Thereafter, this vigorous civic crusade was continued by Chamberlain's relatives and associates. Birmingham acquired a Welsh water supply, its bishopric, and its university. In 1889, it was raised to the rank of city; in 1896, its mayor became lord mayor; and in 1911, it was enlarged into Greater Birmingham, "the second city in the Empire."[5]

But this is only the municipal side of the story. For, in 1876, having already established himself as the dominant force in the National Education League, Joseph Chamberlain resigned the mayoralty and was returned unopposed as one of the town's three Liberal M.P.s at a by-election. As in the Council House, so in the Commons, he was regarded as an advanced radical — hostile to the aristocracy and the monarchy, master of the Birmingham caucus, and the architect of the new National Liberal Federation.[6] He remained an M.P. for the next thirty-eight years, transferring to West Birmingham, one of the seven single member constituencies created by the Third Reform Act. For much of that time, Chamberlain was the city's most celebrated public figure, and this was either despite, or because of, the many changes in his politics: separating from Gladstone over Home Rule, creating a new electoral organization to supersede the Liberal caucus, becoming a Unionist and embracing imperialism, and resigning from Balfour's government to campaign for Tariff Reform. Throughout these unexpected turns and developments, Chamberlain's Birmingham "duchy" held firm. Such sustained dominance of a British city by one man was distinctly unusual.[7]

All this is well known. When Birmingham men and women talked, as they did by the 1900s, of the "Chamberlain tradition," they were referring to a potent and unique amalgam of personal charisma, civic vigor, electoral success, and national political importance, apparently dating back a quarter of a century. But Chamberlain's "fortress" was for much of that time less secure than this implies. On the municipal front, there was opposition in his own day from the Ratepayers' Association and the Conservatives, and later from the Liberals and the new Labour Party. Nor was it any easier in the constituencies. At the 1880 general election, there was a strong Conservative revival in the city, and Chamberlain was returned with fewer votes than the other two successful Liberal candidates. In 1885, the Conservative vote went up again, and Chamberlain left the veteran M.P. John Bright to rebut the challenge mounted by Lord Randolph Churchill in Birmingham Central.[8] During both of these elections, he was much criticized: for the expense of the Council House, the Art Gallery, and Corporation Street, for his lack of interest in the housing of the poor, and for the dictatorial methods of the caucus. Indeed, the dominant Birmingham Liberal in these years was not Chamberlain, who in age and votes was the junior partner, but John Bright, who had been M.P. for the city since 1857.[9]

During the later part of the 1880s, Chamberlain's local position remained weak, since he did not so much lead slavish Birmingham opinion in a rightward direction as follow it in an uncertain search for a new accommodation with it. His first responses to Gladstone's Home Rule proposals were far less decisive than John Bright's.[10] Once it was clear in 1887 that there would be no reunion with the Gladstonian leadership, Chamberlain was obliged to create a new organization in Birmingham from scratch. There was much animosity from the Liberals (his former friends) whom he was leaving behind and distrust from the Conservatives (his former enemies), who were now expected to make way for their old adversary. Only the disarray of the Birmingham Liberals enabled him to secure victory for himself and his friends in the elections of 1886. Not until the election of 1892 was his local position fully consolidated, and not until 1895 did he become a serious player at Westminster again. And it was only during the early 1900s that the idea of a "Chamberlain duchy" in the West Midlands as a whole, and a "Chamberlain tradition" in Birmingham itself, became generally recognizable.[11]

That Chamberlain, his relatives and associates worked hard for Birmingham's (not always reliable) votes cannot be doubted. Much less appreciated are the other ways in which they sought to stamp their mark on the town and win popular support. The image of Birmingham that they projected during the last quarter of the nineteenth century resembled that of an Italian city-state: proud, free, and independent. They saw their town as a latter-day Renaissance Venice and themselves as latter-day oligarchs, a hereditary patriciate, governing and beautifying their city in the interests of all its inhabitants, with the same skill and virtue, piety and patriotism, wisdom and disinterestedness that Venice had shown in its prime.[12] This self-image did not completely square with the partisan nature of Chamberlainite council and party politics; but nor was it wholly fanciful. For the "civic renaissance" was not just about gas and water: it was also about promoting the arts, elevating the taste of ordinary citizens, and nurturing in them a sense of civic identity. As *The Times* obituarist noted on Chamberlain's death, "he held up the ideal of a self-sufficient community with stately and beneficent public institutions, and a dignified public life."[13]

The most visible expression of this civic gospel were the public buildings constructed during this period: "the projection of values into space and stone."[14] This was partly because of the need to house the expanding municipal bureaucracy, and partly as a way of asserting the importance of the town and the council. But it was also a deliberate attempt at enlightened municipal patronage. "Art," observed John Thackeray Bunce, a friend of Chamberlain's and editor of the *Birmingham Daily Post*, "must . . . permeate and suffuse the daily life, if it is to become a real and enduring influence." There must be "public buildings, ample and stately and rich enough in their ornament to dignify the corporate life," which would promote "a municipal life nobler, fuller, richer than any the world has ever seen." Hence the construction of the Council House between 1874 and 1879 and the City Museum and Art Gallery from 1881 to 1885. And the images projected by these buildings perfectly accorded with Bunce's vision. Above the portico of the Council

2

House was a relief of "Britannia Rewarding the Birmingham Manufacturers," the inscription stone of the Art Gallery bore the words "By the Gains of Industry We Promote Art," and the Art Gallery boasted a campanile modeled on that of San Marco in Venice.[15]

This was a portent of things to come. For while the Council House and Art Galley were mainly neoclassical, the Chamberlainites soon developed their own distinctive architectural style, which was Venetian or Ruskinian Gothic. It was characterized by red brick and terra-cotta, by high, pointed windows, gables, towers, chimneys, and spires, and by elaborate ornamentation in ironwork, glass, marble, granite, and tiles.[16] During the last quarter of the nineteenth century, most of the public buildings in Birmingham were constructed in this manner, including Mason College, the extensions to the Birmingham and Midland Institute and the Central Reference Library, and the Birmingham School of Art. The shops and offices that fronted onto Corporation Street were built in the same style, as were more than thirty board schools, which became as characteristic of Birmingham's inner suburbs as Wren's churches were of the City of London. Even the hardware princes of Edgbaston turned from suburban stucco to Gothic villas, inspired by The Grove, where Archibald Kenrick lived, and by Highbury, the grandest palazzo of them all, constructed for Joseph Chamberlain in 1880.[17]

Most of these buildings were designed by John Henry Chamberlain, who, though no relation, was a Liberal friend of Joseph Chamberlain's, and closely involved with the Birmingham Society of Artists, the Birmingham School of Art, and the Birmingham and Midland Institute. It was said that he "cared for the municipal life of our town with a steadfast and passionate feeling," and he was the de facto official architect to the civic gospel. As such, he successfully projected the image of Birmingham as a latter-day Venice in the most public and enduring way. He was Ruskin's most ardent practicing disciple, and he firmly believed in the social responsibilities of architects, and in the appropriateness of Venetian Gothic for the great buildings of Victorian towns.[18] They established a direct continuity with an earlier golden age of urban life; they were majestic expressions of civic patriotism and municipal high-mindedness; and they enriched and informed the lives of all who saw them. As J. T. Bunce declared in an obituary notice, "to the whole community he spoke . . . by the buildings with which his creative skill had adorned the town," thereby "teaching daily lessons of beauty and refinement to the crowds who daily pass them."[19]

J. H. Chamberlain's buildings were the cathedrals of the new civic gospel: and he also assisted in the celebration of its saints and evangelists. Surrounded by the Town Hall, the Art Gallery, the Reference Library, and Mason College in the center of the city, Chamberlain Square was created, "adorned with monuments commemorating, either by design or association, the achievements of Liberalism in politics, in science, in eloquence or in local work," including statues of such worthies as George Dawson, the most influential preacher of the civic gospel, and Josiah Mason, who founded the local science college, from which the university eventually developed.[20] But pride of place went to the Chamberlain Memorial, a sixty-five foot gothic spire, richly ornamented with mosaics and a portrait medallion of Joseph Chamberlain himself. Designed by his namesake and unveiled in 1880, the year in which Chamberlain resigned from the town council, it proclaimed the Liberal values of municipal enterprise. Nearby, in Council House Square, another commemorative project was also begun, with statues of the radical scientist Joseph Priestley and John Skirrow Wright, a long-serving Liberal councillor.[21]

J. H. Chamberlain's early death in 1883 meant that for the two great public buildings of a later period, the city was forced to turn to London. But Aston Webb, the architect selected for both commissions, designed very much in Chamberlain's established idiom. The Victoria Law Courts, constructed on Corporation Street between 1887 and 1891, were another richly ornamented terra-cotta extravaganza, complete with stained-glass windows depicting episodes in Birmingham's history and celebrating its industries. The courts were much admired, and inspired such neighboring buildings as the General Hospital and the Methodist Central Hall.[22] Twenty years later, Joseph Chamberlain summoned Webb again to design the new university, of which he was chancellor, promoter, and chief fund raiser. In addition to the buildings devoted to education and research, Chamberlain wanted something distinctive — partly as another monument to himself, partly to make the university a landmark in the city, and partly to proclaim that it was a place of general culture belonging to a great European tradition. Not surprisingly, he settled on an Italian campanile — primarily based on that of Siena's cathedral, but also with touches derived from the tower of San Giorgio Maggiore at the entrance to the Grand Canal of Venice.[23]

Like the oligarchs of Renaissance Venice, the Chamberlainites of Victorian Birmingham sought to glorify civic life and advance their civic crusade by staging grand ceremonials against the backdrop of the buildings and spaces they had created.[24] From the time of Chamberlain's mayoralty, the scale and tempo of municipal festivities considerably increased. Between 1874 and 1882, the foundation stones of the Council House and Mason College were laid and the buildings declared open; there was a dinner given to Chamberlain on his resignation as mayor, and there was the inauguration of Chamberlain Square; and there were the laying of the inscription stone of the Art Gallery and the reopening of the Central Reference Library. Each of these occasions was notable for large crowds and speeches on the importance of local civic endeavor. In 1883, there were weeklong celebrations of the silver jubilee of John Bright's first election as Birmingham M.P. There were a procession through five miles of streets, a mass meeting in Bingley Hall, a banquet at the Town Hall, and a civic address and reception. In March 1888, Chamberlain was made the first honorary freeman of the borough, and a year later, there was a public reception to welcome him and his new wife.[25]

As Chamberlain and Birmingham moved from Liberalism to Unionism, the royal family was also brought to the center of the civic stage. The jubilees of 1887 and 1897 were celebrated with loyal extravagance — thanksgiving services, public holidays, addresses, processions, illuminations, and fireworks — and the monarchy became directly involved in ceremonials of civic aggrandizement. From 1858 to 1885, there were no official royal civic visits, but from the mid 1880s on, there was a sudden upsurge. The queen appeared in her Golden Jubilee year to lay the foundation stone of the Law Courts that would bear her name; the prince of Wales visited in 1885 and 1891 to open the Art Galley and the Victoria Law Courts; and the duke and duchess of York laid the foundation stone of the General Hospital.[26] And this new but increasingly close connection between royal visits and civic aggrandizement was recognized in more permanent ways. Council House Square, hitherto a monument to liberalism and nonconformity, was completely transformed. In 1901, a statue of the queen empress was unveiled, and the place was renamed Victoria Square. In 1913, Priestley and Wright were moved to Chamberlain Square, and a statue of Edward VII was unveiled by Princess Louise. Radical and civic Birmingham had been superseded by royal and imperial Birmingham.[27]

Interleaved with these royal occasions were later ceremonials connected with Chamberlain himself—now no longer a politician on the defensive but an international statesman. On his farewell to Birmingham in November 1902, prior to his visit to South Africa, there was a lengthy civic dinner, a horse-drawn procession along a route illuminated by 4,000 torchbearers from the city center to Canon Hill Park, and a great fireworks display, ending in a fire portrait of Chamberlain and his wife. It was this elaborate extravaganza that established Chamberlain's position as "analogous to that of Mr Bright a generation ago," and for decades afterward, it was remembered as "the greatest display of affection ever shown to a politician" in his own city.[28] But even this was surpassed by the celebrations of July 1906 to mark Chamberlain's seventieth birthday and thirtieth anniversary as Birmingham's M.P., which were modeled on the John Bright jubilee of more than twenty years before. There was a civic lunch in the Council House, at which Chamberlain delivered his last panegyric on public service in municipal life. There was an eighty-car procession through seventeen miles of decorated streets. There was a speech in Bingley Hall where Chamberlain reviewed his political life. And there was another torchlight procession, followed by fireworks. This was the most elaborate and inclusive ceremonial ever to have taken place in the city, and half the population of Birmingham had turned out for it.[29]

There were also the occasions marking Birmingham's evolution as a city. On 24 July 1904, the Corporation and guests were taken by train to Rhayader in North Wales to witness the official opening of the Elan Valley Water Supply Scheme by King Edward VII, who knighted the mayor, Alderman Hallewell Rogers. Less than a year later, Charles Gore was enthroned as Birmingham's first bishop before a large congregation in St. Philip's Cathedral. Although this was a religious occasion, Gore's sermon was a Chamberlainite "eulogy of the civic spirit." "Very much," he observed, "of what is best, noblest, most beautiful, most intellectual in the world's history . . . is bound up with the intense life of cities, with men's love for their city."[30] Finally, on 7 July 1909, there was the opening of the new university buildings by King Edward VII and Queen Alexandra: the first time a reigning king had ever set foot in the city. There were seven miles of street decorations and six triumphal arches; there was a civic luncheon, at which the king declared that Birmingham was "the home of the best traditions in municipal life"; the absent and ailing chancellor sent a message; and there were fireworks, illuminations, and medals.[31]

In Joseph Chamberlain's Birmingham, these buildings and these ceremonies were more important than has generally been recognized. They involved Birmingham people in all sorts of ways, creating a powerful sense of excitement, identity, tradition, and inclusion that partly depended on broader national developments but also had local ingredients that were peculiarly its own. They projected an image of the managing oligarchy, at once confident and benevolent, powerful and socially responsible, politically partisan yet community-minded, which was not without its critics and its opponents but seems to have enjoyed an increasingly broad base of support. As the *Birmingham Daily Post* put it on Chamberlain's return from South Africa, it was his "forceful but *non partisan* personality which is so well known in Birmingham."[32] It was not so well known elsewhere. In the aftermath of the Home

Rule split, Chamberlain was the most hated man in British politics. Gladstone thought him "the greatest blackguard I have ever come across," and two decades later, Tories hostile to tariff reform took the same view. "The Chamberlain tradition is that you must give no quarter in politics and that the spoils are to the victors," John Strachey declared.[33]

In Birmingham, "the Chamberlain tradition" generally meant something very different, but however regarded, it was much attenuated after 1906. In the aftermath of his seventieth birthday celebrations, Joseph suffered a stroke, and thereafter he played no public part in municipal or national life. Since 1892, he had been joined in the Commons by his eldest son. But Austen sat for East Worcestershire, which was not Birmingham, and he was fully taken up with events in London. Moreover, in the city itself, Unionist zeal and organization flagged. "I fear," Neville Chamberlain wrote to Bonar Law in 1913, "that one day there will be a very unpleasant awakening to realities." In local government, by contrast, "the Chamberlain tradition" continued into the next generation. Joseph's nephew Norman became a councillor, and in 1911 he wrote an article acclaiming Birmingham as a "city state" still characterized by strong "civic feeling," religious commitment to the public good, and "easy co-operation of classes in matters of common interest."[34] In that year, Norman was joined by his cousin Neville, who was active in business and philanthropy in the city. "I am," he noted on his election, "only following out the traditions in which I have been brought up, and which it is my earnest desire to maintain." Neville became lord mayor in 1915, bringing "a new atmosphere of initiative and energy" into local affairs, especially as regards town planning, the city orchestra, and the municipal bank. And when he was re-elected mayor in 1916, William Cadbury observed that "the municipal career of Joseph Chamberlain would always remain an inspiration to the people of Birmingham. His son had worthily carried on that tradition."[35]

But this is to anticipate, for in July 1914, Joseph Chamberlain died in London. His family refused a burial in Westminster Abbey, and his body was brought back to Birmingham, where he was buried in Key Hill Cemetery, alongside his relatives and other makers of modern Birmingham: Kenricks and Martineaus, Dawson and Dale. Thousands of his fellow citizens lined the streets to see his final journey, and the local press mourned him as "Birmingham's greatest son" no less than as a world statesman. Even *The Times* admitted that during his mayoralty, the city "rose to a level of dignity and autonomous power surpassed by no other civic community in the world."[36] But all that now seemed in the past. Chamberlain's widow remarried in 1916, left the city, and settled in London. Austen inherited Highbury, but insufficient money to keep it up. He sold the orchids and the contents, disposed of the adjoining lands, and eventually gave the house to the corporation. From 1915 to 1918, it was used as a military hospital, and thereafter, it was a home for disabled ex-servicemen and aged women. Another planned commemoration was a large-scale biography of Joseph Chamberlain to be completed by J. L. Garvin "in two years." But nothing came of it for a decade. "Damn Garvin!" Austen raged in 1931, "Why can't he get on?" [37]

II

Nevertheless, Chamberlain's memory and "the Chamberlain tradition" lived on in his city for another generation, kept alive by his two sons. On his father's death, Austen moved to his constituency of West Birmingham, and in 1914 and 1918, he was returned unopposed. His 1922 election posters bore two portraits, of himself and of his father, with the slogan: "You voted for Joe. Vote for Austen." So they did. "I have," Austen told his sister Ida, "not only inherited but made personal to myself much of the old Chamberlain feeling." In 1926, he was made a Freeman, and spoke with pride of his native city: "I was born in Birmingham, I was bred in Birmingham, Birmingham is in my blood and in my bones; and wherever I go and whatever I am, I shall remain a Birmingham man." [38] Meanwhile, his half brother Neville had been elected M.P. for the Ladywood division in 1918, as "the second son of Birmingham's greatest citizen." Although he spent much of the 1920s in office, he remained actively involved in civic affairs. As minister of health, he nudged the corporation toward an innovative project for a new hospital center, next to the university, combining treatment and teaching. In 1925, he attended the unveiling of a bust of his father to celebrate the municipal jubilee of the gas department. He spoke, "both as a citizen and a son," of the importance of civic endeavor, and concluded that "the relations between the city and the various members of my family are unique." [39]

Both Austen and Neville continued to represent Birmingham until their deaths, carrying on "the Chamberlain tradition" at the parliamentary level. But they did not enjoy the local rapport that their father had done. "There was not really much of Birmingham about [Austen]," Harold Macmillan recalled; "sometimes he almost seemed a *grand seigneur*." He had never been in business or in local government in the city, spent his time in Sussex or London, and preferred the Commons or international diplomacy. Stiff and aloof, he was notoriously inattentive to his constituency as an M.P., and in the 1929 election, he scraped in by only forty-three votes. [40] Despite his stronger local roots and greater attentiveness, Neville was little better. His "manner freezes people," Austen wrote in 1925, in words equally applicable to himself. "His workers think he does not appreciate what they do for him. Everybody respects him and he makes no friends." For all his conscientiousness, Neville was ill at ease in Ladywood, the most working-class constituency in the city. His majority fell at the elections of 1922 and 1923, and in 1924, Oswald Mosley came within seventy-seven votes of capturing the seat. In 1929, which was just in time, Neville removed himself to safe, solid, suburban Edgbaston.[41]

It was developments such as these that caused Lord Beaverbrook to opine that "in Birmingham itself, the Chamberlain dominion is worn out." This was an exaggeration, but there was some truth in it. For it was not just that Austen and Neville failed to catch the imagination of Birmingham's citizens in the way their father had done: it was also that the clan itself was much depleted in these years. Joseph's brothers were all dead; two members of the next generation, John Chamberlain and Norman Chamberlain, were killed on active service during the war; and another cousin, Arthur Jr., retired from business in Birmingham to become a Devon country gentleman. Of Joseph's three surviving daughters, Hilda and Ida (who were Neville's sisters) moved away to Hampshire when Highbury was closed as the family home, and Beatrice (Austen's sister) died in the influenza epidemic of 1918. This was a serious diminution of Birmingham-based talent and energy, and Norman's death was a particularly severe blow. Had he lived, he would almost certainly have been an interwar lord mayor, and he would probably have joined Austen and Neville in national politics. But his death meant there was no Chamberlain left to carry on the family tradition in local government during the interwar years.[42]

At the same time, the city itself was becoming a different place. The enlargement of Birmingham's boundaries significantly altered its character: it was diminishingly a "great village" with a strong sense of community and increasingly a great metropolis, with more segregated housing and a much expanded administration. Its constituency politics changed, too: in the aftermath of the Fourth Reform Act, the number of Birmingham M.P.s was increased from seven to twelve, and more seats to contest meant a larger organization to fund and facilitate the fighting. Birmingham's economy was also evolving as small workshops were gradually replaced by larger factories and new industries such as electrical engineering, aluminum, and car manufacturing, often owned by companies that were nationally rather than locally based. One result was that conditions of work improved, and the city

missed the worst unemployment of the interwar depression.[43] Another was
the growth in the strength and success of the Labour Party. During and after
World War I, its organization was much strengthened, and in the elections
of 1924 and 1929, Labour scored its first victories, breaching the hitherto im-
pregnable bastion of Chamberlainite Unionism. In 1924, Labour captured its
first seat, and in 1929, it won six of the twelve Birmingham constituencies, its
best results in the country.[44]

Taken together, these developments in the Chamberlain clan and in the
city of Birmingham significantly altered the tone and the tempo of municipal life, which became less operatic and more prosaic. The brief flowering
of the creative arts in the service of the civic gospel during the late nineteenth century spawned no interwar successor, the Venetian idiom of a
latter-day city-state vanished from public speech and public buildings, and
the civic spectaculars built around the Chamberlain family virtually disappeared.[45] Most local effort after 1918 was centered on the monuments and rituals associated with Remembrance Day, and also on royal visits, which were
themselves often associated with the city's attempts to commemorate World
War I. The financing and construction of Birmingham's war memorial was
very protracted, with debates over what it ought to be, where it ought to be,
how much it should cost, and how it should be paid for. Eventually, the foundation stone of the Hall of Memory was laid by the prince of Wales in 1923,
and it was opened by Prince Arthur of Connaught two years later. But while
such occasions brought the citizenry together, there was nothing specially
Chamberlainite about them, and nothing about them that was unique to
Birmingham.[46]

Such municipal effort as there was during the 1920s centered on planning
a new civic center, complete with City Hall, Mansion House, Municipal
Offices, a Natural History Museum, and a Public Library, with the Hall of
Memory as the focal point. As Birmingham grew, there was a need for more
office space for local government, and also for a public space larger than
Chamberlain Square and Victoria Square. The purchase of land, along
Broad Street and to the northwest of the old city center, was begun in 1922.[47]
A competition was announced in October 1926, and the winning entry was
by Maximilian Romanoff of Paris, whose extravagant plan took little heed of
existing buildings and thoroughfares. He had "no personal knowledge of
Birmingham, and no sort of personal regard for its traditions, its general character or its resources," and his scheme was "a clean break with the past" — a
piece of grandiose monumentality that had more in common with Hitler's

Berlin, Mussolini's Rome, or FDR's Washington than with the Birmingham of Joseph and John Henry Chamberlain. In the end, the scheme was declared to be too expensive, and it was never implemented.[48]

For all the continuation by Austen and Neville of the "Chamberlain tradition," it is clear the 1920s represented a falling away from the intensity and involvement of the prewar era. But there was a revival during the 1930s. The Labour challenge was much weakened—partly because of the failure of the 1929 administration, and also because of the Labour Party split following the formation of the National Government. In the general elections of 1931 and 1935, the Birmingham Unionists swept the board, recapturing the seats they had lost in 1929, and both Austen and Neville were safely returned—Austen with an increased majority in Birmingham West, and Neville more comfortably in Edgbaston than he had ever been in Ladywood.[49] When campaigning in 1935, Austen met people who had borne torches in the processions in 1903 and cherished his father's memory. As a visiting journalist explained: "Joe Chamberlain's spirit is not dead. Indeed, it is still a potent political force. . . . Labour canvassers are still told, 'My father voted for Joe Chamberlain and what was good enough for him is good enough for me.' It is as if Joe were still alive."[50]

At the same time, the individual reputations of the Chamberlains also revived, beginning with Joseph's. Between 1932 and 1934, Garvin produced the first three volumes of his much-delayed official life, covering its most successful period up to 1900. He told the story of the Birmingham mayoralty and the civic renaissance, the struggle with Gladstone over Home Rule, and the early years at the Colonial Office, culminating in the Boer War.[51] Then, in 1936, came an unprecedented opportunity for civic homage: the centenary of Joseph Chamberlain's birth. In London, there was a rally at the Albert Hall, which dwelt on the continuing relevance of his imperial vision. But in Birmingham, the celebrations were more domestic. There was a special meeting of the City Council in the Town Hall; the vice-chancellor of the university delivered an oration; the council passed a resolution recording its appreciation of Chamberlain's "distinguished and valuable services" to the city; Neville replied that his father had set local government "on a new pedestal of dignity and honour"; wreaths were laid on the Chamberlain Memorial and on his grave; and there was a civic reception for those who had "grown up under his shadow."[52]

During the same decade, Austen's standing also improved somewhat. After 1929, he was out of office and spent more time in his constituency. From sheer financial necessity, he also turned to writing. His first effort, *Down*

The Years, consisted of "random recollections of men and events," and it was rightly remarked that his father was "present in every line of the book." The second, *Politics from Inside,* was even more filial in content, consisting of the letters Austen had written to his stepmother to keep his father informed during his period of incapacity from 1906 to 1914. Both books tied him more closely to Joe — and thus to Birmingham — than ever before.[53] Within a year, however, Austen was dead. "National figure as he was," opined the *Post,* "he never ceased to be a man of Birmingham." This was pious exaggeration: as evidenced by the fact that Austen's remains were buried in London rather than beside his father in his home city. But the lord mayor acclaimed him for "the way in which, through the whole of his life, he identified himself with his native city," and at the memorial service in the cathedral, he was eulogized as "a Birmingham man, carrying on the great Birmingham tradition."[54]

But while Austen was dead, his younger brother was "still with us and carrying on the great Birmingham and Chamberlain tradition." On the formation of the National Government, Neville had become chancellor of the exchequer, and in 1932, he introduced a scheme of protection that he described as the fulfillment of the tariff reform program that his father had conceived but failed to carry through, and that he laid before the Commons "in the presence of one and by the lips of the other of the two immediate successors to his name and blood." "How proud father would have been of Neville," Austen wrote, "and how it would have moved him that Neville should complete his work."[55] As a result, Neville was given the freedom of Birmingham, following his father and his brother, and in May 1937, scarcely ten weeks after Austen's death, he became prime minister. Soon afterward, he was given a civic banquet, and in his speech, he recalled the great reception given to his father on his seventieth birthday, spoke of his work on Birmingham city council, and reiterated his pride in the fact that "I was born and bred in Birmingham." "It reminded me of the old days," he noted, "when the people used to run after Father's carriage."[56]

By agreeable coincidence, this meant that Neville Chamberlain was prime minister when Birmingham marked the centenary of its incorporation in 1938. Although no one could have known it, these celebrations were the last local hurrah of "the Chamberlain tradition," politically, architecturally, and ceremonially. In 1935, a second competition for a civic center had been won by Cecil Howitt of Nottingham with a design of orthodox, neo-Georgian monumentality, "reminiscent of the Cunard offices in New York." The foundation stone was laid in the centenary year, and the lord mayor described it as the most important occasion "since Joseph Chamberlain laid the stone of the present Council House." [57] The year 1938 also witnessed the completion of the new Birmingham Hospital Centre in Edgbaston: located in Neville Chamberlain's constituency, and completed in considerable part thanks to his efforts. The foundation stone had been laid by the prince of Wales in 1934, and the buildings were opened by the royal visitors in incorporation year. They were described as "a synthesis of the accumulated civic consciousness of a hundred years, handed over with both hands by the Birmingham of today to the Birmingham of tomorrow." But as with the Civic Centre, there was nothing in their style or ornamentation that embodied or articulated this view. [58]

The visit of the king and queen to open the new Birmingham Hospital Centre was the climax of the centenary celebrations themselves. These were staged on a scale that surpassed the royal jubilees of 1887 and 1897, and even those of John Bright and Joseph Chamberlain. Once again, there were street decorations, floodlighting, and fireworks. But there were also broadcasts, souvenir programs, and a newly commissioned history of the city, in all of which pride of place went to Joseph Chamberlain. [59] The main event was a pageant of Birmingham organized by Gwen Lally, who had stage-managed previous spectaculars at Tewkesbury, Coventry, and Warwick. Planned and rehearsed over a period of three months, and involving six thousand performers drawn from all parts of the city, it told the story of Birmingham from the dinosaur to modern times. On 14 July, Neville Chamberlain accompanied the royal visitors to a special performance, and watched the panorama of the city's history unfold in a succession of tableaux, the last one devoted to the greatest figures from Birmingham's past, in which special homage was paid to his own father. That evening, at the centenary civic banquet, Neville proposed the health of the City of Birmingham. [60]

Thereafter, the prime minister's reputation, and that of "the Chamberlain tradition," were inexorably tied to national and international events unfolding in places far away from Birmingham. When Neville returned from Munich later in 1938, bearing "peace with honour," the local press celebrated its "own son's triumph in the role of peacemaker," and there were rumors that, like Austen, Neville would be awarded the Nobel Peace Prize. The lord mayor sent a telegram, "Birmingham is especially proud today," and opened a Thanksgiving Fund in appreciation of the prime minister's efforts. [61] Commemorative souvenirs were issued, including a plate depicting the three Chamberlains as "Britain's most famous political family," inscribed "in appreciation of Mr Neville Chamberlain securing peace for Europe during the crisis of September 1938." And the whole dynasty was memorialized by

Sir Charles Petrie in a book entitled *The Chamberlain Tradition*, which showed "what Great Britain and the British Empire owe to the Chamberlain family" and drew "attention to those qualities which the father and two sons possessed in common": "courage and optimism, foresight and vigour."[62]

But during the next eighteen months, Neville Chamberlain lost his reputation and his job, and there was growing opposition to his foreign policy, even among some local Unionists. Eventually, it was his fellow Birmingham M.P., Leopold Amery, who was a great admirer of Joseph Chamberlain's, and whose son Julian eventually completed Garvin's biography, who quoted the terrible words of Oliver Cromwell[63] in the parliamentary debate that brought Neville down in May 1940. Birmingham's support continued strong to the end, however. In January 1939, addressing the Jewellers' Association, Neville described its "demonstration of loyalty and affection" as "only a continuation of the favours you have always accorded to members of my family."[64] In March, on the eve of his seventieth birthday, he made what turned out to be his last speech in the Town Hall, and throughout the defeats and disappointments of his final months, the *Birmingham Post* remained loyal. On his death in November 1940, the lord mayor paid tribute to one of the city's "most distinguished sons," and at the memorial service, Bishop Barnes eulogized him as "Birmingham's most renowned citizen." But like his brother, and unlike his father, Neville did not return to his home city: instead, he was buried in Westminster Abbey.[65]

III

One of the most remarkable aspects of "the Chamberlain tradition" is the abruptness and completeness with which it disappeared. For the death of Neville Chamberlain was "the end of an era, the end of eight decades in which the Chamberlains and their friends had guided Birmingham through an age of unprecedented growth, prosperity, and good government."[66] Why was this? There can be no doubt that the whole clan suffered by association from the lasting damage done to Neville's reputation by the events of 1939 and 1940, and this may help explain why, at the personal level, the Chamberlain line simply gave out. Neither Austen's son, Lawrence, nor Neville's son, Frank, showed any inclination to carry on the family tradition in local or national politics. As a result, the general election of 1945 was the first since 1874 when there was no Chamberlain to solicit the votes of Birmingham's electorate. But that election was a turning point in other ways too: during the war, there was growing enthusiasm for the Labour Party, and its organization had strengthened, while the Unionists had stagnated. There was a 23 percent swing to Labour in Birmingham, higher than in any other city in Britain, and Labour won ten of the thirteen seats. Although the Tories were later to win back some constituencies, 1945 meant the end of the old-style, locally based Unionism of the Chamberlain era.[67]

Here was the "unpleasant awakening to realities" that Neville Chamberlain had feared over thirty years before.[68] It was the same in local government. The surviving members of the extended Chamberlain clan played their part in Birmingham's social and philanthropic life for another generation; but in the Council House, their dominion passed away, as municipal politics became increasingly partisan confrontations between Labour and Tories that merely mimicked and reflected national trends. At the same time, the creation of a "new" Birmingham was a deliberate rejection of the Victorian and Venetian pretensions of John Henry Chamberlain and his ilk. Much of his city center, including parts of Chamberlain Square itself, was torn down and replaced by concrete blocks devoid of local articulation, "owing nothing to historical precedent," and lacking any civic meaning. Birmingham's buildings, like its politics, were becoming indistinct from those of any large metropolitan area, and so were its much-attenuated civic rituals. The centenary of Joseph Chamberlain's mayoralty was largely ignored, and the hundred and fiftieth anniversary of his birth was barely noticed.[69] "The Chamberlain tradition" has passed into history.

PART III

European Cultural Modernism

9. Building Historical and Cultural Identities in a Modernist Frame

Karl Friedrich Schinkel's Bauakademie in Context

In *Art and Act: On Causes in History—Manet, Gropius, Mondrian* (1976), Peter Gay briefly notes the inspirational and exemplary role that the work of the Prussian architect Karl Friedrich Schinkel (1781–1841) played in the formation and self-consciousness of the architectural modernism of Peter Behrens, Adolf Loos, Mies van der Rohe, Philip Johnson, and especially Walter Gropius and the Bauhaus School. Gay also suggests that the construction of Schinkel as a prophet of modernism by these modernists was based on selective historical memory. The Romantic historicism and accommodation to traditional royal authority that marked Schinkel, at least in part, as an antimodernist who feared and resisted the cultural consequences of market-oriented social relations and liberal democratic politics, was downplayed in order to highlight his achievements in the formation of an architecture suited to the needs of a modern industrial economy and technocratically managed mass society: the innovative adaptation of spatial relations and building materials to changing social functions and the austere sobriety of constructive design freed from historicist ornamentation.[1] Perhaps the wisdom of hindsight, chastened by the knowledge that National Socialist designers of monumental, *Gemeinschaft*-creating public spaces (like Paul Troost and Albert Speer) also revered Schinkel, produced Gay's hesitancy about enrolling Schinkel in the class of authentic modernists. Yet Gay's own definition of modernism would seem to incorporate Schinkel's ambivalence about economic, social, and political "modernization." The great modernists, Gay proposes in the same text, did not ignore the desires for self-transcending, socially integrating cultural meaning produced by the weakening of traditional social bonds in the process of modernization, but incorporated them into a complex, inclusive, undogmatic vision of a society founded on a rational management of outer and inner nature, a democratically shaped consensus regarding the formation of secular public meaning based on testable knowledge ("science"), and a lawfully articulated interdependence of individual freedom and social order.[2] Within this broad definition, perhaps Schinkel was a "modernist," not in spite of, but because of his concern for the creation of a public architecture and urban design that might rescue ethical community, public meaning, and collective memory from the corrosive powers of modernization. Schinkel's Bauakademie, constructed on the banks of the Kupfergraben in central Berlin between 1832 and 1836, is often portrayed as his most modern, original, least historicist, building. In this essay, I argue that it was also, in its very modernism, an experiment in the use of architecture to create historical identity and communal integration, to build and furnish a cultural "home" for the emancipated individual of a modern society. In order to illuminate the historical meaning of the Bauakademie, I shall set it in the context of two earlier architectural projects through which Schinkel hoped to mold modern emancipated subjects into the shape of an ethical community.

Schinkel as Romantic Historicist: The Cathedral of Liberation and the Gothic Shape of Germanic Community

In the decade following the defeat of Napoleon's forces in 1813, Schinkel experimented with both neo-Gothic and neoclassical styles in his attempt to imagine and construct appropriate spatial environments for the lives of nineteenth-century Germans recently set free, not only from the French, but from the traditional legal and social bonds of the ancien régime. The conviction that the profession of architecture was not just a trade but a cultural calling with the status of a fine art, and that its serious pursuit entailed a duty to participate in the general historical mission of transforming an aggregate of individual egos into a community of free agents, was passed on to Schinkel by his mentors and teachers, especially David and Friedrich Gilly. Following in the footsteps of the great eighteenth-century neoclassical humanists and philosophical idealists, Schinkel had begun his architectural career with the desire to create appropriate spatial contexts for an enlightened public order, to produce a built environment for free individuals who affirmed their freedom as self-legislators through stringent devotion to the universal laws defining their moral duties as citizens of an ethical community.[3] However, in the wake of the Napoleonic conquest and occupation of Prussia after the humiliating defeat of the Prussian forces at Jena in 1805, Schinkel was rapidly swept along by the Romantic enthusiasms that attached the ideal of the emancipated, self-determining subject to identification with a linguistically defined national community and its distinctive historical traditions. By the time of his initial appointment in the Prussian Civil Service, as aesthetic assessor in the State Building Administration in 1810, Schinkel had clearly come to identify the emancipation of the German people from foreign domination, the re-creation of the Prussian state as an ethical community of autonomous citizens through domestic social and legal reform, and the spatial representation of the reciprocal dependence of freedom and community with the forms of Gothic architecture, particularly with the monumental structures of the Gothic cathedral.[4]

In two of Schinkel's first submissions for state commissions, in 1810–11, he accompanied his proposed designs with programmatic manifestos proclaiming the distinctive Germanic character of the Gothic style.[5] As the spatial form for the historical expression of the essential identity of the Germanic peoples, Gothic was also the architectural language of national liberation, an assertion of German cultural autonomy against the neoclassicism of the "Latin" peoples. When Schinkel received a commission to design a memorial cathedral to commemorate the victories over Napoleon in 1813–14, it was almost inevitable that he would choose the "Old German," Gothic style, the imagined distinctive style of the "fatherland," to memorialize the awakening of German identity and to represent German freedom.[6]

Schinkel's neo-Gothic designs and the rhetoric that accompanied them were, however, characteristically shaped by his own commitment to the inner reform of Prussian society on the basis of liberal principles. The "freedom" that Schinkel imagined as embodied in a national cathedral was not just freedom from Napoleonic domination and French cultural hegemony but also the freedom of individuals to participate as autonomous subjects or "spiritual" beings in the making of their own world. The pointed-arch structure of the Gothic embodied for Schinkel the polar tensions and restless striving for self-transcendence that characterized the self as a spiritual agency in its constant struggle with the physical limitations of its finite embodiments in space and time. Using the modest, earthy materials of brick and stone to express the self-transcending qualities of the human spirit, Gothic cathedrals were the essential public representation of Germanic culture as an aesthetic work that transformed physical objects into meaningful signs and freed expressive content from merely functional requirements. Pointed-arch con-

struction was seen by Schinkel primarily as a symbolic form. As pure, func-
tionless artifice, it was the clearest expression of the inner structure of spiritual
reality, the idea of freedom constructed in space. The idea of freedom was immanent in the self-conscious manipulation of constructive techniques, like
vaulting, to represent an experience of restless striving toward a sublime point
that could never finally be attained. Self-transcending striving was the soul
of the Gothic organism, the life that coursed through its cosmos.

Schinkel, however, was intent on interpreting this constant movement of
transcendence, this teleology of freedom, as an inner, immanent principle.
The self-transcending movement of the Gothic was definitely not to be seen
as a desire to leave this world. In fact, Schinkel claimed that to look beyond
earthly existence for freedom and fulfillment was to "sin" against the vocation of mankind, to reject the claim of the Germans' cultural mission to make
freedom real within existence, to make actual the "Idea" of their culture in
every dimension of their terrestrial being.[7] Schinkel thus appropriated the
Gothic as an inspiration and external sign of his own chosen historical project of constructing a community of free spirits, not as the sign of a transcendent reality or the symbolic home of a church community that lived only in
hope of otherworldly salvation.

Schinkel presented the Gothic as a progressive, modern style, an affirmation of self-conscious human autonomy and voluntary, consciously willed,
secular community, as a construction of spatial relations that asserted its historical authority by building on and absorbing earlier historical accomplishments. The classical horizontal forms of "natural" affirmation were not simply denied in the soaring, self-transcending dynamics of the Gothic, but constituted the objective foundation of its daring experiments. Cultural creativity
and self-determination emerged from the solid foundation of a confident
affirmation of humanity's natural being. Thus Schinkel's imagined Gothic
structures were furnished with broad, exaggerated pedestals and tended toward pyramidal shapes (figs. 1 and 2). The Gothic method of constituting
unity — the proliferation of differences connected by a distinctive animating
style, or "inner" spirit, rather than an imposed hierarchical order based on
universal principles — mirrored the organic life forms of the natural world.[8]
The use of natural symbolism — from the starry heavens painted between the
branching, arboreal stone vaulting to the "flowers" on the tops of the spires
and gables — affirmed the structural continuity between the natural and the
cultural universes. For Schinkel, the Germanic cultural Idea had not attained
full historical realization in the Middle Ages because this totalizing, synthetic dimension of the Idea of freedom, which appropriated, transformed,

1. Sideview of Karl Friedrich Schinkel's planned Cathedral of Liberation, ca. 1814–15. Kupferstichkabinett-Sammlung der Zeichnungen und Druckgraphik-Staatliche Museen zu Berlin-Preussischer Kulturbesitz-SM23.1. Lost during World War II.

and absorbed its "other" as part of its own self-determination, had not been recognized.

Aside from his emphasis on the upward, liberating dynamics of pointed-arch vaulting and the horizontal grounding of a solidly based pyramidal structure, Schinkel's plan for a modern Gothic cathedral was marked by the prominence given to the domed altar space (fig. 3). An octagonal choir was conceived as a rotunda in which individual subjects could, without the mediation of a priestly class, experience their common participation in the principle of self-transcending freedom that animated their being and motivated their constant self-sacrifice for the interests of the community. For Schinkel in 1814, the place of community identification was a space of individual inwardness. The recognition of identity with others was not forged in the public spaces of daily business, where self-interested egos exchanged with others, but produced through the mediation of a common principle shared by all, through inner participation in the divine "Idea" of the national community. Although the "people" were "gathered" together in the place of mutual identification, "the solemnity [Würdigkeit] of the space disposed everyone to fulfill themselves quietly within themselves."[9] The inward, individual nature of Schinkel's image of cultural identification was articulated in the

2. Frontal perspective of Karl Friedrich Schinkel's planned Cathedral of Liberation, ca. 1814–15. Kupferstichkabinett-Sammlung der Zeichnungen und Druckgraphik Staatliche Museen zu Berlin-Preussischer Kulturbesitz-SM20a.247.

3. Transverse section of the domed altar space or rotunda of Karl Friedrich Schinkel's planned Cathedral of Liberation, ca. 1814–15. Kupferstichkabinett-Sammlung der Zeichnungen und Druckgraphik-Staatliche Museen zu Berlin-Preussischer Kulturbesitz-SM20a.249.

siting of his imagined Gothic cathedrals outside of city centers, elevated above everyday work and social exchange, as monuments of self-recognition and reverence for the sacred identity of the community. The projected Cathedral of Liberation (Befreiungsdom) was sited at the Potsdamer Tor and Leipziger Platz, which at that time placed it on the border between city and country. As a sanctuary and pilgrimage site where individuals would find their identity with one another through an inner identification with the shared cultural Idea that was their common essence, the sacred place of historical commemoration and communal identification was a place set apart for participation in integrating symbolic rituals and separated from the utilitarian and functional activities through which individual egos pursued their particular interests.

The individual's experience of identification with the essential, divine Idea of the cultural community was the foundation for the insertion of individual memory into public memory, for the reading of individual life histories within the framing script of a collective narrative of the people. In the still incomplete, or not fully realized, Gothic monuments of the Middle Ages, this insertion was portrayed as the elevation of the individual soul into the cosmic story of human redemption as recounted in biblical myth and the history of the Church. In the modern era of civic emancipation and national identification, however, this narrative merged with the secular narrative of national development and bound sacred history to the historical struggle of the people to display the fullness of their essential Idea in space and time. In Schinkel's projected cathedral, the very structure of the building signified a historical dialectic in which preclassical and classical forms were transformed into components of the universal Christian-Germanic Idea. Some early sketches made this historical layering of structural space even more explicit, displaying pyramidal structures in which Egyptian bases and Greek temple porticoes were topped with Gothic spires. More specifically, the decorative sculpture of Schinkel's Cathedral of Liberation inserted the present moment into three interlocking and symbolically overlapping narratives: first, the sacred biblical meta-narrative, reaching from Lucifer's defeat by the Archangel Michael to the triumphant rulership of Christ over the earthly globe; second, the emergence of the Germanic cultural nation from tribal solidarity in war against the Romans to self-recognition as an ethnic/linguistic community during the recent wars of national liberation from the French invader; and finally the peculiarly Prussian narrative of the construction of a civic community from a primitive state of externally imposed rational order by heroic soldier kings to the recent emergence of a constitutionally articulated community of self-conscious, self-legislating citizens.

During the period of his participation in the Prussian reform movement and the mobilization of popular forces against the French, Schinkel imagined his architectural vocation in terms of the mobilization and integration of a vaguely defined German cultural nation — the "people" — through spatially defined symbolic processes of self-assertion and self-recognition. The historical moment of Prussian domestic reform and the Wars of Liberation was seen as an epochal historical turning point from a past of paternalistic tutelage and externally enforced order to a future in which the collective national agency of the "people" would become the self-conscious subject of its own history. The complex entanglement of sacred and secular historical narrative that Schinkel hoped to display in and on his memorial cathedral clearly highlighted the entry of the people into its historical majority as it responded enthusiastically to the call to be free, a call both for civil emancipation and political rights and for self-sacrifice in armed resistance against the foreign oppressor. For Schinkel, this process of national self-determination was a clearly articulated but still unfinished project. He planned his cathedral with empty niches for future heroes of national development and as a long-term building project in which the ongoing work of construction would continue to reaffirm the historical mission whose beginnings and claims on the future the building commemorated. The work on the Cathedral of Liberation would symbolize the general task of building a world that would complete the national narrative of awakening, self-sacrifice, victory over the external enemy, and creation of an organically integrated and fully self-determining ethical community.

It was not the ethnically and culturally exclusive vision of Germany as a single unified community (imagined as the idealized Protestant Prussia of the patriotic reformers of 1806–14) but the populist and inclusive elements in Schinkel's conception that aroused the resistance of privileged social groups and traditional political authorities after 1815. The Cathedral of Liberation was never built. It was displaced by a much more modest memorial: a single cast-iron Gothic spire constructed outside of Berlin, on the Kreuzberg, in the early 1820s. In the niches around the spire the battles of the struggle for liberation were represented by individual figures modeled primarily on members of the Prussian Hohenzollern dynasty, wearing the costumes of Greek and old German warriors. The spirit or "Idea" of the people was embodied in traditional authority.

The Carlsbad Decrees of 1819 effectively put an end to the political significance of the populist nationalist movement in public life throughout Germany. Its leaders were jailed or exiled, its sympathizers among academic and bureaucratic reformers were silenced and stripped of significant power, and its cultural proponents in the fine arts were restricted to indirect modes of speech. The Kreuzberg Memorial was, in one of its dimensions at least, a representation of this historical moment of repression and compromise, disillusionment and resignation.

After 1815, Schinkel's projects display a radical shift away from the populist myth of a national folk essence that merely needed to be "awakened" or " liberated" in order for contemporary Germans to appropriate their past and assert control over their future. By 1816, the Gothic had become for Schinkel an object of historical preservation rather than an incomplete cultural form in which the present could and should work out its own cultural goals. The

historical/structural relation between Gothic vertical self-transcending freedom and Greek horizontal stability and natural affirmation was inverted. Beginning with ambitious new plans for the redesign of the center of Berlin in
1816–17, Schinkel evolved a historical vision in which the Gothic religious
building as the sacred symbolic center of a unified national culture was displaced to a subordinate position in a more broadly conceived conception of
the progressive development of the classical tradition and the humanist educational model for constructing civic identities. With this shift there also
emerged a more chastened conception of freedom. Community construction and the liberation of the self as subjective agent did not simply drop out
of Schinkel's work after 1815, but his sense of historical mission took a turn in
which the Gothic style appeared increasingly as an object of nostalgic historical distortion and dangerous misrecognition when applied uncritically to
the present, rather than as an appropriate frame for ethical commitment and
self-recognition.

The Temple of Aesthetic Education: The Tutelary
State and the Discipline of Civic Culture

In early 1823, Schinkel submitted a plan for the construction of a public
museum to house the Prussian royal art collections on the open, northern
side of the pleasure garden (Lustgarten) that marked the end of the boulevard
Unter den Linden leading into the city center from the Brandenburg Gate.
The Lustgarten was bordered on its three closed sides by important symbolic
architectural representations of the traditional Prussian state—the Military
Arsenal (Zeughaus) and the Hohenzollerns' City Palace (Stadtschloss), two
imposing baroque monuments by Andreas Schlueter, and the modest, undis-
tinguished eighteenth-century Royal Cathedral. Schinkel's plan received almost immediate royal approval, construction began in the summer of 1823,
and the building, which eventually came to be known as the Altes Museum,
was dedicated and opened to the public in the summer of 1830. The design
and construction of the Altes Museum marked the culmination of an intense, concentrated period of urban redesign and building, during which
Schinkel transformed the representational center of the Prussian capital in
ways that are still discernible. The most obvious common visual trait of the
structures that marked this transformation—the New Royal Guardhouse
(Neue Wache), the Palace Bridge (Schlossbrücke), the new façade and re-
modeled interior of the Royal Cathedral, the Altes Museum, and the Royal
Theater on the Gendarmenmarkt—was their austere, monumental neoclas-

sical style. At the moment (1816) when Schinkel was finally given the power to actualize his designs in constructed buildings, he shifted his aesthetic commitments in a strikingly radical fashion from the Old German, neo-Gothic forms of Romantic historicism to the neoclassical Greek style favored by the German humanist tradition of the late eighteenth century. Although Schinkel only provided oblique and partial reasons for this "turn" in histori-cal perspective in his public pronouncements, the notes and commentaries of the drafts of his never completed or published *Architektonisches Lehrbuch* (Architectural Textbook) from this period provide evidence of a significant change in his perceptions of civic identity, individual freedom, and the cul-tural function of architecture and art.

First, Schinkel displayed increasing ambivalence about the idea of au-tonomy as the organizing telos of European cultural development. His cri-tique of freedom as infinite self-determination had psychological, social, and aesthetic dimensions. He now insisted that the legitimate human search for identification with the universal or the totality, the quest to be at home in the world, was, or should be, primarily directed toward the stability of perma-nent order in the constantly shifting world of historical appearances. "Not everything must change and go under," he warned, "the human being desires to possess something that is permanent." [10] The loss of the feeling of being grounded in something solid and permanent was not necessarily or primar-ily a "liberation"; it might very well be experienced as a disastrous dissolution of traditional social and ethical bonds, as the triumph of anxiety-prone, rest-less, self-centered activity by isolated individual egos in a civil society regu-lated only by the vagaries of the market. Insofar as restless, open-ended striv-ing was the informing meaning of the Gothic style, this architecture repro-duced and reinforced feelings of anxiety and homelessness. The problems of instability that Schinkel had in his earlier writings discerned in Gothic struc-tures not firmly grounded in "classical" pedestals were now, after 1816, at-tributed to Gothic forms more generally. The freedom embodied in the Old German style was an illusion, and perhaps even a delusional denial of the earthly limitations of finite human existence. The subjective aestheticism of the Gothic suddenly seemed like a dangerous disavowal of the reality of the object. In merging decorative, symbolic, and structural elements, Gothic po-etry in stone hid its own constructive and material conditions under a layer of deceptive artifice. The unreconciled tensions of the pointed arch trans-lated the psychology of restless homelessness into the medium of material objects, producing the vision of a world verging on cosmic chaos.

Against the dangers of neo-Gothic enthusiasms, Schinkel now proposed a

return to the classical humanist ideals of stability and serenity, and of reconciliation with, and resignation to, the object. *Kunstruhe* (aesthetic peace or
serenity) was asserted as the most fundamental of aesthetic values.[11] In architecture, such *Kunstruhe* expressed itself in two primary ways. First, relations between spaces and materials in a structure should follow principles
that articulated horizontal rest and vertical stability. Elements should connect in ways that affirmed the laws of gravity, pressing down at right angles,
distributing weight equally. The dynamic tensions of such relations should
always be subordinated to the general principle of obviously recognized and
experienced stability. Second, Schinkel noted that the stability of *Kunstruhe*
was dependent on hierarchical relations. The Gothic vision of an organic order produced by the flow of a unifying life energy through all components of
a "characteristic" or "individual" unity was rejected in favor of the subordination of individual parts to their limited functions as elements in the general
structure. The tension among equally valued parts was always destructive; the
creation of an authentic ethical consciousness from the experience of spatial
and tectonic relations required structural resolution and reconciliation.[12]

Such rather dogmatic expressions of architecture's cultural and ethical
function were matched by an emphasis on the honest presentation of material and constructive techniques. Transparency in the external display of internal structural principles and building materials was set against the subjective illusions of Gothic artifice. The value of resignation to the limitations
of subjective freedom was expressed by Schinkel in terms of the natural
earthly conditions of human culture, exemplified in antique construction,
not, as in the work of many of his contemporaries, in a renewed assertion of
the reality of a transcendent personal will controlling human affairs. A move,
not to the revealed truths of faith, but to the natural, material limitations of
creativity and production marked Schinkel's "conservative" turn in the decade after 1815. Not neopietist religion but the Goethe cult was Schinkel's refuge from the disappointments of populist Romantic nationalism. Building
churches remained an important dimension of Schinkel's assigned work as a
Prussian civil servant, but as he redefined his own conceptions of the architectural representation of the organizing center of public memory and cultural identification, Schinkel shifted his attention from the Cathedral of Liberation, the building of cultural "awakening" and self-recognition, to the
Temple of Aesthetic Education. The design of the Altes Museum expressed
a general reorientation toward the importance of public sites (the designs for
a new Music Academy and especially of a new Royal Theater were developed
at about the same time) in which the emancipated individual of the new civil

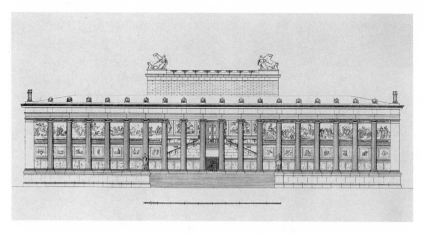

4. Engraving of the Main Façade of the Altes Museum. Karl Friedrich Schinkel, *Collection of Architectural Designs* (New York: Princeton Architectural Press, 1989), facsimile edition of *Sammlung Architektonischer Entwürfe* (1866), engraving #39.

society experienced the ethical power of aesthetic experience. It was in the new temples of art that the isolated ego was to be transformed into an integrated member of an ethical community.

For purposes of comparison with the unbuilt *Befreiungsdom*, the Altes Museum can be divided into three characteristic spaces — the façade, with its colonnade and external staircase, the rotunda, and the galleries. The museum façade contrasts dramatically (in almost a caricatured opposition) with the soaring pyramid of gables, baldachins, and spires of the 1814 cathedral. An open porch, divided into twenty segments by eighteen free-standing Ionic columns, functions as a covered public walkway, punctuated by busts and statues, between the interior of the building and the Lustgarten. Raised on a prominent pedestal, it is entered via a broad stairway, spanning one third of the façade. The horizontal lines of the wide rectangular façade are emphasized by the Prussian eagles above the cornice, which mark off the rhythmic pattern of evenly spaced columns. The flattened rectangular shape of the building is repeated in the boxlike structure above the cornice that hides the curves of the interior rotunda (fig. 4).

Besides its exaggerated horizontal emphasis and insistent rectangularity, the exterior of the museum has one further striking trait: the interior wall of the porch in the center of the façade is pushed back to provide space for an exterior (open to the air, but under the roof of the building) stairway leading from the ground floor to a second-floor balcony from which the visitor can

5. Upper balcony of the main staircase of the Altes Museum with a view through the colonnade into the Lustgarten. Karl Friedrich Schinkel, *Collection of Architectural Designs* (New York: Princeton Architectural Press, 1989), facsimile edition of *Sammlung Architektonischer Entwürfe* (1866), engraving #43.

enter the second-floor galleries or the rotunda balcony or stop to view the Lustgarten through the columns. The staircase articulates the duality of the porch as a boundary area and walkway linking the public activity of the city and the interior space of the Temple of Art, and provides a perspective on the contemporary world framed by classical architectural orders (fig. 5). It also provides a guide for the way in which Schinkel imagined a visit to the museum, separating the two gallery levels in terms of a movement outside into the urban present before reentry into the world of historical art objects.

The second distinctive element of the Altes Museum is the rotunda that dominates its interior space (figs. 6 and 7). Because the main staircase is outside, the entry into the building coincides with a direct entry into the rotunda, a space that Schinkel conceived of, in analogy to the domed altar space of the cathedral, as the sanctuary in which the individual would be drawn into an aesthetic experience that offered the possibility of subjective transformation and self-recognition. This experience was no longer imagined as the identification with the spirit of self-creative freedom pulsing through the

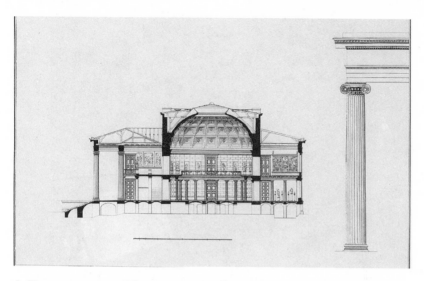

6. Transverse section of Altes Museum. Karl Friedrich Schinkel, *Collection of Architectural Designs* (New York: Princeton Architectural Press, 1989), facsimile edition of *Sammlung Architektonischer Entwürfe* (1866), engraving #40.

historical life of a particular people but as the mastery of natural and historical limitation in the serenely balanced harmonies of aesthetic form, an experience of the secular, "natural" incarnation of the divine in the human through contemplation of and submission to the paradigmatic cultural forms of classical Greece. Against the criticism of the art historian and theorist Alois Hirt, who would rather have used the money and space consumed by the rotunda to expand the museum's collections, Schinkel defended the importance of a "dignified central focus" (*würdiger Mittelpunkt*) that could function as a "sacred space" (*Heiligtum*) in which the most precious, perfect aesthetic objects were displayed. "One must first experience this space," he insisted, "when one enters from the external portico. The perception of a beautiful and exalted space creates a sensitivity and mood for the enjoyment and knowledge [*Genuss und Erkenntnis*] of that which the building preserves more generally." [13] As a built artwork, the museum itself initiated the visitor into an aesthetic experience that opened up the meaning of the artworks on display in the galleries.

The rotunda was conceived on the model of the classical Pantheon, with the addition of an interior balcony supported by free-standing Ionic columns in the cylindrical space of the first floor. Original or restored statues of the

7. The Rotunda of the Altes Museum, facing out toward the Lustgarten. Karl Friedrich Schinkel, *Collection of Architectural Designs* (New York: Princeton Architectural Press, 1989), facsimile edition of *Sammlung Architektonischer Entwürfe* (1866), engraving #44.

Greek gods were placed between the columns. Modern Germans did not find the idea of their own particular cultural identity as they entered the rotunda space, but rather a universal model of the way in which any culture must perfect its historical and natural potentialities in fully articulated aesthetic form. As they viewed their city through the Greek columns of the portico on their way to the painting galleries of the second floor, viewers brought with them a consciousness of a historical mission to build here, in this time and place, under the peculiar conditions of their own historical existence, as the Greeks had built in antiquity.

The second-floor galleries were devoted to what Schinkel and the museum curator, Gustav Waagen, considered the high points of "modern" Christian art, primarily works of the Italian and Northern European Renaissance, culminating in the paintings of the Van Eycks, Dürer, and especially Raphael. The contents of these galleries did not "transcend" the plastic classical art represented on the first floor but were also organized around the rotunda (at the balcony level) in a hierarchy of quality, moving from the center to the periphery, allowing visitors to reenter the world of classical perfection as they wandered through the upper galleries.

The importance of the rotunda in Schinkel's plan was reinforced for the external viewer by its rectangular housing floating above the cornice. The galleries were subordinate to this central space and constructed in a less obvious representational fashion. As Goerd Peschken has pointed out, Schinkel's gallery plans were strikingly modern in their completely functional, variable design.[14] Open columned galleries on the main floor allowed sculpture to be displayed in various arrangements and gave the visitor the option of bypassing certain exhibitions. No designated path guided the visitor through the galleries, although arrangements of proximity to the rotunda did produce a built-in hierarchy. Upstairs, the arrangement of galleries as partitioned halls at right angles to the external walls similarly allowed visitors to choose their itinerary. The specifics of the art-historical narrative were thus left at least somewhat open to individual construction, even though larger epochal shifts and the general meta-historical frame were clearly controlled by the portico, staircase, and rotunda. The portico, staircase and rotunda also marked the Altes Museum as more a work of art than a house of art, as some of Schinkel's critics had complained from the beginning.[15] The art displayed in the building was subordinated to the building's own purpose of creating an aesthetic experience with ethical implications. Schinkel defended his building as a place where the enjoyment of great works of art took precedence over the didactic tasks of learning the history of art, but the experience he intended to produce was also the ground for "teaching" a certain kind of historical narrative, much as the altar space in the Cathedral of Liberation would have constructed the experiential conditions for the assimilation of the idea of the people that informed the narrative of national self-determination.

The narrative of the Altes Museum was a narrative of dialectical relations between cultural principles or "Ideas." In contrast to the cathedral, the museum centered its story on the objective perfection of the Greek individual and social body, not the transcending activity of the spiritual subject. The Christian story appeared in the paintings of the second-floor galleries, not as a fully constructed world, but as a subjectively envisioned project that remained an uncompleted historical task for the present.

After 1816, Schinkel tended to define this present project in terms of discipline, refinement, and control, rather than liberation. He remained convinced that military liberation from foreign domination was for the Germans, as it had been for the Greeks in their Persian wars, the condition of cultural efflorescence. The Prussian eagles along the museum's cornice, and the statuary memorializing heroes of the Wars of Liberation that Schinkel intended for the steps to the portico and the walkway inside it, affirmed this view. The primary focus of the museum was, however, on the task of inner, ethical discipline and control. From the horse-taming Dioscuri on the roof to the mythological narratives of the murals in the portico, Schinkel tried to portray a story of aesthetic peace and cultural unity produced by the cultivated discipline of the barbarian within.

Schinkel was especially concerned with the murals of the portico's interior wall, which he sketched and resketched until the mid 1830s. The trend of his revisions was toward a darker vision, a vision of the transformation of nature into culture that revealed the possibilities of catastrophic collapse, emphasized the heroic self-discipline and self-sacrifice demanded for the creation of a human world out of nature's potentialities, and ultimately accepted the limitations of all attempts to create a permanent cultural order in the face of the impersonal powers of death and regeneration that ordered the natural cosmos. His last two sketches, for the paintings inside the staircase balcony, focused on heroic acts of self-sacrifice required to protect culture against both the violence of external nature and the violence of human barbarism.[16] In Greece, it seemed to Schinkel, the triumph over the external barbarians had led to a victory over the internal demons and the production of an ethical community. This community had, moreover, accepted the natural limitations of human cultural aspiration. His own museum was not so much an expression of a similar reality in Germany, however, as a presentation of the Greek ideal as an ethical task. In the mid 1820s, Schinkel suggested that in the contemporary world, the temporal relationship between art and ethical community might be reversed. The Greeks had recognized who they were in their art, but Germans had to be taught what they should become through the art of their aesthetic educators. The museum was not a reflection of historical accomplishment as much as the proclamation of an ethical task, an active intervention in the historical process, not so much a memorial, or a shrine of self-recognition, as a public school. Art had become an experimental, historical "testing ground" (*Probierstein*) for the production of meaningful community: "Formerly art followed great political events and was a consequence of them. It would perhaps constitute the highest product of a new form of action in the world if the arts went ahead."[17]

8. View from Unter den Linden of the projected Altes Museum in the context of the Lustgarten ensemble — the Arsenal on the left, the Cathedral, Palace Bridge, and Royal Palace on the right (1823). Kupferstichkabinett-Sammlung der Zeichnungen und Druckgraphik-Staatliche Museen zu Berlin-Preussischer Kulturbesitz-20z.250.

The historical narrative that Schinkel was trying to formulate and teach through the spatial relations and visual ornamentation of the Altes Museum becomes clearer from the examination of its place in Schinkel's general design for the center of Berlin. From the very beginning, Schinkel imagined the museum as transforming the Lustgarten ensemble from a royal garden into an urban square and civic center. His first drawings of the projected museum in 1823 reveal the way in which the museum reinterpreted the central pillars of the Prussian state, balancing representations of the dynasty, the army, and the Church with the cultural power of aesthetic education (fig. 8). Unlike the cathedral of 1814, the Altes Museum presented itself as an element in the construction of a public space in which the central components of the community intersected. It expressed a vision of the civic order as a panoramic ensemble that could be internalized through contemplation and cognitive appropriation by the individual. These spatial arrangements were accompanied by certain narrative paradigms into which the individual could insert his or her own life history. After 1816, the dominant story embodied in Schinkel's buildings and urban designs was that of the construction of Prussia as a public order grounded in military discipline and self-sacrifice, on the one hand, and the knowledge and ethical example of a cadre of civil servants, on the other. Schinkel himself had contributed to this story with his Neue Wache and Schlossbrücke. During the 1820s, he tried out various plans for a

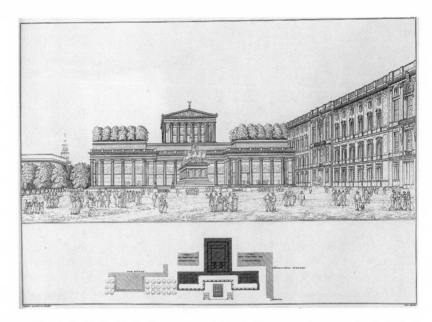

9. Sketch for Frederick the Great memorial in the Lustgarten between the Cathedral and Royal Palace (1829). Karl Friedrich Schinkel, *Collection of Architectural Designs* (New York: Princeton Architectural Press, 1989), facsimile edition of *Sammlung Architektonischer Entwürfe* (1866), engraving #167.

capstone to the narrative articulated in stone and space in the Prussian triumphal way from the Brandenburg Gate to the Lustgarten with plans for a monumental memorial to Frederick the Great. He thus took up themes and plans first adumbrated by his mentors in the 1790s and returned to projects that had first inspired his own commitment to architecture as a public vocation. The significance that Schinkel attached to the Frederician tradition in the formation of civic order is evident in plans for a memorial to Frederick the Great dating from 1829, which would have dwarfed the Royal Cathedral and matched the impact of the museum in the Lustgarten ensemble (fig. 9).

In contrast to the populist conception of a national community expressed in Schinkel's neo-Gothic designs, his neoclassical projects of the 1820s defined the ethical community, not as an expressive product of the liberation of the innate spirit of the people, but as a civic artifice that was historically constructed through the disciplined control of external and internal nature, guided by a trained elite of political administrators and cultural educators. The message written in the stones and the urban environmental siting of the

Altes Museum defined an increasing tension between the people, conceived of as an inherent unity shaped by the evolution of their innate ethnic and linguistic potentialities, and the ideal community embodied in the educational ideals and political vision of the servants of the public order or community as a whole—the class of educated professional state administrators. Two distinct issues were involved in the cultural task of disciplining, refining, and "spiritualizing" the individuals emancipated from traditional communal bonds and inherited systems of meaning during the period of revolution, reform, and national liberation: (1) transformation of the raw productivity of labor in the service of physical needs into an aesthetic creativity expressed as a productive transformation of natural force and matter into a cultural world that mirrored and sustained the values of human autonomy and community, and (2) integration of emancipated individual subjects, pursuing selfish interests in a market-oriented civil society, into a public, ethical community based on moral consensus and self-conscious mutual identification. In social terms, these tasks involved the integration of the new laboring classes (a product of the emancipation of serfs and dissolution of the guild system) and the middle classes operating outside of the circle of the state service class (a product of the expanded market of goods and services) into the community of rational law and cultural meaning embodied in, and propagated by, the state class of historically educated, aesthetically cultivated, civil servants.

Building a Community of Meaning from the Products of Modernization: The Bauakademie as a Model for Modernism

Since his first years in the Prussian civil service, Schinkel had developed exceptionally close ties to a generational contemporary and fellow bureaucrat—Peter Christian Wilhelm Beuth (1781–1853)—who was one of the most active and influential promoters of state support for entrepreneurial initiative, technological innovation, and modern methods of production in post-reform Prussia. As the head of the technical commission for the development of trade and manufacture in the Prussian ministry of finance, Beuth was in charge of using the regulating and educational powers of the state to mobilize the productive powers of individual economic activity in the new market-oriented civil society that had begun to emerge after the dissolution of the feudal and guild restrictions of the old regime. Besides his official positions within the government, he also headed an association for the promotion of new technology and industrial design, which included manufacturers and merchants as well as technocrats and educators from the state-service elites.[18] Like Schinkel, Beuth was intensely concerned with mobilizing and guiding the emancipated individual energies released by the Prussian reform movement in the direction of new forms of subjective, voluntary identification with the historically evolving, spiritual substance of a collective culture. Beuth shared Schinkel's early Romantic enthusiasms for a national culture grounded in the awakening of German ethnic identity and had also accompanied him in his turn toward neoclassical, especially Greek, models of cultural community and aesthetic education after 1815. Schinkel in turn, combined his own primary interests in the social shaping of individual subjects through aesthetic stimuli, with strong inclinations toward technocratic management and rational planning. Since 1819, Schinkel had been a prominent member of Beuth's technocratic commissions and associations. Beuth at the same time incorporated many of Schinkel's perspectives in the creation of his School for Industrial Engineering and Design. Their careers seem to overlap almost completely around 1830, when Beuth became the head of the Prussian General School of Architecture and Schinkel presided over the State Building Commission.

Since 1821, Schinkel and Beuth had collaborated on a project that expressed their shared interests most clearly—the publication of a series of engravings and commentaries intended to encourage aesthetic refinement as well as technical skill in the engineering and building trades—machine-making, metalwork, masonry, woodworking, ceramics, textiles, and so on. The various volumes of *Vorbilder für Fabrikanten und Handwerker* (Models for Manufacturers and Craftsmen) place particular emphasis on the integration of new materials, machine technology, and industrial methods into a vision of production defined by historical knowledge and cultivated aesthetic taste. As Beuth comments in his introduction to the first volume in the series, the aesthetic dimension of the product, as much as its more obvious economic and social utility, constituted the value added to the raw material in the process of production:

How necessary and useful it is to endow your work not only with technical excellence but also with the highest perfection of form. Only work which combines the two can bring the craftsman close to the work of fine art, stamp it with a sense of refinement and give it a more lasting value than the cost of its own materials.[19]

A manual of models of this kind also expressed the belief of Schinkel and Beuth that refining mere work into aesthetic production and sheer technical control into beautiful form occurred through submission to the historical understanding and cultivated sensibilities of the educated leaders of society within the state-service class. It is noteworthy that Schinkel clearly separated the higher pedagogy of his detailed architectural designs and the explanations and theoretical conceptualizations of his never completed architectural textbook from his popular pedagogy in the *Vorbilder*. The workers who shaped the materials according to the designs were not imagined as serious interlocutors in the creation of those designs. The historical and cultural self-consciousness that added meaning to matter and turned produced commodities into components of a human world was an achievement of the educated elite and legitimated their management of individuals in civil society who pursued their self-interests without a clear understanding of the cultural context of their activities.

Schinkel's interest in the technical management of the movements of emancipated individuals in the emerging civil society is perhaps most evident in the designs for revised street patterns and traffic flows that accompanied most of his building projects.[20] In 1817, as he worked on the design for the Neue Wache and the Schlossbrücke, he also conceived a general plan for rearranging the siting of particular social functions and types of production and exchange in concentrated areas of the city and joining them together with efficient arterial streets, bridges, and canals. In such plans, the city seemed more like a rationally organized mechanism of functional parts than a site for the construction of historical and cultural identities. However, Schinkel always sought for ways in which the everyday activities of production and exchange might be connected and elevated into forms of communal meaning and ethical consciousness.

During the summer and fall of 1826, Schinkel joined Beuth for an extended tour of France and Great Britain, and his diary responses to some of the apparent consequences of unrestricted free trade and industrial capitalism express his ambivalence about the emergence of a world shaped by competitive individualism and the correlative demand that material productivity create private profit. Like Beuth, Schinkel was immensely impressed by British innovation in engineering and technology, especially as it effected construction of built environments for the new processes of industrial production and exchange. At the same time, he was appalled by the social consequences of a lack of historical and aesthetic consciousness in much of this new construction. The huge brick factories of the British Midlands inspired him by their technical engineering feats and frightened him by their disdain for the ethical effect of environments determined completely by economic utility. "It gives one a frightfully sinister impression," he wrote. "Colossal masses of building substance are being constructed by builders alone without any regard for architectural principles, solely for utilitarian ends and rendered in red brick."[21] And just as he was impressed by the productivity that blossomed from competitive commodity production in a market society, he was frightened by the signs of social anarchy and uncontrolled economic fluctuation that seemed to characterize a society of emancipated, homeless individuals guided only by the vagaries of market demand. The example of England indicated that architecture and urban design were called upon, more than ever before, to integrate the individual into self-transcending patterns of historical and cultural meaning.

Even before his English journey, Schinkel had made an initial attempt to incorporate the world of buying and selling within the boundaries of the representational, monumental built environment of central Berlin. In the early 1820s, he had designed an extension of the Wilhelmsstrasse near the Brandenburg Gate, breaking through the façades of the north side of Unter den Linden with an open street mall of small shops with adjoining mezzanine apartments. This retail project also provided an uninterrupted traffic flow through Unter den Linden to both the growing working-class suburbs north of the Spree and the older residential and commercial areas of the Friedrichstadt to the south, thus connecting three areas of the city "in the most comfortable and efficient manner."[22] After returning from England, Schinkel conceived a more ambitious attempt to bring the world of the new civil society into the boundaries of the cultivated civic community in the form of a huge U-shaped retail mall right in the middle of the rows of monumental buildings along Unter den Linden, on the site of the old Academy of Arts and royal stables. This *Kaufhaus* was designed to encompass two hundred shops on its first and third floors, with space for residential apartments on the second and fourth levels. The design followed the new framing principles Schinkel had admired in British commercial architecture. It used a skeleton of piers and spanning shallow vaults to create flexible, neutral interior spaces covered by an exterior curtain of brick and glass. However, Schinkel elevated the exterior to a classic monumentality in keeping with the surrounding public buildings by designing the façades in two-story rectangular segments that transformed the pier and vault interior skeleton into large classical planes rhythmically articulated by pilasters and entablatures layered over the brick construction. An ornamental balustrade reiterated and emphasized these proportional harmonies (fig. 10). Behind this slightly deceptive façade, however, the building consisted of an uncentered aggregate of multiple-use spaces that allowed individual agents to construct their own particular itinerary, choose

10. Watercolor of Karl Friedrich Schinkel's planned Retail Mall (*Kaufhaus*) on Unter den Linden (1827). Kupferstichkabinett-Sammlung der Zeichnungen und Druck-graphik-Staatliche Museen zu Berlin-Preussischer Kulturbesitz-SM23b.52.

their own paths in the flow of pedestrian traffic, or relax and converse or stroll in the open courtyard fronting the avenue. The ground-floor shops took on the characteristic of an arcade through the innovative use of canvas awnings supported by removable poles.

Schinkel's attempt to invite the new world of bourgeois commerce into the sphere of the traditional Prussian administrative and cultural elites was rejected by his royal patron as brash and inappropriate. Despite this discouragement, he persisted in his efforts. Signs of a possible return of the social and political turmoil of the revolutionary era during the summer of 1830 (news of the July Revolution in Paris arrived in Berlin during the festivities for the opening of the museum on the Lustgarten) simply increased the intensity of Schinkel's concerns about the civic and cultural consequences of economic and social modernization. In 1830, he began another ambitious project to extend the representational and educational urban space of the Lustgarten and Unter den Linden into the world of labor and commerce. The construction of the museum at the north end of the Lustgarten had entailed a revision of river traffic through the city center as well as a rearrangement of the customs, shipping, and storage facilities that served that traffic. Just to the northwest of the museum, Schinkel designed a consolidated Packhof, or customs and storage station, along the reconstructed banks of an enlarged Kupfergraben to replace the previously dispersed jumble of buildings that had housed these facilities. According to the plan executed in 1830–32, three connected cubelike structures were built in a line along the waterfront. The building closest to the museum and most clearly visible from the Lustgarten and the Schlossbrücke housed the residence and offices of the head

11. Customs and Storage Buildings (*Packhof*) from the Palace Bridge. Karl Friedrich Schinkel, *Collection of Architectural Designs* (New York: Princeton Architectural Press, 1989), facsimile edition of *Sammlung Architektonischer Entwürfe* (1866), engraving #149.

of the state customs administration. Its brick structure was covered with a neoclassical grooved stucco façade, and a classical pediment with an allegorical frieze emphasized the incorporation of commercial activities into the classical proportions of the represented civic relations of the Lustgarten ensemble. The second building, housing general customs offices and meeting rooms, lacked the pediment but continued the rectangular lines and stuccoed exterior of the first. Connected to this intermediary structure by a waterfront colonnade and docking area loomed a massive five-story warehouse of exposed red brick, which, unlike the two administrative buildings, revealed its interior skeletal framing in its arched doorways and window openings. As seen from the vantage point of Schinkel's Schlossbrücke, the Packhof complex suggested how efficient utilitarian structures serving the demands of a commercial society could be composed into an urban panorama that articulated the principles of classical proportion and collective historical memory (fig. 11). In a sense, the Packhof was a statement in stone and space of the state-controlled market expansion and commercial development represented by the German Customs Union (*Zollverein*), which the Prussian Department of Finance was negotiating at precisely this time. But the project that most fully articulated Schinkel's hopes for the transformation of emancipated individual egos produced by modernization into historically self-conscious, aesthetically cultivated members of a consensual, ethical, "modern" community was the construction between 1832 and 1836 of his own "home," not just his private residence (Schinkel lived with his family in a third-floor apartment from 1836 until his death in 1841), but his home as civil servant, urban designer, architect, and building supervisor—the Allgemeine Bauschule, or Bauakademie (General School of Construction and Design, or Building Academy)—on the west bank of the Kupfergraben just south of the Schlossbrücke, backing onto the northeast corner of the Friedrich Werder Square and facing Unter den Linden and the Lustgarten ensemble.

The plan to build a new structure to house both Beuth's Building Academy and Schinkel's Building Commission emerged soon after Beuth was appointed head of the Bauakademie in 1831. The two friends justified their proposal first of all in terms of functional consolidation and rational efficiency. The cramped and dispersed quarters of the old Bauakademie made the centralized organization and oversight of various tasks virtually impossible. Moreover, the old buildings threatened the safe preservation of its heritage of books, engravings, and drawings. Since this library was also a major resource for Schinkel's Building Commission, a shared structure seemed most efficient. The Bauakademie was thus imagined on one level as an efficiently organized, multiple-use space. The design needed to encompass well-lit studio spaces, fireproof storage areas, administrative offices, and residential quarters for the heads of both institutions. Schinkel also proposed a ground-floor level of upscale shops, whose rents would help defray the costs of constructing and maintaining the building.

The appropriate spatial structure for this exemplary embodiment of the relations between state, society, and culture in the post-reform era was imagined and constructed by Schinkel as a simple cube with a skeletal frame composed of massive brick piers connected (with the help of iron clamps) by shallow, segmented brick vaults. This skeleton was constructed first, the floors and roof were added, and only then were the walls filled in, like a shell or curtain over the structural frame. Finally, the windows, doors, and decorative elements were set, as prefabricated components, into their appropriate spaces. The building was a symmetrical square, four stories in height, with eight bays between the brick piers on each side and a small inner courtyard. The four façades were identical, except for the side facing north toward the Schlossbrücke and Lustgarten, which was marked as the front by two large doors in the central bays. But even this apparent focal point was misleading, as the doors led, not to a single central staircase or large foyer, but to separate hallways and stairwells, one to the studios, classrooms, and library of the Bauakademie on the second floor, the other to the administrative offices of the Oberbaudeputation on the third floor. One could imagine a hierarchical order in the organization of the three main stories (the fourth was simply a storage attic, with an inwardly sloping roof for efficient drainage). The com-

12. Main façade of the Bauakademie, showing five of the eight bays, and the two entrances. Karl Friedrich Schinkel, *Collection of Architectural Designs* (New York: Princeton Architectural Press, 1989), facsimile edition of *Sammlung Architektonischer Entwürfe* (1866), engraving #121.

mercial level on the ground floor was superseded by the level of educational training of productive labor in both technical competence and historical aesthetics. Finally, Schinkel's offices on the third floor embodied the elevated sphere of professional expertise and cultural self-consciousness inhabited by members of the state administration. One could read this vertical organization as a narrative of civil society transmuted by the state and its educators into a harmonious, well-proportioned, rationally planned totality. But the levels were functional, not ceremonial, and the spaces of the structure were neutral and available for other purposes (fig. 12).

Schinkel built his "home" almost completely of *gebrannte Erde* ("burnt earth"), or fired clay, which was the primary material of both raw and glazed brick and the terra-cotta ornamentation and moldings. The earthy (natural), populist (social), and north German (historical/cultural) connotations of exposed brick construction had been part of Schinkel's consciousness since his first memorials to the people's sacrifices in the Wars of National Liberation.

The idea of burnt earth resonated with Schinkel's almost alchemical sense of the power of architecture to transmute the simplest and most common of natural materials into beautiful human form. The Bauakademie itself was an expression of the transformation of social utility and rational function into aesthetic and cultural value, of the workplace into the artwork. Presenting its material and structural substance unabashedly on its exterior exposed brick façades, the building sought to display "aesthetic serenity," not through the imposed artifice of historical imitation or decoration, but from within, as the essence of its own constructive principles. Window and door framing echoed the broad and shallow interior vaulting. The great structural piers divided the façades into evenly proportioned wall surfaces like huge classical columns, but also created a rhythm of vertical bays as in a Gothic cathedral. Glazed layers of lilac-colored brick, repeated at every fifth layer of the exposed red brick, emphasized the horizontal, "stratified" (*lagerhaft*) character of the structure, and emphasized the "architectural peace" already present in the broad rectangularity of its four façades.[23] The combination of a "medieval" arched brick vaulting and "classical" piers and entablatures appeared to evolve naturally from constructive principles of the building and the nature of its materials, not as a programmatic historical synthesis of competing cultural styles.

The ornamentation of the Bauakademie echoed and expanded the messages implied in its tectonic relations, spatial proportions, and raw materials.[24] Two important series of terra-cotta panels under the windowsills of the second floor (repeated on each of the four sides) and around the two large north-side entry doors, articulated in sequential images the narrative embodied in the building's structural principles. Schinkel exhibited the window panels independently in 1832 and devoted a full page of his *Sammlung Architektonischer Entwürfe* (Collection of Architectural Designs) to them (fig. 13). He described the panels as representations of "various moments in the developmental history of the art of building."[25] The twenty-four panels, grouped in threes within the eight bays under the windows of the second floor, can thus be seen as an attempt to provide a historical frame for the Bauakademie, to articulate the cultural narrative within which his own building emerged as a culminating meaningful act.

Moving from left to right, the nine panels in the first three bays portray the story of the decline, fall, and resurrection of the spirit or "genius" of the art of building. As in his earlier portrayals of the Idea of the Germanic people in terms of the winged "spirit" of the archangel Michael, or the classical goddesses on the Schlossbrücke, who represented the spiritual agency informing

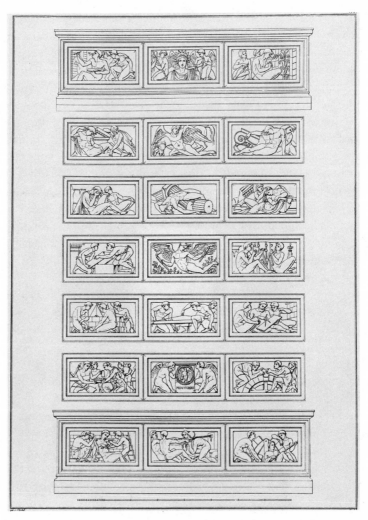

13. Designs for the terra-cotta panels under the first floor windows of the Bauakademie (1832). The engraving shows only seven of the eight sets (the set for the fifth
bay, with Pallas Athene, is missing), and they are not in the order in which they were
finally placed on the building. From top to bottom the sequence of the constructed
sets (left to right on the four sides of the Bauakademie) is 4, 1, 2, 3, 7, 6, 8. Moreover,
the third panel in set 6 was exchanged with the first panel of set 8 in the final place-
ment. Karl Friedrich Schinkel, *Collection of Architectural Designs* (New York: Princeton Architectural Press, 1989), facsimile edition of *Sammlung Architektonischer Entwürfe* (1866), engraving #118.

the processes of defiance, defeat, discipline, resurrection, victory, and spiritualization, the agent of the history that Schinkel inscribed on his Bauakademie was an inner essence or "Idea" visualized as a spiritual (winged) being. The Idea of the building arts is represented as a naked, winged "Greek" youth. Six panels are devoted to the decline and apparent death of this spirit through the historical decline and collapse of the principles of classical architecture. Broken columns and fractured pediments form the background for scenes of mourning and death. The panels in the third bay, however, are marked by a resurrection of the spirit, who flies aloft, a burning torch in each hand, and is flanked by scenes portraying the revival of architectural competence and trained skill in the building arts during the Christian Middle Ages — the laying of foundation stones and the sculpting of the ornamental flowers of a Gothic spire. The six panels of the two middle bays (which are thus situated above the entry doors of the north façade) have a less historical, more systematic content. Each trio centers on a Greek divinity, Apollo to the left and Pallas Athena to the right. Apollo with his lyre, and flanked by representations of painting and sculpture, is presented as the protector of the spirit of architecture as a fine art. Athena, set between scenes of scientific teaching and the technical mastery of construction methods, is presented as the protectrix of the technical knowledge and skills involved in the mastery of natural forms. The laying of the foundation stone of the Bauakademie by two spirits (marked by the date 1832 and a Prussian eagle) is flanked by social scenes from building sites — morning or noon meals with the family and the return of the laborer to the family circle at the end of the working day. The last six panels portray a set of scenes that express active scientific control over matter through technical progress and the discovery of scientific laws and principles that make possible the construction of the human environment according to rules and ideal forms that sustain the natural order. In these last panels, the figures themselves conform to the general model of the classical nude, but the work presented has a pointed-arched form, indicating a strong historical continuity between postclassical building techniques and classical methods and principles.

The panels surrounding the doors provide further clues to the historical and cultural messages Schinkel was trying to embody in the Bauakademie (figs. 14 and 15). Each portal arch is composed of seven panels, which repeat the figuration of the spirit of architectural art as a winged youth with a torch. In these panels, the youth emerges at waist level from an acanthus leaf. This emergence of art from nature, and the repetitious, constantly reproduced transformations of nature into art throughout the evolution of art forms, con-

14. Design for the left portal and door of the Bauakademie. Karl Friedrich Schinkel, *Collection of Architectural Designs* (New York: Princeton Architectural Press, 1989), facsimile edition of *Sammlung Architektonischer Entwürfe* (1866), engraving #120.

stitutes the major theme of the door panels. The side panels on the door on the left (the door to the Architectural School), begin from the bottom with representations of the acanthus plant in both its blossom and seed-cone phases of development. Above this pair appear the archaic architectural forms of the Egyptian and Doric orders, followed by a pair of female nudes

15. Design for the right portal of the Bauakademie. Karl Friedrich Schinkel, *Collection of Architectural Designs* (New York: Princeton Architectural Press, 1989), facsimile edition of *Sammlung Architektonischer Entwürfe* (1866), engraving #122.

holding harvest baskets on their heads in the shape of Ionic and Corinthian capitols. Moving upward, the next pair features a nude male youth discovering the principles of architectural form through an intuitive revelation of the inner forms of organic natural life (the myth of Callicrates discovering the Corinthian Order). Finally, in the upper corners, Schinkel paired two mythical figures (Orpheus and Amphion), who conjure up constructed "artificial" worlds of brick and stone through the creative harmonies of their music.

The panels around the door to the right (leading to the offices of Schinkel's Building Commission) emphasized not so much the evolution of aesthetic form from the principles of natural life, and thus the continuity between nature and culture, as progress in the technical mastery and control of nature. The bottom panels portray a dreaming youth whose imagination soars with his eagle, and an active harvesting youth picking fruit from a tree — perhaps representing the origins of theoretical contemplation and productive labor as basic forms of human mastery over the natural world. The next stage presents a youth balancing on a boat and a maiden riding a panther while playfully balancing two balls in her hands; representations, possibly, of the conquest of the animal kingdoms of sea and land for purposes of human play and enjoyment. At the next level the mastery of nature takes the more abstract form of the representation of writing and formal mathematical calculation by clothed female figures carrying large torches. The portal is completed with scenes of two master builders being crowned with laurel wreaths by the spirits of their professional arts.

The door panels thus present a complex developmental perspective on the relations between art and nature, on the one hand, and art and science, on the other. On the one hand, Schinkel represents architectural forms as emerging from innate tendencies in the natural world. The genius of the arts emerges as the spirit of nature rediscovered and made actual as a self-conscious agency. Organic development and aesthetic construction are portrayed in a continuous line of development, as well as in a systematic relation of analogy. Architecture completes and echoes the natural materials and inherent organic principles from which it creates. The interior side panels around both doors emphasize the theme of culture as a repetition of nature with their series of acanthus plants transforming themselves through various stages of organic growth and maturation.

The panels around the door to Schinkel's Oberbaudeputation, however, also narrate a story of technical control for practical use, of the mastery of natural forces and materials to fulfill human needs and provide the materials for the creation of human value. Whether the relationship of the human spiritual activity (as art or science) to nature was imagined as harmonious continuity or technical mastery, however, Schinkel presented it as an immanent process guided by the genius or spirit of the form inherent in the material, rather than as a transcendent imposition of order on the basis of revelation of a knowledge external to nature or to man as a part of nature. The narrative of the temple of work as art, or art as the production of a human world from the ground of nature, was a secular, immanent narrative. The meta-historical frame of this narrative was developed from a belief that meaning is inherent in nature. Even the meanings established against nature's forces, as a defense against raw and unrefined nature, emerge from within the natural order of being.

The ornamentation of the Bauakademie placed it in at least two significant communicative relations with its built urban environment. On the north side, the terra-cotta panels seemed to be set into a conscious conversation with the murals on the inner wall of the museum façade, whose sketches Schinkel was completing at the same time. In the message inscribed on his own building (where he presided as creator, resident, and patron), his per-spective was oriented toward the future and exemplified the shape of the proj-ect that the history of art had set for the present generation. The strenuous discipline, harsh conflicts, and visions of potential disaster portrayed in the museum murals' version of the historical struggle to create a human world from the recalcitrant materials and energies of nature appeared in the ico-nography of the Bauakademie in a more optimistic light. Even the mastery over nature in the Bauakademie panels emerged as the product of a pro-gressive understanding of the laws and relations inherent in nature. One way of reading this relationship between the two inscriptions is that the Bauaka-demie took up the challenge thrown out by the museum and affirmed the possibility of turning the natural man into a subjectively, voluntarily inte-grated member of the community of constructed meanings.

At the same time, the Bauakademie panels on the south side engaged the figures of the neoclassical frieze circling the middle of the austere cubic form of the Royal Mint on the Friedrich Werder Square. This frieze, conceived by Schinkel's revered teacher Friedrich Gilly in 1800, had exploited classical ref-erences and images to tell a story of the appropriation of natural materials and natural forms for the production of human wealth and the creation of cultural forms that would withstand the onslaught of uncontrolled natural powers.[26] For a few years after 1800, some of the rooms in the upper story of the mint were used to house the nascent Bauakademie. One of the pecu-liarities of Schinkel's panels becomes more comprehensible in this context. The mint frieze tells its story within the frame and formal language of the classical tradition. The narrative of Schinkel's panels begins with the decline and destruction of the classical tradition. The new building emerges as a re-generation of the spirit of architecture from the obsolete husk of a historical form. Although in some ways a tribute itself to the power of classical models, the Bauakademie is also a statement of liberation from the unquestioned authority of Greek forms. It asserts that the spirit of architecture that informed the initial flowering of Greek building could only be regenerated by adapting the essential principles of architecture to the needs, functions, and historical mission of the present, and by adapting and fully appropriating all of the developmental stages that had brought the spirit of architecture from classical Athens to nineteenth-century Berlin. Gilly had helped Schinkel imagine the past as a foreign country that could become a model for the present. But for Schinkel that past lived on in the present through all of the historical forms in which its principles had been transfigured and passed on through time.

The contextual relations of Schinkel's Bauakademie panels point to the larger issue of the ways in which this building, like Schinkel's other urban structures, was built not as an isolated monument but as a part of a broadly conceived urban design. The Bauakademie's decorated portals faced north toward the Zeughaus, the Schlossbrücke, and the Altes Museum. It was clearly visible from the staircase balcony of the museum and thus an important component of the constructed ensemble that Schinkel imagined at the center of Prussia as a civic and cultural community. Its ornamental figures engaged those on the museum and the Schlossbrücke. Yet the Bauakademie, as Schinkel was the first to emphasize, also operated within the urban space as a functional component in the efficient regulation of the flow of people, goods, and services. The construction of the building opened up two new urban arteries — one along the river and one connecting the Friedrich Werder Square to the areas of Alt-Cölln and eastern Berlin across the Kupfergraben and the Spree. Like the Wilhelmsstrasse extension, the Bauakademie centralized certain economic and social functions in one place and opened up smooth and "comfortable" linkages to other areas of the city, thus transforming the city from an aggregate of relatively isolated neighborhoods into a single social organism. The shops on the ground level of the Bauakademie were integrated into the commercial character of the Friedrich Werder Square and its surrounding streets. Along the eastern waterfront façade, the Bauakademie opened up an opportunity to modernize the Kupfergraben embankment and create a tree-lined promenade that joined the triangular park north of the building to complete an important part of an urban landscape ensemble that now reached along the canal to the last warehouses of the Packhof (fig. 16). The representational avenue of Unter den Linden and the symbolic public space of the Lustgarten were crossed by, and integrated into, a cityscape along the artificial waterway of the Kupfergraben that por-

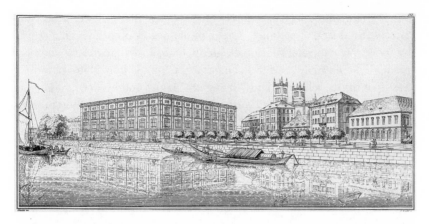

16. The Bauakademie from the Schlossbrücke. Karl Friedrich Schinkel, *Collection of Architectural Designs* (New York: Princeton Architectural Press, 1989), facsimile edition of *Sammlung Architektonischer Entwürfe* (1866), engraving #115.

trayed the new creative forces of commerce, skilled labor, and technocratic management. The individual strolling along the canal and crossing over to the Lustgarten on Schinkel's Schlossbrücke would encounter aesthetically composed "built" views unrolling in both southern and northern directions. In this panorama, as in the buildings themselves, the constructed world was related to a technically mastered natural environment, producing a world of order and freedom in which the individual subject might attain aesthetic serenity.

On the Friedrich Werder side, the Bauakademie was also placed in relation to Schinkel's Friedrich Werder Church, a building that had been in planning and construction stages since the early 1820s but was just completed in 1830. The exposed red brick and terra-cotta decoration of the church, its rectangular blocklike body with its large windowed bays, mirrored important dimensions of the Bauakademie. At the same time, the significance of the Friedrich Werder Church as a religious building opened up the problematic issue of the role of religious or transcendent authority in Schinkel's vision of constructed historical and cultural identities.

During the period between his English journey and the completion of the Bauakademie (1826–36), Schinkel's theoretical positions concerning the relationship between architectural form and the historical evolution of culture seemed to be an elaboration of the views constructed during his shift toward a dogmatic neoclassicism after 1815. The new passages that he composed for the introductory section of his *Lehrbuch* after 1825 still strongly affirm the foundational nature of Greek principles. "European architecture," he wrote, "is equivalent to Greek architecture in its progressive development." [27] Greek architecture had an originary, foundational status because it was itself firmly, self-consciously based on "nature and her forms." All constructed human meanings grew from these natural forms and their progressive transformations, interpretations, and applications. The fine arts of architecture, sculpture, and painting, in Schinkel's view, were closer to the "language of nature" than the culture of the written or spoken word, and they thus established a more secure basis for the construction of a human world that would sustain harmonious relations to the natural forms that were its foundation. The history that most concerned Schinkel during the 1820s was not what he defined as the trivial, genre history of contingent differences in the externalities of costume and custom, but the immanent structural history of the progressive relationship between nature and the human attempt to re-create and represent nature in the artifice of culture. Architectural honesty and wisdom were ultimately tied to the relationship between constructed forms and the objective materials that were the substance of those forms. Buildings should display the ways in which their materials — brick, stone, wood, glass, metal — implicitly suggested certain forms appropriate to their inherent qualities. Progress in architecture was not a series of leaps from one cultural idea to another. What Schinkel envisioned was a continuity in the progressive struggle to re-create the inherent forms of the world as a cultural artifact, to make the nature of being self-conscious and comprehensible, to transform the apparent hostility of the external world into man's "natural" home.

Central to Schinkel's theorizing was the idea that the forms of art should emerge from the immanent progress of the subjective agent's relation to the natural object. Within human culture, objects become communicative symbols. But if art was to fulfill its mission and represent the human world as a home within nature, it must also allow the object to present itself as an object, as a historical being in its own right, as a "carrier of its own nature" ("Träger seiner eigenen Natur"). [28] The natural world was not just the "other" of the cultural order but also its origin. The dialectical struggle between nature and culture was in a sense an immanent progress within nature. In the artifice of architecture, nature finally spoke its own meaning. The landscape was remade in the human form of the cityscape.

Although Schinkel's theories might seem progressive in their secular emphasis and their search for the principles of cultural development within the material foundations of the natural world, they were also conservative in their deep suspicion of any human intervention in the historical process that was not itself grounded in humble submission to, and deep understanding of, the "objective" reality of nature. Goethe remained Schinkel's cultural hero during this period, a model who not only provided him with a critical perspective on the limiting, parochial character of Christian-German constructions of the past and theories of future community building but also helped him justify his resignation to the "given" as a form of higher understanding of universal principles embedded in the natural order of things. For Schinkel, "man" did make his own history. In architectural constructions of form and space, human beings created a cosmos they could call their own, but only as a part of nature and only in submission to nature's rules.

In the 1830s, Schinkel construed the barbarism of the present age primarily as a subjective hubris that denied human finitude within the natural order, aggressively asserted the power of the subject over the object, and imagined historical communities as arbitrary constructions of human imagination and will. The barbarism of the present age was not so much raw brutality, a lack of civilized refinement, as a cultivated barbarism of overrefinement that ignored the natural foundations of cultural creation and alienated culture from its origins. Modern barbarism was expressed in the belief that the world was there to service the needs of the self-interested individual ego, in the "refined avoidance of all laws of society for egoistic purposes."[29]

Schinkel's modernist constructivism was thus severely limited by his metaphysical faith in the dynamic and progressive order of nature as the source of form and law. But nature was not static. As a part and product of nature, human agency, defined as the creative productivity that constantly transformed objects into human meaning, was a part of the dynamic nature/culture relationship that itself defined the reality of nature in historical time. History in Schinkel's vision, so clearly presented both in his built spaces and in the inscriptions he placed on them, was defined as a dynamic process in which human beings transformed the natural world of which they were a part. This process was progressive, moving persistently toward a greater humanization of nature, but it was never free of the conditions that made it possible. The creation of an appropriate built environment for the modern emancipated ego entailed self-conscious possession of the historical development that produced the conditions of the present, and also of the natural principles that were the permanent ground of the process of historical cultural construction itself. Since nature itself was historical, a part of the nature/culture interaction that constituted history, obedience to natural law (which was the highest form of freedom) was obedience to "history" itself. And to obey history was to move from the given to the creation of something new, to construct the future on the foundations of the present. In this sense, classicism and loyalty to "natural" principles of construction and objective materiality were the very foundations of authentic historicism in architecture.[30]

10. The European Modernist as Anglican Moralist

The Later Social Criticism of T. S. Eliot

I

One of the most notable features of the intellectual history of the first few decades of the twentieth century was the hostility toward "modernity," variously understood, expressed by many of the leading figures in those overlapping cultural and artistic developments that we have come to label "Modernism." This reaction, examples of which may be drawn from all the major European societies, did not issue in a single political position, although their animating aversion to the democratization of consumption and culture disposed many of the leading Modernists to adopt some kind of conservative or reactionary stance.[1] Underlying these unstable and not always clearly framed political allegiances, one can usually discern the traces of what Peter Gay, writing of Weimar Germany, has aptly called "the hunger for wholeness." Gay's characterization of the antipathies through which this "hunger" was expressed among German writers and intellectuals of the period could, due allowance being made for the different inflections of various national traditions, stand as a description of a paranoid style of demonizing "modern society" that was widely shared: "the dehumanizing machine, capitalist materialism, godless rationalism, rootless society, cosmopolitan Jews, and that great all-devouring monster, the city."[2]

Among the leading Modernists in other European countries, few would seem, at first sight, to match this profile as neatly as T. S. Eliot, with his constant denigration of liberalism, his antipathy to secular rationalism, his fastidious aversion to "mass society," his political agrarianism, his deep yearning for stability and order, and, not least, his notorious remark in 1934 that, when considering the conditions favorable to a settled society, "reasons of race and religion combine to make any large number of free-thinking Jews undesirable."[3] Given that the general response that Gay identifies can be seen as a yearning to have some form of reassuring and consoling *Gemeinschaft* substituted for the lonely mobilities of an all-devouring *Gesellschaft*, Eliot's writing may seem a particularly revealing embodiment of the dialectical relationship between these two poles. While his social criticism frequently lauds the stability imputed to a lost Eden of "community," the intensity of his poetry rests upon its capacity to distill the experience of a dislocated urban existence: in these terms, *The Waste Land* is *Gesellschaft* as Modernist lyric.

One benefit of considering Eliot in this way is that it reminds us, in the face of accumulated institutional pressure to address him exclusively as part of that selection of British and American writing that has come to constitute "English Literature," of his close engagement with the cultural and political life of continental Europe. Beginning with the year Eliot spent in Paris immediately after graduating from Harvard (1910–11), his contact with the intellectual and political currents of European, especially French, life was always to remain closer than that of most of his English contemporaries. His editorship of *The Criterion* (1922–39) was premised on the value of extending and deepening the notion of a shared European culture.[4] And some of his own closest affinities at the formative stage of his development were with that overtly reactionary and monarchist strain of European political thinking, powerful in such countries as Spain and Italy, that found its most stylish expression in the work of the founder of Action française, Charles Maurras.[5]

This last affinity has in fact been strongly insisted upon in the most recent wave of critical commentary upon Eliot, which has emphasized not just the belligerently Christian and authoritarian features of this tradition but also its Fascist and anti-Semitic tendencies. The most severe, as well as the most widely noted, indictment of Eliot in these terms has certainly been Anthony Julius's *T. S. Eliot: Anti-Semitism and Literary Form*, which attempts to place Eliot's writing, some of the early poetry above all, in a much wider tradition of European anti-Semitism.[6] Perhaps more representative of this general line of interpretation, in part because more temperate and based upon a wider range of Eliot's writings, is Kenneth Asher's *T. S. Eliot and Ideology*, an extended attempt to support the claim that "from beginning to end, Eliot's work, including both the poetry and the prose, was shaped by a political vision inherited from French reactionary thinkers, especially from Charles Maurras."[7] These works have helped to draw attention to features of Eliot's writing that had perhaps been insufficiently attended to by most earlier literary scholars, but, as so often with studies built around a single polemical thesis, they are prone to damaging exaggeration and one-sidedness.

One particular failing arises from the attempt to identify the Maurrassien affinity as the informing emphasis in Eliot's writing "from beginning to end," since this tends to run together phases of his work that are marked by a somewhat different focus and tone. It is noticeable that most of the quotations deployed to support what one might call the Maurrassien reading of Eliot come from the first half of his writing career, culminating in the publication of *After Strange Gods* in 1934. As scholars have long recognized, that short book is itself problematic in several ways, having been written at a time of great inner disturbance in Eliot's life, and combining some of the offhand provokingness of his early literary essays with sentiments he hoped might strike a responsive chord among some members of his audience in Virginia.[8] However, the bulk of his social and political writing dates from the second half of his career, especially the years between 1934 and 1948, the period that saw the publication of his two best-known works of social criticism, *The Idea of a Christian Society* (1939) and *Notes Towards the Definition of Culture* (1948). During these years Eliot also did a substantial amount of occasional and journalistic writing that, unlike many of his late literary essays, has never been republished, and that has received only selective scholarly attention.[9] In addition, he took a more active role than has usually been recognized in several organizations and groups that were part of the mainstream of English public life at the time. In the absence of adequate biographical evidence, speculation about Eliot's intentions is hazardous, but I suspect that during this period he aspired to play a more direct part in shaping influential opinion in England than he had earlier, when his style had been rather that of the irresponsible gadfly, and that this closer involvement in public life had its effect on the nature and style of his social criticism, with the result that its idioms and allegiances may need to be characterized more in terms drawn from the indigenous political tradition.

That there are complexities here not adequately acknowledged in current scholarship may be suggested by quoting two widely differing earlier commentators who place Eliot in company quite other than that recently so much insisted on. Reflecting on the later political writings, J. M. Cameron proposed in 1958 that Eliot's sympathies were not really with the "totalitarian" leanings of Maurras, despite his repeated professions of admiration for the French writer, and Cameron went on to suggest that Eliot "fails to see that his real affinities are . . . with Jefferson and Burke, with Acton and Maitland."[10] To treat Eliot as essentially a late representative of the English Whig tradition was, in some ways, a daring piece of reclassification. Eliot's concerns and characteristic tone, even in his political and social writings, seem far removed from the legal-historical sensibility at the heart of this tradition of political thinking, and in his well-known antipathy to everything he took "liberalism" to represent, Eliot might seem an improbable bedfellow for a figure like Acton, often regarded in the late nineteenth century and after as the conscience of European liberalism's better self. But the more one explores the place of Eliot's polemical writings in public debate in Britain in the late 1930s and 1940s, the more suggestive this reclassification becomes (Cameron himself did not expand upon his comment beyond observing that "the *Maurrassien* note is scarcely struck" in *The Idea of a Christian Society* and "is quite vanished" by the time of *Notes Towards The Definition of Culture*).[11] During this period, Eliot could be sympathetic to almost any form of pluralism in social and political arrangements, most notably in his defense of the differentiation of classes and regions in *Notes*, and more generally in his resistance to assigning further powers to an already alarmingly collectivist state. Above all, his constant insistence on the need for the countervailing power of the Church in modern society could also place him in the company of, say, J. N. Figgis and hence of the thinkers who stand behind Figgis—Acton and Maitland outstanding among them.

My second quotation complicates the question of Eliot's political identity during these years still further. In his historical survey of Anglican social thought, Edward Norman encountered Eliot's political writings from a perspective very different from that of most literary scholars, and he treated the Eliot of the later 1930s, in particular, as part of "Anglican social radicalism."[12] Again, the company seems surprising on first acquaintance, but, as Norman noted, the figure to whom Eliot expressed a particular debt in his writings of this period was R. H. Tawney, acknowledged as the leading "Christian socialist" thinker of the interwar years. Nor is the political classification of such company simply a matter of hindsight: the 1941 Malvern conference on "The Life of the Church and the Order of Society"—at which Eliot delivered a paper on "The Christian Concept of Education" that was later included in the best-selling volume made of the proceedings—was described at the time by the (admittedly conservative) bishop of Winchester as "a gathering of the Left-Wing intelligentsia."[13] Such labels are obviously not to be taken entirely at face value, and classifying Eliot as a fellow-traveler of English Christian socialism is no nearer to being the whole story than is describing him as a late English Whig, but these are in their different ways helpful reminders that the current insistence on his Maurrassien affinities cannot really do full justice to the writings that issued from his much closer engagement with English public life in the years from the mid 1930s to the late 1940s.

In attempting to give a more adequate characterization of Eliot's role as a social critic in this period, this essay is also intended to serve as an illustration of two more general claims. First, reflection on this particular case may suggest certain distinctive features in the position and opportunities of the intellectual in Britain compared to the situation in other European countries at this time. And secondly, I hope this discussion may indicate some of the ways in which, when the characterization of a writer's, even an indisputably "major" writer's, public role is in question, the work of the literary scholar may need to be extended and supplemented by the comparative perspectives of the intellectual historian.

II

In the 1930s, there was no shortage of denunciations of the iniquities of capitalism. These were expressed in a variety of idioms and they issued in diverse remedies, but they concurred in repudiating the elevation of the return on capital into the overriding social goal. Although alternatives to laissez-faire capitalism could be proposed by radically opposed ends of the political spectrum, the repudiation of the principle of profit and private enterprise itself most obviously tended to come from those sympathetic to some form of socialism. In Britain this attitude had deep roots in a tradition of ethical socialism that stretched back to the early nineteenth century and derived much of its moral force from Protestant Christianity, even when not expressed in overtly Christian terms.[14] While Tawney, as mentioned above, was acknowledged in the 1930s as the leading intellectual representative of this tradition, its critical application to contemporary conditions was undertaken by, most notably, the self-described "Christian sociologists" of the Christendom Group.

The Christendom Group had been started in 1920, animated by the idea of addressing contemporary social ills by drawing inspiration from the principles of Christianity, especially as elaborated in the medieval heyday of the natural law tradition. It had from the outset a markedly anti-industrial and anticapitalist emphasis: several of its most prominent members, such as A. J. Penty and Maurice Reckitt, had belonged to the earlier, and (in the idiom of the day) explicitly "Collectivist," Church Socialist League.[15] In the 1920s there was considerable overlap in both ideas and personnel with the Conference on Christian Politics, Economics, and Citizenship (usually referred to as COPEC), whose most energetic representative was William Temple, appointed archbishop of York in 1929 and elevated to the see of Canterbury in 1942. Several members of these organizations were also active in the Guild Socialist movement, which in turn had its own medievalizing strain, and many members of the group were later to be enthusiasts for Major Douglas's "Social Credit" theories. A number of leading Christian intellectual figures were among the authors of a letter in *The Times* in April 1934 expressing enthusiasm for "Social Credit"; the signatories included Hewlett Johnson, the "Red Dean" of Canterbury, perhaps the leading left-wing figure in the Anglican Church at the time.[16]

The quarterly periodical *Christendom: A Journal of Christian Sociology* was founded in 1931, with Maurice Reckitt as editor, and annual summer conferences soon followed. In Britain, the term "sociology" was still sufficiently unestablished and contested for its appropriation in certain special senses not yet to be a wholly quixotic enterprise, and the label "Christian sociology" had considerable currency between the 1920s and the 1940s to indicate a concern with analyzing and promoting a conception of society as a collective moral enterprise. In the late 1930s and the 1940s, this strain of explicitly Anglican social thinking enjoyed a markedly prominent place in public debate in Britain, and several members of this group, such as Reckitt, Canon V. A. Demant, and Philip Mairet, were active in the organizations and publications through which this prominence was gained and exercised.

T. S. Eliot was an active member of this group from the early 1930s to the late 1940s. In the 1920s, his rather limited forays into contemporary public debate had been made as something of a political dandy, where the elegance and strikingness of his attitudes almost seemed to be ends in themselves, regardless of their lack of realism or their limited persuasiveness. But recent Eliot scholarship has perhaps underestimated the extent to which, in the course of the mid and late 1930s, Eliot deliberately involved himself in more conventional and, in some respects, more pragmatic political activity. He came to write as someone who believed that influential sections of English opinion sufficiently shared his premises for it to be worth engaging in the wearying work of committees and discussion groups, worth stating and restating basic principles in pamphlets and newspaper articles, worth trying to identify the areas of least disagreement. This development did not only represent a shift in Eliot's own attitudes and commitments: it was part of a wider cultural change that involved a marked resurgence of explicitly Christian attitudes and groups in English public life during these years.[17] We need to take the measure of Eliot's involvement in these activities if we are not to misconstrue the nature and intended point of his social writings.

Eliot had been received into the Church of England in 1927, and in the course of the 1930s he became a prominent Anglican layman.[18] In these years, he was closely associated with the Christendom Group, addressing its summer conferences, publishing in its journal, and representing it on various Anglican bodies. He expressed his sympathy for the group's ideas in other ways, too. In fact, he was also one of the signatories of the letter supporting Social Credit mentioned earlier: a figure such as Hewlett Johnson is hardly the political company in which one might expect to find Eliot, especially when one remembers that this letter appeared only a few weeks after the publication of *After Strange Gods*, but as I have already suggested, anti-industrialism could make strange bedfellows. From 1934, he was on the editorial committee of the *New English Weekly*, edited by another Christian sociologist, Philip Mairet. Through this association he was led to join the "Chandos group" (which took its name from the restaurant at which meetings were held), a gathering of like-minded Christians, including Demant and Reckitt, committed to formulating "certain absolute and eternal principles of true sociology."[19]

By the mid 1930s, Eliot was recognized not just as a cultural asset to the Anglican Church but as a willing and effective participant in its activities. In 1936 he became a member of the archbishop of Canterbury's committee to prepare a conference, to be held in Oxford the following year, on "Church, Community and State." He read a paper to the conference on "The Ecumenical Nature of the Church and Its Responsibility Towards the World" and became a member of the special section dealing with "the economic order." He took part in further meetings at Lambeth Palace in 1938, where the question of a "lay order" was considered, and in April of that year he was among a group of some twenty Christian public and intellectual figures, subsequently referred to as "the Moot," who held the first of their regular gatherings that continued until 1947. The principal organizer of the Moot was the ecumenical churchman J. H. Oldham, who also recruited Eliot to a meeting of the Council on the Christian Faith and the Common Life in September 1938. Eliot began writing *Idea* in February 1939.[20]

Thereafter, he was involved in, among other activities, the preparations for the Malvern conference of 1941, an event that in some ways represented the high-water mark of the Church's direct influence on political opinion at this time.[21] In 1943 he served as one of the two Anglican representatives involved in preparing an interchurch statement on "religious freedom," in 1947 he was a member of the committee that drew up the report on "Catholicity" in the Church, and so on.[22] When, in a discussion paper for the Moot, he had concluded that "the most important point of operation of a social philosophy may be the education in values of the political classes,"[23] he was expressing a conviction to which he attempted to give particularly practical expression during this period.

Of course, convictions that were held by others with all the vigor of partisanship tended to be hedged in Eliot's mind with obliquities and velleities that resist easy description. But at the heart of his close association with the "Christian sociologists" was a shared antipathy to industrialism (more encompassing than a critique of capitalism as such) and a frequently reiterated lament about the divorce between morality and the market, ultimately between Church and life. At the same time, it is important to see that the political inclinations of this group of Christian writers were neither homogeneous nor unchanging. In particular, the central individuals such as Demant and Reckitt (to whom Eliot repeatedly expressed his indebtedness) came, by the early 1940s, to take a less optimistic view of the possibilities of large-scale social reorganization; if anything, the dangers involved in the fashionable enthusiasm for central planning came to seem more pressing.[24] Demant's influential book *The Religious Prospect*, published in 1939, was severe on the "progressive optimism" of contemporary liberalism, just as in the course of the war Reckitt came to fear that "social radical" enthusiasm would lead to excessive state control. Both Demant and Reckitt came in the 1940s to lay more emphasis on the dogma of Original Sin as setting limits to the effectiveness of merely political change.[25] Nonetheless, they continued to insist on the distance separating the genuinely Christian social thinker from the conventional wisdom of secular thought: "Christian sociologists," wrote Reckitt as late as 1945, must be "at war with prevailing assumptions."[26]

There was an element of self-dramatization in this description given the extent to which public life at the time was still officially, and in some ways actively, Christian. And although Reckitt particularly had in mind the "assumptions" that sustained contemporary economic arrangements, even here the Christian sociologists belonged to a long tradition of anti-industrial thought and feeling that enjoyed widespread support among the English educated classes in the first half of the twentieth century.[27] Eliot himself commented on "the anomaly that the most highly industrialised country in the world should be the one which has the least adapted itself and reconciled itself to its own industrialism."[28] In his journalism of this period in publications like the *New English Weekly* or the *Christian Newsletter*,[29] on whose editorial boards he served, as well as in his more extended exercises in social criticism, Eliot was far from writing as a lone voice crying in the wilderness. Casual asides such as his remark that "readers of *Christendom* do not need to be reminded that the agricultural community is the most stable" indicate the extent to which he was confident of the responses of his implied reader.[30]

This particular form of social radicalism reached its peak in his *The Idea of a Christian Society*, which described itself as an attempt to "criticize our economic system in the light of Christian ethics."[31] There he proposed changes in "our organisation of industry and commerce and financial credit"; he acknowledged the truth in the charge that "what we have is not democracy but financial oligarchy"; he denounced the lowering effect of "mass society organised for profit"; he constantly inveighed against "private profit" and "unregulated industrialism"; he concurred with Demant's complaints about "the subservience of politics to plutocracy"; he even remarked that a possible appeal of totalitarianism was that it did at least subordinate "the financier"; and, in a much-quoted passage, he professed to wonder, in the light of the Munich crisis, whether "our society" was "assembled round anything more permanent than a congeries of banks, insurance companies and industries, and had it any beliefs more essential than a belief in compound interest and the maintenance of dividends?"[32] Throughout, a deep moral conservatism functioned to underwrite a sweeping economic radicalism. Indeed, one could redescribe the place of *Idea* in English political thinking of the period simply by posing the, at first sight implausible, counterfactual question: how little of the book would need to be altered if the title were changed to *The Idea of a Christian Socialist Society*?

More obliquely, the book is also a meditation on the theme of cultural leadership in a modern society. From its title on, it is the most Coleridgean of Eliot's works, and nowhere is this more marked than in its preoccupation with what it tries, not always successfully, to resist calling "the clerisy."[33] In sketching the components of his Christian society, Eliot distinguished the small, self-conscious "Community of Christians" from the larger, and largely unreflective, "Christian Community": the former were to be "the consciously and thoughtfully practising Christians, especially those of intellectual and spiritual superiority." Having emphasized that they could not be the kind of vocational body that Coleridge had had in mind in his idea of a "clerisy"—

to which university teachers and parish priests belonged by virtue of their offices — he goes on:

> The Community of Christians is not an organisation, but a body of indefinite outline; composed of both clergy and laity, of the more conscious, more spiritually and intellectually developed of both. It will be their identity of belief and aspiration, their background of a common system of education and a common culture, which will enable them to influence and be influenced by each other, and collectively to form the conscious mind and the conscience of the nation.

If one replaced the first phrase in this passage with the phrase "Christian intellectuals are not an organisation, but . . . ," the rest of the passage would seem a natural gloss, concluding with the defining role of intellectuals, "form[ing] the conscious mind and the conscience of the nation." Indeed, as Eliot goes on to lament increasing specialization, he observes that literature, theology, politics, and so on are all seen as separate, even by "those who should be the intellectuals." But this term leads a troubled life in Eliot's writing. Having insisted that "the Community of Christians" would contain "both clergy and laity of superior intellectual and/or spiritual gifts," he continued: "And it would include some of those who are ordinarily spoken of, not always with flattering intention, as 'intellectuals.'" At the same time, it was essential that this group should not become any kind of separate intellectual caste: it was desirable that "ecclesiastics," "politicians," and "those who are ordinarily spoken of . . . as 'intellectuals'" should mix.[34] This kind of social integration had, of course, long been the reigning model (and to some extent practice) in Britain — as compared, predictably, with France — and the lack of "flattering intention" in the common use of the label "intellectuals" partly referred to the self-important sense of apartness that this label was taken to connote. In Victorian Britain, the man of letters and the don, like the higher ecclesiastic and the politician, were largely seen as gentlemen among gentlemen. An ambivalence toward this model is frequently discernible beneath the smooth surfaces of Eliot's prose, and *Idea* is one of the places where his distance from comfortable English assumptions is occasionally evident.

Having insisted on the value of religious orders in his conception of a Christian society, he adds a sentence that at first appears to be a non sequitur: "And, incidentally, I should not like the 'Community of Christians' of which I have spoken, to be thought of as merely the nicest, most intelligent and public-spirited of the upper-middle class — it is not to be conceived on that analogy."[35] This sentence, with which the paragraph ends, is formally characteristic of much of Eliot's prose, from the apparent offhandedness of "incidentally" to the abruptness of the last clause and the tacit withholding of any further explanation. When an author disclaims any intention of saying or meaning something, there is always some significance to why it is *that* something, out of the limitless somethings he is not saying, that he chooses to disown. Why should Eliot choose at this point to distance himself from this particular possible misinterpretation? The immediately preceding and succeeding sentences defend — his tone hints at the pleasures of snubbing fashionable prejudices — the role of celibate and contemplative religious orders. The implication could be, therefore, that rather than the social interpretation of his category that he repudiates in the quoted sentence, he is summoning a more unworldly, less conventional set of beings into existence. But those in religious orders clearly constitute only a tiny fraction of the individuals who constitute Eliot's "Community of Christians," so they can hardly be thought to provide the positive illustration of the term that would seem to be necessary to prevent the slackly conventional assumption from usurping it. Yet the incongruously archaic image of the cloistered, celibate monk does figure what Eliot hints is missing in the conventional conception, something to do with giving priority to one's relation with God. And, at the risk of appearing to try to extract too much from this one sentence, I would suggest that Eliot's mind moves instinctively to repudiate *this* particular conception precisely because the "most intelligent and public-spirited of the upper-middle class" had in fact been the source of so much of the reforming and morally earnest activity in English society for several generations.[36] This is the contrast that comes to his mind, because he wants his "Community of Christians" to represent a more strenuous ideal, one carried by a heterogeneous group of individuals who are less at ease in Zion than the traditional leaders of English opinion, less rooted in a particular social class.

The Idea of a Christian Society and Notes Towards the Definition of Culture are almost invariably treated in tandem; indeed, since 1960 they have been available in the United States in a single volume entitled *Christianity and Culture*, the form frequently cited by subsequent scholars.[37] There are, needless to say, deep continuities between the two books, but there are also, I want to suggest, significant shifts in preoccupation and style of argument, shifts that bear directly on the question of how best to characterize the political identity of Eliot's later writings. The changes were partly an expression of a more general decline in the optimistic Anglican social radicalism of the 1930s, partly of a wider anxiety about the growth of "collectivism" during the war and the immediate postwar period. But in provoking the altered tone and argument of *Notes*, a not insignificant part was played by one of the figures whom Peter Gay has singled out as a leading representative of the Weimar spirit in exile, Karl Mannheim.[38]

III

Eliot and Mannheim do not make an obvious couple. Although specialist scholars have long been aware of the links between them, the significance of the relationship for our understanding of Eliot's place in the intellectual history of the period has not, perhaps, been fully appreciated. In 1935, Mannheim, who had fled Germany two years earlier and taken up a teaching post at the London School of Economics, published *Mensch und Gesellschaft im Zeitalter des Umbaus*, which appeared in a revised and enlarged form in 1940 as *Man and Society in an Age of Reconstruction*. It was in this and other work from the late 1930s and early 1940s that Mannheim elaborated his notion of "planning for freedom," an analysis in the abstract conceptual language of German sociology of the need to supersede laissez-faire individualism with democratic planning. Mannheim was working, broadly speaking, within a post-Weberian framework that focused on how something more than the affectless link of individual rationality is needed to hold modern societies together. Here he looked particularly to the role of "the intellectual elite" as formulators and disseminators of the "values" that provide the requisite social glue, and in the course of the 1940s, he became increasingly preoccupied with the ways in which this elite could be effective under the conditions of "mass society."[39] Eliot would seem to have met Mannheim at the second Moot, to which the latter had been introduced by his fellow émigré Adolf Löwe.[40] It is clear from surviving accounts that Mannheim became a focal figure at meetings of the Moot, and several of Eliot's contributions took the form of direct or indirect responses to Mannheim's ideas.[41]

Initially, Eliot broadly endorsed Mannheim's analysis of the ways in which cultural leadership in an age of "mass society" had still to be exercised by cultivated minorities, but he clearly found both the secular frame of Mannheim's account and its tendency to recommend the "organisation" of "values" deeply uncongenial. Mannheim wanted a systematic theoretical structure within which the analysis of individual problems could be located, whereas Eliot (and, it would seem, most other members of the Moot) inclined rather to the pursuit of individual intuitions and practical suggestions.[42] There were similar differences over the conception of an "order" with which the Moot had begun. Mannheim, characteristically, favored the establishment of a highly organized group committed to collective action; Eliot was among those who thought it more appropriate to confine their activities to discussion and informal contacts with influential members of the largely secular surrounding society. Eliot also deprecated the notion that they should have an agreed body of ideas to promote: "It is not the business of clerics [sc., members of a clerisy] to agree with each other; they are driven to each other's company by their common dissimilarity from everybody else, and by the fact that they find each other the most profitable people to disagree with."[43]

Publicly, Eliot treated Mannheim's work with considerable respect. Reviewing *Man and Society* in 1940, he broadly endorsed its premise that "for better or worse, we have a 'mass' society, and if we do not study how to use the techniques for good, then we must certainly be prepared to see them used for evil."[44] He recognized that this analysis focused attention on the role of the "elites," but he was skeptical of Mannheim's faith in the selection of elites in a mass society on the basis of aptitude and achievement alone. When he reviewed Mannheim's *Diagnosis of Our Time* three years later, he also raised doubts about the adequacy of sociology as a basis for the understanding of society.[45] In effect, Eliot was reserving for the "man of letters" the mantle of "the generalist," not imprisoned by a particular professional idiom and standpoint.[46]

The Moot records reveal two recurrent features of Eliot's response to Mannheim: first, he tried constantly to substitute terms and observations drawn from England's distinctive social circumstances in place of Mannheim's general sociological categories; and secondly, he pointed to ways in which Mannheim's examples of the working of *elites* in a democratic society actually presupposed some of the advantages enjoyed by a dominant *class*. An undercurrent in Eliot's response (which occasionally surfaced in public comment, as in his review of *Diagnosis of Our Time*) was his skepticism about sociology's scientific pretensions; both "the man of letters" and "the Christian sociologist" were identities that offered to transcend (and trump) the limitations of the kind of scientistic and mechanical understanding of society that Eliot saw as gaining increasing authority with the wider public.

The surviving records of the Moot largely consist of summaries of the proceedings, but they also contain two typescript discussion papers entitled "Notes on Mannheim's Paper" and "On the Place and Function of the Clerisy," dating from January 1941 and December 1944 respectively, in which Eliot took issue with Mannheim's ideas directly.[47] The first of these contains

one of his earliest attempts, here made in explicit contrast to Mannheim's usage, to grapple with the concept of "culture":

I cannot find that I have ever associated "progress" with what I mean by "culture." I
mean by the latter, something which is always decaying and always has to be reborn:
we try to preserve something which is essentially the same amidst extreme superficial
changes. I do not mean by culture the extension of popular education and of refinement of manners: these forms of progress may even be, in practice, inimical to culture. What I mean by it may be something peculiar to myself: but I think that the
point that it does not mean quite the same thing here that it does in central Europe
is perhaps worth making.[48]

The first published fruits of this train of thinking appear in his articles "towards a definition of culture" in the *New English Weekly* in January 1943,
where, against the implicitly Mannheimian notion of the role of the intellectual elite in promoting culture, he argued that "there is no 'culture' without 'a culture.'"[49]

The later exchange over "the clerisy" shows Eliot uneasy with Mannheim's analysis of the role of intellectuals. Throughout, he implicitly contested any attempt to sacralize or institutionalize intellectuals (a term he stu-
diously avoided here) or to expect them to form a self-contained caste acting
in concert for objects of their own. As we have seen, Eliot was not willing to
posit the existence of "elites" divorced from the larger units of "class." In England, he argued, the clerisy has by and large been part of the upper middle
class, although its members have been conscious of their sense of distance
from the core of that class and have often been highly critical of it. In the
same vein, Eliot did not envisage the clerisy as a whole acting as a single unit:
"Agreement and common action can only be by particular groups of clerics,
and is most effectively exercised against some other groups of clerics." Nor,
finally, would Eliot accept that "culture" is the preserve of the clerisy: "The
maintenance of culture is a function of the whole people, each part having
its own appropriate share of responsibility; it is a function of classes rather
than of elites."[50] In these terms, his earlier notion of "the Community of
Christians" begins to look rather like a self-selected elite.

Eliot could have what he regarded as fruitful disagreement with Mannheim only because there was so much about the nature of modern societies,
and the need for cultural leadership within them, on which they agreed. Indeed, it is clear that the Moot's discussions were premised on the assumption
that it was for a cultural elite to decide what "the people" needed, and to do
it; the model of cultural leadership present in the various proposals was that

of an already established elite using its position and resources to propose "values" *to* the great bulk of the population, not to engage in discussions *with*, still less to receive instruction *from*, them. It is this premise that allows Eliot to use such phrases as the following without any suggestion of self-consciousness: "The necessity for the re-education of the people's sense of values, from above, is one of immediate importance." When he went on to say that, once the war was over, "we shall be told . . . that we have allowed the people to sink into a state of physical, moral and cultural deterioration," the responsibility for these things lies clearly with the "we" who belong to this elite.[51]

Eliot's engagement with Mannheim's ideas was only part of an extended process by which he modulated the strenuous Christian ideal of *Idea* into the more sociological and pragmatic concerns of *Notes*. Attention to the chronology of some of the main stages of this process may be helpful at this point: it makes clear that the argument and, to a large extent, the formulations of the later book had taken shape by the end of the war, and so although Eliot saw the program of the Labour government as confirming his fears about planning, *Notes* was not primarily conceived as a response to that program. Instead, much of it was worked out in the course of his engagement with Mannheim's ideas, and the bulk of the book was drafted by the end of 1945.[52] The final form of the contents was only settled after the typescript had been read by Philip Mairet in 1947,[53] and, following further delays, the book was not actually published until November 1948.

IV

As its calculatedly diffident title suggests, *Notes Towards the Definition of Culture* presented itself as an attempt to clarify the current meanings of the term "culture." For all Eliot's habitual fastidiousness of phrasing, the book leaves the term drifting uncertainly between overlapping and sometimes conflicting senses. Ostensibly, it favored a usage that went beyond the narrow, Arnoldian sense and moved closer to the comprehensive, anthropological sense that had established itself in the first half of the twentieth century, although Eliot's frequent laments about the "decline" of culture betrayed the continuing normative power of his usage. Masquerading as a "sociological" inquiry into the conditions conducive to a flourishing culture (understood as a societywide complex of activities and attitudes), the book actually constituted — and was widely recognized as[54] — a topical restatement of the conservative conception of society as a delicate organic growth whose health depended upon the maintenance of a balanced diversity in social structure, in regional differentiation, and in religious organization.

At the heart of the book were three recurrent arguments, couched in general terms though with obvious local reference. First, Eliot asserted an indissoluble (if still elusive) connection between culture and religion: he denied that the relation could be captured by the flat term "relation," preferring to describe culture as "essentially, the incarnation (so to speak) of the religion of a people."[55] Secondly, he argued that the existence of a flourishing culture depended upon diversity and, indeed, "friction"; any movement toward uniformity threatened this vitality. And thirdly, he challenged the meritocratic doctrine of "elites," insisting on the need for that kind of intergenerational transmission of values that could only be assured by the existence of classes.

These arguments were far from peculiar to Eliot: all had long pedigrees in English intellectual life and public debate. The first was recognizable as, among other things, a more cautious and sophisticated statement of the view that, in the previous two decades, had become particularly associated with the name of Christopher Dawson (one of the three figures to whom, in the preface to *Notes*, Eliot acknowledges "a particular debt").[56] Dawson had begun to make a name for himself in the 1920s with some wide-ranging historical works intended to support the claim that the vitality of civilizations depended on the vitality of their religions. He adumbrated this case in a 1925 article entitled "Religion and the Life of Civilizations" and expanded it in his 1929 book *Progress and Religion*.[57] In the former, he wrote: "The great civilizations of the world do not produce the great religions as a kind of cultural by-product; in a very real sense, the great religions are the foundations on which the great civilizations rest. A society which has lost its religion becomes sooner or later a society which has lost its culture."[58] Eliot read *Progress and Religion* with admiration when it appeared, and wrote to Dawson to solicit an article for *The Criterion*; he later told the poet and painter David Jones, who knew Dawson well, how much the latter's book had influenced his own ideas on religion and culture.[59] In the course of the 1930s, Dawson became a well-known cultural commentator and a prominent figure in the revival of Catholic intellectuals in that decade.[60] When, in 1948, Dawson contributed an essay to a volume, edited by Demant, entitled *Our Culture* (which Eliot reviewed favorably), he could rightly assume that his general position was well known: "I do not think there is any need for me to insist on the fundamental thesis that the present crisis of Western civilisation is due to the separation of our culture from its religious basis. I have been saying little else for the last fifteen years."[61]

The second main argument in *Notes* can perhaps best be seen as the transcription into cultural terms of familiar Whig-liberal arguments about political liberty and social progress. At times Eliot could sound like Burke — "When I speak of the family, I have in mind a bond which embraces a longer period of time than this: a piety towards the dead, however obscure, and a solicitude for the unborn, however remote" — and at times like J. S. Mill — when speaking of "the vital importance for a society of *friction* between its parts," or urging that within the "unity" of Christendom "there should be an endless conflict between ideas, for it is only by the struggle against constantly appearing false ideas that the truth is enlarged and clarified" — and at other moments he could sound like any of a long line of English political thinkers who had deplored the "unsettled" political history of France since the Revolution or who had professed to fear that the alternative to fruitful diversity was to fall into "oriental lethargy."[62] By the early twentieth century, these traditional Whig-liberal arguments had become national rather than sectarian possessions;[63] by the 1940s, they were, for obvious reasons, most frequently appealed to by conservative critics of increasing "collectivism."

If the book's third chief argument struck a somewhat more distinctive note, it was because Eliot was one of the first to recognize the challenge laid down to conservative social thinkers by Mannheim's theory of elites. One relevant aspect of Eliot's tactics here, as in their Moot exchanges, was his attempt to replace the sociologist's abstract categories with terms that stayed close to the distinctive conditions of English society. For example, where Mannheim had spoken of the category of "bourgeois society," Eliot added the gloss, "I think it would be better to say, for this country, 'upper middle class society,'" and similarly where Mannheim treated aristocratic and bourgeois society as two distinct and mutually exclusive stages of social development, Eliot stressed, as "a difference applying particularly to England," the way the upper middle class "would not have been what it was, without the existence of a class above it, from which it drew some of its ideals and some of its criteria, and to the condition of which its more ambitious members aspired."[64] More substantively, he implicitly generalized the English case in his contention that a flourishing culture had depended (and would continue to depend) on the existence, not of elites, but of *the* elite, drawn chiefly "from the dominant class of the time, constituting the primary consumers of the work of thought and art produced by the minority members, who will have originated from various classes, including that class itself."[65] The moral was clear: a classless or egalitarian society, a radical dream regarded by many at the time as at last coming within reach, could not, therefore, be expected to sustain a vital culture.[66]

Notes commanded considerable attention in Britain, not just on account of Eliot's literary standing, but also because it gave topical and stylish expression to certain long-respected forms of argument, bringing them to bear upon issues at the heart of contemporary domestic debate, above all the question of what could be done to promote and diffuse culture, either by government agencies dedicated to the purpose or, in broader terms, through a more egalitarian educational system.

The contrasts between Eliot's two major works of social criticism can be partly characterized in terms of their interestingly different antipathies. In *Idea*, the fundamental defect of modern society is its tendency toward an almost entirely secular view of the world, and the most pressing manifestation of this defect is to be found in the unchallenged preeminence of economic values. In *Notes*, while the increasing secularism of society is still, of course, deplored, the fundamental defect is identified rather as an encroaching uniformity, and here the most pressing manifestation takes the form of the enthusiasm for planning. Conversely, the two works suggest a different degree of accommodation to what are perceived as the deep-seated features of English society.

Hence, in terms of his intellectual affinities and relevant predecessors, the Eliot of *Idea* is something of a cross between Coleridge and Tawney, who are not such an unlikely pairing as they may at first seem, especially if one concentrates on their common antipathy, in the name of Christian ethics, to the dominance of the commercial and the "mechanical." The pedigree of *Notes* may be a little harder to identify, but one possible bloodline would be "out of Burke by Weber," though insofar as one is talking of an actual connection rather than merely an intellectual affinity, one has to acknowledge that it is Weber as mediated by Mannheim. And this general change or shift of emphasis in Eliot's social criticism is mirrored in his treatment of the theme of cultural leadership. In *Idea*, his "Community of Christians" is a heterogeneous and partly self-selected group: in principle, membership is determined by the individual's spiritual and intellectual qualities rather than by social position or occupation, even if, as I have suggested, the traditional role of the English professional class hovered in attendance. But in the early 1940s — chiefly, it would seem, as a result of his critical engagement with Mannheim's thinking — Eliot came increasingly to distrust any notion of an elite that betrayed the presence of atomistic or purely meritocratic assumptions, and to look instead to those groups whose cultural leadership was also rooted in values and attitudes sustained across the generations, partly by unconscious or unattended-to social processes. At the same time, he came to fear what one might call the fundamentally Jacobin tendency of the doctrine of elites — the anxiety, to which Burke gave the most enduring expression, that a society governed by an elite who had nothing in common other than their ability and determination to rise to the top would be a society in which no institution or practice would be safe from a leveling rationalism.[67]

Eliot recognized, of course, that, in a modern "mass" society, the day was long past when the aristocracy or some similar caste could exercise cultural leadership as a right, but implicitly his later social writings assume that sociological theories of "elites" and "intellectuals," based on continental European experience, failed to do justice to the way in which, in English conditions, an educated upper middle class, partly shaped by "pre-bourgeois" values, could continue to provide the living tradition that cannot be planned or created *ex nihilo*. In proposing this general analysis, Eliot was coming down in favor of a model that was, as his conservative philosophical intuitions said it should be, an abstraction from the concrete case of English social conditions during the previous century or so. He was essentially making the case for a version of the Victorian intellectual aristocracy in the new circumstances of mass society. In so doing, he was in effect proposing in the sphere of culture a version of the old Whig ideal of adaptability in the sphere of politics.

The believer in a vital, and hence adaptable, tradition constantly faces the difficulty of having to make delicate discriminations about what is to be acknowledged as a legitimate modulation of established practice and what to be stigmatized as a disruptive innovation. By the mid 1940s, the case could, after all, be made for seeing the Utilitarians and Fabians as representing a central, possibly now dominant, strand in English political thinking, and hence for seeing the current vogue for central direction and planning as an appropriate expression of the native political tradition. A perception of this kind led some conservative thinkers during these years to reach further back and further afield to relativize, and thus relegate, what Michael Oakeshott influentially called "rationalism in politics."[68] Eliot had his share of this disposition,[69] and the tendency of his literary criticism had, of course, been to look to the "unified sensibility" of early seventeenth-century England, or to go even further back to the "unified society" of the age of Dante, in his search for correctives to the disintegration of thought and feeling evident in a literature corrupted by Romanticism and science. But by 1948, he seemed no longer willing to dismiss modern society in toto as "worm-eaten with liberalism." It is revealing of Eliot's greater concern to persuade that shortly before publication, he added a final paragraph to *Notes* that had not been present in the draft submitted to Faber's reader. That draft ended, bleakly, with Eliot brooding on how we are "destroying our ancient edifices to make ready the ground upon which the barbarian nomads of the future will encamp in their mechanised caravans." Prompted possibly by Philip Mairet's misgivings,[70] Eliot then added a further paragraph that referred deprecatingly to the previous ending as "an incidental flourish designed to relieve the feelings of the writer." As published, the text ends with a much soberer, and implicitly more optimistic, affirmation of the need to "consider how far these conditions of culture are possible."[71] By this point, the "hunger for wholeness" might, it seems, be appeased, if not entirely satisfied, by bite-size measures.

V

After 1948 Eliot largely retired from social criticism and controversial writing, becoming what he had long threatened to become, an institution. Perhaps the award of both the Nobel Prize and the Order of Merit in that year gave him little choice. The aldermanic gravity and eirenic reasonableness of his accommodation to liberal democracy in the 1950s seemed far removed from the aggressive antimodernity and stylized provokingness of his social writings leading up to the publication of *After Strange Gods*. Eliot himself hinted that his social and political thinking had changed and developed to a greater extent than had his purely literary ideas; he intended, but never completed, a review of his social thinking to parallel his assessment of his earlier critical work in "To Criticise the Critic."[72] But his prose of the 1950s suggests a mind already at rest, and his later lectures and speeches on cognate themes, such as his 1955 address on "The Literature of Politics," amounted to little more than a wary and sometimes weary restatement of broadly conservative intuitions, too bland really to merit the label "social *criticism*."

In the late 1930s and 1940s, however, his views were still flinty enough to produce sparks, though during these years he was not, as he has sometimes been represented and as he largely had been in the previous decade, an isolated, idiosyncratic figure, attended to only because of his literary eminence. In fact, one can identify several prominent features of public debate in twentieth-century Britain that corresponded to characteristics of Eliot's social writings. First, there was the very deep strain of anti-industrialism, a tradition of thought and feeling that drew energy from sources that might equally well be labeled "radical" or "conservative." Secondly, there was the long-standing expectation, which perhaps enjoyed a final flourish during this period, that the Anglican Church's leading intellectual figures should be able to make its authority and its distinctive perspective on social and economic matters tell in public debate and the formulation of policy. Thirdly, there was the frequently renewed vitality and purchase in English history of a style of political thinking that might, in its broadest allegiances, be called Whig, and of which Pluralism was a late and partial expression. And finally, there was the cultural disposition to treat literature, or, more exactly, literary criticism, as a "generalist" discourse, free from the distorting narrowness of more specialized or technical idioms. These elements, already heterogeneous, were only partially and unevenly expressed in Eliot's social writings during the period from 1934 to 1948, but they help provide more rewarding terms for the analysis of those writings than do those derived from the continental European traditions of reactionary, monarchist, and ultimately fascist, styles of political thinking.

The evolution of Eliot's writing that I have traced also accounts for his greater impact in domestic English cultural debate in the 1940s and 1950s.[73] Had he remained the posturing ultra of the much-quoted preface to *For Lancelot Andrewes*, he would still have been treated with respect on account of his literary standing, but he would not have posed any intellectual *problems* for his opponents.[74] But it is striking to see how those who engaged in the debate about culture in the next generation precisely selected Eliot as the antagonist to be wrestled with. The most striking testimony is provided by the extended, and in some ways surprisingly generous, discussion of his late social writings in Raymond Williams's *Culture and Society*, written in the mid 1950s. Williams discriminated between, on the one hand, the Introduction and the "Notes on Education," which he saw as "the growling innuendoes of the correspondence columns rather than the prose of thought," and, on the other, the central chapters which displayed some of "that brilliance and nervous energy of definition which distinguishes Eliot's literary criticism." He recognized Eliot's role in strengthening the case against more egalitarian social and educational arrangements, on which matters "he now commands considerable attention and support." But, more tellingly still, Williams saw the force of Eliot's arguments against the belief in meritocracy unsupported by any inherited "whole way of life" and against the easy assumption that "culture" could, without dilution, be endlessly diffused: on these questions, concluded Williams, "he has left the ordinary social-democratic case without many relevant answers."[75] Similarly, Richard Hoggart later recalled of this period how *Notes* "stood for so much I did not agree with in conservatism. Yet it was the hardest book I knew, from that side of the cultural debate, to rebut."[76]

To continental European observers, "the cultural debate" referred to here may have seemed by this date a peculiarly British, even parochial, one. The British experience of totalitarianism, war, and the Holocaust had, of course, been radically different from that of most of mainland Europe, but even by the end of the 1930s, as Eliot had noted in winding up *The Criterion*,[77] political conditions in Europe were accentuating the perceived distinctiveness of British circumstances. It was perhaps only the pardonable wishfulness of the exile that led Mannheim, writing to an American correspondent in 1939 about the mood in London, to muse: "The dynamism of the time reminds me a little of the Weimar Republic."[78] Although the author of an appreciative essay on Marie Lloyd might well have responded to the charms of Sally Bowles, the trajectory of Eliot's career surely confirms the growing divergence, rather than convergence, between the cultural situations in Britain and continental Europe in the 1930s and 1940s. More narrowly, I have been arguing that Eliot's political writings increasingly moved away from the manner of the European reactionary tradition he had earlier espoused and closer to certain well-established domestic styles of political argument. In this, perhaps limited, respect, James Cameron's passing observation that Eliot's "real affinities are . . . with Jefferson and Burke, with Acton and Maitland," quoted at the beginning of this essay, seems nearer the mark than the trend of much recent Eliot criticism.

But larger issues of intellectual history are obviously involved in these different characterizations. Peter Gay has observed how the writings of many of those Weimar intellectuals consumed by "the hunger for wholeness" ultimately displayed "a vehement, often vicious, repudiation of reason accompanied by the urge for direct action or for surrender to a charismatic leader."[79] Such extremes of intellectual and political reaction were obviously not unknown in interwar Britain, just as, conversely, Weimar also had its *Vernunftrepublikaners* and others not guilty of this particular *trahison des clercs*. But intellectual traditions and cultural situations help to turn what, in one society, is eccentric or of no consequence into what, in another society, may figure as central or dominant, and vice versa. The identities informing Eliot's later political writings, I have suggested, were essentially those of "the man of letters," "the Anglican moralist," and "the cultural Whig." There is obviously considerable resemblance between these identities and those that, elsewhere and in other idioms, might be termed "the intellectual," "the Catholic social philosopher," and "the antidemocratic reactionary." How best to account for the larger worlds of difference discernible behind the subtle contrasts between these two sets of terms would require another essay, perhaps a series of volumes. For the present, one may borrow from Eliot's own expression of writerly discontent, and conclude of the analysis actually attempted here:

> That was a way of putting it — not very satisfactory:
> A periphrastic study in a worn-out poetical fashion,
> Leaving one still with the intolerable wrestle
> With words and meanings.

11. Céline and the Cultivation of Hatred

Was ist das, was in uns lügt, mordet, stiehlt? Ich mag
dem Gedanken nicht weiter nachgehen.
— Georg Büchner

Le sentiment de la destruction inné dans l'homme:
on dirait que c'est un animal mal doué et homicide
de nature.   —Edmond and Jules de Goncourt

The joy of killing! The joy of seeing killing done —
these are the traits of the human race at large.
—Mark Twain

With these Victorian obiter dicta, Peter Gay launches his pathbreaking study
of aggression among the nineteenth-century bourgeoisie, *The Cultivation
of Hatred* (1993).[1] In Gay's work, the erotic, the belligerent, and the hostile
assume their rightful places as central features of modern European cultural history. In this book, as in so many other studies, Gay, the historian of
the *Aufklärung* and its children —Voltaire, Bernstein, Freud— instructs us to
know our enemy, the enemy within.

His point of view was shared by some very unsavory people, both in the
nineteenth century and after. I want to discuss one of them: the French physician and novelist Louis-Ferdinand Céline. Ideas are not undermined simply by the character of the people who hold them, although the political
stance of some of those, like Céline, who took to heart the words of Büchner,
the Goncourts, and Twain gives one pause about the implications of what
they had to say.

It isn't only what they said, but how they said it that matters. Following the
Victorians, aggression has entered the citadel of literature itself. It is this phe-

nomenon that I want to discuss in these remarks. Prose or poetry as aggression; words as insults; images as weapons to mock the reader were not invented in the nineteenth century, although Baudelaire and Flaubert raised them to a new and disturbingly powerful level. The working out of this angular Victorian legacy in twentieth-century cultural history is my subject, located within the corpus of a writer who knew a thing or two about the cultivation of hatred.

Louis-Ferdinand Destouches, who wrote under the pen name of Céline, completed his medical studies in 1924. The final phase of his passage into the profession was the preparation of a thesis. The subject he chose was the Hungarian physician Ignaz Philipp Semmelweis and his war against filth in the delivery theater. Semmelweis had been scoffed at and rejected in his time. He went insane and committed suicide. "Semmelweis," Céline later said, "is my ideal."[2] Both lived among the sick, the deluded, and the dying. In this, his first extended piece of writing, Destouches/Céline had found his home: in dirt and gynecology of a very scatological kind. He lived in close proximity to both for the rest of his life.

Céline is the poet of the filthy.[3] He reveled in it; celebrated it; mocked those uncomfortable with it. He created a unique literary style to convey his disgust with the filth in men. His work is not so much the literature of decadence as its apotheosis. Closer to Rabelais than to Chekhov among doctors who were also men of letters,[4] Céline offers a vision of darkness and corruption derived from late-nineteenth-century discussions of biological and social pestilence and decline.[5] War to Céline is an embodiment of the viciousness in human nature. It gives sadism and cruelty a respectable, indeed a patriotic and glorious, face. One of these faces is that of the psychiatrist treating men suffering from, or claiming to suffer from, mental illness in wartime. Other physicians and scientists come in for their dose of abuse too. But in his first and most celebrated work, *Voyage au bout de la nuit*, published in 1932,[6] eight years after he had entered the medical profession, it is the psychiatrist who particularly incarnates the sickness of a society whose full hideousness had been exposed by war. Céline the healer is the cultivator of hatred, a soldier, physician, and iconoclast who spewed out his misanthropy in some of the most inspired and repellent passages in twentieth-century literature.

Short-War Illusions

In dealing with Céline, it is never possible to establish a clear, fully documented narrative of events. He loved embroidery and wove lies, half-lies, and complete fabrication into the tapestry of his war service presented in *Journey to the End of the Night.* This is true of other war writers as well; Robert Graves, hardly a misanthropist, remarked famously that only those who told lies about the war were really telling the truth.[7] It is the nature of the lies Céline told that sets him apart from other writers about World War I. Like them, he hated the war; but unlike them, he also hated those who waged it — on both sides — with an unbridled passion.

Destouches grew up in a drab, although not impoverished, part of central Paris. His family lived in the Passage Choiseul, a few streets geographically and light-years away culturally from the Bibliothèque nationale. It was the Paris of small-scale merchants and shopkeepers, most very respectable, some shady.[8] It was just at what Céline later called the point of a wedge of the wealthy, stretching from his home in the 1st *arrondissement* outward to the more fashionable districts of the 8th and then the 16th *arrondissements.*[9] Among the chief characteristics of this world was its rancor — its obsession with money and its hatred of those who (through corruption or influence) commanded it. In no way proletarian, these lower-middle-class people were ideal material for the "socialism of the fools" — anti-Semitism and racism.[10] In due course, Céline became master of both.

Céline recalled this world as suspicious and ill-ventilated, filled with characters who believed that somehow life had cheated them.[11] In his memory, it was a district where the inhabitants guarded their respectability like a jewel, and where most people shared the general preoccupation with personal health and public hygiene, concerns popularized through the research of Pasteur and others.

Disease was indeed everywhere in turn-of-the-century Paris. It was one of the unhealthiest capital cities in Western Europe, well behind both Berlin and London in life expectancy and infant survival rates. *Quartiers* varied substantially, and the Passage Choiseul, although not at all a slum, shared the air and water of unhealthier quarters not far away. A mile to the east, the space occupied today by the Centre Pompidou, a great cultural forum, was in the 1890s the worst *îlot insalubre* (island of disease) in Paris.[12]

This was a stratified district, where small distinctions took on great significance. In 1905, the slight superiority of the Destouches family over their neighbors could be demonstrated by finding the cash to send their son, not to the local school, but to a boarding school, Saint-Joseph-des-Tuileries.[13] Two years later, he was back at the local school, and after passing his primary school examinations, he was sent off first to Germany and then to England to learn the languages. This was just the thing for a future career in business. He worked sporadically in the clothing trade, mostly for businesses with international outlets. His future lay elsewhere, but his English and especially his German would come in handy later in his life.

Compulsory military service followed in 1912. When asked to identify his trade, he responded as many recruits tend to do, in a forward-looking, none too accurate way. He was, he wrote, a jeweler.[14] Now he was a jeweler turned cavalryman, just the branch of service for a respectable young man facing three years in the army. The problem was, though, that the cavalry required its recruits to follow a stiff six-month course of military training and to look after horses as well. This was not the sort of thing Destouches had faced before, and it hit him hard. His fellow soldiers, mostly laconic Bretons, were hardly able to offer him solace. It may be that his later defiance of all authority and liking for a life from which one can clear out at a moment's notice were a reaction not to his baptism of fire but to army discipline.[15]

There is one whiff of defiance in this phase of Destouches's life. In the environs of Rambouillet, a remarkable anarchist ran a school for freethinkers. Sébastian Faure presided over a salon for the unconventional, liberally endowed by the duchess of Uzès. She liked to hunt, and Destouches may have encountered her and Faure in that setting.

A few years later, Faure was convicted of molesting little girls. The charge may have been simply a frame-up of a man who, like a good anarchist, railed against war.[16] Destouches remembered him fondly. It is unclear how well they knew each other, or whether what attracted him were Faure's ideas, his personal tastes, or his defiant style. Possibly all three.

When war broke out, Destouches's unit moved east, facing Metz and Nancy, then in German territory. His unit supported French troops engaged in encounters now dignified with the title of "the Battle of the Frontiers," a series of failed and particularly bloody French offensives in Alsace and Lorraine. The cavalry were used to cover the massive French retreat that followed. In this role, combat was rare. Destouches's regiment lost its first man on 8 September 1914, a full month after the outbreak of the war.

Although they didn't suffer many casualties, they saw them and the detritus of war all around them. "I have never seen and will never see so much horror," Destouches wrote his parents.[17] Bodies left on the battlefield, funeral pyres of the dead, corpses blown to bits by artillery searching for the living. These were the hallucinatory images recalled by the young cavalryman, exhausted by a march interrupted by at best two or three hours of sleep.

When this part of the front stabilized in early October, Destouches's unit was sent north and west to Flanders. This time, near the river Lys, the cavalry were deployed to guard the flanks of the British Expeditionary Force, then being rebuilt after having suffered heavy casualties during the German invasion of Belgium and France. German attacks were beaten off in foggy nights in what Destouches described to his parents as "this strange land where only Flemish is spoken."[18] Further south, near Armentières, the cavalry were in action again, and suffered more casualties. By mid-October, they were back in Belgium, near Poelkappelle on the outskirts of the Allied strong point of Ypres. There, Destouches, sent at night to find another isolated post, was hit in the arm by a ricocheting bullet. He was evacuated on 26 October.

Instead of going to a military hospital, the wounded man found his way to a Red Cross ambulance and was treated in a Red Cross hospital in Haze-brouck. Amazingly, given the chaos of communication and transport, Des-touches got through by phone to his parents, and they arrived at the hospital. Destouches refused morphine or an anesthetic, fearing amputation of his arm when he was unconscious. He preferred the pain to the uncertainty of what he might see when he awakened after an operation. A civilian doctor removed the bullet and sutured the wound.

From his Red Cross hospital, he proceeded to the military hospital in Paris at Val-de-Grâce. There he was awarded the Military Medal. His exploits were immortalized in the patriotic journal *L'Illustré national*. In its issue of November 1914, it saluted Destouches, of the 12th Cavalry Regiment, who had "spontaneously volunteered . . . to deliver an order under heavy fire. After having delivered the order, he was seriously wounded on returning from his mission." The truth was more mundane: he had been hit accidentally, wandering around in the darkness.

In early 1915, he was operated on in a hospital at Villejuif in the suburbs of Paris. The aim was to correct muscle and nerve damage to his right arm, and the operation was a success. Further consultations followed. In March, he underwent electric shock treatment to stimulate recovery of the use of his arm.

That was the full extent of his active military service. Despite later yarns that he did little to contradict, there is no evidence that Destouches suffered from shell shock or that his wound was accompanied by any other trauma. He had received what British soldiers called a "Blighty," the best kind of wound—honorable but in no sense dangerous. He was out of the real war.

And just in time. Destouches's war was not the Great War. He was a cavalryman, removed from the field of battle just as it was about to be revolutionized. By the spring of 1915, in the same sector in Flanders in which he had been wounded, the Germans introduced poison gas to the battlefield; on the other side of Europe, at Gallipoli, French troops joined British in a futile attempt to knock Turkey out of the war. This war was now a world war, fought by machines on a scale no one had dreamed possible. The war of cavalrymen was a thing of the past.

And so was Destouches's part in it. Through a veiled conversation or two on the part of his father, he found a superb posting: as an aide to the French military mission in London. All those English lessons had paid off. His job was to process visa applications for those who wanted to visit France. Many adventures followed, including a marriage, the existence of which Destouches hardly noticed and abandoned with a flick of his wrist. Then came adventure in Africa as an agent of a French company in the Cameroons, formerly under German, then under French control. The heat, the mosquitoes, dysentery, and sheer boredom drove him out of Africa.

Dr. Destouches

In June 1916, back he came to France and a new career. After helping out in the offices of a number of obscure publications, he found his métier. The route to it was characteristically indirect. While the Battle of Verdun was at its height, Destouches found a way to perform war work of a special kind. The Rockefeller Foundation put its resources behind a venture in inter-Allied cooperation: a propaganda campaign to fight tuberculosis.[19] In France, the war against disease was one way to help reverse the country's demographic decline, a constant preoccupation of public health campaigns in this period.[20] The patriotic meaning of public health measures was brought to the population, in schools, in public meetings, through posters, songs, films, dramatic sketches, all paid for by the Rockefeller Foundation.

Several of Destouches's friends joined the enterprise, some for a lark, others for more dubious reasons connected with deferment from military service. Through them he became a public lecturer in this campaign against tuberculosis, "the enemy within." One of its leading figures in Rennes was Dr. Follet, president of the anti-tuberculosis committee of the Department of Ille-et-Vilaine, and professor in the School of Medicine in Rennes. He organized a reception in the city hall to greet the committee, after it had been cheered on by admiring crowds on its way from the train station. There Destouches met Follet's daughter Édith, whom he subsequently married.

With the dowry generously provided by his father-in-law, Destouches moved on from his baccalaureate — reduced in demands due to his military service — to medical studies. These studies occupied Destouches in 1920 and 1921, first in Rennes and then in Paris. Finally, in 1924, he submitted his thesis on Semmelweis and the fight against puerperal fever. The link to

Destouches's work for the Rockefeller Foundation is clear: here was the story of a man who found a way to relieve suffering, a man before his time. But Semmelweis was intriguing for another reason. His was a tragic story, the tale of a man ignored and rejected, a man who died mad and unknown. Destouches the physician was turning into Céline the author, the celebrant of failures and frauds.[21]

Dr. Céline

It is not my intention to traverse the years following Destouches's entry into the medical profession and his emergence as a major writer. Suffice it to say that much of the fictional material out of which his books grew came from his work first for the League of Nations as a "technical officer" in their Health Bureau. This post was funded by the Rockefeller Foundation and gave Destouches the opportunity to visit many countries, including the United States. Further elements of his writing may be traced to his next post, as a medical practitioner in Clichy, a mixed suburb adjacent to the 18th *arrondissement* in Paris. He ran the municipal dispensary there at which every conceivable ailment of those too strapped to pay for a private consultation was paraded before him. Installed in Montmartre in 1929 with his third wife, an American dancer named Elizabeth Craig, he received small grants from his friends in Geneva to study aspects of public health. These grants were a cover for his real mission: to complete a novel, an embryonic project that he described in this way: "without pretension and certainly not literature, my God no. But I have in me a thousand pages of nightmares in reserve, those of war naturally at the head."[22] Out of those nightmares came the *chef d'oeuvre* of Destouches/Céline, *Voyage au bout de la nuit*, published in 1932.

Writing Against the Grain

It is one of the pitfalls of cultural history to read fiction as biography and both as framed in the language of the time; biography is too narrow a focus; the "times," too wide. Fiction has its own optics, a subject far too complex to be examined fully here. All I want to insist upon is that the images and actions in *Voyage* are in no sense the story of Destouches's life. Their appropriate location, *pace* Céline, is within a genre widely developed in the interwar years, that of "war literature."

By 1932, whole libraries of memoirs and fictional accounts of the 1914–18 war had appeared in the languages of all the combatant countries. Bringing the trenches to life in fiction was a growth industry, stimulated by the cinematic success of a number of such books, most notably Erich Maria Remarque's *All Quiet on the Western Front*. Never averse to financial considerations, Céline knew there was a market for accounts of the war by former soldiers.

Many such books took the form of *Voyage au bout de la nuit*. They started with the war and its horrors and then followed the restless and damaged lives of the "front generation" in the interwar years. By the time *Voyage* was published, the world economic crisis and the political turbulence it occasioned made many people return to the question, what had the Great War accomplished? What did it mean?

Here is the point of entry for Céline's distinctive voice. He was not alone in articulating the view that the war had no "meaning" in the sense of fulfilling the war aims of one side or the other. But his aim was entirely different. Other writers had condemned the war as pointless butchery. But they had contrasted the political void of the war with a profound evocation of what the war had meant on the level of the individual soldier. The war had "meant" something profound to Barbusse and Genevoix and Remarque and Graves and Jünger—and to millions who never wrote their memoirs—because of the deep bonds formed between combatants, because of their sense of common suffering, because of their capacity to share sacrifices and preserve their dignity. They were the "men of '14" and wore the badge with pride. At times, Céline quietly shared this mood.

So did dozens of veterans' associations that believed that the lessons of camaraderie had to be applied to postwar society. They, the men who had come to know war at its worst, could educate the young. They could convince them that war was an abomination that must never be allowed to happen again. They could show how the spirit of fellowship learned in uniform could be applied in later years, to help the mutilated men who struggled to rebuild their lives after the war, to come to the aid of the widows and the orphans whose misfortunes came directly out of the war. In countless commemorative ceremonies, and especially on 11 November, these men came together to remember the war and to draw out of it some sense of personal, religious, or aesthetic redemption.[23]

Not Céline. In place of love for one's comrades, compassion for their suffering, and for those who tried to help them during and after the war, Céline offered hatred, contempt, abuse, spleen. His was a misanthrope's vision, full of the conviction that the war had exposed the venality and sadism at the heart of human nature.

He told his story as a first-person narrative. This was the fashion in war literature and has led to a lot of nonsense about war memoirs as "true" or "false."[24] No one should read war literature to find out "what the war was really like." This is especially so in reading Céline, whose experiments in style capture a sense of delirium, of what he liked to call "the vertigo of words." His "truth" is that of a semi-sober barroom conversation between two buddies reflecting on their adventures and grievances. The tone is that of an extended masculine rant about life's injustices and hypocrisies. Exaggerations and general reflections on life abound. No one, Céline suggests, could possibly take all this literally or totally seriously.

Of course, this was a useful defense, a way of distancing himself from statements he made of a dubious or incriminating kind—for example, remarks he uttered at the Institut Allemand in Paris in December 1941 about the need to exterminate the Jews. Such statements could have led to his execution as a collaborator during or after World War II, but he successfully hid behind the veil of his self-induced "vertigo" (and the penchant of the French authorities to treat writers as special cases).[25]

Céline's "truth" was of a different order entirely. For our purposes, it may be useful to concentrate on only two elements of Céline's subversion of the canon of war literature. The first is his discussion of patriotism among soldiers and civilians during the war; the second is his approach to psychiatric care, both during and after the war.

Patriotism as Madness

Céline subverts every element of humanism in the characterization of the men who went to war in 1914. But the force of his invective is amplified by his showing the cruelty, falsehoods, and vapidity of wartime patriotism. It was the wordsmiths of "war enthusiasm" who banished humanity from the scene, and those poor fools who fell into their clutches never got away. This theme tied him to a very different war writer, Henri Barbusse, whose novel *Le Feu*, published in 1917, was the first widely read account of the war to strip away the patriotic patina. Barbusse was a humanist, later a communist, but Céline held his work in high regard. The primary reason was his intolerance of those using elevated language to describe the cruelties of combat. Instead, Barbusse told the unvarnished story of the common soldier in his own rough language. At least in these respects, Céline followed his lead.[26]

Once entrapped in the war, Céline's soldiers divide into two sorts: the raving lunatics on both sides, armed to the teeth, trying to kill him and every other living thing on the battlefield; and the renegades, isolated individuals prepared to do anything to get out of the "muddy fricassee"[27] of flesh at the front. In his descriptions of the killers, he goes well beyond the occasional glimpses of brutality at the front captured in other war novels. His approach resembles that of Blaise Cendrars, whom Destouches knew in Paris, and whose novel *La Main coupée* does not mince words about the cruelties of combat.[28] But in *Voyage*, his two "heroes," Bardamu, the narrator, and his companion throughout the novel and alter ego, Léon Robinson, fear the sadism of their own side as much as the ferocity of the enemy. Bardamu is trapped in a nightmare, wandering around in the dark "with no better prospect than to end in a sea of liquid manure, sickened at the thought that we'd been tortured, duped to the entrails by a gang of vicious lunatics, who had suddenly become incapable of doing anything else than killing and spilling their guts without knowing why."[29]

In a characteristic Célinian aside, echoing in a demonic form the language of the Psalms, Bardamu tells the reader that he learned a lot about men at the front. "Never again will I believe what they say or what they think. Men are the thing to be afraid of, always, men and nothing else."[30]

Here is Céline's recipe: two parts misanthropy and one part anarchy. Because men are innately vicious, it was not the war that had brutalized them; they brought their brutality with them and were ready to spill it out in a torrent strong enough to drown anyone in the vicinity. For that very reason, Bardamu and Robinson, first separately and then together, decide to clear out.

Robinson is a man of all trades, "a kind of engraver," who prefers working on his own, "selling the evening papers in a quiet neighborhood where I was known, around the Bank of France," "kind of unskilled," but ingenious and totally unscrupulous. He strips off his uniform, and tries to get himself taken prisoner by the Germans. Bardamu, totally lost, and leading his horse through the darkness, joins Robinson in their nonviolent search for the enemy. The problem is, though, as Robinson puts it, "It's hard for a man to get rid of himself in a war!"[31] The two men part, still stuck on their side of the line.

We lose sight of Robinson at that point and follow Bardamu back from the front with an arm wound, an absurdly undeserved medal for bravery, and an unshakable resolve never "to go back on duty in the flaming graveyards of no man's land."[32] He considers himself a doomed man, with a "suspended sentence to be murdered" hanging over him.

To avert the decree, he plays his hero/invalid's status for all it is worth in the "putrid carnival" of the home front.[33] His status as a hero wins the favors of a promiscuous American nurse, whose vapidity is matched only by her desirability. Hiding in her bed works for a while. Why? Because

Lying, fucking, dying. A law had been passed prohibiting all other activity. The lies that were told surpassed the imagination, far exceeding the limits of the absurd and the preposterous — in the newspapers, on posters, on foot, on horseback, in carriages. Everybody was doing it. It was like a competition, to see who could lie the most outrageously.[34]

Psychiatry as Madness

And in that competition, Bardamu learns, psychiatrists are front-runners. After having subverted the notion of heroic soldiers stolidly standing the course out of love for their country and their families, it was time to undermine the notion that those in the medical profession engaged in treating soldiers were anything other than sadistic, criminal fools.

After a stroll in a Paris park and a glance at a disused shooting gallery, "the Gallery of the Nations," Bardamu is overcome with the feeling that everyone is shooting at him. Shouting out his fears to all and sundry, he is taken away to a psychiatric hospital for observation and treatment. "I was delirious, driven mad by fear, they said at the hospital. Maybe so. The best thing to do when you're in this world, don't you agree, is to get out of it. Crazy or not, scared or not."[35]

Here the tale takes a new turn, with echoes of more general discussions of traumatic illness among front-line soldiers.[36] The medical corps are there to help evaluate men like Bardamu and to separate the shirkers from the sufferers. But, Céline asks, what's the difference between the two? If the sufferers are cured, they go back to the trenches to endure more suffering. Shirking duty is in this context the only sane thing to do. Here is Bardamu's homely philosophy on this point:

At a time when the world is upside down and it's thought insane to ask why you're being murdered, it obviously requires no great effort to pass for a lunatic. Of course your act has got to be convincing, but when it comes to keeping out of the big slaughterhouse, some people's imaginations become magnificently fertile.[37]

Their job is to convince the psychiatrists that they are mad, but these specialists are the ones most divorced from reality. Bardamu falls into the hands of one such man, Professor Bestombes, who works in a dingy establishment in the southern suburbs, a home for the indigent elderly, who are kept "like insects" in this prison until they die. This is a reworked image of the capital's major mental hospital at Bicêtre.[38] The contrast between the setting, the treatment, and the rhetoric lavishly dished out could not be greater. To the sick, the professor offers whatever medical science can do for them:

Our science is at your disposal! It is yours! All its resources will be devoted to curing you! Help us with your good will! I know we can count on your good will!! We hope, we trust, that each one of you will soon resume his place side by side with his dear comrades in the trenches! Your sacred place![39]

Not if Bardamu has anything to do with it. Here in hospital he is in the midst of a guerrilla war against the state, which has for reasons no one can fathom sentenced him to death at the front. To get him there, he is "counted, watched, serial-numbered."

And treated by electro-convulsive shock therapy, dispensed from machines the doctor has personally purchased. Bardamu gets to know this physician and even tells him that he was not quite "as brave as I should have liked to be and as the undoubtedly sublime circumstances required." Bestombes takes this admission as a sign that recovery is on the way, a conclusion he derives from the work of the French psychiatrist Ernest Dupré, who (the doctor points out) has shown that the mentally ill benefit from "recollection of memories," which "if the cure is properly administered, should soon be followed by a massive break-up of anxiety percepts and the definite liberation of the area of consciousness" that Dupré calls "disencumbering cognitive diarrhea." This outpouring is likely to be accompanied by "intense euphoria, a marked resumption of relational activity" including "conspicuous hyperactivity of the genital functions, amounting in patients who were previously frigid, to a positive sexual frenzy. . . . " Bardamu, no doubt, is on the road to recovery.

The professor tells Bardamu that he is about to read a paper on "the fundamental characteristics of the human mind at the Society for Military Psychology." The war has remedied psychiatric ignorance. "By a process of breaking and entering, painful to be sure, but decisive and providential for science, we have penetrated [man's] most innermost depths!" The quarrel in every mind between altruism and selfishness has been exposed. To heighten altruism, the most sublime concept has been found: patriotism, a notion that (the doctor insists), once imbibed, enables soldiers to cast off "the sophism of self-preservation." Suppress the ego: heighten altruism; that is his morality. "That, Bardamu, is how I mean to treat my patients, electricity for the body, and for the mind massive doses of patriotic ethics, injections as it were of invigorating morality."[40]

This satirical tour de force is vintage Céline. His model for Bestombes
was Gustave Roussy, director of the Paul-Brousse Hospital in Villejuif, who
was the author of articles on shell shock and treated men suffering from that
condition in his hospital. Destouches had been there, too, but not for shell
shock; as I have noted, he was treated for nerve damage in his right arm. He
had been in Val-de-Grâce, too, where the real Ernest Dupré, one of the foremost French authorities on shell shock, was director of psychiatric medicine.[41] But there is no evidence whatsoever that Destouches was treated for
shell shock or any other psychic ailment in either hospital, although he liked
to cultivate the story that he had been trepanned.[42] There is even a photograph of him at Val-de-Grâce, with a bandage covering his face from the top
of his head to the bottom of his chin like a kerchief. A toothache is the likely
explanation, but the image was a wonderful resource for later embroidery.[43]
There were physicians who used electro-convulsive shock treatment in a
controversial way; the case of one man, Clovis Vincent, became a cause
célèbre during the war itself.[44]

But Céline's target is a bigger one: "society" itself, with its sadistic servants
who use high-blown language to cover its cannibalism, its tendency to devour its own. The mockery of Freud's theories of psychotherapy has the same
purpose. In the war of every single man against the state, physicians who
serve the state are the enemy incarnate. Recovery is not rehabilitation but a
return to torture.

What better irony than to follow this section of *Voyage au bout de la nuit*
with the first mention in the novel of Bardamu's entry into the medical profession? If his motto is "homo homini . . . lupus," now is his chance to get in
the first blow. And, ultimately, he does.

Work in a seedy municipal dispensary and a miserably poor private practice in the northern suburbs brings Bardamu in touch with misery, venality,
and cruelty of every kind. Ultimately, he finds a post in another clinic in the
Parisian suburbs, thanks to the intervention of a scientist who works there,
who has been dismissed from the Institut Pasteur for molesting little girls.

At this clinic, Bardamu offers his second set of reflections on psychiatry,
this time of a more general kind. They are useful to summarize, since they
point to the primary reason why he chose mental illness as one of the key
themes of his book. The remarks are first voiced by the director of the clinic,
a mild-mannered rationalist, Baryton. Here is his vision of the world:

I opened my Institution . . . just before the Exposition [of 1900], the big one, Ferdinand . . . we alienists in those days were . . . much less curious, I can assure you, and

less depraved than today! . . . None of us in those days tried to be as crazy as his patients. . . . It was not yet the fashion for the healer to go off his rocker on the pretext that it furthered the cure, an obscene fashion, mind you, like almost everything that comes to us from foreign countries. . . .

The secret is out: cosmopolitan ideas in psychiatry are part of a more general degeneration due to a mixing of races and peoples. Mockingly, Baryton asks Bardamu: "[H]aven't all differences and distinctions been effaced? No more white! No more black! Everything dissolves. That's the new approach! The fashion! If that's the case, why not go mad ourselves? . . . Right this minute! As a starter!" And that is what he proceeds to do.

The rant continues:

Sometimes, Ferdinand, when I listen to certain of our colleagues, and mind you, among the most esteemed, the most sought-after by the clientele and the academics alike, I wonder where they're leading us! It's infernal! Diabolical, prurient, captious, and dishonest, these minions of modern psychiatry are hurling us into the abyss with their superconscious analyses. . . . And the fact is, what with masturbating their intelligence day and night, those ultra-super wise men seem even now to have shut themselves up in the dungeons of the damned.

I say day and night, because you know, Ferdinand, they fornicate themselves all night in their dreams. . . . Need I say more! . . . They dig at their minds! They dilate them! They tyrannize them! . . . All around them there's nothing left but a foul slumgullion of organic debris, a marmalade of madness and symptoms that drip and ooze from every part of them . . . The remains of the mind are all over our hands, and there we are, sticky, grotesque, contemptuous, fetid. Everything's going to collapse, Ferdinand, everything is collapsing. I, old man Baryton, am telling you, and it won't be long now! . . . You'll see the end, Ferdinand, the great débâcle! Because you're still young! You'll see it! Oh, you'll enjoy it, I can promise you! . . . You'll all end up in the nuthouse! *Zoom!* Just one more outburst of madness! One too many! And *wham!* off you go to the loony bin.

"I saw the human mind, Ferdinand, losing its balance little by little and dissolving in the vast maelstrom of apocalyptic ambitions," Baryton adds. From 1900 on, in his opinion, "the world in general and psychiatry in particular have been one frantic race to see who could become more perverse, more salacious, more outlandish, more revolting, more creative. . . . The beast will devour us all, it's a certainty and a good thing too!. . . . Even now its wars and its flaming slobber are pouring in on us from all sides!" [45]

Toppling over the edge into insanity, Baryton decides to become an English gentleman. He leaves the clinic in the hands of Bardamu, who himself admits to living "on the dangerous rim of madness, on the brink, so to speak."[46] And so, our hero has finally arrived at a place where he can control the lunacy around him. He has created his own little society, one where only he decides what the rules are and who is sufficiently sane to enter the world.

The Body in Question

One central theme links Céline's diatribes on war and madness with his preoccupation with decay and corruption. It is his intense awareness of the body, the scene of the crime, as it were. As a physician, he could keep close tabs on the physical pathways of disease and degeneration. As a Don Juan, he revels in female flesh much more than in female companionship. As a soldier, he had taken whatever pleasure he could: "In the shadow of the slaughterhouse, you don't speculate very much about your future, you think only about loving in the days that are left to you, because there's no other way of forgetting your body a little, now that it's about to be skinned alive."[47]

The opposite was true. Céline almost never forgot about his body during the war, precisely because some anonymous force was set on turning it into a corpse. Bardamu believes that his flesh and bones are destined "to serve as a strainer and sorting house for mixed French and German bullets." After perforation, it will be "dripping with worms and infinitely more disgusting than ten pounds of turds on the Fourteenth of July," when future celebrations will be held three feet above the spot where he lies "rotting stupendously with all my deluded flesh."[48]

Voyage au bout de la nuit is a *tour d'horizon* of bodies. First and foremost there are the soldiers' bodies. Then there are the delectable female ones. These are worth possessing for a while, but they aren't really the same species as men. One incident highlights this point of view. In the mental hospital, Bardamu is struck by the patriotism of the nurses. Feeling for the country went straight to their ovaries, Céline writes, because they were programmed to copulate after the war to renew the war-torn world.[49]

His first lover, the American nurse Lola, shares her bed with him as long as she is convinced that he is a hero. Her body is a revelation; it shows that "a country capable of producing bodies so daringly graceful . . . must have countless other vital revelations to offer, of a biological nature, it goes without saying." And so, Céline concludes, "it was in the immediate vicinity of Lola's rear end that I received the message of a new world."[50] As soon as he shares his views about the hideousness of the war, however, she drops him like a stone.

His next lover is Musyne, a violinist turned prostitute, working for a prospering madam, with a lingerie shop and the good fortune to have had her ovaries removed after a bout of gonorrhea. Musyne is a patriot too. They last together until faced with the need to descend into an impromptu bomb cellar in the Paris suburbs during a Zeppelin attack. Bardamu refuses to join her in the cellar, a butcher's larder, "with all that meat hanging on hooks." "I have certain memories," he remarks. Lacking such scruples, Musyne goes into the shelter and out of Bardamu's life.[51]

Like other women in Bardamu's circle, Musyne does not share his nightmares about dismembered limbs. Later, when he meets Lola in New York, he recalls both women and the "intense hatred" he felt for them, a loathing that had "become part and parcel of my being." Certainly they were desirable, but in true misogynic fashion, Céline converts desire into hatred: "Where there's a luxurious body," he opines, "there's always a possibility of rape, of a direct, violent breaking and entering into the heart of wealth and luxury, with no fear of having to return the loot."[52]

Then comes Molly, a Detroit whore with the heart of gold. Bardamu lives with her, and off her earnings, but he has his pride. And his restlessness, which overcomes whatever affection he feels for her. Later on, he has a brief dalliance with a Toulouse woman, Madelon, the fiancée of his friend Robinson. When Robinson drops her and flees back to Paris, she returns to reclaim her man. She knows Bardamu can find Robinson and goes to seek his help. Instead, she gets a slap in the face. Literally. He tells her to go away. And when she does not move, he acts:

She was only a weak woman, so to speak. I had always wanted to slap a face consumed with anger, to see what a face consumed with anger would do under the circumstances. . . . On the streets, in cafés, wherever aggressive, touchy, boastful people quarrel. I'd never have dared for fear of getting hit back and even more of the shame that comes of getting hit. But here for once I had a golden opportunity. . . . I slapped her face twice, hard enough to stun a mule.[53]

Here Céline discloses the link between desire and contempt, between fucking and cruelty, between male bodies taking the chance to inflict pain on weaker women after having spent nearly a lifetime fleeing from the pain men in uniform inflict on one another.

The ugliness of human flesh is a central motif in Céline. It describes a man standing in front of a mirror, riveted by his own ghastly image. It's the same whether at war or at peace. During wartime, people hope that peace will be better, but "then they bite into that rope as if it were a chocolate bar, but it's only shit after all. You don't dare say so at first for fear of making people mad. You try to be nice. When you're good and sick of wallowing in muck you speak up. Then everybody suddenly realizes you were very badly brought up. And there you have it."[54] There indeed: the novelist of putrefaction spews forth his guts in this novel, an ode to decay, a paean to putrefaction.

Conclusion

Eight years after the publication of *Voyage au bout de la nuit*, the Nazis occupied France, and Céline became one of their most outspoken supporters. The reasons why he joined the Nazi camp are numerous. It was a way to shock more people than ever before, to outrage them, to thumb his nose at respectability. But there were other, deeper reasons for his affinity with his country's conquerors.

Initially, Céline behaved like a "loyal" Frenchman. He volunteered as a ship's doctor in 1939 and sailed briefly on the troopship *Chella*. But when the war was lost, he resumed the pose of contempt for conventional patriotism expressed in *Voyage au bout de la nuit*. His position, therefore, may be described as desultory pacifism, the kind that was one part self-preservation, one part loathing of his country.[55] France was moribund anyway. The causes of its predicament were as much biological as political. Céline was a racist, a convinced anti-Semite, who drew upon a long tradition of literary reactions to the theme of degeneracy and decline. His description of the process differs from that offered by many other writers, but his pessimism, like theirs, bears the traces of nineteenth-century forms of biological determinism.

In October 1933, Céline delivered an homage to Émile Zola, the author of *L'Assommoir*. Zola was fascinated by the genetic transmission of degeneration, recorded in tales of personal and collective downfall. His fiction is replete with woe, drunkenness, and insanity inscribed in a family's genes. Here was something to Céline's tastes, and he whipped up a brew of Zola and Freud, the Freud of the death instinct and the pessimism of *Civilization and Its Discontents*.

An unlikely trilogy: Zola, Freud, Céline. But not if we take note of the propensity of writers, doctors, and politicians to use biological metaphors to describe and to analyze social problems.[56] In this context, it is not surprising that Céline compares Zola to Pasteur, another student of disease.[57] If the body politic really had a life resembling that of living organisms, then it was in the process of corruption at all times. Its putrefaction was built into its very nature. And like other organisms, it was beset by invasion by foreign growths, which either succumbed to the body's defenses or overwhelmed them. From this premise, it is but a short step to the view that foreigners and Jews are unassimilable to the body politic, but form tumors, growths that devour the host unless eliminated by radical surgery.[58]

Here Céline was thinking along lines laid out by many other contemporary figures. The biologist Alexis Carrel, Nobel Prize winner in medicine, set up an institute for the improvement of the French race. Eugenics in France faced the out-and-out hostility of the Catholic Church, which was dead set against euthanasia or other forms of "negative eugenics," the restriction or elimination of those deemed "tainted" or carriers of undesirable social or biological characteristics.[59] But Carrel advocated "positive eugenics," the creation and protection of a biologically elite group to lead France in future years.[60]

After the war, Céline complained that the Nazis weren't racist enough. They had used the rhetoric to gather popular support but failed to take any real measures in a racist direction.[61] Is this Céline the joker, the buffoon unaware that he had blood on his hands? Probably not. From the time he grew up in the Passage de Choiseul, through his war service and his years as a medical student writing about Semmelweis, in the League of Nations Health Bureau and in private and municipal medical practice, Destouches/Céline was obsessed with decay. Corruption was everywhere; sometimes it took the form of tuberculosis or typhus; at other times, of venereal disease; then again it was insanity, either caused by the pace of urban life or inscribed in the genes.

Who better than a physician to link the sickness of the individual to the sickness of society as a whole? Céline was a student of diseased people and poisoned social relations, and like others who described society as a living organism, he had ready access to the language of the pathologist, redolent with images of decay and corruption.[62]

From Baudelaire to Zola to Céline, savage, sometimes scatological, indictments of conventional society have been dressed up in biological terms by writers of distinction. Nineteenth-century positivism fed the imagination of the social realists, prepared to describe facets of life from which polite society turned away. Céline had little to teach Baudelaire about contempt for his reader; and he had little to offer that was shocking to the Zola of *Germinal*, in which a venal shopkeeper is castrated by the women he has abused.

What Céline adds to this tradition is first and foremost a genius for the spoken word, an ear for conversation at once elliptical, fragmentary, funny, on occasion, moving. But he also adds his unforgettable portrait, this time not of urban decay—a well-worked theme by 1932—but of war, a war he knew only briefly, but whose atrocities filled his imagination until his dying day. His subject was "war and insanity, those two absolute nightmares."

His comments on psychiatry have a fascination of their own. Just as psychiatric themes were emerging as a powerful source for writers, artists, and thinkers of many kinds, Céline offered a totally subversive account of them. His psychiatrists are liars or charlatans, controlling or manipulating the people in their care. What makes the satire even more powerful is Céline's mockery of the use of language in psychotherapy. Here fiction, lies, myth, narcissism, and malingering all combine in a tale of not one but two surrealist hospitals, one operating during and one after the war. Both are places where language is converted into one more whip to keep the sick in order or in uniform. In the developing discourse on psychiatric care in general and on Freudian ideas in particular, Céline's malicious images and notions bear his characteristic stamp of the profound and the ludicrous.

Céline himself was the ultimate picaro,[63] the wanderer just barely able to outwit and lie to those in authority, with enough foresight to escape from trap after trap and move on to the next set of life-threatening scrapes. His voice is that of the anarchist, the subversive, intent on offering a totally discordant note on the subject of war and insanity.

He rails also against the chorus of commemoration of the dead of the Great War, in art, in ceremony, and especially in literature. Time and again the authors of war literature ask themselves: were there any redeeming features to the Great War? Did any good come out of it? Most answer either equivocally or positively. Céline offers a growl, an obscenity appropriate in his view to the subject. To him the war was a reflection of disease, a disease oozing out of the pores of society, presenting its stench to those unintoxicated by romantic nonsense about the nobility of war, warriors, or the men who tried to heal them. He is the poet of "war and insanity, those two absolute nightmares."[64] War signaled collapse; insanity embodied it. Their horrors foretold the end of days, and—Céline might have added—good riddance to you all.

12. Modern and Postmodern Paganism

Peter Gay and Jean-François Lyotard

The history of that odd hybrid we have come to call "Judeo-Christian" civilization has been haunted by what its defenders have so mightily sought to suppress and forget: the dogged persistence of the cultures and religions that came before.[1] Although widely divergent, these have been collectively defined by a term that none ever in fact chose as a self-description, but that has served their enemies well as a blanket term of opprobrium. That term is, of course, "paganism." Derived from the Latin for "from the country" (*pagus*) and drawing on the Roman soldiers use of *paganus* to stigmatize civilians, it was initially employed by the early Christians to refer to all those non-Jews who were not militants in Christ's army.[2] Although more neutral uses were occasionally adopted, the term's negative connotation was only intensified when the Church Fathers launched their polemics against classical philosophy and culture.

In fact, for well over a millennium, "pagan" served Christendom — as well as Judaism and the newer monotheistic culture of Islam — as a potent label to stigmatize those who departed from the dominant cultural norm. Clustered with its close neighbors "heathen," "idolater," and "infidel," it came to separate those who were saved from those who were damned. When paired with "savage" or "barbarian," it divided those who were civilized from those who were not. Linked with "diabolical" and identified with witchcraft and black magic,[3] it suggested an even more radical distinction between the truly human who possessed a dignity that must be honored and those who fell outside the pale of humanity and could be crushed with impunity. As demonstrated by the vicious persecution of the gypsies, who first wandered into Europe from India in the fourteenth century, "pagan" could become an epithet with very fateful consequences indeed.[4]

No binary opposition can, however, retain its boundaries for very long without some erosion, and that between "pagan" and its various others proved no exception.[5] Indeed, the pollution (or invigoration) of Jewish, Christian, and Islamic culture by paganism is so fundamental a theme of our history that no justice can be done to it in the short compass of an essay. But certain salient features of that story, especially its Christian chapters, must be quickly highlighted before we turn to the true focus of our enterprise, the comparison between modern and postmodern revivals of the pagan legacy as represented respectively by Peter Gay and Jean-François Lyotard.

"What has Athens to do with Jerusalem?" Tertullian contemptuously remarked, but many others continued to ask the same question in a less dismissive manner, ultimately helping to blur the distinction. One early way in which the opposition between the monotheistic religions and the pagan past started to erode was, in fact, through the allegorical reading of the ancient myths as prefigurations of Christian moral teachings, which began with the Neoplatonists in the Church, who were themselves borrowing a tactic from the Stoics, and reached a crescendo with the Jesuits during the Counter-Reformation.[6] Another was the tacit recognition and grudging acceptance of the tenacity of pre-Christian survivals in Christian practices. Thus, it was possible to discern in the medieval cult of local saints and their relics a residue of an earlier worship of local deities, in the same way that holy sites could be understood as reminiscent of Roman *loca sacra*. So too the mobilization of images in Christian worship, although a periodic source of iconoclastic anxiety,[7] could be understood as continuous with the pagan celebration of theophanous divinities.

The risk of such a recognition was, of course, the damage it might do to orthodox Christian belief. In the hands of such seventeenth-century skeptics as Pierre Bayle or such deists as John Toland, the similarities between pagan myth and Christian gospel were, in fact, deliberately brought to the fore to discredit the latter.[8] Catholicism in particular could be reviled as a polytheistic superstition only pretending to believe in one God. By the time folklore and ethnography began to emerge as scholarly disciplines in the nineteenth century, even the central story of the Crucifixion and Resurrection could be situated in the context of a universal pagan belief in a dying and reborn God of nature, as Sir James Frazer famously argued in *The Golden Bough*.

If one way of calling into question the absolute distinction between Christian and pagan was by showing how much of the latter had remained transfigured in the former, another was by reversing the order and finding in what had been stigmatized much to admire. Here perhaps the first sustained rehabilitation came with the renewed respect for classical learning in the Renaissance, when humanist naturalism sought inspiration in Greek and Roman philosophy, architecture, and the visual arts.[9] What one of our protagonists, Peter Gay, was to call "the era of pagan Christianity"[10] from 1300 to 1700 somehow found a way to combine orthodox faith and a new interest in antiquity. Many of the hermetic traditions of astrology, necromancy, and alchemy were combined in a heady way with a Christian spirituality that seemed to need their energizing power. But the equilibrium proved in the long run hard to maintain and by the time of the neoclassical Enlightenment, paganism and freethinking began inexorably to gravitate toward each other, turning revealed religion into a target.[11]

Neoclassicism, to be sure, had a highly selective reading of the pagan past, which identified it largely with its most elevated and ennobling achievements, an attitude that spawned a tradition — increasingly privileging Greece over Rome — whose best known exponents were Johann Joachim Winckelmann in Germany and Matthew Arnold in England. Deliberately aimed at the Lutheran and Puritan attempt to reinforce the boundary between an uncorrupted Christianity and its allegedly idolatrous predecessors, a boundary apparently weakened during the late Middle Ages and Renaissance, it sought to free itself from what it construed as the moralizing, life-denying rigorism derived from an exaggerated fidelity to the competing tradition it called "Nazarene" or "Hebraic."[12] The pagan Greece that "tyrannized" not only Germany, to borrow E. M. Butler's celebrated verb, but also much of English and French thought from the mid-eighteenth century on, found an aesthetic wholeness and reconciliation between nature and culture in the Hellenic world, which helped legitimate that non-anthropocentric respect for nature whose rise Keith Thomas has identified in the early modern period.[13] It could also paradoxically provide both a retreat from vulgar politics into inward-looking individual cultivation (*Bildung*) and a utopian model for the modern state.[14] Inspiration for the latter was readily found in the classical traditions of civic virtue and public rhetoric, which were revived by thinkers like Giambattista Vico, whose *New Science* also did much to urge belief in the truth-telling function of mythopoeic fantasy before Christian gospel and modern science.[15]

The new appreciation for the indigenous folk cultures of Europe, which began in the eighteenth century with Herder and intensified with the Romantic fascination with diversity and particularity, provided, however, a very different model of paganism, which helped it survive the decline in the actual reading of classical and Humanist texts during the late Enlightenment.[16] What can be called the desublimated alternative to neoclassical Hellenism found much to admire in the simplicity, vitality, and authenticity of supposedly "primitive" cultures. Celtic, Teutonic, Baltic, Slavic, and Magyar myths, rituals, and holy sites were rediscovered and incorporated into the developing national consciousness of various modern communities. Druidism, to take a salient example, was actively studied and even revived in eighteenth-century Britain, often for the purposes of inventing usable, if somewhat fanciful, cultural traditions.[17] In France, a positive reevaluation of "nos ancêtres les gaulois" went along with the Revolution's attempt to discredit the aristocracy, which was identified instead with those allegedly foreign pagans known as the Franks.[18]

A similar desublimating reassessment of classical paganism itself began as early as the mid-eighteenth century, when the buried Roman cities of Herculaneum and Pompeii were uncovered.[19] A new taste for the more "primitive" poetry of Homer went along with a fascination for the locales described in his epics.[20] Although it took until the era of Romanticism for the full effect to be felt, these sites revealed an antiquity that was more than the highest examples of timeless beauty; instead, they showed a whole way of life, including the most mundane details of quotidian existence. The archaeological discoveries of Heinrich Schliemann, who unearthed Troy in 1873 and Mycenae in 1874, and Arthur Evans, who uncovered even earlier Minoan sites on Crete after 1900, further excited the imaginations of those, like Sigmund Freud, who were anxious to dig beneath the surface of Winckelmann's idealized aesthetic of "noble simplicity and serene greatness"[21] to find an earlier, "archaic" period. By the late nineteenth century, the so-called "Cambridge School" of anthropology, led by Jane Ellen Harrison and Francis Cornford, sought to show the roots of classical Greece in the esoteric cults of primitive religion.

Often accompanying this excitement went a frank admiration for the fleshly delights of pagan sensuality, sometimes understood as a model of naive innocence, sometimes as a symptom of overripe decay. Present in increasingly desublimated ways from the Pre-Raphaelites (who were themselves sometimes called neo-Pagans) and Walter Pater to Oscar Wilde and Edward Carpenter in Britain, it was also evident among the French Decadents and Austrian Aesthetes. The struggle to give dignity to homosexual practices in particular explicitly borrowed from their honored role in Greek life. So too an appreciation of archaic Greece often resulted in a celebration of an allegedly benign matriarchal civilization ruthlessly suppressed by its patriarchal successor, as was argued by Johann Jakob Bachofen, Otto Gross, and their followers.[22]

The emergence of a less idealized image of Greek culture—ripping off the fig leaves, we might say, that had been added in the period of pagan Christianity—was, in fact, a Europewide phenomenon. In Germany, for example, its beginnings in the visual arts can be traced to the campaign to restore the vivid colors that had faded from the blanched image of neoclassical art with its marmoreal coldness, a cause championed, among others, by the great architect Gottfried Semper in the 1820s and 1830s.[23] In literature, the same impulse has often been discerned in Heinrich Heine's debunking poem "The Gods of Greece," which registers his disillusionment with Goethe's Olympian Hellenism and anticipates Nietzsche's *The Birth of Tragedy*. The latter book celebrates the mythic community reflected in the integration of Apollonian and Dionysian impulses in Attic tragedy, a community whose return Nietzsche saw foreshadowed in Wagner's operas. Although he abandoned the quest when he lost faith in Wagner's mission, attempts to realize it in the years before World War I were made by such militantly anti-Christian publicists as the brothers August and Ernst Horneffer, who promoted an explicitly "pagan life course" based on the values of heroic nationalism.[24]

Whether or not such a revival had any meaningful influence on the fuzzy embrace of a Teutonic pseudo-religion on the part of the Nazis a generation later remains in dispute.[25] But it is clear that the self-proclaimed paganism of such Weimar figures as Ludwig Klages and Alfred Schuler could easily be given, not only an anti-Christian, but also an explicitly anti-Semitic flavor, abetted by the demeaning identification of Judaism with "soulless" patriarchal intellectuality and alienation from nature. The ground had already been prepared by nineteenth-century classicists, who, if Martin Bernal's controversial argument is to be believed, had sought to find an "Aryan" lineage from antiquity to the modern age, thus repressing the African roots of Hellenic civilization.[26] In fact, even the most respectable exponents of philhellenism, such as Werner Jaeger, could turn their love for pagan Greece into an implied apologia for the Third Reich.[27]

However one construes such episodes, it is clear that by the end of the nineteenth century and the beginning of the twentieth, the term "pagan" was available widely again for positive identification in many other, less sinister contexts. In Britain, for example, novelists like Thomas Hardy and D. H. Lawrence sought to draw on its power as an antidote to the repressive dreariness of modern life. In 1908, a group of young nature-worshipping, friendship-extolling, anti-Victorians at Cambridge gathered around the poet Rupert Brooke could self-consciously choose to call themselves "neo-pagans" in order to signal their desire to inhabit groves that were once again sacred.[28] Although World War I put paid to the mobilization of Homeric images of heroic valor for patriotic purposes and hastened the decline of classical studies,[29] other variants of the tradition were still available for later revival. Whether optimistically vitalist or pessimistically entropic—the Decadent imagination, as noted, was often fueled by languid images of a pagan world in delicious, indolent decay—paganism had shown itself to be an especially buoyant floating signifier with remarkable staying power, but no settled meaning.

In our own day, it has, as we know, been reappropriated by a wide variety of nature-venerating, antitechnological groups, whose New Age spirituality is an eclectic amalgam of many different beliefs, customs, and rites. Repudiating the heroic masculinist readings of some earlier revivals, these often take on an explicitly feminist coloration. As in the period of Bachofen and Gross, such goddesses as Isis, Artemis, and Astarte, whose closeness to the earth is extolled as an antidote to the transcendent striving of typically patriarchal religions such as Judaism or Christianity, are put at the center of the pagan pantheon. Although it is difficult to assess the literalness of their belief, many New Age devotees seem determined to reverse the secularization of pagan religion, which allowed it to survive only in aesthetic form in Renaissance and neoclassical Europe, and hope instead to reenchant the world. Even the diabolic variant of paganism, however apocryphal the connection between early modern witchcraft and ancient practices may actually be, has found its adherents, at least so it would seem from the popular press's fascination with Satanism today. More secular celebrants of pop culture's profitable mixture of sex and violence, such as Camille Paglia in her widely discussed *Sexual Personae*, equally exult in the claim that "the latent paganism of western culture has burst forth again in all its daemonic vitality."[30]

To complicate the picture still further, the term has also retained its aura for those who stubbornly hold on to an ennobling notion of Hellenic culture. The right-wing British moral philosopher John Casey, for example, has recently sought to make a case for paganism, not on aesthetic or religious, but on ethical grounds. Casey defends the worldly virtues of pride, courage, magnanimity, temperance, fame, and practical wisdom against the world-denying ones of Christian and Kantian humility, self-abnegation, and fairness.[31] Paganism in this usage becomes a weapon in the struggle against the leveling egalitarianism of the modern age, a justification for accepting the privileges provided by fortune as instances of what Bernard Williams has called "moral luck."[32] Right-wing German hermeneuticians such as Odo Marquard have also found in pagan polytheism and "polymyths," at least in their disenchanted form as histories and stories, an alternative to "philosophy as an or-thological mono-logos,"[33] which is shorthand for Habermasian Critical The-ory. And French radical right-wingers such as Jacques Marlaud have sought to concoct a pagan pedigree for Alain de Benoist and the "nouvelle Droite" by tracing the defense of myth in Henri de Montherlant, Jean Cau, Louis Pauwels, Pierre Gripari, and their ilk.[34] Countering this usage is the persis-tent evocation of the democratic polis of Periclean Athens as a radical anti-dote to the authoritarian implications of Platonic politics, a case that has been perhaps most vigorously made by Hannah Arendt and her followers.

With all of this as a prelude, it may well seem that nothing much can be gained from trying to slow down the whirl of denotations and connotations that have surrounded the history of the vexed term "paganism" and assign it a single, coherent meaning. I would, in fact, agree that no benefit would ac-crue from attempting to privilege one variant of the term over another, for what has made it so powerful a semantic resource is precisely its polysemic indeterminacy. What may be worth attempting, however, is a more modest comparison of the use made of it by two of its most respected recent advo-cates, who are too clever to hope for the magical reenchantment of the world and thus successfully avoid the New Age *Schwärmerei* that often surrounds the term. By comparing the modern paganism of Peter Gay with its post-modern counterpart in Jean-François Lyotard, we may be able to appreciate how at least some of its lessons may still have something to teach us as the second millennium of the Christian era draws to a close.

Writing in defiance of the attempt, most vigorously made by Carl Becker,[35] to reduce the Enlightenment to a secularized variant of medieval Christian thought, Peter Gay provocatively subtitled the first volume of his magisterial work *The Enlightenment: An Interpretation* (1966) *The Rise of Modern Pa-ganism*. Explicitly drawing on Heine's distinction between "Hebrews" and "Hellenes," he sought to situate the "party of humanity" squarely in the lat-ter camp. The greatest figures of the Enlightenment—Montesquieu, Fonte-nelle, Gibbon, Lessing, Rousseau, Diderot, Winckelmann—were virtually all in the thrall of the classical world, moving beyond mere identification with its heroes to an active pagan identity of their own. "The philosophes," Gay claimed, "did not merely quote antiquity, they earned it, and they ex-perienced it."[36] The battle between the Ancients and the Moderns turned out in a way to be a victory for both.

That of the Enlightenment was, however, a distinctly "Mediterranean pa-ganism," which ought not to be confused with the "Teutonic paganism" that

Gay describes as a "strange mixture of Roman Catholic, primitive Greek and folkish Germanic notions."[37] Nor, despite their frequent resort to sensualist rhetoric, should they be thought of as particularly licentious: "these preachers of libertinism," he insisted, "were far less self-indulgent, far more restrained in their habits, than their pronouncements would lead us to believe."[38] Instead, their paganism meant first and foremost an extension of the slow replacement of myth and superstition by reason that had characterized antiquity (Vico, let it be noted, is entirely absent from Gay's account). The philosophes, he claims, primarily admired the ancients "for their realism, their impatience with obfuscation and mystery."[39]

They were, to be sure, explicitly "modern" pagans, by which Gay means that they spurned a pedantic study of antiquity for its own sake, casting off what Diderot called "the spectacles of anticomania."[40] Resistant to any nostalgia, cautiously upholding the ideal of progress, but not naively utopian, the philosophes went beyond the "first Enlightenment" that had taken place in Greece and Rome. Anti-Platonic, they rejected all variants of metaphysics, including the speculative Rationalism that had prevailed in the century before them, as a compromise with religion. Their focus instead was on epistemology and psychology, which allowed them to probe the underlying sources of humankind's need for false consolations.[41] "What made the pagans modern and gave them hope for the future," Gay argues in the second volume of The Enlightenment, "was that they could use science to control their classicism by establishing the superiority of their own, second age of criticism over the first, and thus keep their respect for their ancestors within proper bounds."[42]

Endorsing Ernst Cassirer's celebrated defense of the eighteenth century as an age of analytical critique rather than synthetic system-building,[43] Gay nonetheless makes David Hume, rather than Cassirer's hero Kant, the culminating figure in his narrative. The more militantly antireligious Hume, successfully liberated from the shackles of his Scottish Presbyterian upbringing, was, Gay contends, "the complete modern pagan" who "makes plain that since God is silent, man is his own master: he must live in a disenchanted world, submit everything to criticism, and make his own way."[44]

Reading the Enlightenment in this light meant that Gay had clearly chosen to pursue the second of the two ways through which paganism lost its stigma described above: being elevated over its religious opponents through a reversal of the initial hierarchy. Although Gay admits that the philosophes had exaggerated in their contempt for Christian learning, which had in fact acted as a "transmission belt"[45] of the classical legacy, he endorses their larger thesis: that the Middle Ages undermined the pagan world's healthy progress from myth to reason. For Gay, not only was there little genuinely pagan left in Christianity, but paganism itself was also purged of its original religious substance. The polytheism of antiquity, as Montesquieu and Hume had noted, may have been superior to monotheism to the extent that it promoted the toleration of difference, but its religious content as such was nugatory.

Not surprisingly, Gay's attempt to keep the boundary between paganism and Christianity firmly in place has met with some skepticism. Students of the specifically German *Aufklärung*, such as Peter Hanns Reill, argue that at least its adherents would have been shocked to find themselves called pagans and would have rejected the model of classical learning derived from the Renaissance as overly intellectual and lacking in moral fervor.[46] Defenders of the specifically British contribution to the Enlightenment, such as Hans Kohn, argue for the importance of religious dissenters, most notably John Milton, in preparing the ground.[47] Historians of medieval and early modern culture, such as Amos Funkenstein, agree that Gay had the better of the argument with Becker, but claim nonetheless that "the Enlightenment inherited from Christianity not its apocalypticism, but rather its social and pedagogical drive. . . . From Christianity the Enlightenment inherited its missionary zeal—not from any pagan religion of classical Antiquity, for none of them possessed it."[48] According to Funkenstein, the similarities between the freemasons and traditional churches also demonstrate the Enlightenment's dependence on an ecclesiastical surrogate with its own counterrituals and countersacraments.[49] And from a very different perspective, that of a self-proclaimed contemporary pagan immoralist, Camille Paglia chides Gay for reducing paganism to its Apollonian guise, thus shortchanging its more transgressive Dionysian counterpart, which she follows Nietzsche in insisting must be revived to reenchant culture.[50]

Whatever the justice of these complaints, the abiding power in Gay's argument can perhaps be appreciated if we now turn to our second major figure, Jean-François Lyotard. For there turns out to be a surprising convergence between his postmodernist use of the pagan tradition and that of the resolutely modernist Gay. There are, to be sure, obvious differences between the two; no one, after all, would charge Lyotard with being a worshiper of Apollonian moderation or the scientific spirit. Nor does he share Gay's taste for an elegant and lucid style as the best means of presenting his ideas.[51] The Freud he uses to justify a "libidinal politics" of desire often seems more transgressive than Gay's embattled liberal humanist.[52] And there is symptomatically only a marginal role for the "sublime," that privileged Lyotardian concept, in Gay's consideration of the eighteenth century.[53] But in certain un-expected ways, Lyotard's "lessons in paganism" reinforce those taught in Gay's study of the Enlightenment.

Lyotard's embrace of the pagan ideal, it must first be understood, came in the wake of his "drift" (*dérive*) away from the phenomenological Marxism of his *Socialisme ou Barbarie* period.[54] Although he had been an outspoken critic of French control of Algeria and supported the "events" of 1968,[55] by the 1970s, Lyotard was rapidly modulating his politics of resistance in a new key. In 1977, he collected his essays of the past few years under the title *Rudiments païens* and published a short dialogue with an imaginary interlocutor called *Instructions païennes*. Two years later, the record of his actual conversation with Jean-Loup Thébaud appeared under the title *Au Juste* (*Just Gaming* in its punning English translation).[56]

In these works, Lyotard proposes a pagan politics and philosophy that defines itself in opposition to the redemptive utopianism of the Marxist tradition, which he now detected in *Socialisme ou Barbarie*'s call for worker self-management. Indeed, he challenged any strong hope, Kantian as well as Marxist, for absolute human autonomy.[57] Such grandiose expectations, Lyotard now contended, were only a secularized version of an essentially religious desire for absolute redemption, which paganism had explicitly denied. "When I say 'pagan,'" Lyotard made clear, "I mean godless."[58] Like Peter Gay's, his paganism was thus deliberately impious, "without Olympus and without pantheon, without *prudentia*, without fear, without grace, without debt and *hopeless*."[59] If it drew any inspiration from classical polytheism, it was to deny the single master narrative that accompanied a potentially total-itarian monotheism (an argument that was to be repeated with great effect in Lyotard's celebrated description of postmodernism a few years later).[60] Instead, it favored many local narratives, whose fallible narrators knew they were not omniscient.

Although lacking hope in redemption, paganism was not a denial of the possibility of justice. But it was a justice that operated case by case and judged according to no fixed rules or a priori principles. "When I speak of paganism," Lyotard insisted, "I am not using a concept. It is a name, neither better nor worse than any other, for the denomination of a situation in which one judges without criteria."[61] Very much in the spirit of Gay's skeptical "party of humanity," even if he was anxious to avoid the taint of humanism,[62] Lyotard rejected the certainties of Platonic idealism as well as the speculative rationalism of the seventeenth century in favor of moral and political realism.[63] If his position had any relation to Kant, it was only to the *Critique of Judg-*

ment, "not the Kant of the concepts and the moral law, but the Kant of the imagination, the one who recovered from the sickness of knowledge and rules and converted to the paganism of art and nature."[64]

If paganism meant a certain return to nature from the Olympian realm of transcendence, it did not, however, mean what many of its critics have claimed it did: a pantheistic worship of the world as an immanent totality.[65] Although there is no privileged vantage point outside the world, no single God's-eye view of the whole, no metalevel or metanarrative, self-sufficient immanence was also a mistaken fantasy of full presence. The word *pagus,* Lyotard insisted, signifies the opposite of the village or "home" (here he introduced the highly charged German word *Heim*).[66] Instead, it meant the borderlands, a place of endless negotiation between peoples, all in a kind of exile, a porous boundary through which different intensities clashed without resolution. "The paganism I have in mind," he wrote, "could not be that of instituted ancient religions, even Dionysian ones. Rather, this paganism resides in an infiltration of the social body — at the surface of the social body — of areas left open to imaginations and to so-called disordered, useless, dangerous, and singular concrete enterprises: areas left open to the instincts."[67]

It was thus very much in tension with the French Revolution's version of dechristianization, which merely put another exclusive cult, that of a unified Reason, in the place of the dethroned Church. The Revolution's pseudo-Roman republic — a neoclassicism of masculine heroic virtue, which led to the Terror — was not the paganism Lyotard favored. His instead meant the parodic laughter and the subversive theatricality of the women repressed by Rousseauist austerity and authoritarianism, "the wild, nocturnal, 'unchained' woman whom the powers that be (and Jacobins first of all) try to eradicate."[68]

Lyotard would ultimately come to question the unconstrained libidinal politics informing his work of the 1970s and with it a fully desublimated version of paganism as themselves a variant of romantic enthusiasm. But in *Le Différend (The Differend),* originally published in 1983, he would still positively contrast the *pagus,* the borderland between heterogeneous genres of discourse, with the *Heim,* a zone of internal consensus and self-identity. "The *Volk,*" he wrote, "shuts itself up in the *Heim,* and it identifies itself through narratives attached to names, narratives that fail before the occurrence and before the differends born from the occurrence. Joyce, Schönberg, Cézanne: *pagini* waging war among the genres of discourse."[69]

In his transference of the metaphor of the *pagus* from a libidinal to a discursive context, Lyotard, however, began to introduce a new component in his thought, which relativized his identification with paganism, especially in

its more Dionysian moods. Judaism, he argues in *Just Gaming*, complements
paganism in its hostility to that absolute autonomy and mastery of the modern subject exemplified by the Kantian tradition.[70] Both Judaism and paganism represent the repressed, abject "other" of a Christian civilization that
culminated in humanist hubris and self-assertion. In the case of the Greeks,
"their gods are not masters of the word in the sense in which the Christian
God is a master of the word, that is, their word is not performative as the word
of the Christian God is. It does not create the world. . . . these gods, even
when they have the position of the first speaker, are themselves narrated in
narratives that tell what they are telling."[71]

Although the Jewish God is also normally understood as a single creator
God,[72] Lyotard chose to follow Emmanuel Levinas in stressing the importance of the ethical obligation in Judaism to defer to the other rather than
any ontological description of the created world. There is, he argues, a fundamental incommensurability — in his terminology, a "differend" — between
a prescriptive language game and a descriptive one, a linguistic variant, as we
have seen, of pagan polytheism. In the former, the focus is on the addressee
of the obligation, the subject who is "hostage" to the ethical demands of
the other, not the one who actually does the addressing. It does not matter
whether the one imposing the obligation is God or the finite other, a simple
human being; what does matter is the sense of quasi-heteronomous, asym-
metrical dependence of the one called to duty, a call that comes in the form
of a command, not a conceptual justification.

This is not the place to probe the full implications of Lyotard's complicated appropriation of Levinas's thought.[73] Suffice it to say that it does mean
a replacement of paganism by a new religious piety or a seamless amalgam
of religious and pagan ideals. What it does is allow Lyotard some distance
from another amalgam, that between Christianity and paganism,[74] which he
locates in Heidegger, whose anti-Semitism he probed in the aftermath of the
scandal in France over the philosopher's Nazi past. In a 1988 book entitled
Heidegger et "les juifs" (*Heidegger and "the jews"*), Lyotard cautions that
"Heidegger's god is merely pagan-Christian, the god of bread, wine, earth
and blood. He is not the god of the unreadable book, which only demands
respect and does not tolerate that one liberate oneself from respect and dis-
respect (of good and evil) through the sublation of the sacrifice, the old main-
stay of the dialectic."[75] Judaism, like paganism, is thus figured for Lyotard as
a kind of resistance to the imperative to return home, an uncanny (*unheimlich*) remembrance of the wandering and dispersion that comes before the

alleged original unity and will remain after any realized sublation of alterity and difference.

Introducing the notion of "pagan-Christianity" returns us to Peter Gay, whose account of the Enlightenment, it will be recalled, stresses a repudiation of the Renaissance attempt to integrate the classical past with Christian faith. There are, in fact, other surprising similarities between our two protagonists' impious use of the pagan legacy. Both are antinationalists resolutely hostile to any nostalgia for an alleged world of cultural wholeness before the fall into modern, diasporic alienation. Both insist on a strictly disenchanted reading of the pagan legacy, which they contrast with revealed religion and its secular equivalents, such as the cults of Reason and the People. Both are impatient with romantic notions of full reconciliation with a benign nature, such as those that fuel certain New Age, goddess-worshiping understandings of paganism. Both decry dialectical sublations, whether idealist or materialist, of the alleged contradictions of existence, sublations that do the work of mythic reconciliation. And both are moral realists who resist a utopian notion of perfect justice or naive faith in the perfectibility of the species.[76]

"I believe that modernity is pagan,"[77] Lyotard would, in fact, write in 1978, echoing without acknowledgment the argument of Gay's volumes on the Enlightenment. Although he would emend that formula a year later to say that the variant of modernity that is most pagan is best called "postmodern," because it jettisons the problematic notion of a collective addressee called "the people" and loses its regulative ideal, he is careful to deny that postmodernity is a period concept meant to indicate an era after the end of modernity. Instead, Lyotard, claims, it is an intermittent impulse within the modern period itself. One might even say that the postmodern modern is haunted—benignly haunted, to be sure—by the *unheimlich* return of what it thought it had left behind, the pagan past, an argument that is not so far from Gay's reading of the Enlightenment as a whole.

Lyotard has, to be sure, often lashed out against the universalism of the Enlightenment, decried its alleged metanarrative of progress, and attacked the totalizing intellectuals who claim to speak in its name.[78] As a result he is routinely pitted as the champion of the postmodernist counter-Enlightenment against Jürgen Habermas in contemporary discussions.[79] But when the philosophes are seen through the lenses of a Peter Gay rather than those of, say, a Carl Becker, it is no longer so obvious that his target merits such scorn. For the Enlightenment he and so many other postmodernist thinkers attack may have been far less of a secularized heavenly city than an impious pagan borderland, where critique rather than certainty rules and the boundaries between language games resist becoming completely porous.[80]

Nor, to turn the argument around, is it clear that for all his stress on incommensurable local narratives and a plurality of language games, Lyotard has entirely escaped the cosmopolitan impulse of the Enlightenment, which Gay frankly applauds. Even though he has often written an epitaph for the intellectual, distancing himself from the practice of speaking in the name of voiceless victims, Lyotard's own penchant for giving lessons and prescribing cures — even, tongue only half in cheek, explaining postmodernism "to children"[81] — seems suspiciously familiar.[82] What two of his sympathetic commentators have called "Lyotard's hesitance to dissociate himself entirely from the project of the Enlightenment"[83] is evident in his desire to "perform" philosophy as an intervention in the world, including the world of politics.

In short, if we acknowledge the unlikely alliance of our two impious pagans, Peter Gay and Jean-François Lyotard, it becomes difficult to accept without reservation the conventional contrast between modern and postmodern, which seems so widely assumed in contemporary discourse. For although there have been paganisms that have sought to reverse secularization, reenchant the world, and restore mythos over logos, theirs is a very different brand indeed. It shows us that even the most iconoclastic and critical impulses can find surprising sustenance in the return of the repressed.

PART IV

Culture, Politics, and Society
in Twentieth-Century Germany

PETER JELAVICH

13. Paradoxes of Censorship
in Modern Germany

While Peter Gay was writing his volumes on the Enlightenment, he also composed his interpretive survey of Weimar culture. On the surface, the two subjects seem worlds apart. Even at the height of the *Aufklärung*, "freedom of the pen existed nowhere in Germany."[1] The Weimar Republic, by contrast, enjoyed a constitution that proclaimed: "Censorship will not be exercised." Yet, as Peter Gay knows so well, the relationship between art and power is not clear-cut. The repressive principalities of the eighteenth century could not prevent the flowering of Germany's classical age of literature and philosophy. Conversely, the arts of the Weimar era were never as free as the constitution proclaimed, and they soon were fettered by a tyranny that made all Old Regime despots pale by comparison.

In this essay, I explore the relationship between art and power in modern Germany by focusing on censorship under a number of regimes—the Imperial state, the Weimar Republic, the Third Reich, the Federal Republic, and the German Democratic Republic. I discuss censorship of literature, the visual arts, theater, and film, but I do not deal with journalism or the news media. Nor do I provide an encyclopedic or comprehensive listing of notable censorship cases. Rather, I compare various modes of censorship in these different eras and highlight their (ostensibly) paradoxical effects. By choosing this focus, I by no means wish to imply that censors never were repressive in a straightforward, indeed brutal, manner. Nevertheless, there was considerable unpredictability in the practice of censorship, which could lead to paradoxical outcomes. Often attempts to ban a work made its existence even more visible. Conversely, some of the strategies devised by artists to circumvent censorship were less subversive than they imagined and may even have benefited the status quo. The tussle between censor and censored could turn into a game of wits, a pathetic farce, or a grim tragedy—or all three at once.

An initial paradox we encounter in dealing with censorship is definitional, and results from the fact that states simultaneously engage in censorship and deny its existence. Since the word has negative connotations in the modern era, every state seeks to define it as narrowly as possible, namely, as preventative censorship or precensorship (*Vorzensur*). That is the system whereby a publication, an image, or a script must receive approval from some governmental authority before it can be presented to the public. If we accept this narrow definition of censorship, then we have to concede that except for film, no medium was "censored" in Germany after 1918: that includes not only parliamentary democracies like the Weimar Republic and the Federal Republic but also the Nazi regime and the German Democratic Republic. Obviously, this state-authorized definition of censorship has little value for historians, let alone for the average citizen.

Whereas modern states prefer the narrowest conceivable definition of censorship, in order to deny its existence, authors and artists often promote so broad a meaning that they too destroy the term's utility. There are many artists and writers who claim that every external constraint on their creativity — not only that of the state, but also market pressures and ultimately public taste — is a form of censorship. For them, censorship is just about anything that hampers their careers or hinders appreciation of their works.

Obviously, we need to locate censorship between these two extremes. I prefer a definition that reads something like this: "Censorship is any attempt by a state to influence the arts or the media, with the intent of suppressing opinions or information." This definition is not particularly precise, but at least it emphasizes that censorship proceeds from state institutions, and it includes both direct prohibitions and more indirect forms of curtailing art and knowledge.

In order to discuss censorship, one needs not only some definitional clarity, but also a bit of emotional restraint. Most people educated in classically "liberal" societies — in polities that value freedom of expression — react negatively to the faintest whiff of censorship. Yet it is important not to demonize the phenomenon. I dare say that not a single reader of this essay does not approve of censorship in one form or another. In other words: every one of you is a proponent of censorship. Almost all citizens support legal prohibition of libel and malicious slander, and of especially egregious forms of pornography (such as child pornography). To be sure, one might argue that such laws do not fit my definition of censorship, since they do not entail a government's suppression of unwanted knowledge or beliefs. Rather, they belong to a different purview of state authority, namely, protecting citizens from their unscrupulous compatriots (the slandered from the slanderer, or the child from the pornographer). Suppressing information or beliefs with the aim of augmenting the state's power, one might argue, is censorship; defense of individuals from each other is not. In practice, however, the two realms share many gray zones. Where is one to draw the line between acceptable criticism and libel? Should certain categories of individuals, such as public figures, be protected from potential slander to a greater or lesser degree than ordinary citizens? Such questions involve issues of state authority. That is true as well of many forms of pornography, since, as we shall see, its definition reflects the relative power of groups that compete to define social mores. Few people would deny that there should be laws against slander and pornography; the question is, where to draw the line, and the answer must be decided in the political realm. Censorship is and must remain a perennial and perennially debated phenomenon.

Many modalities of censorship were apparent in the Wilhelmine era. Precensorship of the press had been abandoned in the wake of the revolutions of 1848, but it still applied to the stage. The scripts of all plays, operas and operettas, songs, skits and poems — and after the turn of the century, copies of all films — were required to receive pre-performance approval from the local police. The authorities could accept the entire script, excise limited parts, or ban it completely. They also sent observers to performances to ensure that nothing in the actors' gestures or the singers' intonations added subversive or salacious inflections to the verbal meaning. The only way of avoiding such scrutiny was to sponsor a "closed performance" (*geschlossene Vorstellung*) for specially invited guests. In that case, one had to provide the police with a list of everyone invited, and one could not advertise the performance, sell tickets in advance, or collect admission fees at the door. That loophole was intended to guarantee freedom of expression and performance to private associations (*Vereine*), those bulwarks of German sociability.

Why was precensorship retained for the stage and applied to the new medium of film? The answer lies in the nineteenth-century mind-set in which aesthetic, moral, and social values were intertwined. Performances presented by live actors before a multitude of spectators were considered potentially more dangerous than the printed word, which was less sensual and immediate in its impact and was usually read by a solitary individual. This attitude reflected the fear that the lower classes, lacking bourgeois rationality and self-restraint, might be incited by a subversive performance. In 1893, for example, the Deutsches Theater in Berlin applied for permission to perform Gerhart Hauptmann's new play *Die Weber*, a dramatization of the Silesian weavers' uprising of 1844. The local censors denied the request, arguing that it might incite Social Democratic workers to revolt. The theater managers then took the case to court, where the censors were overruled, since the judge concluded that workers could not afford tickets for the Deutsches Theater: "[I]t is well known that the seats are generally so expensive, and the number of less expensive seats relatively so small, that this theater can be attended in the main only by members of those social circles who are not inclined to violence or disturbance of public order."[2] Subsequently, police in other cities allowed performances of *Die Weber* if theaters promised to keep ticket prices high or not perform the drama on Sundays, the only day that workers would have been free to attend. Like so many other aspects of the legal system, censorship was applied differentially among the social classes.

Printed texts and images, unlike the stage, were not subjected to *Vorzensur*, but that did not imply that total freedom of expression existed in that medium. Printed matter could be seized and its creators punished *after* publication (*Nachzensur*). Texts and images that violated stipulations of the Penal Code could be confiscated and destroyed, and their authors, artists, or responsible editors could be fined or imprisoned. The articles of the Penal Code that were especially pertinent to writers of the Imperial era were those concerning lèse-majesté (94–101), blasphemy (166), and obscenity (184). In short, the hot-button issues, then as now, were politics, religion, and sex.

This leads us to a fundamental paradox of censorship: prohibitions increase interest in whatever is prohibited. Politics, religion, and sex are inherently controversial, but their aura is augmented by the protective walls built around them. This general principle is magnified in specific cases: whenever a particular work is censored, its existence is spotlighted and it receives, as it were, free advertising from the very people that want to make it disappear. In Imperial Germany, censorship cases were widely and heatedly discussed in the news media, and the resulting public interest might lead to increased sales of other, unconfiscated works of the authors affected. At trials, a parade of cultural luminaries invariably took the stand to attest to the artistic worth of the proscribed works, which often persuaded judges to overturn the bans. Thereafter, sales of the confiscated book or journal would soar, or, in the case of plays, performances would sell out. Police officials and judges were well aware of this problem. In 1902, Kurt von Glasenapp, head of Berlin's theater censorship division, complained to the Prussian minister of the interior that over the previous years,

numerous works that I had prohibited were approved by the appeals courts. Experience shows that the public, drawn by curiosity, is especially partial to precisely such plays. Likewise, it became clear that a police prohibition followed by a court annulment of the ban constitutes an exceedingly effective means of advertisement. The box-office successes generated in this manner induced theater directors and authors, who were more interested in sensationalism than art, actively to seek out a ban and a subsequent annulment, especially when they were suffering financial difficulties.[3]

In short, the police knew that censorship could backfire, and playwrights and producers knew that a shaky ban could be turned into a cash cow.

Another paradoxical aspect of censorship is that it often functions as a "creative" force in cultural production. While censorship is generally (and correctly) viewed as an instrument of suppression, it is also a "positive" force that encourages certain styles and genres — often unintentionally and inadvertently. With respect to Imperial Germany, Gary Stark has argued that "censorship did literary naturalism little harm and perhaps considerable good. . . . [C]ensorship actually helped create new forums of expression for the naturalist movement, helped coalesce naturalist authors, and helped popularize their works."[4] The censorship rules of Imperial Germany induced naturalists to found the theatrical societies that made them famous — the Freie Bühne and the Freie Volksbühne — since only in the context of such "closed" associations could censorship be avoided. Formerly a rather disparate group of individuals, the naturalists came together in these societies not only to mount plays but also to publish two important journals, the *Freie Bühne für modernes Leben* and the *Freie Volksbühne*. Stark argues that without the spur of censorship regulations, the naturalists would not have organized themselves so effectively, and the movement would have had less coherence and impact. In short, not only did censorship advertise the naturalists; it also encouraged their cohesion and shaped the organizations through which they became known.

Censorship can also encourage certain genres. Obviously, the intent of censorship is to induce cultural producers to create works that stay within state-sanctioned bounds of political, ethical, and aesthetic norms. Conservative writers and traditionalist artists automatically subscribe to such values and need no encouragement. Censorship is necessary to persuade more cautious types, who personally might be inclined to subvert the norms, to stay within the prescribed bounds; in such cases, the "scissors in the head" ("Schere im Kopf") restrains the pen or the paintbrush. But censorship can also, inadvertently, inspire genres that actively try to undermine the norms that it seeks to uphold. An obvious example is satire, which exists in all societies, but which flourishes in polities that exercise a moderate but noticeable degree of censorship. In such situations, the tabooed topics become especially attractive to certain writers and artists, as well as to many members of the public; they regard a prohibition as a challenge to a legal and cultural duel. This turns into a cat-and-mouse game, with delicious results. In turn-of-the-century Munich, for example, the cartoons in journals like *Simplicissimus* and *Jugend*, the poems and plays of Ludwig Thoma, and the skits of cabarets like the *Elf Scharfrichter* were direct responses to censorship, and they are still a joy to read.

Yet the pleasure that we derive from satire may also be its undoing. While political and social satire seeks to subvert state-sanctioned norms, it can also serve the status quo by functioning as a safety valve for discontent (what Germans call a *Ventilfunktion*). Authors, performers, and their appreciative publics can laugh off their frustrations without actually disturbing any of the powers that be. Ernst von Wolzogen, a politically conservative writer who founded Germany's first cabaret in January 1901, touted this as a blessing: "[T]he paw with splayed claws that is laughingly slapped on the knee is much less harmful than the fist clenched in the pocket." [5] In 1919, a generation later, Kurt Tucholsky, the premier satirist of the Weimar era, likewise noted that "a well-aimed joke is a better lightning-rod for public anger than an ugly riot that cannot be brought under control"; and "a [political] song is a good safety valve, through which powerful emotions dissipate in a harmless manner whenever the boiler is bursting with pressure, as it is today." [6] Whereas Wolzogen was pleased with this effect, it drove Tucholsky increasingly to despair: eventually he came to regard himself as an ineffectual political clown. Satire, nourished on censorship, does not necessarily bite the hand that feeds it.

There are other, more serious reasons why we must not treat censorship too lightly, since its paradoxical effects go only so far. Despite the "creative" potential of censorship, as well as its tendency to backfire, the games it encouraged could take a grave turn and involve substantial costs. The famous "Palestine" issue of *Simplicissimus* that ridiculed the Kaiser's trip to the Near East in 1898 led to six months' fortress arrest for Frank Wedekind and Thomas Theodor Heine, while the publisher, Albert Langen, fled abroad for five years to avoid a similar fate. He derived scant satisfaction from the fact that in the wake of that scandal, circulation of his journal jumped from 26,000 to 67,000 in the space of a few months. And there were worse cases: in 1895, the "blasphemous" play *Das Liebeskonzil* earned Oskar Panizza a year in prison, the harshest sentence meted out to a writer in the Imperial era. Panizza gained no profit from the publicity; the experience destroyed his career and ultimately his life. [7]

However deplorable the conviction of Panizza, it must be said that, in general, Imperial Germany's public prosecutors were not enthusiastic persecutors of writers and artists, since they knew that the results were unpredictable. If the state's officials were circumspect about censorship, then where did the impetus arise to engage in the practice? Here we come to a further paradox of censorship: namely, it often occurs in response to pressure "from below." The most vocal proponents of censorship in modern Germany (and not just Germany) have often been private interest groups and elected politicians. It would not be an exaggeration to say that in Imperial Germany, the federal states hesitated to censor unless encouraged by public pressure. To push the paradox a bit further: after 1871, the more "democratic" the German states were, the more they resorted to censorship; when they behaved more autocratically, they censored less. That provides, to be sure, a striking contrast to the pre-1848 situation, when the states were both authoritarian and extremely censorious. But during the last half of the century, administrators increasingly adopted the liberalism of the educated and propertied middle classes. Nineteenth-century liberalism, in turn, warned that democracy could be inimical to freedom of thought: Alexis de Tocqueville deplored the "tyranny of the majority," and John Stuart Mill echoed the concern. Vox *populi* could cry for the censor as loudly as any *Vormärz* autocrat.

The case of the lex Heinze, the most serious battle over censorship in the Imperial era, is a classic example of this issue.[8] In 1892 the Imperial government presented the Reichstag with a bill that would have tightened the laws against procuring and prostitution (Heinze was a pimp who had been involved in a spectacular murder trial in 1890, hence the bill's nickname). Some parties in the Reichstag—mainly the Catholic Center, but also the Conservatives and the Anti-Semites—attached riders to the bill that would have greatly expanded the legal definition of obscenity, so much so that not only "trash," but also much modern (and even classical) art would have been threatened. At that point, the Imperial government, anxious to avoid a culture war, withdrew the bill, but it was reintroduced by the Center from the floor of the Reichstag at the end of the decade. A furious battle ensued. Within weeks, literally thousands of artists, writers, and their supporters were holding protest meetings in major cities. The affair embarrassed the Imperial government, as well as the Bavarian state, since Munich's art scene seemed particularly threatened. Had a vote been taken on the original bill in the Reichstag, it would have passed, but its opponents skillfully employed obstructionist parliamentary tactics to force a watering-down of the proposal.

That was a tactical defeat for cultural conservatives, but they did not give up the fight. Morality crusaders—and every major city seems to have had its Men's League for Combating Public Immorality (Männerverein zur Bekämpfung der öffentlichen Unsittlichkeit)—constantly pressured local censorship boards to tighten control, and they advocated more stringent enforcement of anti-blasphemy and anti-obscenity laws. The situation in Bavaria was especially tense: although Luitpold, the regent, had appointed liberals to his cabinet, the parliament had a solid Catholic majority that repeatedly called for stiffer censorship. In 1903, parliamentary pressure led to the closing of the *Elf Scharfrichter*, the best cabaret of the Imperial era, and most of Wedekind's plays were kept off Munich's stages as well.

The imposition of censorship by democratic institutions under pressure "from below" became even clearer during the Weimar Republic. Precensorship of the stage was abolished, but it was retained for cinemas, since film was now viewed as the medium with the greatest potential for influencing and inciting the masses. Article 118 of the Weimar Constitution read: "Censorship will not be exercised [Eine Zensur findet nicht statt], but exceptional measures can by law be imposed on film." In 1920, the Reichstag passed a bill formally instituting censorship boards, whose approval was required before any feature film could be screened. The government was even more fearful of radio, the newest mass medium. It rejected the demands of radio fans for "das amerikanische System"—that is, a number of competing private stations. Instead, it retained a state monopoly of the airwaves and installed "political oversight boards" to ensure that the broadcasts were "balanced." Extreme viewpoints, whether of the left or the right, were kept off the air. Hitler's voice was thus not heard on German radio until January 1933.

Even though article 118 abolished "censorship" for every medium except film, it also stipulated that the other arts were guaranteed freedom "within the limits of the general laws"—in other words, the Penal Code and the option of *Nachzensur* were still in effect. To be sure, the paragraphs concerning lèse-majesté were struck, since there no longer was a *Majestät*, and it was expressly forbidden to prosecute people on the basis of their political convictions. However, one could still be brought to trial for defaming the institutions and symbols of the state. The Reichswehr—not notably loyal to the Republic, and under constant criticism for its role in the Great War as well as its attempts to subvert the Treaty of Versailles—was particularly eager to go to court to defend its honor. Democratic forces likewise sought legal protection from abuse. In 1922, after the assassination of Walter Rathenau, the parliament passed a "Law for the Defense of the Republic," which guarded the new democratic symbols and institutions from defamers on the left and the right. Yet it was the old standbys of the Penal Code—blasphemy and pornography—that caused writers and artists the most trouble. They were used on occasion to prosecute artists and writers who had subversive *political* views, since such individuals tended to say wicked things about religion and sex as well. Authors like Carl Einstein, Walter Hasenclever, Kurt Tucholsky, Bertolt Brecht, Carl Zuckmayer, and Johannes R. Becher, and artists like George Grosz, Georg Scholz, and Otto Dix faced legal proceedings; but almost always, they either were acquitted or received token fines.[9]

That being the case, Weimar prosecutors, like their Wilhelmine predecessors, hesitated to bring charges against writers and artists. But once again, their hands were forced by conservative and religious associations, and increasingly by radical right-wing pressure groups. Conservatives and right-wingers knew that chances for conviction were slim—but that was not the point of their efforts. The well-publicized court proceedings provided flash points for right-wing politics. Radical anti-Republican forces could create the impression that blasphemous and obscene art and literature were widespread in the Weimar Republic, and that the democratic state permitted "too much freedom." Acquittal or minor fines gave further cause for ranting and raving against the Republic. In short, the purpose of these manufactured "scandals" was to denigrate the Weimar "system" and to consolidate an anti-Republican voter base. What was paradoxical here was the fact that censorship was demanded, not really in order to suppress offensive art, but to highlight its presence. Indeed, the existence of putatively offensive art actively benefited its opponents, as it allowed them to mobilize their potential supporters through a campaign of invective.[10]

The Nazi Party in particular systematically resorted to this tactic, especially after its massive electoral gains in the Reichstag elections of September 1930. The Nazis' first major political coup in the cultural arena occurred in December 1930, when they launched violent demonstrations against the Hollywood version of *All Quiet on the Western Front*, which was being shown at a cinema on the Nollendorfplatz in Berlin. The film seemed made to order as a target for Nazi resentments: it was based on a best-selling pacifist novel that had been decried by the entire right-wing and conservative press; it had been filmed in the United States, which the Nazis branded as a major source of "degenerate" mass culture; and its producer, Carl Laemmle, was a Jewish émigré from Germany. To be sure, the film had received approval from the Berlin Film Censorship Board; and the Berlin police, under the Social Democratic leadership of the Prussian state, were more than happy to clobber the Nazi demonstrators and protect the cinema. But the Film Censorship Appeals Board caved in to pressure from the Reichswehr, the Foreign Office, and conservative states like Bavaria and Thuringia—as well as the turmoil on the Nollendorfplatz — and banned the film after it had been shown for a week.[11] By exercising "censorship from the streets," the Nazis scored their first big success, as they boasted in the *Völkischer Beobachter*: "When the ruling of the Film Appeal Board was issued, the system of 1918 suffered its first great defeat in the eyes of all, and in a flash its complete impotence was revealed."[12]

The Nazis' denigration of "degenerate" and "un-German" art, with its strongly anti-Semitic overtones, echoed many of the charges that conservative, nationalist, and religious (both Catholic and Protestant) ideologues had voiced throughout the Weimar era. On cultural issues, the Nazis often were in the same camp with traditional conservatives. Yet the latter, however much they despised the Weimar system, generally respected the laws of the land and used newspapers and legal proceedings to make their points. The Nazis felt no such constraints, especially after January 1933. In the months following Hitler's appointment as chancellor, Weimar culture was brutally suppressed. Real and potential opponents of the regime were scared into silence or driven into exile, and their works were banned from libraries, bookstores, theaters, galleries, and museums. Within months, a constantly expanding "blacklist" of undesirable publications was officially established and circulated to librarians and booksellers. These repressive acts were complemented by the founding of the Reich Culture Chamber (Reichskulturkammer) in the fall of 1933. Anyone who wanted to engage in literature, the arts, journalism, film, or broadcasting was required to become a member, and membership was denied to Jews and unrepentant leftists.[13]

After purging politically and "racially" undesirable people and blacklisting unwanted books, the Nazi regime could generally forgo a formal system of precensorship. It was also unnecessary, inasmuch as there were enough committed followers and sycophantic citizens who were willing to act as cultural watchdogs. In particular, the Nazis could tap into resentments among stylistically traditional, as well as downright hack artists and writers, whose passé works had been spurned by trend-setting museums, publishers, and critics during the modernist 1920s. Many such people were more than willing to fill the void created by the cultural purge and to ensure that modernism would not resurface. Since the Nazis could count on policing "from below," they established well-defined channels for denunciation within the cultural bureaucracy. Paragraph 4 of the "Decree of the President of the Reich Chamber of Literature regarding harmful and undesirable writing," which inaugurated the blacklisting of books in autumn 1933, read: "Requests for additions to the list . . . are to be sent to the Reich Chamber of Literature.

The president of the Reich Chamber of Literature will then decide after consultation with the Minister of Popular Enlightenment and Propaganda."[14] Decisions on prohibitions were centralized in the hands of Goebbels, but he was dependent upon information voluntarily submitted "from below." Of course, denunciations also could be made directly to the police or the Gestapo. Fear of denunciation, which activated the "scissors in the head," was the major instrument of cultural control in the Nazi era. A strictly formalized system of precensorship was unnecessary, because the Nazi regime could count on private initiative, the "invisible hand" of denunciation.

In order to heighten public vigilance, the Nazis perfected the tactics they had developed in the Weimar era. As noted above, writers and artists rarely suffered serious hardship from court proceedings in the 1920s, but the highly publicized cases were useful in maintaining resentment against modern art among conservative voters. Under Goebbels's guidance, Nazi students provided an outlet for that outrage in May 1933 by staging book burnings throughout Germany, complete with ritual incantations. The Nazis artificially revived this outrage in 1937 and 1938 — years after their thorough destruction of Weimar culture — by means of their exhibitions of "degenerate art" and "degenerate music."[15] At the former, paintings by the greatest modernist artists of the Weimar era were juxtaposed with works by inmates of mental asylums, and captions stated the amounts that museums had paid for them — a sure means to infuriate taxpayers, even though those taxes had been paid a decade ago. "Jewish," "Bolshevik," and "Negroid" were adjectives used interchangeably to characterize the art and the music denigrated at both exhibitions. These exceedingly crude defamations of modernist culture were intended to fortify the "healthy taste" of the *Volk*. This exemplified a basic principle of Nazi cultural policy: influencing consumers of the arts was even more important than dominating producers of culture. The Nazis wanted to cultivate a populace that would voluntarily reject anything that did not conform to their taste; such a people would not only avoid modernist art, but would denounce its crafters to the authorities. This would have been the most perfect mode of censorship, with a "democratic" overlay to boot: the "healthy taste" of the *Volk* would have become the only required instrument of cultural control. To a certain extent the Nazis achieved their goal of educating a citizenry that despised modernist and critical art, since the public's cultural conservatism during the Adenauer era was not only a holdover from the nineteenth century but also a result of the Nazis' successful implementation of their cultural policies.

The Federal Republic of Germany tried to build on the democratic traditions of the Weimar Republic, while avoiding its weaknesses. Article 5, paragraph 1, of the Basic Law proclaimed freedom of expression in speech, print, and imagery, and repeated the phrase of the Weimar constitution: "Censorship will not be exercised." Once again, the situation was not that simple. Although film was freed from precensorship, for many years it was kept within strict bounds by an "American" system of film industry "self-regulation." Radio and television, the newest mass medium, were retained as state monopolies, a condition that lasted until the 1980s. Moreover, the freedom of expression proclaimed in paragraph 1 was qualified in paragraph 2: "These rights find their limits in the stipulations of the general laws, the laws for the protection of youth, and the rights of personal honor." As in the Weimar era, the "general laws" included provisions against political extremism, which were used to quell neo-Nazi statements as well as communist beliefs, especially during the hottest years of the Cold War. And once again, rambunctious writers and artists could be charged with the blasphemy and obscenity paragraphs of the Criminal Code. They were applied on occasion in the 1950s and early 1960s, with the usual, predictable results: notwithstanding the generally conservative mood of the public at large, the accused writers and artists gained liberals' sympathy and free publicity.

During the 1960s, however, a fundamental shift occurred. Since the ongoing secularization of opinion and the "sexual revolution" made prosecution for blasphemy and obscenity appear increasingly benighted, the pertinent articles were weakened in major revisions of the Penal Code. That opened the doors to a number of sexually provocative and blasphemous artworks that went far beyond the bounds of "good taste." Initially, they might have had a considerable shock effect, but the indignation soon subsided, to be replaced by public uninterest. The arts acquired an almost total carnival license, but paid the price by losing public impact and attention. This fact seemed to prove, indirectly, the fundamental paradox of censorship that I mentioned at the outset: when a state restricts freedom of expression on issues like politics, sex, or religion, it makes them especially appealing to many artists as well as to consumers. Conversely, when the restrictions are rescinded, such themes lose the aura of the forbidden and they become less enticing. Just as the state increases the potency of the arts when it restricts them, it decreases their impact when it grants them total freedom.

Although changing *mentalités* account for the relaxation of censorship during the 1960s, its judicial justification resided in an expansion of a loophole from which the arts had benefited for well over a century. In the Imperial era, courts had granted greater leeway to "art"—as opposed to journalistic prose or literary and pictorial "trash" (*Schund*) — in sexual, religious, and political matters. The most obvious case was the academic nude. The operative words were *Durchgeistigung* and *Veredelung*: as long as a work could claim to "spiritualize" or "ennoble" its subject matter — that is, project it into a realm beyond crude materiality and everyday interest — it had a good shot at claiming to be "art," and thus was granted more "freedom." Of course, that situation reflected the predominance of an idealistic aesthetic, which regarded art as a sphere of disinterested contemplation removed from the quotidian world. It also had a clear class dimension: more freedom could be granted to that type of art because only the bourgeoisie had access to it. That was made clear in the Imperial era by the fact that academic nudes could be viewed in museums or purchased as expensive reproductions, but the police often confiscated the very same images if they were hawked as postcards or cheap lithographs — that is, when they appeared in an inexpensive format accessible to youths and workers.[16] That aesthetic mind-set collapsed over the course of the twentieth century, as academic idealism was blasted by modernism and tainted by the Nazis' embrace; but the social framework in which "art" was a purview of the elite remained. In a series of crucial rulings in the early 1960s, German judges took account of the changed situation. Faced with a number of sexually explicit paintings and novels, they acknowledged that avant-garde art by definition sought to transgress boundaries; that the intended public for such art was limited; and that this public was presumably more open-minded than the "average citizen," whose taste had formerly been the standard for blasphemy and pornography rulings.[17] Art, which had always benefited from looser controls than other forms of expression, was now unfettered and granted almost limitless freedom.[18]

What might sound utopian proved to be a mixed blessing, because it acknowledged that art had little to do with society at large. Alfred Döblin had warned of such a situation back in the Weimar era. He had caused a stir in 1929 when he attacked those people who argued that since "art is sacred," the artist should be allowed to say anything. "Art is not sacred, and artworks should be allowed to be banned," he countered. His point was that if ever authors and artists should enjoy total freedom of expression, then that would be the surest sign that they were not being taken seriously. It would imply that "the artist is an idiot, let him say anything that he wants"; it would mean that "the beast has lost its teeth." Döblin believed, in contrast, that since artists and writers were part of society and should be active in it, they had a right to be treated like everyone else. Indeed, he thanked those judges who continued to prosecute and condemn cultural producers: "We want to be taken seriously. We want to have an impact, and thus we have—a right to be punished."[19] That "right" was largely taken away in the 1960s. Even writers and artists who desperately wanted to create a stir often found that they were shouting in the desert.

The general relaxation of judicial standards in the Federal Republic did not, however, end the debate over censorship. By the 1970s, attention had shifted to those cultural institutions directly controlled or indirectly influenced by the state. These included not only the state-monopolized mass media, namely, radio and television, but also the numerous state and municipal theaters, operas, orchestras, and museums. Of course, Germany had had a long and distinguished tradition of public support of the arts, going back to the premodern days of princely patronage. But by the 1970s, critical attention shifted to state-financed institutions, in part because more overt cases of censorship became rarer, but also because the ballooning of public arts' funding made such institutions even more prominent players on the cultural scene than they had been before. One especially virulent, although not untypical attack was penned by Rolf Hochhuth. In an article entitled "Censorship in the Federal Republic of Germany," he claimed that politicians could forgo direct censorship because they indirectly controlled so many outlets for the arts. Censorship was exercised informally by theater managers, museum directors, and television and radio programmers whose jobs were dependent upon the goodwill and the purse strings of politicians. Hochhuth claimed:

The potentates of the Federal Republic rarely cry out for the public prosecutor when they need a legal advocate to oppose art—for they are still clever enough to avoid playing the censor themselves. They calmly rely upon the art commissars that they have installed in the control towers of the mass media . . . managing directors, artistic directors, department heads above all of television, of municipal arts programs, of theater, of radio. . . . Not the courts, but the state's intellectual officeholders are the actual censors in our Republic . . . : more powerful, more far-reaching, less conspicuous than the judicial ones.[20]

Hochhuth personally knew whereof he spoke: his play Der Stellvertreter—a hard-hitting work about the Vatican's reticence during the Holocaust, and arguably the most important German drama of the 1960s—was never performed in Catholic areas. Moreover, during the 1970s, at the height of the Red Army Faction kidnappings and murders, many artists criticized what they considered governmental overreactions and infringements on civil rights; these protests made some of them non grata with the public media and arts institutions.

Hochhuth's accusations point to more general problems that surface in every society where the arts receive public subsidies. State-funded culture will always, directly or indirectly, be at the mercy of politicians. As Hochhuth noted, they themselves need not make decisions: they simply have to appoint directors that know and respect the limits of what is politically, socially, morally, or economically "acceptable" at the time. Against Hochhuth, one could argue that writers and artists can always turn to private stages, galleries, and now broadcasters to get their messages across. But Hochhuth would reply that the state-financed institutions engage in unfair competition, precisely because they are subsidized; they use tax money to undersell those cultural goods that do not meet the state's standards. Beyond that, state-funded arts encourage conformity even among people who are not currently on their payroll, since potentially critical authors and artists know (or at least suspect) that they will receive no public commissions if they do not moderate their views. The scissors in the head start snipping in anticipation of lucrative public contracts.

Hochhuth may have exaggerated, but his concerns were shared by many artists and writers. Their attitude toward state subsidies is perhaps not paradoxical, but it is at least ambivalent. On the one hand, many an artist is unhappy with the arts market, because the general public is supposedly too benighted to shell out money for art—at least for his art. On the other hand, when an artist receives public funds, she does not want strings attached that would fetter her creativity. As soon as public agencies start to impose stipulations regarding style or (more frequently) content, the cultural community screams: "Censorship!" Avant-garde artists in particular are in a crunch: lacking a sizable paying public, they need to persuade state agencies to sponsor their works, but at the same time they demand a total absence of state oversight and control of their products. Politicians, in turn, are faced with questions like: How can we justify to the average taxpayer the existence of subsidies for the arts, when only a minority of citizens—as producers and viewers—benefit from them? Put more bluntly: in Germany, subsidies for the arts constitute an income transfer from the public at large to the financially better-off classes who attend museums, theaters, and high-cultural events in general. In other words, the poorer classes are forced to pay for the diversions of the richer classes. That situation is dicey enough in a healthy economy; it is a prescription for political and cultural disaster in bad financial times, such as now. Germany's massive post-unification deficits are forcing a reduction of state subsidies to the arts. The result is stunned incomprehension on the part of many artists, mutual name-calling between artists and politicians, and a certain amount of *Schadenfreude* among the public at large.

While the extent of state influence over the arts in the Federal Republic is debatable, there is no question that it is paltry compared to the controls that were exercised in the German Democratic Republic. To be sure, the GDR's potentates officially denied that they engaged in censorship. As late as 1990, Erich Honecker asserted: "But we didn't have any censorship. . . . We were the only socialist nation that let things go their own way."[21] Hermann Kant, as president of the Writers' League, made a similar statement in 1979, but with threatening overtones: "The expression *censorship*, gentlemen, is tainted; knowledgeable people need not be told that. Anyone who applies the word 'censorship' to the state's direction and planning even of the publishing industry is not concerned about our cultural policy—he doesn't want it at all."[22] In his attack on censorship at the Tenth Writers' Congress of the GDR, Günter de Bruyn skillfully navigated around the issue by saying: "I usually call it censorship, but to avoid a fruitless quarrel over terms, I shall call it 'the practice of obtaining permits to publish' [*Druckgenehmigungspraxis*]."[23] Even the "Stasi" (state security police) could not find an appropriate euphemism for "censorship" in its secret reports, although its agents often paired it with "supposed." Thus a Stasi report on Stefan Heym in 1975 noted: "He demanded the abolition of the censorship that supposedly exists in the GDR and he called for artists to have their own publishing houses and mass media, in order to avoid this supposed censorship."[24]

Despite such official denials of censorship, it was very much a reality—and in purely institutional terms, the censorship mechanisms of the GDR were more extensive than those of Nazi Germany. That by no means implies that the GDR was more repressive than Hitler's regime. Nevertheless, the communist state possessed more formalized means of directly controlling its writers and artists than its fascist predecessor, since many cultural institutions that were still in private hands in the Nazi era—publishing houses, newspapers and journals, theaters, cinemas—were socialized in the GDR. Authors, visual artists, and other cultural producers were expected to join the appropriate professional organization, such as the Writers' League (Schriftstellerverband), modeled after similar organizations formed in the Soviet Union in the early 1930s. Furthermore, the GDR instituted a comprehensive system of precensorship. In practice, all works printed, all plays staged, and all films screened had to procure preliminary approval from some state agency. For example, authors had to discuss their manuscripts with one or more "editors" at the state-owned publishing houses. The editors then had to acquire a "license" to print the work from the state publishing office, a subdivision of the Ministry of Culture (that was the *Druckgenehmigungspraxis* to which de

Bruyn referred). Since members of the ruling Socialist Unity Party (SED) held commanding posts in all of these agencies at every level, authorship was in practice subjected to Party supervision.[25]

This de facto precensorship combined with other mechanisms to form a complex carrot-and-stick system. The carrots took various forms, such as a fixed monthly income, and hence protection from the caprices of a "capitalist" marketplace for the arts; other material advantages, such as a nice apartment, a car, or permission to travel abroad; and public esteem. In contrast, criticism of the ruling system could be severely punished. Dismissal from the Writers' League or a similar association was often tantamount to a prohibition to publish or be culturally active. Although there was nominally no censorship, and the constitution of the GDR (like that of the FRG) guaranteed freedom of opinion, there was also (as in the West) a Penal Code that circumscribed those rights. The law books of the GDR prescribed jail terms for activities like "agitation against the state" (*staatsfeindliche Hetze*) or "defamation of the state" (*Staatsverleumdung*). Beyond that, there were the thoroughly extralegal activities of the Stasi. In addition, there were quasi-legal practices like forced emigration, which became the preferred method of getting rid of troublesome writers and artists after 1976, when Wolf Biermann was denied reentry into the GDR after performing in Cologne.

A classic example of the carrot-and-stick system employed by the GDR may be found in a conversation between the writer Reiner Kunze and officials of the Ministry of Culture in the summer of 1975. At that time, Kunze had been offered membership in the Bavarian Academy of Fine Arts. He was requested to come to Berlin from his home in Greiz, and the officials tried to persuade him to turn down the offer. Afterward Kunze recounted the discussion to a supposed friend, actually an informant, who passed his comments on to the Stasi:

In the conversation [at the Ministry of Culture] they first expressed great admiration for his achievements, and then they tried to negotiate with him. . . . On the material side, they offered him a plush apartment in Berlin, a weekend retreat near Berlin and a car manufactured in the West. . . . But when he declined these offers and insisted on accepting membership in the [Bavarian] Academy, they thanked him for his visit and — by implication — told him: We cannot guarantee you an accident-free trip back to Greiz — which he interpreted as a threat to murder him.[26]

Obviously, Kunze lived to tell the tale, but he emigrated permanently to the West two years later.

Censorship and other state steering mechanisms profoundly influenced the culture of the GDR, but in what manner and to what degree has been a subject of much debate since 1989. In particular, there is disagreement over the extent to which criticism or opposition was possible within the GDR. Despite the extensive means for cultural control, the authorities sometimes had to be circumspect for the same reason as censors in other eras: their attempts to suppress a work might turn it into a cause célèbre, especially if the West German media got word of it. Like their counterparts in earlier eras, East German writers, artists, directors, and filmmakers became quite adept at playing cat-and-mouse games: for example, authors might lace their drafts with obviously "unacceptable" passages that would distract their "editors" from less obvious criticisms, which would be spared the scissors. "Reading between the lines" became a favorite public pastime — but was it dangerous to the state? Slipping one past the authorities might have given satisfaction and amusement to author and reader — but that hardly affected the status quo and, like satire in all ages, might have been a mere diversion, a safety valve for discontent. Many serious writers and artists did not, however, go in for such games. They openly and deliberately tried to expand the boundaries of criticism, but their results were equally questionable. One could legitimately claim that a writer like Christa Wolf acted subversively insofar as she appealed for individuality and subjectivity; since she lived in a state that sought to direct the lives of its citizens as much as possible, every call for individuality was nonconformist, almost by definition. But was that really so threatening? One could argue, conversely, that even if her books had changed the habits of some or even many citizens, that would not have been truly subversive, since people who cultivate their own individuality are not normally active opponents of the state. The *Nischengesellschaft* of the GDR — the "niche-society" in which authenticity was reserved for private circles — confirmed the state's continued dominance of the public sphere. By the 1980s, formerly committed writers, aware of their limited powers, drifted off into massive cynicism (Heiner Müller), or portrayed their lives in wistfully Chekhovian and self-deluded terms (Wolf's *Sommerstück*, Volker Braun's *Die Übergangsgesellschaft*).

More recently, an even more disturbing question was asked of GDR literature: namely, to what extent was the opposition actually manipulated by the state? Were there seemingly nonconformist groups that were secretly sponsored by the Stasi in order to assemble opponents at venues where they could be more effectively observed? I am referring, of course, to the debate about "Prenzlauer Berg" — the heart of East Berlin's young avant-garde, centered around the poet Sascha Anderson, who turned out to be a Stasi informer. The issue erupted in autumn 1991, when Wolf Biermann, in his speech upon receiving the Georg Büchner Prize, let loose the notorious phrase about "the untalented babbler Sascha Asshole [Sascha Arschloch], a Stasi informer, who still tries to be cool and play the muses' son and hopes that his dossiers will never see the light of day." I personally find the ensuing sentence even more provocative: "The Ministry of State Security placed its creatures everywhere at the head of the opposition in order to be better able to break it up."[27]

"Everywhere at the head of the opposition" is surely an exaggeration. But although I tend to be suspicious of Foucaultian arguments, there were indeed times when the government of the GDR created its own opposition in order to better exert its rule. A benign example is cabaret.[28] In the mid 1970s, the regime decided that every district (*Bezirk*) of the GDR should have a professional cabaret, so the number of troupes was increased from four to a dozen. The GDR's cabarets were very popular and invariably sold out, because they were a forum for what appeared to be subversive humor. Yet there were limits to the topics that could be satirized. One could joke about the lack of consumer goods, the inability to travel abroad, and even the foibles of Party careerists (as long as they remained unnamed "types" rather than recognizable individuals); but the Soviet Union and upper-level Party functionaries were definitely taboo topics. The laughter at the cabarets was loud and genuine, but it took place in venues that were explicitly designed to be safety valves for discontent.

Cabaret was not the only safety valve. A Stasi report on one of Kunze's private conversations in February 1976 recorded: "In his opinion the seeming liberalization of the cultural-artistic life of the GDR results de facto in a complete incapacitation and exclusion of the real producers of culture from social developments. The system of little safety valves [*Ventilchen*] has become so perfected, that the people can no longer see what is actually happening in and with the arts."[29] It is thus not totally amiss to suspect that the Prenzlauer Berg scene was tolerated, or even encouraged, as a *Ventilchen*. The state would have derived several benefits from such a ploy: For one, Prenzlauer Berg served as an assembly point for all potential nonconformists, and thus their observation was facilitated. Second, the Prenzlauer Berg poets adopted a stance that was nonconformist but ultimately unthreatening. Insofar as they avoided the official cultural associations of the GDR—for example, they refused to become members of the Writers' League—they could not engage in internal opposition within official structures, as did authors like Christa Wolf and Stefan Heym. Third, they cultivated abstruse styles of art and literature, which denied their works the broader appeal enjoyed by writers in the older

critical-realist tradition. And fourth, this generational divide could also benefit the state, since the youngsters branded the cohorts of Wolf and Heym as
stylistically passé.

If this case had been the rule in the GDR, then there would have been a
perfect paradox. On the one hand, there would have been a state whose overt
attempts at censorship had often gone awry. At the Tenth Writers' Congress
of the GDR, Christoph Hein alluded to the perennial paradox of censorship:
"Censorship is paradoxical, because it always achieves the opposite of its declared intent. The censored object does not disappear. . . . Censorship then
operates simply like a ploy for increasing sales."[30] On the other hand, there
would have been an artistic community that considered itself subversive,
oblivious to the fact that its opposition was always already planned by the
authorities. A censorship that, far from suppressing, actually spotlights what
it wants to hide; an opposition whose attacks must always miss the true mark,
because the targets were consciously provided by the state—the absurdity
of that situation would have been unparalleled in the annals of German
censorship.

Such paradoxes did appear now and then in the GDR, but they were exceptions. For there were genuine oppositional movements in the GDR,
whose criticisms were meant seriously and treated harshly by the authorities.
The state could and did employ repressive measures that could destroy artworks, artistic creativity, and even human lives—if not physically, then
psychologically and emotionally. Even in cases that hardly could be called
tragic, the censorship and steering mechanisms fundamentally perverted
cultural production in the GDR. After the fall of the Wall, the poet Richard
Pietraß admitted: "The hide-and-seek game with the censors and the powerful awakened and refined our verbal skills, but it simultaneously domesti-
cated and deformed, so that we experienced the end of the GDR as cheeky
cripples. Amid the inseparable fusion of scandal and fame, we were the victims of censorship and its silent beneficiaries."[31] The degree to which the
artists and writers of the GDR were molded by their political environment
can be measured by the fact that so many of them cannot find a voice or a vision in the expanded Federal Republic. In his post-unification poem "Property," Volker Braun observed "my country goes to the west" and concluded:
"my whole text becomes incomprehensible" ("unverständlich wird mein
ganzer Text").

The writers and artists of the former GDR must now come to terms, one
way or the other, with their new situation. In February 1994, speaking to a
packed audience at the Dresden Opera House, Christa Wolf appealed for

"the ability to recognize and endure the paradox in which we live."[32] Four years earlier, at an emergency meeting of the Writers' Congress of the soon-to-be-defunct GDR, Wolf had quoted Heinrich Heine, who had written during the revolution of 1848: "How should a person write without censorship, who has always lived under censorship?" Heine's question was intended ironically, and Wolf took it in that spirit, since she proceeded to say: "Why should we all at once collectively lose our heads, give up ourselves, our history, our courage and our self-consciousness, also our time-tested experience in making the best of contradictions among the rulers — simply because the powers that we confront have changed?"[33]

THOMAS A. KOHUT

14. The Creation of Wilhelm Busch as a German Cultural Hero, 1902–1908

It is not a matter of indifference who the favorite
humorist of a nation is.
— Josef Hofmiller, 1908 [1]

Although nearly every German is familiar with Wilhelm Busch, the nine-teenth-century humorist is largely unknown outside the German-speaking world. In part, this can be attributed to the difficulty of translating the deceptively simple, ironic verses that accompany his often violent picture stories; in part, to the rootedness of his humor in a uniquely German cultural context. Given Busch's deep cultural resonance for Germans (certainly comparable to that of his contemporary Mark Twain for Americans), it is surprising that — with the notable exception of Peter Gay — historians have paid relatively little attention to this influential and representative artist, poet, and philosopher. [2]

This essay is concerned less with Wilhelm Busch himself than with his reception in early twentieth-century Germany. Specifically, I explore Busch's sudden elevation to the status of a national cultural hero between 1902 and 1908, although drawings and poems produced decades earlier had already made him the most beloved humorist of nineteenth-century Germany. This essay, then, is related to the work of numerous literary scholars and a handful of historians on literary reception and to the burgeoning historical literature on public ritual, festival, and commemoration. [3] Pioneered by historians of early modern Europe and influenced by literary theorists like Mikhail Bakhtin and cultural anthropologists, these historical studies have generally been written from a functionalist perspective. I am not concerned primarily with the social and political function of the Busch celebrations, however, but focus instead on their experiential meaning. Attending first to a series of contradictions that characterized the creation of Wilhelm Busch as a German cultural hero and then analyzing the most striking paradox of the published response to the humorist between 1902 and 1908, I seek ultimately to use the Busch reception to understand something about the way those celebrating him in Germany during the crucial decade before the outbreak of World War I experienced themselves and the world in which they lived.

The "Busch-Enthusiasm" and Its Contradictions

Lacking precise sales figures for books published in the nineteenth century, it is difficult to assess an author's relative popularity with confidence. Nevertheless, the figures we do possess for the works of Wilhelm Busch reveal him to be one of the most popular authors — perhaps *the* most popular author — of late nineteenth- and early twentieth-century Germany. By his death in January 1908, more than one and a half million copies of his work published in book form had been sold. His two most popular works, *Max und Moritz* and *Die fromme Helene*, had sold 426,000 and 199,000 copies respectively.[4] And yet, despite the steady and increasing popularity of his work, Busch received remarkably little critical attention before 1902, with three notable exceptions. In 1878, Paul Lindau published a thoughtful analysis of Busch's humor in *Nord und Süd*.[5] In 1881, Theodor Vischer produced a relatively critical assessment of Busch's artistic and literary significance, in which he condemned Busch for attempting social satire and exhibiting pornographic tendencies after 1869 (he cited as evidence Busch's treatment of the beard of Antonius of Padua during one of the seduction scenes in the story of that name).[6] And, in 1886, partially in response to Vischer, Eduard Daelen published a flamboyant celebration of Busch as a genius of "titanic" proportion, in the process transforming Busch into a political artist, the counterpart to Bismarck in the national-cultural crusade against Catholicism.[7] Apart from these three studies, however, relatively few assessments or analyses of Busch's work were published in Germany before 1902.[8] Nor was Busch cited in encyclopedias or biographical dictionaries or in histories of nineteenth-century literature, illustration, or children's stories.[9] All that would change in April 1902.

Suddenly it was discovered that Busch was alive and had reached his seventieth birthday. A wave of "Busch-Enthusiasm" swept Germany as he and his work became the focus of intense public interest and critical attention.[10] Well over a thousand congratulatory messages were sent to Busch in the rural village of Mechtshausen, including telegrams from the Kaiser and the grand duke of Baden, and Busch was the subject of at least sixty-six articles in German newspapers, literary journals, and popular magazines — this despite the fact that eighteen years had passed since the publication of his last *Bildergeschichte* or picture story, *Maler Klecksel*. Numerous articles and even a handful of books on Busch appeared over the next five years, culminating in another surge of public interest on the humorist's seventy-fifth birthday in 1907. Busch's death nine months later, in January 1908, produced a final outpouring of public affection, with dozens of articles expressing the nation's gratitude and sense of loss. Messages of condolence from Wilhelm II and Chancellor Bülow were sent to the Busch family, and the humorist's simple funeral in Mechtshausen was attended by political dignitaries, representatives of Germany's cultural establishment, and members of the press. All in all, between 1902 and 1908, well over 150 publications on Busch appeared in Germany. Although subsiding after his death, the "Busch-Enthusiasm" only came to an end with the outbreak of war in August 1914.[11]

The explosion of interest in Busch was experienced by his contemporaries as unprecedented. According to some, it was the celebration of Busch in 1902 that secured for him the status of an important literary and artistic figure, and, indeed, thereafter sections on Busch were to be found in nearly every encyclopedia and literary history published in Germany.[12] In the judgment of many of those celebrating him in the first decade of the twentieth century, Wilhelm Busch had become *the* greatest German humorist.

Busch's sudden celebrity can be explained in a number of ways. With his most popular works published nearly twenty years before, Busch had long ago withdrawn from the competition for critical acclaim. Now, having reached the ripe old age of seventy, he had become venerable, a grand old man who could be celebrated without controversy. Moreover, the public curiosity about Wilhelm Busch in 1902 and beyond can be explained as an attempt to discover a new Busch story in Wilhelm Busch himself. Although little was known about him before 1902, now it was asserted that Busch's works could not be understood without a knowledge of the remarkable personality that had produced them.[13] Indeed, the philosophical depths and unique complexities lying behind the humorous surface of Busch's stories were simply reflections of a philosophically deep and uniquely complex personality lying behind the image of the cheerful *Spaßmacher*, or wag.[14] In the absence of new Busch creations, then, Busch's personality had become a work of art and a source of entertainment.[15] A third explanation of the Busch-Enthusiasm is that, in rediscovering the seventy-year-old Busch in 1902, a "Wilhelm Busch generation," born in the late 1850s and early 1860s, discovered that it was in its prime. The authors of these articles had grown up with Busch's stories (stories that had appeared in a sequence adapted to their own development),[16] and many wrote as if personally connected to him.[17] He had been an "uncle,"[18] our "true companion," "tablemate and fellow citizen,"[19] "our German family friend,"[20] with whom "so many have a personal and cordial relationship."[21] In 1886, Johannes Proelß had written that most Germans have "certainly never thought to imagine what the personality of this man might actually be like."[22] Now, to one journalist on Busch's death in 1908, it seemed that "the image of the man has grown with us, within us."[23] In celebrating Busch, then, a generation celebrated its maturity and mourned its youth, a "green golden age," Theodor Herzl wrote in 1902, only to add, "that has been lost."[24]

And yet there was more to the Busch-Enthusiasm than this. In an era characterized by a nationalism that was as nervous as it was strident, Busch emerged in these articles as "a national artist, through and through,"[25] "the pride of the German name,"[26] "a hero, a universally revered national possession," deserving "a place of honor in the Valhalla of our leading cultural lights."[27] "Attempt it, German people, to blaze a path to this treasure, who liberates and delights!" Fritz von Ostini wrote of Busch on his death in a poem published in *Jugend* and widely reprinted.[28] To Ferdinand Avenarius, writing two years later in *Kunstwart*, Busch seemed "in many essentials, for many people, precisely in our time: *an exemplary human being.*"[29] In an era described variously by the Busch celebrants as "pessimistic," "humorless," "anxious," "complicated," "depressing," "decadent," "degenerate," or "in decline,"[30] Busch's works offered philosophical perspective and comfort, and his personality served as a model to be emulated.[31] He was presented as a symbol of the best of what was or what ought to be, as the embodiment of values and ideals that seemed lost, not yet achieved, or ephemeral.

Consistent with a generation mourning its lost youth, a large measure of nostalgia for a simpler, less uncertain time was manifest in the celebration of Busch that began in 1902. In these articles Busch was consistently presented as a preindustrial figure, living in rustic nests of "cozy comfort [*Behaglichkeit*] and tranquillity . . . that know neither the steam of the locomotive nor the smoke of the factory chimney,"[32] far from where "the great wide world pursues its hasty, work-filled, numbed, and joyless existence."[33] Busch in this image (literally depicted by Wilhelm Schulz in *Simplicissimus* in 1908) was

1. "Wilhelm Busch †,"
by Wilhelm Schulz.
Simplicissimus 27
(January 1908): 732.

2. "To the Master Wilhelm
Busch on his 75th Birthday,"
by A. Schmidhammer.
Jugend, no. 16 (1907).

a benevolent old man, sitting in his rural cottage garden surrounded by flowers and bees, smoking a pipe, with pretzels, coffeepot, and cup on a wooden table, a look of contentment on his wise old face—the kind of scene gleefully destroyed in Busch's own stories (figure 1).[34] A comparable drawing in *Jugend* the previous year, entitled "Dem Meister Wilhelm Busch zum 75. Geburtstage," showed a huge circle of various types of people and species of animal all gathered happily around a grandfatherly Wilhelm Busch reading *Max und Moritz*, with a strapping "youth" leaning over his shoulder (figure 2).[35] Although consciously drawn in "the Master's" style, this peaceable kingdom, which presented Busch as an integrating figure whose works brought harmony and peace, eliminated the natural violence, strife, and discord that fill so many of his works. In general, the Busch celebrants sought to convey an image of the humorist compatible with nostalgic cozy comfort, or *Behaglichkeit*.[36] Thus it was important to deny that Busch might in fact be contemptuous of humanity, a thorough pessimist, or a committed disciple of Schopenhauer.[37] Instead, Busch was presented again and again as the "comforter" or "benefactor" or "the cure for the cares" "of the German people."[38] His old-fashioned, rural *Behaglichkeit* soothed Germans whose nerves had been frayed by the pace and uncertainty of urban, industrial society.[39]

Frequently linked with the recently deceased Bismarck,[40] Busch was presented as a man of a past but better era, who had fled the urban marketplace and national celebrity for the rural isolation of Wiedensahl and Mechtshausen.[41] Even the country pigs depicted in Busch's stories were celebrated by Paul Ernst as a representation of an older, better world destroyed by industrialization (see figure 3). That breed, which became extinct before the 1860s, "was more estimable but sturdier than the pigs of today—a moving symbol for the people. The *Behaglichkeit* of that time, the honest guilelessness and naïveté, is disappearing more and more."[42] As if to Wilhelm Busch personally, one journalist wrote in the *Breslauer Zeitung* in 1902: "In more than one way you are the embodiment of that which they [the German people] have lost without being able to attain it again." You, he continued, represent the simplicity, tranquillity, and stability of the "little German world . . . that . . . suddenly became the great new Germany." Nevertheless the author believed that Busch could still serve as an example for the Germans to follow: "And as you connect the present to a long-lost childlike time, . . . you open up a way for them out of the present, to where it will be better, in happier, more naively experienced times."[43] A similar, if less confused and con-

3. "Sie stößt, mit schrecklichem Gebrumm,
Das Kind, den Tisch und Nachbarn um."

"She shoves, with a most terrible rumble,
Causing neighbors, child, and table to tumble."

From "Der Bauer und sein Schwein," by Wilhelm Busch. Originally published in
Münchener Bilderbogen, 316 and 317 of 1862.

siderably more critical, assessment was made by Josef Hofmiller on Busch's
death:

It is not without sentimentality that, at the time when the young empire impetuously
stretches and strains, the Germans swoon over Busch and Reuter: over the agrarian
idyll, over the cozy comfort of the rural village [*Landstädtchenbehaglichkeit*], over
the happiness of the musty German parlor. . . . The real life of the age was never
captured by Busch. No rumbling and roaring from the new realms of work and
expanding power penetrated the isolation of Wiedensahl. A young world was in
the making, but many Germans wanted nothing to do with it, closed their eyes, and
enveloped themselves in the narrow horizon of Low German Philistinism [*platt-
deutscher Spießbürgerlichkeit*].[44]

Nevertheless, Hofmiller's verdict was only partially accurate. For, despite
the nostalgia, a series of contradictions in these articles called the value of
the past into question. Busch, the craftsman-artist,[45] who throughout his life
sketched with a goose quill and preferred to use old-fashioned, self-prepared
sepia ink,[46] was celebrated for his depiction not only of extinct livestock but
of that section of the German *Mittelstand* consisting of those "little people

who now for the most part are in the process of dying out, who more and more are facing their destruction. It is the class that owns its own small business or practices its handicraft, and whose comfortable [behäbige] existence has been rendered more and more impossible by large-scale industry and the department store. That is, for example, the village or small-town miller."[47] At the same time, Busch images were being mass-produced, allowing, according to the author of the article "What Does Wilhelm Busch Mean to Us?" in the Süddeutsche Uhrmacher-Zeitung (The South German Clockmakers' Newspaper), "the bright sunshine of humor to light up the room."[48] For children, there were clocks bearing the likenesses of Max and Moritz ("it is most amusing when the Max and Moritz clock runs and the two rascals turn their heads from right to left, as if on the lookout for opportunities to play new pranks") or of Hans Huckebein and the young Fritz ("here too both figures move; Fritz slides along the branch toward the bird, which turns its head suspiciously towards the boy"). For adults, there were Max and Moritz lighters and Hans Huckebein cigar cutters.[49] Busch's work was reproduced on paper bags, porcelain, clothes, in kaleidoscopes, as a pattern for curtains and couch cushions, as statues, baking forms, forms for frozen foods, and wall decorations.[50] Busch and his works had become mass-produced symbols of the handicraft era.

A similar paradox characterized the effort to present Busch as a sustaining alternative to the prevailing "Zeitalter der Öffentlichkeit," or era of publicity.[51] He was extolled by these authors for his flight from the ovations, for his rejection of the "hero worship of our time,"[52] with no apparent awareness that by celebrating Busch they fostered the contemporary pathos and ostentation they manifestly were rejecting.[53] Busch was praised for his reserve and modesty, for being so unlike the self-promoting celebrities of the day — "that, despite his successes, he never lifted a finger to inform the world about his person or affairs,"[54] "especially today when one often learns more about a personality than about his works and when advertising is almost always the artist's unpleasant companion"[55] — with no apparent awareness that by promoting popular curiosity about him they fostered the very spirit of contemporary voyeurism they manifestly were condemning.[56] Without irony, F. Wippermann noted in "Wilhelm Busch und das katholische Haus" that Busch's quiet withdrawal "from the gossipy and curious world . . . increased the interest [Teilnahme] that the German people harbor for their favorite."[57] Without shame, the reporter for the Hamburger Nachrichten at Wilhelm Busch's funeral complained that the presence of the press was "undignified," "distasteful," and "greedy," adding lamely that he was professionally obliged to cover this intimate event.[58]

Emphasizing the apolitical character of his work, those celebrating Busch yearned for an allegedly apolitical past.[59] In the satirical journals *Jugend*, *Lustige Blätter*, and *Simplicissimus*, this yearning was expressed by transforming Busch's *Bildergeschichten* into political cartoons.[60] On one level, these cartoons paid homage to Busch as an ancestor of the Wilhelmian satirists. On another level, because their humor lay precisely in the politicization of Busch's decidedly apolitical characters, these cartoons actually emphasized that the authentic Busch had become dated and that political satire had replaced his *Bildergeschichten* as popular entertainment.[61] The gulf separating Busch from contemporary Germany was indicated by a 1907 *Simplicissimus* cartoon in which Max and Moritz were sentenced to forty years in prison for their pranks, despite an impassioned imaginary defense put forward by their creator. Testifying to a world that seemed to have become harsh, crass, and conservative, the author wondered plaintively whether, over the forty years that had passed since he created them, Busch might not have become convinced of the guilt of Max and Moritz himself.[62] Characters like "Die fromme Helene" as a prostitute, depicted with a hint of George Grosz, or "Fipps, der Antisemit" were used, Busch was used, to make fun of and criticize Wilhelmian Germany as base and tawdry, but in a way that transformed them and him into coarse Wilhelmians (figures 4 and 5).[63] A cartoon in *Lustige Blätter* in 1906 of a promiscuous and polymorphous-perverse "Julchen" expressed a surface yearning for the simpler, more naive era of the mid 1870s when Busch had produced the story of that name.[64] And yet the cartoon simultaneously sensationalized and vulgarized the very image to which it was appealing. Ostensibly using Busch to decry contemporary decadence, it transformed Busch into a decadent and a source of titillation (see figures 6–8).[65] In sum, while those celebrating Busch overtly avowed the preferability of the past, they covertly confirmed the inescapability of the present and pandered to the very features of contemporary life they manifestly found so objectionable.

The efforts to assess Busch's place in history made in a number of these articles exhibit the same confusion about Busch and his relation to the contemporary world and the same ambivalence about the relationship between present and past. Busch is generally presented in these assessments as a transitional figure, standing "on the threshold of a new era, which only came after him, of which he had a presentiment."[66] He partook of both the old and the new and played a role in making the transition from Romanticism to Ma-

Da war ein Herr von Lindenschmidt,
Der lange schon an Asthma litt,
Weil er — was Mancher ja entschuldigt —
Wein, Weib und Sang zu stark gehuldigt;
Der jetzt ganz wieder die Natur
Nur noch in Taxametern fuhr,
Der kam zu Lenchen bittend um
Ein heilsam Privatissimum.
Und da der Saal voll Beter grade,
So heilt man in der Remenate.

4. Busch's "Die fromme Helene" as a prostitute with one of her clients, from "Helene heilt." *Lustige Blätter,* no. 16, *Busch-Nummer* (1902).

Zwei Nickel zahlt man an der Kasse,
Und auf den rötlichen Manasse
Schwingt Fipps der Affe seinen Spietsch
Der fulminant antisemitsch.
Es meinten die, die dort verkehren,
Den Drescher-Affen muß man hören,
Wie der mit seinem Maulwerk laut
Die Jüden kurz und klein verhaut;
Und was dabei besonders wichtig:
Der Affe selber mauschelt richtig.

5. Busch's "Fipps, der Affe" as "Fipps, der Antisemit." *Lustige Blätter* 21, no. 52, *Jahres-Buschiade* (1906): 25.

Zulchen, ihn gesehen habend,
Wünscht ihm einen guten Abend.
D'rauf spricht er: „Wie Sie mich schau'n,
Bin ich Gentleman und Clown.
Nachts — das sollten Sie 'mal sehen,
Kräh' ich, wie die Hähne krähen!"

Gern wollt' ihn nun Zulchen küssen,
Hätt' ihn gern ins Ohr gebissen,
Doch da nahte and'rerseits
Sonja Gribojeff bereits.
Möppel vor der Dichterin
Flieht ins Blumenhäuschen hin,
Wohin Fred, der Bräutigam,
Auch vorhin die Zuflucht nahm.

6. "Listen! Juggling seven apples,
Along strolled Mr. Little Mapples.
Julchen, having watched him from afar,
Wished him cordially: 'Bon soir.'
'As you can see,' he told her, beaming
    down,
'I am a gentleman and a clown.
You should see how I at night,
Crow with all a rooster's might!'

Gladly would Julchen him have kissed,
And in his ear have gladly bit,
But there approaching readily,
Came Sonja Gribojeff steadily.
From the poetess, Mapples fled
Into the flower shed ahead,
Where Julchen's bridegroom, Fred,
Had himself already fled."

Sonja spricht: „Wie Sie mich schauen,
Schwärm' für Männer ich und Frauen.
Ganz egal, ob sie's, ob er's ist,
Ach wie schön, wenn man pervers ist!"
Gerne wollt' nun Zulchen küssen,
Hätte gern sogar gebissen,
Doch da nahte and'rerseits

7. "'As you can see,' says Sonja with elan,
'I swoon for woman and for man.
I don't care if it's a he or she,
Oh how lovely is perversity!'
Gladly would Julchen her have kissed,
And in her ear have gladly bit,
But there approaching readily,
Came Count Sperner steadily.'"

6–8. Scenes from "Das Blumenhaus," in *Lustige Blätter* 21,
no. 52, *Jahres-Buschiade* (1906): 6.

Herr Graf Sperner schon bereits.
Julchen ihn geseben habend,
Wünscht dem Grafen guten Abend,
Frägt ihn: „Möchten Sie mich küssen?"
Doch er mag davon nichts wissen.
Julchen wird nun sehr energisch,
Da empfiehlt er sich auf törkisch,
Flüchten will er gradeaus
Ins — besetzte — Blumenhaus.
Julchen stürmt ihm wütend nach,
Lachen — Lärmen — Trubel — Krach.

Ferne mit Laternenfeuer,
Naht der Großpapa, Herr Soyer;

8. "Julchen, having watched him from
   afar,
   Wished the Count cordially: 'Bon soir.'
   Asked him: 'Would you like me to kiss?'
   But that the Count took quite amiss.
   Julchen became most energetic now,
   And he retreated with a craven bow.
   He sought to flee straight ahead
   Into the — already occupied — flower
   shed.
   Julchen stormed in anger after him,
   Laughter — shouting — Hubbub — Din."

"In the distance, with lantern fire,
Approached the Grandpapa, Herr
   Hire;"
Etc.

terialism,[67] or from Romanticism to Realism,[68] or from an older Pessimism to modern Optimism,[69] or from an older Optimism to modern Pessimism.[70] When connected with the view of Busch as simultaneously contemporary and outmoded, these assessments testify to their authors' sense of living in a transitional era and their uncertainty about its stability, inevitability, or desirability.

Mass Appeal and Mass Misunderstanding

No contradiction in the published response to Busch is more striking than the simultaneous celebration of the fact that he was universally beloved and insistence that he was universally misunderstood in Germany. Already in 1901, Wilhelm Jänecke-Stade asserted both that Busch's popularity testified to his greatness and that Busch was not popularly appreciated, apparently without any sense that this paradox required explanation.[71] Frequently, the very authors who proclaimed that Busch was misunderstood acclaimed his popularity and that his appeal transcended generation, class, and region.[72] Especially to be celebrated was the fact that Busch's work was popular and profound, that he had achieved public and critical success, that he appealed to the masses and the intelligentsia alike.[73] Indeed, one of the features of Busch's genius was his *Volkstümlichkeit*, that he could be understood immediately by the people and required no cultural interpreters to be appreciated.[74]

Not only did the claim that Busch was generally misunderstood contradict the celebration of his popularity, the ubiquity of the claim rendered it paradoxical. Again and again, in article after article, author after author insisted that Wilhelm Busch was not understood or appreciated by the Germans.[75] To be sure, there was a range of opinions about his meaning. A handful of authors claimed that Busch was nothing more than a harmless *Spaßmacher*; a handful, that he was a pessimistic nihilist. Despite the insistence that Busch was misunderstood by populace and critics alike, the vast majority agreed that he was a serious philosopher, a humorist, not a comic or satirist, whose deep knowledge of humanity and the world had produced wise resignation, even pessimism.[76] Still, whether through the catharsis of laughter, Busch's paternal forgiveness, or the transcendent perspective he brought to his work, that resignation or pessimism produced wholesome, refreshing amusement, and, above all, comfort and contentment. Thus, although there was some disagreement over his meaning, and more over how he was misunderstood,[77] there was widespread agreement that he *was* misunderstood.[78]

These articles, then, were impressively elitist. The masses celebrated Busch and either did not know why or did so for the wrong reasons. Only the author of the article, Busch himself, and perhaps a handful of others appreciated Busch's true significance. The published response to Busch between 1902 and 1908 suggests that one appeal of his works was the powerful sense of superiority they produced, based, it would often seem, upon an imagined exclusive personal relationship with the humorist. The reader of Busch's work identified not with the characters but with the author who portrayed them. Busch's attitude toward those characters, it was maintained, was that of a benignly indifferent God who observed their trials and tribulations with dispassionate amusement. Or Busch was a puppeteer; his characters, the puppets.[79] But only "the select few" were able to see the strings.[80] Most Germans could not and laughed unwittingly at the suffering of Busch's characters, not realizing that they were themselves the butt of his humor.

The sense of superiority manifest in Josef Hofmiller's insistence that Busch "was never grasped in his essence by the multitude acclaiming him"[81] was directed on the part of socialist authors less at the German people in general than at the German bourgeoisie. "Busch was always an authority on and a ridiculer of the German petty bourgeois," Stefan Großmann wrote in 1902 in the Viennese *Arbeiter-Zeitung*. "The German burghers laughed at Herr Knopp and did not recognize that it was often they whom he had by the collar."[82] Indeed, for the natural philosopher Wilhelm Bölsche, writing in the *Sozialistische Monatshefte* in 1908, a defining feature of the Philistine was that he did not recognize his own status:

Busch indisputably had a small community that loved him and a quite enormous one that deified him. This latter was the community of the Philistines, the Knopps and Uncle Noltes, whom he had tarred and feathered and who had failed to notice anything. The Philistine always has the same fortunate characteristic. He takes much amiss . . . but he never takes it amiss when the Philistine as such is mocked; for he never sees himself as a Philistine; as long as he is the genuine article, he never feels this label applies to him.

Like the other writers claiming Busch was misunderstood, Bölsche clearly did not entertain the possibility that he might fit his definition of a Philistine himself. Instead, he self-confidently proclaimed Busch to be *the* satirist of the German middle class and one of the "great sages, interpreters, and liberators of world literature."

Against the excellent uncle who creeps under his feather bed in full possession of the assurances of the Philistine even the flea is a revolutionary. . . . For satire it is enough, however, that, against this Knoppdom, even a monkey is a genius, an individualist, a courageous hero on freedom's barricades. One day, as you wait quietly content for the barber to crimp your wig, the spirit of progress will sit behind you and curl your ears with hot glowing shears. . . . Fipps the Monkey will always triumph in world history, even if in the book a stupid Philistine shot picked him off the tree.[83]

Like Marx's *Communist Manifesto*, which despite its most famous sentence was directed squarely at the middle class, Bölsche's article confirms that self-contempt was a defining characteristic of the late nineteenth- and early twentieth-century bourgeoisie.[84] Indeed, the receptivity of that class to socialist ideas can be traced in part to the sense of superiority they engendered, enabling bourgeois socialists to elevate themselves above their class. Bölsche actually renders the proletariat insignificant in his article on Busch. Consis-

tent with his philosophy, he reduces the working class to a natural phenomenon—animals, insects, and children—and assigns the decisive historical
role to the bourgeoisie, which, through inner contradiction, hypocrisy, and
Philistinism, will simply destroy itself.

In contrast to Bölsche, a number of the Busch celebrants recognized that
they were being laughed at, that indeed Busch was laughing at himself, a recognition only serving to elevate them to Busch's transcendent position. "Did
he at all stand above the people as he depicted them?" Albert Dresdner asked
in 1908. "Yes, he stood above them, in that he saw through and beyond them,
in that he was immeasurably superior to them in spirit and in judgment. But
whoever reads his verses attentively . . . will detect everywhere how Busch,
the wag, says: 'My children, in essence I am as you are. . . . When I make fun
of you, I make fun of myself. Only, I know what it is that I am, and you do
not. That I can step outside myself, and you cannot.'"[85] Because they could
knowingly laugh at themselves, authors like Dresdner were "superior" in relation to their benighted contemporaries as Busch was "superior" in relation
to the characters he had created. Busch's humor, then, had the elitist and exclusionary character of an in-joke.[86] And yet, looking back from the last decade of the twentieth century, it seems to have been an in-joke that nearly
everybody in the century's first decade was in on.

The elitist appeal of Busch's humor as presented in these articles is also
manifest in the conviction, so characteristic of the nineteenth and early twentieth centuries, that truth lay hidden beneath the surface,[87] or, finally to quote
Wilhelm Busch himself, thanking those who had congratulated him on his
seventy-fifth birthday in 1907,

> Nur eins erschien mir oftmals recht verdrießlich:
> Besah ich was genau, so fand ich schließlich,
> Daß hinter jedem Dinge höchst verschmitzt,
> Im *Dunkel* erst das wahre Leben sitzt.[88]

> One thing alone most vexing to me seemed:
> On close examination, in the end I deemed
> That behind each thing, with most cunning art,
> There alone the true life sits, within the *dark*.

Indeed, it was Busch's genius, these authors believed, to have penetrated beneath *Schein*, appearance, to discover *Sein*, being, or, in a frequently used
metaphor, to strip off the mask exposing the reality beneath. And yet Busch
did not transform *Sein* into *Schein*. His work had a surface and a hidden
depth, as did Busch himself. Too often his ignorant contemporaries mistook

surface for reality both in Busch's work and in his personality.[89] Like Busch, the authors of these articles could strip away the mask, exposing the superficiality of the popular response to him. Now, in general, the notion that the truth lies hidden is elitist, for only "the select few" have the insight or courage to penetrate beneath the surface. And it is a notion specifically confirming the function of a cultural elite that can expose the hidden truth to masses all too ready to mistake *Schein* for *Sein*. The authors of these articles were, of course, writers, poets, journalists, and editors of the feuilleton sections of newspapers, who, in an era of burgeoning, commercialized mass culture, sought perhaps to assert their exclusive identity and function as the mediators of culture.[90] And yet, Franz Diederich, who shared the assumption that "it is from within that the outer form, the outer life expression is shaped," believed that "today we strive ever more consciously for a culture of expression that, in reflecting essence [*Wesensspiegelung*], does not distort the inner state. So perhaps that too lies behind this growing pleasure taken in Busch in our times."[91]

We do not need to rely on Diederich's testimony on the broad cultural resonance of this reading of Busch, however, to conclude that the elitist satisfaction engendered by Busch's works was not restricted to a relatively small number of literati seeking to justify their social position and cultural role. After all, these writers were addressing an extremely large and diverse group of readers,[92] for these articles appeared in widely read German newspapers and journals ranging from *Vorwärts* to the publication of the Pan-German League, from *Gartenlaube* to *Simplicissimus*, from *Jugend* to *Die allgemeine deutsche Lehrerzeitung*, from *Die Arbeiter Zeitung* to *Die Welt des Kaufmanns*. None of the authors appear to have sought to enlighten Busch's readers as to their misunderstanding of him.[93] The clear implication was that author and reader shared the correct interpretation of Busch, shared, indeed, Busch's understanding of himself. It was the others who misunderstood. The purpose of these articles, then, was not pedagogical but conspiratorial. They sought to establish an insider relationship between writer and reader (and ultimately the humorist himself) based upon their shared superior understanding of the massively misunderstood Busch.

The elitism manifest in the Busch reception was a defining feature of Wilhelmian Germany. It characterized the aristocratic conception of the state and its relation to society of the leaders of the Reich, the anxious social and cultural superiority of the *Bildungsbürgertum*, even the contempt of those in opposition to the Wilhelmian state and social order for middle-class Philistines, the idiocy of rural life, or the Lumpenproletariat. The leading ideologies of the era were based upon elitist conceptions of the superiority of the Germanic people, of German culture, of Germany's imperial and colonial mission, even of the special historical role assigned the German proletariat. It is probably no accident that historians have been so ready to employ the term "elites" in writing about this period, for they have (largely unwittingly) appropriated a way of thinking characteristic of the Wilhelmian era itself.

Although the authors celebrating Busch offered their readers the pleasures of elitism, they also testified to the inherent insecurity of the elitist position. Lacking the stability of the traditional *Ständestaat* or even of the naturally functioning exploitation of the class society, elitist conceptions always contained the threat of the loss of elite status. On the one hand, there was the fear that the elite would be overwhelmed by the mass. In the response to Busch, the conception of elite understanding and mass misunderstanding carried with it the danger that the latter would prevail, despite the best efforts of the Busch celebrants, contributing to the submersion of traditional high culture by modern popular culture. On the other hand, there was the fear of being mistaken, of discovering that one did not belong to the elite but to the uncomprehending mass. In the response to Busch, the conception of elite understanding and mass misunderstanding carried with it the danger that one was not in on the joke but its unwitting butt. A similar instability is manifest in the extremist, "all or nothing" thinking of this era, in the flamboyant predictions of greatness and glory and the dire premonitions of decline and doom. For history might reveal that, instead of being the bastion upholding Prussian values and a hierarchical social order, the state would give way to leveling bourgeois democracy or even be overthrown by proletarian revolution; that, instead of being the vanguard of triumphant socialist revolution, the German working-class movement would be destroyed or disintegrate; that, instead of being racially superior, the Germanic people would prove unworthy; that, instead of being the supreme world empire, the Reich would sink to the status of a satrapy; that, instead of being the culmination of Western civilization, German culture would be overwhelmed by inferior foreign cultures or, worst yet, succumb to internal degeneration. These drastic hopes and fears contributed to the adventurism of Wilhelmian foreign policy and the decision of the leaders of the Reich to opt for war in 1914 as a last desperate gamble to secure greatness and prevent collapse, as well as to the enthusiasm with which that policy and decision were greeted by broad sections of the urban population, particularly by those Germans whose views were represented in the creation of Wilhelm Busch as a national cultural hero.[94]

In 1907, in one of the few articles critical of Busch and his popularity, Karl Scheffler wrote: "What an entire people, what an era laughs about is not a trivial matter; the innermost life uncovers itself in the laughter."[95] Although we are less comfortable today in generalizing about the zeitgeist than were Scheffler and his contemporaries, this essay seeks to shed light, if not upon the zeitgeist, then upon the experience of Germans in the first decade of the twentieth century. In so doing, it attempts to avoid impressionistic speculation or having to generalize from the testimony of individual intellectuals by grounding the exploration of their experience in the voluminous published response to Wilhelm Busch between 1902 and 1908.

In retrospect, that response seems contradictory, even paradoxical. Busch represented both an irretrievably lost past and a model for the future. He was both bygone and relevant. In fact, he was relevant precisely because he was bygone, but he was made relevant only by updating him. On the one hand, he was counterposed to ostentatious public celebration, to the celebrity personality as an object of public curiosity, to the public's fascination with politics. In holding Busch up as dismayed by the fuss made over him, as modest and retiring, as apolitical, these authors rejected contemporary forms of popular entertainment. On the other hand, they upheld the very features of contemporary culture they were condemning. They celebrated Busch's rejection of modern celebrity and promoted his aversion to modern self-promotion. Lamenting modern public voyeurism, they focused public attention on his personality. Presenting him as an apolitical alternative to the modern preoccupation with politics, they politicized him. The claim that Busch was misunderstood by the masses endorsed an elitist conception of culture; the praise for Busch's popularity and accessibility endorsed a populist conception. The attempt to uphold elite against mass culture was further undermined by the ubiquity of the claim of ubiquitous misunderstanding. Here too they had it both ways. Through an appreciation of Busch that was simultaneously widespread and exclusive, they created *mass elitism*.

It would be easy to look back at the Busch-Enthusiasm between 1902 and 1908 with the superiority characteristic of so many of the articles written in his honor. Adopting a more empathic perspective, one can say that in an era of economic, social, and cultural transformation, the Busch celebrants manifestly rejected the present even as they revealed their inability or unwillingness to avoid fulfilling its demands. They manifestly wished to remain attached to the past even as they revealed that they had moved irredeemably beyond it. Those celebrating Busch in the years preceding the outbreak of World War I expressed and spoke to a sense of being trapped in dissatisfaction with who one was and how one lived. That dissatisfaction and the attempts to break out of it would have historical consequences transcending the celebration of any single German humorist, even one as remarkable as Wilhelm Busch.

15. When the Ordinary Became Extraordinary

German Jews Reacting to Nazi Persecution, 1933–1939

With the Nazi seizure of power, Jews became the official pariahs of Germany. Between 1933 and 1938, Jewish daily life gradually became enveloped by lawlessness, ostracism, and a loss of rights. As Jews went about their lives, most became increasingly aware of the uneven yet steady growth of hostility and danger around them. Still, for most Jews daily life consisted of the commonplace — trying to make a living, nurture their families, and achieve at school, activities that continued at least until November 1938. They tried to lead "normal" lives while experiencing outward oppression and inward tension and frustration. They tried to cope with practical solutions, sometimes burying themselves in the details. And they assessed their situation by how much they had to suffer while doing their daily tasks. The routine nature of their tasks and the apparent ordinariness with which Jews continued their daily existence notwithstanding, their internal equilibrium was shattered.

On the national policy level, the status of Jews deteriorated between 1933 and 1938. On the individual, experiential level, the lives of Jews were affected unevenly. There were many mixed signals and complicated situations to which individuals responded with hope, fear, or confusion. For example, in 1933, a ten-year-old observed Nazis marching with placards reading: "Germans, don't buy from Jews. World Jewry wants to destroy Germany. Germans, defend yourselves." But in 1935, her father was still decorated for active service in the past war, receiving a citation signed by the chief of police of Berlin.[1] Moreover, Jewish experiences differed according to where they lived: Berliners were able to go about their business and schooling with far less interference than Jews in villages and small towns. Experiences also differed according to age and class. Parents might continue in their occupations, but their children's present and future in Germany looked bleak. Many young people got out; many of the elderly were trapped. Wealthier Jews could insulate themselves from certain situations, but only for a time. And, gender, too, created distinctive experiences and reactions.

Women took on traditional as well as novel roles in this process. They remained the ones to calm the family, to keep up the normal rhythms of life. But gender roles also blurred as women and men tried to salvage some peace of mind by accommodating to their new predicament. And gender roles were dramatically reversed when women, rather than men, had to intercede for their families with state officials and when they pushed for their families to flee Germany.

Private Responses to Expulsion from the "Racial Community"

Families and Individuals

Jews generally reacted to Nazi policies as these affected them on an individual basis: that is, not all Jews felt the full weight of the Nazis' anti-Semitic policies; rather, they felt the weight of particular decrees or humiliations. Individuals thus responded to the increasing frustrations in daily life in a variety of ways, depending on the extent to which particular Nazi policies touched them. In 1940, Harvard University researchers analyzed the ways in which ninety people who had lived in Germany during the early years of Nazi rule had faced the new and mounting hardships. These included: flight into the family and into one's self; the increased importance of Jewish friendships; a change in life philosophy; "an endless procession of petty conformities to the harrowing demands of the Nazi persecutors"; the lowering of ambitions; and increased planning and action.[2]

The Harvard study found heightened in-group feelings among those persecuted by the Nazis, noting: "Most dramatic are the many instances of return to the healing intimacy of the family after bitter experiences of persecution on the street, in the office, or in prison."[3] Later memoirs and interviews affirm that "[l]ife centered more around the family then."[4] In the face of daily stress, ostracism by former non-Jewish friends, and the threat of increased fanaticism, many Jews sought the relative safety and comfort of their families, both nuclear and extended. This emphasis on the family had both positive and negative results. Someone who had been a young adult at the time later commented:

If I search for the special element associated with . . . existence as an outcast, then what I think of first is a positive gain . . . the increase in the intensity of family life. . . .

Yet there was a loss here too: in that entire period of ten years. . . . I only made two new friendships.[5]

Children were even more dependent on the family. They were not only aware of the social ostracism directed toward all Jews but experienced rejection directly from other children. The more hearty responded like the young teenager Peter Gay, who could associate with his cousins and absorb himself in soccer magazines to "escape to a playful reality . . . even for a few hours each week, away from the harsher reality of Nazi broadcasts, Nazi posters, Nazi teachers, Nazi fellow-students."[6] Other children were so deeply hurt that their wounds lasted a lifetime. Marion Gardner, born in 1931, wrote: "It didn't take long until one got used to not being allowed to be together with other Germans. . . . I was lonely, and until today . . . it is hard for me to make friends."[7] A mother noted that when her daughter's friends no longer came to their home, "Loneliness enveloped us more and more each day."[8]

Jews turned to each other for friendship and comfort. This was usually not difficult, since most Jews, even those who felt genuinely integrated into a non-Jewish social world, maintained a circle of Jewish friends and colleagues. Given the atmosphere outside, Jews often limited their social life to their own homes or organizations, staying away from public theaters, concerts, and museums but still occasionally frequenting movie houses.[9] Many turned with new zest to their remaining friends.[10] Mally Dienemann, the wife of Rabbi Max Dienemann of Offenbach am Main, marveled at the close friendships she witnessed: "Those who remained behind, whose circle got increasingly smaller, closed ranks all the more tightly. Friendship once again became the essence of life."[11]

Yet, in the strained circumstances affecting the entire Jewish community, shadows hovered over social evenings with Jewish friends. Such evenings were hardly relaxing: "As the prisoners in Dostoyevsky's *House of the Dead* speak only of the freedom that they might enjoy in perhaps 20 years, perhaps never, so the people in our circle spoke only of freedom beyond Germany, which they one day hoped to reach."[12] The topic of conversation inevitably turned to the worsening situation for Jews, the emigration of friends and children, and details of visas, foreign lands, and foreign climates, "of an existence where they would no longer be frightened to death when the doorbell rang in the morning, because they would be certain: it is only the milkman!"[13] Moreover, when groups of Jews gathered in private homes, they feared that they were being watched by suspicious neighbors, or worse, the Gestapo.

Upper-middle-class Jews had more options. They could act as though a certain normalcy were attainable, even when this was a self-deception. For example, they took vacations outside of Germany. When fewer German hotels accepted Jewish clientele, Ruth Glaser's parents sent her to Switzerland for a vacation.[14] Others enjoyed France, Italy, and Eastern Europe.[15] Also, daily strains could be alleviated if one had the financial means. Non-Jewish domestic servants could be asked to shop in markets that no longer welcomed Jews, and those able to afford it could even order food by telephone and pay delivery charges to avoid aggravation.[16]

Religion provided solace to many Jews. Observant Jews continued their adherence to Jewish laws and their celebration of Jewish holy days, sometimes even risking attention and possible eviction by building a backyard sukkah.[17] The bar mitzvah of a son, or the rare confirmation of a daughter, was cause for celebration, even amid the hatred surrounding them. A substantial number of Jews even became more religious.[18] Rather than a dramatic change of heart, this probably was the accentuation of "dominant preexisting philosophical tendencies."[19] That is, some Jews who had not practiced in the past began to take religious traditions more seriously. Ruth Glaser described her confirmation in 1935 with ten other girls in white dresses — the first time in Düsseldorf that girls had ever been confirmed. She reflected on how identities were shifting: "First one was a German and then a Jew. Now that we were reminded every day that we were Jewish, we became more aware of it. It became a comfort and something to hold onto and fight for."[20] Religion offered some a realm in which they could feel at home, safe from outside enmity. Synagogue attendance increased dramatically as Jews, depicted as evil and inferior by the government and media, sought balm for their raw nerves and affirmation of their identity. Joachim Prinz, a rabbi in Berlin, called his sermon on the night before the boycott of 1 April 1933 an "attempt at collective therapy."[21]

Other Jews turned toward Zionism, which had been a minority position within Jewish circles. In 1933, this changed and "a mass movement emerged out of the elite movement of German Zionism."[22] New subscribers purchased the Zionists' *Jüdischer Rundschau* looking for moral support. In the first few months of 1933, thousands of people streamed into the Palestine Office of the Zionist Organization in search of a new homeland. Between April 1933 and September 1934, the Haluz societies, or the German branch of the worldwide Zionist worker-pioneer organization, grew from 500 to over 15,000 members.[23]

Jews did not only turn to Jewish family, friends, religion, or new ideologies to counter deprivations. Many gradually accommodated to hostility, hoping that the Nazis would go no further and grateful for small loopholes or exceptions. Insidiously and incrementally, abuse became "normal" to some and familiar to all. A German-Jewish refugee to the United States reflected upon this process:

I don't think one can ever see if something is on a steady acceleration. . . . the terror is steady and you live with it and you go right along with it. And you really crack only if it suddenly increases.[24]

A mother of four whose children had emigrated and were urging her to leave recalled that "we within the borders of Germany had once more adjusted ourselves to the prevailing conditions."[25] Some acclimated to changed circumstances because they had thicker skin and some because they held different interpretations and perceptions of the malicious behavior or dangers confronting them. Others tried to deaden their feelings, a recurrent theme in the diary of Victor Klemperer, who noted the "unbelievable human capacity to endure and get accustomed" to the increasing cruelties of daily life.[26] Although coping with strained situations is an important human response, this adjustment may have exhausted some, distorting their perspective and harming their ability to make sound judgments about the overall situation.

People who had been out of the country for a couple of years often recognized the increasing danger more clearly than those living in Germany, who had gradually become accustomed to daily restrictions. Bella Fromm's daughter, returning from the United States for the Olympics in the summer of 1936, told her mother: "I could not breathe here anymore." In 1937, a seventeen-year-old whose parents had insisted that he flee, while they stayed, reported on his return for a visit:

It was 1937 and my parents wanted me back home for my summer vacation! This decision shows the supreme trust my parents, together with their fellow Jews, had in their government, despite what they saw happening around them. It showed how they had somehow accepted and adjusted themselves to the new conditions. Evidently they felt little risk in having their child return to a land that was about to explode.[27]

The Household

In the face of progressively worsening living conditions, it was women who were supposed to "make things work" in the family. Jewish housewives tried, where possible, to prepare less expensive meals, to repair their homes and clothing themselves, and to make do with less help around the house. The Nuremberg Laws (which forbade Jews to hire female "Aryan" household help under the age of 45) left most middle-class Jewish women entirely to their own devices in running a household with greater problems, in shopping for food in increasingly hostile stores, and in doing these tasks with ever-shrinking resources. Moreover, many took on paid work for the first time in their lives. Finally, Jewish women attempted to comfort frightened children and encourage family members in the face of harassment and unhappiness.

Women's organizations urged women to preserve the "moral strength to survive" and pointed to biblical heroines as role models.[28] Increasingly, it became apparent that biblical role models would not suffice in providing Jewish women with either the spiritual courage or the practical help they needed. Jewish newspapers began to deal more openly (and perhaps more honestly) with the issues plaguing families, particularly women. For example, as some families moved into smaller apartments, while others took in boarders in order to make ends meet, tighter living quarters caused strain. The League of Jewish Women acknowledged this but characteristically urged women to absorb it.[29]

Cooking played a prominent role among issues causing stress because of tight budgets, limited household help, and the difficulties for religious Jews of acquiring kosher meat. Jewish newspapers advised housewives to consider vegetarian menus because they were cheaper, healthier, and avoided the kosher meat problem.[30] After the Nuremberg Laws, the *Central Verein Zeitung*, the newspaper of one of the major Jewish organizations, ran articles entitled "Everyone Learns to Cook" and "Even Peter Cooks. . . . "[31] These articles emphasized how children, particularly daughters, could help their mothers.[32] "Daughter exchanges," another alternative to help overworked mothers, provided a half year's training in housework without pay to two young women who switched households.[33] In addition, some Jewish families hired young female relatives to help out, usually in exchange for some pocket money, room, and board.[34]

Jewish husbands were expected to pitch in—but only minimally. This seems to have been a particularly sensitive point for women and men alike. When Erna Becker-Kohen found grocery shopping more and more difficult due to the hostility of neighbors and government regulations, her non-Jewish husband took over that burden. She was especially grateful to him for this role reversal, because he had hated going shopping before the Nazis came to power, considering it "unmanly."[35] The League of Jewish Women suggested that since women had to do more for their families and were often the sole support of families as well, men should begin to do some housework.[36] But male—and female—resistance to such role reversals continued.[37] Moreover, some league members had little faith in men's competence, even if they showed themselves willing: "Jewish women can not count on the practical support of husbands (Jewish men are not as handy as Aryan husbands)."[38] Most commonly, husbands were only asked to limit their expectations[39] and to restrain their criticisms if meals were not what they used to be; to try praising their wives once in a while; to close their eyes to some imperfections ("a husband must also adapt").[40] Thus, gender privilege persisted, somewhat modulated, within the family, although conditions had changed profoundly, forcing many previously sheltered women to take on the entire burden of the household for the first time — often as they took on their first jobs as well.

To lighten household chores, the League of Jewish Women preached "Spartan simplicity" and Jewish newspapers proclaimed the "gospel of scientific management," ceaselessly urging women to rationalize their households by organizing, streamlining, and cutting back on their tasks.[41] As late as 1938, women could also read articles suggesting that they purchase time- or energy-saving kitchen utensils.[42] Furthermore, advice columns counseled women to hire daily or hourly help where possible.[43] In what must have been desperation, they urged hiring young men to help in the household.[44] Yet rationalizing the household or hiring unconventional helpers was, at best, a partial answer to domestic stresses. Articles in Jewish newspapers addressed overworked, overwrought mothers. Written in the tradition of the psychoanalytic discourse of the 1920s and reworked by Jews in the dismal 1930s, these articles show psychological and pedagogic sensitivity. They focus on deteriorating mother-child relationships. With titles like "Mommy, do you have time for me?" and "Mommy is so nervous!" they pleaded with mothers not to neglect their small children in their overcrowded days and to repress their outward nervousness by "pull[ing themselves] together if at all possible."[45]

These newspaper articles stand in stark contrast to many retrospective accounts. Whereas news articles chronicle stress, memoirs and interviews record action, accentuating the coping *behavior* that preoccupied Jews more than their feelings. Although feelings are not absent in memoirs, making them so painful to read at times, they are the backdrop to a frenzy of activity. Newspapers, on the other hand, in offering "solutions" to crises, actually document the enormous stress weighing on Jewish families, particularly housewives. It is hard to imagine that training daughters, streamlining work, taking on extra tasks, and repressing nervousness made life any easier. But, then again, maybe exertion and repression *did* help one, not only to survive, but to be able, in later years, to write a memoir of such anguishing times. Letters to a Jewish newspaper in August 1938 by women who worked both outside and inside the home affirm the stress and despair women experienced, but focus on action: "'you have to do it' is the eleventh commandment for us all now."[46]

311

The psychological blow of Nazism affected all Jews deeply. In December 1935, Dora Edinger, a leader of the Jewish women's movement, acknowledged in a letter that it was "hard to bear, even though I had long anticipated it rationally. Again and again, it is something entirely different to know something and to experience it."[47] The League of Jewish Women acknowledged that "increased burdens oppress Jewish women," but urged that all new hardships should be met as "duties . . . with calm and presence of mind." Its leaders called on Jewish women to maintain the home and family and the honor of the Jewish community.[48]

Trying to protect themselves and their families from the gloom around them, women often engaged in denial of their immediate hardships. They did this through what psychologists called "adoption of temporary frames of security," for example, in practical efforts, some even taking solace in additional housework burdens.[49] Although, in a few cases, such distraction may have kept the family from realizing just how significant the increasing deprivations were, some denial was necessary in order to preserve personal and family stability. Moreover, most people function on several levels at the same time. People could occupy themselves with the details of daily life while still studying a language useful for emigration, pushing a reluctant spouse to consider emigration, or filling out the mountains of forms necessary to apply to emigrate.

Finding safety in the routines of housework was generally a female form of escapism. This usually lasted longer than the male version—escape by submerging in occupational activities, since many men lost their jobs and businesses. Women also joined voluntary organizations, studied foreign languages, or learned new skills in an effort to help the community and to "deaden [their] worries."[50] In retrospect, many women realized what they had been doing. Alice Baerwald made herself so busy setting up a Zionist youth emigration program in Danzig that she "forgot to dismantle my own life."[51] Mally Dienemann's response when asked how one survived psychologically in Germany was: "[O]ne studied languages intensely and read a great deal, and with this intellectual diversion and preparing for new careers in handicrafts, one tried to deaden one's worries."[52] But these were not only distractions or practical necessities; they "set our mind and spirit free."[53]

Gallows humor may have helped Jews as well. Many remarked upon the frustrations of language training. If one studied Spanish or Portuguese to go to Latin America, sudden barriers to entry arose and one had to prepare for another country. If one turned to Hebrew, obstacles to acquiring the necessary certificates were certain to develop, and one had to change to yet another language. Thus, a joke made the rounds of one town: "'What language are you learning?' 'The wrong one, of course.'"[54] Children, too, turned to humor. A twelve-year old in a home for "non-Aryan" children where lunch consisted of potatoes and vegetables, called to his friends: "Now we're all vegetarians, so from behind, we're 'arians'!" ("Wir werden jetzt alle Vegetarier,— dann sind wir doch von hinten—'Arier'!").[55] Later, such humor expressed more serious defiance. In 1941, Edith Wolff opposed the regime by writing postcards to Nazi headquarters and bureaucrats echoing a joke making the rounds of Berlin: "Germany is now called Braunschweig: one half is brown [*braun* = Nazi uniforms] and the other half is silent [*schweig* = silence]."[56]

Role Reversals Among Jewish Women and Men

Their normal lives and expectations overturned, Jewish families embarked on new paths and embraced new strategies that they would never have entertained in ordinary times. For women, this meant new roles as partners, as breadwinners, as family protectors, and as defenders of their businesses or practices. These were roles that were often strange to them, but ones that they had to assume if they were to save their families and property.

While managing their households entirely on their own or with minimal help, many women also retrained for vocations that would be useful in emigration. Some women prepared for several possible jobs and studied several different languages at once, assuming that they would need to be versatile should they emigrate. One woman studied English and took lessons in sewing furs, making chocolate, and doing industrial ironing. A mother and her daughter took courses in Spanish, English, baking, and fine cookery. Then they asked their laundress to accept them as her apprentices. This was not only a new role for them but a reversal of their previous class position.[57] Many Jewish women who had never worked outside the home before suddenly needed paid employment. While some sought employment with strangers, others began to work for their husbands, who could no longer afford to pay employees. By 1938, there were "relatively few families in which the wife [did] not work in some way to earn a living."[58] Later that year, Hannah Karminski, an officer of the League of Jewish Women, remarked: "The picture of a woman who provides her family's basic sustenance is typical."[59] Still, the hope was that "work for married women is only and may only be an expedient in an emergency."[60] By proclaiming the crisis nature of women's new position, Jews, both male and female, could dream of better times and ignore the even more unsettling issue of changing gender roles in the midst of turmoil.

Role reversals were most pronounced where women found themselves representing or defending their men, as was increasingly the case. As early as 1933, a non-Jewish colleague suggested to Dr. Ernst Mueller and his wife Liselotte that because Ernst "had such a Jewish nose," she should appeal to a prominent non-Jewish doctor, Dr. Kleine at the Robert Koch Institute, on behalf of her husband. Discouraged by political events, Ernst agreed that his wife should represent him. When Dr. Kleine interviewed Liselotte, he asked why her husband had not come himself, and she began to cry, explaining the circumstances. The doctor thereupon invited them both to dinner. "When I told Ernst about the dinner invitation, he felt as if a miracle had happened. How quickly one's outlook changes! A short time before he would not have considered it a miracle to be invited by a non-Jewish doctor."[61]

Many incidents have been recorded of women who saved family members from the arbitrary demands of the state or from the Gestapo. In these cases, it was always assumed that the Nazis would not break gender norms: they might arrest or torture Jewish men, but would not harm women. Thus women took on a more assertive role in the public sphere than ever before.[62] In one small town, a Jewish family decided to send two of its women to the city hall in order to ask that part of their house not be used as a Nazi meeting place. They were successful.[63] Other women interceded for family members with German emigration or finance officials. In some cases they not only broke gender barriers but also normal standards of legality. Many memoirs report that Nazi officials had to be bribed and that, despite their original shock over this, women quickly caught on.[64] Some women actually took responsibility for the entire family's safety, a reversal of previous roles with their husbands. Liselotte Mueller traveled to Palestine to assess the situation there. Her husband, who could not leave his medical practice, simply told her: "If you decide you would like to live in Palestine, I will like it too." She chose Greece. Her husband, who was older and more educated than she was and in other circumstances had been the decision maker, agreed.[65] Ann Lewis's mother went to England to negotiate her family's emigration with British officials and her medical colleagues. This decision was based on her fluency in English, her desire to meet members of her psychoanalytic profession herself, and her husband's profession — as a medical doctor he was not welcome in Britain but she still was. She, who had always been "reserved with strangers," and for whom asking favors "did not come easily," had to ask for letters of recommendation from British psychiatrists and to apply to the Home Office for residence and work permits. And, although her husband had been the one to choose England, it was she who decided where the family would reside.[66]

Women had to call upon assertiveness they did not know they possessed. After traveling to the United States to persuade reluctant distant relatives to give her family an affidavit, one woman had to confront the U.S. consulate in Stuttgart, which insisted that there was no record of her. She showed her receipts, but the secretary just shrugged. At closing time, she refused to leave, insisting that her husband's, mother's, and children's lives depended on their chance to go to the United States. She would spend as many days and nights in the waiting room as necessary until they found her documents. After much discussion, the consul ordered a search of the files, and the documents were discovered. Today, her daughter refers to her mother as the "first sit in." [67]

Women often faced routine danger and dramatic situations, requiring both bravery and luck. Twenty-year-old Ruth Abraham urged her parents to move to Berlin to escape the hostility in their small town. The Nazis permitted this move only provided the father promised to appear at Gestapo headquarters weekly. Ruth always accompanied her father to these perilous interrogations. When her uncle was arrested in Düsseldorf, she hurried from jail to jail until she found out where he was. Then she appealed to a judge who seemed attracted to her. He requested that she come to his home in the evening, where he would give her a release form. Knowing that she risked a sexual demand or worse, she entered his home. The judge treated her politely and signed the release. She comments in her memoir: "I must add that I look absolutely 'Aryan,' that I have blond hair and blue eyes, a straight nose and am tall." Later, these traits would save her life in hiding; now, she was able to gain the interest or sympathy of men who did not want to believe that she was Jewish. [68]

The judge's treatment of Abraham notwithstanding, traditional sexual conventions could be quite menacing. Despite increasing propaganda about "racial pollution" or "racial defilement" (*Rassenschande*), Jewish women recorded frightening incidents in which "Aryans," even Nazis, made advances to them. In one small town, a young single woman became troubled about her safety on the streets at night. "In daylight they reviled me as a Jewish woman and at night they wanted to kiss me. The whole society disgusted me." [69] Another woman wrote of the perils of sexual encounters:

During the Hitler era I had the immense burden of rejecting brazen advances from SS and SA men. They often pestered me and asked for dates. Each time I answered: "I'm sorry, that I can't accept, I'm married. . . . " If I had said I was Jewish, they would have turned the tables and insisted that I had approached them. [70]

Sometimes overcoming the stereotypes of female passivity or sexual availability meant confronting still other obstacles rooted in gender conventions.

A social worker from Breslau attempted to have her new husband released from prison in June 1938. Convinced of his innocence, she appealed to his friend, a lawyer, for help. This man warned her that "when a woman is married for six weeks only, she does not know anything of the previous life of her husband." She wrote: "All these shocks undermine your self-confidence and . . . confidence in the world and in the goodness of men."[71] She held tenaciously to her opinion that the wrong man had been arrested, proved it, and was able to save her husband.

Women's new roles may have increased stress in some cases, but in general both women and men appreciated the importance of the new behavior. Edith Bick summed up the situation: "[I]n the Hitler times . . . I had to take over, which I never did before. Never." Her husband "didn't like it," but "he not only accepted it. He was thankful."[72] As conditions worsened, role reversals became ever more common. Women forced themselves to behave in "unwomanly" ways, some putting up a strong front when men lost it. One woman struggled to retain her self-control for the sake of her children as her husband sank into a deep depression. He could no longer sleep:

> He stopped eating, as he said no one had the right to eat when he did not work and became . . . so despondent that it resulted in a deep depression. . . . He feared we would all starve . . . and all his self-assurance was gone. . . . These were terrible days for me, added to all the other troubles, and forever trying to keep up my chin for the children's sake.

They decided to send the children away, because it was not good for them to see their father in such a state and they were also being constantly humiliated at school.[73]

Many women remarked upon the issue of self-control—its loss or its retention. They saw self-control as an attempt to retain their families' dignity and equilibrium in the face of dishonor and persecution. Probably men rarely describe this kind of behavior because they took it for granted, while women, previously allowed and encouraged to be the more "emotional" sex, were particularly conscious of their own efforts at self-control and of their husbands' fragility.[74]

The Emigration Quandary

Assessing and Deciding

As emigration became more and more crucial, women usually saw the danger signals first and urged their husbands to flee Germany. I have discussed the reasons for this and the ensuing family tensions elsewhere,[75] but Peter Wyden's summary of the debates within his own and other Jewish families in Berlin can be seen as representative:

It was not a bit unusual in these go-or-no-go family dilemmas for the women to display more energy and enterprise than the men. . . . Almost no women had a business, a law office, or a medical practice to lose. They were less status-conscious, less money-oriented than the men. They seemed to be less rigid, less cautious, more confident of their ability to flourish on new turf and, if necessary (at least this was true in my cocky mother's case), to find another man who would support them or make an effective partner.[76]

The Berlin artist Charlotte Salomon, who painted a stunning exploration of her life during 1941–42 while awaiting her fate in southern France, also summed up this predicament in her typically ironic way. In one painting, she depicted her short grandmother looking up to her tall grandfather, whose head is above the frame of the painting. The caption reads: "Grossmama in 1933: 'Not a minute longer will I stay here. I'm telling you let's leave this country as fast as we can; my judgment says so.' Her husband almost loses his head."[77]

Notwithstanding the gender differences in picking up signals and yearning to leave, it is crucial to recognize that these signals occurred in stages that could fool both women and men. Alice Nauen recalled her own behavior, which, I would argue, can be generalized to many others.[78] She and her friends "saw it was getting worse. But until 1939 nobody in our circles believed it would lead to an end" for German Jewry.[79] Moreover, these signals were often profoundly *mixed*, again bewildering both men and women. When Hanna Bernheim's sister who had emigrated to France returned for a visit in the mid 1930s, the sister wanted to know why the Bernheims remained in their south German town rather than flee. Hanna Bernheim replied:

First of all it is so awfully hard for our old, sick father to be left by all his four children. Second there are so many dissatisfied people in all classes, professions and trades. Third there was the Roehm Purge and an army shakeup. And that makes me believe that people are right who told us "Wait for one year longer and the Nazi government will be blown up!"[80]

Random kindnesses, the most obvious "mixed signals," gave some Jews cause for hope. One woman wrote that every Jewish person "knew a decent German" and recalled that many Jews thought "the radical Nazi laws would never be carried out because they did not match the moderate character of the German people."[81]

That men and women often *assessed* the dangers differently reflected their different contacts and frames of reference. But *decisions* seem to have been made by husbands — or, later, by circumstances. Despite some important role reversals, both men and women generally held fast to traditional gender roles in actual decision-making unless they were overwhelmed by events.

The common prejudice that women were "hysterical" in the face of danger or exaggerated fearful situations, worked to everyone's disadvantage. Charlotte Stein-Pick had begged her father to flee in March 1933. Her husband brought her father to the train station only moments before the SS arrived to arrest the older man. Not knowing about the SS visit, her husband returned home to say: "[A]ctually, it was entirely unnecessary that your parents left, but I supported you because you were worrying yourself so much."[82] Stein-Pick also overheard a private conversation in a train on 6 November 1938 in which the participants discussed what was about to happen to Jewish men in two days.

When I arrived home I implored my husband and a friend who lived with us to leave . . . immediately. . . . But my counsel was in vain. They believed my nerves had given way: how should these people have known anything and one could not have built camps big enough.[83]

Another husband believed his wife to be completely overwrought when she suggested — in 1932 — that he deposit some money in a Swiss bank. Cabaret artists were already joking about people taking trips to visit their money in Switzerland, but her husband refused. In this case, the belief that women were not supposed to mix into business matters further complicated the situation, making her suggestions even less likely to be heeded.[84]

Not only were men inclined to trust their own political perceptions more than their wives', but their role and status as breadwinners and heads of households both contributed to their hesitancy to emigrate and gave them the authority to say no. Else Gerstel fought "desperately" with her husband of twenty-three years to emigrate. Fearful that he would not find a job abroad, he refused to leave, insisting: "[T]here is as much demand for Roman law over there as the Eskimos have for freezers." "I was in constant fury," she wrote, representing their dispute as a great strain on their marriage.[85]

A combination of events usually led to the final — by then, joint — decision to leave and, as conditions worsened, women sometimes took the lead. In early 1938, one daughter reported, her mother "applied to the American authorities for a quota number without my father's knowledge; the hopeless number of 33,243 was allocated. It was a last desperate act and Papa did not even choke with anger anymore." (Her parents and young brother were deported and killed.)[86] Still another woman responded to narrowly escaping battering by a Nazi mob in her small hometown by convincing her husband to "pack their things throughout the night and leave this hell just the next day."[87] After the November Pogrom, there were wives who broke all family conventions by taking over the decision-making when it was unequivocally clear to them that their husbands' reluctance to leave Germany would result in even worse horrors. Else Gerstel recalled that although her husband had been arrested on 9 November, he did not have to go to a camp and still "had no intention of leaving Germany, but I sent a telegram to my brother Hans in New York . . . 'please send affidavit.'"[88]

Facing Closed Doors and Poverty

One of the chief objectives of Nazi policies toward the Jews between 1935 and September 1939 had been to foster emigration, once called "the territorial final solution." A series of plans, with such titles as "Syrian Project," "Madagascar Plan," "Ecuador Project," and "Haavara Transfer," were devised to deposit Germany's unwanted Jews around the globe.[89] The government urged individual emigration as well. Jewish agencies, in particular the Hilfsverein der deutschen Juden, the Hauptstelle für jüdische Wanderfürsorge, and the Palästina Amt, advised Jews on emigration possibilities, obtaining visas, and financial aid, and the Jewish press ran articles detailing emigration possibilities. Jews had to confront a bewildering array of countries, requirements, and details. Peter Wyden remembered that the language around his house changed between 1935 and 1937:

Our future had come to depend on three new guideposts: "the quota"—the total number of German refugees permitted to enter the United States under the miserly immigration laws; "the affidavit"—the document from an obscure umpteenth cousin . . . guaranteeing that he would support us if we became destitute; and "the visa"—which would be our stamped admission ticket into the promised land. . . . Beyond [these words] everyone learned about the "Zertifikat" from the British authorities to enter Palestine; the Reich Flight Tax that had to be paid to the Nazis as an exit fine . . . and the "certificate of harmlessness" required before one could cross the border.[90]

Profound obstacles to emigration existed. During the worldwide depression of the 1930s, foreign countries restricted immigration. In July 1938, the thirty-two nations assembled at the Evian Conference "regretted" that they could not take in more Jews. The New York Herald Tribune concluded: "Powers Slam Doors Against German Jews."[91] Those few countries with open doors needed farmers, not middle-class professionals and business people. Also, the German-Jewish age distribution limited emigration, since German Jews were disproportionately old.[92] No country wanted middle-aged and elderly people, who often decided not to become burdens on their children or relatives.

The Nazis created another major obstacle by restricting the amount of currency and property Jews could take with them. The plunder of Jewish property was part and parcel of all emigration proceedings. The Nazis "pressured Jews to leave the country, but the privilege of leaving was expensive."[93] The Reich Flight Tax (*Reichsfluchtsteuer*), originally instituted by the Brüning government in 1931 to prevent capital flight, threatened to impoverish prospective emigrants. Raised to punitive heights for emigrating Jews by the Nazis,[94] the Reich Flight Tax provided the German government with 1 million marks in 1932–33 and 342 million marks in 1938–39. In all, the German treasury may have gained as much as 900 million marks from it alone.[95] Many people had to sell all of their belongings simply to meet this particular tax requirement. Gerdy Stoppleman, for example, sent her husband, recently released from Sachsenhausen concentration camp, ahead to England while she stayed behind to pay the tax. She recalled, "To be able to pay the . . . tax I sold our furniture, valuable paintings and carpets, etc., dirt cheap. Many a home of true Aryans, S.A. and S.S. became exceedingly well furnished."[96]

In 1936, the Nazis forbade Jews to send money abroad, and later their bank accounts were even more stringently blocked. This meant that emigrants could not transfer the remainder of their (after-tax) money abroad but had to deposit it in "blocked accounts in marks for prospective emigrants." From these accounts, they could buy foreign currency—at a very unfavorable exchange rate, amounting to a further punitive tax. Until 1935, the exchange rate stood at half the official market rate of the mark; thereafter, the government steadily pushed it downward. By 1939, Jews could buy foreign currency worth only 4 percent of the value of their blocked German money. The Nazis forbade all transfers of money when war broke out.[97] Emigrating Jews thus lost 30 to 50 percent of their capital in the years 1933–37 and 60 to 100 percent between 1937 and 1939.[98] For many, it became harder and harder to leave, because new laws every few months robbed them of the means to start a new life elsewhere.[99] Under these conditions individuals and families hesitated to hurry abroad, and yet the more they hesitated, the more conditions deteriorated.

What these laws meant in terms of people's everyday reality can be seen in the memoirs of Ann Lewis, whose parents tried to leave in 1937. By then the sum my parents received in sterling was less than a quarter of what it would have been at the official rate. When the transfer to their English bank had been completed their 27,000 marks had become only £450 instead of the £2,160 which they would have obtained if their funds had been exchanged at what was then the normal rate.

Due to this poor transfer rate, her parents decided to buy everything they could in Germany, because they would barely have the means for subsistence once they arrived in England.

Nothing would be bought in England that could possibly be brought from Germany, and that applied not only to furniture and other household goods but also to items such as soap and other toilet articles . . . stationery, medical supplies, and of course enough clothes to last us for the next few years.[100]

Jews also faced plunder by individual corrupt bureaucrats. Gestapo agents, civil servants, packers, and even individuals in foreign consulates demanded bribes and tributes of every sort.[101] "We have come to see what you may take with you when you leave," said two Gestapo agents, transparent in their greed. Lola Blonder responded: "Feel free to look around." She added in her later memoirs:

They looked and took whatever little objects they liked—from the wall . . . from the tables . . . I was used to this by now. Whenever a group of Nazis visited, they helped themselves to . . . valuables. Robbing, robbing! Every day robbing me![102]

The story of how individual Germans enriched themselves from the theft of Jewish property still needs to be told. Many government officials were highly corrupt, seemingly relishing their new roles, hardly banal bureaucrats who were just "taking orders."

Material booty collected by the government and individuals was still not the worst of it. The government also limited Jewish mobility in 1937 by the issuance of passports for emigration only. The regime forbade information trips intended to assess the possibilities available in another country, and only people who were ill or visiting children studying abroad could leave and return.[103] Perhaps the major barrier to emigration for most was not having relatives or friends abroad who could sponsor admission into a country of refuge. For those with no contacts, applying abroad for positions as domestic servants became an important route of escape—especially, but not only, for women. Mountains of paperwork had to be completed in order to find such refuge, and the committees in charge of these matters sternly demanded "qualifications," that is, certificates guaranteeing domestic skills, so that their reputations would be enhanced in order to assist others. Besides photos, autobiographies, school transcripts, and health certificates, individuals needed proof that they were experienced at or capable of domestic service.[104] Then, after one had been accepted by a potential employer, the required emigration paperwork began.

Despite all hindrances, Jewish emigration was far from negligible, although it took an uneven course. About 37,000 Jews left Germany in 1933.[105] More discrimination, however, was not matched by more emigration. In 1934, only 23,000 fled. Many middle-class Jewish émigrés abroad were sliding into poverty, and some 10,000 had returned by early 1935. Return emigration halted after the Nazis threatened returnees with internment in a concentration camp in 1935. By the end of that year (after the Nuremberg Laws), about 21,000 had emigrated.[106] Another 25,000 left Germany in 1936, followed by 23,000 in 1937. With increasing persecution in 1938, another 40,000 emigrated. The first wave of refugees fled to neighboring countries, probably hoping to return home at some point or to continue abroad if necessary. The proportion of the total number of emigrants who fled overseas grew dramatically as conditions in Europe worsened in the later 1930s.[107]

Statistics give the false impression that Jews smoothly managed to leave Germany and enter the country of their choice, hiding individual stories that describe complicated emigration attempts, failures, and new attempts. For example, one family in Leipzig first decided to go to Palestine. The father, who had owned a silverware shop, trained to become a painter. By the time he received his diploma from the Leipzig League of Painters, however, there were too many applications to Palestine. The family next considered Chile and the Dominican Republic, but these did not work out either. Finally, the father wrote to a sister in Brooklyn, from whom his family received a U.S. affidavit in 1937.[108] And, as indicated by the joke about language training quoted above , accounts are legion of Jews having to switch languages in the middle of their studies because emigration to that spot had just become impossible.[109] Still, before 1938, a significant proportion — about one quarter — of German Jews left, answering the question posed by one husband to his wife, "Could you really leave all this behind you to enter nothingness?"[110] with a resounding affirmative.

Fleeing after the Pogrom

The Harvard psychologists who studied refugee memoirs determined that almost 40 percent of memoir writers did not give up psychologically until 1938 or 1939. The November Pogrom decisively tipped the balance toward emigration for those who were still confused or uncertain. For those in camps, the only way out was proof of readiness to emigrate. And, for those not in camps, the violence influenced their decisions.[111] It was only after the brutality of the Pogrom that Jews were finally convinced that they faced physical danger. After November 1938, "essentially everyone tried to find a possibility of emigrating."[112]

Still, immigration restrictions in foreign countries and Nazi bureaucratic and financial roadblocks stymied Jews. Countries of potential refuge thwarted Jewish entry. Elizabeth Freund, describes the many attempts by her and her husband to leave Germany:

It is really enough to drive one to despair. . . . We have filed applications for entry permits to Switzerland, Denmark, and Sweden . . . in vain, though in all these countries we had good connections. In the spring of 1939 . . . we obtained an entry permit for Mexico for 3,000 marks. But we never received the visa, because the Mexican consulate asked us to present passports that would entitle us to return to Germany, and the German authorities did not issue such passports to Jews. Then, in August 1939 we did actually get the permit for England. But it came . . . only ten days before the outbreak of war, and in this short time we were not able to take care of all the formalities. . . . In the spring of 1940 we received the entry permit for Portugal. We immediately got everything ready and applied for our passports. Then came the invasion of Holland, Belgium and France. . . . A stream of refugees poured into Portugal, and the Portuguese government recalled . . . all of the issued permits. . . . It was also good that in December 1940 we had not . . . paid for our Panamanian visas, for we noticed that the visas offered us did not . . . entitle us to land in Panama.

Freund was frustrated with friends who urged them to leave Germany: "As if that were not our most fervent wish." She agonized:

There are no more visas for the U.S.A. My husband has made one last attempt and asked our relatives in America by wire for the entry visas for Cuba. . . . No other country gives an entry permit to German Jews any longer, or is still reachable in any way.[113]

Once they received permission to *enter* a foreign country, Jews still had to acquire the papers to *exit* Germany. "Getting out . . . is at least as difficult as getting into another country and you have absolutely no notion of the desperation here," wrote 66-year-old Gertrud Grossmann to her uncomprehending son abroad. Getting the required papers took months of running a bureaucratic gauntlet, which many women whose husbands remained in camps faced alone. They met officials who could arbitrarily add to the red tape at whim: "[T]here was no rule and every official felt like a god."[114] Mally Dienemann, whose 63-year-old husband languished in Buchenwald, raced to the Gestapo to prove they were ready to emigrate. Next, she rushed to the passport office to retrieve their passports.

After I had been sent from one office to another. . . . I had to go to . . . the Emigration Office in Frankfurt, the Gestapo, the Police, the Finance Office, [send] a petition to Buchenwald, a petition to the Gestapo in Darmstadt, and still it took until Tuesday of the third week, before my husband returned. . . . Next came running around for the many papers that one needed for emigration. And while the Gestapo was in a rush, the Finance Office had so much time and so many requests, and without certification from the Finance and Tax offices . . . one did not get a passport, and without a passport a tariff official could not inspect the baggage.[115]

Finally arriving in Palestine in March 1939, Rabbi Dienemann died from his ordeal. By 1939, new arbitrary laws slowed emigration still more. Peter Gay recalled "the energetic efforts my parents made to flee Nazi Germany . . . and the steps my father undertook, bold, illegal and dangerous, to take us to safety in late April 1939, the last refugees allowed to land in Havana."[116] This situation deteriorated to such an extent by 1940 that Gertrud Grossmann wrote her son who had left in 1938: "Your emigration was child's play compared to today's practically insurmountable difficulties."[117]

Who Remained in Germany?

That women wanted to leave Germany well before their men does not mean that more women than men *actually* left. On the contrary, fewer women than men left Germany. Why was this so? In part, there were still compelling reasons to stay. First, women could still find jobs as teachers in Jewish schools or as social workers, nurses, and administrators in Jewish social service institutions, or as clerical workers for the Jewish community. Hedwig Burgheim, for example, found challenging and important work. In 1933, she was forced to resign as director of a teacher-training institute in Giessen. Thereafter she directed the Leipzig Jewish community's School for Kindergarten Teachers and Domestic Services, which trained young people for vocations useful in lands of emigration. After the November Pogrom, her own attempts at emigration having failed, she taught at the Jewish school in Leipzig and, by 1942, headed the Jewish old age home there. Along with its residents, she was deported in early 1943, and she died in Auschwitz. Dr. Martha Wertheimer, a journalist before 1933, also found her skills in demand thereafter. She plunged into Jewish welfare work and also escorted many children's transports to England. Ultimately, she wrote a friend in New York that, despite efforts to emigrate, she was no longer waiting to escape: "[A] great dark calm has entered me, as the saying of our fathers goes '*Gam zu le'tovah*' ('this, too, is for the best'). . . . It is also worthwhile to be an officer on the sinking ship of Jewish life in Germany, to hold out courageously and to fill the life-boats, to the extent that we have some."[118]

While the employment situation of Jewish women helped keep them in Germany, that of men helped get them out. Some men had business con-nections abroad, facilitating their immediate flight, and others emigrated alone in order to establish themselves and then send for their families. A handful of men, some with wives, received visas to leave Europe from groups hoping to save eminent intellectuals and artists. Women's organizations agreed that, if there was no choice, wives should not "hinder" husbands from emigrating alone, but they argued that it was often no cheaper for men to emigrate without their wives.

Before the war, more men than women faced immediate physical danger, another reason to leave rapidly. After the November Pogrom, in a strange twist of fortune, the men interned in concentration camps were released only upon showing proof of their ability to leave Germany immediately. Families—mostly wives and mothers—strained every resource to provide the documentation to free these men and send them on their way while some of the women remained behind. Alice Nauen recalled how difficult these emigration decisions were for Jewish leaders:

Should we send the men out first? This had been the dilemma all along. . . . If you have two tickets, do you take one man out of the concentration camp and his wife who is at this moment safe? Or do you take your two men out of the concentration camp? They took two men out . . . because they said we cannot play God, but these are in immediate danger.

Even as women feared for their men, they believed that they themselves would be spared serious harm by the Nazis. In retrospect, Ruth Klüger re-flected on this kind of thinking and the resulting preponderance of women caught in the trap: "[O]ne seemed to ignore what was most obvious, namely how imperiled precisely the weaker and the socially disadvantaged are. That the Nazis should stop at women contradicted their racist ideology. Had we, as the result of an absurd, patriarchal short circuit, perhaps counted on their chivalry?"[119]

Parents sent sons into the unknown more readily than daughters. Bour-geois parents worried about a daughter traveling alone, believing boys would be safer. Also, families assumed that sons needed to establish economic fu-tures for themselves, whereas daughters would marry. As more and more sons left, daughters remained as the sole caretakers for elderly parents. One female commentator noted the presence of many women "who can't think of emigration because they don't know who might care for their elderly mothers . . . before they could start sending them money. In the same families, the sons went their way." Leaving one's aging parent—as statistics indicate, usually the mother—was the most painful act imaginable. Ruth Glaser described her own mother's agony at leaving her mother to join her husband, who had been forbidden reentry into Germany: she "could not sleep at night thinking of leaving her [mother] behind." Men, too, felt such grief, but proportionately more left nonetheless. Charlotte Stein-Pick wrote of her husband's anguish: "This abandonment of his old parents depressed him deeply. . . . He never got over this farewell. . . . To be sure, he saw that we could never have helped them, only shared their fate. I almost believe he would have preferred it." [120]

As early as 1936, the League of Jewish Women noted that far fewer women than men were leaving and worried that Jewish men of marriageable age would intermarry abroad, leaving Jewish women behind in Germany with no chance of marrying. As late as January 1938, one of the main emigration organizations, the Hilfsverein, announced that "up to now, Jewish emigration . . . indicates a severe surplus of men." Blaming this on the "nature" of women to feel closer to family and home and on that of men toward greater adventurousness, it promised that women's emigration would become a priority. Yet, only two months later, the society announced it would expedite the emigration of only those young women who could prove their household skills and were willing to work as domestics abroad. Jewish organizations also provided less financial support to emigrating women than to men. [121]

The growing disproportion of Jewish women in the German-Jewish population also resulted because there were more Jewish women than men in Germany to start. In 1933, 52.3 percent of Jews were women, resulting from such factors as male casualties during World War I, greater marrying out and conversion among Jewish men, and greater longevity among women. In order to stay even, a greater absolute number of women would have had to emigrate. The slower rate of female than male emigration, however, meant that the female proportion of the Jewish population rose from 52.3 percent in 1933 to 57.5 percent by 1939. In 1939, one woman wrote:

Mostly we were women who had been left to ourselves. In part, our husbands had died from shock, partly they had been processed from life to death in a concentration camp and partly some wives who, aware of the greater danger to their husbands, had prevailed upon them to leave at once and alone. They were ready to take care of everything and to follow their husbands later on, but because of the war it became impossible for many to realize this intention and quite a few of my friends and acquaintances thus became martyrs of Hitler.[122]

A large proportion of these remaining women were elderly. Age, even more than being female, worked against timely flight. Together they were lethal. Between June 1933 and September 1939, the number of Jews in Germany under the age of 39 decreased by about 80 percent. In contrast, the number of people over 60 decreased by only 27 percent. By 1939, the proportion of people over 60 had increased to 32 percent of the Jewish population, and by 1941, two-thirds of the remaining Jews were past middle age. In Berlin alone, the number of old age homes increased from 3 in 1933 to 13 in 1939 and to 21 in 1942. Already in 1933, the elderly had consisted of a large number of widows, the ratio being 1,400 Jewish women over the age of 65 to 1,000 men. By 1937–38, 59 percent of the recipients of Jewish Winter Relief aged 45 and over were female. In 1939, 6,674 widowers and 28,347 widows remained in the expanded Reich.[123] When Elisabeth Freund, one of the last Jews to leave Germany legally in October 1941, went to the Gestapo for her final papers, she observed: "All old people, old women" waiting in line.[124]

Historians who study the Nazis tend to argue that their Jewish policy was either part of a methodical plan (the intentionalist approach) or haphazard, contradictory, and the result of internal bureaucratic dynamics (the functionalist approach). Most recently, the debate has focused on the peculiar character of German anti-Semitism: its wish to "eliminate" Jews, which led to their extermination by "willing executioners." [125] These debates stem from the bias of looking at the killers. When one examines the hapless *victims* of these policies, the debates pale; they are not something the victims lived. What is striking in the victims' accounts is not whether the Nazis intended the destruction of the Jews out of unmitigated and unparalleled hatred of them or whether they backed into it, but the speed *and* the ambiguities of the attack against Jewish life and the speed *and* the ambivalence with which Jews adapted in the years before 1938. Jews thought about and prepared for emigration, all the while wishing they would not have to leave their homeland. Although there were many deprivations and humiliations, until November 1938, the majority of Jews attempted to adjust to the new circumstances, clinging to mixed signals, hoping that the regime would fall or that its anti-Semitic policies would ease. Hindsight may make everything seem inevitable, but, at the time, even the November Pogrom did not provide a clear indicator of the genocide to come.

Still, between 270,000 and 300,000 Jews managed to flee Germany—
about three-fifths of German Jewry. These facts notwithstanding, it has been
common, in hindsight, to criticize German Jews for not having emigrated
quickly enough, for hoping that they could remain in Germany, for loving
Germany too much, for not seeing the writing on the wall. This is a profound
and cruel distortion. Condemning Jews for not having left in time fails to acknowledge how unimaginable Nazism was to most contemporary observers,
or how earnestly Jews tried to emigrate after the November Pogrom, when the
danger was apparent. Although many German Jews did love Germany and
did not want to leave at first, many more could not leave. Those who could
not were trapped by their obligations or their economic and social circumstances. In any case, perceptions by Jews of their predicament—either before or after 1938—were *never* the crucial factors affecting emigration. A bureaucratic gauntlet and Nazi plunder, creating the specter of abject poverty
abroad, discouraged many, but most important, as we know, the potential
lands of refuge heartlessly slammed their doors.

Freud and the History
of Psychoanalysis

16. Opposite the Pantheon

Fantasy about a Picture Postcard
Sent by Sigmund Freud

The slightly yellowed picture postcard from Rome shows the Pantheon and a part of the Piazza della Rotonda with its obelisk-surmounted fountain, manifestly photographed at a time when market stalls were still allowed there. Added drama seems to have been imparted to some of the heavy shadows by retouching. On the other hand, some characteristic details are missing. Of the portico, only the eight monolithic granite columns of the façade can be seen, one of these moreover being almost completely masked by the fountain. As a result, the depth of the pronaos, which has sixteen columns in all, is lost, giving a two-dimensional effect. Although the inscription on the architrave is invisible, it is echoed by the picture's caption: "Roma—Pantheon di Agrippa." In the right-hand margin, the second and subsequent lines running obliquely presumably so as to gain a little more space for the laconic communication, the following words appear in Sigmund Freud's handwriting:

Eden Hotel
1. 9. 23
Eben mit Anna hier ange-
komen   Herzlich Papa

Eden Hotel
1. 9. 23
Just arrived here with
Anna   Fondly Papa

On the date line, the year is followed by an apparently deleted, raised character that cannot be unequivocally deciphered.

On the back of the card, aside from stamps and the postmark—which shows that it was mailed on the same day—there is only the address of Freud's youngest son:

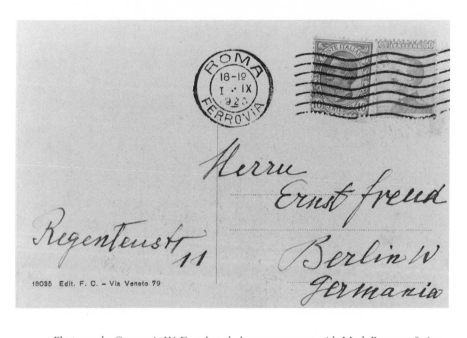

Herrn
Ernst Freud
Berlin W
Germania

On the left, in the space actually intended for the message, we find just the recipient's street address:

Regentenstr

11

The street address would have fitted perfectly well on the right-hand side. Could it have been written on the left so as to conceal the conspicuous blankness of the space there?

This conjecture is open to criticism as being overhasty; it was after all something of a habit of Freud's to write on the picture side of postcards. Again, it might initially be imagined that he wrote the actual message on the front of the card because the Eden Hotel, at which he had taken rooms with his youngest daughter, on what was to be his last visit to Rome, was situated on the Piazza della Rotonda.

Not so, however. That venerable establishment, in which Freud had stayed on previous occasions, was — and still is — located far away on the Via Ludovisi, nearer the Villa Borghese. Freud does indeed seem to have related his own and his daughter's arrival to the building illustrated, the Pantheon, perhaps at first by a split-second preconscious process of perception and mental filing akin to a daydream. He may have become fully aware of this reference only while writing, and if so have taken fright, not least because his son might have interpreted it as meaning that he had been relegated to an inferior position or ousted from his father's affections. Freud may therefore have inserted the words "Eden Hotel" into the corner left blank by the slope of the remaining lines *subsequently*, in order to suggest the "more harmless" reading of the card's message contemplated above — in the hope that his son in far-off Berlin was unaware of the topographical relationship between the Pantheon and the Eden Hotel.

The Pantheon is situated in the heart of the old city and, despite the stripping of its materials for use in other buildings, pillage, and defacement, it is still the best-preserved memorial to imperial Rome. As the inscription on the architrave records, it was erected by Marcus Agrippa, the son-in-law of Augustus, in the first century B.C.; destroyed by fire, it was rebuilt by Hadrian in the form that has come down to us today. As an archaeological phenomenon, it is exceptional, if only because, in this circular building that is almost completely hidden from the outside by the façade of the pronaos, the visitor can feel secure under an intact antique roof and take delight in the harmony of the unique dome. Through the thirty-foot oculus in the immaculate coffered vault, he may observe the radiance of the present-day heavens set in an ancient frame.

For centuries this grandiose domed building presented a challenge in Rome. Its height was not exceeded until Michelangelo built the dome of St. Peter's. Envy of the admired model may have motivated the destructive action of the baroque pope Urban VIII in having the bronze ceiling of the portico removed and used in the construction of Bernini's high altar in St. Peter's.

When Freud arrived here in 1923, the building already embodied *both* meanings of the word "pantheon." It had originally been a temple sacred to the seven planetary divinities, whose statues once stood in the interior niches. An element of the early polytheistic meaning persists in the fountain-and-obelisk also depicted on the card. By 609 A.D., Pope Boniface IV had transformed the Pantheon into a church, S. Maria ad Martyres, and as it were made the second meaning more applicable, for the onetime home of the ancient gods now became the resting place of the bones of Christian martyrs transferred from the Catacombs — memorable figures, albeit not yet in the sense of being outstanding individuals. However, Freud of course knew that the rotunda housed the mortal remains of a number of artists, including Raphael — even if not Leonardo — and thus conformed perfectly to the second denotation of the word "pantheon," as a hall of honor for the great, like the classicistic Panthéon of Paris today.

Already in 1897, Freud had confessed to his friend Wilhelm Fliess: "My longing for Rome is, by the way, deeply neurotic. It is connected with my high school hero worship of the Semitic Hannibal. . . . "[1] The extent of this preoccupation, in which he identified with the Carthaginian general, who never set eyes on Rome, is documented in his own famous sequence of dreams about the city reported in *The Interpretation of Dreams*. One of them shows an unconcealed link with the theme of Moses: "Another time someone led me to the top of a hill and showed me Rome half-shrouded in mist; it was so far away that I was surprised at my view of it being so clear. . . . the theme of 'the promised land seen from afar' was obvious in it."[2] Again: "I was clearly making a vain attempt to see in my dream a city which I had never seen in my waking life."[3]

When he at last dared to set foot there in September 1901 — that is to say, *after* the publication of his magnum opus — Freud discovered for himself ancient Rome in particular. This certainly included the Pantheon, as we know from an enthusiastic card dated 3 September of that year to his wife Martha, who was then relaxing in Thumsee — not this time a picture postcard but just a plain *cartolina postale* — in which he writes: "Noon opposite the Pantheon — so that's what I've been afraid of for years!"[4] Even if he goes on to describe his visit that morning to St. Peter's, as well as to the Sistine Chapel and Raphael's Stanze, while also mentioning that "churches" would "probably" be on his sightseeing agenda for that afternoon, there can be no doubt that it was above all ancient Rome that captivated him, rather than the "second," Christian Rome.[5] He was thereby in his own way actualizing the link with Hannibal that is also emphasized in *The Interpretation of Dreams*: "To my youthful mind Hannibal and Rome symbolized the conflict between the tenacity of Jewry and the organization of the Catholic church."[6] Including that final journey, he went to Rome in all seven times for shorter or longer periods, on each occasion finding a happiness and renewed vigor that are described eloquently in his letters.

In February 1923, Freud had noticed a growth in his mouth. It was not until April that he consulted a rhinologist, who then performed a botched operation. Although the fact of the tumor's malignancy was at first concealed from him or disputed, Freud seems to have "known" the truth. This is clear from the following extract from a letter written in English to Ernest Jones at the end of April, the same month in which *The Ego and the Id* appeared: "I detected 2 months ago a leukoplastic growth on my jaw and palate right side, which I had removed on the 28th. I am still out of work and cannot swallow. I was assured of the benignity of the matter but as you know, nobody can guarantee its behaviour when it be permitted to grow further. My own diagnosis had been epithelioma, but was not accepted. Smoking is accused as the etiology of this tissue-rebellion."[7] Although he may have momentarily welcomed the well-meaning deception, the subsequent X-ray and radium treatments must have made him thoroughly distrust the spurious diagnosis, even if he did not show it. Looking back, he declared to Sándor Ferenczi in August 1924: "I knew after all from the beginning that I had an epithelioma. . . ."[8] Indeed, on reading this letter, Ferenczi may have recalled that Freud had informed him seven years before, in connection with a brief period of abstention from tobacco, of a transitory swelling of the palate, which had already given rise to the conjecture "Carcinoma?"[9]

The decision to travel to Rome with Anna was made within a week of that first operation. She too must have suspected that her father's illness was cancer. Although Felix Deutsch, whom Freud occasionally consulted as a doctor at this time, had informed the members of the committee of the seriousness of the situation, he had said nothing about it to Anna. When she asked him whether they could stay longer in Rome if they both liked it there, he reacted with horror and made her promise that they would return punctually. As she later declared, Anna Freud had at once interpreted Deutsch's alarmed reaction correctly: the radical life-saving operation by the renowned oral surgeon Hans Pichler was scheduled to be performed immediately after their return. Repeated drastic surgery was in fact to prove necessary before a halt could be called to the pathological process.

In June — that is, before their departure — Freud was stricken by the loss of his favorite grandchild Heinele, the younger son of his daughter Sophie, who had herself been abruptly carried off by influenza a few years earlier. Not yet five years old, the graceful child, who was manifestly highly gifted, had died suddenly of miliary tuberculosis. When the boy was still in a coma, Freud had an unexpectedly violent depressive reaction. "I find this loss very hard to bear," he wrote. "I don't think I have ever experienced such grief. . . . "[10] While taking the cure at Bad Gastein, he wrote to his son-in-law Max Halberstadt, Heinele's father, on 7 July 1923: "Here I have spent some of the blackest days of my life mourning for the child. Finally I have pulled myself together and am now able to think of him calmly and talk about him without tears. All sensible consolations having failed, the only thing that has helped is the argument, appropriate solely to me, that at my age I should in any case not have seen much of him."[11] And in the same vein, he wrote to Max Eitingon and Oscar Rie in August, shortly before his departure: "I am still being tormented in my snout and obsessed by impotent longing for the dear child"; he "meant the future to me and thus has taken the future away with him."[12] The pain, complaint, anger, and protest no doubt arose mainly from the senselessness of that child's death, the destruction of a still slumbering potential, the violation of what was felt to be the natural order of dying of the generations. However, Freud himself surmised that the shock of his own cancer might have contributed to the intensity of these feelings. His depression over Heinele was also a displaced reaction to the brutal confrontation with his own mortality. The child imago may have stood in his unconscious for the unlimited, open-ended time horizon. From this point of view, it had been the diagnosis of cancer, of which he had "known" at least preconsciously, that had "taken the future away with [it]."

In traveling to Rome, the *eternal*, imperishable city, he was thus seeking refuge; for the last time with an intact body—for he surely realized that the intrusive operation in his mouth would constitute a severe handicap for the rest of his life—Freud would be strolling among the familiar sites, talking freely to his daughter and able to forget for a few moments, or days, what had just happened and what lay ahead. No doubt he also showed her the Moses of Michelangelo, which forms an almost equilateral triangle with the Pantheon and the Eden Hotel in the topography of Rome and which he had once before reflected upon to help him cope with an earlier crisis.

While still in Rome, he wrote to Eitingon, manifestly with great satisfaction: "Anna is savoring it to the full, finds her way about brilliantly, and is equally receptive to all sides of Roman polydimensionality."[13] In almost identical terms, Anna Freud confirmed to Lou Andreas-Salomé in a letter also composed in Rome: "Papa . . . has introduced me to everything so well, and made me feel at home among all the beauties, antiquities and other sights that now after the second week I feel that I quite belong, and as if I had been with him on all the other numerous occasions that he has been here."[14]

Had this masterly guided tour of Rome, whether or not by design, reinforced Anna's identification with her father? At the time she was not yet 28 years old and in the full bloom of youth. Conversely, Freud may have identified with her youthfulness, causing his daydreams to take flight. Arriving with her at the Pantheon may have had a twofold preconscious meaning. It may have given him the courage to move into the "Egyptian pantheon"[15] as it were in the form of the vulture-headed divinity described in his study of Leonardo, a being with the narcissistic perfection accruing from the possession of both male and female sex characters; or perhaps, more probably, it inspired in him the idea of a father-daughter syzygy in which he would find a permanent place in the pantheon of the great through his work and its continuation in hers. From this point of view, he might well have recalled with satisfaction a remark in a letter from Ludwig Binswanger received on 27 August 1923, just before he left for Rome, to the effect that the daughter's style was "already no longer distinguishable from that of the father."[16]

Freud could not then have known how many years he still had ahead of him and how creative, for all his torments, they would be. At any rate, the twofold unity of father and daughter intensified in the ensuing period, not least because the daughter's paradoxical analysis by the father was resumed in 1924. Reminiscences of their trip to Rome together are to be found in letters and works. While in Milan in April 1927, Anna Freud wrote the following short sentence to her father as if in passing: "Thought a lot about Rome."[17] And in the new edition of *The Interpretation of Dreams* prepared for the *Gesammelte Schriften*, the first quasi-collected edition of Freud, conceived in the shadow of his cancer, he completed a note on the Rome dreams that had appeared in the 1909 second edition, in which he had already informed the reader that he had learned how even wishes long deemed unattainable could in fact be fulfilled with "a little courage"; now, in 1925, he added the following words, which dispelled any residual vagueness: "and thereafter became a constant pilgrim to Rome."[18]

However, the main reminiscence is to be found in one of those late works that Freud in 1923 could never have hoped to write, *Civilization and Its Discontents*. It is surely no coincidence that it features in the context of ideas about the "problem of preservation in the sphere of the mind"—that is, the "view, that in mental life nothing which has once been formed can perish. . . . "[19] The concluding passage of these reflections is here reproduced in full, if only because, at the end of our intellectual game, it presents us again with the Pantheon illustrated in the picture postcard:

Now let us, by a flight of imagination, suppose that Rome is not a human habitation but a psychical entity with a similarly long and copious past—an entity, that is to say, in which nothing that has once come into existence will have passed away and all the earlier phases of development continue to exist alongside the latest one. This would mean that in Rome the palaces of the Caesars and the Septizonium of Septimius Severus would still be rising to their old height on the Palatine and that the castle of S. Angelo would still be carrying on its battlements the beautiful statues which graced it until the siege by the Goths, and so on. But more than this. In the place occupied by the Palazzo Caffarelli would once more stand—without the Palazzo having to be removed—the Temple of Jupiter Capitolinus; and this not only in its latest shape, as the Romans of the Empire saw it, but also in its earliest one, when it still showed Etruscan forms and was ornamented with terracotta antefixes. Where the Coliseum now stands we could at the same time admire Nero's vanished Golden House. On the Piazza of the Pantheon we should find not only the Pantheon of to-day, as it was bequeathed to us by Hadrian, but, on the same site, the original edifice erected by Agrippa; indeed, the same piece of ground would be supporting the church of Santa Maria sopra Minerva and the ancient temple over which it was built. And the observer would perhaps only have to change the direction of his glance or his position in order to call up the one view or the other.[20]

Commencing a new paragraph, Freud concludes:

There is clearly no point in spinning our phantasy any further, for it leads to things that are unimaginable and even absurd. If we want to represent historical sequence in spatial terms we can only do it by juxtaposition in space: the same space cannot have two different contents. Our attempt seems to be an idle game. It has only one justification. It shows us how far we are from mastering the characteristics of mental life by representing them in pictorial terms.[21]

Could that attempt also have had a completely different aim: to luxuriate once more, again as if in a daydream, in the indelible memories of his glorious last visit to Rome with Anna, and to place on record the wish he had set up against his death anxiety, that no iota of his work and its polydimensionality should perish?

———

In the fall of 1976, two volumes of pictures devoted to Sigmund Freud appeared. The first, entitled *Berggasse 19: Sigmund Freud's Home and Offices, Vienna 1938*, was published by Basic Books; it contains the photographs taken by Edmund Engelman just before Freud's emigration to London, with an introductory essay by Peter Gay. The second, *Sigmund Freud: Sein Leben in Bildern und Texten*,[22] came from Suhrkamp; this book had originally been planned by Freud's youngest son, Ernst, but after he died in 1970, when the work on it was just beginning, the project was brought to fruition by myself in agreement with his widow, Lucie Freud. The two volumes had come into being independently of each other — that is, each without the knowledge of the initiators of the other. So when both were published almost simultaneously, there was at first a mutual feeling of not only agreeable surprise.

However, my initial displeasure soon gave way to joyful astonishment at how different the two books had turned out to be and how well they dovetailed with each other: our volume brought together pictorial material from a wide variety of sources spanning every phase of Freud's life and work, coupled with an accompanying text made up of extracts from his writings and letters so as to make a kind of illustrated autobiography in the form of a mosaic; whereas Engelman's photographs were a static snapshot of the Berggasse residence, already bedecked with a swastika flag, in effect capturing a dramatic, tragic moment, and were made to speak by Peter Gay's masterly essay likening them to a manifest dream — rare and fascinating raw material, which, however, called for interpretation. It was Gay, the historian uniquely familiar with psychoanalysis, who added the dimension and the dynamic of the pre-1938 period by eloquently demonstrating that an intellectual revolution that had changed our epoch down to the very structures of everyday life had taken place in this seemingly conventionally bourgeois laboratory in the almost half a century that had elapsed since 1891, the year Freud had moved in. "[H]is living quarters, which these photographs permit us to enter, offer a suggestive contrast to the ideas he generated there. It is only after one has reconstructed the mental atmosphere and scientific pieties of the late nineteenth century that the full measure of Freud's revolution emerges. Yet he made his revolution in the most unrevolutionary of surroundings. Its banners and slogans are all invisible."[23]

This introduction, with its ironic-sounding title "Freud: For the Marble Tablet," is in fact Peter Gay's first essay to center on the founder of psychoanalysis. The text is of supple elegance and produces an effect as of multifocal refraction: the profuse things discernible in the illustrations—family photographs, bookshelves, pictures on the wall, carpets, and above all the antique statuettes, bronzes, and terra-cotta figures—are described and explained, as is Freud's natural, empathic prose. However, Gay's telling formulations at the same time convey something of the singularity of the analytic process—for example, "the psychoanalyst becomes the detective of absences: of subjects dropped, overtures rejected, silences prolonged"[24]—so enabling the reader to appreciate the eccentric effort, or indeed paradox, of Freud's self-analysis. Years before Bruno Bettelheim, criticism is leveled at the English translations of Freud, and long before the performances of the present-day Freud-bashers, Gay already notes that it is becoming customary "to discredit Freud's discoveries by denigrating his character."[25]

After this essay, Peter Gay published an impressive series of books, by which, with his continued reflection about Freud and his texts, he has enriched not only Freud research but also the history of modernist culture and the debate on historical methods. His crowning work, which appeared in 1988, is *Freud: A Life for Our Time*.[26] An attentive reading of the essay that opens *Berggasse 19* will—on the level of content as well as of form—reveal it as a sketch, a kind of map projection, for the future great biography.

There is in fact also a link between the two works and my fantasy about the Pantheon postcard. In the context of his considerations on the meaning of Freud's passion for collecting, Gay refers in his essay to the former's frequent use of archaeological metaphors, quoting that passage from *Civilization and Its Discontents* on the problem of preservation in the mental sphere for which he adduces Rome, the many-layered eternal city, for comparison.[27] It is the very quotation with which my intellectual game ends. By his careful reconstruction of the history of Freud's illness and treatment, for which Gay opened up new sources, his biography so to speak supplies the factual background against which my fantasy about the Pantheon postcard can stand out. I am thinking of the ninth chapter, "Death Against Life," in which he places the section on Freud's cancer, "Intimations of Mortality," immediately before the section headed "Anna." By adopting this order, Gay is indicating that he too considers the two themes to be intimately linked to each other. He may therefore agree with my interpretation and perhaps even read it as a small variation on those two moving pieces of his own great biography of Freud.

Translated by Philip Slotkin

17. Retrogression

Helene Deutsch's Account
of the "Dark Continent"

"The sexual life of adult women," Freud wrote in 1926, "is a 'dark continent.'" [1] By the time those words appeared in print, Helene Deutsch was already launched on her exploration of it. During the following decade, before her emigration to the United States, she fashioned a story that amounted to a narrative of retrogression.

"Retrogression" — a backward or reversed movement, a return to a less advanced state, a reversal of development — conjures up the world of late-nineteenth-century biology, the world of Charles Darwin and Ernst Haeckel. It was a world of permeable disciplinary boundaries, a world in which biological categories or terms might serve a variety of theoretical functions in the social or human sciences, homology, analogy, and metaphor among them. [2] Freud himself did not hesitate to borrow from biology or even to engage in biological speculation — although biological determinism was not a feature of his thought. (Given his Lamarckianism, how could it have been?) Retrogression, then, like its first cousin, regression, was a concept that would have been familiar to the psychoanalytic community in general and to Helene Deutsch in particular.

By the mid 1920s, Deutsch could be reckoned a pillar of that community: by then she figured as a member of the Viennese old guard. [3] She had arrived in the Austrian capital in 1907 just as she was turning twenty-three. Born in Przemyśl, a fortress town near the Carpathian Mountains, she was the youngest child of a lawyer, a Jew who had assimilated to the intelligentsia and had prospered. (There were two older sisters and an unpromising older brother in the family as well.) At the age of fourteen, having finished the official schooling available to her, Helene launched a campaign to acquire the *Abitur* and with it the possibility of university training. Over the next decade, she earned her medical degree — six women entered Vienna's School of

Medicine along with her, only two of whom finished — and then pursued a specialty in psychiatry. Doing so entailed a brief stint in Munich working under Emil Kraepelin and the better part of six years in Vienna under Julius Wagner-Jauregg at the university's Clinic for Psychiatry and Nervous Diseases. Thanks to the war and the shortage of male physicians, Deutsch rose to the position of assistant in charge of the women's division, a post to which, as a woman, she was not legally entitled. She had engaged in experimental work in Munich and again at the beginning of her association with Wagner-Jauregg, but each time her enthusiasm soon dwindled. By war's end, she had had ample hands-on psychiatric experience; intellectually, she was still lacking a purpose.

In the course of her education, Deutsch encountered Freud's writings and attended meetings of the Vienna Psychoanalytic Society, which, during the war, convened on an irregular basis. In early 1918, she was elected to membership. Was she in the process of becoming a psychoanalyst, and if so, what did that process entail? Of formal instruction and supervision, there was none; in fact, no prescribed program existed in Vienna until 1924, when Deutsch herself was appointed the first director of the Training Institute, a position she held until her departure for the United States in 1935. Of personal analyses, which, though not yet a requirement, were becoming common, she had two, the first with Freud, the second in Berlin with Karl Abraham.

Deutsch was not forthcoming about her double experience as analysand. It is safe to assume, however, that in both instances conflicts about motherhood, marriage, and professional ambitions brought her to treatment. By the time she began analysis with Freud — it went on for less than a year in late 1918 and early 1919 — she had been married to Felix Deutsch for six years, and they had a nineteen-month-old son. (To provide milk for their child, Felix had brought two goats to Vienna. During her analysis, Helene shared the goats' milk with Freud's wife.) According to her account, she managed to "avoid mentioning conflicts" involving her "motherhood";[4] according to her biographer, "details about her small child and her difficulties with her nursemaid" bored her analyst.[5] As for her marriage, she was frequently restless in it, and whether or not to divorce was a crucial question in her seeking Abraham's help in 1923–24. This time treatment lasted a little more than a year. Shortly after she began it, Freud wrote his disciple in Berlin, telling him that the Deutsches' marriage ought not to be disrupted by Helene's analysis. Abraham showed the letter to his patient, and the marriage remained intact. Whatever inadequacies she felt as a mother, whatever doubts she entertained about her marriage, she would have to handle on her own.

Her professional activities were another matter. Here Freud offered encouragement. He expressed no discomfort with what Deutsch thought of as masculine strivings and thus provided a model of tolerance. (In this connection, she recalled a dream in which she had a double set of genitals. Apparently, Freud did not pursue its interpretation.)[6] He considered her marked identification with her father — in her childhood Helene had adored her father and hated her mother — as a source of strength to be reinforced. She viewed it as the source of a never-resolved transference as well.[7] Throughout her subsequent career, she imagined Freud as her audience; she felt that in him she had found "the center" of her "intellectual sphere."[8]

In the Service of Femininity

> In conformity with its peculiar nature, psycho-analysis does not try to describe what a woman is — that would be a task it could scarcely perform — but sets about enquiring how she comes into being, how a woman develops out of a child with a bisexual disposition. In recent times we have begun to learn a little about this, thanks to the circumstance that several of our excellent women colleagues in analysis have begun to work at the question. . . . The ladies, whenever some comparison seemed to turn out unfavourable to their sex, were able to utter the suspicion that we, the male analysts, had been unable to overcome certain deeply-rooted prejudices against what was feminine, and that this was being paid for in the partiality of our researches. We, on the other hand, standing on the ground of bisexuality, had no difficulty in avoiding impoliteness. We had only to say: "This doesn't apply to *you*. You're the exception; on this point you're more masculine than feminine."[9]

Herewith Freud offered an olive branch to his female disciples. Given his admission that bisexuality "remained surrounded by many obscurities," given his inability to find a place for it in his instinct theory, his remarks should not be construed as suggesting an approach to a vexing question.[10] Rather, he was suggesting a rhetorical strategy that those disciples might adopt in order to address a largely male audience on matters of female psychology. It was a suggestion that Deutsch had already shown herself willing to accept.

What in her texts brings to mind a "bisexual" (that is, masculine as well as feminine) stance? The answer is: the persona of the narrator. In *Psychoanalysis of the Sexual Functions of Women* (1925), Deutsch's first book, that narrator seemed distant and detached. Most of the time, she avoided the first-person pronoun altogether. For example:

[P]sychological findings, insofar as they are based on the psychology of the conscious, will not be referred to here, for it is the purpose of this book to explain what was bound to remain mysterious to the psychology of the conscious.

It was the purpose of the book, Deutsch further elaborated, to explain what had, likewise, up until now remained mysterious to the psychology of the unconscious:

The hidden contents of the male mind have obviously been more accessible to the male because of the closer kinship. . . . [U]nderstanding of mental processes in women has lagged behind. . . . In particular, little analytic attention has been paid to the generative processes, though these form the centre point of the mental life of the sexually mature woman. Kant's saying that woman does not betray her secret still applies.

Those hidden contents of the male mind had presumably been accessible to the narrator. That was not all. Now the female mind — more specifically "woman's psychological relations to the physiological processes of sexual life" — was in the course of betraying its secret.[11] Male and female alike were within the narrator's grasp, who thus implicitly claimed kinship with both.

At the same time Deutsch claimed membership in the psychoanalytic community and addressed the text to her fellow members. The narrator assumed on the part of the reader "a thorough knowledge of psychoanalysis" and of the method that allowed it to reach unconscious mental contents.[12] Her task, then, was to persuade her audience that hers was an account of female development in a distinctly psychoanalytic idiom.[13]

Two texts foreshadowed Deutsch's *Psychoanalysis of the Sexual Functions of Women*: Freud's paper on "The Infantile Genital Organization" (1923) and Abraham's "A Short Study of the Development of the Libido, Viewed in the Light of Mental Disorders" (1924). Freud's piece bore the subtitle "An Interpolation into the Theory of Sexuality" and reflected his continuing effort to enlarge and modify his *Three Essays*. (The first edition appeared in 1905, and the last, the sixth, in 1925.) Not until 1915, with the publication of the third edition, did he interpolate a section on pregenital organizations of the libido, that is, "preliminary stages" that constituted a "sexual regime of a sort."[14] In the 1923 paper he expanded on the role the genitals themselves came to play in the sexual life of children. What distinguished the infantile stage of genital organization from the adult variety was the fact that "for both sexes, only one genital, namely the male one," mattered.[15] The phallus had now gained primacy.

Abraham's study represented a further interpolation, a fleshing out of the anal and the oral. At the same time, as its subtitle suggested, it represented a contribution to a long-standing (and never solved) psychoanalytic problem: the choice of neurosis. From the beginning of his career, Freud had tried to explain why one rather than another neurotic outcome had resulted, why, for example, a patient developed hysteria rather than an obsessional neurosis. He had initially linked the age at which a traumatic sexual seduction had occurred to a specific neurosis. Although he came to replace childhood sexual trauma with infantile sexuality, he did not abandon his efforts to provide an etiological account. In piecemeal fashion, he undertook the task of connecting sexual development to mental disorders. It was this unfinished business that Abraham was taking up.

For Abraham's purposes, Freud's two pregenital stages were inadequately elaborated. Abraham readily concurred with his mentor that both obsessional neurosis and melancholia had similar features and that they shared "a common relation to the anal . . . organization of the libido"—that is, he agreed that in both instances, the anal acted as a fixation point, "formed in the course of development," to which the libido retreated at the onset of the neurotic illness. These two illnesses had dissimilar features as well; and if, Abraham argued, they nonetheless took "their inception" from the same level of libidinal organization, it followed that the stage in question contained heterogeneous elements that had not yet been sorted out. The work of sorting led Abraham to postulate two anal stages, an earlier one of expelling the object (of the libidinal aim) and destroying it, and a later one of retaining and controlling the object. Further investigation into melancholia produced an additional differentiation, this time of the oral stage. The earlier, or sucking, oral stage, Abraham considered pre-ambivalent; in the later, or cannibalistic, oral stage, ambivalence toward the object entered the scene. With these refinements at his disposal, Abraham was confident of locating "a more definite connection between certain kinds of illness and certain levels of the libido" than had previously been feasible.[16] But, as he was quick to acknowledge, gaps remained. The theory of libidinal development remained very much a work in progress.

Meanwhile, that is, until psychoanalysts should "have collected a greater number of thorough analyses to confirm and amplify the theoretic assumptions" he had made, Abraham thought it might "not be superfluous to consider the *prima facie* arguments" in their favor. Here he pointed to "a striking parallel between the organic and the psychosexual development of the individual." In the embryos of certain animals, for example, the "orginal mouth-opening" (the blastopore) closed up at the "anterior end" and became "enlarged at the posterior end." This "direct derivation of the anus from the blastopore," he concluded, stood as the "biological prototype" of the progress from the oral to the anal that occurred in the second year of extrauterine existence.[17] Such embryological analogies he used as a crutch—and nothing more.

"It was only the discovery of the phallic level or organization," Deutsch wrote, "that enabled us completely to explain the origin and significance of the 'masculinity complex.'"[18] The phallic level may have been Freud's concept; its significance as "progress," it owed to Deutsch.

Her little girl, even more than Freud's, started out as a little man. Deutsch pictured her as the proud possessor of an "organ of absolutely sterling value"—the clitoris—to which large quantities of pleasure were attached.[19] Deutsch also equipped her with a primary paternal identification equivalent to the one Freud, in other texts, ascribed to the boy.[20] The two went together. For the little girl, the clitoris had the significance of a penis and served as the vehicle for this identification. It also served as a vehicle for activity. Thanks to the clitoris, the little girl was richly endowed with masculine attributes.

What happened to little girls when they discovered the anatomical distinction between the sexes? In Freud's account, on catching sight of the boys' genitals, girls immediately noticed "the difference, . . . and its significance too."[21] They made their judgment and decision "in a flash." They had "seen it" and knew that they were "without it" and wanted "to have it."[22] They fell "victim to 'envy for the penis.'"[23] Deutsch elaborated. Some girls regarded "the castration . . . as a punishment," and in them it produced "inferiority feelings." Some "felt it to be an injustice suffered," and in them it produced "intensive tendencies to exact revenge." And then there were those who, like Freud's little boys, responded with denial: they energetically maintained that everyone had a penis. This kind of girl clung to "the assumption of real possession" of it, did not "accept the sexual difference," and continued to see herself as like father. As a consequence the clitoris retained "its fully satisfying sexual role," and the vagina remained permanently without sensation.[24] Here was the masculinity complex in its purest form.

But it was the impure variety that Deutsch never failed to encounter in clinical practice. "Psychoanalytic experience," she wrote, forced her and her colleagues — her rhetorical "us" — "more and more to the conclusion that the 'masculinity complex' in women" was "a permanent component of their psychical structure." Permanent — and non-pathological; for "only under definite conditions," which Deutsch left unclear, did its presence lead to "neurotic phenomena." Its permanence could be explained by invoking a "residue of a past state of development," that is, the phallic phase. Seen in this light, the masculinity complex served as a memorial to "a biogenetically conditioned masculine phase," which, Deutsch added, "must be regarded as . . . progressive."[25]

In a girl "the final phase of infantile organization," Deutsch explained, "represented progress towards the 'female attitude,'" but was "nevertheless a regression from the point of view of libido development."[26] Upon abandoning the clitoris, the little girl — or her libido — took up components of the anal phase; she took up again an interest in fecal matter. In the meantime, feces had acquired symbolic meaning: they had come to stand for baby. Here Deutsch was being faithful to Freud. She parted company from her mentor, however, in embedding this wish for an "anal child" in a tale of "retrogression."[27]

She continued her story: clitoral sexuality and father were linked — hence "giving up the clitoris" entailed giving up the thought of possessing what father possessed (never completely accomplished);[28] anal child and mother were linked — hence wishing for a fecal baby entailed identifying with mother. Note that the maternal identification — in contrast to the paternal — did not rest on anatomy: the little girl did not move from clitoris to vagina; the vagina itself remained undiscovered. The identification derived from an understanding of coitus; that is, the understanding that to have a child — anal or otherwise — the little girl had to assume the mother's position in intercourse. And that position in turn entailed passivity and masochism.

What happened when the wish for a fecal baby was disappointed, when the little girl was obliged to give up hope a second time? At this point Deutsch interpolated reflections on superego formation. It took place, she argued, in two phases. The first, following the "renunciation of the clitoris," elevated the identification with father to the "higher plane" of the superego. The second, following the abandonment of the wish for a fecal baby, elevated the identification with mother to that same higher plane. Father and mother identifications both found their way into the superego, and with complementary functions: "father" was responsible for the ban on incest; "mother" was responsible for "idealized maternity and a definite sexual morality and sexual inhibition characteristic of the moral woman."[29] The little girl was in the course of adopting a "female attitude," and along the way she had accepted a plethora of sexual inhibitions.

Deutsch had concentrated her attention on the aim — active or passive, sadistic or masochistic — of the libido; she had said little about its objects. Whereas in Freud's account of superego formation, the superego was the precipitate of abandoned object-choices and could be read as a history of those choices, in her account the superego vouchsafed no such history.[30] Sexual object-choice would have to be fitted into a narrative framework that had already been set.

In a footnote subsequently added to her paper "Homosexuality in Women" (1932), Deutsch explained what had prompted her to publish her material. She had been analyzing female homosexuals — "more or less thoroughly" — for over a decade;[31] she had collected data on eleven such cases and had planned to report her findings to the International Psycho-Analytical Congress in 1931, but the world economic crisis led to its postponement. That same year, Freud had produced his essay "Female Sexuality," in which he specifically addressed the question of how, when, and why the little girl detached herself from her mother, that is, the question of object-choice. Deutsch had thus missed two opportunities to have her work recognized as crucial to understanding that question.[32] It was high time to publish.

In his essay Freud had struck a diffident pose. Everything about the girl's earliest attachment to her mother, he wrote, had been difficult for him to grasp — "so grey with age and shadowy and almost impossible to revivify — that it was as if it had succumbed to an especially inexorable repression." Perhaps, he added, women in analysis with him clung to their "attachment to . . . father" — an attachment that, after their turning from mother, had been a refuge for them — and hence his impression of inexorable repression. By the same token, women analysts, thanks to the maternal transference they elicited from their female patients, were well placed to correct his impression. Deutsch took care to accept Freud's implicit invitation: she took care to portray herself, in her clinical role, as a "suitable mother-substitute"[33] — so much so that at one point in the text she failed to distinguish between the real mother and the analyst as maternal figure.[34] (Note that there are two personae, not one, in this text. There are the persona of the narrator and the persona of the practicing psychoanalyst.) The practitioner, in contrast to the narrator, had nothing "bisexual" about her.

That practitioner was most clearly in evidence in Deutsch's first case. The patient had come to her under dramatic circumstances. "For years she had suffered from fits of depression." They "had become more and more frequent" and more and more severe. "On quite a number of occasions the patient had made unsuccessful attempts to commit suicide; the last of these had brought her to death's door"—and to Deutsch's as well, thanks to a referral from the attending physician. During treatment the patient recalled a scene just after this last attempt (by poisoning): "She woke up out of deep unconsciousness, still strapped to a stretcher, and saw the physician bending over her with a kindly smile. She was conscious that he had saved her life (as was actually the case), and she thought: 'Yes, this time: but all the same you cannot really help me.'"[35]

When the analysis began, the patient was married. She had never been hostile to men; "she had many men friends and did not object to being admired and courted" by them. Still "she had never really fallen in love with a man"—not even her husband.[36] She had been disappointed in his lack of sexual passion and masculine activity; she had been most disappointed when she had been in an anxious state about her household staff, and he failed to protect and support her with sufficient vigor. Marriage notwithstanding, Deutsch regarded her patient as homosexual.

When the patient started treatment, Deutsch wrote, she appeared to be a case of inversion—"manifest, but not actively practiced." She was "perfectly aware that her capacity for love and her sexual fantasies were confined to her own sex" and she "experienced quite unmistakable sexual excitations when embracing and kissing certain women with whom she was in love." That love, however, went no further. "She could not explain why her homosexuality did not take a more active and urgent form; she only knew that her inhibitions were too strong, and rationalized them on grounds of social timidity, her duty to her family, and her dread of 'bondage.'" About a year after leaving treatment, the patient saw her analyst again. With evident pleasure she reported an "uninhibited sexual relation with another woman."[37]

During the analysis itself, during the fits of depression that the patient experienced in it, she reported dreams containing "nearly all the known symbolism relating to the mother's body: there were dreams of dark holes and openings into which the patient crept, dreams of cosy dark places which seemed to her known and familiar and where she lingered with a sense of rest and deliverance. . . . Again and again, one particular dream picture appeared: the patient saw herself wrapped up like a baby in swaddling clothes."

The dream led to a memory of a dangerous operation her mother had undergone and to her "having seen her mother wrapped up . . . and carried on a stretcher to the operating theater." The memory, in turn, led to a revival of "murderous hatred for her mother," which "now became the focal point of the analysis."[38]

Another dream — about eight months further along in the treatment — led to another memory. In the dream, the patient "saw herself sitting behind the bars in a police station, having been accused of some sort of sexual misconduct. Apparently she had been brought in from the street under suspicion of being a prostitute. The police inspector, a kindly man, stood on the other side of the bars without helping her." The childhood memory went back to roughly the patient's fifth year, to the time when her masturbatory practices had drawn her mother's attention and disapproval:

What happened, according to the patient, was that her mother, not knowing what else to do, resorted to the following plan: she tied the child's hands and feet, strapped her to the cot, stood beside it and said: "Now go on with your games!" This produced a twofold reaction in the little girl. On the one hand it evoked a feeling of furious anger with her mother. . . . On the other hand it gave rise to a violent sexual excitement, which, in spite of her mother's presence or perhaps in defiance of her, she tried to gratify by rubbing her buttocks against the mattress.

To the child's mind the most terrible thing about this scene was that her father, whom her mother summoned, remained a passive witness of it and did not try to help his little daughter whom he loved tenderly.

The scene, Deutsch continued, met with repression (now being undone), and so too did the child's sexuality and her "hatred for her mother, which in real life she never again betrayed in the same degree."[39]

Deutsch took pains to spell out for her readers how she had construed the scene's significance:

I do not regard . . . [it] as traumatic in the sense that it produced the subsequent psychic attitude of the patient. . . . The reproach against her mother that she had forbidden masturbation would certainly have arisen in her mind even *without* this scene. The reaction of hatred toward her mother was perceptible also in other situations of childhood and was in accordance with the patient's sadistic constitution. The same was true of her reproach against her father for failing to protect her from her mother. But the scene brought all these trends to the boiling point, so to speak, and thus became the prototype of later occurrences.[40]

After working through her hostility to her mother — that is, after overcoming her hostility to her analyst in the "transference situation" — the patient allowed her father, for the first time, to appear "on the stage of the analytic play. With him came all the impulses belonging to the Oedipus complex, beginning with the vehement reproach, which the patient had never been able to get over, that he had not been active enough in his love for his daughter." At this point the analysis ended — on Deutsch's urging. In hopes that the revival of the father relation — "above all, . . . the renewed animation and correction of *this* relation" — would produce a "more favorable . . . outlook for the patient's libidinal future," Deutsch sent her patient to "an analyst of the fatherly type. Unfortunately, the transference never went beyond respect and sympathy, and after a short time the patient broke off the analysis."[41] The task of "animation and correction" proved beyond the capacities of male and female analyst alike. The latter, not unhappily, settled for homosexuality: in her view it was far better to love a homosexual object than never to love at all.

Deutsch the narrator presented Deutsch the practicing psychoanalyst as modest in her therapeutic goals; she also presented her as judicious in her research aims. She had collected analytic material about her patient — the first of her eleven cases; she had posed to herself the question of how to account for her patient's object-choice; and then, for more than a decade, she lived with a problem "she could not solve." Tact, tolerance, patience: these were her trademarks as therapist and researcher. When Deutsch the narrator, her credibility enhanced by her self-representation as practitioner, turned to drawing "theoretical conclusions . . . important for the understanding of feminine sexuality in general and of feminine homosexuality in particular," she spoke with confidence and authority.[42]

She naturally paid heed to what Freud had written. According to her mentor, one line of development, starting from the castration complex, led the little girl "to cling with defiant self-assertiveness . . . to the hope of getting a penis . . . [and] to her threatened masculinity" — with "a manifest homosexual choice of object" as a possible result.[43] Deutsch's patient displayed ample penis envy. Moreover, the "analysis revealed phases, both in her childhood (before the time of the fateful experiences described) and also at puberty, in which unmistakable signs could be detected of a very marked development of activity, with a masculine bias. Especially at puberty she manifested quite plainly interests which were rather unusual in a girl of her period and social sphere." But, her analyst wrote, penis envy was not "the central part" of her personality. Similarly, Deutsch added, "neither her character nor her attitude toward men indicated that she belonged to the type of woman who has a 'masculinity complex.'"[44] Deutsch resisted the temptation to follow Freud in regarding her patient's homosexuality as an expression of her masculinity. Instead, she concluded that her patient did not fit his pattern.

Deutsch took a different tack. Homosexuality, she conjectured, might be a matter not of development gone awry but rather of development arrested. She asked herself—and her reader—whether it would be appropriate "to speak of a primal fixation," to speculate that in her homosexual patients "the libido had always known but *one* object, the mother." Their sexual practices were suggestive. With the first patient "her homosexual relation took the form of a perfectly conscious mother-and-child situation, in which sometimes the one and sometimes the other played the part of mother." In subsequent cases, "all the women in question stood in a mother-and-child relation to their homosexual love object and more or less consciously recognized this fact. In all cases the forms of sexual gratification were the same: sleeping in close mutual embrace, sucking one another's nipples, mutual genital and, above all, anal masturbation, and cunnilingus, mainly in the form of sucking, practiced intensively by both parties." Deutsch was prepared to grant that in certain instances a primal fixation might be at work, "but these were quite special cases, in which the whole neurosis had the character of a general psychic infantilism."[45] Not one of her eleven, she maintained, fit this pattern.

The pattern that did fit, Deutsch claimed, was one of "retrogression to the mother-child attitude." (Once again, as in accounting for femininity in the first place, she invoked retrogression.) From what had her patients regressed? From the Oedipus complex, Deutsch answered: it was discovered "in its entirety" in all her cases. And so too was frustration, disappointment, and rejection by the father, which her patients experienced as the loss of the love object. Deutsch imagined them saying to themselves, "'If my father does not want me and such a blow is dealt to my self-love, who will love me now if not my mother?'" In these circumstances, the libido turned back to experiences enjoyed earlier. As Deutsch's homosexual patients retreated, they took with them "from the phallic phase the wish for activity"—more specifically the wish to masturbate. A "sanctioning of activity and permission to masturbate" constituted "a motive common to all forms of [female] homosexuality."[46]

The original prohibition had come at the hands of the mother. The childhood scene recollected by Deutsch's first patient represented that prohibition in graphic—indeed lurid—form. It functioned not only as prologue to later occurrences in the patient's sexual life but also as prologue to Deutsch's understanding of her own therapeutic task as well. (In contrast to Deutsch, who stressed the reaction to this prohibition "as the girl's strongest motive for turning away" from her mother, Freud emphasized "the reproach that her mother did not give her a proper penis.")[47] A "sanctioning of activity and permission to masturbate": such could be granted by a "suitable mother-substitute," be she female lover or female analyst. So it had been with Deutsch's patient.

Psychoanalysis, Freud wrote, had set itself the task of inquiring how a woman came into being. Retrogression was the tale told by Deutsch in reply. It was a tale, at least initially, of successive deprivations, with the unattached woman figuring as the most deprived of all. Penis and fecal baby: these losses were common to the female lot. Heterosexual women might some day acquire a real child; homosexual women might some day be the child; chaste women had nothing — unless, of course, their chastity derived from a masculinity complex in its purest form, in which case they might fantasize that they possessed a penis.

In the Service of Masculinity

In 1930 Deutsch published a second book; two years later, it appeared in English under the title *Psycho-Analysis of the Neuroses*. It consisted of eleven lectures, delivered by her in her capacity as director of the Training Institute, addressed specifically to future analysts, and replete with case illustrations.

The case that drew most inventively on Deutsch's "insight into the mental processes of the woman in her procreative function" was that of a fifteen-year-old girl whose "neurosis had broken out in puberty in the form of severe fits and twilight states." Deutsch commented that nowadays one did not often meet such patients in analytic practice, and in fact she did not see the girl in her own consulting room; the patient lived in a sanitarium during the treatment. Both Deutsch and the patient relied on sanitarium personnel for information about what happened during the girl's seizures; the patient remembered nothing. The treatment itself did not last long: "for external reasons" the analysis was "broken off after a few months, before we," that is, Deutsch and the patient working together, "were able to penetrate to the bottom of . . . infantile experiences. . . . The making conscious of puberty conflicts," however, "succeeded in restoring the girl to health, at any rate for the time being."[48] It also succeeded in elucidating the thoughts and emotions common to hysterical fits and twilight states alike.

In reconstructing the meaning of her patient's hysterical attacks, Deutsch kept Freud's precepts in mind. For example:

Hysterical symptoms are — like other psychical structures — an expression of the fulfillment of a wish. . . .

Hysterical symptoms are the realization of an unconscious phantasy which serves the fulfillment of a wish. . . .

Hysterical symptoms may take over the representation of various unconscious impulses which are not sexual, but they can never be without a sexual significance.[49]

Unconscious impulses of a destructive variety had been easy to detect, but their "sexual significance" less so. The patient's violent rage had not been completely hidden from her, not even before the analysis; it had been suppressed, "until finally the inability to control it provoked the motor discharge of the seizure." Against whom had it been aimed? The patient quite consciously loved her mother and hated her father, and it was he, she readily admitted, who was the target of her rage. Yet she did not appreciate that her current attitude was simply "a return to a state of feeling which had formerly been present—namely, a primary, excessive love for the mother and a furious protest against the interfering father." She did not appreciate that this return constituted a "reaction to the normal Oedipus relationship" and "represented a complete inversion of the real emotional" situation. And it was here that Deutsch located the unconscious impulses, sexual and destructive alike, which combined in the hysterical fit.[50]

All the patient's accusations against her father, Deutsch reported, and all her "rationalizations of her rage took as their ground his neglect of the family and his brutality to her mother." "Neglect," Deutsch pointed out to patient and reader alike, was "identical with 'refusal of love,' and . . . the word 'brutality' was an expression of the patient's view of parental intercourse . . ." Deutsch had difficulty getting her patient to confirm this latter interpretation. She persevered: "[T]he concept of the sexual act as an act of violation was peculiarly noticeable" (how, she left unspecified) in her patient's "defense mechanisms." It was noticeable in her history as well: "[D]uring the war the little girl had really been witness to violations." Here was "an actual kernel for the violation fantasy."[51] And here was a fantasy that Deutsch regarded as typical of puberty.

She had now established that the "convulsions procured" the patient "the motor discharge of an attack of rage . . . ; and they represented coitus as well." Still more, it "became clear in the course of the analysis" that they also dramatized "the act of birth." Not the mother, but the patient herself "should be violated by the father and give birth to a child": so Deutsch interpreted.[52] Here was wish whose fulfillment was expressed in the patient's hysterical fit.

The patient's wish—as interpreted by Deutsch—and Deutsch's theoretical formulation mirrored each other. The patient condensed coitus and childbirth into one; Deutsch expanded the sex act to include childbirth: in her view, orgasm and parturition belonged to the same sequence, divided by an interval of nine months. That expansion allowed Deutsch to bring in retrogression and give it free rein.

> When the erotogenic susceptibility to stimulation
> has been successfully transferred by the woman
> from the clitoris to the vaginal orifice, it implies that
> she has adopted a new leading zone for the purposes
> of her later sexual activity.[53]

> The final task of the completely achieved female attitude is not the satisfaction in the sex act of the infantile wish for a penis, but the successful discovery
> of the vagina as an organ of pleasure.[54]

The first quotation comes from Freud's *Three Essays*; the second, a faithful reproduction, from Deutsch's *Psychoanalysis of the Sexual Functions of Women*. According to Freud "a wave of repression at puberty" overtook "clitoridal sexuality" and along with it a female's "childish masculinity."[55] Deutsch phrased the process in terms of a woman's giving up the "claim of the clitoris to be a penis surrogate";[56] but in her hands this renunciation did not entail the extinction of the female's masculinity. In elaborating her version of the sex act, she managed to revivify that masculinity. In so doing she turned the narrator's "bisexual" (that is, masculine as well as feminine) stance to more than rhetorical account; in effect the medium became the message.

Deutsch started with the standard version, that is, with sexual intercourse, and even with this unpromising point of departure, she managed to preserve a modicum of masculinity for the woman. She started with the vagina, more precisely, with the vexed question of how the exchange of clitoris for vagina took place. The beginning of an answer, she claimed, lay in a direct transfer of libido from the one to the other. This "libidinal component" remained "'male-oriented' even in its vaginal application." The clitoris had "exercised its 'masculinity' in identification with the paternal penis," an identification based on the equation clitoris = penis; the vagina exercised its masculinity "under the aegis of identification with the partner's penis," an identification derived from the introduction into the body from the outside of a real penis which "in wish fulfillment" became an "organ of the woman's own body."[57] Had Deutsch been satisfied by a sex act so conceived, a woman's masculinity would have been a matter of identification with a male figure (and his organ).

Deutsch began again with the standard version and now found in it a serviceable point of departure for her story of retrogression. She began again with the exchange of clitoris for vagina, this time with indirect transfer of libido to the vagina from the body as a whole. The equation penis = nipple did the trick. Just as the mother's nipple concentrated the infant's body libido in its mouth, so too the partner's penis concentrated the woman's body libido in her vagina. The penis performing like a nipple activated another equation, one "prefigured in the whole anatomical structure," that of vagina = mouth. The vagina, in turn, performing like a mouth, constituted the "really passive feminine attitude." The woman had reached "the highest level of libidinal organization (the vaginal phase)." And she had done so by an "intensive mobilization of regressive trends," by the repetition of the lowest, that is, Abraham's pre-ambivalent oral stage.[58] Had Deutsch been satisfied by a sex act conventionally construed, retrogression would have facilitated symbolic trading in body parts, but that trading would not have revivified a woman's masculinity. Retrogression, symbolic bodily equations, and a reconceptualization and expansion of the sex act: all three were necessary to make a woman's masculinity something other than a matter of identification.

The sex act begun in coitus, according to Deutsch, reached its conclusion — for a woman — only with parturition. (How to regard the sex act when the woman did not conceive, Deutsch failed to specify.) What then of the interval in between, which figured as part of her expanded version? Here she once again introduced retrogression, alerting her readers to anticipate reactivated traces of "pre-female" or "bisexual" phases, that is, of developmental phases "common to male and female" alike. Coitus reactivated the pre-ambivalent oral phase. Pregnancy reactivated not only oral phases, pre-ambivalent and ambivalent, but anal ph...es as well. Orality manifested itself in "various 'cravings,'" in "characteristic hunger alternating with complete loss of appetite"; the ambivalence associated with the later oral phase turned up, above all, in morning sickness. Anality manifested itself in the "pregnant woman's very typical temporary character changes . . . e.g., stubbornness, capriciousness, particular cleanliness, thrift bordering on meanness, and a kind of collecting mania"; ambivalence turned up in the symptoms of early labor, and if intense enough, that ambivalence could lead to miscarriage. The equation vagina = mouth — and the child, then, as something ingested — paved the way for the revival of the classic Freudian equation feces = baby; feces, after all, were "orally introduced in food."[59] Freud's equation, as Deutsch and her audience fully appreciated, included a middle term: feces = penis = baby. Retrogression was in the course of revivifying a woman's masculinity.

357

"In the tremendous disturbance of the libidinal economy" that took place in pregnancy, Deutsch wrote, "the path of regression once entered upon" led "to all abandoned libidinal trends being sought out"—the phallic included. With the beginning of the fifth month of pregnancy, with the child's first stirrings in the womb, it lost its anal meaning, and its phallic significance came to the fore. In the happiest circumstances the child as penis figured as a component of the woman's ego. And as long as those circumstances obtained, the woman experienced "increased self-feeling, self-satisfaction"; she reached her "physical and psychical prime." The equation child = penis thus offered the woman "a direct substitute" for the male organ earlier missed.[60]

Such circumstances could not last:

The stimulus proceeding from the foetus becomes intolerable and presses for discharge. In this final struggle all the hostile impulses that have been mobilized in the course of the pregnancy reach their greatest intensity. In the physical respect this struggle manifests itself in the contracting activity of the musculature and its tendencies to retain and to expel. The latter finally gain the upper hand. The introjected object is projected into the outside world, and by the route by which it was introjected in coitus.

Coitus had been merely the start, and it was pleasurable, Deutsch suggested, "chiefly because of the psychological fact" that it represented "an attempt at and a beginning of the act of parturition." The "orgastic activity of the vagina" Deutsch regarded as tantamount to a "missed labour." The orgastic activity of the vagina she also considered "analogous to that of the penis"— in a "much moderated form."[61] Childbirth knew no moderation. It occasioned, she claimed, the most intense sexual pleasure and a novel equation: vagina = penis.

The sex act had reached its climax and conclusion, but Deutsch's tale of symbolic trading in body parts had a sequel. It followed immediately upon the climactic event and entailed a repetition of sexual intercourse—"with a reversal of roles. . . . As the penis took control of the vagina in coitus," so did "the erect mammary gland now take control of the infant's mouth. The part of the seminal fluid" was "played by the flow of milk." Here Deutsch offered a clinical vignette:

A young mother with a very ambivalent relationship to her child had to give up breast-feeding even though she wished to continue and possessed an amply functioning mammary apparatus. What happened was that in the interval between the child's feeding times the milk came gushing out, with the result that the breast was empty when the child was put to it. The practices to which she resorted to circumvent this unhappy state of affairs recalled the behaviour of a man suffering from premature ejaculation who desperately tries to accelerate the sex act but is always overtaken with the same lack of success — she was invariably too late.[62]

Once more nipple equaled penis.

Deutsch's tale of retrogression had a sequel as well. Menopause, she wrote, represented "a retrogressive phase in the history of the libido." Under the pressure of failure — and the vagina inevitably failed, that is, it experienced "greater difficulty in object-finding" — it gave up the struggle, and a regressive attachment to "the clitoris as a centre of excitation" occurred — in short, a regression to the phallic phase. Biology, Deutsch argued, now revived a "bisexual constitution," and women reentered a phase in which male and female did not exist.[63] Biology now gave its seal of approval to what had all along been a psychological possibility.

Deutsch's equations, as she admitted, might be "complicated and . . . seem far-fetched,"[64] but they provided a woman with penis surrogates during her reproductive years when her clitoris had renounced that particular function. No surrogates, no masculinity: a bodily representation figured as an essential requirement. And although both the bodily representation and a woman's masculinity ranked as psychological, they were construed as leaning on biology. "Among lower animals," Deutsch wrote, one found "processes in which the close connection between the mouth and genital apparatus" was plain; "similarly, the connection between . . . execretory processes . . . and the genital function" was extremely frequent. Like Abraham, she drew an analogy between "actual phylogenetic forms of development . . . and pre-genital phases of the libido."[65] Like him, she used biology as a crutch — in her case to justify symbolic trading in body parts.

Female analysts, Freud had argued, might take comfort in the notion that they were more masculine than feminine. In his view, their masculinity made them exceptional; in Deutsch's view, that masculinity was the rule among women. Her tale of retrogression, having initially transformed the Freudian "child with a bisexual disposition" into a woman, subsequently restored the woman's masculinity. In this fashion, Deutsch suggested that with regard to gender, there might be no bedrock.

PETER LOEWENBERG

18. A Stoic Death

Sigmund Freud, Max Schur,
and Assisted Dying
in Contemporary America

To every thing there is a season,
and a time to every purpose under the heaven:
A time to be born, and a time to die. . . .
　　　　　　　　　　　—Ecclesiastes 3:1–2

Es gibt ein Recht, wonach wir einem Menschen das
Leben nehmen, aber keines, wonach wir ihm das
Sterben nehmen: dies ist nur Grausamkeit.

There is a justice by which we take a man's life, but
none by which we may take his death: that is mere
cruelty.　　　　　　　　—Friedrich Nietzsche

The reformist impulse of the philosophes survived
in Freud and continues to do so in the psychoanalytic profession.　　　　　　　—Peter Gay (1997)

Auden's line memorializing Freud: "To us he is no more a person now but a
whole climate of opinion"[1] is certainly truer today than six decades ago when
it was written. Psychoanalysis has infused every aspect of our modern culture, has impregnated and fertilized the thought, discourse, literature, theater, and media of the literate world. Freud had a prescription for cultural
change from the earliest years of psychoanalysis, a model that still works and
commends itself to us. As early as chapter 7 of *The Interpretation of Dreams*,
Freud reckoned with "the possibility that the ego may have a greater share

than was supposed in the construction of dreams."[2] In 1905, he wrote of the pubertal "detachment from parental authority, a process that alone makes possible the opposition, which is so important for the progress of civilization, between the new generation and the old."[3] In his structural theory, the ego is the structure of the mind that deals with time and culture and synthesizes sociocultural forces in the person and his or her adaptation to reality. Psychoanalytic ego psychology is the theoretical framework of choice for conceptualizing cultural change because it is time-specific and therefore social and historical.

Freud said in 1933: "What distinguishes the ego from the id quite especially is a tendency to synthesis in its contents, to a combination and unification in its mental processes which are totally lacking in the id. . . . To adopt a popular mode of speaking, we might say that the ego stands for reason and good sense while the id stands for the untamed passions."[4] The functions of the ego include dealing with reality, adapting and coping with the vicissitudes of life, nature, the sadism and mendacity of other humans, and the pressures of our animal drives and our socialized conscience. Not only does the superego internalize outside objects, but the ego is also formed and conditioned by its relationship with culture. Freud was explicit about this: "We have repeatedly had to insist on the fact that the ego owes its origin as well as the most important of its acquired characteristics to its relation to the real external world."[5]

Psychoanalysis offers tools of perception for exploring contemporary cultural change because, as Freud said, it is cultural in its foundation: "Where id was, shall become ego. It is the work of culture like the draining of the Zuider Zee" ("Wo Es war, soll Ich werden. Es ist Kulturarbeit etwa wie die Trockenlegung der Zuydersee").[6]

Currently, there is a change in a Freudian direction taking place in American culture; our culture is catching up with Freud on an issue on which he was ahead of his time. This is our social and legal culture's attitude toward death. American society, as expressed in our courts and popular referenda, has in the past decade been engaged in a fierce clash on fundamental beliefs about life, death, current informal practices, personal autonomy, and the law. Sixty-five *amicus curiae* briefs filed on this issue demonstrate that it generates passions unmatched since the abortion wars of twenty years ago.[7] With due circumspection, indicative of high ambivalence, there is a discernible movement in our culture toward upholding the individual's right to determine the time and manner of his or her death, and to meet the desire to die with dignity.

Most people in our society no longer die of acute infectious diseases as our grandparents did. Modern Americans die in new ways. The majority of us will die of extended decline degenerative diseases — cancer, atherosclerosis, heart disease, chronic pulmonary disease, liver, kidney, or other organ disease, or degenerative neurological disorders.[8] The issues of dying are currently related to the acceleration of medical technology, which, as the Supreme Court stated in the *Cruzan* case (1990), is today "capable of sustaining life well past the point where natural forces would have brought certain death in earlier times."[9] Due to expensive technological systems of life support and prolongation, which were not available to health-care professionals as recently as twenty-five years ago, patients, families, and treating physicians are faced with dilemmas that Hippocrates never knew. The demographic and fiscal dimensions of the problem are enormous. With the shifting age structure of our population, there is a substantially increased demand for medical care by the elderly population. U.S. health expenditure as a percentage of gross domestic product rose from 5.3 percent in 1960 to 13.2 percent by 1991.[10] U.S. government medical care expenditure on the age group over 60 totaled 50 percent in 1980. The International Monetary Fund estimates that by the year 2000, it will be 54.4 percent; by 2010, 55.6 percent; and by 2025, 64.6 percent.[11] Using 1980 as the base year, the projected increases in real government expenditures on medical care will be 130 percent by the year 2000, and 180 percent by 2025.[12] In each case the U.S. figures are comparatively the world's highest.

Most medical decisions in America are also financial decisions. The issues of assisted suicide, selective management of severely disabled newborns, and the right to die for chronically afflicted adults are complicated by the ascendancy of corporate health management organizations whose imperative is cost containment. Medical decisions are made on a cost-benefit rather than a patient-benefit basis. Financial constraint in the terminal phase of life is one of the crucial differences between the United States and every other developed nation. Western Europe, in particular, has systems of national health care that provide at-home physician care, home nursing, long-term nursing homes, dietitian counseling, physical therapy and rehabilitation, and psychological counseling, which make the costs to the patient largely irrelevant. American patients facing death, as well as their families, physicians, and caretakers, must always consider the financial costs of the timing and manner of death. The United States is also by far the most litigious society in the world. In managing the dying of patients, physicians practice defensive medicine to avoid the risks of malpractice litigation and criminal prosecution.

The court majority in *Cruzan* assumed that the U.S. Constitution "would grant a competent person a constitutionally protected right to refuse lifesaving hydration and nutrition."[13] Withholding and withdrawing treatment is no longer legally controversial and is now widely practiced. Yet allowing a person to die of thirst, to starve to death, or suffocate for lack of oxygen may be a cruel and sadistic policy. Dr. Joel Potash of Syracuse, New York, tells of a bedridden patient with kidney cancer that had metastasized to the bones who asked for assistance in dying. Dr. Potash encouraged him to starve himself, because that is now the only legal recourse. The patient replied: "Eating is one of my few pleasures. I can't."[14] Karen Ann Quinlan remained alive in a coma for nine years, fed by nasogastric tube, *after* the New Jersey Supreme Court ruled that the respirator could be turned off.[15] Informal and illegal aid in dying may be ineffective, failing in its purpose because the patient and his or her helpers do not have the requisite expertise in techniques, physiology, pharmacology, and dosages. Clandestine legal disobedience also encourages cynical disregard of the law, always poor public policy.

Timothy E. Quill, professor of internal medicine at the University of Rochester, asks: "Do people at the end of their lives have to undergo more suffering than they feel they can endure? Who is to say they do, particularly since we have used medical technology to keep them alive longer and longer?"[16] Justice Stephen Reinhardt of the Ninth Circuit Court of Appeals, writing for the court majority in 1996, was eloquent: "A competent terminally ill adult, having lived nearly the full measure of his life, has a strong liberty interest in choosing a dignified and humane death rather than being reduced at the end of his existence to a childlike state of helplessness, diapered, sedated, incontinent. How a person dies not only determines the nature of the final period of his existence, but in many cases, the enduring memories held by those who love him."[17]

What are the psychodynamic considerations that bear upon the problem of assisted death? We are aware of feelings of helplessness in people who are ill, let alone in those with a terminal diagnosis. The insight that every human exchange simultaneously engages past and present internalized objects is a radical discovery unique to psychoanalysis. We know the authority of transference both to physicians or caretakers and to institutions such as hospitals.[18] The doctor-patient relationship is not a contractual relationship between equals when the patient is in pain or is in the process of dying. We should not underestimate the coercive power of modern medicine as a "total" institution that controls information, demands "compliance," and has the inherent and inevitable conscious and unconscious role of structuring advice, counsel, and the presentation of alternatives to a person in need.[19] Modern hermeneutics and psychoanalytic theories of intersubjectivity are relevant here.[20] There is no "neutral" counsel or intervention. The very act of raising a possible course of action alters the clinical situation. We know the role of anxiety at the prospect of physical pain and at the threat of psychological and physical abandonment.

We may well adapt Freud's observation "The ego is first and foremost a bodily ego"[21] to "All anxiety is first and foremost bodily anxiety." In the regressed and dependent state of chronic pain and illness, is a truly voluntary choice possible? The difference between "voluntary" and "involuntary" is not always clear. "Informed consent" is not always sufficient protection, because it does not always neutralize the sources of compulsion. At what point do the question, "Is it your wish to die?" and the second consultation become pro forma? As analysts, we listen for the ambiguity of manifest communications. A person asking for death may actually be looking for hope, for reassurance that life still holds something worthwhile, and that they are still needed and wanted. We need to bear in mind what we know of human ambivalence and of changes in mood over time. A request for aid in suicide is always to some extent ambivalent. Today, many physicians, including many psychiatrists, know neither how to listen to patients nor how to listen to their own countertransference.[22] Unexamined countertransference is evident, for example, in Dr. Paul Nitschke, a specialist who administered lethal barbiturates in the Territory of Northern Australia, where voluntary euthanasia was legal. He said in an interview: "You can't help but feel like an executioner. You can't get around that. You walk in that room, and you know that there will be one less person when you walk out."[23] We speak the language of voluntarism, maximizing choices and options, "enablement," and patient empowerment. As Herbert Hendin asks in his skeptical study of euthanasia in the Netherlands, "but who is being empowered?"[24] "The outcome in . . . cases is often determined by whether family or physicians choose to hear the wish to continue living or only to support the wish to die."[25]

The American medical profession received tremendous power in acquiring a monopoly in the dispensing of narcotics in the Pure Food and Drug Act (FDA) of 1906, the beginning of federal drug regulation, and the Harrison Act of 1914. Yet American medicine is generally withholding and retrograde in palliative pain management. As the *Wall Street Journal* recently editorialized: "The medical profession has to bear some of the responsibility for letting pain management slip so low in their priorities."[26]

While immediate family may be too conflicted, ambivalent, or guilty to aid a dying patient, doctors may also not be the optimal persons to assist in dying. The trusted physician who made house calls and was a presence from birth to death for generations of family life is a thing of the past. Today, extended family, friends, relatives, and spiritual and psychological counselors have often known the patient longer and more intimately than the attending physician at death.[27] Psychoanalysts, cultivated in listening to multiple levels of meaning, are uniquely qualified to relate and respond to the dying. There should always be a psychoanalytically trained professional who is attuned to hearing and understanding the degree of ambivalence that the dying person may be conveying present on the administering team.

We should think psychoanalytically and developmentally of dying as a phase and process in the human life cycle, as the other end from infancy and early childhood, which have been intensively studied. Psychoanalysis has conceptually structured the tasks of infancy, childhood, latency, adolescence, and, to a lesser extent, adulthood.[28] Our task as psychoanalysts should now be to formulate the complex amalgam of aging and the awareness of the nearness of death manifested by the inevitable, but often denied, evidences of diminished responses, depletion and organic decline, such as loss of memory, in our intrapsychic, interpersonal, and physiological selves. Some of the phase-specific psychological markers of aging are concern with legal arrangements for death such as wills, gifts, legacies, and trusts, seeking forms of immortality such as naming buildings and foundations, decisions to repair breaches with family members and friends, providing for children and grandchildren, fantasies of retirement as a return to the Garden of Eden, where man and woman may play in a timeless world and need not toil.

We should not dismiss the heuristic value of Freud's expression of the sense of life as consisting "of a continuous descent towards death."[29] Freud wrote of death as "a matter of expediency, a manifestation of adaptation to the external conditions of life" and of "the death instinct" that seeks "to lead what is living to death."[30]

After World War I, Karl Binding (1841–1920) of Leipzig and Alfred Hoche (1865–1943) of Freiburg, an early psychiatric opponent of Freud on the sexual etiology of hysteria,[31] coauthored *Die Freigabe der Vernichtung lebensunwerten Lebens* (On Sanctioning the Destruction of Unworthy Life),[32] a book that Heinz-Peter Schmiedebach interprets as continuing the "aggressive attitude [toward 'war neurosis' patients] evoked during the war but now disguised as academic reflections."[33] Binding and Hoche argued for an active voluntary public euthanasia program because society should not care for "lives that have a negative value" (*Leben negativen Wertes*).[34] There is a monstrous historical irony in Hoche's prediction of 1920:

There was a time, which we now regard as barbaric, in which as a matter of course those who were born or became unfit for life were eliminated. Then came the still current phase in which finally the maintenance of every worthless existence was regarded as the highest moral demand. A new time will come that from the standpoint of a higher morality will cease constantly to actually implement at great expense the demands of an exaggerated concept of humanity and an overestimation of the value of the very principle of existence.[35]

Since the Third Reich, euthanasia has been in bad repute, because it is associated with programs under which those defined as "unfit" by the Nazi state, the mentally retarded, handicapped, mentally ill, or chronically ill, were medically murdered.[36] In this century, in a developed Western country, doctors killed those who were deemed "racially undesirable," "genetically undesirable," "deficient people" (*Defekt-Menschen*), "empty human shells" (*leeren Menschenhülsen*), "burdensome beings" (*Ballast-Existenzen*), because they were viewed as having no value to society. The fear of involuntary experimentation and death by those who are socially marginal in America — the poor, the disabled, the ethnically stigmatized — is not without historical precedent. The issue of potential abuses is a real one. Concern that the legalization of assisted dying must never become a mandate to kill for the good of society is legitimate.[37]

Appropriate safeguards and measures to determine patient intent as accurately as possible are mandatory. For clarity's sake, we need to distinguish between, first, establishing the right of a person to autonomy over one's body and, second, that right's implementation. It is an extreme violation of patients' autonomy to force them to live in a vegetative state that they were desperate to avoid. Not legalizing assisted dying is socially harmful and against the expressed wishes of many people. As the legal scholar Ronald Dworkin pungently puts it: "Making someone die in a way that others approve, but he believes a horrifying contradiction of his life, is a devastating, odious form of tyranny."[38] Once the right to one's body is established, a second stage occurs in which the measures of regulation and patient protection are carefully worked out. Expert and experienced medical ethicists have thoughtfully drafted potential provisions for such oversight, so I shall not here engage with legal and bureaucratic recipes for review.[39]

The conflict in our culture's attitudes toward dying and death is captured by two of the twentieth century's greatest writers, one from a Protestant, the other from a Catholic culture. At the beginning of the century, before the wonders of antibiotics, Thomas Mann, ever the supreme ironist, presents Frau Consul Buddenbrook addressing her doctors:

"I want—I cannot—let me sleep! Have mercy, gentlemen—let me sleep!" . . . But the physicians knew their duty: they were obliged, under all circumstances, to preserve life just as long as possible; and a narcotic would have effected an unresisting and immediate giving-up of the ghost. Doctors were not made to bring death into the world, but to preserve life at any cost. There was a religious and moral basis for this law, which they had known once, though they did not have it in mind at the moment. So they strengthened the heart action by various devices, and even improved the breathing by causing the patient to retch.[40]

James Joyce presumed to draw upon all of the essential traditions of our cultural past and he did so successfully. His modern Ulysses, a man who has no religion, half-Irish, half-Hungarian, part-Jew, "Everyman or Noman,"[41] who was baptized both a Protestant and a Roman Catholic, is on 16 June 1904 in Dublin riding a funeral carriage with three acquaintances:

—As decent a little man as ever wore a hat, Mr. Dedalus said. He went very suddenly.
—Breakdown, Martin Cunningham said. Heart.
He tapped his chest sadly. . . .
—He had a sudden death, poor fellow, he said.
—The best death, Mr. Bloom said.
Their wide eyes looked at him.
—No suffering, he said. A moment and all is over. Like dying in sleep.
No one spoke.[42]

Nothing creates more social awkwardness than the sudden simultaneous silence of everyone present. Speechlessness is the response of Joyce's good, believing Dubliners faced with Bloom's classical humane view of death.

America's great social experiment with assisted dying is Oregon's Death with Dignity Act, which went into effect after a popular referendum in November 1997. The election saw the highest voter turnout for a nonpresidential election in 34 years (59.69 percent); in this case there was no election of officials, only two ballot propositions. After a hard fought and costly campaign, including appeals to the U.S. Supreme Court, the people of Oregon by a margin of 3 to 2 overwhelmingly voted to establish the right to assisted dying. The percentage, 60 percent / 40 percent, does not adequately present the nature of the landslide; it was 666,275 versus 445,830 votes.[43] The meaning of the size of the Oregon majority is that this is a very personal issue, more than a political, ideological, or a religious one. It is an issue that voters decided in the privacy of their experience and their consciences and in the secrecy of the ballot box. This was also a case which defied the conventional political wisdom that the side with the most money to spend and the greatest media saturation will win. The organized opposition of the Catholic Church, the Mormon Church, and the fundamentalist Christian churches together raised over $4 million and outspent the proponents of the law by 4 to 1.[44] The single major contributor to advocates of "Death with Dignity" was the philanthropist George Soros.

The timing of the Oregon vote was propitious because it came on the heels of a Supreme Court decision urging the states to experiment with legislation and referenda. In his majority opinion in *Washington v. Glucksberg* Chief Justice Rehnquist held: "Throughout the nation, Americans are engaged in an earnest and profound debate about the morality, legality, and practicality of physician-assisted suicide. Our holding permits this debate to continue, as it should in a democratic society."[45] The court said, we will not do it—the states and the people must decide. The court showed appropriate judicial restraint—why should the judgment of *these* nine individuals determine public policy on such a vital personal issue?

The people of Oregon were the first to act on the court's mandate. In American history the vanguard of political and social innovations, such as women's suffrage (Wyoming, 1869; then the next eight states in order: Colorado, Utah, Idaho, Washington, California, Arizona, Kansas, Oregon); the presidential primary by popular election, initiative, referendum, and recall; railroad and utility regulation, have often come from the West. Other states are now considering legislation modeled after Oregon's Death with Dignity Act. This is the kind of private issue, analogous to homosexuality and adultery, or a position on the sexual privacy and personal life of the president, on which the majority of Americans are more tolerant, rational, and mature in their personal values than are the legislators, the media, and the political class inside the Washington Beltway, who issue pronouncements that do not accurately reflect public opinion. Surveys in Oregon showed that up to 50 percent of Roman Catholics voted to allow assisted dying.[46] The stance people will take before a network camera, or what they will disclose on the record to a media interviewer, or a neighbor at church, is not necessarily what they will do in a voting booth on what they perceive to be a personal issue. Upon passage of the law, Dr. Glen Gordon, a former president of the Oregon Medical Association, said: "I've been a surgeon in practice for 50 years, so I speak from

experience when I say many patients would have liked to have had this option available to them. Fifteen years ago, we heard arguments over refusing
life support. Now it's accepted. The move toward helping patients at the end
of their lives is expanding."[47]

Let us examine the Oregon Plan and its operation during its first year.
The Oregon Death With Dignity Act provides multiple safeguards, alternative options, referral for counseling, and the right to rescind "at any time and
in any manner."[48] The law requires the patient to make a written request to
die on a single page form entitled "Request for medication to end my life in
a humane and dignified manner," a copy of which goes to the state. One witness must be neither a relative nor benefit from the death in any way; the patient's attending physician does not qualify as a witness. The initial oral and
written request to die must be reiterated after no less than a fifteen-day waiting period. There is a mandatory minimum of 48 hours between the patient's
last written request and the writing of a prescription. Two doctors must cer-
tify that the patient is of sound mind and has a terminal illness with less than
six months to live. The patient must be informed of "feasible alternatives, including, but not limited to, comfort care, hospice care and pain control."
The law provides for counseling referral and explicitly states: "No medication to end a patient's life in a humane and dignified manner shall be prescribed until the person performing the counseling determines that the person is not suffering from a psychiatric or psychological disorder, or depression causing impaired judgment."[49] This is not the Doctor Kevorkian model
of physician assisted dying. Doctors under the Oregon law do not give lethal
injections—they may prescribe drugs that would be self-administered, with
notification to the state. The circumstances of the patient's death are also
certified to the state.

Oregon's Death with Dignity Act has now been in effect for over a year.
The flood of applications and abuses that the doomsayers predicted has not
occurred. The Oregon Health Division announced that only fifteen persons
obtained prescriptions for lethal medications under the act in its first full
year of operation. Eight other people also received prescriptions under the
law, but six died from their terminal illnesses before taking the drugs and two
did not take the medication as of 1 January 1999. There were 29,000 deaths
in Oregon last year, in a population of over 3,200,000. Their physicians
judged all fifteen persons as capable of making and communicating health-
care decisions. All received a medical evaluation by a second physician to
confirm the diagnosis and terminal prognosis, and all complied with the
mandated fifteen-day waiting period between the first and second requests

for a prescription for lethal medication. The average age of those obtaining prescriptions was 69 years. Cancer was the underlying terminal illness for thirteen persons and the other two had heart or lung disease. Eight were men and seven were women. All of the people who used the act were white. The average time to unconsciousness was 5 minutes, with the overall range from 3 to 20 minutes; and the average time to death was 26 minutes, with the range from 15 minutes to ½ hour. Dr. Peter Rasmussen, a Salem, Oregon, cancer specialist was present at two occasions in which terminally ill patients died after taking a chocolate pudding laced with barbiturates. "One of the potential advantages is you can plan it—people who have relatives far away can gather everybody together. I've seen it happen and it was a very positive, joyful experience," he said.

For some of the people who wished to use the law, the safeguards were too demanding, it took too long, and the promised relief came too late. Many people are concerned with the potential for victimization of the poor, the underprivileged, the street people, and the derelicts of society whom no one cares about or represents. The Oregon state report stated: "Physician-assisted suicide was not disproportionately chosen by terminally ill patients who were poor, uneducated, uninsured, fearful of the financial consequences of their illnesses or who lacked end-of-life care."[50] Due to many scrupulous safeguards, assisted dying in America will be a middle- and upper-class privilege, as are the Health Management Organizations. Just as HMOs in the United States work best for those who know how to use them to get the referrals and consultations that they need, the first year's experience indicates that the beneficiaries of Oregon's "Death with Dignity" law will be the upper and middle classes—those who have legal counsel and personal physicians, those who know how to use documents, bureaucracies, and reporting laws as instruments to reach desired ends.

I wish to set this important trend in contemporary American public policy and society in the context of psychoanalytic humanism and Sigmund Freud's position on assisted dying. As early as 1899, in his correspondence with Wilhelm Fliess forty years before his death, Freud objected to what he termed

one of the most aggravating features of our modern medicine. The art of deceiving a sick person is not exactly highly necessary. But what has the individual come to, how negligible must be the influence of the religion of science, which is supposed to have taken the place of the old religion, if one no longer dares to disclose that it is this or that man's turn to die? . . . I hope that when my time comes, I shall find someone who will treat me with greater respect and tell me when to be ready.

"Shakespeare says, after all, 'You owe Nature a death,'" Freud adds, adapting a line from Part I of Shakespeare's *Henry IV*, where Prince Hal tells Falstaff: "Why, thou owest God a death" (5.1). A postscript to this letter evokes Freud's engagement with the Stoic values of Hellenic culture: "I am deep in Burckhardt's *History of Greek Civilization*."[51]

During World War I, Freud conducted the deepest part of his self-analysis, working through filicidal feelings he thought had long ago been resolved, and he gave us two profound works on death, "Thoughts for the Times on War and Death" (1915) and its companion piece, "Mourning and Melancholia" (1917). In the former he wrote: "Towards the actual person who has died we adopt a special attitude — something almost like admiration for someone who has accomplished a very difficult task."[52] This is because we do not truly comprehend death and cannot emotionally conceive of it as applied to ourselves. As Freud put it in 1919: "No human being really grasps it, and our unconscious has as little use now as it ever had for the idea of its own mortality."[53] For the Greeks in its original meaning, *eu-thanatos* meant a good death, one in the person's interest, and better than the death that person would have had if left to nature. It was in this sense that, when James Jackson Putnam died painlessly in his sleep in 1918, Freud said to Sándor Ferenczi, "He had an enviable end."[54] Ferenczi wrote to Freud about their mutual friend Anton von Freund, who was terminally ill with cancer: "He wanted to persuade . . . [his surgeon] to subject him to an illusory operation and to narcotize him to death."[55] And again five months later: "The doctors must fulfill his demand for euthanasia; he has complete justification for it."[56] Freud replied: "Euthanasia is not easy if one doesn't want to kill the patient directly."[57] In 1927, Freud wrote of "the great necessities of Fate, against which there is no help [which we must] learn to endure with resignation."[58]

Both Felix Deutsch, his physician, and the "Committee," Freud's most trusted disciples, withheld from him the diagnosis of cancer. Years later, when Ernest Jones told him of the Committee's deception, Freud "with blazing eyes . . . asked '*Mit welchem Recht?*'" (By what right?).[59] He reproached Deutsch, who resigned as his personal physician, because the diagnosis was initially withheld from him and he was deceived.[60] Freud wrote to Deutsch invoking his Stoic ideal:

I could always adapt myself to any kind of reality, even endure an uncertainty due to a reality — but being left alone with my subjective insecurity, without the fulcrum or pillar of the *ananke*, the inexorable, unavoidable necessity, I had to fall prey to the miserable cowardice of a human being and had to become an unworthy spectacle for others.[61]

During the next sixteen years, Freud underwent thirty-three operations of the mouth. As ever greater areas of the jaw, palate, and cheek were removed in increasingly radical operations, he had to learn to live with a huge prosthesis, which he termed "the monster." Deutsch notes that Freud "never complained about his misfortune to me; in these years he simply treated the neoplasm as an uninvited, unwelcome intruder whom one should not mind more than necessary."[62]

Freud was without a personal physician after 1923. In 1928, on the recommendation of Marie Bonaparte, he engaged Max Schur. He presented Schur with two conditions, first, "that he always be told the truth and nothing but the truth," and second, "when the time comes, you won't let me suffer torment unnecessarily" (*Versprechen Sie mir auch noch: Wenn es mal soweit ist, werden Sie mich nicht unnötig quälen lassen*).[63] In 1939, Schur was in America, taking his New York State Medical Boards in the last week of June. He recrossed the Atlantic by ship in early July, arriving in London on 8 July 1939. When, on 21 September, Freud took Schur's hand and said: "My dear Schur, you remember our first talk. You promised then not to leave me in the lurch when my time comes. Now it is nothing but torture and makes no sense anymore" (*Lieber Schur, Sie erinnern sich wohl an unser erstes Gespräch. Sie haben mir damals versprochen mich nicht im Stiche zu lassen wenn es so weit ist. Das ist jetzt nur noch Quälerei und hat keinen Sinn mehr*). Schur indicated he had not forgotten.[64] Freud thanked him and asked Schur to "talk it over with Anna, and if she thinks it's right, then make an end of it." Schur redeemed his promise, giving Freud three centigrams of morphine, which he repeated, and then gave him a final morphine injection the next day.[65] Freud never awoke.

We can only speculate and wonder at the awesome psychodynamic meaning to Schur of experiencing Freud, the father of psychoanalysis, who had conceptualized the oedipal wish to murder the father, say to him, "Please kill me, you must put me to death."[66] The deep level of personal empathy between Schur and Freud, not only physician and patient but also close friends, constitutes the exemplar of humane assistance in death. Norbert Elias beautifully expresses it:

It can be one of the last great joys for dying people to be cared for by family members and friends — last proof of love, a last sign that they mean something to other people. That is a great support — to find a resonance of feeling in others for whom one feels love or attachment, whose presence arouses a warm feeling of belonging. This mutual affirmation of people through their feelings, the resonance of feeling between two or more people, plays a central part in giving meaning and a sense of fulfillment to a human life — reciprocal affection, as it were, to the last.[67]

What Peter Gay terms Freud's "stoic suicide" is a part of his legacy to the world and to us. His resignation to fate and his acceptance of unalterable reality never wavered or faltered. With the exception of an occasional aspirin, he took no drugs until the very end, so that he could think clearly. He continued his psychoanalytic work until July 1939. He died on 23 September, believing in life, and that death was the necessary outcome of life. Death is natural, undeniable, and unavoidable. Freud's unflinching attitude toward death, forthright, without sentimentality or self-pity, but with a full consciousness of reality, represents the best of what psychoanalysis means for man's attitude toward himself: stoic acceptance. This life is all there is, and there is little you can do about it. Man must die, and that fact should not be obviated or denied. We must live with that realization and die, if possible, with a minimum of suffering and without illusions. Freud saw the single human, in his body and with his drives, facing the coercion and constraint of culture. Freud's contract with Max Schur was a model of how a rational person in possession of his mental faculties could choose to ask for aid in terminating his suffering. Our culture is now catching up with Freud.

We hear Freud's personal philosophy of life and death, but this is also a psychoanalytical attitude of sanctifying the claims of the individual against the coercive power of society, which is always controversial but widely shared in our culture. Freud did not like America. He termed it "a gigantic mistake." He attributed to America both prudery and vulgarity, the commercialization and bowdlerization of culture and of psychoanalysis.[68] He intuited that American culture is particularly filled with denial of aging and death. We do not handle death well. Our values of the adoration of youth, vitality, and beauty allow no place for the realities of old age and mortality. Freud's most acerbic views of America were omitted from the published version of the 1927 "Postscript" to "The Question of Lay Analysis" (1926). The three deleted pages have only recently been published. Certain of Freud's remarks reflect on our subject. He speaks of

the Americans' horror of authority, their inclination to assert personal independence in the few fields which are not yet occupied by the implacable pressure of public opinion . . . the American has no time. Time is indeed money, but it is not entirely clear why it has to be transformed into money in such a hurry. It would, after all, retain its monetary value even if it went more slowly, and it might be thought that, the more time one were first to invest, the more money would eventually result. . . . He has a passion for large numbers, for the magnification of all dimensions, but also for cutting the investment of time to an absolute minimum. I believe the word for this is "record." So he wants to learn analysis in 3 or 4 months, and, of course, the analytic treatments must not last any longer than this.[69]

Freud's thoughts on time are cogent current considerations about managed care and dying. The psychoanalytic consideration is that assisted dying is a subtle, complicated, and highly individual issue, and that there should be someone present with time and clinical competence to listen, interpret, and respond. This is directly contra the fast closure, cost containment/cost effective, "quick fix" considerations of managed care.

The "right to be let alone" is a theme of American resistance to the conforming power of culture that Freud should have treasured as being the essence of psychoanalysis. As early as 1914 Justice Benjamin N. Cardozo said: "Every human being of adult years and sound mind has a right to determine what shall be done with his own body."[70] The humane physician Walter Alvarez wrote:

Some day when I myself lie dying, I hope that I will have by me some wise and kindly physician who will keep interns from pulling me up to examine my chest, or constantly puncturing my veins, or putting a tube down my nose, or giving me enemas and drastic medicines. I am sure that at the end I will very much want to be let alone.[71]

In a famous judicial dissent written at the time Freud was composing *Civilization and Its Discontents*, Justice Louis D. Brandeis cast the authors of our Constitution as protecting the privacy and sensibilities of the single person against the state.[72] In a position the majority of the present Supreme Court would not agree with, but which Freud, with his vision of the single individual in lifelong struggle with the imperatives of culture, would have endorsed, Brandeis said:

[The authors of the Constitution] recognized the significance of man's spiritual nature, of his feelings and of his intellect. They knew that only a part of the pain, pleasure and satisfaction of life are to be found in material things. They sought to protect Americans in their beliefs, their thoughts, their emotions and their sensations. They conferred, as against the government, the right to be let alone — the most comprehensive of rights, and the right most valued by civilized men.[73]

This is a liberal ideology to which Freud would have subscribed, because it is inherent in psychoanalysis. I am arguing in the Lockean liberal political tradition of self-ownership of one's body as an expression of a natural right. John Locke (1632–1704) was, not coincidentally, among his other pursuits, a practicing physician. In the immortal language of his *Second Treatise of Government* (1690), Locke made the case, which powerfully influenced the authors of the Declaration of Independence and the American Constitution a century later, for the recognition of self-ownership as a natural right that

all men are naturally in . . . a *state of perfect freedom* [italics in the original] to order their actions, and dispose of their possessions and persons, as they think fit, within the bounds of the law of nature, without asking leave, or depending upon the will of any other man . . . he be absolute lord of his own person and possessions, equal to the greatest, and subject to no body.[74]

We are not owned by the state and it should not determine what we may or may not do with our bodies at the time of our meeting death.[75] This means permitting individuals to express their will about themselves and for the legal culture and the state to honor that expression. A liberal, tolerant society should allow matters of dying to be decided by individual conscience, which in contemporary discourse is a quasi-religious code for personal choice. As Ronald Dworkin puts it: "Government has no proper business poking around in this realm, stomping on these highly personal and spiritual concerns with the jackboots of criminal law as has been the case with doctor-assisted suicide."[76]

As a historian, I trust I shall not be considered a hopeless romantic if I suggest that we ought to allow each person to be the author of the story of the end of his or her life, their own leave-taking from loved ones and from this world.[77] None of us had any choices in the circumstances and the surround of our birth. People should be permitted — in consultation, if they wish, with their family, physician and medical attendants, spiritual advisors, and psychological and legal counselors — to write their own narrative and rituals of the conclusion of their life, as Freud did. I know this is possible and feasible in contemporary America because I have seen it happen. In May 1997, my 74-year-old cousin, who had lymphoma of the lung, refused intubation, saying: "If this is to prolong life, I want it, but if it will merely prolong my death, it is now time to go." With her husband, children, and grandchildren present, she received a gradually increasing morphine drip until she lost consciousness and descended into a sleep from which she did not awake. Her son expressed to me the immeasurable gratification it was for him to have been able to give his mother the precious gift of the dignified death she wished.

Ironically, the same modern technology that artificially prolongs life also provides devices enabling patient-controlled analgesia (PCA), which allow patients to determine the dosage of their own intravenous pain medication, usually an opioid, by means of a programmable pump.[78] PCA gives the patient control of pain relief rather than waiting for the nurse or someone else to come to administer an injection, thus curbing anxiety and requiring less medication.[79]

A realistic problem is the reluctance of families and physicians to discuss with patients their wishes and instructions about the kind of care they want at the end of life.[80] Few people have signed living wills, even among those who believe in them.[81] Life, and each day of living, is immeasurably precious. We have not cultivated the art of dying, any more than we have cultivated its integral correlate, the art of living.

Bibliography of Writings
by Peter Gay

A. BOOKS

The Dilemma of Democratic Socialism: Eduard Bernstein's Challenge to Marx. New York: Columbia University Press, 1952. Reprinted with a new Postscript, Collier Books, 1962.

Voltaire's Politics: The Poet as Realist. Princeton: Princeton University Press, 1959. Second edition with a new Preface, Yale University Press, 1988.

The Party of Humanity: Essays in the French Enlightenment. New York: Knopf, 1964.

The Enlightenment: An Interpretation. Vol. 1: *The Rise of Modern Paganism.* New York: Knopf, 1966. Norton reprint, 1977.

A Loss of Mastery: Puritan Historians in Colonial America. Berkeley and Los Angeles: University of California Press, 1966.

Age of Enlightenment. New York: Time-Life Books, 1966.

Weimar Culture: The Outsider as Insider. New York: Harper & Row, 1968.

The Enlightenment: An Interpretation. Vol. 2: *The Science of Freedom.* New York: Knopf, 1969. Norton reprint, 1977.

The Bridge of Criticism: Dialogues Among Lucian, Erasmus, and Voltaire on the Enlightenment — On History and Hope, Imagination and Reason, Constraint and Freedom — And on Its Meaning for Our Time. New York: Harper & Row, 1970.

Modern Europe. With R. K. Webb. New York: Harper & Row, 1973.

Style in History. New York: Basic Books, 1974.

Art and Act: On Causes in History — Manet, Gropius, Mondrian. New York: Harper & Row, 1976. Originally presented as seven lectures at the Cooper Union for the Advancement of Science and Art, New York, March–April 1974.

Freud, Jews, and Other Germans: Masters and Victims in Modernist Culture. New York: Oxford University Press, 1978.

The Bourgeois Experience: Victoria to Freud. Vol. 1: *Education of the Senses.* New York: Oxford University Press, 1984.

Freud for Historians. New York: Oxford University Press, 1985.

The Bourgeois Experience: Victoria to Freud. Vol. 2: *The Tender Passion.* New York: Oxford University Press, 1986.

A Godless Jew: Freud, Atheism, and the Making of Psychoanalysis. New Haven: Yale University Press, 1987.

Freud: A Life for Our Time. New York: Norton, 1988.

Reading Freud: Explorations and Entertainments. New Haven: Yale University Press, 1990.

The Bourgeois Experience: Victoria to Freud. Vol. 3: *The Cultivation of Hatred.* New York: Norton, 1993.

The Bourgeois Experience: Victoria to Freud. Vol. 4: *The Naked Heart.* New York: Norton, 1995.

The Bourgeois Experience: Victoria to Freud. Vol. 5: *Pleasure Wars.* New York: Norton, 1998.

My German Question: Growing Up in Nazi Berlin. New Haven: Yale University Press, 1998.

Mozart. New York: Viking, 1999.

B. CHAPTERS IN BOOKS

"International Police Force: University of Nebraska (Forum of the Air)." In *University Debaters' Annual: Constructive and Rebuttal Speeches Delivered in Debates of American Colleges and Universities During the College Year 1943–1944*, ed. Edith M. Phelps, 207–22. New York: H. W. Wilson Co., 1944.

"Light on the Enlightenment." In *The Present-Day Relevance of Eighteenth-Century Thought*, ed. Roger P. McCutcheon, 41–42. Washington, D.C.: American Council of Learned Societies, 1956.

"Carl Becker's Heavenly City." In *Carl Becker's Heavenly City Revisited*, ed. Raymond O. Rockwood, 27–51. Ithaca, N.Y.: Cornell University Press, 1958.

"Voltaire's *Idées républicaines*: A Study in Bibliography and Interpretation." In *Studies on Voltaire and the Eighteenth Century*, ed. Theodore Besterman, 6 (Geneva: Institut et Musée Voltaire, 1958), 67–105.

"*Encyclopédie* and Enlightenment: 'Changing the General Way of Thinking,' 1745–1764." In *Major Crises in Western Civilization*, vol. 2: *1745 to the Nuclear Age*, 7–10. New York: Harcourt, Brace, 1965.

"The Social History of Ideas: Ernst Cassirer and After." In *The Critical Spirit: Essays in Honor of Herbert Marcuse*, ed. Kurt H. Wolff and Barrington Moore, Jr., 106–20. Boston: Beacon Press, 1967.

"The Enlightenment as Medicine and as Cure." In *The Age of the Enlightenment: Studies Presented to Theodore Besterman*, ed. W. H. Barber, J. H. Brumfitt, R. A. Leigh, R. Shackleton, and S. S. B. Taylor, 375–86. Edinburgh and London: Oliver & Boyd, 1967.

"Burckhardt's *Renaissance*: Between Responsibility and Power." In *The Responsibility of Power: Historical Essays in Honor of Hajo Holborn*, ed. Leonard Krieger and Fritz Stern, 183–98. Garden City, N.Y.: Doubleday, 1967.

"The Enlightenment." In *The Comparative Approach to American History*, ed. C. Vann Woodward, 34–46. New York: Basic Books, 1968.

"Jonathan Edwards: An American Tragedy." In *Jonathan Edwards: A Profile*, ed. David Levin, 231–51. New York: Hill & Wang, 1969.

"Weimar Culture: The Outsider as Insider." In *The Intellectual Migration: Europe and America, 1930–1960*, ed. Donald Fleming and Bernard Bailyn, 11–93. Cambridge, Mass.: Harvard University Press, Belknap Press, 1969.

"Law, Order, and Enlightenment." In *Is Law Dead?* ed. Eugene V. Rostow, 21–31. New York: Simon & Schuster, 1971.

"Voltaire." In *The Horizon Book of Makers of Modern Thought*, 181–89. New York: American Heritage, 1972.

"Why Was the Enlightenment?" In *Eighteenth-Century Studies Presented to Arthur M. Wilson*, ed. Peter Gay, 61–71. Hanover, N.H.: University Press of New England, 1972.

"For Beckmesser." In *From Parnassus: Essays in Honor of Jacques Barzun*, ed. Dora B. Weiner and William R. Keylor, 42–54. New York: Harper & Row, 1976.

"Freud: For the Marble Tablet." In *Berggasse 19: Sigmund Freud's Home and Offices, Vienna 1938 — The Photographs of Edmund Engelman*, 13–54. New York: Basic Books, 1976.

"The Applied Enlightenment?" In *The Idea of America: A Reassessment of the American Experiment*, ed. E. M. Adams, 11–38. Cambridge, Mass.: Ballinger Publishing, 1977.

"The Burden of Prophecy." In *A View of a Decade*, 27–38. Exhibition catalogue, 10 September–10 November 1977, Museum of Contemporary Art, Chicago.

"Freud and Freedom: On a Fox in Hedgehog's Clothing." In *The Idea of Free-*

dom: *Essays in Honour of Isaiah Berlin*, ed. Alan Ryan, 41–59. Oxford: Oxford University Press, 1979.

"On the Bourgeoisie: A Psychological Interpretation." In *Consciousness and Class Experience in Nineteenth-Century Europe*, ed. John M. Merriman, 187–203. New York: Holmes & Meier, 1979.

"The Enlightenment as a Communication Universe." In *Propaganda and Communication in World History*, ed. Harold D. Lasswell, Daniel Lerner, and Hans Speier, vol. 2: *Emergence of Public Opinion in the West*, 85–111. Honolulu: University Press of Hawaii, 1980.

"Foreword." In *Theodor Fontane: Short Novels and Other Writings*, ed. Peter Demetz, vii–ix. New York: Continuum Books, 1982.

"Freud's America." In *America and the Germans: An Assessment of a Three-Hundred-Year History*, ed. Frank Trommler and Joseph McVeigh, vol. 2: *The Relationship in the Twentieth Century*, 303–14. Philadelphia: University of Pennsylvania Press, 1985.

"Introduction." In Shepard Bancroft Clough, *The Life I've Lived: The Formation, Career, and Retirement of an Historian*, ix–xi. Washington, D.C.: University Press of America, 1985.

"A Gentile Science?" In *For Want of a Horse: Choice and Chance in History*, ed. John M. Merriman, 63–67. Lexington, Mass.: Stephen Greene Press, 1985.

"Reading Freud Through Freud's Reading." In *Freud in Our Time: A Seventy-Fifth Anniversary Symposium*, ed. William A. Koelsch and Seymour Wapner, 22–38. Clark University Monographs in Psychology and Related Disciplines, no. 4. Worcester, Mass.: Clark University, 1988.

"Psychoanalysis in History." In *Psychology and Historical Interpretation*, ed. William McKinley Runyan, 107–20. New York: Oxford University Press, 1988.

"The Bite of Wit: Humor, Sadism, Aggression in Wilhelm Busch," "History, Biography, Psychoanalysis," and "On Writing the Freud Biography." In E. Fox Keller, Peter Gay, E. H. Gombrich et al., *Three Cultures: Fifteen Lectures on the Confrontation of Academic Cultures*, 73–88, 89–100, 109–20. The Hague: B. V. Universitaire Pers Rotterdam, 1989.

"Introduction." In *Sigmund Freud and Art: His Personal Collection of Antiquities*, ed. Lynn Gamwell and Richard Wells, 15–19. New York: Harry N. Abrams, 1989.

"Psychoanalyzing the Psychoanalyst: Writing the Freud Biography." In *Essays in European History Selected from the Annual Meetings of the Southern Historical Association, 1986–1987*, ed. June K. Burton, 5–17. Lanham, Md.: University Press of America, 1989.

"The Father's Revenge." In *The Don Giovanni Book: Myths of Seduction and Betrayal*, ed. Jonathan Miller, 70–80. London: Faber & Faber, 1990.

"Experiment in Denial: A Reading of the *Gartenlaube* in the Year 1890." In *Traditions of Experiment from the Enlightenment to the Present: Essays in Honor of Peter Demetz*, ed. Nancy Kaiser and David E. Wellbery, 147–64. Ann Arbor: University of Michigan Press, 1992.

"Foreword." In Charles Hanly, *The Problem of Truth in Applied Psychoanalysis*, vii–xiii. New York: Guilford Press, 1992.

"The Manliness of Christ." In *Religion and Irreligion in Victorian Society: Essays in Honor of R. K. Webb*, ed. R. W. Davis and R. J. Helmstadter, 102–16. New York: Routledge, 1992.

"Goethe in Love." In *The Spectrum of Psychoanalysis: Essays in Honor of Martin S. Bergmann*, ed. Arlene Kramer Richards and Arnold D. Richards, 185–98. Madison, Conn.: International Universities, 1994.

"Erikson's Truth." In *The Flora Levy Lecture in the Humanities 1990*, ed. Albert W. Fields and James A. Marino, 1–23. 1994.

"Freud." In *Past Imperfect: History According to the Movies*, ed. Mark C. Carnes, 170–73. New York: Henry Holt, 1995.

"Epilogue: The First Sex." In *Between Sorrow and Strength: Women Refugees of the Nazi Period*, ed. Sibylle Quack, 353–65. Cambridge: Cambridge University Press, 1995.

"The Cost of Culture: On Liebermann, Lichtwark, and Others." In *From the Berlin Museum to the Berlin Wall: Essays on the Cultural and Political History of Modern Germany*, ed. David Wetzel, 31–42. Westport, Conn.: Praeger, 1996.

C. ARTICLES IN JOURNALS AND MAGAZINES AND PUBLISHED LECTURES

"The Enlightenment in the History of Political Theory." *Political Science Quarterly* 69 (September 1954): 374–89.

"Three Stages on Love's Way: Rousseau, Laclos, Diderot." *Encounter* 9 (August 1957): 8–20.

"Carl Becker's Heavenly City." *Political Science Quarterly* 72 (June 1957): 182–99.

"The Unity of the French Enlightenment." *History* 3 (September 1960): 7–28.

"The Seven Prisoners in the Bastille: History in the Age of the Counter-Cliché." *Yale Review* 50 (March 1961): 350–56.

"Rhetoric and Politics in the French Revolution." *American History Review* 66 (April 1961): 664–76.

"An Age of Crisis: A Critical View." *Journal of Modern History* 33 (June 1961): 174–77.

Stephen Donadio, "Columbia: Seven Interviews." *Partisan Review* 35 (summer 1968): 354–92.

"A Program in Practice: America's Meaning for the Enlightenment." *University Review* 1 (May 1969): 14–15.

"The History of History." *Horizon* 11 (autumn 1969): 112–19.

"The Weimar Renaissance." *Horizon* 12 (winter 1970): 4–15.

"The Enlightenment." *Horizon* 12 (spring 1970): 40–45.

"The Message of the Enlightenment." *Dialogue* 4 (1971): 82–88.

"The Berlin-Jewish Spirit: A Dogma in Search of Some Doubts." *The Leo Baeck Memorial Lecture*, 15. New York: Leo Baeck Institute, 1972.

"How the Modern World Began." *Horizon* 15 (spring 1973): 4–15.

"History and the Facts." *Columbia Forum*, n.s., 3 (spring 1974): 7–14.

"Musings in Munich." With Ruth Gay. *American Scholar* 44 (winter 1974–75): 41–51.

"Mondrian." *Horizon* 17 (winter 1975): 64–79.

"Encounter with Modernism: German Jews in German Culture, 1888–1914." *Midstream: A Monthly Jewish Review* 21 (February 1975): 23–65.

"Hermann Levi and the Cult of Wagner." *Times Literary Supplement*, 11 April 1975, 402–4.

"America the Paradoxical." *Virginia Law Review* 62 (June 1976): 843–57.

"Thinking About the Germans: I." *New York Times*, 3 August 1976, A29.

"Thinking About the Germans: II." *New York Times*, 4 August 1976, A33.

"At Home in America." *American Scholar* 46 (winter 1976–77): 31–42.

"Aimez-vous Brahms? Reflections on Modernism." *Salmagundi* 36 (winter 1977): 16–35.

"Craft, Competence, and Countertransference: The Historian as the Scientist of Memory." In "Celebrating the Inauguration of Henry J. Copeland as Ninth President of the College of Wooster," 24–35. 3–7 October 1977.

"The New Yale President's Professors." *New York Times*, 21 December 1977, A21.

"Victorian Sexuality: Old Texts and New Insights." *American Scholar* 49 (summer 1980): 372–78.

"Freud's Jewish Identity." *Iliff Review* 38 (winter 1981): 41–50.

"Second Thoughts: Peter Gay on 'Voltaire's Politics.'" *Times Literary Supplement*, 12 June 1981, 673–74.

"Aggression and Culture: A Psychoanalytic Perspective." *Syracuse Scholar: An Interdisciplinary Journal of Ideas* 2 (fall 1981): 26–35.

"Mind Reading: The Forgotten Freud." *Harper's*, September 1981, 83–86.

"Freud's Jewish Identity." *Iliff Review* 38 (winter 1981): 41–50.

"Liberalism and Regression." *Psychoanalytic Study of the Child* 37 (1982): 523–45.

"Six Names in Search of an Interpretation: A Contribution to the Debate over Sigmund Freud's Jewishness." *Hebrew Union College Annual* 53 (1982): 295–307.

"Philosophy of History." *Philosophy and Human Enterprise: USMA Class of 1951 Lecture Series: 1982–1983*, 3–25.

"The Historian as Psychologist." The Sixth Annual O. Meredith Wilson Lecture in History, University of Utah (5 May 1982). University of Utah, 1983.

"The Discreet Pleasures of the Bourgeoisie." *American Scholar* 53 (winter 1983–84): 91–99.

"Address." In *Three Hundred Years of German Immigration: President Karl Carstens' Visit to Yale University* (14 October 1983), 4–25. New Haven: Yale University Press, 1984.

"The Intellectual Emigrés." *Humanities* 4 (November 1985): 1–4.

"The Age of Self-Scrutiny: A Reading of the Nineteenth Century." *Halcyon: A Journal of the Humanities* 8 (1986): 1–17.

"Symposium: Gay on Freud." *Psychohistory Review* 5 (fall 1986): 81–104.

"The Jewish Freud." Letter to the editor. *New York Review of Books* 33 (15 January 1987): 51–52.

"Freud, God, and the Enlightenment." *Explorations*, special ser., *The Age of Enlightenment* 1 (1987): 1–9.

"Patterns of Order: Imposed or Intrinsic?" *Groniek* 100 (1988): 147–48.

"Psychoanalysis in History." *Poetics Today: Interpretation in Context in Science and Culture* 9 (1988): 239–47.

"The German-Jewish Legacy — and I: Some Personal Reflections." *American Jewish Archives: The German-Jewish Legacy in America, 1938–1988*, 40 (November 1988): 203–10.

"The Legacy of Sigmund Freud." *Memories* 2 (August–September 1989): 32–34, 36.

"The Theory of Progress Today." Luncheon address. *Les Droits de l'Homme and Scientific Progress*, Conference Summary (25–28 October 1989), 45–47. Washington, D.C.: Smithsonian Institution, 1989.

"The Bite of Wit." *Proceedings of the American Philosophical Society*, 135 (September 1991): 327–31.

"Sigmund Freud?" *The Jewish Standard*, 21 February 1992, 3.

"Mensur: The Cherished Scar." *Yale Review* 80 (April 1992): 94–121.

"Response to Juliet Mitchell, 'From King Lear to Anna O. and Beyond: Some Speculative Theses on Hysteria' and to T. J. Clark, 'The Look of Self-Portraiture.'" *Yale Journal of Criticism* 5 (spring 1992): 121–24.

"Erikson's Truth." In *The Flora Levy Lecture in the Humanities 1990*, ed. Albert W. Fields and James A. Marino, 1–23. 1994.

"The 'Legless Angel' of 'David Copperfield': There's More to Her Than Victorian Piety." *New York Times Book Review*, 22 January 1995, 22–4.

"Leave-takings, Codas and Fond Goodbyes." *New York Times Book Review*, 13 July 1997, 31.

D. ESSAYS, PUBLISHED LECTURES, AND INTERVIEWS IN FOREIGN LANGUAGES

"Ideologie und Literatur: Festansprache (Frankfurter Buchmesse)." In *Börsenblatt für den Deutschen Buchhandel* 26 (9 October 1970): 2272–76.

"Der 'Berlinisch-jüdische Geist': Zweifel an einer Legende." *Monat* 31 (February–March 1979): 5–18.

"Psychoanalyse und Geschichte—oder Emil und die Detektive." In *Wissenschaftskolleg—Institute for Advanced Study—zu Berlin Jahrbuch 1983/84*, 135–44.

"Probleme der kulturellen Integration der Deutschen 1849 bis 1945." In *Die Rolle der Nation in der deutschen Geschichte und Gegenwart: Beiträge zu einer internationalen Konferenz in Berlin (West) vom 16. bis 18. Juni 1983*, ed. Otto Büsch and James J. Sheehan, 181–92. Berlin: Colloquium, 1985.

"Hunger nach Ganzheit." In *"Neue Erziehung, Neue Menschen": Ansätze zur Erziehungs- und Bildungsreform in Deutschland zwischen Kaiserreich und Diktatur*, ed. Ulrich Herrmann, 35–45. Weinheim and Basel: Beltz, 1987.

"Was ist Kultur?" In *Deutschlands Weg in die Moderne: Politik, Gesellschaft und Kultur im 19. Jahrhundert*, ed. Wolfgang Hardtwig and Harm-Hinrich Brandt, 45–63. Munich: Beck, 1993.

"Freud et la guerre." In Jean Jacques Becker, Jay M. Winter et al., *Guerre et Cultures: 1914–1918*, 111–17. Paris: Armand Colin, 1994.

"Amerika: Eine Liebesaffäre." In *Der Aquädukt: 1763–1988: Ein Almanach aus dem Verlag C. H. Beck im 225. Jahr seines Bestehens*, 107–13. Munich: Beck, 1988.

"Skriptinterview." With Henk Bas and Rosalien Blommestein. *Skript* 6 (September 1984): 200–209.

"'Ik heb niet zoiets als het Licht gezien': Jan Blokker in Gesprek met Peter Gay." *De Volkskrant*, 25 October 1985, 5–11.

"De psychoanalyse in de geschiedschrijving: Je kunt Clio niet op de divan leggen." *De Volkskrant*, 25 October 1985, 12–25.

"Freuds Amerika." In *Amerika und die Deutschen: Bestandsaufnahme einer 300jährigen Geschichte*, ed. Frank Trommler, 639–49. Opladen: Westdeutscher Verlag, 1986.

"'Ik denk dat historici een luxe zijn, een fantastische luxe!': Een interview met de cultuurhistoricus Peter Gay." With Anke van Beckhoven, Wilfred van Buuren, and Oscar Steens. *De Tijdgenoot: Tijdschrift voor cultuurgeschiedenis & literatuur* 2 (December 1988): 33–41.

"Freud, Shakespeare und Looney." *Psyche* 45, no. 8 (August 1991): 649–74.

"Berlins Liebermann—Liebermanns Berlin." *"Berliner Lektionen"* 1992 (addresses at the Berliner Festspiele, 1992), 29–47. Gütersloh: C. Bertelsmann, 1992.

"In Deutschland zu Hause . . . Die Juden der Weimarer Zeit." In *Die Juden im Nationalsozialistischen Deutschland: The Jews in Nazi Germany, 1933–1943*, 31–43. N.d.

"Die Lust des Hanno Buddenbrook." In *Lebenskunst und Lebenslust: Ein Lesebuch vom guten Leben*, ed. Dieter Thomä, 40–43. Munich: Beck, 1996.

"Töne der Liebe." In *Das 19. Jahrhundert: Ein Lesebuch zur deutschen Geschichte: 1815–1918*, ed. Wolfgang Piereth, 257–59. Munich: Beck, 1997.

E. TRANSLATIONS

Cassirer, Ernst. *The Question of Jean Jacques Rousseau*. Translated and edited with an Introduction and additional notes by Peter Gay. New York: Columbia University Press, 1954. Reprint, Bloomington: Indiana University Press, 1963; 2d ed., with a new Postscript, New Haven: Yale University Press, 1989.

Neumann, Franz. "Anxiety and Politics" (1954). Translated by Peter Gay, in Neumann, *The Democratic and the Authoritarian State: Essays in Political and Legal Theory*, ed. Herbert Marcuse, 270–300. Glencoe, Ill.: Free Press, 1957.

Voltaire. *Philosophical Dictionary*. Translated with an Introduction and Glossary by Peter Gay. Preface by André Maurois. New York: Harcourt, Brace & World, 1962.

——. *Voltaire's Candide: A Bilingual Edition*. Translated and edited by Peter Gay. New York: St. Martin's Press, 1963.

F. INTRODUCTIONS AND TRANSLATED WORKS

Cassirer, Ernst. *Rousseau, Kant, and Goethe*. Translated by James Gutmann, Paul Oskar Kristeller, and John Herman Randall, Jr. New York: Harper Torchbooks, 1963. Introduction to the Torchbook Edition by Peter Gay. Reprint, Princeton: Princeton University Press, n.d.

Ségur, Philippe-Paul, comte de. *Napoleon's Russian Campaign*. Translated from the French by J. David Townsend. With a new introduction by Peter Gay, xvii–xxi. New York: Time Inc., 1965.

Lanson, Gustave. *Voltaire*. Translated by Robert A. Wagoner. Introduction by Peter Gay, 1–11. New York: John Wiley & Sons, 1966.

Bracher, Karl Dietrich. *The German Dictatorship: The Origins, Structure, and Effects of National Socialism*. Translated by Jean Steinberg. Introduction by Peter Gay, vii–ix. London: Weidenfeld & Nicolson, 1971.

La Tour du Pin Gouvernet, Henriette Lucie Dillon, marquise de. *Memoirs of Madame de La Tour du Pin*. Edited and translated by Felice Harcourt. Introduction by Peter Gay, 4A–4D. New York: McCall Pub. Co., 1971.

Staël, Madame de. *Ten Years of Exile*. Translated by Doris Beik. Introduction by Peter Gay, xix–xxix. New York: Saturday Review Press, 1972.

Rousseau, Jean Jacques. *On the Social Contract*. Translated and edited by Donald A. Cress. Introduction by Peter Gay, 1–11. Indianapolis: Hackett, 1987.

G. EDITED ANTHOLOGIES

With Shepard B. Clough and Charles K. Warner. *The European Past*. Vol. 1: *Reappraisals in History from the Renaissance Through Waterloo*. Vol. 2: *Reappraisals in History since Waterloo*. New York: Macmillan Co., 1964.

John Locke on Education. Classics in Education, no. 20. New York: Teachers College, Columbia University, 1964.

Deism: An Anthology. Princeton: D. van Nostrand, 1968.

Historians at Work. Vol. 1, with Gerald J. Cavanaugh: *Herodotus to Froissart*. New York: Harper & Row, 1972.

Historians at Work. Vol. 2, with Victor G. Wexler: *Valla to Gibbon*. New York: Harper & Row, 1972.

The Enlightenment: A Comprehensive Anthology. New York: Simon & Schuster, 1973.

Historians at Work. Vol. 3, with Victor G. Wexler: *Niebuhr to Maitland.* New York: Harper & Row, 1975.

Historians at Work. Vol. 4, with Gerald J. Cavanaugh: *Dilthey to Hofstadter.* New York: Harper & Row, 1975.

The Freud Reader. New York: Norton, 1989.

H. EDITED AND COLLECTED WORKS

Eighteenth-Century Studies Presented to Arthur M. Wilson. Edited by Peter Gay. Hanover, N.H.: University Press of New England, 1972.

The Columbia History of the World. Edited by John A. Garraty and Peter Gay. New York: Harper & Row, 1972.

I. REVIEW ESSAYS AND BOOK REVIEWS

The Conservative Mind from Burke to Santayana, by Russell Kirk. *Political Science Quarterly* 68 (December 1953): 586–88.

The Social Contract, Jean-Jacques Rousseau. *Political Science Quarterly* 70 (September 1955): 442–45.

Jean-Jacques Rousseau: A Critical Study of His Life and Writings, by F. C. Green. *Political Science Quarterly* 71 (June 1956): 292–93.

Diderot: The Testing Years, 1713–1759, by Arthur M. Wilson, and *Progress in the Age of Reason,* by R. V. Sampson. *Political Science Quarterly,* 72 (December 1957): 622–24.

A Diderot Pictorial Encyclopedia of Trades and Industry, Manufacturing and the Technical Arts, by Denis Diderot. *Political Science Quarterly* 75 (March 1960): 150–51.

The Calas Affair: Persecution, Toleration, and Heresy in Eighteenth-Century Toulouse, by David D. Bien. *Political Science Quarterly* 76 (June 1961): 309–11.

Selected Letters of Voltaire, trans. and ed. Theodore Besterman. *New York Review of Books* 2 (16 April 1964): 10.

The Age of Voltaire, by Will and Ariel Durant. *Book Week: The Sunday Herald Tribune,* 10 October 1965, 2–3.

Madness and Civilization: A History of Insanity in the Age of Reason, by Michel Foucault. *Commentary* 40 (October 1965): 93–96.

"Roots of Kultur." Review of *The Decline of the German Mandarins: The Ger-*

man Academic Community 1890–1933, by Fritz K. Ringer. *New Republic*, 22 February 1969, 27–29.

"Last of a Dying Species." Review of *Experiences*, by Arnold Toynbee. *New Republic*, 17 May 1969, 21–22.

"Neglected Books." Review of *French Ecclesiastical Society under the Ancien Régime: A Study of Angers in the Eighteenth Century*, by John McManners. *Amerian Scholar* 39 (spring 1970): 324, 326.

The Wish to be Free: Society, Psyche, and Value Change, by Fred Weinstein and Gerald M. Platt. *American Historical Review* 76 (December 1971): 132–33.

La Naissance de l'historiographie moderne, by Georges Lefebvre; *Perspectives on the European Past: Conversations with Historians*, by Norman F. Cantor; and *The Historian's Workshop: Original Essays by Sixteen Historians*, ed. L. P. Curtis, Jr. *American Historical Review* 77 (December 1972): 1403–5.

"Art in History" (review essay). *The American Scholar* 41 (autumn 1972): 660, 662, 664, 666, 668, 670, 672–73.

"George Lichtheim: 1972–1973" (review essay). *Partisan Review* 40 (1973): 461–66.

Art and Architecture of the Eighteenth Century in France, by Wend Graf Kalnein and Michael Levey. *Journal of the Society of Architectural Historians* 33 (October 1974): 265–66.

Allan Nevins on History, compiled and introduced by Ray Allen Billington. *New Republic* 173 (11 October 1975): 29–30.

Rousseau: The Self-Made Saint, by J. H. Huizinga, and *Voltaire and the Century of Light*, by A. Owen Aldridge. *New York Times Book Review*, 17 October 1976, 22, 24.

"A Guardian of the Shrine." Review of *Cosima Wagner: Die Tagebücher*, ed. Martin Gregor-Dellin and Dietrich Mack, vol. 1: 1869–1877, and *Richard Wagner: Das braune Buch, Tagebuchaufzeichnungen, 1865–1882*, ed. Joachim Bergfeld. *Times Literary Supplement*, 28 January 1977, 94.

"Urns into Chamber Pots." Review of *Karl Kraus and the Soul-Doctors*, by Thomas Szasz. *Times Literary Supplement*, 27 May 1977, 647.

"In the Worship of R." Review of *Cosima Wagner, Die Tagebücher*, ed. Martin Gregor-Dellin and Dietrich Mack, vol. 2: 1878–1883. *Times Literary Supplement*, 24 March 1978, 344.

"Hannah Arendt on Our Minds." Review of *The Life of the Mind*, vol. 1, by Hannah Arendt. *Washington Post Book World*, 26 March 1978, G1, G3.

"Performing for Hitler." Review of *A Confidential Matter: The Letters of Richard Strauss and Stefan Zweig, 1931–1935*, trans. Max Knight. *Times Literary Supplement*, 26 May 1978, 593.

"The Hannah Arendt of the Left." Review of *Injustice: The Social Bases of Obedience and Revolt*, by Barrington Moore, Jr. *New York Times Book Review*, 30 July 1978, 9, 21.

"A Genius of Self-Regard." Review of *Hermann Hesse: Pilgrim of Crisis*, by Ralph Freedman. *New York Times Book Review*, 21 January 1979, 3, 24–25.

"Aesthetic of the New." Review of *Selected Papers*, by Meyer Schapiro, vol. 2: *Modern Art: Nineteenth and Twentieth Centuries. Washington Post Book World*, 18 February 1979, E1, E4.

"Equal Billing." Review of *The Brothers Mann: The Lives of Heinrich and Thomas Mann, 1871–1950 and 1875–1955*, by Nigel Hamilton, and *From the Magic Mountain: Mann's Later Masterpieces*, by Henry Hatfield. *New York Times Book Review*, 5 August 1979, 7, 21.

"Isaiah Berlin: Historian of Ideas." Review of *Against the Current: Essays in the History of Ideas*, by Isaiah Berlin. *Washington Post Book World*, 10 February 1980, 3.

"Man of Myriad Minds." Review of *Voltaire: A Biography*, by Haydn Mason. *New Republic* 185 (15 August 1981): 37–38.

"A Homeland for Heroes." Review of *Evangelist of Race: The Germanic Vision of Houston Stewart Chamberlain*, by Geoffrey G. Field, and *Idealism Debased: From Völkisch Ideology to National Socialism*, by Roderick Stackelberg. *Times Literary Supplement*, 4 September 1981, 997.

"Painted Life." Review of *Charlotte: Life or Theater?* by Charlotte Salomon. *New York Times Book Review*, 8 November 1981, 14, 44–45.

"A Life of Thomas Mann." Review of *Thomas Mann: The Making of an Artist, 1875–1911*, by Richard Winston. *New York Times Book Review*, 3 January 1982, 9, 21–22.

"What We Don't Know about Mozart." Review of *Mozart*, by Wolfgang Hildesheimer. *London Review of Books* 5 (17 March 1983): 12.

"The Past Recaptured." Review of *Weimar Etudes*, by Henry Pachter. *Dissent* 30 (spring 1983): 261–63.

"Charismatic Manipulator." Review of *Brecht*, by Ronald Hayman. *New York Times Book Review*, 27 November 1983, 14, 18.

"A Revisionist View of Freud in Retreat." Review of *The Assault on Truth: Freud's Suppression of the Seduction Theory*, by Jeffrey Moussaieff Masson. *Philadelphia Inquirer Books/Leisure*, 5 February 1984, 1, 8.

"All Together Now: The Nineteenth Century's Stars and Lesser Lights." Review of *Nineteenth-Century Art*, by Robert Rosenblum and H. W. Janson. *Art and Antiques*, June 1984, 99–100.

"Prophet of the Full Life." Review of *Ruskin*, by George P. Landow, and *John Ruskin: The Early Years 1819–1859*, by Tim Hilton. *Times Literary Supplement*, 14 June 1985, 655–56.

"Learning from England." Review of *Little Germany: Exile and Asylum in Victorian England*, by Rosemary Ashton. *Times Literary Supplement*, 5 September 1986, 961.

"Personal Sources of a Theory." Review of *Freud's Discovery of Psychoanalysis: The Politics of Hysteria*, by William J. McGrath, and *Freud's Self-Analysis*, by Didier Anzieu. *Times Literary Supplement*, 3 October 1986, 1085.

"Make It Modern, Make It Plastic." Review of *The New Art . . . The New Life: The Collected Writings of Piet Mondrian*, trans. and ed. Harry Holtzman and Martin S. James. *New York Times Book Review*, 1 March 1987, 13–14.

"To the Editor" (on Dr. Max Eitingon). *New York Times Book Review*, 6 March 1988, 2, 33.

"Recognising Mozart." Review of *Mozart the Dramatist: The Value of His Operas to Him, to His Age and to Us*, by Brigid Brophy; *1791: Mozart's Last Year*, by H. C. Robbins Landon; and *Mozart: Studies of the Autograph Scores*, by Alan Tyson. *London Review of Books* 10 (7 July 1988): 15–16.

"Hochjuden." Review of *Jewish High Society in Old Regime Berlin*, by Deborah Hertz. *London Review of Books* 11 (5 January 1989): 27.

"Kissing Cure." Review of *The Clinical Diary of Sándor Ferenczi*, ed. Judith Dupont. *London Review of Books*, 11 (31 August 1989): 14.

"A Master Diplomat and a Good Hater." Review of *Bismarck and the Development of Germany*, by Otto Pflanze (3 vols.). *New York Times Book Review*, 26 January 1992, 12.

"Freud verstehen: Zu einem Essay von Ilse Grubrich-Simitis." Review of *Freuds Moses-Studie als Tagtraum*, by Ilse Grubrich-Simitis. *Psyche* 47 (October 1993): 973–83.

Hannah Arendt: Essays in Understanding, 1930–1954, ed. Jerome Kohn. *Dimensions: A Journal of Holocaust Studies* 8 (1994): 37, 40.

"They Weren't Thinking of England." Review of *The Making of Victorian Sexuality*, by Michael Mason. *Times Literary Supplement*, 20 May 1994, 22.

"Why Cooking Has Progressed More Than Sex." Review of *An Intimate History of Humanity*, by Theodore Zeldin. *New York Times Book Review*, 15 January 1995, 7.

"On Not Believing the Unbelievable." Review of *Bound upon a Wheel of Fire: Why So Many German Jews Made the Tragic Decision to Remain in Nazi Germany*, by John V. H. Dippel. *New York Times Book Review*, 23 June 1996, 13.

Jews, Germans, Memory: Reconstruction of Jewish Life in Germany, ed. Michael Bodemann. *Modernism/Modernity* 4 (April 1997): 205–8.

The Ufa Story: A History of Germany's Greatest Film Company, 1918–1945, by Klaus Kreimeier. *Dimensions: A Journal of Holocaust Studies* 11, no. 1 (1997): 35–38.

"Coping Gladstones." Review of *The Two Mr. Gladstones: A Study in Psychology and History*, by Travis L. Crosby. *Times Literary Supplement*, 16 May 1997, 12.

The Rise and Fall of Weimar Democracy, by Hans Mommsen. *The Historian* 60 (fall 1997): 178–79.

J. FOREIGN EDITIONS AND TRANSLATIONS
OF BOOKS BY PETER GAY

Das Dilemma des demokratischen Sozialismus: Eduard Bernsteins Auseinandersetzung mit Marx. Translated by Erwin Schuhmacher. Nuremberg: Nest, 1954.

Le Siècle de lumières: 1685 à 1800. 1974.

Voltaire politico: Il poeta come realista. Translated by Gino Scatasta. Bologna: Il Mulino, 1991.

O Estilo na história: Gibbon, Ranke, Macaulay, Burckhardt. Translated by Denise Bottmann. São Paolo: Companhia das Letras, 1990.

Style in History. Japanese ed. Tokyo, 1977.

História Universal. 5 vols. Translated by Jordi Beltrá, José Cano, Ignacio Herro, Jordi Mustieles, and Horacio Vazquez. 1981.

Die Republik der Außenseiter: Geist und Kultur in der Weimarer Zeit, 1918–1933. Translated by Helmut Lindemann. Introduction by Karl Dietrich Bracher. Frankfurt: Fischer, 1970; Fischer Taschenbuch, 1987.

Weimar Culture. Japanese ed. Misuzu Shobo, 1970.

Weimar Culture. London: Secker & Warburg, 1969. Harmondsworth: Penguin Books, 1974.

A cultura de Weimar. Translated by Laura Lúcia de Costa Braga. Rio de Janeiro: Paz e Terra, 1978.

La cultura de Weimar: La inclusión de lo excluido. Translated by Nora Catelli. Barcelona: Argos Vergara, 1984.

Freud, Juden und andere Deutsche: Herren und Opfer in der modernen Kultur. Translated by Karl Berisch. Hamburg: Hoffmann & Campe, 1986.
Freud, Jews, and Other Germans. Japanese ed. Translated by Keiko Kawachi. Tokyo: Shisaku-sha, 1987.
Freud, Juden und andere Deutsche. Munich: dtv Sachbuch, 1989.
Freud, gli ebrei e altri tedeschi: Dominatori e vittime nella cultura modernista. Translated by Salvatore Maddaloni. Rome: Laterza & figli, 1990.
Freud voor historici. Translated by Walter van Opzeeland. Foreword by Arthur Mitzman. Amsterdam: Wereldbibliotheek, 1987.
Storia e psicoanalisi. Translated by Gino Scatasta. Bologna: Il Mulino, 1989.
Freud para historiadores. Translated by Osmyr Faria Gabbi Júnior. São Paolo: Paz e Terra, 1989.
Freud für Historiker. Translated by Monika Noll. Tübingen: Edition Diskord, 1994.
Freud for Historians. Japanese ed. Translated by Atsuhiko Narita and Kouji Moriizumi. Tokyo: Iwanami Shoten, 1995.
"Ein gottloser Jude": Sigmund Freuds Atheismus und die Entwicklung der Psychoanalyse. Translated by Karl Berisch. Frankfurt: Fischer, 1988.
Un ebreo senza Dio: Freud, l'ateismo e le origini della psicoanalisi. Translated by Valeria Camporesi. Introduction by Pier Cesare Bori. Bologna: Il Mulino, 1989.
Un Juif sans Dieu: Freud, l'athéisme et la naissance de la psychanalyse. Translated by Kim Tran. Paris: Presses universitaires de France, 1989.
Um Judeu sem Deus: Freud, ateísmo e a construção da psicanálise. Translated by Davi Bogomoletz. Rio de Janeiro: Imago Editora, 1992.
A Godless Jew. Japanese ed. Tokyo: Misuzu Shobo, 1992.
Un Judío sin Dios: Freud, el ateísmo y la construcción del psicoanálisis. Translated by Cristina Pina. Prologue by Antonio Barrutia. Buenos Aires: Ada Korn, 1993.
Freud: A Life for Our Time. London: Dent, 1988. London: Papermac, 1989.
Freud: Una vita per i nostri tempi. Translated by Margherita Cerletti Novelletto. Preface by Arnaldo Novelletto. Milan: Bompiani, 1988.
Freud: Eine Biographie für unsere Zeit. Translated by Joachim A. Frank. Frankfurt: Fischer, 1989; Fischer Taschenbuch, 1995.
Freud: Zijn leven en werk. Translated by Bert van Rijswijk. Baarn, Neth.: Tirion, 1989.
Freud: Una vida de nuestro tiempo. Translated by Jorge Piatigorsky. Mexico City: Paidós, 1989. 2d ed., 1990.
Freud. Translated by Mirja Rutanen. Helsinki: Otava, 1990.

Freud: Une vie. Translated by Tina Jolas. Introduction by Catherine David. Paris: Hachette, 1991. 2 vol. paperback reprint also in *Collection Pluriel.*
Freud. Translated by Margareta Edgardh. Viborg, Denmark: Bonnier, 1991.
Freud. Hebrew ed. Tel Aviv: Dvir Publishing, 1993.
Freud: Uma vida para o nosso tempo. Translated by Denise Bottmann. São Paolo: Companhia das Letras, 1995.

Notes

CHAPTER 1

1. Richard Hofstadter, *The Paranoid Style in American Politics and Other Essays* (New York: Vintage Books, 1967), vii, cited by Peter Gay in *Freud, Jews, and Other Germans: Masters and Victims in Modernist Culture* (New York: Oxford, 1978), preface, vii, in regard to his own work.

2. Peter Gay, *Style in History* (New York: Basic Books, 1974), x.

3. Carl Becker, *The Heavenly City of the Eighteenth-Century Philosophers* (New Haven: Yale University Press, 1932); J. L. Talmon, *The Origins of Totalitarian Democracy* (London: Secker & Warburg, 1952); Irving Babbitt, *Rousseau and Romanticism* (Boston: Houghton Mifflin, 1919). For Gay's critiques of these texts, see "Carl Becker's Heavenly City" and "Reading about Rousseau," reproduced in Peter Gay, *The Party of Humanity: Essays in the French Enlightenment* (New York: Knopf, 1964), 188–210, 279–82, 223–25.

4. Peter Gay, *The Enlightenment: An Interpretation*, vol. 1: *The Rise of Modern Paganism* (New York: Knopf, 1966), 429.

5. As is clear from Gay's first article on the eighteenth century, "The Enlightenment in the History of Political Theory," *Political Science Quarterly* 69 (Sept. 1954): 374–89.

6. Ibid., 389.

7. "The historian, as historian, must first establish what he conceives the movement to have been," he commented. "It is only after this that he is ready to argue, as a political being, that it was something valuable. It would be naive to deny the political passions that underlie the arguments over historical facts: the historian who undertakes to clear the Enlightenment of what he regards as misinterpretations is usually an admirer of the Enlightenment" (Gay, *Party of Humanity*, 185).

8. Peter Gay, Introduction to Ernst Cassirer, *Rousseau, Kant, Goethe*, trans. James Gutman, Paul Oskar Kristeller, and John Herman Randall, Jr. (New York: Harper Torchbooks, 1963), x.

9. "Sigmund Freud, the thinker who above all others is supposed to have destroyed the foundation of Enlightenment rationalism, was the greatest child of the Enlightenment our century has known" (Gay, *Party of Humanity*, 270). See also id., *The Enlightenment: An Interpretation*, vol. 2: *The Science of Freedom* (New York: Knopf, 1969), 166.

10. Ibid.

11. Ives Hendrick, "Instinct and the Ego During Infancy," *Psychoanalytic Quarterly* 11 (1942): 40, 41. See also Hendrick, "Work and the Pleasure Principle," *Psychoanalytic Quarterly* 12 (1943): 311–29; and "The Discussion of the 'Instinct to Master,'" *Psychoanalytic Quarterly* 12 (1943): 561–65.

12. Peter Gay, *The Bourgeois Experience: Victoria to Freud*, vol. 4: *The Naked Heart* (New York: Norton, 1995), Introduction, 3.

13. Other historians at this time also felt the need to ground the study of past ideas in lived experience. See Robert Darnton, "In Search of the Enlightenment: Recent Attempts to Create a Social History of Ideas," *Journal of Modern History* 43 (1971): 113–32, and H. S. Hughes, "European Intellectual History, 1884–1984: The Socialization of Ideas," *International Forum* (Seoul) 9 (1986–87): 31–40.

14. Gay's first use of the phrase "the social history of ideas" can be found in *Party of Humanity*, ix–xii. For his fullest discussion, see "The Social History of Ideas: Ernst Cassirer and After," in *The Critical Spirit: Essays in Honor of Herbert Marcuse*, ed. Kurt H. Wolff and Barrington Moore, Jr. (Boston: Beacon Press, 1967), 106–20.

15. Peter Gay, *The Bridge of Criticism: Dialogues Among Lucian, Erasmus, and Voltaire on the Enlightenment— On History and Hope, Imagination and Reason, Constraint and Freedom—And on Its Meaning for Our Time* (New York: Harper & Row, 1970); François-Marie Arouet de Voltaire, *Voltaire's Candide: A Bilingual Edition*, trans. Peter Gay (New York: St. Martin's Press, 1963), and *Philosophical Dictionary*, trans. with an introduction and glossary by Peter Gay (New York: Harcourt, Brace & World, 1962); Ernst Cassirer, *The Question of Jean Jacques Rousseau*, trans. and ed. with an introduction and additional notes by Peter Gay (New York: Columbia University Press, 1954); *The Enlightenment: A Comprehensive Anthology*, ed. with introductory notes by Peter Gay (New York: Simon & Schuster, 1973); *Deism: An Anthology*, ed. Peter Gay (Princeton: D. van Nostrand, 1968); *John Locke on Education*, ed. Peter Gay, Classics in Education, no. 20 (New York: Teachers College, Columbia University, 1964).

16. Peter Gay, "Weimar Culture: The Outsider as Insider," *Perspectives in American History* 2 (1968): 11–93; id., *Weimar Culture: The Outsider as Insider* (New York: Harper & Row, 1968).

17. In addition to his *Weimar Culture* (1968), see Peter Gay (with Ruth Gay), "Musings in Munich," *American Scholar* 44 (winter 1974–75): 41–51; Peter Gay, *Art and Act: On Causes in History—Manet, Gropius, Mondrian* (New York: Harper & Row, 1976); and id., *Freud, Jews, and Other Germans*. See also Peter Gay, "The Intellectual Emigrés," *Humanities* 4 (Nov. 1985): 1–4; id., "Experiment in Denial: A Reading of the *Gartenlaube* in the Year 1890," in *Traditions of Experiment from the Enlightenment to the Present: Essays in Honor of Peter Demetz*, ed. Nancy Kaiser and David E. Wellbery (Ann Arbor: University of Michigan Press, 1992), 147–64; id., "Was ist Kultur?" in *Deutschlands Weg in die Moderne: Politik, Gesellschaft und Kultur im 19. Jahrhundert*, ed. Wolfgang Hardtwig and Harm-Hinrich Brandt (Munich: Beck,

1993), 45–63; and id., *The Bourgeois Experience, Victoria to Freud*, vol. 5: *Pleasure Wars* (New York: Norton, 1998).

18. Gay, *Freud, Jews, and Other Germans*, xiv.

19. Ibid., 19–26, 258–61.

20. See his impassioned and tightly argued preface and introduction to *Freud, Jews, and Other Germans* (1978).

21. Ibid., preface, ix.

22. Gay, "Weimar Culture: The Outsider as Insider," in *The Intellectual Migration: Europe and America, 1930–1960*, ed. Donald Fleming and Bernard Bailyn (Cambridge, Mass.: Harvard University Press, 1969), 11.

23. Gay, *Freud, Jews, and Other Germans*, 6.

24. See Gay, "*Bourgeoisophobes*," in *The Bourgeois Experience: Victoria to Freud*, vol. 5: *Pleasure Wars* (1998), 24–45.

25. Gay, "History, Biography, Psychoanalysis," in Evelyn Fox Keller, Peter Gay, E. H. Gombrich et al., *Three Cultures: Fifteen Lectures on the Confrontation of Academic Cultures* (The Hague: B. V. Universitaire Pers Rotterdam, 1989), 95.

26. Peter Gay, *Bourgeois Experience*, vol. 3: *The Cultivation of Hatred* (New York: Norton, 1993), 526. See also id., "On the Bourgeoisie: A Psychological Interpretation," in *Consciousness and Class Experience in Nineteenth-Century Europe*, ed. John Merriman (New York: Holmes & Meier, 1979), 179–203.

27. This reinterpretation was based in part on a reading of diaries and other personal documents uncovered by Gay and his wife Ruth, who was then a librarian in Yale's manuscript and archives division.

28. See also Peter Gay, "Aggression and Culture: A Psychoanalytic Perspective," *Syracuse Scholar: An Interdisciplinary Journal of Ideas* 2 (fall 1981): 26–35.

29. As Gay acknowledges, the lacuna in the set is a volume on Victorian religious belief and practices.

30. Peter Gay, "Liberalism and Regression," reproduced in *The Psychoanalytic Study of the Child* 37 (1982): 523–45.

31. Ibid., 524.

32. Peter Gay, "At Home in America," *American Scholar* 46 (winter 1976–77): 31. Our brief biographical sketch draws heavily on this article, supplemented by interviews with Gay conducted by Robert L. Dietle in February and March 1997.

33. On the struggle of German-born Jews to emigrate in the later 1930s, see Marion A. Kaplan, "When the Ordinary Became Extraordinary: German Jews Reacting to Nazi Persecution, 1933–1939," Chapter 15 of this volume.

34. Two of Gay's paternal aunts remained behind and were murdered in extermination camps.

35. Peter Gay, "Thinking About the Germans: I," *New York Times*, 3 Aug. 1976, 29.

36. Peter Gay, introduction to Karl Dietrich Bracher, *The German Dictatorship: The Origins, Structure, and Effects of National Socialism*, trans. Jean Steinberg (New

York: Praeger, 1970), vii. See also id., "At Home in America," 31–42; and id., "The German-Jewish Legacy—and I: Some Personal Reflections," in *American Jewish Archives*, vol. 40: *The German-Jewish Legacy in America, 1938–1988* (Nov. 1988), 203–10.

37. Dedication to Peter Gay, *A Loss of Mastery: Puritan Historians in Colonial America* (Berkeley and Los Angeles: University of California Press, 1966). We thank Helmut Smith for first suggesting the significance of this dedication.

38. Gay, "At Home in America," 31–42.

39. Ibid., 36.

40. On the transplantation of European intellectuals to North America, see Laura Fermi, *Illustrious Immigrants: The Intellectual Migration from Europe, 1930–41* (Chicago: University of Chicago Press, 1968); *Intellectual Migration*, ed. Fleming and Bailyn (1969); *The Legacy of the German Refugee Intellectuals*, special issue, *Salmagundi* (fall 1969–winter 1970); and H. Stuart Hughes, *The Sea Change: The Migration of Social Thought, 1930–1965* (New York: McGraw-Hill, 1975).

41. Richard Hofstadter, *Anti-Intellectualism in American Life* (New York: Vintage Books, 1963), 394.

42. For evocations of the time and place, see Terry A. Conney, *The Rise of the New York Intellectuals: Partisan Review and Its Circle* (Madison: University of Wisconsin Press, 1986), and Alan M. Wald, *The New York Intellectuals* (Chapel Hill: University of North Carolina Press, 1987), as well as the many memoirs and autobiographies of group members.

43. Nathan G. Hale, Jr., *The Rise and Crisis of Psychoanalysis in the United States: Freud and the Americans, 1917–1985* (New York: Oxford University Press, 1985), chs. 11–16.

44. See Richard Pells, *The Liberal Mind in a Conservative Age: American Intellectuals in the 1940s and 1950s* (New York: Harper & Row, 1985).

45. Richard Hofstadter, *The Age of Reform from Bryan to FDR* (New York: Knopf, 1955), and id., *Anti-Intellectualism in American Life*, both of which won Pulitzer Prizes.

46. Martin Jay, *Dialectical Imagination: A History of the Frankfurt School and the Institute of Social Research, 1923–1950* (Boston: Little, Brown, 1973), 39–40, 44, 114–15, 219–20.

47. Quoted in H. Stuart Hughes, "Franz Neumann Between Marxism and Liberal Democracy," in *Intellectual Migration*, ed. Fleming and Bailyn, 448.

48. Quoted in ibid., 459.

49. Franz Neumann, *Behemoth: The Structure and Practice of National Socialism, 1933–1944* (London: Oxford University Press, 1942); id., *The Democratic and the Authoritarian State: Essays in Political and Legal Theory*, ed. with a preface by Herbert Marcuse (Glencoe, Ill.: Free Press, 1957).

50. Before his death in an automobile accident in September 1954, Neumann's study of Freud was beginning to inform his work. His interest in psychoanalysis was

made explicit in a public lecture entitled "Anxiety and Politics" that Neumann delivered at the Free University of Berlin. Neumann asked Gay to translate the essay into English, and it was later included in Neumann's *The Democratic and the Authoritarian State*, 270–300.

51. Gay, "History, Biography, Psychoanalysis," in *Three Cultures*, 93.

52. Marcuse, "The Social Implications of Freudian 'Revisionism,'" *Dissent* 3 (summer 1955): 221–40.

53. See Robert S. Hartman, "Cassirer's Philosophy of Symbolic Forms," in *The Philosophy of Ernst Cassirer*, ed. Paul Arthur Schlipp (New York: Tudor Publishing Co., 1949), 291.

54. Quoted in Gay, *The Enlightenment: An Interpretation*, 1: xi.

55. The phrase "objectivity of the imagination" comes from Peter Gay, "The Social History of Ideas: Ernst Cassirer and After," in *The Critical Spirit: Essays in Honor of Herbert Marcuse*, ed. Kurt H. Wolff and Barrington Moore, Jr. (Boston: Beacon Press, 1967), 107.

56. Gay, *Style in History*, 198–99.

57. Gay, "History, Biography, Psychoanalysis," in *Three Lectures*, 94.

58. For an overview of Hofstadter's career, see *The Hofstadter Aegis: A Memorial*, ed. Stanley Elkins and Eric McKitrick (New York: Knopf, 1974), 300–367. For Gay on Hofstadter, consult *Historians at Work*, vol. 4: *Dilthey to Hofstadter*, ed. Peter Gay and Gerald J. Cavanaugh (New York: Harper & Row, 1975), 383–89.

59. See *The European Past*, ed. Peter Gay, Shepard B. Clough, and Charles K. Warner, vol. 1: *Reappraisals in History from the Renaissance Through Waterloo*; vol. 2: *Reappraisals in History since Waterloo* (New York: Macmillan, 1964); and *The Columbia History of the World*, ed. John A. Garraty and Peter Gay (New York: Harper & Row, 1972). See also the two-volume textbook Gay later co-authored with R. K. Webb: *Modern Europe to 1815* (New York: Harper & Row, 1973) and *Modern Europe since 1815* (New York: Harper & Row, 1973).

60. In "History, Biography, Psychoanalysis" (1989), 90, Gay traces his later interdisciplinarity in part to the eclectic disciplinary background of his early years.

61. Ruth Gay, *Jews in America: A Short History* (New York: Basic Books, 1965); id., *The Jews of Germany: A Historical Portrait*, with an introduction by Peter Gay (New Haven: Yale University Press, 1992); Ruth Gay, *Unfinished People: Eastern European Jews Encounter America* (New York: Norton, 1996).

62. Peter Gay, interview with Robert L. Dietle, Mar. 1997.

63. Gay's final year at Columbia was marred by campuswide political unrest. The events of 1968 divided the faculty and the department and for many professors further created the sense of an end of an era at the university.

64. For a photograph of the house, see Gay, *Art and Act*, 140.

65. Erich Fromm, *Escape from Freedom* (New York: Farrar & Rinehart, 1941); Richard Hofstadter, "The Paranoid Style in American Politics," *Harper's Magazine* (1963), reprinted in *Paranoid Style in American Politics and Other Essays*, ch. 1.

66. Peter Gay, "Rhetoric and Politics in the French Revolution," *American Historical Review* (1961), reprinted in *Party of Humanity*, ch. 6.

67. Peter Gay, *Freud for Historians* (New York: Oxford University Press, 1985), esp. 148–55, 181–87.

68. Many of Gay's chapter headings in the series—"A Profession of Anxiety," "Readers in Conflict," "Social Science as Cultural Symptom," "Regression to Polarities"—also reveal a psychologized perspective on his historical material.

69. Gay, *Bourgeois Experience*, vol. 1: *Education of the Senses*, 8.

70. Gay, *Freud for Historians*. See also Peter Gay, "Psychoanalysis in History," in *Psychology and Historical Interpretation*, ed. William McKinley Runyan (New York: Oxford University Press, 1988), 107–20, and "Symposium: Gay on Freud," *Psychohistory Review* 5 (fall 1986): 81–104.

71. Clearly, his work in these two areas overlapped. In *The Bourgeois Experience*, Gay frequently cites Freud as a cultural witness. Conversely, in *Freud: A Life for Our Time*, he periodically uses psychoanalytic modes of analysis in discussing his subject. On the last point, see Gay, "Psychoanalyzing the Psychoanalyst: Writing the Freud Biography," in *Essays in European History Selected from the Annual Meetings of the Southern Historical Association*, ed. June K. Burton (Lanham, Md.: University Press of America, 1989), 5–17.

72. Peter Gay, "Freud: For the Marble Tablet," in *Berggasse 19: Sigmund Freud's Home and Offices, Vienna 1938—The Photographs of Edmund Engelman* (New York: Basic Books, 1976), 13–54.

73. Peter Gay, personal communication to Robert L. Dietle, fall 1985.

74. Peter Gay, *Reading Freud: Explorations and Entertainments* (New Haven: Yale University Press, 1990); *The Freud Reader*, ed. id. (New York: Norton, 1989).

75. See Judith Miller, "New York Public Library Starts Center to Support Humanities Scholarship," *New York Times*, 30 July 1997, B3.

76. To be sure, other scholars of Gay's generation, outside this group, also contributed. Foremost among these historians are H. Stuart Hughes and Frank Manuel.

77. Eric J. Hobsbawm, *The Age of Extremes: A History of the World, 1914–1991* (New York: Oxford University Press, 1994), ix.

78. A comparative, book-length study of the circle would be welcome.

79. Nor do these sections exhaust the themes animating his work. Consider additionally Gay's writings on the history of history and the history of modern European Jewry. In the first category, see his *Loss of Mastery* (1966); "Burckhardt's *Renaissance*: Between Responsibility and Power," in *The Responsibility of Power: Historical Essays in Honor of Hajo Holborn*, ed. Leonard Krieger and Fritz Stern (Garden City, N.Y.: Doubleday, 1967), 183–98; "The History of History," *Horizon* 11 (autumn 1969): 112–19; *Historians at Work*, vol. 1: *Herodotus to Froissart*, ed. Peter Gay and Gerald J. Cavanaugh (New York: Harper & Row, 1972); *Historians at Work*, vol. 2: *Valla to Gibbon*, ed. Peter Gay and Victor G. Wexler (New York: Harper & Row, 1972); *Style in History* (1974); "History and the Facts," *Columbia Forum*, n.s., 3 (spring 1974): 7–14; *Histori-*

ans at Work, vol. 3: *Niebuhr to Maitland*, ed. Peter Gay and Victor G. Wexler (New York: Harper & Row, 1975); and *Historians at Work*, vol. 4: *Dilthey to Hofstadter*, ed. Peter Gay and Gerald J. Cavanaugh (New York: Harper & Row, 1975).

In the second category, see Gay's *Freud, Jews, and Other Germans* (1978), introduction, chs. 2, 3, 4; "Six Names in Search of an Interpretation: A Contribution to the Debate over Sigmund Freud's Jewishness," *Hebrew Union College Annual* 53 (1982): 295–307; *A Godless Jew: Freud, Atheism, and the Making of Psychoanalysis* (New Haven: Yale University Press, 1987); and "The German-Jewish Legacy—and I," *American Jewish Archives*, 1988: 203–10.

CHAPTER 2

1. Peter Gay, *The Enlightenment: An Interpretation*, vol. 2: *The Science of Freedom* (New York, 1969), 189. In the first volume, Hobbes appears chiefly as an Erastian and an alleged atheist. See Gay, *The Enlightenment: An Interpretation*, vol. 1, *The Rise of Modern Paganism* (New York, 1966), 316, 349, 402.

2. Gay, *Science of Freedom*, 189.

3. This essay draws heavily on Quentin Skinner, "*Scientia Civilis* in Classical Rhetoric and in the Early Hobbes," in *Political Discourse in Early Modern Britain*, ed. Nicholas Phillipson and Quentin Skinner (Cambridge, 1993), 67–93, and Quentin Skinner, *Reason and Rhetoric in the Philosophy of Hobbes* (Cambridge, 1996) but at the same time incorporates some important corrections and additions to my earlier arguments. For helping me to get clearer about the issues, and for reading successive drafts, I am especially indebted to Susan James and Karl Schuhmann. Note that all translations are my own unless otherwise specified.

4. Thomas Hobbes, *The Elements of Law Natural and Politic*, ed. Ferdinand Tönnies, 2d ed., introduction by M. M. Goldsmith (London, 1969), xvi. This edition will henceforth be cited as *The Elements of Law*. I have corrected Ferdinand Tönnies's numerous transcription mistakes by reference to the best surviving manuscript, B.L. Harl. MS 4235.

5. Thomas Hobbes, *De Cive: The Latin Version*, ed. Howard Warrender (Oxford, 1983), 77–78. Despite Warrender's claims to the contrary in his "Editor's Introduction" (ibid., pp. 4–8), the English version of *De Cive* was not made by Hobbes. Noel Malcolm, in Thomas Hobbes, *The Correspondence*, ed. id. (Oxford, 1994), 229n, has now identified the translator as the poet Charles Cotton. Since Cotton's version is misleading at several crucial points, I have preferred to make my own translations.

6. Thomas Hobbes, *Leviathan, or The Matter, Forme, & Power of a Commonwealth Ecclesiasticall and Civill*, ed. Richard Tuck (Cambridge, 1991), 129. Note too that, when Hobbes appends his diagram of the sciences to chapter 9 of *Leviathan*, he initially subdivides the basic category of science into natural and civil elements. See *Leviathan*, 61.

7. Thomas Hobbes, *Leviathan, sive De Materia, Forma, & Potestate Civitatis Ec-*

clesiasticae et Civilis, in *Thomae Hobbes Malmesburiensis Opera Philosophica Quae Latine scripsit, Omnia* (Amsterdam, 1668), 122.

8. For an outline of this aspect of humanist culture in Renaissance England, see Skinner, *Reason and Rhetoric in the Philosophy of Hobbes.*

9. For a discussion of these elements in the classical theory of written eloquence, see ibid., esp. 40–51.

10. On the fivefold character of the Renaissance *studia humanitatis*, and its individual elements as grammar, rhetoric, poetry, history, and moral philosophy, see P. O. Kristeller, "Humanism and Scholasticism in the Italian Renaissance," in *Renaissance Thought and Its Sources*, ed. M. Mooney (New York, 1979), 85–105. On the Elizabethan Grammar School curriculum, the standard work remains T. W. Baldwin, *William Shakspere's Small Latine & Lesse Greeke*, 2 vols. (Urbana, Ill., 1944). See also Kenneth Charlton, *Education in Renaissance England* (London, 1965), Joan Simon, *Education and Society in Tudor England* (Cambridge, 1979), and Skinner, *Reason and Rhetoric in the Philosophy of Hobbes*, esp. 26–40.

11. For the overwhelming concentration on these linguistic skills, see Kenneth Charlton, *Education in Renaissance England* (London, 1965), 116–19, and Anthony Grafton and Lisa Jardine, *From Humanism to the Humanities: Education and the Liberal Arts in Fifteenth- and Sixteenth-Century Europe* (London, 1986), 143–45. For a survey of grammar and rhetoric teaching in this period, see W. Keith Percival, "Grammar and Rhetoric in the Renaissance," in *Renaissance Eloquence: Studies in the Theory and Practice of Renaissance Rhetoric*, ed. James J. Murphy (Berkeley and Los Angeles, 1983), 303–30.

12. See, e.g., the 1566 statutes of Norwich Grammar School printed in H. W. Saunders, *A History of the Norwich Grammar School* (Norwich, 1932), esp. 147.

13. For an excellent discussion of Hobbes's later hostility to classical education and its allegedly subversive implications, see Martin Dzelzainis, "Milton's Classical Republicanism," in *Milton and Republicanism*, ed. David Armitage, Armand Himy, and Quentin Skinner (Cambridge, 1995), esp. 3–7.

14. See Cicero, *De inventione*, ed. and trans. H. M. Hubbell (London, 1949), 1.2.2, pp. 4–6, on the need for men as the *materia* of cities to congregate *in unum locum* and act together in a manner at once *utilis* and *honestus* if they are to realize their highest *opportunitas.*

15. See ibid. on how some *magnus vir* must have *compulit* this *materia.*

16. Ibid., p. 4.

17. Ibid., pp. 4–6. Cf. Cicero, *De oratore*, ed. and trans. E. W. Sutton and H. Rackham (London, 1942), 1.36.165, vol. 1, pp. 112–14.

18. On these activities as the highest duties of citizenship and at the same time as the characteristic abilities of the orator, see Skinner, *Reason and Rhetoric in the Philosophy of Hobbes*, esp. 66–87.

19. On the Ciceronian ideal of a union between reason and eloquence, and the revival of this ideal in the Renaissance, see Jerrold E. Seigel, *Rhetoric and Philosophy*

in Renaissance Humanism: The Union of Eloquence and Wisdom, Petrarch to Valla (Princeton, 1968).

20. Cicero, *De inventione* 1.1.1, p. 2: "civitatibus eloquentiam vero sine sapientia nimium obesse plerumque, prodesse nunquam."

21. Ibid. 1.1.1 and 1.2.3, pp. 2 and 6: *sapientia* is *tacita*, so that "sapientiam sine eloquentia parum prodesse civitatibus."

22. See ibid. 1.2.3, p. 6, on *ratio atque oratio*, and cf. 1.4.5, p. 12, on how, if *eloquentia* is added to *sapientia*, "ad rem publicam plurima commoda veniunt."

23. Ibid. 1.1.1, p. 2: "urbes constitutas . . . cum animi ratione tum facilius eloquentia."

24. See ibid. 1.5.6, p. 14, on *civilis scientia* and the fact that "Eius quaedam magna et ampla pars est artificiosa eloquentia quam rhetoricam vocant," and that "Officium autem eius facultatis videtur esse dicere apposite ad persuasionem finis persuadere dictione."

25. Cicero, *De oratore* 3.26.104, vol. 2, p. 82: "Summa autem laus eloquentiae est amplificare rem ornando."

26. Ibid. 3.27.104, vol. 2, p. 82: "vel cum conciliamus animos vel cum concitamus."

27. For an account of the *genus deliberativum*, see Skinner, *Reason and Rhetoric in the Philosophy of Hobbes*, esp. 41–44, 93–95, 114–15, and references there.

28. See Cicero, *De inventione* 1.2.2, pp. 4–6, on the "magnus videlicet vir et sapiens" who recognized "quanta ad maximas res opportunitas in animis inesset hominum."

29. Ibid. 1.2.3, p. 6: "fidem colere et iustitiam retinere discerent et aliis parere sua voluntate consuescerent."

30. Ibid. 1.2.2, p. 6: "primo propter insolentiam reclamantes."

31. See ibid. 1.2.3, p. 6, on *sapientia* as *tacita* and *inops dicendi*, and on the need for "homines ea que ratione invenissent eloquentia persuadere."

32. Ibid. 1.1.1, p. 2: "multas urbes constitutas, plurima bella restincta, firmissimas societates, sanctissimas amicitias intelligo cum animi ratione tum facilius eloquentia comparatas."

33. For an account of the *genus iudiciale*, see Skinner, *Reason and Rhetoric in the Philosophy of Hobbes*, esp. 41–45, 95–97, 116–17, and references there.

34. Quintilian, *Institutio oratoria*, ed. and trans. H. E. Butler, 4 vols. (London, 1920–22), 2.17.32, vol. 1, p. 338: "duos sapientes aliquando iustae causae in diversum trahant, (quando etiam pugnaturos eos inter se, si ratio ita duxerit, credunt)."

35. Ibid. 2.16.10, vol. 1, p. 322: "in utramque partem valet arma facundiae."

36. Cicero, *De oratore* 3.27.107, vol. 2, pp. 84–86: "de virtute, de officio, de aequo et bono, de dignitate, utilitate, honore, ignominia, praemio, poena similibusque de rebus in utramque partem dicendi animos et vim et artem habere debemus."

37. Ibid. 1.10.44, vol. 1, p. 32: "Missos facio mathematicos, grammaticos, musicos, quorum artibus vestra ista dicendi vis ne minima quidem societate contingitur."

38. Ibid., pp. 32–34: "ut in iudiciis ea causa, quamcumque tu dicis, melior et pro-

babilior esse videatur; ut in concionibus et sententiis dicendis ad persuadendum tua plurimum valeat oratio; denique ut prudentibus diserte stultis etiam vere dicere videaris."

39. Warrender, "Editor's Introduction," in Hobbes, *De Cive: The Latin Version*, 8–13; cf. ibid., 77–84.

40. Ibid., 77.

41. See ibid. on "Cicero, caeterique Philosophi Graeci, Latini," and cf. 77–78 on *scientia civilis* and on this form of *scientia* as "dignissima certe scientiarum."

42. See ibid., 77–78, on *scientia civilis* as a *doctrina officiorum*. Cicero had entitled his major treatise on moral philosophy *De officiis*. See Cicero, *De officiis*, ed. and trans. Walter Miller (Oxford, 1913).

43. See Hobbes, *De Cive: The Latin Version*, 77–78 on *scientia civilis* as a *scientia justitiae*.

44. This aspect of Hobbes's argument has largely been overlooked by recent commentators, who have generally assumed that for Hobbes all sciences must take the same anti-teleological form. But for a valuable corrective, see Noel Malcolm, "Hobbes's Science of Politics and His Theory of Science," in *Hobbes oggi*, ed. Andrea Napoli (Milan, 1990), 145–57. I am tempted to go further than Malcolm and add that Hobbes's Baconian conception of *scientia propter potentiam* gives a purposive orientation to his view of natural science as well.

45. On men as the *materia* of cities, see Hobbes, *De Cive: The Latin Version*, 79, para. 9. See, too, the title of the 1668 Latin *Leviathan* with its allusion to men as the *materia* of *civitates*.

46. Hobbes, *De Cive: The Latin Version*, 79–80; cf. Malcolm, "Hobbes's Science of Politics and His Theory of Science," esp. 147, 149, and 151–52.

47. See Hobbes, *De Cive: The Latin Version*, 78–79 on *civitates* being founded *vivendi causa* (para. 4) and in order to enable us, by means of right reasoning, to follow the *via regia pacis*.

48. Ibid., 79: "qua re utilius nihil excogitari potest." And see also ibid.on the *materia* and *forma* of cities.

49. Ibid., 79–80: "qualis sit natura humana, quibus rebus ad civitatem compaginandam apta vel inepta sit, & quomodo homines inter se componi debeant, qui coalescere volunt, recte intelligatur."

50. See ibid., 81, on the indispensability of following the dictates of *ratio*.

51. For an excellent analysis, concentrating on this aspect of *The Elements*, see David Johnston, *The Rhetoric of Leviathan: Thomas Hobbes and the Politics of Cultural Transformation* (Princeton, 1986), esp. 26–65, an account to which I am much indebted.

52. The Epistle Dedicatory of *The Elements* is signed "May 9th 1640." See Hobbes, *The Elements of Law*, ed. Tönnies, xvi.

53. Ibid., xv.

54. Ibid., 75, 99.

55. Ibid., xv.

56. Ibid., 89, 92.

57. Ibid., 116.   58. Ibid., 64.

59. Ibid., 22, 66.

60. Quintilian, *Institutio oratoria* 6.2.13–19, vol. 2, pp. 422–26.

61. Hobbes, *The Elements of Law*, ed. Tönnies, 1–2.

62. See Euclid, *The Elements of Geometrie*, trans. H. Billingsley (London, 1571).

63. Hobbes, *The Elements of Law*, ed. Tönnies, xv, xvi.

64. Ibid., xv.   65. Ibid., xvi.

66. Ibid., 1.   67. Ibid., 171.

68. Ibid., 176.   69. Ibid., 183.

70. See Hobbes, *De Cive: The Latin Version*, 76: "neque specie orationis, sed firmitudine rationum."

71. See ibid. 2.2, p. 100, and 15.4, p. 221, on "dictamina rectae rationis"; 3.19, p. 115, on how "ratio iubet"; 3.27, p. 118, and 15.14, p. 227, on how "ratio dictat"; and 15.15, p. 229, on how "ratio imperat."

72. Ibid. 13.9, p. 198: "opiniones non imperando, sed docendo, non terrore poenarum, sed perspicuitate rationum animis hominum inseruntur."

73. See ibid., *Epistola Dedicatoria*, p. 75 on the claim that such an argument can always be "utraque pars . . . tueatur."

74. Ibid. 10.12, p. 178: "contrariis sententiis orationibusque pugnant."

75. See ibid. 12.10, p. 191, speaking of topics "ad disserendum."

76. See ibid. 2.1, p. 98, on the methods "qui locum contra disputandi non relinquunt."

77. Hobbes is very emphatic that his conclusions in *De Cive* are not merely probable but demonstrated. See, e.g., ibid. 7.4, p. 152, and 15.1, p. 219.

78. Ibid., *Epistola Dedicatoria*, pp. 75–76: "commodo usus sit docendi principio . . . inde virtutis moralis officiorumque civilium Elementa, in hac opella, evidentissima connexione videor mihi demonstrasse."

79. The manuscript is preserved in the Bibliothèque Nationale as Fonds Latin MS 6566A. It is dated and discussed by Jean Jacquot and Harold Whitmore Jones in their introduction to Thomas Hobbes, *Critique du "De mundo" de Thomas White* (Paris, 1973), 12–13, 43–45.

80. B.N., Fonds Latin MS 6566A, fo. 451ʳ (cf. Hobbes, *Critique du "De mundo" de Thomas White*, ch. 39, para. 7, p. 432): "eos qui vere philosophantur, id est, eos qui certa via et fixo demonstrationis tramite incedunt."

81. B.N., Fonds Latin MS 6566A, fo. 451ᵛ (cf. Hobbes, *Critique du "De mundo" de Thomas White*, ch. 39, para. 7, p. 432): "eos qui philosophiam prae se ferunt sed vere tantummodo logicam, hoc est in utrumque disserendi facultatem in materia philosophica exercent."

82. B.N., Fonds Latin MS 6566A, fo. 451ᵛ (cf. Hobbes, *Critique du "De mundo" de Thomas White*, ch. 39, para. 7, p. 432): "Nam 'incedere via certa & fixo demonstrationis tramite,' id solius logicae est disserere autem in utramque partem posse, id a rhetoricae disciplina oritur."

83. B.N., Fonds Latin MS 6566A, fo. 452^r (cf. Hobbes, *Critique du "De mundo" de Thomas White*, ch. 39, para. 7, p. 433): "Certe ego, etsi omnia quae dixerim viderentur mihi demonstrata esse."

84. See Hobbes, *De Cive: The Latin Version*, 12.12, p. 192, for the claim that *sapientia* "oriturque partim a rerum ipsarum contemplatione, partim a verborum in propria & definita significatione acceptorum intelligentia."

85. Ibid.: "sententiae & conceptuum animi perspicua & elegans."

86. See ibid., p. 193, on true *Eloquentia* as a product of mastering the *Ars logica*, not the *Ars rhetorica*.

87. Ibid.: "eloquentia potens, separata a rerum scientia."

88. For suggestions about the influence of epistemological skepticism on the development of Hobbes's thought, see Arrigo Pacchi, *Convenzione e ipotesi nella formazione della filosofia naturale di Thomas Hobbes* (Florence, 1965), esp. 63–69, 97–100, and 179–83, and Anna Maria Battista, *Alle origini del pensiero politico libertino: Montaigne e Charron* (Milan, 1966), esp. 22, 53, 135, 145, and 172–75. The argument has been much taken up by more recent commentators. See Anna Maria Battista, "Come giudicano la 'politica' libertini e moralisti nella Francia del seicento," in *Il libertinismo in Europa* (Milan, 1980), 25–80; Marshall Missner, "Skepticism and Hobbes' Political Philosophy," *Journal of the History of Ideas* 44 (1983): 407–27; L. T. Sarasohn, "Motion and Morality: Pierre Gassendi, Thomas Hobbes and the Mechanical World-View," ibid. 46 (1985): 363–79; Victoria Kahn, *Rhetoric, Prudence and Skepticism in the Renaissance* (Ithaca, N.Y., 1985), esp. 154 and 181; Richard Tuck, *Hobbes* (Oxford, 1989), esp. 64, 93, and 102; Iain Hampsher-Monk, *A History of Modern Political Thought: Major Political Thinkers from Hobbes to Marx* (Oxford, 1992), esp. 4–6; Donald W. Hanson, "Science, Prudence, and Folly in Hobbes's Political Theory," *Political Theory* 21 (1993): 643–64, esp. 644–45; Richard E. Flathman, *Thomas Hobbes: Skepticism, Individuality, and Chastened Politics* (London, 1993), esp. 2–3, 43–47, and 51–52. But for an excellent corrective, see Tom Sorell, "Hobbes Without Doubt," *History of Philosophy Quarterly* 10 (1993): 121–35.

89. Thomas Hobbes, *De Cive: The English Version* (Oxford, 1983), 26.

90. He paused only in 1646 to make some revisions and additions to *De Cive*, the second edition of which appeared in 1647.

91. "Illustrations of the State of the Church during the Great Rebellion," *The Theologian and Ecclesiastic* 6 (1848): 172. Cf. B. D. Greenslade, "The Publication Date of Hobbes's 'Leviathan,'" *Notes and Queries* 220 (July 1975): 320.

92. "Illustrations of the State of the Church during the Great Rebellion," 223.

93. For these claims, see, respectively, Tuck, *Hobbes*, 28; D. D. Raphael, *Hobbes: Morals and Politics* (London, 1977), 13; Arnold A. Rogow, *Thomas Hobbes: Radical in the Service of Reaction* (New York, 1986), 126; and Howard Warrender, *The Political Philosophy of Hobbes: His Theory of Obligation* (Oxford, 1957), viii. For similar suggestions, see Jean Hampton, *Hobbes and the Social Contract Tradition* (Cambridge, 1986), 5, and Deborah Baumgold, *Hobbes's Political Theory* (Cambridge, 1988), 3, 11.

94. It has already been challenged in Johnston, *Rhetoric of Leviathan*, and Tom Sorell, *Hobbes* (London, 1986), two important books to which I am much indebted. I must also emphasize my debt to several valuable articles on contiguous themes, especially Frederick G. Whelan, "Language and Its Abuses in Hobbes' Political Philosophy," *American Political Science Review* 75 (1981): 59–75; Jeffrey Barnouw, "Persuasion in Hobbes's *Leviathan*," *Hobbes Studies* 1 (1988): 3–25; Conal Condren, "On the Rhetorical Foundations of *Leviathan*," *History of Political Thought* 11 (1990): 703–20; and Jeremy Rayner, "Hobbes and the Rhetoricians," *Hobbes Studies* 4 (1991): 76–95.

95. Hobbes, *Leviathan*, ed. Tuck, 37; cf. "perspicue demonstrare" in the 1668 Latin *Leviathan*, 39.

96. Hobbes, *Leviathan*, ed. Tuck, 110.

97. Ibid., 254.

98. A point excellently made in Missner, "Skepticism and Hobbes' Political Philosophy," esp. 419–21. For analogous points, see Whelan, "Languague and Its Abuses in Hobbes' Political Philosophy," 71; Johnston, *Rhetoric of Leviathan*, 98, 101–4; and Condren, "On the Rhetorical Foundations of *Leviathan*," 703–5.

99. But the seeds of Hobbes's later doubts can be traced to his account of the distinction between reason and right reason in chapter 30 of his *Critique* of White's *De mundo*, where he concedes that "it is to be doubted whether the reason of any one man can always be right, although everyone thinks their own reasoning is right alone." See B.N., Fonds Latin MS 6566A, fo. 348ᵛ (cf. Hobbes, *Critique du "De mundo" de Thomas White*, ch. 30, para. 22, p. 359): "dubitatur an ullius hominis ratio recta semper esse possit, putantque singuli suam solam rectam esse."

100. Hobbes, *De Cive: The Latin Version*, 14.19, *Annotatio*: "qui recte ratiocinari non solent, vel non valent, vel non curant."

101. Hobbes, *Leviathan*, ed. Tuck, 32.

102. John Dee, "Mathematical Preface" to Euclid, *Elements of Geometrie*, trans. Billingsley, sig. A, 1ᵛ.

103. Hobbes, *Leviathan*, ed. Tuck, 36; cf. the 1668 Latin *Leviathan*, 37–38, on geometry as an "ars magica."

104. Hobbes, *Leviathan*, ed. Tuck, 48.

105. Ibid., 304.

106. Ibid., 454.

107. See Cicero, *De inventione* 1.1.1, p. 2, on *ratio* and how "sine eloquentia parum prodesse civitatibus."

108. Ibid.: "urbes constitutas . . . cum animi ratione tum facilius eloquentia."

109. Quintilian, *Institutio oratoria* 5.14.29, vol. 2, p. 364.

110. Ibid., *Proemium*, 10, vol. 1, p. 10: "vir ille vere civilis . . . non alius sit profecto quam orator." See also Cicero, *De oratore* 1.8.34, vol. 1, p. 26.

111. Hobbes, *Leviathan*, ed. Tuck, 62; cf. 61.

112. Ibid., 181.

113. Ibid., 483. For commentary on this passage, see Gary Shapiro, "Reading and

Writing in the Text of Hobbes's *Leviathan*," *Journal of the History of Philosophy* 18 (1980): 157; Whelan, "Language and Its Abuses in Hobbes' Political Philosophy," 71; Johnston, *Rhetoric of Leviathan*, 130–2; Barnouw, "Persuasion in Hobbes's *Leviathan*," 3–4; Charles Cantalupo, *A Literary Leviathan: Thomas Hobbes's Masterpiece of Language* (Lewisburg, Pa., 1991), 20–23, 241–49; Raia Prokhovnik, *Rhetoric and Philosophy in Hobbes's Leviathan* (London, 1991), 120–22.

114. Hobbes, *Leviathan*, ed. Tuck, 483.

115. Ibid., 483–84.

116. Ibid., 1–2.

117. Ibid., 483.

118. Ibid., 177.

119. Ibid., 493.

120. Ibid., 483.

121. Ibid., 175–76.

122. Ibid., 484.

123. Ibid., 119–20, on the dangers posed by rhetoric to civil peace, and 132, 181, on the irrational impact of orators in public assemblies.

CHAPTER 3

1. I want to acknowledge the help of careful readings by John C. O'Neal (Hamilton College), Ron Rosbottom (Amherst College), and Peter Gay. This essay originated as a presentation to a forum sponsored by Williams College's Center for the Humanities and Social Sciences (Dec. 1993).

2. Bernard Grosperrin, *La Représentation de l'histoire de France dans l'historiographie des lumières* (Lille: Université de Lille, 1982), ch. 1 Citations are of Jean-Jacques Rousseau, *Emile, or On Education*, trans. Allan Bloom (New York: Basic Books, 1979), followed by reference in brackets to the Bibliothèque de la Pléiade edition of Rousseau's *Œuvres complètes*, ed. B. Gagnebin et al., vol. 4 (Paris: Gallimard, 1969). For what follows, see 110–12 [348–51].

3. Ibid., 110 [348].

4. The story is drawn from Plutarch's life of Alexander. The child conflates Alexander's taking of poison with his own recent experience of having to take bad-tasting medicine. Ibid., 110–11 [349–50].

5. Ibid., 111 [350].

6. Ibid., 111–12 [350].

7. On Rousseau's use of the theater as metaphor in *Emile* and its similarities to his *Lettre à d'Alembert*, see Suzanne Gearhart, *The Open Boundary of History and Fiction: A Critical Approach to the French Enlightenment* (Princeton: Princeton University Press, 1984), 271–78. Marc Eigeldinger, "La Vision de l'histoire dans l'*Emile*," in *L'Histoire au dix-huitième siècle*, Colloque d'Aix-en-Provence, Centre Aixois d'Etudes et recherches sur le XVIIIème siècle (Aix-en-Provence: EDISUD, 1980), also discusses history in *Emile*, but largely in relationship to his reflections on the past in other works, not in relation to the questions of knowing and teaching.

8. *Emile*, 237 [526]; for what follows, see 236–49 [526–41].

9. What follows is a classic example of that rhythm of search for transparency and

encounter with obstacles delineated brilliantly by Jean Starobinski, *La Transparence et l'obstacle* (Paris: Plon, 1957).

10. *Emile*, 238 [526–27].

11. Ibid., 238 [527].

12. "The ancient historians are filled with views which one could use even if the facts which present them were false. But we do not know how to get any true advantage from history. Critical erudition absorbs everything, as if it were very important whether a fact is true, provided that a useful teaching can be drawn from it. Sensible men ought to regard history as a tissue of fables whose moral is very appropriate to the human heart." Ibid., 156n [415].

13. Ibid., 238 [528].   14. Ibid., 239–41 [528–31].

15. Ibid., 239 [529].   16. Ibid., 242 [532].

17. Ibid., 247–48 [540–41].

18. The text used here is from François-Marie Arouet de Voltaire, *Œuvres complètes*, vol. 33 (Oxford: Voltaire Foundation, 1987). Translations are my own.

19. Ibid., 164.

20. E.g., François-Marie Arouet de Voltaire, *Le Pyrrhonisme de l'histoire* (1769) and *La Défense de mon oncle* (1767).

21. Voltaire, *Œuvres complètes*, 33: 170.

22. Ibid., 176.

23. Ibid., 177.

24. Ibid., 178. Voltaire adds a caveat as a bow to the censor: "unless this has been attested by men moved by the divine spirit."

25. Ibid., 178.   26. Ibid., 179.

27. Ibid., 180.   28. Ibid., 182.

29. Ibid., 184.   30. Ibid., 185–86.

31. Jean Le Rond d'Alembert, *Œuvres*, vol. 2, part 1 (rpt., Geneva: Slatkine, 1967), 1. Translations are my own.

32. Ibid., 2–3.   33. Ibid., 3–4. Emphasis in original.

34. Ibid., 4.   35. Ibid., 4–5.

36. Ibid., 5. Emphasis in original.

37. Ibid., 5–6. For example: "So many princes, whose characters people claim to have portrayed, *as if they had been their courtiers*, and whose policies they describe for us, *as if they had sat in on their councils*, would have a good laugh if they returned to earth, at the portrayals of them and the ideas attributed to them. At the Peace of Utrecht, the *politiques* of England heatedly argued among themselves as to whether Queen Anne had been right to support the peace. At this same moment a Cambridge professor was writing dissertations to prove that I-don't-know-what Greek emperor of the Byzantine empire had been right or not (I forget which) to make peace with the Bulgarians." Emphasis in original.

38. Ibid., 7.

39. Ibid., 7.

40. Ibid., 8.

41. Ibid., 8. This suggestion was commonplace among some educational reformers of the eighteenth century. See Grosperrin, *La Représentation de l'histoire de France dans l'historiographie des lumières*, 30–31.

42. Ibid., 8.

43. On the role of antiquity in Enlightenment thought, see esp. Peter Gay, *The Enlightenment: An Interpretation*, vol. 1: *The Rise of Modern Paganism* (New York: Knopf, 1965). For examples of the role of antique categories in Enlightenment thought about history, see Roger Schmidt, "Roger North's Examen: A Crisis in Historiography," *Eighteenth-Century Studies* [henceforth cited as *ECS*] 26, no. 1 (fall 1992): 57–76; Philip Hicks, "Bolingbroke, Clarendon, and the Role of the Classical Historian," *ECS* 20, no. 4 (summer 1987), 445–71; Cathérine Volpilhac-Auger, *Tacite et Montesquieu* (Oxford: Voltaire Foundation, 1985); and esp. George H. Nadel, "Philosophy of History Before Historicism," *History and Theory: Studies in the Philosophy of History* [henceforth cited as *HT*] 5 (1964): 291–315.

44. The best account of the development of Renaissance historical rhetoric is Nancy Struever, *The Language of History in the Renaissance* (Princeton: Princeton University Press, 1970). William J. Bouwsma, "Three Types of Historiography in Post-Renaissance Italy," *HT* 4 (1963): 302–14, is suggestive on the ways different styles of rhetoric fit different political situations in Italy, and is therefore suggestive for the eighteenth-century French case.

45. Nadel, "Philosophy of History Before Historicism."

46. In addition to the statements from Voltaire, Rousseau, and d'Alembert, see David Hume, "Of the Study of History," in *Essays Moral, Political and Literary* (Oxford: Oxford University Press, 1963); Edward Gibbon, "Essay on the Study of Literature," in *Miscellaneous Works*, ed. Lord John Sheffield (London: Blake, 1837), 625–70; Philip Hicks, "Bolingbroke, Clarendon, and the Role of the Classical Historian," *ECS* 20, no. 4 (summer 1987): 445–71; and the numerous citations of Nadel, "Philosophy of History Before Historicism."

47. On the development of value-free scientific and aesthetic categories in the Enlightenment, see esp. Ernst Cassirer, *The Philosophy of the Enlightenment* (Boston: Beacon Press, 1951), and Peter Gay, *The Enlightenment: An Interpretation*, vol. 2: *The Science of Freedom* (New York: Knopf, 1969). These developments were not, of course, wholly complete, as science was still closely related to questions of theodicy and human utility, and much art criticism still focused on the moral content of the art, even in the writings of someone as experimental as Diderot. In this context Voltaire's insistence on distinguishing *histoire naturelle* from true *histoire* is not an innocent judgment.

48. Philip Hicks, "Bolingbroke, Clarendon, and the Role of the Classical Historian," *ECS* 20, no. 4 (summer 1987): 445–71, provides the best summary of this *topos* in the context of his discussion of Bolingbroke's failed attempt to adopt this model.

49. On the creation and trajectory of the office of royal historiographer, see Orest

Ranum, *Artisans of Glory: Writers and Historical Thought in Seventeenth-Century France* (Chapel Hill: University of North Carolina Press, 1980). On Lenglet-Dufrenoy, see the accounts of Geraldine Sheridan, "Censorship and the Booktrade in France in the Early Eighteenth Century: Lenglet Dufresnoy's *Méthode pour étudier l'histoire*," *Studies in Voltaire and the Eighteenth Century* [henceforth cited as VS] 241 (1986): 95–107, and Lester A. Segal, "Nicolas Lenglet Du Fresnoy: Tradition and Change in French Historiographical Thought of the Early Eighteenth Century," VS 98 (1972): 69–117. On the role of the historiographer in the battle over the history of the monarchy, see Keith Michael Baker, *Inventing the French Revolution* (Cambridge: Cambridge University Press, 1990), chs. 2 and 3. See also Thomas Kaiser, "Rhetoric in Service of the King: The Abbé Dubos and the Concept of Public Judgment," *ECS* 23, no. 2 (winter 1989–90): 182–99, on the royalist Dubos and his conceptualization of the need for a new fact-oriented rhetoric in the battle for public opinion.

50. François-Marie Arouet de Voltaire, "Historiographe," in *Œuvres complètes*, vol. 33 (Oxford: Voltaire Foundation).

51. On the "métier" of historian in eighteenth-century France, see Henri Duranton, "Le Métier d'historien au dix-huitième siècle," *Revue d'histoire moderne et contemporaine* 23 (1976): 481–500, and "L'Académicien au miroir: L'Histoire idéale d'après les éloges de l'Académie des Inscriptions et des Belles-Lettres," in *L'Histoire au dix-huitième siècle*, Colloque d'Aix-en-Provence, Centre Aixois d'Etudes et recherches sur le XVIIIème siècle (Aix-en-Provence: EDISUD, 1980), 449–78.

52. On censorship, see Georges Benrekassa, "Savoir politique et connaissance historique à l'aube des lumières," VS 151 (1976): 261–85, and Sheridan, "Censorship and the Booktrade in France in the Early Eighteenth Century." Phyllis Leffler, "French Historians and the Challenge to Louis XIV's Absolutism," *French Historical Studies* 14 (1985): 1–22, shows how Boulainvilliers could work around censorship. François Furet, *In the Workshop of History* (Chicago: University of Chicago Press, 1984), ch. 7, also provides insight into Boulainvilliers's methods.

53. Grosperrin, *La Représentation de l'histoire de France dans l'historiographie des lumières*, 50–117, describes individually the many such publications. The most popular were those of Père Gabriel Daniel and Jean-François Lenglet-Dufrenoy. On the nature of the *artes historicae*, see also Jean-Pierre Guicciardi, "La Dialectique de la vérité et de l'erreur dans quelques *Artes Historicae*," in *L'Histoire au dix-huitième siècle*, Colloque d'Aix-en-Provence, Centre Aixois d'Etudes et recherches sur le XVIIIème siècle (Aix-en-Provence: EDISUD, 1980), 3–28.

54. Furet, *In the Workshop of History*, 80. For what follows, see esp. ibid., ch. 5, "The Birth of History in France"; Nadel, "Philosophy of History Before Historicism"; and, esp., Grosperrin, *La Représentation de l'histoire de France dans l'historiographie des lumières*.

55. Furet, *In the Workshop of History*, 84.

56. Etienne Bonnot de Condillac, "De l'étude de l'histoire," in *Œuvres* (Paris: Huel, 1798), 21: 1–145.

57. Grosperrin, *La Représentation de l'histoire de France dans l'historiographie des lumières*, 71–117, reviews many of these.

58. Ibid., 774–77.

59. On the role of censorship in composition of histories, see Ranum, *Artisans of Glory*; Sheridan, "Censorship and the Booktrade in France in the Early Eighteenth Century"; Duranton, "Le Métier d'historien au dix-huitième siècle"; and esp. Benrekassa, "Savoir politique et connaissance historique à l'aube des lumières."

60. On the creative role of the rhetorical view of history, see esp. Struever, *Language of History in the Renaissance*; and see Felix Gilbert, *Machiavelli and Guicciardini* (Princeton: Princeton University Press, 1965) on its two greatest practitioners.

61. On the Renaissance approach to the past, see Peter Burke, *The Renaissance Sense of the Past* (New York: St. Martin's Press, 1969).

62. On the French school, see Donald R. Kelley, "Ancient Verses on New Ideas: Legal Tradition and the French Historical School," *HT* 9 (1970): 173–94, and J. G. A. Pocock, *The Ancient Constitution and the Feudal Law: A Study of English Historical Thought in the Seventeenth Century* (Cambridge: Cambridge University Press, 1957). The work of Joseph M. Levine, "Ancients, Moderns, and History: The Continuity of English Historical Writing in the Later Seventeenth Century," in *Studies in Change and Revolution: Aspects of English Intellectual History, 1640–1800*, ed. Paul J. Korshin (Menston: Scolar Press, 1972) provides parallel accounts for the British case.

63. The classic study of someone so motivated is Lionel Gossman, *Medievalism and the Ideologies of Enlightenment: The World and Work of La Curne de Saint-Palaye* (Baltimore: Johns Hopkins Press, 1968) on the medievalist work of Saint-Palaye. On the image of the antiquarian, see Duranton, "L'Académicien au miroir."

64. On the relationship of this question to the battle of Ancients and Moderns, see Levine, "Ancients, Moderns, and History."

65. See, e.g., the criticism, coupled with grudging gratitude, in Jean Le Rond d'Alembert, *Preliminary Discourse to the Encyclopedia of Diderot*, trans. Richard Schwab (Indianapolis: Bobbs-Merrill, 1963), 63–64. Gibbon, the one major Enlightenment figure who thought he saw the way to combine fruitfully the labors of the erudite with the graceful style of the rhetorician, took d'Alembert to task for these words in his youthful "Essay on the Study of Literature" (cited n. 46 above). On the antiquarians and on Gibbon's relationship to them, see esp. Arnaldo Momigliano, *Studies in Historiography* (New York: Harper, 1965), chs. 1–2.

66. On the history of skepticism, see Richard Henry Popkin, *The History of Scepticism From Erasmus to Descartes* (The Hague: Van Gorcum, 1960). On the relationship of the *érudits* and *antiquaires* to Pyrrhonism, see Momigliano, *Studies in Historiography*, ch. 1.

67. See esp. Ian Hacking, *The Taming of Chance* (Cambridge: Cambridge University Press, 1990); Lorraine Daston, *Classical Probability in the Enlightenment* (Princeton: Princeton University Press, 1988); Barbara Shapiro, *Probability and Certainty in Seventeenth-Century England* (Princeton: Princeton University Press, 1983);

and id., *"Beyond Reasonable Doubt" and "Probable Cause": Historical Perspectives on the Anglo-American Law of Evidence* (Berkeley and Los Angeles: University of California Press, 1991).

68. John Craig, *Craig's Rules of Historical Evidence; from Joannis Craig, Theologiae Christianae principia mathematica (Londinium impensis Timothei Child. 1699)*, HT suppl. 4 (The Hague: Mouton; Middletown, Conn.: Wesleyan University Press, 1964).

69. Daston, *Classical Probability in the Enlightenment*, 33–34.

70. See R. M. Burns, *The Great Debate on Miracles* (Lewisburg, Pa.: Bucknell University Press, 1981). Also, this was the period that saw the development of the concept of "beyond reasonable doubt" in Anglo-Saxon jurisprudence. See Shapiro, *"Beyond Reasonable Doubt" and "Probable Cause."*

71. For what follows, see esp., Erica Harth, *Ideology and Culture in Seventeenth-Century France* (Ithaca, N.Y.: Cornell University Press, 1983), ch. 4; Georges May, *Le Dilemme du roman au dix-huitième siècle* (Paris: Presses universitaires de France, 1963), ch. 5; John F. Tinkler, "Humanist History and the English Novel in the Eighteenth Century," in *Studies in Philology* (Chapel Hill: University of North Carolina Press, 1988); Everett Zimmerman, "Fragments of History and *The Man of Feeling*," ECS 23, no. 3 (spring 1990): 283–300; Stuart Peterfreund, "Sterne and Late Eighteenth-Century Ideas of History," *Eighteenth-Century Life* 7, no. 1 (1881): 25–53; Hamilton Beck, "The Novel Between 1740 and 1780: Parody and Historiography," *Journal of the History of Ideas* 46 (1985): 405–16; Marlou Switten, *"L'histoire* and *la poésie* in Diderot's Writings on the Novel," *Romanic Review* 47 (1956): 259–69.

72. On the very suggestive role of the categories of classical rhetoric, John F. Tinkler, "The Rhetorical Method of Francis Bacon's *History of the Reign of King Henry VII*," HT 26 (1987): 32–52, is most helpful.

73. See Switten, *"L'histoire* and *la poésie* in Diderot's Writings on the Novel"; Peterfreund, "Sterne and Late Eighteenth-Century Ideas of History"; and Beck, "The Novel Between 1740 and 1780," on the growing self-reflexivity.

74. Harth, *Ideology and Culture in Seventeenth-Century France*, 145. For a reprint of the 1683 edition, see Du Plaisir, *Sentiments sur les lettres et sur l'histoire avec des scrupules sur le style*, ed. Philippe Hourcade (Geneva: Droz, 1975).

75. As summarized in May, *Le Dilemme du roman au dix-huitième siècle*, 141–42.

76. As quoted in Switten, *"L'histoire* and *la poésie* in Diderot's Writings on the Novel," 261. The translation is my own.

77. See Suzanne Gearhart, "Rationality and the Text: A Study of Voltaire's Historiography," VS 140 (1975): 21–43; id., *Open Boundary of History and Fiction* (cited n. 7 above), and Hayden White, "The Irrational and the Problem of Historical Knowledge in the Enlightenment," in *Tropics of Discourse* (Baltimore: Johns Hopkins University Press, 1978), 135–49.

78. See Dennis F. Essar, "The Language Theory, Epistemology, and Aesthetics of Jean Le Rond d'Alembert," VS 149 (1976), for the fullest description of d'Alembert's habits of mind.

CHAPTER 4

Research for this paper was supported by grants from the National Institutes of Health, the Culpeper Foundation, and the Senate of the University of California. I wish to express my gratitude for their generosity.

1. Peter Gay, *The Party of Humanity: Essays in the French Enlightenment* (New York: Knopf, 1964).

2. Peter Gay, *The Enlightenment: An Interpretation*, vol. 1: *The Rise of Modern Paganism*; vol. 2: *The Science of Freedom* (New York: Knopf, 1966–69).

3. Jacques Tenon, *Mémoires sur les hôpitaux de Paris* (Paris: Pierres, 1788); for the English version, see Dora B. Weiner, ed. and annot., *Tenon's Memoirs on Paris Hospitals* (Canton, Mass.: Science History Publications, 1997).

4. See Dora B. Weiner, trans. and ed., *The Clinical Training of Doctors: An Essay of 1793 by Philippe Pinel* (Baltimore: Johns Hopkins University Press, 1980).

5. For information about these periodicals, see *Dictionnaire des journaux, 1600–1789*, ed. Jean Sgard, Jean-Daniel Candaux et al. (Paris: Universitas, 1991).

6. Letter to his brother Pierre, dated 12 Jan. 1783 in *Lettres de Pinel*, ed. Casimir Pinel (Paris: Masson, 1859), 41–43.

7. Pierre Chabbert, "Philippe Pinel à Paris (jusqu'à sa nomination à Bicêtre)," in *Aktuelle Probleme aus der Geschichte der Medizin: Proceedings of the XIX International Congress of the History of Medicine* (Basel: Karger, 1966), 589–95. See also id., "L'Œuvre médicale de Philippe Pinel," in 96ème Congrès national des sociétés savantes, *Comptes-rendus* (Paris: Bibliothèque Nationale, 1974), 1: 153–61.

8. Pierre Chabbert, "Un Rival heureux de Pinel: Desmarescaux," *Monspeliensis Hippocrates* 4 (1961): 17–23.

9. Michel Caire, "Philippe Pinel en 1784: Un Médecin "étranger" devant la Faculté de médecine de Paris," *Histoire des sciences médicales* 29, no. 3 (1995): 243–51.

10. Chabbert, "Philipe Pinel à Paris," 591.

11. Lettre à Desfontaines, *Lettres de Pinel*, ed. C. Pinel, 45.

12. Philippe Pinel, *Traité médico-philosophique sur l'aliénation mentale ou la manie*, 1st ed. (Paris: Richard, Caille & Ravier, An IX [1800–1801]), 54–57.

13. Société royale de médecine, *Histoire et mémoires*, 10 vols. (Paris: Pierres, 1776–89), 5: 17, and *Gazette de santé*, 1784, no. 19: 75.

14. Philippe Pinel, "Recherches et observations sur le traitement moral des aliénés," *Mémoires de la société médicale d'émulation* 2 (An VII [1798–99]): 218 n. 1.

15. See Roselyne Rey, "*Gazette de santé*," in *Dictionnaire*, ed. Sgard et al. (cited n. 5 above), 1: 495–99.

16. *Gazette de santé*, 1785, "Avertissement."

17. Pinel, "Lettre à Desfontaines," 46, 48.

18. See Dora B. Weiner, "Health and Mental Health in the Thought of Philippe Pinel: The Emergence of Psychiatry During the French Revolution," in *Healing and*

History: Essays for George Rosen, ed. Charles E. Rosenberg (New York: Dawson Science History Publications, 1979), 59–85.

19. *Gazette de santé*, 1788, no. 51: 201–2.

20. Ibid., 1787, no. 25.

21. Ibid., 1787, no. 30: 117–18.

22. Pedro Marset Campos, "El punto de partida de la obra psiquiátrica de Pinel: Análisis de la producción psiquiátrica de Ph. Pinel anterior al 'Traité sur la manie' (1784–1801)" (M.D. thesis, Valencia, 1971); id., résumé of thesis, in *Medicina española* 65 (1971): 390–404; and id., "Veinte publicaciones psiquiátricas de Pinel olvidadas: Contribución al estudio de los orígenes del 'Traité sur la manie,'" *Episteme* 6 (1972): 163–95.

23. Pierre Chabbert and Philippe Mangin, "Les Premières publications de Philippe Pinel consacrées à la médecine mentale," in *Actes du XXVII Congrès international d'histoire de la médecine* (Barcelona, 1980), 42–47, and Jacques Postel, "Les Premières expériences psychiatriques de Philippe Pinel à la Maison de santé Belhomme," *Revue canadienne de psychiatrie* 28 (1983): 571–76.

24. Marset, "Veinte publicaciónes," 167–73.

25. Philippe Pinel, "Lettre sur l'impotence," *Gazette de santé*, 1786, no. 45: 179–80; id., "Considerations sur l'empire de la coutume . . . ," ibid., 1788, no. 32: 125–27.

26. David Stuart, *Disputatio medica de mania* (Edinburgh: Balfour, Auld & Smellie, 1770).

27. *Gazette de santé*, 1785, no. 3: 10–12.

28. "Observations communiquées par M. Régis Rey de Cazillac," ibid., 1785, no. 22: 85–86.

29. "Remarques sur les effets physiques que produisent certaines affections morales, telles que la crainte et la tristesse souvent renouvellées," ibid., 1786, no. 28: 109–10.

30. "Observation sur une mélancolie nerveuse dégénérée en manie," ibid., 1786, no. 9: 34–35.

31. *Gazette de santé*, 1785, no. 43: 171–72.

32. The phrase was coined by Esquirol in *Des établissements d'aliénés en France, et des moyens d'améliorer le sort de ces infortunés. Mémoire présenté à Son Excellence le Ministre de l'Intérieur en septembre 1818* (Paris: Huzard, 1819), 12.

33. *Gazette de santé*, 1787, no. 5: 17–18.

34. Ibid., 1787, no. 26: 102–3.

35. Ibid., 1787, no. 51: 205–6. On Pinel's presumed indebtedness to Smyth, see Othmar Keel, *La Généalogie de l'histopathologie: Une Révision déchirante, Philippe Pinel, lecteur discret de J. C. Smyth (1741–1821)* (Paris: Vrin, 1979), critically reviewed by Dora B. Weiner in *Archives internationales d'histoire des sciences* 33 (1983): 386–89.

36. *Gazette de santé*, 1787, no. 44; and no. 48: 189–190.

37. Ibid., 1788, no. 12, 47–48.

38. Ibid., 1787, no. 37, 145–46.

39. Rey, "*Gazette de santé*," 499.

40. The article on the *Journal de médecine, chirurgie et pharmacie* by Roselyne Rey appears under the journal's original title, *Recueil périodique d'observations de médecine, de chirurgie et de pharmacie*, in the *Dictionnaire des journaux*, ed. Sgard et al. (cited n. 5 above), 2: 1063–67.

41. "Avis à MM. les souscripteurs," *Gazette de santé*, 1789, no. 52.

42. "MM. de la classe d'anatomie ont présenté MM. Broussonet, Chambon et Pinel: Les Premières voix ont été pour M. Broussonet, les deuxièmes pour M. Chambon," *Procès-verbaux de l'Académie des sciences*, 104: 108.

43. This copy is in the Bibliothèque de l'Institut de France.

44. Philippe Pinel, "Sur le mécanisme des luxations de l'humérus," 15.

45. Philippe Pinel, "Sur une nouvelle méthode de classification des quadrupèdes, fondée sur la structure mécanique des parties osseuses qui servent á l'articulation de la mâchoire inférieure," *Journal de Physique* 41 (1792): 401–14 (according to a personal communication from Charles C. Gillispie of Princeton, the method used in this memoir prefigures the thought of Cuvier, who may well have known it).

46. Philippe Pinel, "Nouvelles observations sur la structure et la conformation des os de la tête de l'éléphant," ibid. 43 (1793): 47–60; and id., with Deyeux, "Observations sur le cerveau ossifié d'un bœuf," ibid. 42 (1793): 462–70.

47. A. N. Millin, P. Pinel, and A. Brongniart, *Rapport fait à la Société d'histoire naturelle de Paris sur la nécessité d'établir une ménagerie, le 14 décembre 1792* (Paris: Boileau, 1792), 4 pp.

48. *Journal de physique* 39 (1791): 138–51. In this connection, see Silvia Collini and Antonella Vannoni, "La Società d'histoire naturelle e il viaggio di d'Entrecasteaux alla ricerca di Lapérouse: Le istruzioni scientifiche per i viaggiatori. I. Documenti di Jean Baptiste Lamarck e Philippe Pinel. II. Documenti inediti di L. C. M. Richard, Lezerme e E. F. Fourcroy," *Nuncius* 10 (1995): 257–91; 11 (1996): 227–75. See also Dora B. Weiner, "The Scientific Origins of Psychiatry in the French Revolution," in *Proceedings of the 1st European Congress on the History of Psychiatry and Mental Health Care*, ed. Leonie de Goei and Joost Vijselaar (Rotterdam: Erasmus Publishing, 1993), 314–30.

49. William Cullen, *Institutions de médecine pratique, traduites sur la quatrième et dernière édition de l'ouvrage anglais de M. Cullen, Professeur de médecine pratique dans l'Université d'Edimbourg, etc., Premier médecin du roi pour l'Ecosse*, trans. Philippe Pinel, 2 vols. (Paris: Duplain, 1785).

50. F. G. Boisseau, in *Biographie du Dictionnaire des sciences médicales*, s.v. "Cullen."

51. Philippe Pinel, *Nosographie philosophique, ou Méthode de l'analyse appliquée à la médecine* (Paris: Brosson, 1798; 2d ed., 3 vols., 1802–3; 3d ed., 1807; 4th ed. 1810; 5th ed., 1813; 6th ed., 1818).

52. Chabbert, "Philippe Pinel à Paris," 593.

53. Philippe Pinel, *Gazette de santé*, 1785, no. 43: 169–70.

54. Giorgio Baglivi, *Opera omnia* (Lyon: Anisson & J. Posuel, 1714).

55. Arturo Castiglioni, *A History of Medicine*, trans. E. B. Krumbhaar (New York: Knopf, 1947), 548.

56. Giorgio Baglivi, *Opera omnia medico-practica*, trans. and ed. Philippe Pinel, 2 vols. (Paris: Duplain, 1788).

57. Philippe Pinel, letter to Desfontaines, 27 Nov. 1784.

58. Philippe Pinel, *Traité médico-philosophique sur l'aliénation mentale*, 2d ed. (Paris: Brosson, 1809), 383.

59. This is a manuscript of 29 folios, "Registre d'entrée s'échelonnant de 1804 à 1810 de la maison de santé du Dr. Belhomme [sic] rue de Charonne." A detailed analysis is forthcoming. The best study of the maison Belhomme is René Bénard, "Une Maison de santé psychiatrique sous la révolution: La Maison Belhomme," *Semaine des hôpitaux* (32) 1956: 3990–4000. Bénard discovered a police register naming 112 persons lodged in Belhomme's home between 5 Aug. 1793 and 7 Feb. 1795. Archives de la Préfecture de Police, AB 316 (3994 n. 2). See also Archives nationales, D V 5 no. 58, F 7 4706 and 4774.

60. Postel, "Premières expériences," 571–76.

61. Sergio Moravia, "La Société d'Auteuil et la révolution," *Dix-huitième siècle* 6 (1974): 181–91; still useful for individual anecdotes, Antoine Guillois, *Le Salon de Madame Helvétius* (Paris: Calmann-Lévy, 1894).

62. The literature on Ideology is huge. Among the best sources are Sergio Moravia, *Il pensiero degli Idéologues: Scienza e filosofia in Francia, 1780–1815* (Florence: Nuova Italia, 1974); id., "Les Idéologues et l'âge des Lumières," *Studies on Voltaire and the Eighteenth Century* 154 (1976): 1465–86; and Georges Gusdorf, *La Conscience révolutionnaire: Les Idéologues* (Paris: Payot, 1978).

63. On Cabanis, see Martin S. Staum, *Cabanis: Enlightenment and Medical Philosophy in the French Revolution* (Princeton: Princeton University Press, 1980); Sergio Moravia, "'Moral'–'Physique': Genesis and Evolution of a 'Rapport,'" in *Enlightenment Studies in Honour of Lester Crocker*, ed. J. Bingham and V. W. Topezio (Oxford: Voltaire Foundation, 1979), 163–74; F. Colonna d'Istria, "La Logique de la médecine d'après Cabanis," *Revue de métaphysique et de morale* 24 (1917): 59–73; and id., "L'Aliénation mentale d'après Pinel," *Revue scientifique* 20 (1899): 619–25.

64. In 1788 in the *Journal de Paris*, under the rubric "Médecine": "Ne doit-on pas veiller avec un nouveau soin sur sa santé aux approches du printemps?" 28 Mar., 386–87; "Remarques diététiques sur l'usage de la poire," 2 Nov., 1307–8.

In 1789: "Observations sur le régime moral qui est plus propre à rétablir, dans certains cas, la raison égarée des maniaques," 17 Feb., 211–12.

In 1790 in the *Journal gratuit*, neuvième classe (Santé): "Exemple d'une fièvre lente nerveuse," nos. 1–2, 15–20; "Reflexions médicales sur l'état monastique," no. 6, 89–93; "Suite pratique sur les variétés de l'impression des médicaments, relativement aux divers degrés de sensibilité et d'irritabilité des individus," no. 21, 13 Dec., 321–27.

65. See n. 45 above.

66. *La Médecine éclairée par les sciences physiques ou Journal des découvertes relatives aux différentes parties de l'art de guérir* 2 (1791): 23–24.

67. Ibid., 39–42; 3 (1792): 60–64, 126–28.

68. Philippe Pinel, "Recherches sur l'étiologie, ou la mécanisme de la luxation de la mâchoire inférieure," *La Médecine éclairée* 3 (1792): 183–92.

69. Philippe Pinel, "Reflections sur la buanderie," *La Médecine éclairée* 2 (1791): 12–21.

70. Philippe Pinel, "Observations sur une espèce particulière de mélancolie qui conduit au suicide," *La Médecine éclairée* 1 (1791): 154–59, 189–91.

71. Philippe Pinel, *Traité médico-philosophique sur l'aliénation mentale*, 1st ed. (cited n. 12 above), 187–88, 146–48, 241–42.

72. Jacques Postel, "Philippe Pinel: 'Observations sur une espèce particulière de mélancolie qui conduit au suicide,'" *Information psychiatrique* 54 (1978): 1137–41.

73. Introduction, *La Médecine éclairée* 1 (1791): 44–45.

74. *Abrégé des transactions philosophiques de la Société royale de Londres*, ed. Jacques Gibelin, 12 vols. (Paris: Buisson, 1790–91), 1: xxiv–xxv.

75. *Abrégé des transactions philosophiques de la Société royale de Londres*, vol. 5, *Chimie*, ed. Philippe Pinel (Paris: Buisson, 1791), Introduction, i.

76. *Abrégé des transactions philosophiques de la Société royale de Londres*, vol. 7, *Médecine et chirugie*, ed. Philippe Pinel (Paris: Buisson, 1791), *Avant-propos*, 7.

77. Philippe Pinel, "Dose et doser," in *Encyclopédie méthodique: Médecine* (1792), 5: 512.

78. Ibid.

79. Philippe Pinel, "Dose et doser," in *Dictionnaire des sciences médicales* (1814), 10: 151–69.

80. *La Médecine éclairée* 3 (1792): 117.

81. *Journal de Paris*, 1790, no. 18 (Jan. 18): 70–72; *L'Esprit des journaux* 19 (Feb. 1790): 365–68.

82. Philippe Pinel, *Lettres*, ed. C. Pinel, 10–12.

83. For an English version, see Dora B. Weiner, "Philippe Pinel's 'Memoir on Madness' of December 11, 1794: A Fundamental Text of Modern Psychiatry," *American Journal of Psychiatry* 149, no. 6 (1992): 725–32.

84. See Dora B. Weiner, *Comprendre et soigner: Pinel (1745–1826) et la médecine de l'esprit* (Paris: Arthème Fayard, 1999).

85. See Dora B. Weiner, *The Citizen-Patient in Revolutionary and Imperial Paris* (Baltimore: Johns Hopkins University Press, 1993), esp. ch. 9.

CHAPTER 5

1. Peter Gay, *The Education of the Senses*, vol. 1 of *The Bourgeois Experience: Victoria to Freud* (New York, 1984), 495.

2. Jeanne Veyrin-Forrer, "L'Enfer vu d'ici," in id., *La Lettre et le texte: Trente an-nées de recherches sur l'histoire du livre* (Paris, 1987), 393–421. See also Anne Stora-Lamarre, *L'Enfer de la IIIe République: Censeurs et pornographes (1881–1914)* (Paris, 1990).

3. Patrick J. Kearney, *The Private Case* (London, 1981), and Walter Kendrick, *The Secret Museum: Pornography in Modern Culture* (New York, 1987).

4. Guillaume Apollinaire, Fernand Fleuret, and Louis Perceau, *L'Enfer de la Bi-bliothèque Nationale* (Paris, 1919), and Pascal Pia, *Les Livres de l'Enfer du XVIe siècle à nos jours* (Paris, 1978).

5. In addition to the works of Kearney and Kendrick cited in n. 3, see Peter Wag-ner, *Eros Revived: Erotica of the Enlightenment in England and America* (London, 1988), 5–7, and Lynn Hunt, "Introduction," in *The Invention of Pornography: Ob-scenity and the Origins of Modernity, 1500–1800*, ed. id. (New York, 1993), 13–16.

6. The best general history of erotic literature is still Paul Englisch, *Geschichte der erotischen Literatur* (Stuttgart, 1927). For examples of more recent scholarship, see *Invention of Pornography*, ed. Hunt, and Carolin Fischer, *Education érotique: Pietro Aretinos "Ragionamenti" im libertinen Roman Frankreichs* (Stuttgart, 1994).

7. Robert Darnton, *The Forbidden Best-Sellers of Pre-Revolutionary France* (New York, 1995); id., *The Corpus of Clandestine Literature in France, 1769–1789* (New York, 1995); Michel Delon, "De *Thérèse philosophe* à *La Philosophie dans le boudoir*, la place de la philosophie," *Romanistische Zeitschrift für Literaturgeschichte* 7 (1983): 76–88; Roland Mortier, "Libertinage littéraire et tensions sociales dans la littérature de l'ancien régime: De la *Pícara* à la *Fille de joie*" and "Les Voies obliques de la pro-pagande 'philosophique,'" in id., *La Cœur et la raison: Recueil d'études sur le dix-huitième siècle* (Oxford, 1990), 403–13 and 414–26.

8. *Thérèse philosophe ou mémoires pour servir à l'histoire du Père Dirrag et de Mademoiselle Eradice*, in *L'Enfer de la Bibliothèque Nationale* (Paris, 1986), 5: 69. For reasons of convenience, this and the following texts are quoted from the reprints in this series, cited henceforth as *L'Enfer*, which are listed in the bibliography.

9. *L'Enfer*, 6: 198–99.

10. Ibid., quotations from 147 and 207. The narrator, a rich courtesan of humble birth, gives the following instructions to her maid about how to make love with an aristocrat: "You are about to unite the Third Estate with the nobility: uphold the cause of your order, and . . . prove that you have the right stuff to do battle with him" (196).

11. *L'Enfer*, vol. 7, quotations from 267–69 and 263–64.

12. *L'Enfer*, 3: 362.   13. *L'Enfer*, 7: 638.

14. *L'Enfer*, 3: 57.   15. *L'Enfer*, 4: 140.

16. Catharine MacKinnon, *Only Words* (Cambridge, Mass., 1993), 17.

17. *L'Ecole des filles*, in *L'Enfer*, 7: 274.

18. Andrea Dworkin, *Pornography: Men Possessing Women* (New York, 1981), 68.

19. *L'Enfer*, 7: 460–61.

20. Ibid., 224.

21. Ibid., 468–69.

22. After beginning a regular regime of masturbation, Thérèse notes, "The shadows covering my mind dissipated; little by little, I became accustomed to thinking, to reasoning seriously" (*L'Enfer*, 5: 87).

23. *L'Enfer*, 3: 409 and 394.

24. MacKinnon, *Only Words*, 17.

25. *L'Enfer*, 1: 38.

26. *L'Enfer*, 3: 387: "Country curates, monks, clerks, doctors, schoolboys, *petits bourgeois*, artisans, workers, chambermaids, lackeys, kitchen help, stable boys, porters, domestic servants of all kinds want to read, either to amuse themselves or to develop their minds."

27. *L'Enfer*, 6: 35.

28. See, e.g., the elaborate description of the library in *La Cauchoise*: *L'Enfer*, 3: 436–41.

29. Jean-Marie Goulemot, *Ces livres qu'on ne lit que d'une main: Lecture et lecteurs de livres pornographiques au XVIIIe siècle* (Paris, 1991), 134, 153–55.

30. MacKinnon, *Only Words*, 24.

31. Goulemot, *Ces livres qu'on ne lit que d'une main*, 24.

32. Fischer, *Éducation érotique*, 16–22.

33. Darnton, *Corpus of Clandestine Literature*, 21–22, 191–208.

34. Goulemot, *Ces livres qu'on ne lit que d'une main*, 154.

35. *Thérèse philosophe*, in *L'Enfer*, 5: 62. See also *La Messaline française*: "the most admirable *chute de reins*" (*L'Enfer*, 5: 310); and *Eléonore, ou l'heureuse personne*: "He admired her fat and fleshy back, kissed one after another the dimples that love, searching for a nesting place, had carved in it" (*L'Enfer*, 6: 86).

36. *L'Enfer*, 4: 279.

37. *L'Enfer*, 5: 96. "What eyes! What a mouth! You have admirable coloring. I could devour your arms," a lascivious priest trying to seduce a country girl exclaims in *Les Progrès du libertinage* (*L'Enfer*, 4: 285).

· 38. *Margot la ravaudeuse*, in *Romans libertins du XVIIIe siècle*, ed. Raymond Trousson (Paris, 1993), 732.

39. *Les progrès du libertinage*, *L'Enfer*, 4: 373.

40. *Vénus en rut*, *L'Enfer*, 6: 119. The love of fat applied to all parts of the body and particularly the hands. "Fresh coloring, superb teeth, a small, white, fat hand, [and] general chubbiness [*embonpoint*]" typify the ideal beauty in *Eléonore, ou l'heureuse personne* (*L'Enfer*, 6: 41).

41. *L'Enfer*, 6: 113.

42. *L'Enfer*, 7: 37. See also *Histoire de Marguerite, fille de Suzon, nièce de D**B******, *L'Enfer*, 3: 357, where a predatory nobleman lays siege to a peasant girl, declaring, "Your teeth, whiter than ivory, give you the most perfect beauty."

43. *L'Enfer*, 7: 113.

44. Ibid., 120.

45. Ibid., 120.
47. *L'Enfer*, 3: 318.
49. *L'Enfer*, 4: 254.
51. Ibid., 478.
53. Ibid., 102.

46. *L'Enfer*, 4: 103.
48. Ibid., 328.
50. *L'Enfer*, 7: 435–47.
52. *L'Enfer*, 3: 96.
54. Ibid., 236.

CHAPTER 6

This chapter is an expansion of a paper given in September 1996 to the Seminar on Religion at the Australian National University. I am grateful to Dr. Benjamin Penny for arranging that seminar and to the Humanities Research Centre and Professor Iain McCalman, its director, for the fellowship that gave me the leisure and encouragement to pursue this line of research. I want also to thank Dr. G. M. Ditchfield and Dr. David L. Wykes for their critical reading of an early draft of the chapter.

This essay was completed before it was possible for me to see Robert Bruce Mullin, *Miracles and the Modern Religious Imagination* (New Haven, 1996). Mullin does not deal with the English Unitarians, but I regret not having been able to take his general argument into account.

1. For the slim basis of these estimates, R. K. Webb, "Views of Unitarianism from Halley's Comet," *Transactions of the Unitarian Historical Society* 18 (1986): 180–83. The religious census of 1851 recorded the attendance of 26,512 on the morning of 30 March (information from Dr. G. M. Ditchfield).

2. H. S. Perris, in *Inquirer*, 19 Dec. 1903.

3. *Enlightenment and Religion: Rational Dissent in Eighteenth-Century Britain*, ed. Knud Haakonssen (Cambridge, 1996), passim.

4. The article on Priestley, which had appeared anonymously in the *Monthly Repository* in 1833, is the first entry in the four volumes of Martineau's *Essays, Reviews, and Addresses* (London, 1891).

5. Hennell to Harriet Martineau, 13 Apr. 1860, Birmingham University Library HM 428.

6. "Church-Life? or Sect-Life? A Second Letter to the Rev. S. F. Macdonald . . . ," reprinted in Martineau, *Essays, Reviews, and Addresses*, 2: 381–420. The anticipation of Troeltsch is noted by H. L. Short, "Presbyterians under a New Name," in C. G. Bolam et al., *The English Presbyterians, from Elizabethan Puritanism to Modern Unitarianism* (London, 1968), 267. Short's brief essay remains the most concise and perceptive account of modern Unitarianism.

7. See, e.g., a thoughtful little paper by the Rev. D. G. Banham, "The Problem of Miracles," *Faith and Freedom* 33 (1979): 12–18.

8. William Adams, *Essay on Mr. Hume's Essay on Miracles* (1752); George Campbell, *A Dissertation on Miracles* (1762); Richard Price in the last of his *Four Dissertations* (1768). *A Dissertation on Miracles* (1771), a general treatise on the subject by the

popular Independent (Congregationalist) minister Hugh Farmer, never mentions Hume, but no contemporary could have read the essay as anything but a rebuttal.

9. *Letters to a Philosophical Unbeliever* (1780, 1787), in *The Theological and Miscellaneous Works, &c. of Joseph Priestley . . .* , ed. J. T. Rutt, 4 (1818): 368. Letters IX and X, 367–82, contain a general refutation of Hume's views on religion.

10. *Letters to a Philosophical Unbeliever*, part 2 (1787), Letter VII, in *Works*, ed. Rutt, 4: 475–80. See also *Institutes of Natural and Revealed Religion* (1772–74), part 2, ch. 2, ibid., 2: 109–22.

11. See A Believer in Miracles, "Mr. Hume's Objection to Miracles Considered," *Monthly Repository* 4 (1809): 145–48; a letter from Eliezer Cogan, 11 (1816): 644–47, with a supporting letter from A.B.C., 703–4; again, A Believer in Miracles, 12 (1817): 17–20; Cogan, 31–32; A.B.C., 95–96; Cogan, 16 (1821): 1–3; Bereanus, 463–66; Philalethes, 585–89; Cogan, 699–700. Cogan also deals with Hume's objection to arguments (particularly from design) for the existence of God, 17 (1822): 65–68.

12. A key to the authorship of articles in the *Theological Repository* is printed in an appendix to Herbert McLachlan, *The Story of a Nonconformist Library* (Manchester, 1923), 185–89.

13. Joseph Estlin Carpenter, *The Bible in the Nineteenth Century* (London, 1903), 5 n. 1.

14. For an extreme instance, see Joseph Priestley's quarrel with William Newcome, later archbishop of Armagh, about the number of miles Jesus traveled in a day (Priestley, *Works*, 20: 169–71).

15. The introduction, the letter, and an extended account of the course, including tabular references across the four synoptic gospels, are reprinted in John Jebb, *Works*, ed. John Disney (London, 1787), 1: 5–136.

16. *Harriet Martineau's Autobiography* (London, 1877), 1: 39.

17. *Monthly Repository* 1 (1806): 88–89. The book was *Plain and Useful Selections from the Books of the Old and New Testament, according to the most approved modern Translations* (London, 1806) by Theophilus Browne, another Cambridge don whose heterodoxy led to his departure. Browne said he followed a plan he had taken (rather to the reviewer's surprise) from Isaac Watts, cutting out genealogies, expositions of Jewish rituals, histories of wars and evil rulers, lesser prophecies, and "narrations involving circumstances not the most delicate."

18. See n. 14 above.

19. Belsham's statement of purpose is in his reply (signed B.) to the *Quarterly Review* (which, like all orthodox periodicals, took a very severe view of the Improved Version) in the *Monthly Repository* 4 (1809): 373. Martineau, *Autobiography*, 1: 38. Belsham's *Epistles of St. Paul* was published in four volumes in 1822.

20. Martineau identifies Carpenter in "The Bible: What It Is, and What It Is Not" (Liverpool, 1839), 16. See p. 125 in this volume.

21. The lengthy review of the Improved Version is in *MR* 4 (1809): 97–102, 152–

59, 216–21, 274–81, 384–88. To the last of these and continuing over two further issues (388–90, 566–68, 677–79) is appended a tabular presentation of points at which the Improved Version differs from Griesbach. Discussion continues over all of 1809 and subsequent years, notably in the exchanges in 1809 between Theologus and Primitivus.

22. Belsham on the Virgin Birth, "Remarks on Mr. Proud's Pamphlet," *Monthly Repository* 1 (1806): 587. Compare Richard Wright, the celebrated Unitarian missionary, *An Essay on the Miraculous Conception of Jesus Christ* (London, 1808). Belsham preaching at Warrington on the Pentateuch, *Reflections upon the History of the Creation in the Book of Genesis . . . August 19, 1821* (London, 1821). For reactions, see *Monthly Repository* 16 (1821): 646–47 (of particular interest as an unreserved acceptance of the Creation account in Genesis by another former Cambridge don, the radical William Frend), 712–13 (Belsham's reply); 17 (1822), 111–13 (a brief formal review), 24–26, 96–98, 230–35, 278–84. See the delightful essay on Belsham (1898) by Alexander Gordon in *Addresses Biographical and Historical* (London, 1922), 283–310, which quotes Belsham's 1819 letter to John Kenrick about the gospels.

23. Merton A. Christensen, "Taylor of Norwich and the Higher Criticism," *Journal of the History of Ideas* 20 (1959): 179–94.

24. One cannot be too superior on this point. In a letter to James Martineau, 9 Oct. 1882 (Dr. Williams's Library MS 24.153 [27]), J. H. Thom, a preeminent leader of the New School, confessed that his mind was not attuned to metaphysics: "I very often feel, even in reading Kant, as if dealing with shadows, or that I have made a reality of the wrong ghost."

25. John Williams, *Memoirs of the Reverend Thomas Belsham . . .* (London, 1833), 703–4.

26. A similar, though more complex and less dramatic, instance could be found in the genesis and content of, and response to, Charles Christian Hennell's *An Inquiry Concerning the Origin of Christianity* (1838) and *Christian Theism* (1841). The *Inquiry* was published in a German translation the next year, with a preface by Strauss. Hennell, in business as a merchant, had been raised and educated as a Unitarian and remained a regular attender at the Gravel-Pit Chapel, Hackney. From his sister's marriage to the Coventry ribbon manufacturer Charles Bray came the circle in which George Eliot won her liberation from Evangelical orthodoxy; she took over a failed project initiated by Hennell to translate Strauss into English. Hennell was closely associated with Philip Harwood as a theological adviser and in the Beaumont Institution.

27. *Church History* 50 (1981): 415–35.

28. The Bridport background is admirably sketched in Basil Short, *A Respectable Society: Bridport, 1593–1835* (Bradford-on-Avon, 1976). Dodd's comments (420–21) are well taken.

29. Richard Garnett, *The Life of W. J. Fox, Public Teacher and Social Reformer,*

1786–1864 (London, 1910) is outdated; the best subsequent authority is Francis E. Mineka's splendid history, *The Dissidence of Dissent: The Monthly Repository, 1806–1838*, which Fox edited from 1827 to 1836.

30. Henry Crabb Robinson, diary, 6 Aug. 1841, Dr. Williams's Library.

31. What can be known about Harwood's life is summarized in my entry in the forthcoming *New Dictionary of National Biography*. See also M. M. Bevington, *The Saturday Review, 1855–1868* (New York, 1941).

32. William Hincks, *Anti-Supernaturalism Considered* (London, 1841). Thomas Wood, *The Mission of Jesus Christ: A Lecture Preached in Brixton Unitarian Chapel, October 18, 1840* (London, 1840). Compare the reply by J. H. Hutton, *Jesus Christ Our Teacher and Lord by Divine, Not by Self, Appointment* (London, 1841) and John Kentish, *Notes and Comments on Passages of Scripture* (London, 1844), passim.

33. See the glowing review, signed W. G. W., in the *Christian Reformer*, a conservative journal, n.s., 2 (1846): 513–23.

34. The lecture was published separately in Liverpool in 1839, but is more readily available in the collection of the lectures published the same year under the general title *Unitarianism Defended*. On pp. 15–18 and in Note A, Martineau offers a trenchant critique of the Improved Version.

35. James Drummond and C. B. Upton, *The Life and Letters of James Martineau* (London, 1902), 1: 166–9. He specifically rejects the blighting of the fig tree (see p. 117 above) as so contrary to Christ's character as to be unbelievable.

36. Preface to third edition (London, 1845), vii–viii. Tony Cross, "Moving Martineau off the Miracles: The Role of Joseph Blanco White," *Faith and Freedom* 48 (1995): 133–36.

37. To J. H. Hutton, 12 July 1885, Drummond and Upton, *Life*, 2: 79–81. The disparagement of older Unitarianism as Deism plus miracles was not new. In the first of his letters to S. F. Macdonald in 1859, which he called "On the Unitarian Position" (reprinted in *Essays, Reviews, and Addresses*, 2: 371–80; see esp. 378). Martineau referred to the "miraculously-confirmed Deism which often passes under the Unitarian name," a remark that brought a sharp rebuke in the *Christian Reformer* (n.s., 15: 612–13): "One of the least desirable forms in which Unitarianism can be professed is Deism *without the miracles*. The miracles of the New Testament are accepted by Unitarian Christians as proofs of the truth and illustrations of the nature of Christianity. In this view, any statement which represents Unitarianism as a mere belief in God and in certain miracles confirmatory of his Deity, is defective and injurious."

38. William Hincks, *Inquirer*, 28 Dec. 1844.

39. Other prominent representatives of the Old School were the ministers Edward Higginson, Edward Tagart, and Robert Brook Aspland, the last two serving as successive secretaries of the British and Foreign Unitarian Association. There is a vast collection of letters to the Rev. John Gordon (father of the minister and historian Alexander Gordon) from nearly all the major participants in the conflict in the Unitarian College MSS, John Rylands University Library, Manchester.

40. It is possible that the article "Thoughts on Miracles" in the *Christian Reformer*, n.s., 14 (1858): 389–96, signed S. is by Bache; the sentiments are certainly congruent.

41. My chapter, "The Limits of Religious Liberty: Theology and Criticism in Nineteenth-Century England," in *Freedom and Religion in the Nineteenth Century*, ed. Richard J. Helmstadter (Stanford, 1997), 121–49, sets the Unitarian quarrel in the 1860s in remarkable parallel to similar confrontations among Anglicans and Quakers.

42. William Binns, *Christianity in Relation to Modern Thought* (London, 1864), passim. Binns was self-taught and had worked as a booking clerk on the Midland Railway.

43. *Unitarian Herald*, 16 Sept. 1864. The three editors in addition to Wright were John Relly Beard, William Gaskell, and Brooke Herford. In 1865, Gaskell and Herford took the paper over. See also the editorial "Belief in the Bible," 20 May 1864, and Bache's letter "On Fellowship Between Those Who Differ About Miracles," 14 Apr. 1865. In the *Theological Review* in 1875 (12: 14–35), Wright returned to the subject, offering a specifically Unitarian twist. If the psychological and psychosomatic explanations he favored seemed to reduce Jesus to exorcist or thaumaturge, it would damage Him no more than does His submission to ordinary laws governing body and mind. Only by seeing Him as human, can He remain real, a man "with all human appetites and passions strong within him . . . with no help against temptation but his own brave will and tender conscience, with no communion with God but such as every child of God may gain." Christians can then follow Him as brothers, not slaves. Thus "we can gratify all the instincts of the heart, yet not sacrifice one of the conclusions of the intellect."

44. J. H. Thom, "The Question of Miracles," *Theological Review* 2 (1865): 45–74. For the exchange between Beard and Bache, Beard's letters to John Gordon, no. 6, 27 Aug. [1864]; no. 64 [1865]; no. 79, 23 Jan. [1865], Unitarian College MSS, John Rylands University Library. The general lack of dating of these letters can be remedied here by internal evidence.

45. G. Dawes Hicks, "The Religious Teacher and Theologian" in the memorial introduction to the posthumous publication of Drummond's *Pauline Meditations* (London, 1919), xxxv–xxxviii. A temperate but trenchant turn-of-the-century critique of the question is an essay by Walter Lloyd, published first in 1893 as "Miracles of the Old and New Testament" in *Religion and Modern Thought*, ed. T. W. Freckelton, and republished as "The Miracles of the Bible" in *The Transient and Permanent in Religion*, a collection of essays from various nineteenth-century sources published by the British and Foreign Unitarian Association in 1908.

46. What follows is an impression derived from reading the leading articles that in some way deal with miracles between 1876 and 1910. A convincing count according to some clear criterion would be difficult because of variation in the subject (e.g., Roman Catholic miracles) and sources where given (e.g., American Unitarian writers), but I think the result, impressionistic though it is, is fair.

CHAPTER 7

This essay has benefited from Peter Gay's inspirational scholarship, from the comments of Roy Porter, Julia Sheppard, and Michael Neve, and from the expert assistance of Caroline Overy.

1. Waldo Hilary Dunn, *James Anthony Froude, A Biography*, 2 vols. (Oxford: Clarendon Press, 1961–63), 1: 73 (quoting Froude's previously unpublished autobiographical manuscript).

2. Owen Chadwick, *The Secularization of the European Mind in the Nineteenth Century* (Cambridge: Cambridge University Press, 1975), 6.

3. C. Kegan Paul, *Memories* (London: Routledge & Kegan Paul, 1971; reprint of 1899 ed).

4. Gordon Haight, *George Eliot: A Biography* (Oxford: Oxford University Press, 1968), 40 ff.

5. James Moore, "Of Love and Death: Why Charles Darwin 'gave up Christianity,'" in *History, Humanity and Evolution: Essays for John C. Greene*, ed. James R. Moore (Cambridge: Cambridge University Press, 1989), 195–230; more generally, see Bernard Lightman, *The Origins of Agnosticism: Victorian Unbelief and the Limits of Knowledge* (Baltimore: Johns Hopkins University Press, 1987).

6. Lytton Strachey, *Eminent Victorians* (London: Chatto & Windus, 1918), 51; see also Richard Shannon, *Gladstone*: vol. 1: *1809–1865* (London: Methuen, 1982), 227 ff.

7. Peter Gay, *The Enlightenment: An Interpretation*, vol. 1: *The Rise of Modern Paganism*; vol. 2: *The Science of Freedom* (New York: Knopf, 1966–69).

8. Peter Gay, *The Bourgeois Experience: Victoria to Freud*, vols. 1 and 2 (New York: Oxford University Press, 1984, 1986), vols. 3, 4, and 5 (New York: Norton, 1993, 1995, 1998) (henceforth cited as Gay, *BE*). The most extended discussion of religion is in *BE*, 2: 284–312. For Gosse, see *BE*, 4: 131 ff.

9. Susan Budd, *Varieties of Unbelief: Atheists and Agnostics in English Society, 1850–1960* (London: Heinemann, 1977).

10. Ford K. Brown, *Fathers of the Victorians* (Cambridge: Cambridge University Press, 1961); Boyd Hilton, *The Age of Atonement: The Influence of Evangelicalism on Social and Economic Thought, 1785–1865* (Oxford: Clarendon Press, 1988).

11. David Newsome, *Two Classes of Men: Platonism & English Romantic Thought* (London: John Murray, 1974), 86.

12. Francis William Newman, *Phases of Faith*, ed. U. C. Knoepflmacher (Leicester: Leicester University Press, 1970). This is a facsimile of the sixth edition of 1860, which I shall use here.

13. Gay, *BE*, 4, part 2, n. 8; Linda Peterson, *Victorian Autobiography: The Tradition of Self-Interpretation* (New Haven: Yale University Press, 1986).

14. A. O. J. Cockshut, *Truth to Life: The Art of Biography in the Nineteenth Century* (London: Collins, 1974). The most recent major account of Newman's life is Ian

Ker, *John Henry Newman: A Biography* (Oxford: Oxford University Press, 1988). See also Gay, *BE*, 4, part 3, n. 8.

15. I. Giberne Sieveking, *Memoir and Letters of Francis W. Newman* (London: Kegan Paul, 1907).

16. Basil Willey, "Francis W. Newman," in *More Nineteenth-Century Studies* (1956; Cambridge: Cambridge University Press, 1980), 51.

17. William Robbins, *The Newman Brothers: An Essay in Comparative Intellectual Biography* (London: Heinemann; Cambridge, Mass.: Harvard University Press, 1966).

18. Maisie Ward, *Young Mr. Newman* (London: Sheed & Ward, 1948), 8.

19. Quoted in Robbins, *Newman Brothers*, viii n. 17.

20. Strachey, *Eminent Victorians*, 16 n. 6.

21. *The Notebooks of Samuel Butler*, ed. Henry Festing James (London: Hogarth Press, 1985), 187.

22. Quoted in Sieveking, *Newman*, 139, n. 15, from George Grey Butler.

23. On temperance, see Brian Harrison, *Drink and the Victorians* (London: Faber & Faber, 1971); on antivivisection, see Richard D. French, *Antivivisection and Medical Science in Victorian Society* (Princeton: Princeton University Press, 1975); on the campaign against the Contagious Diseases Acts, see Paul McHugh, *Prostitution and Victorian Social Reform* (London: Croom Helm, 1980); on vegetarianism, see Colin Spencer, *The Heretic's Feast: A History of Vegetarianism* (London: Fourth Estate, 1993; Hanover, N.H.: University Press of New England, 1995).

24. Sieveking, *Newman*, 118 n. 15.

25. Ibid., 107–8.

26. Richard Jenkyns, *The Victorians and Ancient Greece* (Oxford: Basil Blackwell, 1980), 196–98.

27. J. A. Froude, as quoted in A. L. Rouse, *Froude the Historian: Victorian Man of Letters* (Gloucester: Alan Sutton, 1987), 120.

28. Gertrude Himmelfarb, *Victorian Minds* (New York: Knopf, 1968), 307. The comparison is with Robbins's double biography *The Newman Brothers* (cited n. 17 above).

29. Ker, *John Henry Newman*, 46 n. 14.

30. *John Henry Newman, Autobiographical Writings*, ed. Henry Tristram (London: Sheed & Ward, 1955), 194.

31. Ker, *John Henry Newman*, 126 n. 14.

32. Ibid., 120.

33. Piers Brendon, "Newman, Keble and Froude's *Remains*," *English Historical Review* 88 (Oct. 1972): 697–716.

34. Owen Chadwick, *The Victorian Church, Part 1* (London: Adam & Charles Black, 1970), 534.

35. Ibid., 537.

36. Dunn, *James Anthony Froude*, 1: 134 n. 1.

37. Francis Newman, *Phases of Faith*, 73 n. 12.

38. F. W. Newman, *Personal Narrative, in Letters, Principally from Turkey, in the Years 1830–3* (London: Holyoake, 1856).

39. "F. W. Newman and His Evangelical Critics," *Westminster Review* 70 (Oct. 1858): 376–435; "Francis William Newman," *Christian Examiner*, n.s., no. 1 (1866): 332–59. There is no copy of *Personal Narrative* either in the UCL Library or in Dr. Williams Library, which has virtually a complete set of his publications, including some with his own annotations. I have used the copy in the British Library.

40. Henry Groves, *"Not of the World": Memoir of Lord Congleton* (London: Shaw, 1884), 11.

41. Newman, *Personal Narrative*, 12 n. 38.

42. Ibid., 68.

43. Anthony N. Groves, *Journal of Mr. Anthony N. Groves, Missionary, During a Journey from London to Baghdad, Through Russia, Georgia, and Persia. Also, A Journal of Some Months' Residence at Baghdad* (London: James Nisbet, 1831), 302.

44. Ibid., 83.

45. Groves, *"Not of the World,"* n. 40; *Memoir of the Late Anthony Norris Groves Containing Extracts from His Letters and Journals*, compiled by his widow (London: James Nisbet, 1856).

46. Groves, *"Not of the World,"* 37 n. 40.

47. Newman, *Personal Narrative*, 83 n. 38.

48. Ibid., 29.

49. Newman, *Phases of Faith*, 32–33 n. 12.

50. Newman, *Personal Narrative*, 31 n. 38.

51. Ibid., 74, 78.

52. Anthony N. Groves, *Journal of a Residence at Bagdad During the Years 1830 and 1831* (London: James Nisbet, 1832), 302.

53. Newman, *Phases of Faith*, 64 n. 12.

54. Frank McLynn, *Burton: Snow upon the Desert* (London: John Murray, 1990); *The Letters of Gustave Flaubert*, ed. and trans. Francis Steegmuller, 2 vols. (London: Faber & Faber, 1980–82).

55. Tennyson, *In Memoriam A. H. H.*, xcvi.

56. *The Victorian Crisis of Faith*, ed. Anthony Symondson (London: S.P.C.K., 1970).

57. For discussions, in addition to works already cited, see Vernon F. Storr, *The Development of English Theology in the Nineteenth Century, 1800–1860* (London: Longmans, 1913); Bernard M. G. Reardon, *From Coleridge to Gore: A Century of Religious Thought in Britain* (London: Longman, 1971).

58. Newman, *Phases of Faith*, 174 n. 12.

59. Robbins, *Newman Brothers*, 67 n. 17.

60. Sieveking, *Newman*, 343 n. 15.

61. Newman, *Phases of Faith*, 72 n. 12.

62. Ibid., 7, 34–35.

63. Robbins, *Newman Brothers*, 60 n. 17.

64. By contrast, the middle Froude son became a distinguished engineer.

65. Ward, *Young Mr Newman*, 360 n. 18.

66. F. W. Newman, *Contributions Chiefly to the Early History of the Late Cardinal Newman* (London: Kegan Paul, 1891), vii.

67. Ibid., 2 (emphasis in original).

68. Ibid., 9.

69. Ibid., v.

70. Frank J. Sulloway, *Born to Rebel: Birth Order, Family Dynamics, and Creative Lives* (Boston: Little, Brown, 1996)

CHAPTER 8

An earlier version of this essay was presented to the seminar in modern British political history at Cambridge University. I am most grateful to the participants for their many helpful and constructive suggestions. My thanks also to Chuck Abdella and Ian Bennett for essential research assistance.

1. Peter Gay, *The Bourgeois Experience: Victoria to Freud*, 5 vols. (New York, 1984–97).

2. The standard lives are as follows: J. L. Garvin and Julian Amery, *The Life of Joseph Chamberlain*, 6 vols. (London, 1932–69); P. Marsh, *Joseph Chamberlain: Entrepreneur in Politics* (London, 1994); Sir Charles Petrie, *The Life and Letters of the Rt. Hon. Sir Austen Chamberlain*, 2 vols. (London, 1939–40); D. Dutton, *Austen Chamberlain: Gentleman in Politics* (London, 1987); *The Austen Chamberlain Diary Letters*, ed. R. C. Self (Cambridge, 1995); Sir K. Feiling, *Neville Chamberlain* (London, 1947); D. Dilks, *Neville Chamberlain*, vol. 1: *Pioneering and Reform, 1869–1929* (Cambridge, 1984).

3. B. S. Benediktz, *Guide to the Chamberlain Collection* (Birmingham, 1978), 6. For three examples of family pride, see Arthur Chamberlain, *The Book of Business* (privately printed, 1899), dedicated to "my children in particular and to all my descendants in general"; Austen Chamberlain, *Notes on the Families of Chamberlain and Harben* (privately printed, 1915); Neville Chamberlain, *Norman Chamberlain: A Memoir* (privately printed, 1923). See also D. H. Elletson, *The Chamberlains* (London, 1966).

4. A. Briggs, *History of Birmingham*, vol. 2: *Borough and City, 1865–1938* (Oxford, 1952), esp. 67–134, 164–99; id., *Victorian Cities* (Harmondsworth, 1968), 184–240; D. Fraser, *Power and Authority in the Victorian City* (Oxford, 1979), 101–10, 151–73; E. P. Hennock, *Fit and Proper Persons: Ideal and Reality in Nineteenth-Century Urban Government* (London, 1973), 17–57; L. V. Jones, "Public Pursuit or Private Profit? Liberal Businessmen and Municipal Politics in Birmingham, 1865–1900," *Business History* 25 (1983): 240–59.

5. E. V. Hiley, "Birmingham City Government," in *Birmingham Institutions*, ed. J. H. Muirhead (Birmingham, 1910), 138; *Birmingham Daily Post* (henceforth cited as *BDP*), 30 Nov. 1888, 1 Feb. 1889, 10 Nov. 1905, and 20 June 1911.

6. J. Chamberlain, "The Caucus," *Fortnightly Review*, n.s., 24 (1878): 721–41; P. Auspos, "Radicalism, Pressure Groups and Party Politics: From the National Education League to the National Liberal Federation," *Journal of British Studies* 20 (1980): 184–204; F. H. Herrick, "The Origins of the National Liberal Federation," *Journal of Modern History* 17 (1945): 116–29; T. R. Tholfsen, "The Origins of the Birmingham Caucus," *Historical Journal* 2 (1959): 161–84.

7. *British Parliamentary Election Results, 1885–1918*, ed. F. W. S. Craig, 2d. ed. (Aldershot, Hants, and Brookfield, Vt., 1989), 75. Chamberlain was returned unopposed in 1886, 1900, and (twice) 1910.

8. *BDP*, 18 and 19 Jan. 1906; Dilks, *Neville Chamberlain*, 7, 15; D. Cannadine, *Lords and Landlords: The Aristocracy and the Towns, 1774–1967* (Leicester, 1980), 190–94; C. Green, "Birmingham's Politics, 1873–1891: The Local Basis of Change," *Midland History* 2 (1973): 84–98; *British Parliamentary Election Results, 1832–1885*, ed. F. W. S. Craig, 2d. ed. (Aldershot, Hants, and Brookfield, Vt., 1989), 46. For one contemporary example of local anti-Chamberlain propaganda, see Birmingham Reference Library (henceforth cited as BRL MS) 89151, Anon., "Joseph and His Brethren" (1880).

9. R. Quinault, "John Bright and Joseph Chamberlain," *Historical Journal* 28 (1985): 623–46. H. Pelling, *Popular Politics and Society in Late Victorian Britain* (London, 1968), 3, has described Chamberlain's improvement scheme as "Municipal Stalinism": "Municipal Haussmannism" might be a better phrase. For the conditions of life for ordinary people, see R. Woods, "Mortality and Sanitary Conditions in the 'Best Governed City in the World'—Birmingham, 1870–1910," *Journal of Historical Geography* 4 (1978): 35–56.

10. R. Quinault, "Joseph Chamberlain: A Reappraisal," in *Later Victorian Britain, 1867–1900*, ed. T. R. Gourvish and A. O'Day (London, 1988), 76–81.

11. M. C. Hurst, *Joseph Chamberlain and West Midland Politics, 1886–1895*, Dugdale Society Occasional Papers, no. 5 (1962); id., "Joseph Chamberlain, the Conservatives and the Succession to John Bright, 1886–89," *Historical Journal* 7 (1964): 64–93; K. W. D. Rolf, "Tories, Tariffs and Elections: The West Midlands in English Politics, 1918–1935" (Ph.D. diss., Cambridge University, 1974), 65–67; H. Pelling, *Social Geography of British Elections, 1885–1910* (London, 1967), 175–203.

12. J. Pemble, *Venice Rediscovered* (Oxford, 1995), esp. 87–109; E. Muir, *Civic Ritual in Renaissance Venice* (Princeton, 1981), 13–23. See also Feiling, *Neville Chamberlain*, 3: "If Manchester might think itself the Florence, the Venice of this second British Renaissance was Birmingham." All the Chamberlains were frequent visitors to Venice.

13. *The Times*, 4 and 7 July 1914; R. Hartnell, "Art and Civic Culture in Birmingham in the Late Nineteenth Century," *Urban History* 22 (1995): 229–37.

14. C. Schorske, *Fin-de-Siècle Vienna: Politics and Culture* (New York, 1980), 24–27 and 62.

15. J. T. Bunce, "Art in the Community," *Fortnightly Review*, n.s., 22 (1877): 340–54; C. Cunningham, *Victorian and Edwardian Town Halls* (London, 1981), 5–6, 8–10, 18–19, 83–85, and 208–9; R. Dixon and S. Muthesius, *Victorian Architecture* (London, 1978), 149.

16. Metropolitan opinion considered Birmingham's buildings from this period extravagantly overornamented: see, e.g., *The Builder*, 27 Nov. 1897, 440; *The Builder's Journal*, 2 Oct. 1907, 163.

17. T. Anderton, *A Tale of One City: The New Birmingham* (Birmingham, 1900), 95–96; B. Morris, "The Harborne Room," *Victoria and Albert Museum Bulletin* 4 (1968): 82–95; *VCH Warwickshire*, vol. 7 (London, 1964), 44–45; N. Pevsner and A. Wedgwood, *The Buildings of England: Warwickshire* (Harmondsworth, 1966), 100, 118–19, 121, 124, 140–41, 145, 187, and 207; Marsh, *Joseph Chamberlain*, 75, 87, 102, and 139–40.

18. Pemble, *Venice Rediscovered*, 122–24, 131–36; M. W. Brooks, *John Ruskin and Victorian Architecture* (London, 1987), 233–53; J. Mordaunt Crook, "Ruskinian Gothic," in *The Ruskin Polygon*, ed. J. Dixon Hunt and F. M. Holland (Manchester, 1982), 65–93; id., *The Dilemma of Style: Architectural Ideas from the Picturesque to the Post Modern* (London, 1987), 69–97, 133–60; BRL MS 78126, "A Catalogue of the Works of Mr John Ruskin, as Collected by J. H. Chamberlain" (1878).

19. J. H. Chamberlain, *On the Office and Duties of Architecture* (Birmingham [1858]); id., *Exotic Art* (Birmingham [1883]); J. T. Bunce, *In Memoriam, John Henry Chamberlain* (Birmingham [1884]); BRL MS 382842, "Newspaper Cuttings Relating to J. H. Chamberlain" (1883–84), esp. *BDP*, 23 and 24 Oct. 1883.

20. *BDP*, 6 Oct. 1881; 21 Sept. and 2 Oct. 1885.

21. *VCH Warwickshire*, vol. 7, frontispiece; *BDP*, 24 Apr. 1880.

22. *BDP*, 22 July 1891; Dixon and Muthesius, *Victorian Architecture*, 176–77; *VCH Warwickshire*, 7: 45; Pevsner and Wedgwood, *Warwickshire*, 117–19.

23. A. P. D. Thomson, "The Chamberlain Memorial Tower, University of Birmingham," *University of Birmingham Historical Journal* 3 (1952): 167–79; E. W. Ives, *Image of a University: The Great Hall at Edgbaston, 1900–1909* (Birmingham, 1988); Pevsner and Wedgwood, *Warwickshire*, 169–70.

24. Muir, *Renaissance Venice*, 4, 60, 74–75, 183, 250, and 300; Marsh, *Joseph Chamberlain*, 641–42. "The Chamberlain tradition" in Birmingham is but one example, albeit perhaps the most famous and best developed, of the close relationship between urban ceremonial, civic power, and local politics in Britain from the last quarter of the nineteenth century to the outbreak of World War II. For some other examples, see D. Cannadine, "The Brief Flowering of a Civic Religion," *The Listener*, 26 July 1984, 14–15; id., "The Transformation of Civic Ritual in Modern Britain: The Colchester Oyster Feast," *Past & Present*, no. 94 (1982): 107–30; id. and E. Hammerton, "Conflict and Consensus on a Ceremonial Occasion: The Diamond Jubilee in

Cambridge," *Historical Journal* 24 (1981): 111–46; T. B. Smith, "In Defense of Privilege: The City of London and the Challenge of Municipal Reform, 1875–1890," *Journal of Social History* 27 (1993–94): 59–83.

25. *BDP*, 17 and 18 June 1874; 24 Feb. 1875; 10 Nov. 1879; 2, 26, and 27 Oct. 1880; 20 July 1881; 2 June 1882; 8 May, 4, 6, 12, 14, 15, and 16 June 1883; 6, 7, 8, 12, and 29 Mar. 1888; 9 Jan. 1889; *Pall Mall Gazette "Extra", The Bright Celebration*, 18 June 1883.

26. *BDP*, 4 Nov. 1874; 5 Aug. 1885; 23 and 24 Mar. 1887.

27. Briggs, *History of Birmingham*, 336–37; W. Corfield, "Birmingham Statues and Memorials," in *Extracts from "Notes and Queries," March 14 to May 9, 1914*, ed. id. (London, 1914), 332; *BDP*, 11 Jan. 1901; 15 Mar. and 24 Apr. 1913.

28. BRL MS 174049, "Mr Chamberlain's Visit to South Africa: Newspaper Cuttings on His Farewell and Return to Birmingham" (1902–3), esp. *Birmingham Daily Gazette, BDP*, and *Birmingham Daily Mail*, all for 18 Nov. 1902. On Chamberlain's return from South Africa to Birmingham, a memorial clock was unveiled in his constituency (*BDP*, 1 Feb. 1904).

29. BRL MS 243171, *The Chamberlain Celebrations, July 7 & 9, 1906: Official Programme*; BRL MS 194741, *Chamberlain Souvenir, 1836 to 1906* (1906); BRL MS 199541, *Chamberlain Celebration, 1906, Programme of the Congratulatory Meeting, Bingley Hall, Birmingham, 9 July 1906* (1906); *BDP*, 7 and 9 July 1906; BRL MS 202060, "Commemoration of Mr Joseph Chamberlain's Seventieth Birthday, Newspaper Cuttings, etc." (1906); Garvin and Amery, *Joseph Chamberlain*, 6: 897–907; Marsh, *Joseph Chamberlain*, 641–47.

30. *BDP*, 11 and 27 June, 21 and 22 July 1904; 27 Sept. 1889; 6 and 25 Feb., 3 Mar. 1905. For the background, see P. J. Morrish, "The Struggle to Create an Anglican Diocese of Birmingham," *Journal of Ecclesiastical History* 31 (1980): 59–88.

31. BRL MS 218653, City of Birmingham, *Authorised Programme of the Royal Visit to Birmingham for the Opening of Birmingham University* (1909); *BDP*, 17 and 29 May, 5, 8, 9, 11, 15, 22, 24, and 30 June, and 7, 8, and 9 July 1909.

32. *BDP*, 1 Feb. 1904.

33. Marsh, *Joseph Chamberlain*, 278; D. Dutton, "Life Beyond the Grave: Joseph Chamberlain, 1906–14," *History Today*, May 1984, 26; id., *Austen Chamberlain*, 49.

34. Rolf, "Tories, Tariffs and Elections," 135–36; Elletson, *The Chamberlains*, 202–10; N. Chamberlain, "Municipal Government in Birmingham," *Political Quarterly* 1 (1914): 89–119; *BDP*, 12 Feb. 1912; 3 Nov. 1913.

35. Feiling, *Neville Chamberlain*, 52, 62; Dilks, *Neville Chamberlain*, 76–79, 105–8, 123–80; *BDP*, 10 Nov. 1916.

36. *BDP*, 4, 6, and 7 July 1914; *The Times*, 4 and 7 July 1914; Marsh, *Joseph Chamberlain*, 666–67.

37. Marsh, *Joseph Chamberlain*, 667–68; BRL MS 259694, "A Catalogue of the Collection of Orchids Formed by the Late Right Hon. Joseph Chamberlain . . . to Be Sold on 15 and 16 Apr. 1915"; BRL MS 259695, "A Catalogue of the Collection of Stove and Greenhouse Plants, Formed by the Late the Right Hon. Joseph Chamber-

lain . . . to Be Sold on 22 April 1915"; BRL MS 259773, "Highbury, Moor Green, Birmingham, Catalogue of Surplus Household Furniture . . . to Be Sold 28 and 29 April 1915"; BRL MS 626472, "Correspondence Between Sir Austen Chamberlain and Others Concerning the Disposal of Part of the Highbury Estate, 1923–24"; D. Ayhurst, *Garvin of the Observer* (London, 1985), 51–55 and 235; Self, *Austen Chamberlain*, 136 and 397; Dutton, *Austen Chamberlain*, 4.

38. Hurst, *Joseph Chamberlain and Midland Politics*, 3; Rolf, "Tories, Tariffs and Elections," 86; Self, *Austen Chamberlain*, 201; *Birmingham Post* (henceforth cited as *BP*), 23 Feb. 1926; BRL MS 325935, "Presentation of the Freedom of the City to the Rt. Hon. Sir Austen Chamberlain, Monday 22 Feb. 1926."

39. Rolf, "Tories, Tariffs and Elections," 87; BRL MS 384453, "City of Birmingham Gas Department, Proceedings at the Unveiling of the Bust of the Late Mr Joseph Chamberlain . . . on 8th December 1925."

40. Dutton, *Austen Chamberlain*, 165; Self, *Austen Chamberlain*, 14–15, 198–99; H. Macmillan, *The Past Masters: Politics and Politicians, 1906–1939* (London, 1975), 128.

41. Dilks, *Neville Chamberlain*, 397; Rolf, "Tories, Tariffs and Elections," 88, 145; Self, *Austen Chamberlain*, 259–60.

42. Elletson, *The Chamberlains*, 218, 265, 271–75. Neville wrote his cousin's memoir, *Norman Chamberlain*, so "that future generations of the family should realise how greatly Norman had contributed to the family fame" (v).

43. Rolf, "Tories, Tariffs and Elections," 48; E. Hopkins, "Working Class Life in Birmingham Between the Wars, 1918–1939," *Midland History* 15 (1990): 129–50.

44. *BP*, 11 Nov. 1924 and 10 Nov. 1925; R. P. Hastings, "The General Strike in Birmingham, 1926," *Midland History* 2 (1974): 250–73; id., "The Birmingham Labour Movement, 1918–1945," ibid. 5 (1979–80): 78–84; *British Parliamentary Election Results, 1918–1949*, ed. F. W. S. Craig (Glasgow, 1969), 80–91.

45. E. J. Hobsbawm, "Mass-Producing Traditions," in *The Invention of Tradition*, ed. id. and T. Ranger (Cambridge, 1983), 303–4; Hartnell, "Art and Culture in Birmingham," 236–37.

46. Briggs, *History of Birmingham*, 336–37; *BP*, 31 Jan., 10 and 21 Feb., 28 Mar., 14 and 17 Oct. 1919; 1 July 1920, 12 June 1923, 15 May, and 6 July 1925.

47. W. H. Bidlake, "Birmingham as It Might Be," in *Birmingham Institutions*, ed. Muirhead, 598–601; *BP*, 1 Apr. 1922 and 12 June 1923.

48. *BP*, 12 Oct. 1926 and 15 Aug. 1927; Anon., "Birmingham Civic Centre Competition," *The Architect and Building News* 118 (1927): 297–301; W. Dougill, "Birmingham Civic Centre Competition: A Criticism of the Designs," *Town Planning Review* 13 (1928): 19–29.

49. Craig, *British Parliamentary Election Results, 1918–1949*, 83, 90; Hastings, "Birmingham Labour Movement," 82, 84–87.

50. Self, *Austen Chamberlain*, 493; Hastings, "Birmingham Labour Movement," 80; *The Observer*, 3 Nov. 1935.

51. Ayerst, *Garvin*, 235–38; Rolf, *Austen Chamberlain*, 418, 420, and 425.

52. L. S. Amery, *My Political Life*, vol. 3: *The Unforgiving Years, 1929–1940* (London, 1955), 201; *BP*, 17 Mar., 8 and 9 July 1936; E. M. Rudland, "Centenary of the Right Honourable Joseph Chamberlain, 1836–1936," in id., *Three Poems* (Birmingham, 1937), unpaginated.

53. Sir Austen Chamberlain, *Down the Years* (London, 1935), 5; id., *Politics from Inside: An Epistolary Chronicle, 1906–1914* (London, 1936), 15; *BP*, 12 Nov. 1936.

54. Self, *Austen Chamberlain*, 520; *BP*, 17, 18, and 20 Mar. 1937; E. M. Rudland, "The Rt. Hon. Sir Austen Chamberlain, Died 16 March 1937," in id., *Three Poems*.

55. Self, *Austen Chamberlain*, 399–400 and 405–6; *BP*, 5 Feb. 1932 and 20 Mar. 1937.

56. BRL MS 391766, "Special Council Meeting to be Held in the Town Hall, to Admit to the Hon. Freedom of the City Barrow Cadbury, the Rt. Hon. Neville Chamberlain, Alderman John Henry Lloyd, Friday 6 May 1932"; *BP* 7 May 1932, 28 Nov. 1933, and 29 May and 5 July 1937; N. Chamberlain, *The Struggle for Peace* (London, 1939), 19–20; Feiling, *Neville Chamberlain*, 306.

57. *BP*, 11 and 17 July 1935, 23 May 1936, and 28 June 1938; Sir Reginald Blomfield, "Birmingham Civic Centre Competition," *The Architect and Building News*, 19 July 1935, 75; W. T. Benslyn, "Birmingham Municipal Offices Competition," *The Builder*, 19 July 1935, 99; Cadbury Brothers, *Our Birmingham*, 2d ed (Birmingham, 1950), 56; Pevsner and Wedgwood, *Warwickshire*, 116–17.

58. *BP*, 24 Jan. 1930, 24 Oct. 1934, and 24 June 1938; *Birmingham Mail*, 14 July 1938.

59. C. Gill and C. Grant Robertson, *A Short History of Birmingham* (Birmingham, 1938), esp. 53–63; BRL 496108, *Birmingham Gazette, Centenary Supplement*, 11–16 July 1938, esp. 18–19; BRL 484281, *Birmingham, 1838–1938: Centenary Souvenir and Guide to the City* (1938); BRL 489614, "'Build Us a City': A Programme in Celebration of the Birmingham Charter Centenary" (BBC Radio, devised and produced by Robin Whitworth); BRL 493289, "City of Birmingham, Centenary Celebrations, 1838–1938, Visit of their Majesties the King and Queen, Thursday 14th July 1938." (In the event, the king and queen were unable to attend, and their places were taken by the duke and duchess of Gloucester.)

60. BRL MS 506373, "City of Birmingham: Centenary Celebrations: Pageant Committee: Notices of Meetings, Agendas etc, 1937–8"; BRL MS 486185, "Pageant of Birmingham, 1938: Costume Designs Drawn Under the Direction of Jean Campbell" (4 vols.); BRL MS 493287, *Pageant Progress: The News Bulletin of the Pageant of Birmingham*, nos. 1–4, 1 Apr. to 1 July 1938; BRL MS 83218 "Birmingham, 1838–1938: Charter Centenary Celebrations: Official Programme, July 11–16 1938"; BRL MS 494493, "Newspaper Cuttings Relating to the Pageant of Birmingham, 1938"; BRL MS F920.008 K113, "Gwen Lally, Autobiography of a Pageant Master, Newspaper Cuttings from the *Birmingham Weekly Post*, 17 Feb. to 31 March 1939."

61. *BP*, 30 Sept. and 1 Oct. 1938; E. M. Rudland, "To Mrs Neville Chamberlain" and "The Rt. Hon. Neville Chamberlain," both in id., *Mrs Neville Chamberlain and*

Other Poems (Birmingham, 1938), 3, 5. The poem about Neville Chamberlain was originally published in the *Daily Express* on 29 Sept. 1938.

62. Sir Charles Petrie, *The Chamberlain Tradition* (London, 1938), esp. v, 32, 275–77. For Petrie's later, and rather less effusive, views of the family, see Sir Charles Petrie, *A Historian Looks at His World* (London, 1972), 64–65.

63. "You have sat here too long for any good you have been doing. Depart, I say, and let us have done with you. In the name of God, go!"

64. Amery, *My Political Life*, 3: 358–65; Chamberlain, *Struggle for Peace*, 381.

65. Chamberlain, *Struggle for Peace*, 381, 413–20; *BP*, 4 Sept. 1939, 10 and 11 May 1940.

66. A. Sutcliffe and R. Smith, *History of Birmingham*, vol. 3: *Birmingham, 1939–1970* (Oxford, 1974), 14.

67. Hastings, "Birmingham Labour Movement," 87–89; R. B. McCallum and A. Readman, *The British General Election of 1945* (Oxford, 1947), 265; Sutcliffe and Smith, *Birmingham*, 82. For the later history, see R. Waller and B. Criddle, *The Almanac of British Politics*, 5th ed. (London, 1996), 77–92.

68. Rolf, "Tories, Tariffs and Elections," 135–36. It can also be argued, at a deeper level, that the whole "Chamberlain tradition" had presumed a greater degree of social harmony than generally existed, and had assumed that Birmingham carried more weight in the councils of the nation than it usually did. From this perspective, what is most extraordinary about "the Chamberlain tradition" is not that it collapsed so suddenly but that it had survived so long and so successfully. For some useful hints, see C. Behagg, "Myths of Cohesion: Capital and Compromise in the Historiography of Nineteenth-Century Birmingham," *Social History* 11 (1986): 375–84; A. Sutcliffe, "The 'Midland Metropolis': Birmingham, 1890–1980," in *Regional Cities in the UK, 1890–1980*, ed. G. Gordon (London, 1986), 25–39; D. Smith, *Conflict and Compromise: Class Formation in English Society, 1830–1914: A Comparative Study of Birmingham and Sheffield* (London, 1982); H. Berghoff, "Regional Variations in Provincial Business Biography: The Case of Birmingham, Bristol and Manchester, 1870–1914," *Business History* 37 (1995): 64–85.

69. *VCH Warwickshire*, 7: 46; Hartnell, "Art and Culture in Birmingham," 237; *BP*, 14 July 1986.

CHAPTER 9

This chapter is based on research completed while the author was a fellow at the Center for Advanced Study in the Behavioral Sciences in Palo Alto, California. I am grateful for financial support provided by the Andrew W. Mellon Foundation.

1. Peter Gay, *Art and Act: On Causes in History—Manet, Gropius, Mondrian* (New York: Harper & Row, 1976), 166–69.

2. Ibid., 108–9.

3. On the austere and monumental neoclassicism of the 1790s in Prussia, a Franco-Prussian style obviously stimulated by visions of civic community emerging from the French Revolution, see David Watkin and Tilman Mellinghoff, *German Architecture and the Classical Ideal* (Cambridge, Mass.: MIT Press, 1987), 59–83.

4. For an overview of the development of Schinkel's Gothic enthusiasms during this period, see esp. Georg Friedrich Koch, "Schinkels architektonische Entwürfe im gotischen Stil, 1810–1815," *Zeitschrift für Kunstgeschichte* 32, no. 3/4(1969): 262–316.

5. Karl Friedrich Schinkel, "Entwurf zu einer Begräbniskapelle für ihre Majestät die hochselige Königen Luise von Preussen," in *Aus Schinkels Nachlass*, ed. Alfred von Wolzogen, 4 vols. (Berlin, 1862–64), 3: 157; and id., "Architektonischer Plan zum Wiederaufbau der eingeäscherten St. Petrikirche in Berlin," reprinted with drafts and accompanying letters in *Karl Friedrich Schinkel, Lebenswerk: Berlin I: Bauten für die Kunst, Kirchen und Denkmalpflege*, ed. Paul Rave (Berlin: Akademie des Bauwesens, 1941), 167–86.

6. Karl Friedrich Schinkel, "Über das Projekt des Baus eine Cathedrale auf dem Leipziger Platz zu Berlin, als Denkmal für die Brefreiungskriege," in *Aus Schinkels Nachlass*, ed. von Wolzogen, 3: 189–97. Wolzogen wrongly dates the two versions of this memorandum as 1819; it is reprinted with the corrected dates of summer 1814 and Jan. 1815 in Rave, *Karl Friedrich Schinkel, Lebenswerk: Berlin I*, 187–201.

7. Karl Friedrich Schinkel, "Lehrbuchstudien und Architekttheoretische Skripten der Hochromantischen Zeit, um 1810–1815," in id., *Das Architektonische Lehrbuch*, ed. Goerd Peschken (Berlin: Deutscher Kunstverlag, 1979), 27.

8. Schinkel's critical opposition to an "absolute order" imposed on nature through symmetrical organization of uniformities, in favor of a "relative, individual order" that represented a "characteristic" unity emerging organically from an historically individual principle goes back to his first attempts to articulate his architectural principles in book form—the notes for an architectural text gathered during his Italian journey of 1803–5. See the materials and discussion in Schinkel, *Lehrbuch*, ed. Peschken, 18–20.

9. Ibid., 33.

10. Ibid., 70.

11. Ibid., 70–71.

12. Ibid., 71: "Der Streit hat Etwas Vernichtendes, das ethische Gefühl will bei jedem Streit ein Resultat. Ein fortwährender Streit und Kampf zwischen ganz gleichen Kräften hat kein menschliches Interesse, weil das Gleiche sich vereinigen soll, alsdann Ruhe und Festigkeit erhält."

13. Karl Friedrich Schinkel, "Votum zu dem Gutachten Herren Hofrat Hirt (Feb. 23, 1825)," cited in Rave, *Karl Friedrich Schinkel, Lebenswerk: Berlin I*, 35.

14. Goerd Peschken, *Baugeschichte Politisch: Schinkel; Stadt Berlin, Preussische Schlösser* (Braunschweig: Vieweg, 1993), 24–45.

15. Good discussions with extensive documentation of the debates over the purpose of the museum in the Prussian administration can be found in Steven Moyano,

"Quality vs. History: Schinkel's Altes Museum and Prussian Arts Policy," *Art Bulletin* 72 (1990): 585–608; and Reinhard Wegner, "Die Einrichtung des Alten Museums in Berlin: Anmerkungen zu einem neu entdeckten Schinkeldokument," *Jahrbuch der berliner Museen* 1989: 265–287.

16. There is an insightful attempt to decode the frescoes, which were destroyed either during the war or in the "restorations" that followed, in Helmut Boersch-Supan, "Zur Entstehungsgeschichte von Schinkels Entwürfen für die Museumsfresken," *Zeitschrift des deutschen Vereins für Kunstwissenschaft* 35, no. 1/4 (1981): 36–46.

17. Schinkel, *Lehrbuch*, ed. Peschken, 71: "Ehemals ging diese Kunst den politisch grossen Ereignissen nach und war Folge davon. Es wäre vielleicht die höchste Blüthe einer neuen Handlungsweise der Welt wenn die schöne Kunst voran ginge."

18. There is an interesting chapter on Beuth's technocratic perspectives and policies in Eric Dorn Brose, *The Politics of Technological Change in Prussia: Out of the Shadow of Antiquity, 1809–1848* (Princeton: Princeton University Press, 1993), 98–132.

19. Quoted in Barry Bergdoll, *Karl Friedrich Schinkel: An Architecture for Prussia* (New York: Rizzoli, 1994), 172–74.

20. Schinkel's concerns for general urban and environmental design are documented and discussed in Hermann G. Pundt, *Schinkel's Berlin: A Study in Environmental Planning* (Cambridge, Mass.: Harvard University Press, 1972).

21. Karl Friedrich Schinkel, *Reise nach England, Schottland und Paris im Jahre 1826*, ed. Gottfried Riemann (Munich: C. H. Beck, 1986), 244.

22. Commentary to plate #19, "Die neue Anlage der verlängerten Wilhelmsstrasse in Berlin," in Karl Friedrich Schinkel, *Sammlung Architektonischer Entwürfe* (Berlin: Ernst & Korn, 1866), reprinted with an introduction by Hermann Pundt and translations of the commentaries as Karl Friedrich Schinkel, *Collection of Architectural Designs* (New York: Princeton Architectural Press, 1989). My translation.

23. Schinkel, *Sammlung Architektonischer Entwürfe*, commentary to plates 115–22.

24. For a detailed description of the Bauakademie's decorative bas-reliefs, see Paul Ortwin Rave, *Genius der Baukunst: Eine Klassisch-Romantische Bilderfolge an der Berliner Bauakademie* (Berlin: Gebr. Mann, 1944).

25. Schinkel, *Sammlung Architektonischer Entwürfe*, commentary to plates 115–22.

26. Alste Oncken, *Friedrich Gilly 1772–1800*, reprint (1935; Berlin: Gebr. Mann, 1981), 91–92.

27. Schinkel, *Lehrbuch*, ed. Peschken, 114, from which all quotations and paraphrases in the remainder of this paragraph are taken.

28. Ibid.

29. Ibid., 117.

30. Ibid., 119: "Mit Freiheit sich aus Vernunft-Gründen oder aus poetischen Gefühl einem hohen Gesetz unterwerfen ist Etwas erhabenes und schönes, aber kein Ge-

setz passt für alle Fälle oder bleibt im Fortgange der unendlichen Verhältnisse gleich gültig. Höhere Einsicht oder Eingebung für den Geist und als Wesen der Dinge lässt hier die Freiheit rechtfertigen, von dem bisher gültigen Gesetz abzugehen und ein neues, aber von höherem Grade, an die Stelle zu setzen."

CHAPTER 10

1. This is a large topic: for a helpful overview, see *Modernism, 1890–1930*, ed. Malcolm Bradbury and James McFarlane (1976; Harmondsworth: Penguin Books, 1991); for the English case in a European setting, see Michael Long, "The Politics of English Modernism: Eliot, Pound, and Joyce," in *Visions and Blueprints: Avant-garde Culture and Radical Politics in Early Twentieth-Century Europe*, ed. Edward Timms and Peter Collier (Manchester: Manchester University Press, 1988).

2. Peter Gay, *Weimar Culture: The Outsider as Insider* (1969; Harmondsworth: Penguin Books, 1974), 100.

3. T. S. Eliot, *After Strange Gods: A Primer of Modern Heresy* (London: Faber, 1934), 20.

4. For a brief characterization, see Stefan Collini, "The Dream of a European Literary Review: T. S. Eliot and *The Criterion*," in *Les Revues européennes de l'entre-deux-guerres*, ed. Nicole Racine and Michel Trebitsch (Paris: IMEC / Editions de la MSH, forthcoming).

5. Among earlier studies that emphasize this affiliation, see particularly Roger Kojecky, *The Social Criticism of T. S. Eliot* (London: Faber, 1971), and William M. Chace, *The Political Identities of Ezra Pound and T. S. Eliot* (Stanford: Stanford University Press, 1973).

6. Anthony Julius, *T. S. Eliot: Anti-Semitism and Literary Form* (Cambridge: Cambridge University Press, 1995). For an example of one of the more substantial, as well as one of the more sober, responses to Julius's book, see Louis Menand, "Eliot and the Jews," *New York Review of Books*, 6 June 1996, 34–41.

7. Kenneth Asher, *T. S. Eliot and Ideology* (Cambridge: Cambridge University Press, 1995), 2–3. In his conclusion, Asher repeats the claim with specific reference to the writings to be considered in this essay: "The Christian community Eliot seeks to establish in the thirties and forties is based on the Maurrassien vision" (162). Another recent account of Eliot's political identity that draws attention to its reactionary European affinities more generally is Michael North, *The Political Aesthetic of Yeats, Eliot, and Pound* (Cambridge: Cambridge University Press, 1991).

8. The book was a revised version of the Page-Barbour lectures given at the University of Virginia; it was a condition of the lectures that they be published. Eliot's later unease with the book is a possible inference from the fact that he would never allow it to be reprinted.

9. Donald Gallup's marvelous *T. S. Eliot: A Bibliography* (New York: Harcourt, 1969) provides a full listing. To date, none of the proposals for a scholarly edition of Eliot's prose has reached fruition.

10. J. M. Cameron, "T. S. Eliot as a Political Writer," in *T. S. Eliot: A Symposium for his Seventieth Birthday*, ed. Neville Braybrooke (London: Hart-Davis, 1958), 145.

11. Ibid., 146. *The Idea of a Christian Society* (London: Faber, 1939) and *Notes Towards the Definition of Culture* (London: Faber, 1948), Eliot's main two works of social criticism, are henceforth cited both in the text and in the notes that follow here as *Idea* and *Notes* respectively.

12. E. R. Norman, *Church and Society in England, 1770–1970* (Oxford: Oxford University Press, 1976), 13; see 315–92 for a detailed discussion of this movement.

13. Quoted in ibid., 366. Norman himself comments that "the Right" was not present at Malvern. Paul Addison notes in *The Road to 1945: British Politics and the Second World War* (London: Cape, 1975), 186–87, that under the guidance of William Temple, then archbishop of York, the conference passed a resolution "to the effect that the private ownership of the principal industrial resources of the community *might* be a stumbling block to Christian lives."

14. See Norman Dennis and A. H. Halsey, *English Ethical Socialism: Thomas More to R. H. Tawney* (Oxford: Oxford University Press, 1988), and, more generally, Raymond Williams, *Culture and Society, 1780–1950* (London: Chatto, 1958).

15. See the discussion in Norman, *Church and Society*, 248–49 and 318–19, where the Christendom Group is described as "the leading Socialist movement in the Church of England" in this period.

16. See *The Times*, 4 Apr. 1934; the list of signatories included Lascelles Abercrombie, Bonamy Dobrée, Aldous Huxley, Edwin Muir, Hamish Miles, Herbert Read, and I. A. Richards.

17. For general accounts of the renewed political and intellectual vigor of the Anglican Church, in particular, between the mid 1920s and the late 1940s, see Norman, *Church and Society*, and Adrian Hastings, *A History of English Christianity, 1920–1985* (London: Collins, 1986). The impact is confirmed, from another perspective, by Addison, *Road to 1945*, esp. ch. 6.

18. Looking back on the late 1940s and early 1950s in *T. S. Eliot: A Friendship* (London: Routledge, 1988), 167, E. W. F. Tomlin later described him as "the most renowned [layman] in the whole Anglican Communion."

19. Quoted in Peter Ackroyd, *T. S. Eliot* (London: Sphere, 1985 [1984]), 222.

20. The above paragraphs are based upon the works by Hastings and Norman previously cited, as well as on Kojecky, *Social Criticism*, 156–58, and Ackroyd, *T. S. Eliot*, 242, 249.

21. "The two pamphlets containing the Malvern proceedings sold, together, more than a million copies" (Addison, *Road to 1945*, 187). Temple's *Christianity and the Social Order*, which restated a similar position, sold 139,000 copies as a Penguin Special in 1942.

22. Hastings, *English Christianity*, ch. 10, esp. 446.

23. T. S. Eliot, "Notes on Social Philosophy," paper prepared for a meeting of the Moot, quoted by Kojecky, *Social Criticism*, 179. The paper is undated; Kojecky says it was prepared for the meeting of July 1940; the guide to the Moot papers in the

Clarke Collection, London Institute of Education, suggests 1942. On the papers of the Moot, see n. 47 below.

24. In *Church and Society*, 364–65, Norman observes that from the late 1930s on, a mood of greater "realism" was evident in Christian commentators: "Social radicalism in the Church was, therefore, in eclipse. And it is important to notice that the reason was not a change of generation, but a feeling of disillusionment amongst the writers who had previously created 'Christian Sociology.'" He specifically mentions Demant and Reckitt as illustrative of this change.

25. See ibid., 363, 376, and 381–83.

26. *Prospect for Christendom: Essays in Catholic Social Reconstruction*, ed. Maurice Reckitt (London: Faber, 1945), 8. Eliot's essay in this collection, "Cultural Forces in the Human Order," provided the basis for the first chapter of *Notes*.

27. This hardly needs to be documented, but for evidence of various kinds one might turn to Martin Wiener, *English Culture and the Decline of the Industrial Spirit, 1850–1980* (Cambridge: Cambridge University Press, 1981), or D. L. LeMahieu, *A Culture for Democracy: Mass Communication and the Cultivated Mind in Britain Between the Wars* (Oxford: Oxford University Press, 1988); a different illustration of the continuing centrality of this issue to public debate in England was, in my view, provided by the controversy surrounding C. P. Snow's "two cultures" thesis: see Stefan Collini, introduction to C. P. Snow, *The Two Cultures* (Cambridge: Cambridge University Press, 1993), esp. xxii–xlii.

28. T. S. Eliot, "The English Tradition: Address to the School of Sociology," *Christendom* 10 (1940): 227.

29. The latter had been established in 1939, with Oldham as editor, as the organ of the Council on the Christian Faith and the Common Life and soon had almost 10,000 subscribers (see Kojecky, *Social Criticism*, 161); Eliot occasionally acted as editor in Oldham's absence.

30. T. S. Eliot, "The English Tradition: Some Thoughts as a Preface to Study," *Christendom* 10 (1940): 105.

31. The book was published on 26 Oct. 1939 and was more successful than Eliot had anticipated; the first printing sold out almost immediately, and the book sold 6,000 copies by Christmas (Tomlin, *Eliot: A Friendship*, 122–23).

32. *Idea*, 10–11, 15, 39, 61, 68, 64.

33. An attempt to revivify Coleridge's term had just been made by Middleton Murry in *The Price of Leadership*, a work cited by Eliot, *Idea*, 35, 74.

34. Eliot, *Idea*, 42, 40, 35, 37.

35. Eliot, *Notes*, 60–61.

36. For a recent reassessment of the role of this stratum, see *After the Victorians: Private Conscience and Public Duty in Modern Britain*, ed. Susan Pedersen and Peter Mandler (London: Routledge, 1994).

37. T. S. Eliot, *Christianity and Culture* (New York: Harcourt, 1960); this is the edition cited in, e.g., Asher's *T. S. Eliot and Ideology*.

38. Gay, *Weimar Culture*, xii.

39. The best account of the development of Mannheim's thinking on this topic is David Kettler, Volker Meja, and Nico Stehr, *Karl Mannheim* (London: Tavistock, 1984), 129–50. See also Gunter W. Remmling, *The Sociology of Karl Mannheim* (London: Routledge, 1975); A. P. Simonds, *Karl Mannheim's Sociology of Knowledge* (Oxford: Oxford University Press, 1978); and Colin Loader, *The Intellectual Development of Karl Mannheim* (Cambridge, Cambridge University Press, 1985).

40. See Loader, *Intellectual Development*, 151.

41. See, e.g., Alec R. Vidler, *Scenes From a Clerical Life: An Autobiography* (London: Collins, 1977), 116–19 (Vidler had been a member of the Moot).

42. Kettler et al., *Mannheim*, 154.

43. T. S. Eliot, "On the Place and Function of the Clerisy" (typescript discussion paper for meeting of the Moot in December 1944), Moot papers, Clarke Collection, London Institute of Education. This paper is printed as an appendix in Kojecky, *Social Criticism*; the quotation is at 244. On the records of the Moot, see n. 47 below.

44. T. S. Eliot, review of *Man and Society in an Age of Reconstruction*, by Karl Mannheim, *Spectator*, 7 June 1940, 782.

45. T. S. Eliot, "Planning and Religion," *Theology* 46 (1943): 102–6.

46. In his obituary notice of Mannheim, Eliot gracefully avoided these differences, but in private he could sometimes be more forthright: "Of the numerous central Europeans here," he wrote to Allen Tate in March 1945, "there are two I recommend: Eric Meissner and Michael Polanyi. Most of the others hold views which I distrust. Karl Mannheim is a very good fellow, but if you have read his 'Man and Society' (Harcourt publish it, I think) you will know that I regard his ideas as dangerous" (Eliot to Allen Tate, 13 Mar. 1945, Tate Papers, Princeton University). Eliot's letter supplementing Mannheim's obituary appeared in *The Times*, 25 Jan. 1947, 7. I am grateful to Mrs. Valerie Eliot and to Faber & Faber for permission to quote from unpublished Eliot material.

47. The records of the Moot are scattered in several private and public collections, not all of them accessible to all researchers. Roger Kojecky was evidently given access to, and freedom to quote from, these records in some form; an example of more limited access is reported in Kettler et al., *Mannheim*, 149. I have consulted the material available in the papers of Sir Fred Clarke at the London Institute of Education and of A. D. Lindsay at Keele University; quotation, unless otherwise specified, is taken from Kojecky, *Social Criticism*.

48. T. S. Eliot, "Notes on Mannheim's Paper," 2, Moot Papers, London Institute of Education.

49. T. S. Eliot, "Notes Towards a Definition of Culture, I," *New English Weekly*, 21 Jan. 1943, 117.

50. Eliot, "On the Place and Function of the Clerisy"; quotations from Kojecky, *Social Criticism*, 245, 244.

51. T. S. Eliot, "Some Notes on Social Philosophy" (paper prepared for the Moot meeting of July 1940), typescript in Moot papers, Clarke Collection, London Institute of Education, quoted in Kojecky, *Social Criticism*, 179. It seems possible that these discussions directly affected Mannheim's own thinking. Kettler et al. refer to his notes for a never-published study of "intellectuals," in which Mannheim discussed the emergence in England of the social type of "the gentleman," who, though he did not pursue abstract speculation for its own sake, was nevertheless conscious that his greater knowledge and culture gave him a responsibility to the larger public. For this reason, Mannheim became convinced that structural problems of "mass society" would be less destructive in England than elsewhere, and that there was a correspondingly greater chance of influencing this influential elite with his own ideas. Rather than having to face the problem, intractable in the circumstances of most European countries, of how to bring "the intellectuals" to power, the task in England seemed to Mannheim to be rather that of bringing the intellectually inclined "gentleman" to recognize his role as a member of the "planning elite." Unfortunately, the date of the composition of these notes is not given. See Kettler et al., *Mannheim*, 137–38.

52. *Idea* was published in October 1939; Eliot's careful reading of Mannheim's *Man and Society* took place in the spring of 1940; he prepared a short paper on "Social Philosophy" for the Moot meeting in July 1940; his "Notes on Mannheim's Paper" was written for the Moot in Jan. 1941; his four articles on "culture" (which were to make up the first chapter of *Notes*) were published in the *New English Weekly* in January and February 1943; in August 1943, he wrote five letters for circulation to the Moot, largely dealing with the role of "the superior individuals of the ruling class"; in the winter of 1943–44, he and Mairet conducted a seminar entitled "Towards the Definition of Culture" at St. Anne's House, a "centre of Christian discourse" in London; his paper on "The Place and Function of the Clerisy" was completed by November 1944; the essay "Cultural Forces in the Human Order" (a reworking of the *New English Weekly* pieces), which appeared in *Prospects for Christendom* and was an early version of the first chapter of *Notes*, was completed early in 1945, and his article on "The Class and the Elite," essentially a draft of the chapter of that title in *Notes*, appeared in the *New English Review* in October 1945.

53. Mairet sent Eliot extensive comments on earlier drafts, and also wrote a reader's report for Faber; these materials are bound in with the typescript of *Notes* held in the Eliot Collection, King's College, Cambridge. The book is dedicated to Mairet "in gratitude and admiration."

54. E.g., Christopher Dawson spoke of Eliot as "stating what would have been a truism to Burke and Fitzjames Stephen" ("Mr T. S. Eliot on the Meaning of Culture," *The Month* 1 [1949]: 154).

55. Eliot, *Notes*, 28.

56. Ibid., 9.

57. For Dawson's career, see Christina Scott, *A Historian and His World: A Life of Christopher Dawson, 1889–1970* (London: Sheed & Ward, 1984).

58. Quoted in ibid., 89.

59. Ibid., 93.

60. Norman remarks that although Dawson was a Catholic, "his appeal to his generation was nowhere greater than in the Church of England" (*Church and Society*, 364–65). When Dawson's *Beyond Politics* appeared in 1939, it met with wide praise; Demant was particularly enthusiastic — see his review-essay reprinted in his *Theology of Society: More Essays in Christian Polity* (London: Kegan Paul, 1947).

61. Quoted in Scott, *Dawson*, 128; for Eliot's favorable opinion of the volume, see "Our Culture," *New English Weekly*, 4 Mar. 1948, 203–4.

62. Eliot, *Notes*, 44, 58, 82, 46, and 45.

63. From an extensive historiography, see J. W. Burrow, *Whigs and Liberals: Continuity and Change in English Political Thought* (Oxford: Oxford University Press, 1988); Dennis Smith, "Englishness and the Liberal Inheritance after 1886," in *Englishness: Politics and Culture, 1880–1920*, ed. Robert Colls and Philip Dodd (Beckenham: Croom Helm, 1986); Julia Stapleton, *Englishness and the Study of Politics: The Social and Political Thought of Ernest Barker* (Cambridge: Cambridge University Press, 1994).

64. Eliot, *Notes*, 39, 40.

65. Ibid., 42.

66. The typescript was a little more outspoken than the published version here; Eliot finally omitted a paragraph referring to "some of Dr Mannheim's disciples" (notably F. C. Happold and H. C. Dent) who appeared to believe that planning could ensure that the right kind of elite would emerge, and commenting: "It is, I fear, Dr Mannheim who has let this wind out of the bag" (Eliot Collection, King's).

67. In addition, as he confided to Philip Mairet in 1941: "I am not naturally sympathetic to the 'carrière ouverte', at least not to the career *wide* open — because I think it makes for instability and leads to the advancement of fellows with nothing in view *but* the career" (Eliot to Mairet, 5 Jan. 1941; HRHRC, Texas).

68. Michael Oakeshott, *Rationalism in Politics and Other Essays* (London: Methuen, 1961); the relevant essays mostly appeared in the *Cambridge Journal* in the mid and late 1940s. The similarities here between Eliot and such conservative thinkers were remarked at the time, e.g., by G. H. Bantock, "Mr Eliot and Education," *Scrutiny* 16 (1949): 66n.

69. It manifested itself in, e.g., Eliot's 1948 review of Middleton Murry's *Free Society*, in which he insists, in Oakeshottian vein, that forms of government cannot be transplanted: "And the concept of 'freedom' abstracted from the history of Britain and then re-applied to Britain *mechanically* might also have unfortunate effects" (*Adelphi* 24 [1948]: 247).

70. Mairet's comments on the typescript indicate that he thought the ending of the book, as drafted, was too polemical; Eliot Collection, King's.

71. Eliot, *Notes*, 108–9.

72. T. S. Eliot, *To Criticise the Critic, and Other Writings* (London: Faber, 1965), 26; see also the preface added to the paperback edition of *Notes* in 1962.

73. In 1956, Raymond Williams observed of *Notes*: "certainly, in England, it has

had an important political effect" ("T. S. Eliot on Culture," *Essays in Criticism* 6 [1956]: 302). For the attention accorded to Eliot's views on culture, see Robert Hewison, *Culture and Consensus: England, Art and Politics since 1940* (London: Methuen, 1995).

74. "The general point of view [of the essays in the volume] may be described as classicist in literature, royalist in politics, and anglo-catholic in religion" (T. S. Eliot, *For Lancelot Andrewes: Essays on Style and Order* [London: Faber, 1928], 7).

75. Raymond Williams, *Culture and Society, 1780–1950* (1958; Harmondsworth: Penguin Books, 1963), 227, 237; the article cited in n. 73 above was an earlier version of this chapter.

76. Richard Hoggart, *An Imagined Life: Life and Times, 1959–1991* (1992; Oxford: Oxford University Press, 1993), 73.

77. T. S. Eliot, "Last Words," *Criterion* 18 (Jan. 1939): 269–75.

78. Mannheim to Louis Wirth, 6 Apr. 1939, quoted in Kettler et al., *Mannheim*, 130 ("as is also shown," added Mannheim with unself-conscious egotism, "by the growth of my following among students and the general public").

79. Gay, *Weimar Culture*, 100.

CHAPTER 11

1. Peter Gay, *The Bourgeois Experience: Victoria to Freud*, vol. 3: *The Cultivation of Hatred* (New York: Norton, 1993; London: Harper Collins, 1994), xi.

2. Louis-Ferdinand Céline, *Semmelweis et autres écrits médicaux; textes réunis et présentés par Jean-Pierre Dauphin et Henri Godard. Cahiers Céline* 3 (Paris: Gallimard, 1977), 8.

3. On this theme, see Mary Douglas, *Purity and Danger: An Analysis of Concepts of Pollution and Taboo* (New York: Praeger, 1966).

4. Jack Green, "Physicians Practicing Other Occupations, Especially Literature," *Mount Sinai Journal of Medicine* 60, no. 132 (1993).

5. Daniel Pick, *Faces of Degeneration: A European Disorder, c. 1848–c. 1918* (Cambridge: Cambridge University Press, 1989).

6. Louis-Ferdinand Céline, *Voyage au bout de la nuit* (Paris: Gallimard, 1932); all citations in this chapter are from the remarkable English translation by Ralph Manheim, *Journey to the End of the Night* (London: John Calder, 1983).

7. As cited in Paul Fussell, *The Great War and Modern Memory* (New York: Oxford University Press, 1975), 132.

8. Nicholas Hewitt, "*Mort à crédit* et la crise de la petite bourgeoisie," *Australian Journal of French Studies* 13 (1976): 110.

9. Céline, *Voyage*, 72.

10. Peter G. J. Pulzer, *The Rise of Political Anti-Semitism in Germany and Austria* (New York: Wiley, 1964).

11. Louis-Ferdinand Céline, *Mort à crédit* (Paris: Gallimard, 1952).

12. See Jay Winter and Jean-Louis Robert, *Capital Cities at War: Paris, London, Berlin, 1914–1919* (Cambridge, Cambridge University Press, 1996), chs. 2, 16.

13. Philippe Alméras, *Céline: Entre haines et passion* (Paris: Robert Laffont, 1994), 13.

14. Ibid., 22.

15. See his account in *Casse-pipe* (Paris: F. Chambriand, 1949), translated under the title *Cannon-fodder* by K. de Coninck and B. Childish (Rochester, Kent: Hangman Books, 1988).

16. Alméras, *Céline*, 32.

17. As cited in ibid., 36.

18. As cited in ibid., 38.

19. Léon Murard and Patrick Zylberman, "L'Autre Guerre, 1914–1918: La Santé publique en France sous l'œil de l'Amérique," *Revue historique* 276, no. 2 (Oct.–Dec. 1986): 367–97; and Léon Murard and Patrick Zylberman, "La Mission Rockefeller en France et la création du Comité national de défense contre la tuberculose (1917–1923)," *Revue d'histoire moderne et contemporaine* 24 (1987): 257–81.

20. M. S. Teitelbaum and J. M. Winter, *The Fear of Population Decline* (London: Academic Press, 1986), ch. 2.

21. Philippe Roussin, "La Médecine, la littérature, et la maladie," *Bulletin de la bibliothèque L.-F. Céline de l'Université Paris VII et de la Société d'Études céliniennes* 5 (1981): 9.

22. As cited in Alméras, *Céline*, 104–5.

23. On this general theme, see Jay Winter, *Sites of Memory, Sites of Mourning: The Place of the First World War in European Cultural History* (Cambridge: Cambridge University Press, 1996).

24. Jean Norton Cru, *Témoins: Essai d'analyse et de critique des souvenirs de combatants édités en français de 1915 à 1928* (Nancy: Presses universitaires de Nancy, 1993); see also the wrongheaded statements in C. Barnett, "A Military Historian's View of the Great War," *Essays by Diverse Hands: The Journal of the Royal Society of Literature,* 1978: 1–18.

25. On Céline's "vertigo" and escape from justice after World War II, see Alméras, *Céline*, 229–30. On his "dizziness," see Julia Kristeva, *Powers of Horror: An Essay on Abjection*, trans. Leon S. Roudiez (New York: Columbia University Press, 1982), 141. On his anti-Semitism, see Alice Yaeger Kaplan, *Reproductions of Banality: Fascism, Literature and French Intellectual Life*, Theory and History of Literature, vol. 36 (Minneapolis: University of Minnesota Press, 1986), 107ff.

26. Alméras, *Céline*, 124.

27. Céline, *Voyage*, 50.

28. Blaise Cendrars, *La Main coupée* (Paris: Denoël, 1928).

29. Céline, *Voyage*, 36.   30. Ibid., 20.

31. Ibid., 47.   32. Ibid., 50.

33. Ibid., 53.   34. Ibid., 54.

35. Ibid., 60.

36. See the discussion in chapter 5 of Jay Winter and Blaine Baggett, *The Great War and the Shaping of the Twentieth Century* (New York: Viking/Penguin, 1996).

37. Céline, *Voyage*, 62.

38. I am grateful to Nick Hewitt for his advice on this and other points.

39. Céline, *Voyage*, 83.

40. Ibid., 90.

41. Marie-Christine Bellosta, *Céline, ou l'art de la contradiction* (Paris: Presses universitaires de France, 1990), 132–36.

42. Milton Hindus, *The Crippled Giant: A Literary Relationship with Louis-Ferdinand Céline* (Hanover, N.H.: University Press of New England, 1986), 10.

43. Céline, *Voyage*, 400. This time it is Robinson who makes the claim. In later years, Céline himself used it to present a defense against extradition from Denmark to France to face accusations of treason. See Alméras, *Céline*, 316ff.

44. See Marc Roudebush, "Shell Shock in France During the Great War in Voyage to the End of a Mind: Céline, War and Psychiatry," in *Traumatic Pasts*, ed. M. Micale and P. Lerner (Cambridge: Cambridge University Press, 2000).

45. Céline, *Voyage*, 370–71.　　46. Ibid., 373.

47. Ibid., 79.　　48. Ibid., 66.

49. Ibid., 85 and 87.　　50. Ibid., 54.

51. Ibid., 80.　　52. Ibid., 193.

53. Ibid., 411.

54. Ibid., 212. On Céline and bodies, see Kristeva, *Powers*, 149ff.

55. Thanks are due to Nick Hewitt for setting me straight on this point. See also Hindus, *Crippled Giant*, 63.

56. Pick, *Faces of Degeneration*; and George Mosse, *Toward the Final Solution: A History of European Racism* (New York: H. Fertig, 1978).

57. Céline, "Hommage à Zola," in *Céline et l'actualité littéraire, 1932–1957: Textes réunis et présentés par Jean-Pierre Dauphin et Henri Godard*, Cahiers Céline 1 (Paris: Gallimard, 1976), 83.

58. Annie Montaut, "Regard médical, mensonge théorique et anti-sémitisme: Une Écriture," *Bulletin de la bibliothèque L.-F. Céline de l'Université Paris VII et de la Société d'Études céleniennes* 9 (1983): 59.

59. Teitelbaum and Winter, *Fear of Population Decline*, chs. 2–3.

60. Alexis Carrel, *L'Homme cet inconnu* (Paris: Les petits-fils de Plon et Nourrit, 1935).

61. Alméras, *Céline*, 337.

62. Hindus, *Crippled Giant*, 35.

63. On the *picaro*, see Richard Bjornson, *The Picaresque Hero in European Fiction* (Madison: University of Wisconsin Press, 1977); Michael André Bernstein, *Bitter Carnival: Ressentiment and the Abject Hero* (Princeton: Princeton University Press, 1992), 123; and Henri Godard, *Poétique de Céline* (Paris: Gallimard, 1985), 335–36.

64. Céline, *Voyage*, 365.

CHAPTER 12

1. For one consideration of this dynamic, which focuses on nineteenth-century France, see Eugen Weber, "Religion or Superstition?" in id., *My France: Politics, Culture, Myth* (Cambridge, Mass.: Harvard University Press, 1991).

2. For a recent account, see Prudence Jones and Nigel Pennick, *A History of Pagan Europe* (London: Routledge, 1995), 1. For an account that traces the origin of the concept, if not the word, to Moses and his Egyptian predecessor Akhenaton, see Jan Assmann, "The Mosaic Distinction: Israel, Egypt, and the Invention of Paganism," *Representations* 56 (fall 1996). He argues that they were the first to distinguish between true and false, or genuine and counterreligions.

3. The claim that early modern witchcraft was a survival of pre-Christian pagan customs was made most insistently by the Egyptologist Margaret Murray in such works as *The Witch Cult in Western Europe* (Oxford: Clarendon Press, 1921). It has been successfully challenged by Norman Cohn, *Europe's Inner Demons* (London: Heinemann, 1975).

4. Jones and Pennick, *History*, 197f.

5. It might be noted that one of those "others" was secular rationalism, which has often been contrasted with pagan myth. For a powerful attempt to undermine this distinction, see Hans Blumenberg, *Work on Myth*, trans. Robert M. Wallace (Cambridge, Mass., MIT Press, 1985).

6. For a discussion, see Jean Seznec, *The Survival of the Pagan Gods: The Mythological Tradition and Its Place in Renaissance Humanism and the Arts* (Princeton: Princeton University Press, 1995); see also his excellent article on "Myth in the Middle Ages and the Renaissance" in the *Dictionary of the History of Ideas* (New York: Scribner, 1973), vol. 3.

7. Its persistence is demonstrated in such recent works as Jacques Ellul, *The Humiliation of the Word*, trans. Joyce Main Hanks (Grand Rapids, Mich.: Eerdmans, 1985).

8. For a wide variety of such texts, including Bayle's "Jupiter" in *The Dictionary Historical and Critical* and Toland's "Origin of Idolatry" from his *Letters to Serena*, see *The Rise of Modern Mythology, 1680–1860*, ed. Burton Feldman and Robert B. Richardson (Bloomington: Indiana University Press, 1972), part 1.

9. Robert Weiss, *The Renaissance Discovery of Classical Antiquity* (Oxford: Blackwell, 1969).

10. Peter Gay, *The Enlightenment: An Interpretation*, vol. 1: *The Rise of Modern Paganism* (New York: Knopf, 1966), ch. 5.

11. There were, to be sure, nineteenth-century attempts to reconcile classical and Christian values, especially in Britain. But as Richard Jenkyns notes in *The Victorians and Ancient Greece* (Cambridge, Mass., Harvard University Press, 1980), 68, "some of the greatest Victorians experienced, not always consciously, a conflict between their passion for ancient Greece and their Christianity."

12. Arnold, to be sure, often tried to integrate and balance the "Hellenic" and the

"Hebraic." For an account of his efforts, see Joseph Carroll, *The Cultural Theory of Matthew Arnold* (Berkeley and Los Angeles: University of California Press, 1982), 69 f.

13. "Since the Anglo-Saxon times the Christian church in England had stood out against the worship of wells and rivers. The pagan divinities of grove, stream and mountain had been expelled, leaving behind them a disenchanted world, to be shaped, moulded and dominated," Keith Thomas notes in *Man and the Natural World: A History of the Modern Sensibility* (New York: Pantheon Books, 1983), 22. He points to many reasons why this attitude was modified, if not reversed, but one was the rediscovery of the classical arcadian pastoral tradition. For the slightly later development of the same sensibility in France, see D. G. Charlton, *New Images of the Natural in France* (Cambridge: Cambridge University Press, 1984), ch. 2.

14. E. M. Butler, *The Tyranny of Greece over Germany* (Boston: Beacon Press, 1958); Henry Hatfield, *Aesthetic Paganism in German Literature* (Cambridge, Mass.: Harvard University Press, 1964) and *Clashing Myths in German Literature: From Heine to Rilke* (Cambridge, Mass.: Harvard University Press, 1974); Josef Chytry, *The Aesthetic State: A Quest in Modern German Thought* (Berkeley and Los Angeles: University of California Press, 1989); and Suzanne L. Marchand, *Down from Olympus: Archaeology and Philhellenism in Germany, 1750–1970* (Princeton: Princeton University Press, 1996).

15. On Vico and classical rhetoric, see John D. Schaeffer, *Sensus Communis: Vico, Rhetoric, and the Limits of Relativism* (Durham, N.C.: Duke University Press, 1990).

16. Robert Darnton, "History of Reading," in *New Perspectives on Historical Writing*, ed. Peter Burke (University Park, Pa.: Pennsylvania State University Press, 1991), 144.

17. Prys Morgan, "From a Death to a View: The Hunt for the Welsh Past in the Romantic Period," in *The Invention of Tradition*, ed. Eric Hobsbawm and Terence Ranger (Cambridge: Cambridge University Press, 1983).

18. For an account of the still potent adoption of Gallic ancestry as a symbol of French identity, see Eugen Weber, "Nos ancêtres les gaulois," in *My France*. It should be noted that aristocratic dynasties themselves often evoked an alleged ancestor in the pagan world to establish their pedigree. Here they could draw on the euhemerist reading of the ancient gods, which interpreted them as actual historical figures who had been transformed over time into deities.

19. Hugh Honour, *Romanticism* (New York: Harper & Row, 1979), 206 f.

20. Jenkyns, *Victorians and Ancient Greece*, 8.

21. Schliemann was one of Freud's explicit heroes, collecting antiquities was his passion, and he often compared psychoanalysis to the discovery of Troy. He was, however, ambivalent about the classical legacy, which meant that at times he upheld a traditional model of sublimated culture as an alternative to fruitless rebellion. For a reading that argues his "choice was for Winckelmann and the classical balance of ancient Greece rather than the continued political antagonism and strife symbolized by

Rome and medieval Europe," see William J. McGrath, *Freud's Discovery of Psychoanalysis: The Politics of Hysteria* (Ithaca, N.Y.: Cornell University Press, 1986), 228.

22. For one account of the power and variety of this matriarchal ideology in pre–World War I Vienna, see Jacques Le Rider, *Modernity and the Crises of Identity*, trans. Rosemary Morris (New York: Continuum Books, 1993), chs. 6, 7, and 8.

23. For Semper's role in the debate over polychromy on Greek buildings, see Harry Francis Mallgrave, *Gottfried Semper: Architect of the Nineteenth Century* (New Haven: Yale University Press, 1996).

24. For an account, see Steven E. Aschheim, *The Nietzsche Legacy in Germany, 1890–1990* (Berkeley and Los Angeles: University of California Press, 1992), 223–29.

25. Ibid. shows that the so-called *Glaubensbewegung*, which tried to revive Nordic religion, was easily assimilated into Nazism (226). But according to John Yeowell, *Odinism and Christianity under the Third Reich* (London: The Odinic Rite, 1993), worshippers of Odin were persecuted by the Nazis. In *Perceptions of Jewish History* (Berkeley and Los Angeles: University of California Press, 1993), 328, Amos Funkenstein notes the discontinuities between pagan anti-Judaism in the classical world and its more virulent Christian successors and claims that because of its general tolerance of different religions, "whatever 'paganism' may mean, in its historical manifestations it was certainly not less humane than Christianity — or Judaism."For a general assessment of the relations between paganism and *völkisch* thought, see Stefanie v. Schnurbein, *Religion als Kulturkritik: Neugermanisches Heidentum im 20. Jahrhundert* (Heidelberg: Carl Winter Universitätsverlag, 1992).

26. Martin Bernal, *Black Athena: The Afro-Asian Roots of Classical Civilization* (London: Free Association Press, 1987). See also, however, the rebuttal of Bernal's thesis in Mary R. Lefkowitz, *Not Out of Africa: How Afrocentrism Became an Excuse to Teach Myth as History* (New York: Basic Books, 1996).

27. For an account of Jaeger's compromised role in the 1930s before his emigration, see Marchand, *Down from Olympus*, ch. 9.

28. Paul Delany, *The Neo-Pagans: Friendship and Love in the Rupert Brooke Circle* (London: Hamish Hamilton, 1987).

29. Jenkyns, *Victorians and Ancient Greece*, ch. 13.

30. Camille Paglia, *Sexual Personae: Art and Decadence from Nefertiti to Emily Dickinson* (New York: Vintage Books, 1991), 25.

31. John Casey, *Pagan Virtue: An Essay in Ethics* (Oxford: Clarendon Press, 1990).

32. Ibid., 201, cites Bernard Williams, *Moral Luck* (Cambridge: Cambridge University Press, 1981), positively.

33. Odo Marquard, "In Praise of Polytheism (On Monomythic and Polymythic Thinking)," in *Farewell to Matters of Principle: Philosophical Studies*, trans. Robert M. Wallace (New York: Oxford University Press, 1989), 104.

34. Jacques Merlaud, *Le Renouveau païen dans la pensée française* (Paris: Le Labyrinthe, 1986).

35. Carl L. Becker, *The Heavenly City of the Eighteenth-Century Philosophers*

(New Haven: Yale University Press, 1932). See Gay's polemic in *The Party of Humanity: Essays in the French Enlightenment* (New York: Knopf, 1964).

36. Ibid., 46. Not all of the members of "the party of humanity" were, of course, equally indebted to the classical legacy. In his review of Gay's book in the *American Historical Review* 73, no. 3 (Feb. 1968), Franklin L. Ford claims that neither Lessing nor Rousseau really qualifies.

37. Gay, *Enlightenment*, 9.

38. Ibid., 8.

39. Ibid., 126.

40. Cited in ibid., 70.

41. It is not difficult to discern the continuities between Gay's reading of the Enlightenment and his later defense of Freud as a scientific researcher more indebted to cosmopolitan traditions of enlightened inquiry and cultivated *Bildung* than to the peculiarities of his Viennese Jewish milieu. Psychoanalysis, he writes in *Freud, Jews and Other Germans: Masters and Victims in Modernist Culture* (Oxford: Oxford University Press, 1978), "demonstrated that it was more than possible, it was necessary, to be rational about irrationality" (71). In *The Bridge of Criticism: Dialogues Among Lucian, Erasmus, and Voltaire on the Enlightenment — On History and Hope, Imagination and Reason, Constraint and Freedom — And on Its Meaning for Our Time* (New York: Harper & Row, 1970), Gay already has Voltaire call Freud "our most distinguished representative in the twentieth century" (91).

42. Peter Gay, *The Enlightenment: An Interpretation*, vol. 2: *The Science of Freedom* (New York: Norton, 1969), 125. Lyotard often pits local narratives against the denotative language game of universalizing science, but he is not above drawing on the lessons of computerization for postmodernism when it suits his purposes. Gay, for his part, acknowledges the importance of the historical narrative during the Enlightenment, which, for all its faults, was more than merely Bolingbroke's "philosophy teaching by example."

43. Ernst Cassirer, *The Philosophy of the Enlightenment*, trans. Fritz C. A. Koelln and James P. Pettegrove (Boston: Beacon Press, 1951).

44. Gay, *Enlightenment*, 1: 419. In *Weimar Culture: The Outsider as Insider* (New York: Harper & Row, 1968), Gay echoes this sentiment, noting: "What Gropius taught, and what most Germans did not want to learn, was the lesson of Bacon and Descartes and the Enlightenment: that one must confront the world and dominate it, that the cure for the ills of modernity is more, and the right kind of modernity" (101).

45. Ibid., 225.

46. Peter Hanns Reill, *The German Enlightenment and the Rise of Historicism* (Berkeley and Los Angeles: University of California Press, 1975), 174f. See also David Sorkin, *Moses Mendelssohn and the Religious Enlightenment* (Berkeley and Los Angeles: University of California Press, 1996). Sorkin's current work extends to other examples of religious enlighteners, such as the Anglican William Warburton, the Lutheran Siegmund Jacob Baumgarten, and the Catholic Anselm Desing.

47. Hans Kohn, "The Multidimensional Enlightenment," *Journal of the History of Ideas* 31, no. 3 (July–Sept. 1970): 469.

48. Amos Funkenstein, *Theology and the Scientific Imagination: From the Middle Ages to the Seventeenth Century* (Princeton: Princeton University Press, 1986), 357.

49. In *Living the Enlightenment: Freemasonry and Politics in Eighteenth-Century Europe* (New York: Oxford University Press, 1991), Margaret C. Jacob, a more recent student of the subject, has a less critical reading of the implications of the masons for Gay's thesis, noting the frequent masonic evocation of a pagan pedigree for their rituals and beliefs. "[P]erhaps we can better understand why some historians have seen in the Enlightenment the rise of modern paganism," Jacob concludes (p. 153). The paganism in question was more Egyptian than Greek, however, a pedigree ignored by Gay. See the discussion in Assmann, "Mosaic Distinction."

50. Paglia, *Sexual Personae*, 681.

51. See Peter Gay, *Style in History* (New York: Basic Books, 1974).

52. Lyotard, however, has grown more skeptical over the years about the emancipatory potential in primary process. Such later essays as "Figure Foreclosed" of 1984, in *The Lyotard Reader*, ed. Andrew Benjamin (Oxford: Basil Blackwell, 1989), signify a more austere reading of the legacy of psychoanalysis.

53. Gay has a short discussion of Burke's *Philosophical Enquiry into the Origin of our Ideas of the Sublime and the Beautiful* in volume 2 of *The Enlightenment: An Interpretation*, but calls it a "young man's book, energetic, facile, a little irresponsible, and sometimes embarrassing" (305).

54. Jean-François Lyotard, *Dérive à partir de Marx et Freud* (Paris: Union générale d'éditions, 1973). For his account of the change, see "A Memorial of Marxism: For Pierre Souyri," in Lyotard, *Peregrinations: Law, Form, Event* (New York: Columbia University Press, 1988). He was a member of the Socialisme ou Barbarie group, led by Cornelius Castoriadis and Claude Lefort, from 1954 to 1966 (the last two years as a member of the faction around the journal *Pouvoir Ouvrier*).

55. For his writings during this period, see Jean-François Lyotard, *Political Writings*, trans. Bill Readings and Kevin Paul Geiman (Minneapolis: University of Minnesota Press, 1993).

56. Jean-François Lyotard, *Rudiments païens: Genre dissertatif* (Paris: Union générale d'éditions, 1977), several essays of which are translated in Lyotard, *Toward the Postmodern*, ed. Robert Harvey and Mark S. Roberts (Atlantic Highlands, N.J.: Humanities Press, 1993); *Instructions païennes* (Paris: Galilée, 1977), translated in *The Lyotard Reader*, ed. Benjamin; *Au Juste: Conversations* (with Jean-Loup Thébaud) (Paris: Christian Bourgeois, 1979), translated by Wlad Godzich as *Just Gaming* (Minneapolis: University of Minnesota Press, 1985). For discussions of his paganism, see Bill Readings, *Introducing Lyotard: Art and Politics* (London: Routledge, 1991); id., "Pseudoethica Epidemica: How Pagans Talk to the Gods," *Philosophy Today* (winter 1992); and Steven Best and Douglas Kellner, *Postmodern Theory* (New York: Guilford, 1991), 160f.

57. Lyotard and Thébaud, *Just Gaming*, 31.

58. Lyotard, "Lessons in Paganism," 123.

59. Lyotard, "The Grip (Mainmise)," in *Political Writings*, trans. Readings and Geiman, 156. This text, from 1990, shows the continuing importance of the pagan ideal in Lyotard's later work, even if it is not as frequently emphasized.

60. Jean-François Lyotard, *The Postmodern Condition: A Report on Knowledge*, trans. Geoff Bennington and Brian Massumi (Minneapolis: University of Minnesota Press, 1984). The original appeared in 1979. It can, however, be argued that polytheism was a form of what Jan Assmann has called "cosmotheism," which means that different religious figures were assumed to be variants of a single God, e.g., the sun (see Assmann, "Mosaic Distinction," 49). If so, paganism did not valorize incommensurability as much as Lyotard claims, but rather intercultural translatability.

61. Lyotard and Thébaud, *Just Gaming*, 16.

62. Jean-François Lyotard, *The Inhuman: Reflections on Time*, trans. Geoffrey Bennington and Rachel Bowlby (Stanford: Stanford University Press, 1991). On the general climate of antihumanism that nurtured his thought, see Richard Wolin, "Antihumanism in the Discourse of Postwar French Theory," in *Labyrinths: Explorations in the Critical History of Ideas* (Amherst, Mass.: University of Massachusetts Press, 1995).

63. Gay, *Enlightenment*, 1: 178. Lyotard, *Instructions païennes*, 84. The English translation in *The Lyotard Reader* mistranslates *réalisme* as "reason," which makes Lyotard say that "reason is pagan" (152).

64. Lyotard, "Lessons in Paganism," 133. There is now a substantial literature on the political implications of this reading of Kant. See, most recently, Kimberly Hutchings, *Kant, Critique and Politics* (New York: Routledge, 1996).

65. This accusation is leveled against paganism, e.g., by such defenders of Judeo-Christian transcendence as Thomas Molnar, *The Pagan Temptation* (Grand Rapids, Mich.: Eerdmans, 1987), and "Paganism and Its Renewal," *Intercollegiate Review* 31, no. 1 (fall 1995).

66. Lyotard and Thébaud, *Just Gaming*, 42.

67. Lyotard, "Futility in Revolution," 99.

68. Ibid., 113.

69. Jean-François Lyotard, *Le Différend* (Paris: Editions de Minuit, 1983), trans. as *The Differend: Phrases in Dispute* by Georges Van Den Abbeele (Minneapolis: University of Minnesota Press, 1988), 151. Readings speculates in *Introducing Lyotard*, xxxiii, that the term "paganism" was "largely dropped by the time of *The Differend*, perhaps because it tends to romanticize the problem of political judgment (it's hard to stop paganism from becoming another religion)."

70. Lyotard and Thébaud, *Just Gaming*, 38. Lyotard also posits the Cashinahua Indians of Brazil as comparable critics of absolute autonomy.

71. Ibid., 39.

72. Lyotard, however, argued that "in primitive Judaism, the theme of 'nature cre-

ated' is quite absent; God is not the author of a visible world. It is only later that the Book of Genesis is adopted, and it is full of borrowings from the cult of Baal" ("Figure Foreclosed," *The Lyotard Reader*, 94). It may also be noted that Jewish thought developed a respect for a plurality of textual meanings, if not of gods. "Rabbinic thought developed the doctrine of poly*semy* as opposed to poly*theism*: the multiple meanings that may be heard or read within the Word, rather than the many gods which may be seen," Susan A. Handelman notes in *The Slayers of Moses: The Emergence of Rabbinic Interpretation in Modern Literary Theory* (Albany, N.Y.: SUNY Press, 1982), 34.

73. See his essay "Levinas's Logic," in *The Lyotard Reader*. For a discussion of his debt to Levinas on the issue of the primacy of vision, which has links to our general theme through the idolatry that is often associated with paganism, see my *Downcast Eyes: The Denigration of Vision in Twentieth-Century French Thought* (Berkeley and Los Angeles: University of California Press, 1993), ch. 10.

74. In his essay "Figure Foreclosed" of 1984, reprinted in *The Lyotard Reader*, he stresses the importance of Judaism for psychoanalysis, especially its refusal of sublation, mediation, and reconciliation. Calling the moment of equilibrium between Apollonian and Dionysian impulses praised by Nietzsche only a fleeting instant in Greek culture, he claims that "in the nocturnal, figurative and plastic current, we can recognize the old religiosity of reconciliation, which will transmit to Christianity its remnants of mediation and which will give Catholicism its pagan allure" (75). A more attractive paganism, Lyotard suggests, will be pluralist, non-totalized, and agonistic.

75. Jean-François Lyotard, *Heidegger et "les juifs"* (Paris: Galilée, 1988), trans. as *Heidegger and "the jews"* by Andreas Michel and Mark S. Roberts (Minneapolis: University of Minnesota Press, 1990), 22–23.

76. In *The Enlightenment*, Gay is at pains to say that a dualist view of history, involving an alternation between Hellenic and Hebraic moments, "rather than the celebrated theory of progress, characterizes the Enlightenment" (33).

77. Lyotard and Thébaud, *Just Gaming*, 16.

78. See, e.g., ibid., 11, and "Tomb of the Intellectual," in Lyotard, *Political Writings*.

79. See, e.g., Richard Rorty, "Habermas and Lyotard on Postmodernity," in *Habermas and Modernity*, ed. Richard J. Bernstein (Cambridge, Mass.: MIT Press, 1985); and Peter Dews, introduction to Jürgen Habermas, *Autonomy and Solidarity: Interviews*, ed. id. (London: Verso, 1986). It might be noted in passing that there is no rhetoric of secularized paganism in Habermas's defense of the Enlightenment. In *The Philosophical Discourse of Modernity*, trans. Frederick Lawrence (Cambridge, Mass: MIT Press, 1987), he writes: "In the mysticism of the New Paganism, the unbounded charisma of what is outside the everyday does not issue in something liberating, as it does with the aesthetic; nor in something renewing, as with the religious—it has at most the stimulus of charlatanry" (184). This statement is made in the context of a discussion of Derrida, whose escape from pagan mysticism Habermas credits to his roots in Jewish monotheism.

80. More radical students of deconstruction, such as Samuel Weber, in fact chide Lyotard for resisting the complete dedifferentiation of language games. See his afterword to Lyotard and Thébaud, *Just Gaming*, 103. The result of such a dedifferentiation would be what I have called elsewhere a "night in which all cows are piebald," a formulation that Bill Readings justly resists with reference to Lyotard ("Pseudo-ethica Epidemica," 381).

81. Lyotard, *Le Postmoderne expliqué aux enfants: Correspondance, 1982–1985* (Paris: Galilée, 1986).

82. A number of commentators remark on Lyotard's covert reliance on totalizing claims, e.g., William Righter, *The Myth of Theory* (Cambridge: Cambridge University Press, 1994), ch. 9; Kerwin Lee Klein, "In Search of Narrative Mastery: Postmodernism and the People Without History," in *History and Theory: Studies in the Philosophy of History* 34 (1995). Indeed, the conversation in Lyotard and Thébaud's *Just Gaming* ends in (embarrassed?) laughter when Lyotard's interlocutor notes: "Here you are talking like the great prescriber himself" (100).

83. Harvey and Roberts, introduction to Lyotard, *Toward the Postmodern*, xiv.

CHAPTER 13

1. Peter Gay, *The Enlightenment: An Interpretation*, 2 vols. (New York: Knopf, 1966–69), 2: 71. See also Gay, *Weimar Culture: The Outsider as Insider* (New York: Harper & Row, 1968).

2. "Urteil des Preußischen Oberverwaltungsgerichts—2. Oktober 1893," reprinted in *Gerhart Hauptmanns "Weber"—Eine Dokumentation*, ed. Helmut Praschek (Berlin: Akademie-Verlag, 1981), 277. See also Manfred Brauneck, *Literatur und Öffentlichkeit im ausgehenden 19. Jahrhundert: Studien zur Rezeption des naturalistischen Theaters in Deutschland* (Stuttgart: Metzler, 1974), 50–62.

3. Glasenapp to minister of the interior, 15 May 1902, in Brandenburgisches Landeshauptarchiv, Pr. Br. Rep. 30 Berlin C, Präs. Tit. 74, Th 804, f. 289–289r.

4. Gary Stark, "The Censorship of Literary Naturalism, 1885–1895: Prussia and Saxony," *Central European History* 18 (1985): 327. I have some doubts about Stark's conclusions that censorship was actually beneficial to the naturalists; that certainly was not the case in Bavaria. See Peter Jelavich, "The Censorship of Literary Naturalism, 1890–1895: Bavaria," ibid., 344–59.

5. *Vossische Zeitung*, 16 Dec. 1900.

6. Kurt Tucholsky, "Politische Satire" and "Politische Couplets," in *Gesammelte Werke* (Reinbek: Rowohlt, 1985), 2: 171, 93.

7. I discuss the censorship of Panizza, Wedekind, and others in Peter Jelavich, *Munich and Theatrical Modernism: Politics, Playwriting and Performance, 1890–1914* (Cambridge, Mass.: Harvard University Press, 1985).

8. See Robin Lenman, "Art, Society, and the Law in Wilhelmine Germany: The Lex Heinze," *Oxford German Studies* 8 (1973–74): 86–113; and Wolfgang Hütt, *Hin-*

tergrund: Mit den Unzüchtigkeits- und Gotteslästerungsparagraphen des Strafgesetz-buches gegen Kunst und Künstler 1900–1933 (Berlin: Henschelverlag, 1990), 9–25, 81–103.

9. At this point I should reemphasize that I am speaking here only of art and literature. The Weimar era witnessed some truly repressive cases aimed at political reporting and journalism: the trial and conviction of Carl von Ossietzsky, for example, was a horrendous and willful miscarriage of justice. For a comprehensive account of censorship in the Weimar era, see Klaus Petersen, *Zensur in der Weimarer Republik* (Stuttgart: Metzler, 1995).

10. Needless to say, this strategy is neither dead nor limited to Germany: its latter-day practitioners are politicians like Pat Buchanan and Jesse Helms in the United States.

11. See *Der Fall Remarque: "Im Western nichts Neues": Eine Dokumentation*, ed. Bärbel Schrader (Leipzig: Reclam, 1992).

12. *Völkischer Beobachter*, 20 Dec. 1930.

13. See Alan Steinweis, *Art, Ideology, and Economics in Nazi Germany: The Reich Chambers of Music, Theater, and the Visual Arts* (Chapel Hill: University of North Carolina Press, 1993).

14. Hütt, *Hintergrund*, 271.

15. See the catalogues of two recent exhibitions about these exhibitions: *"Degenerate Art": The Fate of the Avant-Garde in Nazi Germany*, ed. Stephanie Barron (Los Angeles: Los Angeles County Museum of Art, 1991); and *Entartete Musik: Zur Düsseldorfer Ausstellung von 1938: Eine kommentierte Rekonstruktion*, ed. Albrecht Dümling and Peter Girth (Düsseldorf: Tonhalle Düsseldorf, 1988).

16. On the *Kunstkartenprozesse*, see Gary Stark, "Pornography, Society, and the Law in Imperial Germany," *Central European History* 14 (1981): 222–26; and Ludwig Leiss, *Kunst im Konflikt: Kunst und Künstler im Widerstreit mit der Obrigkeit* (Berlin: de Gruyter, 1971), 245–67.

17. See Sieghart Ott, *Kunst und Staat: Der Künstler zwischen Freiheit und Zensur* (Munich: dtv, 1968), 122–37.

18. In order to be confiscated these days, one must either promote neo-Nazi ideas or publish egregiously sadistic works in comic book or other "popular" formats that might appeal to youths. Readers who feel compelled to see a sampling of such works can turn to *"Ab 18"—zenisert, diskutiert, zerschlagen: Beispiele aus der Kulturgeschichte der Bundesrepublik Deutschland*, ed. Roland Seim and Josef Spiegel (Münster: Kulturbüro Münster, 1995).

19. Alfred Döblin, "Kunst ist nicht frei, sondern wirksam: ars militans," in *Preußische Akademie der Künste: Jahrbuch der Sektion für Dichtkunst 1929* (Berlin: Fischer, 1929), 98, 99, 101.

20. Rolf Hochhuth, "Zensur in der Bundesrepublik Deutschland," in *Rolf Hochhuth: Dokumente zur politischen Wirkung*, ed. Reinhart Hoffmeister (Munich: Kindler, 1980), 305–6, 310.

21. Cited in Konrad Francke, "'Deine Darstellung ist uns wesensfremd': Romane der 60er Jahre in den Mühlen der DDR-Zensur," in *"Literaturentwicklungsprozesse:" Die Zensur der Literatur in der DDR*, ed. Ernest Wichner and Herbert Wiesner (Frankfurt a.M.: Suhrkamp, 1993), 102.

22. *Protokoll eines Tribunals*, ed. Joachim Walter (Reinbek: Rowohlt, 1991), 106.

23. Cited in *Zensur in der DDR: Geschichte, Praxis und Ästhetik der Behinderung von Literatur*, ed. Ernest Wichner and Herbert Wiesner (Berlin: Literaturhaus Berlin, 1991), 32.

24. Erich Loest, *Die Stasi war mein Eckermann, oder: mein Leben mit der Wanze* (Göttingen: Steidl-Verlag, 1991), 20.

25. For an author's account of how one manuscript failed to make it through this system, see Erich Loest, *Der vierte Zensor: Vom Entstehen und Sterben eines Romans in der DDR* (Cologne: Edition Deutschland Archiv, 1984).

26. Reiner Kunze, *Deckname "Lyrik": Eine Dokumentation* (Frankfurt a.M.: Fischer Taschenbuch, 1990), 48.

27. Wolf Biermann, "Der Lichtblick im gräßlichen Fatalismus der Geschichte: Rede zur Verleihung des Georg-Büchner-Preises," in *Machtspiele: Literatur und Staatssicherheit im Fokus Prenzlauer Berg*, ed. Peter Böthig and Klaus Michael (Leipzig: Reclam, 1993), 300.

28. Practitioners of GDR cabaret discussed their work in *Kabarett heute: Erfahrungen, Standpunkte, Meinungen*, ed. Horst Gebhardt (Berlin: Henschelverlag, 1987).

29. Kunze, *Deckname "Lyrik,"* 50.

30. Wichner and Wiesner, *Zensur in der DDR*, 34–35.

31. Richard Pietraß, "Lyrisch Roulette: Zensur als Erfahrung," in *"Literaturentwicklungsprozesse,"* ed. Wichner and Wiesner, 198.

32. Christa Wolf, "Abschied von Phantom—Zur Sache: Deutschland," in *Auf dem Weg nach Tabou: Texte 1990–1994* (Cologne: Kiepenheuer & Witsch, 1994), 336.

33. Christa Wolf, "Heine, die Zensur und wir," in *Reden im Herbst* (Berlin: Aufbau, 1990), 168.

CHAPTER 14

1. Josef Hofmiller, "Wilhelm Busch," *Süddeutsche Monatshefte* 5 (Apr. 1908): 418–32. I want to express my appreciation to Herwig Guratsch, Ingrid Haberland, and Monika Herlt of the Wilhelm-Busch-Gesellschaft in Hannover for their assistance with research for this essay and for reproducing the drawings that appear in it. I would like to thank John Downey and Regina Kunzel for their thoughtful readings of the chapter, as well Ute Daniel, Alexandra Garbarini, Karl-Heinz Lüdeking, Mark Micale, and Harry Payne for their criticisms and suggestions. My deepest gratitude goes to Peter Gay for his help with an early version of this essay and, above all, for his support and example.

2. Peter Gay, *The Bourgeois Experience: From Victoria to Freud*, vol. 3: *The Cultivation of Hatred* (New York: Norton, 1993), 408–23. See also Gay's "Hermann Levi: A Study in Service and Self-Hatred," in *Freud, Jews, and Other Germans: Masters and Victims in Modernist Culture* (New York: Oxford University Press, 1978), 189–230, esp. 205–6.

3. For an introduction to literary reception, specifically, and reading, generally, from a historical perspective, see Robert Darnton, "History of Reading," *New Perspectives on Historical Writing*, ed. Peter Burke (University Park, Pa.: Pennsylvania University Press, 1992), 140–67. For an introduction to the historical investigation of festival, with an emphasis on nineteenth-century Germany, see Manfred Hettling and Paul Nolte, "Bürgerliche Feste als symbolische Politik im 19. Jahrhundert," in *Bürgerliche Feste: Symbolische Formen politischen Handelns im 19. Jahrhundert*, ed. Hettling and Nolte (Göttingen: Vandenhoeck & Ruprecht, 1993), 7–36.

4. "Wilhelm Buschs ungeheuere Popularität," *Münchener neueste Nachrichten*, 9 Apr. 1908 (transcript in the Wilhelm Busch Museum, Hannover); and Albert Vanselow, *Die Erstdrucke and Erstausgaben der Werke von Wilhelm Busch. Ein bibliographisches Verzeichnis* (Leipzig: Adolf Weigel, 1913). The correspondence between Busch and his publisher Otto Bassermann, housed in the Wilhelm Busch Museum, Hannover (henceforth abbreviated WBM), also contains detailed information about the sales of Busch's works. These figures probably do not begin to reveal the extent of Busch's readership, for a single copy of his work was almost certainly read by more than one person, i.e., by an entire family.

5. "Wilhelm Busch," *Nord und Süd: Eine deutsche Monatsschrift* 4 (1878): 257–72.

6. Friedrich Theodor Vischer, "Satirische Zeichnung: Gavarni und Töpffer. Mit einem Zusatz über neuere deutsche Karikatur. Zusatz: Über neuere deutsche Karikatur. Die Fliegenden Blätter," in *Kritische Gänge*, 2d ed., ed. Robert Vischer (Munich: Meyer & Jessen, 1922).

7. Eduard Daelen, *Über Wilhelm Busch und seine Bedeutung: Eine lustige Streitschrift* (Düsseldorf: Felix Bagel, 1886). Twenty-seven years later, Daelen returned to this theme in "Bismarck und Wilhelm Busch: Ein patriotischer Rückblick," *Reclams Universum*, 27 Mar. 1913, 629–34.

8. Other, mainly cursory, treatments of Busch published before 1902 include Karl Albert Regnet, "Wilhelm Busch," *Über Land und Meer: Allgemeine Illustrierte Zeitung* 31 (1875): 466; Julius Stettenheim, "Die Kinder des 19. Jahrhunderts mit 33 Busch-Illustrationen," *Vom Fels und Meer* 1 (Oct. 1884–Mar. 1885): 656–65; Johannes Proelß, "Aus Wilhelm Buschs Leben," *Frankfurter Zeitung*, 7 and 8 Sept. 1886; Richard Moritz Meyer, "Didaktik des 18./19. Jahrhunderts," *Jahresberichte für neuere deutsche Literaturgeschichte*, 1891–93; Eduard Fuchs, "Der Humor der deutschen Kunst," *Allgemeine Kunst-Chronik* 18 (1894); Paul Ernst, "Wilhelm Busch," *Das Magazin für Literatur* 63 (1894); Richard Moritz Meyer, "Didaktik," ibid. (1895); Johannes Schlaf, "Ein Vorgänger von Wilhelm Busch," *Sontagsbeilage No. 37 zur Vossischen Zeitung*, 10 Sept. 1899, 294–96; Schlaf, "Wilhelm Busch in neuer Aus-

gabe," *Die Zeit* (Vienna), no. 272 (Dec. 1899): 168–69; P. W., "Wilhelm Busch," *Geraer Zeitung*, no. 9 (1900); Eduard Fuchs, *Die Karikatur der europäischen Völker: Von Altertum bis zur Neuzeit*, 2d ed., vol. 2 (Berlin: A. Hofmann, 1901–4). Two other treatments of Busch, by Wilhelm Jänecke-Stade and *Simplicissimus* in 1901, are cited below.

9. Nineteenth-century editions of *Brockhaus* and *Meyers Konversations-Lexikon* and the *Künstler Lexica* of H. A. Müller and A. Taubert have no sections on Busch, nor is Busch mentioned in Konrad Lange's *Die künstlerische Erziehung der deutschen Jugend* (Darmstadt: Arnold Bergstraeßner, 1893); in A. Merget's *Geschichte der deutschen Jugendliteratur* (Berlin: Plahn'schen Buchhandlung, 1882); in Wilhelm Scherer's *Geschichte der deutschen Literatur*, either the first or the second editions (Berlin: Weidmannsche Buchhandlung, 1882, 1884); in S. Seydlitz's article "Kinderbücher" in *Kunstwart* 4 (Dec. 1890); in Friedrich Vogt and Max Koch's *Geschichte der deutschen Literatur* (Leipzig and Berlin: Bibliographischen Institut, 1897); or in Wolgast's *Über Bilderbuch und Illustration* (Hamburg: Conrad Kloss, 1894). Two significant studies of Busch were published in France, however, Arsène Alexandre's *L'Art du rire et de la caricature* (Paris: Librairies-Imprimeries Réunies, 1893) and John Grand-Carteret's *Les Mœurs et la caricature en Allemagne, en Autriche, en Suisse* (Paris: Ancienne Librairie Hinrichsen, 1885).

10. Victor Blüthgen, "Ein Altmeister deutschen Humors," *Gartenlaube*, no. 46 (1904).

11. The number of citations in this chapter gives a sense of the extent and scope of the published "Busch-Enthusiasm."

12. The recognition accorded Busch on his seventieth birthday was explicitly acknowledged by Friedrich Vogt and Max Koch as having confirmed Busch's artistic significance, prompting them to include a section on him in their 1904 and 1910 editions of *Geschichte der deutschen Literatur* where he had not been mentioned in the 1897 edition. Similarly, Scherer and Walzel's *Geschichte der deutschen Literatur* published in 1921 contained a section on Busch where the first two editions of the book had not. Other *lexica* and surveys containing sections on Busch after 1902 include Gießler's *Führer durch das deutsche Literatur des 20. Jahrhunderts* (Weimar, 1913); Koester's *Geschichte der deutschen Jugendliteratur in Monographien* (Hamburg: Alfred Janssen, 1906); Krüger's *Deutsches Literaturlexikon* (Munich, 1914); Rothert's *Allgemeine Hannover'sche Biographie* (Hannover: Sponholz, 1912); Wille's *Unserer großen Dichter und Schätze aus ihren Werken* (Berlin: Märkische Verlagsanstalt, 1911); and Witkowski's *Die Entstehung der deutschen Literatur seit 1830* (Leipzig: R. Voigtländer, 1912).

13. The sudden interest in Busch as a personality can also be understood as a manifestation of the tradition of literary biography in Germany, which connected an author's work and personality. See René Wellek, *A History of Modern Criticism, 1750–1950*, vol. 4: *The Later Nineteenth Century* (London: Cape, 1970), 303–5. In

general, the Busch reception discussed here can and should be understood within the context of the history of German literary criticism.

14. There was a sudden interest in Busch's previously neglected poetry, which now became a way to approach this fascinating, if retiring, personality.

15. Ferdinand Avenarius, "Wilhelm Busch," *Kunstwart* 15 (2 Apr. 1902): 92–93; Paul Block, "Beim Einsiedler von Mechtshausen: Ein Besuch bei Wilhelm Busch," *Berliner Tageblatt*, 9 Mar. 1902, reprinted in *Wilhelm Busch: Ernstes und Heiteres*, ed. Otto Nöldecke (Berlin: Verlagsanstalt Hermann Klemm, 1938), 181–82; Carl Hagemann, "Busch, der Dichter (zu seinem siebzigsten Geburtstage)," *Süddeutsche Rundschau*, 15 Apr. 1902, a slightly different version of this article was published in the *Rhein.-Westf. Zeitung*, 15 Apr. 1902; Ernst Heilborn, "Wilhelm Busch: Zu seinem 70. Geburtstag," *Die Nation* 29 (1901–2): 438–41 (transcript WBM); Wilhelm Jänecke, "Zu Wilhelm Buschs 70. Geburtstage," *Hannoverscher Courier*, 13 Apr. 1902 (transcript WBM); Gustav Keyßner, "Wilhelm Busch: Zum 70. Geburtstag (15. April)," *Münchner neueste Nachrichten*, nos. 173 and 175 (Apr. 1902); Max Osborn, "Wilhelm Busch," *Westermanns illustrierte deutsche Monatshefte* 93 (Nov. 1902): 265–84; Max Osborn, "Wilhelm Busch," *Neue deutsche Rundschau* 13 (Apr. 1902): 437–40 (transcript WBM); Johannes Trojan, "Dem Jubilare Wilhelm Busch," *Die Woche*, 12 Apr. 1902, reprinted in *Wilhelm Busch: Ernstes und Heiteres*, ed. Nöldecke, 211–12; Trojan, "Bei Wilhelm Busch zu Gaste," *Der Tag*, 15 Apr. 1902, reprinted in ibid., 194–203; H. L., "Wilhelm Busch. (Zu seinem 70. Geburtstag)," *Vorwärts*, 15 Apr. 1902 (transcript WBM); Ernst Schur, "Wilhelm Busch (Zum 75. Geburtstag), *Unterhaltungsblatt des Vorwärts*, 13 Apr. 1907 (transcript WBM); Eduard Engels, "Neues von Wilhelm Busch," *Die Propyläen* 1 (15 Apr. 1904): 417–20; Karl Freye-Friedenau, "Wilhelm Busch," *Hannoverland*, Feb. 1908 (transcript WBM); Hofmiller, "Wilhelm Busch" (1908); Dr. Owlglaß, "Wilhelm Busch in memoriam," *März* (Munich), no. 2 (Jan. 1908), reprinted in *Wilhelm Busch: Ernstes und Heiteres*, ed. Nöldecke, 270; Rothert, "Wilhelm Busch," *Allgemeine hannoversche Biographie*, 1: 94–105.

16. Thus *Max und Moritz* (1865) was published during their childhood; the more erotic and feisty works like *Der heilige Antonius von Padua* (1870) and *Die fromme Helene* (1872) were published during their adolescence; the Knopp trilogy (1875–77) was published during their late adolescence and young adulthood; *Balduin Bählamm* (1883) and *Maler Klecksel* (1884) were published during their adulthood; and *Eduards Traum* (1891) and *Der Schmetterling* (1895) were published during their full maturity.

17. Franz Diederich, "Wilhelm Busch," *Deutsche Heimat* 5 (13 Apr. 1902): 29–40; Georg Hermann, *Wilhelm Busch* (Berlin: Gose & Tetzlaff, 1902), 40 and 42; Keyßner, "Wilhelm Busch" (1902); Heinrich Seidel, "Dem Jubilare Wilhelm Busch," *Die Woche*, 12 Apr. 1902, reprinted in *Wilhelm Busch: Ernstes und Heiteres*, ed. Nöldecke, 212–14; Ludwig Thoma and Thomas Theodor Heine, "Zu Wilhelm Buschs siebzigstem Geburtstag. Extra-Nummer: Max und Moritz," *Simplicissimus* (1902); Eduard Engels, "Neues von Wilhelm Busch," *Die Propyläen* 1 (15 Apr. 1904): 420; "Wilhelm

Busch," *Berliner Illustrirte Zeitung*, 19 Jan. 1908, 35; Ludwig Thoma, "Wilhelm Busch," *Simplicissimus*, 27 Jan. 1908, 732.

18. Eduard Engels, "Wilhelm Busch," *Magdeburgesche Zeitung*, 15 Apr. 1902; Theodor Herzl, "Busch," *Neue freie Presse*, 13 Apr. 1902 (transcript WBM).

19. Georg Hermann, "Wilhelm Busch: Zu seinem 70. Geburtstag (15 April)," *Vossische Zeitung*, 14 Apr. 1902 (this same article appeared one day earlier in the *Königlich privilegirte Berlinische Zeitung* [transcript WBM]); Hermann's article of the same title in the *Hannoverscher Courier*, 15 Apr. 1902.

20. Ludwig Thoma, "Wilhelm Busch: Ein Nachruf," *Frankfurter Zeitung*, 9 Jan. 1908.

21. Freye-Friedenau, "Wilhelm Busch" (Feb. 1908).

22. Proelß, "Aus Wilhelm Buschs Leben" (transcript WBM). According to Max Osborn, writing in *Westermanns illustrierte deutsche Monatshefte* (Nov. 1902), Busch, as a personality, in contrast to his works, "had almost already lost his connection as an individual to the general public" before 1902 ("Wilhelm Busch," 267). Indeed, it was asserted in 1902 that the lack of popular knowledge about Busch as a person before his seventieth birthday had led to the widespread assumption that he had died years before: Kurt Aram, "Wilhelm Busch (Zu seinem 70. Geburtstag, 15 April 1902)," *Frankfurter Zeitung*, 13 Apr. 1902; "Zu Wilhelm Buschs 70. Geburtstag," *Daheim*, 19 Apr. 1902, 2–3; Hagemann, "Busch, der Dichter," *Rhein.-Westf. Zeitung* (1902); Rudolf Presber, "Wilhelm Busch: Der Philosoph," *Das litterarische Echo* 4 (Feb. 1902): 583–91 (transcript WBM); Gustav Zieler, "Wilhelm Busch (Zu seinem 70. Geburtstag)," *Beilage zur Norddeutsche Allgemeinen Zeitung*, 16 Apr. 1902 (transcript WBM); Paul Zschorlich, "Ein lachender Philosoph," *Die Zeit*, 17 Apr. 1902, 90–91. See also Schur, "Wilhelm Busch" (1907); Traugott Friedemann, "Wilhelm Busch und seine letzte Gabe," *Akademische Turnzeitung* 24 (summer and winter semester 1907–8): 493–95.

23. "Wilhelm Busch," *Frankfurter Zeitung*, 10 Jan. 1908 (transcript WBM).

24. Herzl, "Busch," 2.

25. Daelen, "Bismarck und Wilhelm Busch" (1913), 630.

26. Hans Land, "Wilhelm Busch," *Reclams Universum*, 5 July 1906 (transcript WBM).

27. Ernst von Wolzogen, untitled article following Busch's death in *Die Woche*, 18 Jan. 1908. It is little wonder that this article, in which Wolzogen declared that Busch would be celebrated "as long as the German spirit has not been completely dissolved in the pap [*Brei*] of a rootless cosmopolitanism," would be reprinted in 1938 in *Wilhelm Busch: Ernstes und Heiteres* edited by Otto Nöldecke, who sympathized with the Nazis. It should be stressed, however, that Wolzogen's chauvinistic rhetoric is rarely encountered in the Busch reception after 1902, perhaps partially attributable to the fact that many of the literati who celebrated Busch appear to have been Jewish or of Jewish ancestry. Daelen's "Bismarck und Wilhelm Busch" (1913) voiced similarly chauvinistic sentiments, but without anti-Semitic overtones.

28. Fritz von Ostini, "Wilhelm Busch," *Jugend*, no. 3 (1908).

29. Ferdinand Avenarius, "Wilhelm Busch (Zu seinem Nachlaß)," *Kunstwart* 24 (1910): 198.

30. Karl Scheffler, "Zur Psychologie der modernen Karikatur," *Rheinlande* 2 (1902): 19–28; Siegmar Schultze, "Ein neues Buch vom alten Wilhelm Busch," *Internationale Literatur- und Musikberichte* 11 (12 May 1904): 73–74; Cornelius Veth, "Wilhelm Busch," *Kunst und Künstler* 5 (1907): 304–12; Friedrich Vogt and Max Koch, *Geschichte der deutschen Literatur, von den ältesten Zeiten bis zur Gegenwart*, 2 vols. (Leipzig and Vienna: Bibliographischen Instituts, 1904 [also 1910]), 2: 458; Hans Land, "Wilhelm Busch" (1906); Karl Scheffler, "Wilhelm Busch," *Morgen: Wochenschrift für deutsche Kultur*, 30 Aug. 1907, 355–58 (transcript WBM); Arthur Kutscher, "Wilhelm Buschs Kunst," *Die deutsche Hochschule* 2 (1907–8), (transcript WBM); Busch obituary in the *Norddeutsche allgemeine Zeitung* (1908); Richard M. Meyer, review of Nöldecke, *Wilhelm Busch* in the *Das litterarische Echo* 12 (1 July 1910): 1367–69.

31. "Ehrungen zu Wilhelm Buschs 70. Geburtstag," *Allgemeine Zeitung*, 21 Apr. 1902 (transcript WBM); Hermann, *Wilhelm Busch* (1902); Jänecke, "Zu Wilhelm Buschs Geburtstage" (1902); two poems to celebrate Busch's birthday in *Jugend*, 24 Mar. 1902; Heinrich Kraeger, "Wilhelm Busch: Zum 70. Geburtstage," *Illustrierte Zeitung* (Leipzig), 10 Apr. 1902, 539–40; Schultze, "Ein neues Buch vom alten Wilhelm Busch" (1904); Vogt and Koch, *Geschichte der deutschen Literatur* (1904 and 1910); *Jugend* (1908); Wolzogen, *Die Woche* (1908); Wilhelm Conrad Gomoll, "Wilhelm Busch und sein Nachlaß," *Die Post*, 15 May 1910 (transcript WBM).

32. Osborn, "Wilhelm Busch" (Nov. 1902), 268.

33. Engels, "Neues von Wilhelm Busch" (1904), 418.

34. *Simplicissimus*, 27 Jan. 1908, 732. The number of articles that pointedly mention Busch's interest in beekeeping are too numerous to cite individually. The importance of this fact to these writers clearly derived from their sense of nostalgia. Beekeeping nostalgia even made it into socialist publications: Stefan Großmann, "Wilhelm Busch: Zum 75. Geburtstag: 15 April 1907," *Die neue Gesellschaft* 4 (17 Apr. 1907): 79–84; Schur, "Wilhelm Busch," *Vorwärts* (1907); Wilhelm Bölsche, "Über Wilhelm Busch," *Sozialistische Monatshefte*, Mar. 1908, 349–53 (transcript WBM).

35. *Jugend*, no. 16 (1907).

36. As with beekeeping, the number of articles that mention Busch's *Behaglichkeit* or claim that Busch's works engendered this emotion are too numerous to cite individually.

37. In these accounts, Busch either was not pessimistic at all (Avenarius, "Wilhelm Busch" [1902]; Diederich, "Wilhelm Busch" [1902]; Wilhelm Schöllermann, "Wilhelm Busch: Ein Gruß zu des Künstlers 70. Wiegenfest," *Archiv für Buchgewerbe* 39 [1902], [transcript WBM]; "Wilhelm Busch," *Moderne Kunst* 22 [1908]; Karl Ettlinger, "Die Zerstörung der W. Busch-Legende," *Berliner Tageblatt*, 8 Nov. 1909 [transcript WBM]; Alfred Biese, *Deutsche Literaturgeschichte*, vol. 3: *Von Hebbel bis*

zur Gegenwart [Munich: Beck, 1910] [transcript WBM]), or he was a pessimist but his works were not pessimistic (*Illustrierte Zeitung* [Leipzig], 16 Jan. 1908), or he was a pessimist but underneath affirmed life through humor (Wilhelm Jänecke-Stade, "Wilhelm Busch als Philosoph," *Hannoverscher Courier*, 26 July 1901 [transcript WBM]; Osborn, "Wilhelm Busch" [Apr. 1902]; Presber, "Wilhelm Busch: Der Philosoph" [1902]; Zieler, "Wilhelm Busch" [1902]; C. L. A. Pretzel, "Wilhelm Busch," *Volksbildung* 37 [1907]: 123–25 [transcript WBM]; Veth, "Wilhelm Busch" [1907]; Busch obituary in the *Norddeutsche Allgemeine Zeitung* [1908]; Karl Storck, "Pessimismus und Humor: Zum Tode von Wilhelm Busch," *Der Turmer* 10 [Feb. 1908]: 734–38 [1908]), or he was not a pessimist but resigned (Arthur Kutscher, "Wilhelm Buschs Humor," *Niedersachsen* 12 [1 Apr. 1907]: 238–40), or he was not a pessimist but a skeptic (Aram, "Wilhelm Busch" [1902]), or he combined pessimism with a *"behagliche* love of life" (F. Wippermann, "Wilhelm Busch: Zu seinem 75. Geburtstage," *Hochland* 4 [May 1907]: 245–47 [transcript WBM]), or he had never been a Schopenhauerian (Diederich, "Wilhelm Busch" [1902]; Richard Muther, "Wilhelm Busch," *Der Tag: Illustrierte Zeitung*, 15 Apr. 1902; Schöllermann, "Wilhelm Busch" [1902]; Franz Diederich, "Aus Wilhelm Buschs Selbstschau," *Die Welt des Kaufmanns* 5 [Apr. 1909], 193–98 [transcript WBM]), or he had been a Schopenhauerian but had come to reject the philosopher (Paul Wertheimer, "Wilhelm Busch," *Die Reichswehr* [Vienna], 15 Apr. 1902), or he was a Schopenhauerian but not completely (Hermann, "Wilhelm Busch" [1902]; Georg Hermann, *Die deutsche Karikatur im 19. Jahrhundert* [Bielefeld and Leipzig: Velhagen & Klasing, 1901]), or he was a Schopenhauerian but no pessimist (Engels, "Wilhelm Busch" [1902]; Zschorlich [1902]; Engels, "Neues von Wilhelm Busch" [1904]; Friedemann, "Wilhelm Busch" [1907–8]), or he was a pessimist but still a "comforter . . . of the German people" (Richard Moritz Meyer, *Die deutsche Literatur des neunzehnten Jahrhunderts*, 3d ed. [Berlin: Georg Bondi, 1906] [transcript WBM]).

38. P. W., "Wilhelm Busch" (1900); Fuchs, *Die Karikatur* (1901–4); Jänecke-Stade, "Wilhelm Busch als Philosoph" (1901); Avenarius, "Wilhelm Busch" (1902); "Wilhelm Busch," a poem "von einer fröhlichen Geburtstagsfeier im 'Malkasten' in Düsseldorf" (Apr. 1902), reprinted in *Wilhelm Busch: Ernstes und Heiteres*, ed. Nöldecke, 214–15; letters to Wilhelm Busch on his 70th birthday (Apr. 1902), ibid., 204–6; Otto Grauthoff, "Wilhelm Busch: Zum 70. Geburtstage des Meisters. 15. April 1832–15. April 1902," *Börsenblatt für den deutschen Buchhandel* 69 (25 Mar. 1902); Jänecke, "Zu Wilhelm Buschs Geburtstage" (1902); "Zu Wilhelm Buschens 70. Geburtstag," *Jugend*, no. 14 (24 Mar. 1902); Keyßner, "Wilhelm Busch" (1902); Adolf Klinger, "Wilhelm Busch: Zum 70. Geburtstage," *Österreichs Deutsche Jugend*, no. 19 (June 1902): 134–35; *Lustige Blätter*, no. 16 (1902), *Busch-Nummer*; Muther, "Wilhelm Busch" (1902); J. Norden, "Wilhelm Busch," *Die Gegenwart* (1902), no. 15, 237–38; Eduard Pötzl, "Der echte Humor," *Die Woche* 15 (12 Apr. 1902); Presber, "Wilhelm Busch: Der Philosoph" (1902); Schöllermann, "Wilhelm Busch" (1902); Julius Stinde, "Der angewandte Busch," *Die Woche* 15 (12 Apr. 1902): 646; Alexander Freiherr von Gleichen-

Rußwurm, "Das deutsche Sinngedicht," *Das litterarische Echo* 7 (1 Oct. 1904): 1–7; "Neues von Wilhelm Busch," *Vossische Zeitung*, 20 Apr. 1904; Land, "Wilhelm Busch" (1906); Meyer, *Die deutsche Literatur* (1906); Arthur Kutscher, "Wilhelm Busch," *Hannoversches Tageblatt*, 14 Apr. 1907 (transcript WBM); Kutscher, "Wilhelm Buschs Humor" (1907); Wippermann, "Wilhelm Busch" (1907); Kutscher, "Wilhelm Buschs Kunst" (1907–8); "Wilhelm Busch," *Berliner Illustrirte Zeitung* (1908); E. K., "Erinnerungen an Wilhelm Busch," *Enten-Saison*, 5 Feb. 1908, 6–11; Eugen Schick, "Wilhelm Busch," *Der Deutsche* 7, no. 15 (1908): 471–74; Wolzogen, *Die Woche* (1908).

39. Peter Gay, *The Bourgeois Experience: Victoria to Freud*, vol. 1: *Education of the Senses* (New York: Oxford University Press, 1984), 45–68.

40. Paul Block describes Busch as having "great, bright Bismarck-eyes" in "Beim Einsiedler von Mechtshausen" (1902); Trojan, "Bei Wilhelm Busch zu Gaste" (1902); Wilhelm Poeck, "Das Niederdeutsche in Wilhelm Busch," *Schleswig-holsteinische Rundschau* 2 (Apr. 1907): 13–15; Max Cornicelius, "Wilhelm Busch," *Blätter für Volksbibliotheken und Lesehallen*, 1910: 37–46; Fritz von Ostini, "Wilhelm Busch," *Kleines Busch Album* (Berlin-Grünewald: Hermann Klemm, 1911), 51; Daelen, "Bismarck und Wilhelm Busch" (1913).

41. Block, "Beim Einsiedler von Mechtshausen" (1902); "Zu Wilhelm Buschs 70. Geburtstag," *Daheim* (1902); Heilborn, "Wilhelm Busch" (1902); Hermann, *Wilhelm Busch* (1902); Jänecke, "Zu Wilhelm Buschs 70. Geburtstage" (1902); Kraeger, "Wilhelm Busch" (1902); Muther, "Wilhelm Busch" (1902); Norden, "Wilhelm Busch" (1902); Hermann Meyer, "Ein Besuch bei Wilhelm Busch," *Magdeburgische Zeitung*, no. 175 (1902); Trojan, "Bei Wilhelm Busch zu Gaste" (1902); Graphicus, "Wilhelm Busch. Zu seinem 75. Geburtstage," *Journal für Buchdruckerkunst*, 11 Apr. 1907, 146–48; Herbert Eulenburg, "Wilhelm Busch," *Schattenbilder: Eine Fibel für Kulturbedürftige in Deutschland* (Berlin: Bruno Cassirer, 1917), reprint of an article from 1907–8; "I. K.," "Wie ich Wilhelm Busch die letzte Ehre erwies," *Hamburger Nachrichten*, 13 and 14 Jan. 1908; Ostini, "Wilhelm Busch" (1908); Diederich, "Aus Wilhelm Buschs Selbstschau" (1909).

42. Paul Ernst, "Wilhelm Busch," *Das Magazin für Literatur* 63 (1894) (transcript WBM).

43. "Zu Wilhelm Buschs 70. Geburtstage," *Breslauer Zeitung*, no. 259 (probably 14 Apr. 1902), (transcript WBM).

44. Hofmiller, "Wilhelm Busch" (1908).

45. Joachim Benn, "Palmström," *Deutsche Monatshefte* 13 (1913): 352–53.

46. Friedrich Bohne, *Wilhelm Busch: Gesamtausgabe in vier Bänden*, 4 vols. (Wiesbaden: Emil Vollmer, 1968), 4: 576.

47. Fritz Winther, *Wilhelm Busch als Dichter, Künstler, Psychologe und Philosoph*, University of California Publications in Modern Philology, no. 2 (Sept. 1910), 34.

48. "Was ist uns Wilhelm Busch? Zu seinem Todestage, 9 Januar," *Süddeutsche Uhrmacher-Zeitung*, 1 Jan. 1911, 16–17.

49. Ibid.

50. "Wilhelm Buschs ungeheuere Popularität" (1909); Arthur Kutscher, "Wilhelm Busch," in two parts, *Weserland* 4 (Aug. 1914): 49–52, and 9 (1914–15): 116–20.

51. Max Osborn, "Wilhelm Busch: Zu seinem fünfundsiebzigsten Geburtstage," *Illustrierte Zeitung*, 11 Apr. 1907, 612.

52. Freye-Friedenau, "Wilhelm Busch" (1908).

53. Busch was celebrated as an anti-Wilhelmian, belonging to the better Bismarck era—in a quintessentially Wilhelmian manner. In "Die Wilhelm Busch Feier in Schilda (Ein April Scherz)," published in the *Münchner neueste Nachrichten* on 18 Apr. 1902, "Y" used the Busch birthday celebrations to mock the Wilhelmian enthusiasm for pomp and ceremony as empty self-aggrandizement. See also Muther, "Wilhelm Busch" (1902). Perhaps the best example of a "Wilhelmian celebration" of Busch as an anti-Wilhelmian is Eduard Daelen's "Bismarck und Wilhelm Busch" (1913). The monument to Busch erected in Wiedensahl after his death gave the German people the opportunity, one author maintained, to fulfill their debt of honor to him: "Ein Denkmal für Wilhelm Busch," *Daheim*, 27 Sept. 1913. See also Keyßner, "Wilhelm Busch" (1902); *Lustige Blätter*, no. 16 (1902), *Busch-Nummer*; Osborn, "Wilhelm Busch" (Nov. 1902); Theodor Pixis, "Wilhelm Busch in München: Erinnerungen aus den fünfziger und sechziger Jahren," *Die Woche*, 12 Apr. 1902, reprinted in *Wilhelm Busch: Ernstes und Heiteres*, ed. Nöldecke, 210–11 (see also the letter from Georg Hirth to Busch reprinted in ibid., 204–5); Seidel, "Dem Jubilare Wilhelm Busch" (1902); Thoma and Heine, "Zu Wilhelm Buschs siebzigstem Geburtstag" (1902); Wertheimer, "Wilhelm Busch"(1902); Zieler, "Wilhelm Busch" (1902); Bölsche, "Über Wilhelm Busch" (1908); Ostini, foreword to the catalog to the first major exhibition of drawings and oil paintings by Busch in Munich in 1908, reprinted in *Wilhelm Busch: Ernstes und Heiteres*, ed. Nöldecke, 251–55; Ostini, "Wilhelm Busch" (1911), 14.

54. "Zu Wilhelm Buschs 70. Geburtstag," *Daheim* (1902), 3.

55. Schur, "Wilhelm Busch" (1907).

56. Diederich, "Wilhelm Busch" (1902), 31; Heilborn, "Wilhelm Busch" (1902); Ettlinger, "Die Zerstörung der W. Busch-Legende"(1909); Wilhelm Conrad Gomoll, "Vom Meister des Lachens," *Die Post*, no. 323 (1913) (transcript WBM).

57. "Wilhelm Busch und das katholische Haus," *Die Bücherwelt* 6 (Jan. 1909).

58. I. K., "Wie ich Wilhelm Busch die letzte Ehre erwies" (1908).

59. The Busch birthday celebration of 1902, one author wrote in the *Leipziger neueste Nachrichten*, "is something unique . . . in Germany, especially in our era rent by political and social conflict," and he welcomed the fact that the occasion had at least provided "a respite from the political debate": "W. Busch zu seinem 70. Geburtstage," 21 Apr. 1902 (transcript WBM). As Mary Lee Townsend has revealed in her thoughtful and entertaining book *Forbidden Laughter: Popular Humor and the Limits of Repression in Nineteenth-Century Prussia* (Ann Arbor: University of Michigan Press, 1992), a lively culture of political humor existed in Prussia in the years leading up to the Revolution of 1848.

60. In "Max und Moritz (Frei nach Wilhelm Busch)," *Simplicissimus* 6 (1901), Thomas Theodor Heine and Ludwig Thoma use the two Busch characters to ridicule the trial for lèse-majesté of those responsible for the "Palestina" issue of the magazine. *Lustige Blätter's* 1902 *Busch-Nummer* contains imitation Busch cartoons that satirize the Lex Heinze, the defeat of the Bülow tariff in the Reichstag, and the British in the Boer War. That same year, in "Zu Wilhelm Buschs siebzigstem Geburtstag: Extra-Nummer. Max und Moritz" in *Simplicissimus*, Heine and Thoma mock Krupp and the arms race using Busch characters. In the 1906 *Jahres-Buschiade* of *Lustige Blätter* 21, no. 52, Busch is used to spoof militarism, the Pan-German League, the dismissal of the Prussian minister of agriculture, Podbielski, and Colonial Minister Dernburg. The *Wilhelm Busch-Nummer* of *Simplicissimus* 12 (15 Apr. 1907) uses Fipps der Affe to represent the Social Democratic Party harassing, among others, the Kaiser, Bülow, the aristocracy, and the Lutheran Church. In 1908, *Jugend* used Busch to make fun of the Bülow Bloc.

61. Apart from Busch's picture-stories of the 1870s, produced during the Franco-Prussian war and the Kulturkampf against Catholicism, his work seems manifestly apolitical, despite Gerd Ueding's imaginative, if unpersuasive, effort to transform Busch into a 1968 radical in *Wilhelm Busch: Das 19. Jahrhundert en miniature* (Frankfurt a./M.: Suhrkamp Taschenbuch, 1977).

62. *Simplicissimus* 12 (15 Apr. 1907), *Wilhelm Busch-Nummer.*

63. See *Lustige Blätter*, no. 16 (1902), *Busch-Nummer*; ibid. 21, no. 52 (1906), *Jahres-Buschiade*. See also the political cartoons cited in n. 60.

64. *Lustige Blätter* 21, no. 52 (1906), *Jahres-Buschiade*.

65. The same issue of *Lustige Blätter* contains an imitation Busch poem, "Der Pogrom," and cartoon, "Aus unseren Kolonien," in which Busch's ironic and subtle humor is replaced by a crude, politicized trivialization of human suffering. The 1907 *Wilhelm Busch-Nummer* of *Simplicissimus* includes an updated version of Busch's "Naturgeschichtliches Alphabet" by "Peter Schlemihl" with decidedly racist overtones.

66. Schur, "Wilhelm Busch"(1907). See also Benn, "Palmström" (1913).

67. Johannes Schlaf, "Wilhelm Busch in neuer Ausgabe," *Die Zeit* (Vienna), no. 272 (Dec. 1899): 168–69; Diederich, "Wilhelm Busch" (1902).

68. Fritz Stahl, "Wilhelm Busch. (Zu seinem 70. Geburtstag)," *Der Zeitgeist*, supplement to the *Berliner Tageblatt*, 14 Apr. 1902 (transcript WBM); Wilhelm Poeck, "Wilhelm Busch wird fünfundsiebzig," published both in *Salon-Feuilleton*, 9 Apr. 1907, 4–5, and in the *Deutsche Tageszeitung, Unterhaltungsblätter*, no. 87 (1907).

69. Franz Diederich, "Wilhelm Busch," *Kulturfragen* 3 (1907): 152–58 (transcript WBM).

70. Scheffler, "Wilhelm Busch" (1907).

71. "Wilhelm Busch als Philosoph" (1901). See also Zieler, "Wilhelm Busch" (1902).

72. Avenarius, "Wilhelm Busch" (1902); Rudolf Berger's interpellation to the Aus-

trian minister of education regarding the thirty-year ban on Busch's "Der heilige Antonius von Padua," published by the Alldeutscherverband in Vienna (Apr. 1902) and
reprinted in *Wilhelm Busch: Ernstes und Heiteres*, ed. Nöldecke, 216–17; Diederich,
"Wilhelm Busch" (1902); Grauthoff, "Wilhelm Busch" (1902); Keyßner, "Wilhelm
Busch" (1902); Kraeger, "Wilhelm Busch" (1902); Osborn, "Wilhelm Busch" (Nov.
1902); Stinde, "Der angewandte Busch"(1902); "Wilhelm Busch," *Berliner Illustrirte
Zeitung* (1908); E. K., "Erinnerungen an Wilhelm Busch" (1908).

73. Wertheimer, "Wilhelm Busch" (1902); "Neues von Wilhelm Busch," *Vossische Zeitung* (1904); Schur, "Wilhelm Busch" (1907); "Dem Meister Wilhelm Busch
zum 75. Geburtstage," *Jugend* (1907); Kutscher, "Wilhelm Buschs Kunst" (1907–8);
Albert Dresdner, "Wilhelm Busch," *Die Propylaen* 5 (22 Jan. 1908) (transcript WBM).

74. "Zu Wilhelm Buschs 70. Geburtstag," *Daheim* (1902); Hermann, "Wilhelm
Busch" (1902); Kraeger, "Wilhelm Busch: Zum 70. Geburtstage" (1902); Engels,
"Neues von Wilhelm Busch" (1904); Richard Schaukal, *Wilhelm Busch*, vol. 21 of *Die
Dichtung*, ed. Paul Remer (Berlin and Leipzig, 1905); Friedemann, "Wilhelm Busch
und seine letzte Gabe" (1907–8); Kutscher, "Wilhelm Busch" (1907); Thoma, "Wilhelm Busch: Ein Nachruf" (1908); *Braunschweiger Zeitung*, 13 Jan. 1908; Biese,
Deutsche Literaturgeschichte (1910). This claim, too, appears paradoxical. If Busch
could be understood without critical mediation, why was it necessary to publish articles explaining his significance, including his *Volkstümlichkeit*?

75. Indeed, it was even claimed that Busch's retreat to Wiedensahl was an expression of his disgust at the failure of the Germans to understand his work.

76. Indeed, there appears to have been considerably more consensus about
Busch's meaning between 1902 and 1914 than exists today. Compare only the studies
of Busch published in 1977, Gerd Ueding's *Wilhelm Busch* and Walter Pape's *Wilhelm Busch* (Stuttgart: J. B. Metzlersche Verlagsbuchhandlung, 1977).

77. For a great many authors, their contemporaries thought Busch to be a harmless *Spaßmacher* when he was in fact a serious philosopher. A handful argued the opposite. For a great many, their contemporaries thought Busch to be a time-bound
satirist when he was in fact a universal humorist. A handful argued the opposite. For
many, their contemporaries thought Busch to be an optimist when he was in fact a
pessimist. A handful argued the opposite.

78. Aram, "Wilhelm Busch" (1902); "Zu Wilhelm Buschs 70. Geburtstage," *Breslauer Zeitung* (1902); Stefan Großmann, "Ein deutscher Humorist: Zu Wilhelm
Buschs siebzigstem Geburtstage, 15. April 1902," *Arbeiter-Zeitung* (Vienna), no. 103
(1902); Josef Hofmiller, "Wilhelm Busch, der Pessimist: Zu seinem 70. Geburtstag,"
Allgemeine Zeitung (Munich), 15 Apr. 1902, 1–2; Osborn, "Wilhelm Busch" (Apr.
1902); "Wilhelm Busch," *Vorwärts* (1902); Zieler, "Wilhelm Busch" (1902); "Neues
von Wilhelm Busch," *Vossische Zeitung* (1904); Diederich, "Wilhelm Busch" (1907);
Graphicus, "Wilhelm Busch" (1907); Großmann, "Wilhelm Busch" (1907); Georg
Hermann, "Einige Bemerkungen über Wilhelm Busch," *Die Gegenwart: Wochen-*

schrift 31, no. 36 (1907): 247–49 (transcript WBM); Kutscher, "Wilhelm Buschs Humor" (1907); Paul Landau, "Wilhelm Busch (Zu seinem 75. Geburtstag)," *Hamburger Nachrichten*, 12 Apr. 1907 (transcript WBM); Karl Quenzel, "Wilhelm Busch," *Deutsche Kultur* 3 (July 1907), (transcript WBM); Scheffler, "Wilhelm Busch" (1907); Wippermann, "Wilhelm Busch"(1907); Gustav Zieler, "Ein Gedächtnismal für Wilhelm Busch," *Frankfurter Generalanzeiger*, no. 88 (1907) (transcript WBM); Bölsche, "Über Wilhelm Busch" (1908); Freye-Friedenau, "Wilhelm Busch" (1908); Max Hochdorf, "Busch," *Sozialistische Monatshefte*, Mar. 1908 (transcript WBM); Hofmiller, "Wilhelm Busch" (1908); Hermann Löns, "Wilhelm Busch," *Schaumburg-Lippischen Landeszeitung*, 10 Jan. 1908, reprinted in *Wilhelm Busch: Ernstes und Heiteres*, ed. Nöldecke, 263–68; Ostini, "Wilhelm Busch," *Jugend* (1908); Owlglaß, "Wilhelm Busch in memoriam" (1908); Otto Volkmann, "Wilhelm Busch," *Biographisches Jahrbuch und deutscher Nekrolog*, ed. A. Bettleheim, 1908: 74–97 (transcript WBM); Wolzogen, *Die Woche* (1908); Ettlinger, "Die Zerstörung der W. Busch-Legende" (1909); Wippermann, "Wilhelm Busch" (1909); Otto Volkmann, *Wilhelm Busch der Poet: Seine Motive und Quellen; Untersuchungen zur neueren Sprach- und Literaturgeschichte*, ed. Oskar F. Walzel, 5 (1910); Ostini, "Wilhelm Busch" (1911); Witkowski, *Die Entwicklung der deutschen Literatur* (1912); Vanselow, *Die Erstdrucke* (1913), vii; Karl Voll, "Wilhelm Busch," *Süddeutsche Monatshefte* (1913), (transcript WBM); "Ein Denkmal für Wilhelm Busch," *Daheim* (1913); Peter Panter, "Busch Briefe," *Die Schaubühne*, 16 Apr. 1914, 460–61; C., "Wilhelm Busch," *Berg-Quell*, 30 May 1914, 145–46; Kutscher, "Wilhelm Busch" (1914–15). Even after the war, Carl Neumann in *Wilhelm Busch* (Bielefeld and Leipzig: Velhagen & Klasing, 1919), Wilhelm Scherer and Oskar Walzel, *Geschichte der deutschen Literatur mit einem Anhang: Die deutsche Literatur von Goethes Tod bis zur Gegenwart* (Berlin: Askanischer Verlag, 1921), and Egon Friedell, in "Wilhelm Busch und der deutsche Bürger," *Der Querschnitt* 10 (Oct. 1931) (reprinted in *Kulturgeschichte der Neuzeit*), continued to insist that Busch was misunderstood by the Germans, despite their love for him.

79. Engels, "Wilhelm Busch" (1902); Osborn, "Wilhelm Busch" (Apr. 1902); Osborn, "Wilhelm Busch" (Nov. 1902); Trojan, "Bei Wilhelm Busch zu Gaste" (1902); Trojan, "Dem Jubilare Wilhelm Busch" (1902); "Wilhelm Busch," *Vorwärts* (1902); Engels, "Neues von Wilhelm Busch" (1904); Kutscher, "Wilhelm Buschs Humor" (1907); Kutscher, "Wilhelm Busch" (1907); Wippermann, "Wilhelm Busch" (1907); Ostini, "Wilhelm Busch," *Jugend* (1908).

80. Landau, "Wilhelm Busch" (1907).

81. Hofmiller, "Wilhelm Busch" (1902). Incidentally, comments like this one reveal that German self-hatred predates 1945 and that its appeal—then as since the exposure of the horrors of the Third Reich—rests in the sense of superiority it engenders.

82. "Ein deutscher Humorist." See, also, Großmann, "Wilhelm Busch" (1907); Hochdorf, "Busch" (1908).

83. Bölsche, "Über Wilhelm Busch" (1908).

84. Like the others celebrating Busch in socialist publications, Bölsche was himself thoroughly bourgeois. Indeed, his father had been editor of the *Kölnische Zeitung*. The forthcoming and final volume of Peter Gay's *The Bourgeois Experience: From Victoria to Freud* series, *Taste Wars*, is devoted to the cultural attitudes of the middle classes in Europe during this period.

85. "Wilhelm Busch." See also Richard Schaukal, *Wilhelm Busch* (1905), passim; and Meyer, *Die deutsche Literatur* (1906).

86. As Harry C. Payne has pointed out, humor in general has an exclusionary dimension, engendering an elitist satisfaction among those who get the joke at the expense of those who do not. Indeed, the process of "getting" a joke transforms the listener from ignorant outsider to knowing insider.

87. See, here, K. Ludwig Pfeiffer's article, "Suggestiveness or Interpretation: On the Vitality of Appearances," in *Reflecting Senses: Perception and Appearance in Literature, Culture, and the Arts*, ed. Walter Pape and Frederick Burwick (New York: W. de Gruyter, 1995), 15–32.

88. Wilhelm Busch, "Dank und Gruß" (1907).

89. Hermann, *Die deutsche Karikatur* (1901); Jänecke-Stade, "Wilhelm Busch als Philosoph" (1901); Hofmiller, "Wilhelm Busch" (1902); Diederich, "Wilhelm Busch" (1902); Großmann, "Ein deutscher Humorist" (1902); "Tagebuch des Leutnants von Versewitz: Zu Wilhelm Buschs 70sten Geburtstage," *Jugend* (1902); Kraeger, "Wilhelm Busch" (1902); Muther, "Wilhelm Busch" (1902); Norden, "Wilhelm Busch" (1902); Osborn, "Wilhelm Busch" (Apr. 1902); id., "Wilhelm Busch" (Nov. 1902); Presber, "Wilhelm Busch: Der Philosoph" (1902); Schöllermann, "Wilhelm Busch" (1902); Alfred Semerau, "Wilhelm Busch: Zu seinem 70. Geburtstage," *Leipziger Zeitung*, 15 Apr. 1902 (transcript WBM); Wertheimer, "Wilhelm Busch" (1902); Zieler, "Wilhelm Busch" (1902); Zschorlich, "Ein lachender Philosoph" (1902); Adolph Kohut, *Das Ewig-Weibliche bei Wilhelm Busch* (Leipzig: B. Elischer Nachfolger, 1904); "Neues von Wilhelm Busch," *Vossische Zeitung* (1904); Graphicus, "Wilhelm Busch" (1907); Kutscher, "Wilhelm Buschs Humor" (1907); Kutscher, "Wilhelm Busch" (1907); Kutscher, "Wilhelm Buschs Kunst" (1907–8); Landau, "Wilhelm Busch" (1907); Hans Müller-Brauel, "Hannoverland," *Das litterarische Echo* 9 (15 June 1907): 1355–58; Poeck, "Wilhelm Busch wird fünfundsiebzig" (1907); Willy Pastor, "Wilhelm Busch," *Eckart: Ein deutsches Literaturblatt*, no. 6 (1907–8) (transcript WBM); "Wilhelm Busch," *Allgemeine Zeitung* (Munich), 10 Jan. 1908 (transcript WBM); Friedrich Düsel, "Wilhelm Buschs Nachruhm," *Das nationale Deutschland*, 7 Feb. 1908 (transcript WBM); Busch obituary in *Evangelische Wacht* (Osnabrück), 19 Jan. 1908; Gottlieb, "Wilhelm Busch," *Der Tag* (1908) (transcript WBM); J. Höffner, "Wilhelm Busch," *Daheim* 44 (1908): 18–21; Hofmiller, "Wilhelm Busch" (1908); Busch obituary in *Norddeutsche allgemeine Zeitung* (1908); Ostini, "Wilhelm Busch," *Jugend* (1908); Storck, "Pessimismus und Humor"(1908); Volk-

mann, "Wilhelm Busch" (1908); Biese, *Deutsche Literaturgeschichte* (1910); Josef Hofmiller, *Zeitgenossen* (Munich, 1910), 170–81; Ostini, "Wilhelm Busch" (1911).

90. Jürgen Habermas, *Strukturwandel der Öffentlichkeit: Untersuchung zu einer Kategorie der bürgerlichen Gesellschaft* (Frankfurt a./M.: Suhrkamp Taschenbuch, 1990), 103–5. Habermas's notion that the literary critic came to represent the artist to the public and the public to the artist would seem relevant to the Busch reception between 1902 and 1908, although here the critics seem to have represented the public not to the artist but to the other critics. See also Russell A. Berman, "Literaturkritik zwischen Reichsgründung und 1933," in *Geschichte der deutschen Literaturkritik (1730–1980)*, ed. Peter Uwe Hohendahl (Stuttgart: J. B. Metzlersche Verlagsbuchhandlung, 1985), 205–74, esp. 210–27.

91. "Aus Wilhelm Buschs Selbstschau," *Die Welt des Kaufmanns* 5 (Apr. 1909): 193–98 (transcript WBM).

92. In analyzing the historical significance of literary production, it is important to keep in mind that writing is not merely self-expression but also communication with an audience. See Hans Robert Jauss, "Literary History as a Challenge to Literary Theory," in *Toward an Aesthetics of Reception* (Brighton: Harvester Press, 1982), 3–45.

93. With one exception—Frieda Schulz's "Persönliches von Wilhelm Busch," *Deutsche Zeitung*, 12 Apr. 1902—the articles celebrating Busch between 1902 and 1908 appear to have been written by men.

94. That the German empire was in danger of becoming a "satrapy," presumably of the English, was claimed by Kaiser Wilhelm II. See Thomas A. Kohut, *Wilhelm II and the Germans: A Study in Leadership* (New York: Oxford University Press, 1991), 218. For more on this extremist, all-or-nothing thinking in Wilhelmian Germany and its consequences, see Roger Chickering, *We Men Who Feel Most German: A Cultural Study of the Pan-German League* (Boston: Allen & Unwin, 1984); Elisabeth Fehrenbach, *Wandlungen des deutschen Kaisergedankens 1871–1918* (Munich: Oldenbourg, 1969); Fritz Fischer, *Griff nach der Weltmacht* (Düsseldorf: Droste, 1961); Fischer, *Krieg der Illusionen* (Düsseldorf: Droste, 1969); Paul M. Kennedy, *The Rise of the Anglo-German Antagonism, 1860–1914* (London: Allen & Unwin, 1980); Wolfgang Mommsen, "The Topos of Inevitable War in Germany in the Decade before 1914," in *Germany in the Age of Total War*, ed. Volker Berghahn and Martin Kitchen (London: Croom Helm, 1981), 23–45; Michael Salewski, "'Neujahr 1900': Die Säkularwende in zeitgenössischer Sicht," *Archiv für Kulturgeschichte* 53 (1971): 342–50; Woodruff D. Smith, *The Ideological Origins of Nazi Imperialism* (New York: Oxford University Press, 1986); Jonathan Steinberg, "The Copenhagen Complex," *Journal of Contemporary History* 1 (1966): 23–46; id., *Yesterday's Deterrent: Tirpitz and the Birth of the German Battle Fleet* (London: MacDonald, 1965); and Klaus Wernecke, *Die Wille zur Weltgeltung: Aussenpolitik und Öffentlichkeit am Vorabend des Ersten Weltkrieges* (Düsseldorf: Droste, 1970).

95. "Wilhelm Busch," *Morgen*, 30 Aug. 1907, 355–58.

CHAPTER 15

1. Inge Deutschkron, *Outcast: A Jewish Girl in Wartime Berlin* (New York, 1989), 7, 14.

2. G. W. Allport, J. S. Bruner, and E. M. Jandorf, "Personality under Social Catastrophe: Ninety Life-Histories of the Nazi Revolution," *Character and Personality: An International Psychological Quarterly* 10, no. 1 (Sept. 1941): 14–15.

3. Ibid., 14.

4. "Laura Pelz," in Douglas Morris, "The Lives of Some Jewish Germans Who Lived in Nazi Germany and Live in Germany Today: An Oral History" (B.A. thesis, Wesleyan University, 1976).

5. Rudolf Lennert, "Zugehörigkeit, Selbstbewusstsein, Fremdheit," *Neue Sammlung* 3, 26 (1986): 393, quoted by Frank Stern, *The Whitewashing of the Yellow Badge: Antisemitism and Philosemitism in Postwar Germany*, trans. William Templer (Oxford, 1992), 37.

6. Peter Gay, "The German-Jewish Legacy — and I: Some Personal Reflections," in *The German-Jewish Legacy in America, 1938–1988*, ed. Abraham J. Peck (Detroit, 1989), 19.

7. Marion Gardner in *"Vergessen kann man das nicht": Wittener Jüdinnen und Juden unter dem Nationalsozialismus*, ed. Martina Kliner-Lintzen and Siegfried Pape (Bochum, 1991), 299.

8. Verena Hellwig, Harvard MS, 30. The Harvard manuscripts are in the collection BMS GER 91, Houghton Library, Harvard University, and were written for a contest on the subject "Mein Leben in Deutschland vor und nach dem 30. Januar 1933." Publication of all citations is by permission of the Houghton Library.

9. Lisa Brauer, memoirs, Leo Baeck Institute, New York (henceforth cited as LBI), 38.

10. Allport et al., "Personality under Social Catastrophe," 14.

11. Mally Dienemann, Harvard MS, 25.

12. Reiner in *Sie durften nicht mehr Deutsch sein: Jüdischer Alltag in Selbstzeugnissen 1933–1938*, ed. Margarete Limberg and Hubert Rübsaat (Frankfurt a./M., 1990), 156. See also *Jewish Life in Germany: Memoirs from Three Centuries*, ed. Monika Richarz, trans. Stella and Sidney Rosenfeld (Bloomington, Ind., 1991), 402.

13. Reiner in *Sie durften nicht mehr Deutsch sein*, ed. Limberg and Rübsaat, 156.

14. Ruth Glaser, memoirs, LBI, 15–16.

15. Lisa Grubel (vacation in 1937), memoirs, LBI, 15.

16. Mrs. Elly Busse, of Bern, Switzerland, told Atina Grossmann that she phoned stores in order to avoid showing the *J* on her identification card, even though she was an "Aryan" married to a Jew (Apr. 1993).

17. Barbara Händler-Lachmann, Harald Händler, and Ulrich Schütt, *Purim, Purim, ihr liebe Leut, wisst ihr was Purim bedeut?: Jüdisches Leben im Landkreis Mar-*

burg im 20. Jahrhundert (Marburg, 1995). See photo of the Hahn family eating in their sukkah in 1936, 125.

18. About one-third of the respondents to the Harvard study turned to religion for comfort; 68 percent considered themselves Jewish, and some of the Christians were converts from Judaism (Allport et al., "Personality under Social Catastrophe").

19. Ibid., 16.

20. Ruth Glaser, memoirs, LBI, 16–17.

21. Joachim Prinz, "A Rabbi under the Hitler Regime," in *Gegenwart im Rückblick*, ed. Kurt Grossmann and Herbert Strauss (Heidelberg, 1970); Max Nussbaum, "Ministry under Stress: A Rabbi's Recollection of Nazi Berlin, 1935–40," in ibid.

22. Benno Cohn, "Einige Bemerkungen über den Deutschen Zionismus nach 1933," in *Zwei Welten*, ed. Hans Tramer (Tel Aviv, 1962), 45.

23. Norman Bentwich, *Jewish Youth Comes Home: The Story of the Youth Aliyah, 1933–1943* (London, 1944), 25; Cohn, "Einige Bemerkungen," 48.

24. Alice Nauen, interview, Research Foundation for Jewish Immigration, New York, 10. For many Germans, awareness of the regime's cruel intentions also came "drip by drip, rather like an anesthetic. . . . It was only after it hit you personally that you knew what was going on" (Christabel Bielenberg, interview in *The World at War* [Thames Television], "A New Germany" [1977]).

25. Elizabeth Bamberger in *Women of Exile: German-Jewish Autobiographies since 1933*, ed. Andreas Lixl-Purcell (Westport, Conn., 1988), 92.

26. Victor Klemperer, *Ich will Zeugnis ablegen* (Berlin, 1995), 1: 24, 26, and 66; 2: 104, 191, and 654.

27. Bella Fromm, *Blood and Banquets: A Berlin Social Diary* (London, 1942), 197; Charles Marks, memoirs, LBI, 8.

28. *Blätter des Jüdischen Frauenbundes* (henceforth cited as *BJFB*), Feb. 1935, 12.

29. *BJFB*, July 1938, 13.

30. *Israelitisches Familienblatt* (henceforth cited as *IF*), June 25, 1936.

31. *Central Verein Zeitung* (henceforth cited as *CV*), Feb. 27, 1936. See also *IF*, 19 Mar. 1936.

32. "Junge Mädels lernen der Mutter helfen," *CV*, 9 Apr. 1936; "Häusliche Erziehung," *IF*, 21 May 1936.

33. *IF*, 19 Mar. 1936.

34. Ruth Glaser, memoirs, LBI, 16.

35. Erna Becker-Kohen, diary/memoirs, LBI, 31.

36. *BJFB*, Oct. 1938, 4, 14.

37. "Der Ehemann im Haushalt," in *IF*, 19 May 1938, 19, cited in Sibylle Quack, "Changing Gender Roles and Emigration: The Example of German Jewish Women and Their Emigration to the United States, 1933–1945," in *People in Transit: German Migrations in Comparative Perspective, 1829–1930*, ed. Dirk Hoerder and Jörg Nagler (New York, 1995), 394.

38. *BJFB*, Dec. 1935, 8.
39. *IF*, 19 May 1938, 19.
40. Ibid.
41. *BJFB*, June 1935, 9–10. Scientific management is discussed by Mary Nolan in *Visions of Modernity: American Business and the Modernization of Germany* (New York, 1994), 42 and ch. 10. Nolan stresses the importance of household rationalization under the Weimar Republic, but for bourgeois Jewish women the ideology—and necessity—probably first arose in the Nazi era. See also *CV*, 27 May 1936.
42. *CV*, 17 Mar. 1938, 11.
43. *IF*, Mar. 19, 1936; *Frankfurter Israelitisches Gemeindeblatt*, Nov. 1935, 73–74.
44. *IF*, 26 Mar. 1936.
45. "Mutti, hast du Zeit für mich?" *CV*, 27 Feb. 1936; "Mutti ist so nervös!" *CV*, 16 Sept. 1936.
46. *CV*, 25 Aug. 1938, 8.
47. Letter in the Ottilie Schönewald collection, LBI, IV, 1.
48. *BJFB*, Oct. 1935, 2.
49. Allport et al., "Personality under Social Catastrophe," 14.
50. Ibid.; Mally Dienemann, Harvard MS, 25.
51. Alice Baerwald, Harvard MS, 65.
52. Mally Dienemann, Harvard MS, 25.
53. Lisa Brauer, memoirs, LBI, 38: "being confined to our quarters all the time and not able to go anywhere for entertainment, we had lots of time on our hands. So we studied both English and Spanish. It did not mean just a hobby for us, it set our mind and spirit free."
54. Mally Dienemann, Harvard MS, 25.
55. Edith Wolff, Yad Vashem, Ball-Kaduri Collection, 01/247, 22.
56. Ibid., 14, 21–22.
57. Abraham, LBI, 2; job training in *Community of Fate: Memoirs of German Jews in Melbourne*, ed. John Foster (Sydney and London, 1986), 28–30; mother and daughter in Brauer, LBI, 53. In "Epilogue: The First Sex," *Between Sorrow and Strength: Women Refugees of the Nazi Period* (Cambridge, 1995), 353, Peter Gay tells of how his mother, who had never worked outside the home and struggled with tuberculosis, tried to become a seamstress in 1936 in order to help support the family in emigration.
58. Praising women's flexibility and versatility, the writer notes that women were also sole supports in many families. *IF*, 13 Jan. 1938, 13–14. See also *IF*, 14 July 1938, 12.
59. *CV*, 25 Aug. 1938.
60. *IF*, 14 July 1938, 12.
61. Liselotte Kahn, memoirs, LBI, 21.
62. See, e.g., Jacob Ball-Kaduri, memoirs, LBI, 30; Lisa Brauer, memoirs, LBI, 43, 57.
63. Jacob Ball-Kaduri, memoirs, LBI, 30.

64. See, e.g., Lisa Brauer, memoirs, LBI, 43, 57, on bribes to a shipping company official and to officials at the Finance Dept.

65. Liselotte Kahn, memoirs, LBI, 23.

66. Ann Lewis, memoirs, LBI, 264.

67. Lore Steinitz about her mother, Irma Baum. Note to the author entitled "The first 'sit in'" (7 Jan. 1995), also deposited at the Leo Baeck Institute.

68. Ruth Abraham, memoirs, LBI, 2.

69. Gerta Pfeffer in *Sie durften nicht mehr Deutsch sein*, ed. Limberg and Rübsaat, 141.

70. Rosy Geiger-Kullmann, memoirs, LBI, 72. Echoing these fears, the League of Jewish Women worried that its railroad station shelters might become unavailable to young women, who might be accosted by men who would take advantage of their situation. Bundesarchiv, Coswig: 75C Jüd. Frauenbund Verband Berlin, folder 37— "Protokoll der Arbeitskreistagung vom 2 Nov. 1936, Gefährdung der Jugendlichen."

71. Kate Behnsch-Brower, memoirs, LBI, 4–5.

72. Edith Bick interview, Research Foundation for Jewish Immigration, 18.

73. Hilde Honnet-Sichel, Harvard MS, 72–73.

74. An extreme example of this happened during the deportations when a nurse walked into a double suicide. Terribly upset, she wanted to share her feelings with her husband but could not "because of his own depressions." She did confide in her girlfriend. Frieda Cohn, Yad Vashem, Ball-Kaduri Collection, 01/291, 5.

75. Marion Kaplan, "Jewish Women in Nazi Germany Before Emigration," in *Between Sorrow and Strength: Women Refugees of the Nazi Period*, ed. Sibylle Quack (Cambridge, 1995), 11–50.

76. Peter Wyden, *Stella: One Woman's True Tale of Evil, Betrayal, and Survival in Hitler's Germany* (New York, 1992), 47.

77. Mary Felstiner, *To Paint Her Life: Charlotte Salomon in the Nazi Era* (New York, 1994), 74.

78. Alice Nauen, interview, Research Foundation for Jewish Immigration, 10.

79. Ibid., 8.

80. Hanna Bernheim, Harvard MS, 53.

81. Charlotte Hamburger, memoirs, LBI, 41, 46. She decided to flee after her husband and children faced public abuse.

82. Charlotte Stein-Pick, memoirs, LBI, 2.

83. Ibid., 38.

84. Elizabeth Bamberger, memoirs, LBI, 5.

85. Else Gerstel, memoirs, LBI, 71.

86. Ilse Strauss, memoirs, LBI, 8: 44.

87. Hanna Bernheim, Harvard MS, 45.

88. Else Gerstel, memoirs, LBI, 76.

89. Karl A. Schleunes, *The Twisted Road to Auschwitz: Nazi Policy Toward German Jews, 1933–1939* (Urbana, Ill., 1970), 183–84, 197–98.

90. Wyden, *Stella*, 48, 88.

91. Rita Thalmann and Emmanuel Feinermann, *Crystal Night: 9–10 November 1938* (New York, 1974), 22.

92. In 1933 over 35 percent of the Jewish population were over 50; by 1938 more than half were over 50 and about 20 percent were over 65. See Schleunes, *Twisted Road*, 186, and *Aus Nachbarn wurden Juden: Ausgrenzung und Selbstbehauptung 1933–1942*, ed. Hazel Rosenstrauch (Berlin, 1988), 70.

93. Wyden, *Stella*, 48.

94. Avraham Barkai, *From Boycott to Annihilation: The Economic Struggle of German Jews, 1933–1943*, trans. William Templer (Hanover, N.H., 1989), 99–100.

95. Michael Marrus, *The Unwanted: European Refugees in the Twentieth Century* (New York, 1985), 131.

96. Gerdy Stoppleman, memoirs, LBI, 6.

97. Barkai, *From Boycott to Annihilation*, 99–100.

98. Marrus, *Unwanted*, 131.

99. Hilde Honnet-Sichel in *Sie durften nicht mehr Deutsch sein*, ed. Limberg and Rübsaat, 184.

100. Ann Lewis, memoirs, LBI, 269–70.

101. Nazi officials in Hamburg, e.g., were aware of the bribes paid by Jews to foreign consulates. On the one hand, they wanted to regulate these payments (the unintended result of which would be to hinder Jewish emigration) and, on the other, they wanted to expedite Jewish emigration. Hamburg Staatsarchiv, Oberfinanzpräsident, 314–15, 9UA2: "Auswanderung jüdische Emigranten, 1936–1941."

102. *We Shall Not Forget! Memories of the Holocaust*, ed. Carole Garbuny Vogel (Lexington, Mass.: 1994), 12.

103. *Das Sonderrecht für die Juden im Ns-Staat: Eine Sammlung der gesetzlichen Massnahmen und Richtlinien—Inhalt und Bedeutung*, ed. Joseph Walk (Heidelberg, 1981). See Nov. 16, 1937.

104. Bundesarchiv Potsdam, Coswig, 75C Hil HICEM Prag 5 *Coordinating Committee for Refugees*: Domestic Bureau (Fragebogen, 1939).

105. It is estimated that about 60,000 to 65,000 refugees in total left Germany in 1933 and that about 40 percent of these went to France: Rita Thalmann, "L'Immigration allemande et l'opinion publique en France de 1933 à 1936," in *La France et l' Allemagne, 1932–1936* (Paris, 1980), 149–50.

106. Herbert Strauss, "Jewish Emigration from Germany: Nazi Policies and Jewish Responses" (I), in *Leo Baeck Institute Year Book* (henceforth cited as *LBIYB*) (1980), 357.

107. Yehuda Bauer, *My Brother's Keeper* (Philadelphia, 1974) 138–39. France absorbed much of the first wave of refugees in 1933 (about 21,000, not all of whom were Jewish.) Shortly thereafter, Paris began to restrict the flow, fearful of becoming a dumping ground for refugees. Later, the government turned toward repatriation, resettlement, and internment. See Marrus, *The Unwanted*, 146–47. In "L'Immigration allemande," 149–72, Thalmann speaks of 25,000 German refugees in France in 1933.

108. Shlomo Wahrman, *Lest We Forget: Growing up in Nazi Leipzig, 1933–1939* (New York, 1991), 77–78.

109. See, e.g.,: "L.I. Resident Recalls How as Small Girl She and Parents Hid from Nazi Attacks," *Jewish Week* (Long Island, N.Y.), 19 Nov. 1978. Although they had applied for entry to the United States, Evelyn Pike's parents first studied Spanish, hoping to go to Cuba. When this failed, they studied Portuguese, hoping to go to Brazil. They wound up in Shanghai.

110. Pressing her husband to leave Germany, Marta Appel recorded his reactions: "Like all other men, he . . . couldn't imagine leaving one's beloved homeland and the duties that fill a man's life. 'Could you really leave all this behind you to enter nothingness?' . . . 'I could,' I said, without a moment's hesitation. Quoted in *Jüdisches Leben in Deutschland: Selbstzeugnisse zur Sozialgeschichte 1918–1945*, ed. Monika Richarz, vol. 3 (Stuttgart, 1982), 237.

111. Psychologists who studied refugee memoirs observed that almost 40 percent of memoir writers did not give up psychologically until 1938 or 1939. Allport et al., "Personality under Social Catastrophe," 4.

112. Ibid.; "everyone" in *Davidstern und Weihnachtsbaum: Erinnerungen von Überlebenden*, ed. Bernd-Lutz Lange (Leipzig, 1992), 27.

113. Freund in Richarz, *Life*, 413–15.

114. Letter from Gertrud Grossmann, 17 Jan. 1939 (thank you to Atina Grossmann for sharing these letters); "god" in Bernheim, Harvard MS, 51.

115. Dienemann, Harvard, MS, 35. See also Fromm, *Blood*, 238.

116. "On Not Believing the Unbelievable," *New York Times Book Review*, 29 June 1996, 13.

117. Letter from Gertrud Grossmann, 22 Feb. 1940.

118. Burgheim, LBI archives; *In mich ist die grosse dunkle Ruhe gekommen: Martha Wertheimer Briefe an Siegfried Guggenheim (1939–1941)*, ed. Hanno Loewy (Frankfurt a./M.: Frankfurter Lern- und Dokumentationszentrum des Holocaust, 1993), 6, 9, 13, 15, 22, 37.

119. Alice Nauen (whose father was secretary of the Hilfsverein in Hamburg), interview, Research Foundation for Jewish Immigration, 15; Ruth Klüger, *Weiter leben* (Göttingen, 1992), 83.

120. "The sons" in *BJFB*, April 1937, 5; Glaser, memoirs, LBI, 26, 71; Stein-Pick, LBI, p. 46.

121. League in *BJFB*, Dec. 1936, 1; Hilfsverein in CV, Jan. 20, 1938, 5 and 3 Mar. 1938, 6; financial support in *Informationsblätter*, Jan./Feb. 1938, 6–7.

122. "Martyrs" in Lixl-Purcell, *Women*, 92. Women were also a majority of the Jewish populations of German-dominated Europe: Raul Hilberg, *Perpetrators, Victims and Bystanders* (New York, 1992), 127; *IF*, no. 9 (27 Feb. 1936); Bruno Blau, "The Jewish Population of Germany, 1939–1946," *Jewish Social Studies* 12, no. 2 (1950): 165.

123. On age, see Strauss, "Jewish Emigration" (I), 318–19 and Blau, "Population," 165; old age homes in Wolf Gruner, "Die Reichshauptstadt und die Verfolgung der Berliner Juden 1933–1945," in *Jüdische Geschichte in Berlin: Essays und Studien*,

ed. Reinhard Rürup (Berlin, 1995), 242, 251; Winter Relief in Clemens Vollnhals, "Judische Selbsthilfe bis 1938," in *Die Juden in Deutschland, 1933–1945*, ed. Wolfgang Benz (Munich, 1988), 405, and *BJFB*, Oct. 1938, 4.

124. Disproportionate number of elderly women in Richarz, *Leben*, 61; *JWS*, 1937, 96–97, 161–63, 200–201; Klemperer, *Zeugnis*, 1: 475; *IF*, 16 Jan. 1936; Freund, memoirs, LBI, 146.

125. Daniel J. Goldhagen, *Hitler's Willing Executioners: Ordinary Germans and the Holocaust* (New York, 1996).

CHAPTER 16

1. *The Complete Letters of Sigmund Freud to Wilhelm Fliess, 1887–1904*, trans. and ed. Jeffrey Moussaieff Masson (Cambridge, Mass.: Harvard University Press, 1985), 285.

2. Freud, *The Interpretation of Dreams* (1900), in *The Standard Edition of the Complete Psychological Works of Sigmund Freud*, translated under the general editorship of James Strachey, 24 vols. (London: Hogarth Press, 1953–74) (henceforth cited as *SE*), 4: 194.

3. Ibid.

4. A copy of the card was kindly made available to me by Michael Molnar of the Freud Museum in London.

5. Cf. *Complete Letters of Sigmund Freud to Wilhelm Fliess, 1887–1904*, 449.

6. Freud, *Interpretation of Dreams*, in *SE* 4: 196.

7. *The Complete Correspondence of Sigmund Freud and Ernest Jones, 1908–1939*, ed. R. A. Paskauskas (Cambridge, Mass.: Harvard University Press, 1993), 521.

8. Translated from the manuscript of Ingeborg Meyer-Palmedo's transcription.

9. Ibid., letter of 6 Nov. 1917.

10. Letter to Katá and Lajos Levy of 11 June 1923. In *Letters of Sigmund Freud, 1873–1939*, ed. Ernst L. Freud, trans. T. and J. Stern (London: Hogarth Press, 1970, paperback ed. first published in 1961), 349.

11. This letter, which has not to my knowledge been previously published, is in the Freud Collection at the Library of Congress, Washington, D.C. I am indebted for the information to Albrecht Hirschmüller, from whose transcription the excerpt has been translated. It is presented here with the kind permission of Sigmund Freud Copyrights, Colchester.

12. Both letters quoted in Peter Gay, *Freud: A Life for Our Time* (New York: Norton, 1988), 422.

13. Ibid., 425.

14. Quoted in Sigmund Freud and Lou Andreas-Salomé, *Letters*, ed. E. Pfeiffer, trans. W. and E. Robson-Scott (London: Hogarth Press, 1972), 233 n. 160.

15. Freud, *Leonardo da Vinci and a Memory of His Childhood*, in *SE* 11: 93.

16. Sigmund Freud and Ludwig Binswanger, *Briefwechsel 1908–1938*, ed. G. Fichtner (Frankfurt a./M.: S. Fischer, 1992), 188.

17. Translated from the manuscript of the correspondence between Sigmund and Anna Freud transcribed by Ingeborg Meyer-Palmedo.

18. Freud, *Interpretation of Dreams*, in SE 4: 194 n. 1.

19. Freud, *Civilization and Its Discontents*, in SE 21: 69.

20. Ibid., 70.

21. Ibid., 70f.

22. Published in English as *Sigmund Freud: His Life in Pictures and Words*, ed. Ernst Freud, Lucie Freud, and Ilse Grubrich-Simitis (New York: Harcourt Brace Jovanovich, 1978; paperback ed., New York: Norton, 1985).

23. Peter Gay, "Freud: For the Marble Tablet," in *Berggasse 19: Sigmund Freud's Home and Offices, Vienna 1938* (New York: Basic Books, 1976), 33.

24. Ibid., 29.

25. Ibid., 42.

26. Peter Gay, *Freud: A Life for Our Time* (New York: Norton, 1988).

27. Gay, "Freud: For the Marble Tablet," 20.

CHAPTER 17

1. Freud, *The Question of Lay Analysis: Conversations with an Impartial Person* (1926), in *The Standard Edition of the Complete Psychological Works of Sigmund Freud*, translated under the general editorship of James Strachey, 24 vols. (London: Hogarth Press, 1953–74) (henceforth cited as SE), 20: 212. For a concise and masterly review of Freud's account of the "dark continent," see Peter Gay, *Freud: A Life for Our Time* (New York: Norton, 1988), 501–22.

2. See Peter Weingart, "Biology as Social Theory: The Bifurcation of Social Biology and Sociology in Germany, circa 1900," in *Modern Impulses in the Human Sciences 1870–1930*, ed. Dorothy Ross (Baltimore: Johns Hopkins University Press, 1994), 255–71. Freud encountered the concept of retrogression in the work of his Darwinian professor, Carl Claus: see Lucille B. Ritvo, *Darwin's Influence on Freud: A Tale of Two Sciences* (New Haven: Yale University Press, 1990), 156–58.

3. See Richard F. Sterba, *Reminiscences of a Viennese Psychoanalyst* (Detroit: Wayne State University Press, 1982), 29. For biographical information I have drawn on Helene Deutsch, *Confrontations with Myself: An Epilogue* (New York: Norton, 1973), and Paul Roazen, *Helene Deutsch: A Psychoanalyst's Life* (New Brunswick, N.J.: Transaction Publishers, 1992). See also Marie H. Briehl, "Helene Deutsch," in *Psychoanalytic Pioneers*, ed. Franz Alexander, Samuel Eisenstein, and Martin Grotjahn (New York: Basic Books, 1966), 282–98. For useful commentary, see Brenda S. Webster, "Helene Deutsch: A New Look," *Signs* 10 (1985): 553–71; Nellie L. Thompson, "Helene Deutsch: A Life in Theory," *Psychoanalytic Quarterly* 56 (1987): 317–53; and Janet Sayers, *Mothers of Psychoanalysis: Helene Deutsch, Karen Horney, Anna Freud, Melanie Klein* (New York: Norton, 1991), 25–81.

4. Deutsch, *Confrontations with Myself*, 133.

5. Roazen, *Helene Deutsch*, 156.

6. Deutsch, *Confrontations with Myself*, 134.

7. "In fact," she wrote, "the whole transference situation could have come out of a textbook on psychoanalysis. By a remarkable coincidence, my father left Vienna to go home to Poland at the end of the war on the very same day in August 1918 that I began analysis with Freud" (ibid., 132).

8. Ibid., 131.

9. Freud, *New Introductory Lectures on Psycho-Analysis* (1933), in SE 22: 116–17 (emphasis in the original).

10. Freud, *Civilization and Its Discontents* (1930), in SE 21: 106n.

11. Helene Deutsch, *Psychoanalysis of the Sexual Functions of Women* (1925), ed. Paul Roazen, trans. Eric Mosbacher (London: Karnac, 1991), 3.

12. Ibid., 2.

13. In her otherwise favorable review of the book, Karen Horney expressed the hope that the clinical material on which it was based would soon be published: see Karen Horney, review of *Zur Psychologie der weiblichen Sexualfunktionen*, by Helene Deutsch, *International Journal of Psycho-Analysis* 7 (1926): 92–100.

14. Freud, *Three Essays on the Theory of Sexuality* (1905), in SE 7: 197–98.

15. Freud, "The Infantile Genital Organization (An Interpolation into the Theory of Sexuality" (1923), in SE 19: 142.

16. Karl Abraham, "Short History of the Development of the Libido, Viewed in the Light of Mental Disorders" (1924), in *Selected Papers of Karl Abraham*, trans. Douglas Bryan and Alix Strachey (London: Hogarth Press, 1927; reprint, London: Karnac, Maresfield Reprints, 1979), 424, 482.

17. Ibid., 498, 500. Freud picked up Abraham's comments about the embryonic blastopore: see Freud, *Three Essays*, 199 n. For the most extravagant biogenetic fantasy in psychoanalytic literature, see Sándor Ferenczi, *Thalassa: A Theory of Genitality* (1924), trans. Henry Alden Bunker (London: Karnac, Maresfield Library, 1989).

18. Deutsch, *Psychoanalysis of the Sexual Functions of Women*, 15.

19. Ibid., 11.

20. See Freud, *Group Psychology and the Analysis of the Ego* (1921), in SE 18: 105–6, and *The Ego and the Id* (1923), in SE 19: 31. Freud objected to Deutsch's account of the little girl's identification with her father: see Freud, "Female Sexuality" (1931), in SE 21: 242.

21. Freud, *New Introductory Lectures*, 125; see also Freud, *Three Essays*, 195.

22. Freud, "Some Psychical Consequences of the Anatomical Distinction between the Sexes" (1925), in SE 19: 252.

23. Freud, *New Introductory Lectures*, 125.

24. Deutsch, *Psychoanalysis of the Sexual Functions of Women*, 25, 27.

25. Ibid., 20, 24.

26. Ibid., 27.

27. For her use of the word "retrogression," see ibid., 106; see also Helene Deutsch, "Homosexuality in Women" (1932), in Helene Deutsch, *Neuroses and Character Types*:

Clinical Psychoanalytic Studies (New York: International Universities Press, 1965), 184, 185, and 187.

28. Deutsch, *Psychoanalysis of the Sexual Functions of Women*, 13.

29. Ibid., 12, 14.

30. See Freud, *The Ego and the Id*, 29. Deutsch's notion of the superego echoes Freud's discussion of the ego-ideal in his *Group Psychology and the Analysis of the Ego*, 111–16.

31. Deutsch, "Homosexuality in Women," 165. For an illuminating discussion of this paper, see Teresa de Lauretis, *The Practice of Love: Lesbian Sexuality and Perverse Desire* (Bloomington: Indiana University Press, 1994), 58–65.

32. Freud subsequently acknowledged Deutsch's contribution: see Freud, *New Introductory Lectures*, 131.

33. Freud, "Female Sexuality," 226, 227.

34. See Deutsch, "Homosexuality in Women," 185.

35. Ibid., 167, 168. Deutsch had reported on this patient in an earlier paper: see Helene Deutsch, "On the Psychology of Mistrust" (1921), in Helene Deutsch, *The Therapeutic Process, the Self, and Female Psychology: Collected Psychoanalytic Papers*, ed. Paul Roazen, trans. Eric Mosbacher (New Brunswick, N.J.: Transaction Publishers, 1992), 137–39. She subsequently reused this material: see Helene Deutsch, *The Psychology of Women: A Psychoanalytic Interpretation*, vol. 1 (New York: Grune & Stratton, 1944), 341–46.

36. Deutsch, "Homosexuality in Women," 166.

37. Ibid., 166, 171.

38. Ibid., 168, 169.

39. Ibid., 169 (emphasis in the original).

40. Ibid., 169–70 (emphasis in the original).

41. Ibid., 171 (emphasis in the original).

42. Ibid., 171, 181.

43. Freud, "Female Sexuality," 229–30.

44. Deutsch, "Homosexuality in Women," 170.

45. Ibid., 171, 172–73, and 188 (emphasis in the original).

46. Ibid., 181, 184, and 187.

47. Freud, "Female Sexuality," 234.

48. Helene Deutsch, "Hysterical Conversion Symptoms: Fits, Trance States" (1930), in Deutsch, *Neuroses and Character Types*, 70–71, 62, and 69.

49. Freud, "Hysterical Phantasies and Their Relation to Bisexuality" (1908), in *SE* 9: 163–64.

50. Deutsch, "Hysterical Conversion Symptoms," 68, 70.

51. Ibid., 67, 70.

52. Ibid., 70.

53. Freud, *Three Essays*, 221.

54. Deutsch, *Psychoanalysis of the Sexual Functions of Women*, 61.

55. Freud, *Three Essays*, 220–21.

56. Deutsch, *Psychoanalysis of the Sexual Functions of Women*, 67.

57. Ibid., 65.

58. Ibid., 65, 66, and 87.

59. Ibid., 83, 87, and 88. See also Freud, "On Transformations of Instinct as Exemplified in Anal Erotism" (1917), in *SE* 17: 127–33.

60. Deutsch, *Psychoanalysis of the Sexual Functions of Woman*, 84, 88, and 92.

61. Ibid., 65, 81, 92–93.

62. Ibid., 100–101.

63. Ibid., 106, 109, and 117.

64. Helene Deutsch, "The Psychology of Women in Relation to the Functions of Reproduction" (1925), in Deutsch, *The Therapeutic Process, the Self, and Female Psychology*, 8.

65. Deutsch, *Psychoanalysis of the Sexual Functions of Women*, 84.

CHAPTER 18

I acknowledge with thanks the assistance of Harry Brickman, Esther Dreifuss-Kattan, David James Fisher, Joshua Hoffs, Alfred and Ruth Goldberg, Albert D. Hutter, and Dorothy Wolpert, who read and commented on earlier versions of this essay. Shauna Mulvihill of the Department of History, UCLA, provided computer support, and Whitney L. White provided expert research assistance.

Nietzsche epigraph: *Menschliches, Allzumenschliches*, in *Friedrich Nietzsche: Werke in Drei Bänden*, ed. Karl Schlechta (Munich: Carl Hanser, 1962), vol. 1, stanza 88, 500.

Gay epigraph: Peter Gay, paper presented to conference on "Psychoanalysis and Culture," New York Psychoanalytic Institute and Society, New York City, 15 March 1997 (MS, courtesy of the author), 15.

1. W. H. Auden, "In Memory of Sigmund Freud," in *Collected Poems*, ed. Edward Mendelson (New York: Random House, 1976), 217.

2. Freud, *The Interpretation of Dreams* (1900), in *The Standard Edition of the Complete Psychological Works of Sigmund Freud*, translated under the general editorship of James Strachey, 24 vols. (London: Hogarth Press, 1953–74) (henceforth cited as *SE*), 5: 558; id., *Studienausgabe*, ed. Alexander Mitscherlich, Angela Richards, and James Strachey, 10 vols. (Frankfurt a./M.: Fischer, 1969–89) (henceforth cited as *Stud.*), vol. 2: *Die Traumdeutung* (1972), 532.

3. Freud, "Three Essays on the Theory of Sexuality" (1905), in *SE* 7: 227; id., "Drei Abhandlungen zur Sexualtheorie," in *Stud.* 5: 130.

4. Freud, "New Introductory Lectures on Psycho-Analysis," *SE* 22: 76; id., "Neue Folge der Vorlesungen zur Einführung in die Psychoanalyse (1933)," in *Stud.* 1: 513.

5. Freud, "An Outline of Psychoanalysis" (1940), in *SE* 23: 201; id., "Abriss der Psychoanalyse," in *Gesammelte Werke* (London: Imago, 1941), 17: 132.

6. My translation from "Neue Folge der Vorlesungen" (1933), in *Stud.* 1: 516; "New Introductory Lectures," *SE* 22: 80.

7. See Ronald Dworkin, Thomas Nagel, Robert Nozick, John Rawls, Thomas Scanlon, and Judith Jarvis Thomson, "Assisted Suicide: The Philosophers' Brief," *New York Review of Books* 44, no. 5 (Mar. 27, 1997).

8. Margaret P. Battin, "Suicidology and the Right to Die," in *Suicidology: Essays in Honor of Edwin S. Schneidman*, ed. Antoon A. Leenaars (Northvale, N.J.: Jason Aronson, 1993), 378.

9. *Cruzan v. Director, Missouri Department of Health*, 497 U.S. 261 (1990), at 237.

10. U.S. Department of Health and Human Services, Public Health Service, Centers for Disease Control and Prevention, National Center for Health Statistics, *Health, United States, 1992* (Hyattsville, Md.: Public Health Service, 1993), 161. As cited in *Statistical Record of Health and Medicine*, ed. Charity Anne Dogan (New York: Gale Research, 1995), 933.

11. Peter S. Heller, Richard Hemming, Peter W. Kohnert et al., *Aging and Social Expenditure in the Major Industrial Countries, 1880–2025*, International Monetary Fund Occasional Paper no. 47 (Washington, D.C.: International Monetary Fund: September 1986), 45. As cited in *Statistical Record of Health and Medicine*, ed. Charity Anne Dogan (New York: Gale Research, 1995), 931.

12. U.S. Senate Special Committee on Aging, the American Association of Retired Persons, Federal Council on Aging, and the U.S. Administration on Aging, *Aging America: Trends and Projections* (Washington, D.C.: U.S. Department of Health and Human Services, 1991), 270. As cited in *Statistical Record of Health and Medicine*, ed. Charity Anne Dogan (New York: Gale Research, 1995).

13. *Cruzan v. Director* (1990), at 242.

14. Elizabeth Rosenthal, "When a Healer Is Asked, 'Help Me Die,'" *New York Times*, 13 Mar. 1997, A1, A15.

15. *In re Quinlan*, 70 NJ 10, 355 A2d 647.

16. "In the Name of Mercy: The Anti-Kevorkian Dr. Timothy Quill Makes His Case for Assisted Suicide in His Own Words," *People* 47, no. 13 (7 Apr. 1997), 138.

17. *Compassion in Dying v. State of Wash.*, 79 F3d 790 (9th Cir. 1996), 813–14. Reversed by the U.S. Supreme Court in *Washington v. Glucksberg*, 117 S. Ct. 2258 (1997).

18. Norman Reider, "A Type of Transference to Institutions," *Bulletin of the Menninger Clinic* 17, no. 2 (Mar. 1953): 58–63.

19. Erving Goffman, *Asylums: Essays on the Social Situation of Mental Patients and Other Inmates* (Garden City, N.Y.: Doubleday, 1961).

20. Joseph M. Natterson, *Beyond Countertransference: The Therapist's Subjectivity in the Therapeutic Process* (Northvale, N.J.: Jason Aronson, 1991); Natterson and Raymond J. Friedman, *A Primer of Clinical Intersubjectivity* (Northvale, N.J.: Jason Aronson, 1995).

21. Freud, *The Ego and the Id*, in *SE* 19: 26; id., *Das Ich und das Es* (1923), in *Stud.* 3: 294.

22. A rare exception is the countertransference analysis of John M. Hassler who discerningly writes of "the underanalysis of the conflict of aging in almost all patients": "Turning Forty in Analysis," in *The Race Against Time: Psychotherapy and Psychoanalysis in the Second Half of Life*, ed. Robert A. Nemiroff and Calvin A. Colarusso (New York: Plenum Press, 1985), 97–115. The quotation is from 113–14.

23. Seth Mydans, "Legal Euthanasia: Australia Faces a Grim Reality," *New York Times*, 2 Feb. 1997. The Australian parliament in March 1997 overturned the voluntary euthanasia law of the Northern Territory.

24. Herbert Hendin, *Seduced by Death: Doctors, Patients, and the Dutch Cure* (New York: Norton, 1977), 43.

25. Ibid., 157.

26. *Wall Street Journal*, 1 Apr. 1997, A18.

27. William Winslade puts it well: "It seems to me that in some circumstances a family member, a nurse, a friend or other caretaker, perhaps with a physician's guidance, might be an appropriate or even better person to respond to a request for assisted suicide or assisted voluntary euthanasia. The critical moral factor is the special relationship of intimacy, affection, trust, and concern that gives another the moral standing to participate in such a profound interpersonal event. Of course one must also possess the knowledge and skill to assist another in a competent manner, but this is not limited to physicians or even health professionals": "Assisted Suicide and Euthanasia: Comments on 'Euthanasia in the Netherlands Cancer Institute' and Some Personal Thoughts" (MS, courtesy of the author).

28. Among the exceptions in the psychoanalytic literature that do treat the end of life and dying as a phase, see Stanley H. Cath, "The Awareness of the Nearness of Death, Depletion, and the Senescent Cell Antigen: A Reconsideration of Freud's Death Instinct on the New Frontier Between Psychodynamic Theory and Biology," in *New Dimensions in Adult Development*, ed. Robert A. Nemiroff and Calvin A. Colarusso (New York: Basic Books, 1990), 288–305, and *Race Against Time*, ed. Nemiroff and Colarusso (cited in n. 22 above). See also Daniel J. Levinson et al., *The Seasons of a Man's Life* (New York: Knopf, 1978), and *Themes of Work and Love in Adulthood*, ed. Neil J. Smelser and Erik H. Erikson (Cambridge, Mass.: Harvard University Press, 1980), although neither of these books deals systematically with dying. The early Erikson is much better than the later one at conceptualizing the substance of the psychosocial stages. While his formulations of the tasks of infancy and childhood among "The Eight Ages of Man" are rigorous, Erikson's stages of "adulthood" and "maturity" with categories of "generativity" and "ego integrity" are conceptually thin and sentimental: Erikson, "Eight Ages of Man," in *Childhood and Society* (New York: Norton, 1950, 1963), 247–74. In Erikson's *Identity and the Life Cycle: Selected Papers* (New York: International Universities Press, 1959, 1967), "wisdom," which is a category difficult to operationalize, is ascribed to the eighth stage of life. I would in some cases offer "mellowness" as a substitute.

29. Freud, *The Ego and the Id* (1923), in SE 19: 47; id., *Das Ich und das Es*, in *Stud.* 3: 313.

30. Freud, *Beyond the Pleasure Principle* (1920), in *SE* 18: 46; id., *Jenseits des Lust-prinzips*, in *Stud.* 3: 255.

31. In 1910 Hoche presented a paper entitled "A Psychical Epidemic Among Doctors" that held that "psychoanalysis was an evil method born of mystical tendencies and full of dangers for the standing of the medical profession." See Ernest Jones, *The Life and Work of Sigmund Freud* (New York: Basic Books, 1953–57) (henceforth cited as Jones, *Freud*), 2: 116.

32. Karl Binding und Alfred Hoche, *Die Freigabe der Vernichtung lebensunwerten Lebens: Ihr Mass und ihre Form* (Leipzig: F. Meiner, 1920, 1922) (henceforth cited as Binding and Hoche).

33. Heinz-Peter Schmiedebach, "The Mentally Ill Patient Caught Between the State's Demands and the Professional Interests of Psychiatrists," in *Medicine and Modernity: Public Health and Medical Care in Nineteenth-and Twentieth-Century Germany*, ed. Manfred Berg and Geoffrey Cocks (Washington, D.C.: German Historical Institute; New York: Cambridge University Press, 1997), 116.

34. Binding and Hoche, 41.

35. Ibid., 62.

36. Alexander Mitscherlich and Fred Mielke, *Das Diktat der Menschenverachtung: Eine Dokumentation vom Prozess gegen 23 SS-Ärzte und deutsche Wissenschaftler* (Heidelberg: L. Schneider, 1947), trans. Heinz Norden, as *Doctors of Infamy* (New York: Henry Schuman, 1949); *Medizin ohne Menschlichkeit: Dokumente des Nürnberger Ärzteprozesses* (Frankfurt a./M.: Fischer, 1949, 1962, 1978, 1991); *Wissenschaft ohne Menschlichkeit: Medizinische und Eugenische Irrewege unter Diktatur, Bürokratie und Krieg* (Heidelberg: L. Schneider, 1949), trans. James Cleugh as *The Death Doctors* (London: Elek, 1962); Robert Proctor, *Racial Hygiene: Medicine under the Nazis* (Cambridge, Mass.: Harvard University Press, 1988); Michael H. Kater, *Doctors under Hitler* (Chapel Hill: University of North Carolina Press, 1989); Hans-Walter Schmuhl, *Rassenhygiene, Nationalsozialismus, Euthanasie: Von der Verhütung zur Vernichtung "lebensunwerten Lebens" 1890–1945* (Göttingen: Vandenhoeck & Ruprecht, 1987); and *Medizin im Dritten Reich*, ed. Johanna Bleker and Norbert Jachertz (Cologne: Deutscher Ärzte-Verlag, 1989; 2d ed. 1993).

37. "One need only consider the situation in which idealistic young Americans, working in a mental hospital as conscious objectors to war and violence, reached the point where they 'helped to kill' deteriorated mental patients": Robert Jay Lifton, *The Nazi Doctors: Medical Killing and the Psychology of Genocide* (New York: Basic Books, 1986), 498.

38. Ronald Dworkin, *Life's Dominion: An Argument about Abortion, Euthanasia, and Individual Freedom* (New York: Random House, 1993), 217.

39. Charles Baron et al., "A Model State Act to Authorize and Regulate Physician-Assisted Suicide," *Harvard Journal on Legislation* 33 (winter 1996). See also James Vorenberg and Sidney Wanzer, "Assisting Suicide," *Harvard Magazine* 99, no. 4 (Mar.–Apr. 1997): 30–31, 89. William J. Winslade calls for an elaborate system of prior review, postmortem review, and judicial oversight. See his "Physician-Assisted

Suicide: Evolving Public Policy," in *Physician-Assisted Suicide*, ed. Robert Weir, 224–39 (Bloomington: Indiana University Press, 1997). I am grateful to Professor Winslade for sharing this prepublication essay and other manuscript materials with me. See also Steven Miles, Demetra M. Pappas, and Robert Koepp, "Considerations of Safeguards Proposed in Laws and Guidelines to Legalize Assisted Suicide," in ibid., 205–23.

40. Thomas Mann, *Buddenbrooks* (Berlin: S. Fischer Verlag, 1901), trans. H. T. Lowe-Porter (New York: Knopf, 1924), 480.

41. James Joyce, *Ulysses* (Paris, 1922; New York: Random House, 1961), 727.

42. Ibid., 95.

43. Elections Division, Secretary of State, State of Oregon, Eugene, Oregon.

44. *New York Times*, 6 Nov. 1997, A22.

45. *Washington v. Glucksberg*, Rehnquist, CJ, for the majority, cited in n. 17, above.

46. *New York Times*, Oct. 26, 1997, 19.

47. *New York Times*, Nov. 6, 1997, A22.

48. Oregon Revised Statutes, 1996 Supplement, secs. 27.800–127.897. See also Death with Dignity Preliminary Summary, Oregon Health Division, 18 Aug. 1998.

49. See text of the Oregon Death with Dignity Act and the patient request form in Margaret P. Battin, Rosamond Rhodes, and Anita Silvers, eds., *Physician Assisted Suicide: Expanding the Debate* (New York: Routledge, 1998), Appendix D, 443–48.

50. *New York Times*, Feb. 18, 1999, A1–A17.

51. Freud to Fliess, 6 Feb. 1899, in *Briefe an Wilhelm Fliess 1887–1904* (Frankfurt a.M.: Fischer, 1986), letter 191, 376; *Letters to Fliess*, 343–44.

52. Freud, "Thoughts for the Times on War and Death" (1915), in *SE* 14: 290; id., "Zeitgemässes über Krieg und Tod," in *Stud.* 9: 50.

53. Freud, "The Uncanny" (1919), in *SE* 17: 242; id., "Das Unheimliche," in *Stud.* 4: 264.

54. Freud to Ferenczi, 24 Jan. 1919, in *The Correspondence of Sigmund Freud and Sándor Ferenczi*, vol. 2, 1914–1919, trans. Peter T. Hoffer, ed. Ernst Falzeder, Eva Brabant et al. (Cambridge, Mass.: Harvard University Press, Belknap Press, 1996), no. 787, p. 328.

55. Ferenczi to Freud, 19 June 1919, ibid., no. 815, p. 359.

56. Ferenczi to Freud, 28 Nov. 1919, ibid., no. 823, p. 370.

57. Freud to Ferenczi, 11 Dec. 1919, ibid., no. 825, p. 372.

58. Freud, "The Future of an Illusion" (1927), in *SE* 21: 50; id., "Die Zukunft einer Illusion," in *Stud.* 9: 183.

59. Jones, *Freud*, 3: 93.

60. Ibid., 96.

61. Felix Deutsch, "Reflections on Freud's One Hundredth Birthday," *Psychosomatic Medicine* 18, no. 4 (July–Aug. 1956): 282.

62. Ibid., 282.

63. Max Schur, *Freud: Living and Dying* (New York: International Universities Press, 1972), 408.

64. Ibid., 529.

65. I here rely on Peter Gay, *Freud: A Life for Our Time* (New York: Norton, 1988) (henceforth cited as Gay, *Freud*), 739–40n, which corrects Max Schur's published account in *Freud: Living and Dying*, which was watered down for publication after consulting an attorney on the question of euthanasia. Gay uses what Schur terms "the correct version," his unpublished "The Medical Case History of Sigmund Freud" (27 Feb. 1954) in the Max Schur Papers, Library of Congress. Gay also interviewed Schur's wife, Helen, and Freud's nephew, Harry Freud.

66. Fritz Meerwein points out that Freud had the skill and means to commit suicide on his own. I do not think the fact that a person does not wish to die alone and seeks help necessarily contradicts a wish to end what has become a torturous struggle. Fritz Meerwein, "Selbstaggression, Selbstzerstörung . . . ," in *Züricher Hochschulforum*, ed. Hans-Jorg Braun (Zurich: Artemia, 1985), 6: 192–93. I am indebted to Esther Dreifuss-Kattan for drawing to my attention this essay.

67. Norbert Elias, *Über die Einsamkeit der Sterbenden* (Frankfurt a./M.: Suhrkamp, 1982), trans. Edmund Jephcott as *The Loneliness of Dying* (Oxford: Blackwell, 1985), 87.

68. See Peter Gay's excellent survey of Freud's attitudes to America in the chapter "The Ugly Americans" in Gay, *Freud*, 553–70.

69. Ilse Grubrich-Simitis, *Zurück zu Freuds Texten* (Frankfurt a./M.: Fischer, 1993), trans. Philip Slotkin as *Back to Freud's Texts: Making Silent Documents Speak* (New Haven: Yale University Press, 1996), 177–79 passim.

70. *Schloendorff v. Society of New York Hospital*, 211 NY 125, 129–130; 105 NE 92, 93 (1914).

71. Walter C. Alvarez, "Care of the Dying," *Journal of the American Medical Association* 150, no. 2 (13 Sept. 1952): 86–91; quotation from 91. I thank Harold Vanderpool for supplying me with this article.

72. See also Samuel D. Warren and Louis D. Brandeis, "The Right to Privacy," 4 *Harvard Law Review* 5 (1890): 193–220, a magnificent early article in which they define "the more general right of the individual to be let alone. It is like the right not to be assaulted or beaten, the right not to be maliciously prosecuted, the right not to be defamed. . . . The principle which protects . . . an inviolate personality. . . . The decisions indicate a general right to privacy for thoughts, emotions, and sensations, these should receive the same protection, whether expressed in writing, or in conduct, in conversation, in attitudes, or in facial expression . . . as a part of the more general right to the immunity of the person—the right to one's personality."

73. *Olmstead v. United States*, 277 U.S. 478, 48 S. Ct. 572 (1928) (Brandeis, J., dissenting).

74. John Locke, *Second Treatise of Government* (1690), ed. C. B. Macpherson (Indianapolis: Hackett Publishing, 1980), § 4, 123, pp. 8, 65, passim in this edition; see also §§ 87, 95, pp. 46, 52.

75. Locke opposed suicide because human life belongs to God: "Man . . . has not liberty to destroy himself . . . for men being all the workmanship of one omnipotent,

and infinitely wise maker; all the servants of one sovereign master, sent into the world by his order, and about his business; they are his property whose workmanship they are, made to last during his, not one another's pleasure" (ibid., § 6, p. 9). Locke also believed that atheism and Catholicism should be legislated against as inimical to the state.

76. Ronald Dworkin, "Ethics: The Critical Question Is Whether a Society Will Choose Coercion or Responsibility," *Los Angeles Times*, 5 Mar. 1997, B9.

77. In the reflections that follow I am grateful for the stimulation of the ideas of Professor Thomas Laqueur in his lecture "How Suicide Became a Medical Practice," Conference on "Doctors and Death in the Modern Era," University of California, San Francisco, 14 Feb. 1997.

78. Acute Pain Management Guideline Panel, *Acute Pain Management: Operative or Medical Procedures and Trauma. Clinical Practice Guideline*, AHCPR Pub. no. 92–0032 (Rockville, Md.: U.S. Department of Health and Human Services, Public Health Service, Agency for Health Care Policy and Research, Feb. 1992), 20–21, 51, 59. I am indebted to Janet Hild for drawing this source to my attention.

79. Louis Jolyon West, "Reflections on the Right to Die," in *Suicidology*, ed. Leenaars (cited n. 8 above), 374–75.

80. Esther B. Fein, "Failing to Discuss Dying Adds to Pain of Patient and Family," *New York Times*, 5 Mar. 1997, A1, A14, A15.

81. Dworkin, *Life's Dominion*, 180.

Index

Index

Index

Index

Index

Index

Pick, Daniel, 444n, 446n

Pietraß, Richard, 284, 456n

Pinel, Casimir, 414n, 418n

Pinel, Louis, 69, 72

Pinel, Philippe: and Bicêtre Hospice, 68, 86; and Diest prize, 69–70, 86; "A Doctor Surveys the Effects of the French Revolution," 84–85; education, 66–67; and *Gazette de santé*, 71–76; and hygiene, 72–73; and mental illness, 73–75; memoirs presented to Académie des sciences, 77–78; and mesmerism, 70, 73; publications in medical press, 81–86; "Memoir on Madness: A Contribution to the Natural History of Man," 86; moral treatment, 85; *Nosographie philosophique, ou Méthode de l'analyse appliquée à la médecine*, 79, 416n; *Traité médico-philosophique sur l'aliénation mentale ou la manie*, 70–71, 79, 84, 414n, 417–18nn

Piquér, Andrés, 86

Pixis, Theodor, 464n

Pliny, 72

Plutarch, 47, 53, 72, 408n

Pocock, J. G. A., 412n

Poeck, Wilhelm, 463n, 465n, 468n

Pötzl, Eduard, 462n

Polanyi, Michael, 441n

Polybius, 47

Pompadour, Madame de, 94

Pompeii, 252

Popkin, Richard Henry, 412n

pornography: and anti-clericalism, 92–94, 107; and the Enlightenment, 92–109; as evidence of mentalities, 102–9; feminist views of, 96–97, 99–102; history of, 88–91; library collections, 89–90; and male dominance, 97–98; and philosophy, 92, 98–99; and sexual equality, 95–96; and social criticism, 91–92, 99, 107

Portal, 82

Porter, Roy, 426n

Postel, Jacques, 82, 415n, 417–18n

Potash, Joel, 363

Praschek, Helmut, 454n

Prelinger, Ernst, 19

Prenzlauer Berg (Berlin), 282–83

Pre-Raphaelites, 252

Presber, Rudolf, 460n, 462nn, 468n

Pretzel, C. L. A., 462n

Priapus, 91

Price, Richard, 116, 421n

Priestley, Joseph, 114, 116–17, 153, 422nn

Prinz, Joachim, 308, 471n

Proctor, Robert, 483n

Les Progrès du libertinage, 100, 102

Proelß, Johannes, 289, 457n, 460n

Prokhovnik, Raia, 408n

Prussian Reform Movement, 169, 174–75, 188

Pulzer, Peter G. J., 444n

Pundt, Hermann G., 437nn

Pure Food and Drug Act (1906), 364

Putnam, James Jackson, 371

Pyrrhonian skepticism, 37, 57, 59–60

Quack, Sibylle, 471n, 473n

Les Quarante manières de foutre, 91

Quenzel, Karl, 467n

Quill, Timothy E., 363

Quinault, R., 430nn

Quinet, Edgar, 124

Quinlan, Karen Ann, 363

Quintilian, 30, 33, 36, 40–41; *Institutio oratoria*, 28, 403nn, 405n, 407nn. See also Cicero; civil science; Hobbes, Thomas

Rabelais, 94

Racine, Nicole, 438n

Ragionamenti (Aretino), 101

Rahv, Philip, 14

Rainey, Lawrence, 397n

Ranger, Terence, 433n, 448n

Ranum, Orest, 410–11n, 412n

Raphael, D. D., 406n

Rasmussen, Peter, 370

Rathenau, Walter, 272

Rational Dissent, 113, 114

Rave, Paul Ortwin, 436nn, 437n

Rawls, John, 481n

Rayner, Jeremy, 407n

Readings, William, 451n

Index

Index

Library of Congress Cataloging-in-Publication Data

Enlightenment, passion, modernity : historical essays in European
    thought and culture / introduced and edited by Mark S. Micale and
    Robert L. Dietle.
        p.   cm. — (Cultural sitings)
    Issued as a testimonial volume in honor of Peter Gay.
    Many essays were presented as lectures at a conference in
Professor Gay's honor at Williams College, Williamstown, Mass.,
Oct. 2–3, 1998.
    Includes a bibliography of writings by Peter Gay (p.   ),
bibliographical references (p.   ), and index.
    ISBN 0-8047-3116-0 (cloth : alk. paper). — ISBN 0-8047-3117-9
(pbk. : alk. paper)
    1. Europe — History — 20th century.   2. Enlightenment — Europe.
3. Philosophy — History.   4. Europe — Intellectual life.
5. Psychoanalysis — history.   I. Micale, Mark S., 1957– .
II. Dietle, Robert L.   III. Gay, Peter, 1923– .   IV. Series.
D424.E55   2000
940.5 — dc21   99-39589

Original printing 2000
Last figure below indicates year of this printing:
09 08 07 06 05 04 03 02 01 00